THE OXFORD HANDBOOK OF

MAX WEBER

THE OXFORD HANDBOOK OF

MAX WEBER

Edited by

EDITH HANKE,
LAWRENCE A. SCAFF,

and

SAM WHIMSTER

OXFORD

UNIVERSITY PRESS

OXFORD

UNIVERSITY PRESS

Oxford University Press is a department of the University of Oxford. It furthers
the University's objective of excellence in research, scholarship, and education
by publishing worldwide. Oxford is a registered trade mark of Oxford University
Press in the UK and certain other countries.

Published in the United States of America by Oxford University Press
198 Madison Avenue, New York, NY 10016, United States of America.

Library of Congress Control Number: 2019952443

ISBN 978-0-19-067954-5

1 3 5 7 9 8 6 4 2

Printed by Sheridan Books, Inc., United States of America.

Contents

INTRODUCTION

PART I THE ECONOMY: CAPITALISM IN A GLOBALIZED WORLD

PART II SOCIETY AND SOCIAL STRUCTURE

PART V CULTURE

PART VI SCIENCE AND KNOWLEDGE

About the Editors

Edith Hanke is *Generalredakteurin* of the *Max Weber-Gesamtausgabe* at the Bavarian Academy of Sciences and Humanities in Munich. Her work centered on Leo Tolstoy and his significance for c. 1900 German cultural debates. She edited Max Weber's "Sociology of Domination" for the *Max Weber-Gesamtausgabe* (I/22-4 and I/23) and is currently engaged in research on Max Weber's worldwide proliferation and reception.

Lawrence A. Scaff is professor emeritus of political science and sociology at Wayne State University, Detroit. He is the author of *Fleeing the Iron Cage* (University of California Press, 1989), *Max Weber in America* (Princeton University Press, 2011; German translation Duncker & Humblot, 2013), and *Weber and the Weberians* (Palgrave Macmillan, 2014).

Sam Whimster is professor emeritus of sociology in the Global Policy Institute, London, and a fellow of the Academy of the Social Sciences. He is the editor of the journal *Max Weber Studies* and the author of *Understanding Weber* (Routledge, 2007; Portuguese translation 2007). He edited, with Hans Henrik Bruun, *Max Weber: Collected Methodological Writings* (Routledge, 2012). He is co-author of *Federal Central Banks* (Forum Press, 2018).

Contributors

Andreas Anter is professor of political science at the Faculty of Economics, Law and Social Sciences at the University of Erfurt, Germany. After his studies of political science and sociology in Münster, Freiburg, and Hamburg and his PhD in Hamburg (1994), he taught political theory and domestic politics at the Universities of Hamburg, Leipzig, and Bremen. He is the author of *Max Weber's Theory of the Modern State* (2014), *Max Weber und die Staatsrechtslehre* (2016), and *Theorien der Macht zur Einführung* (4th ed., 2018).

Robert J. Antonio is professor of sociology at the University of Kansas. He specializes in social theory and is currently working on projects related to capitalism's crisis tendencies, especially concerning the intersection of increased economic inequality, ecological risk, and democratic and authoritarian responses. Among his recent publications are "Ethnoracial Populism: An Alternative to Neoliberal Globalization?" in *Social Epistemology* (2019); (with Alessandro Bonanno) "From Fordism to Brexit & Trump: Is Authoritarian Capitalism on the Rise?" in *Blackwell Companion to Sociology* (2019); "Immanent Critique and the Exhaustion Thesis: Neoliberalism and History's Vicissitudes" in *The Palgrave Handbook of Critical Theory* (2017); and "Plundering the Commons: The Growth Imperative in Neoliberal Times" in *Sociological Review* (2013).

Johann P. Arnason is emeritus professor at La Trobe University, Melbourne, where he taught sociology from 1975 to 2003, and affiliated with the Department of Historical Sociology, Faculty of Human Studies, Charles University, Prague, where he taught from 2007 to 2015. His research interests center on social theory and historical sociology, with particular emphasis on the comparative analysis of civilizations. Recent publications include *Anthropology and Civilizational Analysis: Eurasian Explorations* (edited, with Chris Hann; 2018); "Elias and Eisenstadt: The Multiple Meanings of Civilization," in *Social Imaginaries* (2015); and "Theorizing the History of Religions: The Weberian Agenda and Its Unresolved Issues," in *Social Imaginaries* (2017).

Stefan Breuer is emeritus professor of sociology at Hamburg University. He has published widely on critical theory, the evolution of the state, and the radical right in Germany. His publications on Max Weber include *Bürokratie und Charisma. Zur politischen Soziologie Max Webers* (1994), *Max Webers tragische Soziologie* (2006), and "*Herrschaft*" *in der Soziologie Max Webers* (2011). English translations of his essays have been published in *Law and State, Journal of Historical Sociology, History of the Human Sciences, Max Weber Studies,* and *Max Weber, Democracy and Modernization,* edited by Ralph Schroeder.

John Breuilly is emeritus professor of nationalism and ethnicity at the London School of Economics. Recent publications include *The Oxford Handbook of the History of Nationalism* (2013); "Modernisation and Nationalist Ideology," in *Archiv für Sozialgeschichte* (2017); "Modern Empires and Nation-States," in *Thesis Eleven* (2017); and "Popular Nationalism, State Forms and Modernity," in *Nations, Identities and the First World War: Shifting Loyalties to the Fatherland* (2018). A revised version of his edition of *19th Century Germany: Politics, Culture and Society, 1780–1918* will be published in 2019. He is writing a book on how nationalism "traveled" the world.

Hinnerk Bruhns is director of research emeritus at CNRS, affiliated to the Centre de recherches historiques (EHESS/CNRS) in Paris. He joined the CNRS in 1985 and the EHESS in Paris in 1982. Previously he was attached to the Universities of Aix-en-Provence (1971–1975) and Bochum (1976–1979). From 1979 on, he has been active as administrator of international research cooperation programs in German and French public research organizations, and from 1997 to 2008 he was deputy director of the Foundation Maison des Sciences de l'Homme. Recent publications include *Max Weber und der Erste Weltkrieg* (2017) and *Max Webers historische Sozialökonomie/L'économie sociale de Max Weber entre histoire et sociologie* (2014).

Hans Henrik Bruun is adjunct professor at the Department of Sociology, University of Copenhagen. His *Science, Values and Politics in Max Weber's Methodology* (1972, new edition 2010) remains a standard reference work on Weber's methodology. He was translator and co-editor of *Max Weber: Collected Methodological Writings* (2012) and recently published the first complete Danish translation of Weber's *The Protestant Ethic and the Spirit of Capitalism.*

Sérgio da Mata is associate professor at Ouro Preto University, Brazil. He earned his PhD from the University of Cologne. He is author of *Chão de Deus* (2002), *História & Religião* (2010), and *A fascinação weberiana. As origens da obra de Max Weber* (2013). His edited collections include *Contributions to Theory and Comparative History of Historiography: German and Brazilian Perspectives* (2015; with Luísa Pereira and Luiz Fernandes). He has authored numerous articles on Max Weber, German historicism, and German philosophical anthropology. His current project explores the intellectual history of Joachim Ritter's *Collegium philosophicum* at the University of Münster and its meaning for the Weberian tradition in postwar Germany. He is a recipient of fellowships from the Deutsches Akademisches Austauschdienst, the Alexander von Humboldt Stiftung, and the Deutsche Schillergesellschaft.

Joshua Derman is associate professor of humanities at the Hong Kong University of Science and Technology. His research focuses on modern German history and, in particular, the international dimensions of German political and social thought. His book *Max Weber in Politics and Social Thought: From Charisma to Canonization* (2012) is the first comprehensive history of Weber's early impact in Germany and the United States.

Laura R. Ford is an assistant professor of sociology at Bard College. With a background in both law and sociology, her research and teaching interests include law and religion, economic sociology, social theory, the history and development of intellectual property, and historical sociology. Recent publications include articles in *Qualitative Sociology*, *Max Weber Studies*, *Theory & Society*, and the *Cardozo Public Law, Policy & Ethics Journal*.

Rosario Forlenza is a fellow at the Remarque Institute, New York University. He is a historian of modern Europe and has worked at the University of Cambridge, Princeton University, Columbia University, and the University of Padova. Recent books include *Italian Modernities: Competing Narratives of Nationhood* (co-authored with Bjørn Thomassen; 2019) and *On the Edge of Democracy: Italy 1943–1948* (2019).

Peter Ghosh is a fellow in history of St. Anne's College, Oxford. He has published an intellectual biography of Weber, *Max Weber and the Protestant Ethic: Twin Histories* (2014) and two books of essays: *A Historian Reads Max Weber* (2008) and *Max Weber in Context* (2016).

Claudius Härpfer is a postdoctoral researcher and lecturer at the Department of Social Sciences of Goethe-University Frankfurt, Germany. He works on the history of sociology, the philosophy of the social sciences, and network theory. His publications include "Weber and Simmel on the Formation of Norms, Rules and Laws" in *Journal of Classical Sociology* (with Tom Kaden; 2017), *Max Webers vergessene Zeitgenossen* (with Gerhard Wagner; 2016), and "Neo-Kantianism and the Social Sciences: From Rickert to Weber" in *New Approaches to Neo-Kantianism*, edited by Nicolas de Warren and Andrea Staiti (with Gerhard Wagner; 2015).

Gangolf Hübinger is a Viadrina senior fellow at the B/Orders in Motion Center and a retired professor of modern history at the European University Viadrina in Frankfurt (Oder). He has published extensively on intellectual and cultural history, the history of the social sciences and humanities, and religious culture and political movements in the nineteenth and twentieth centuries. He is a co-publisher of the complete editions of Max Weber and Ernst Troeltsch. Recent publications include *Max Weber: Stationen und Impulse einer intellektuellen Biographie* (2019) and *Engagierte Beobachter der Moderne: Von Max Weber bis Ralf Dahrendorf* (2016).

Geoffrey Ingham is life fellow, Christ's College, Cambridge University. His main interests are in the historical sociology and political economy of money and finance, on which he has published widely in journals including *The British Journal of Sociology*, *Acta Sociologica*, *Archives Européenes de Sociologie*, and *Cambridge Journal of Economics*. His major recent books are *The Nature of Money* (2004) and *Capitalism, with Postscript on the Financial Crisis* (2011). In 2013, Jocelyn Pixley and Geoffrey Harcourt edited a Festschrift entitled *Financial Crises and the Nature of Capitalist Money: Mutual Developments from the Work of Geoffrey Ingham*.

Thomas Kemple is professor of sociology at the University of British Columbia in Vancouver, Canada. In addition to articles in *Theory, Culture & Society* and the *Journal of Classical Sociology*, his most recent works include *Intellectual Work and the Spirit of Capitalism* (2012), *The Anthem Companion to Georg Simmel* (co-edited with Olli Pyyhtinen; 2017), *Simmel* (2018), and *Writing the Body Politic: A John O'Neill Reader* (co-edited with Mark Featherstone; 2019).

Sung Ho Kim is professor of political science at Yonsei University, Seoul, Korea. He also taught political, social, and legal theories at the University of California, the University of Chicago, Harvard University, and Keio University (Japan). He is a recipient of the Leo Strauss Award of the American Political Science Association. He authored the "Max Weber" entry for the *Stanford Encyclopedia of Philosophy* and (with C. Hahm) *Making We the People* (2015). His earlier monograph, *Max Weber's Politics of Civil Society* (2004), explored Weber as a liberal and democratic theorist.

Brandon Konoval is on faculty at the University of British Columbia, where he holds a cross-appointment at the UBC School of Music and in the UBC Arts One Program. His research addresses the relationship between music, mathematics, and early modern science, as well as the genealogies of inequality, morality, and sexuality developed by Rousseau, Nietzsche, and Foucault. Recent publications include contributions to *Nietzsche-Studien* (2013), *Perspectives on Science* (2014, 2018), *I Tatti Studies in the Italian Renaissance* (2019), and *Modern Intellectual History* (2017, 2019), as well as a chapter on music and disciplinary culture in *Foucault on the Arts and Letters* (2016).

Scott Lash is visiting professor, School of Creative Media, City University of Hong Kong, and senior research associate at the Centre on Migration Policy and Study at Oxford University. He has written twelve books translated into fifteen languages. His recent books are *Experience: New Foundations for the Human Sciences* (2018) and *China Constructing Capitalism: Economic Life and Urban Change* (co-author; 2014).

Stefan Leder is professor emeritus of Arabic and Islamic studies at Martin Luther University in Halle, Germany, and directed the Orient-Institut Beirut (Lebanon), a research institute in the humanities and social sciences (2007–2017). His current work concerns the discursive contexts and theoretical framing of traditions of political thought in the MENA region and beyond. His related English publications include "Sunni Resurgence, Jihād Discourse and the Impact of the Frankish Presence" and "Towards a Historical Semantic of the Bedouin" (both available online: www.menalib .de/en/), as well as "Religious Texts and the Islamic Purity Regime" in *Discourses of Purity in Transcultural Perspective (300–1600)* (2015).

Kenichi Mishima is professor emeritus for comparative studies of civilizations and for social philosophy at the University of Osaka. He studied philosophy, German literature, and comparative studies of literature and civilization at the University of Tokyo. He also worked as a professor at the University of Tokyo and Gakushuin University. His research focuses on critical theory of society, theory of multiple modernities, German idealism, and critics of modernity. Recent publications have appeared in *Critical Asian Studies* (2016) and *Nova Acta Leopoldina* (2017).

Kari Palonen is professor emeritus of political science at the University of Jyväskylä, Finland. His books deal with the concept of politics (*A Struggle with Time*, 2006), the principles of conceptual history (*Politics and Conceptual Histories*, 2014), textual analysis of politics (*Debates, Rhetoric and Political Action*, 2017, with Claudia Wiesner and Taru Haapala), and parliamentary procedure and rhetoric (*Parliamentary Thinking. Procedure, Rhetoric and Time*, 2018). His Weber books include *Das Webersche Moment* (1998), *Eine Lobrede für Politiker* (2002), *Objektivität als faires Spiel* (2010), *A Political Style of Thinking* (2017), and the collection *Max Webers Begriffspolitik* (2019).

Jos C. N. Raadschelders is professor and associate dean of faculty at the John Glenn College of Public Affairs, The Ohio State University. He is also affiliated with the Institute of Public Administration, University of Leiden, the Netherlands. His research interests include the nature of the government and its study, comparative government, administrative history, and anything else that captures his attention. He is a fellow of the National Academy of Public Administration.

Ralph Schroeder is professor in social science of the Internet at the Oxford Internet Institute at the University of Oxford. His publications include *Social Theory after the Internet: Media, Technology and Globalization* (2018), *Knowledge Machines: Digital Transformations of the Sciences and Humanities* (2015; co-authored with Eric T. Meyer), *An Age of Limits: Social Theory for the Twenty-First Century* (2013), *Rethinking Science, Technology and Social Change* (2007), and *Max Weber and the Sociology of Culture* (1992).

John Scott is an honorary professor at the Universities of Essex, Exeter, and Copenhagen. He was formerly professor of sociology at the Universities of Essex and Leicester and pro-vice chancellor for research at the University of Plymouth. He has been president of the British Sociological Association and chair of the Sociology Section of the British Academy and in 2013 was awarded the CBE for Services to Social Science. His work covers theoretical sociology, the history of sociology, elites and social stratification, and social network analysis. His most recent books include *British Social Theory: Recovering Lost Traditions before 1950* (2018), *Envisioning Sociology. Victor Branford, Patrick Geddes, and the Quest for Social Reconstruction* (with Ray Bromley; 2013), and *The Emerald Guide to Max Weber* (2019).

Hira Singh is associate professor in the Department of Sociology at York University, Toronto, Canada. He has taught sociology at the Delhi School of Economics, University of Delhi, and various other universities in Canada, including Wilfrid Laurier, Victoria, St. Thomas University, and University of New Brunswick. He was a participant in the debate "Feudalism in Pre-colonial, Non-European Societies," sponsored by the *Journal of Peasant Studies*. His previous publications include *Colonial Hegemony and Popular Resistance* (1998), *Recasting Caste: From the Sacred to the Profane* (2014; translated in Hindi and Marathi 2018), and essays in prominent journals.

Lutfi Sunar is associate professor in the Department of Sociology at Istanbul Medeniyet University, Turkey. His major research interests are classical sociological theory, orientalism, social change, and stratification. He has published various articles in international journals. Among his recent books are *Marx and Weber on Oriental Societies* (2014), *Eurocentrism at the Margins: Encounters, Critics and Going Beyond* (as editor, 2016), *Debates on Civilization in the Muslim World: Critical Perspectives on Islam and Modernity* (as editor, 2016), *Toplumsal Değişim* (2018), and *Sosyal Tabakalaşma* (2018).

Barbara Thériault is full professor at the Department of Sociology and at the Canadian Centre for German and European Studies at the University of Montreal. She is in charge of the "Feuilleton" section of *Sociologie et sociétés*. She teaches classical German sociology and translates German feuilletons into French (Simmel, Kracauer, Elias, Roth, Tucholsky). At the center of her current research are two interests: contemporary Germany and sociological writing. Within one concrete project—an ethnography of a German mid-sized town, written in the form of feuilletons—she brings them both together. In 2018 she was writer-in-residence in Lviv, Ukraine.

Bryan S. Turner is professor of sociology and director of the Institute for Religion, Politics and Society at the Australian Catholic University; emeritus professor at the Graduate Center CUNY, USA; and an honorary professor at Potsdam University, Germany, where he is the director of the Centre for Social Citizenship. In 2009 he was awarded a doctor of letters from the University of Cambridge. He won the Max Planck Award in 2015. His interests include the sociology of religion with special reference to law and religion, political sociology with special attention to citizenship and human rights, and social and political theory. He was the chief editor of the five-volume *Wiley Blackwell Encyclopedia of Social Theory* (2018).

Stephen P. Turner is currently distinguished university professor in the Department of Philosophy, University of South Florida. He has written extensively on Max Weber, especially on aspects of his methodological writings, in *Max Weber and the Dispute Over Reason and Value: A Study in Philosophy, Ethics, and Politics* (1984) and *Max Weber: The Lawyer as Social Thinker* (both with the late Regis Factor). His *Cognitive Science and the Social: A Primer* was published in 2018. He has recently co-edited, with Christopher Adair-Toteff, *The Calling of Social Thought: Rediscovering the Work of Edward Shils* (2019).

Eduardo Weisz is professor at the University of Buenos Aires, where he is in charge of the Max Weber research group. He has published and edited several books on different aspects of Weber's legacy, including *Max Weber en Iberoamérica* (edited with Álvaro Morcillo; 2016) and *Racionalidad y tragedia* (2011).

ABBREVIATED TITLES FOR MAX WEBER'S TEXTS

AJ	*Ancient Judaism*
ASAC	*The Agrarian Sociology of Ancient Civilization*
CMW	*Collected Methodological Writings*
CS	*Critique of Stammler*
E&S	*Economy and Society: An Outline of Interpretive Sociology*
Essential	*The Essential Weber: A Reader*
FMW	*From Max Weber: Essays in Sociology*
GARS	*Gesammelte Aufsätze zur Religionssoziologie*
GEH	*General Economic History*
GPS	*Gesammelte Politische Schriften*
HCP	*History of Commercial Partnerships*
MWG	*Max Weber-Gesamtausgabe*
PED	*The Protestant Ethic Debate: Max Weber's Replies to his Critics, 1907–1910*
PESC	*The Protestant Ethic and the Spirit of Capitalism*
PolW	*Political Writings*
RaK	*Roscher and Knies*
RC	*The Religion of China*
RI	*The Religion of India*
RR	*The Russian Revolutions*
RSFM	*The Rational and Social Foundations of Music*
Selections	*Weber Selections*
Soc Rel	*Sociology of Religion*
WL	*Gesammelte Aufsätze zur Wissenschaftslehre*

CHRONOLOGY OF MAX WEBER'S LIFE

(all German titles are translated into English)

Year	City	Important Events in Weber's Life
1864	Erfurt, Prussia	April 21: Max born, the first child of Max Weber Sr. and Helene Weber (née Fallenstein). He is the eldest of seven siblings, the youngest of whom, Lili, is two years old. Weber Sr. was a paid advisor to the city council and was involved in the defense of the town during the Austro–Prussian war. Helene Weber was brought up in Heidelberg in a large villa (the Fallenstein villa that today is the Max-Weber-Haus) across the river Neckar with direct views of the castle. Georg Fallenstein, Helene's father, built the villa in 1847, and under his leadership it became a center of liberal-democratic nationalism and anti-Prussian politics.
1869	Charlottenburg, Berlin, Prussia	The Weber family, including Alfred Weber born in 1868, moves to Berlin. Max Weber Sr. is appointed as municipal official and later elected as a National Liberal delegate for the Prussian Lower House and the German Reichstag.
1882	Heidelberg, Baden	April: Max Weber matriculates from Charlottenburg Royal Empress-Augusta-Gymnasium and begins studies in Roman and German legal history, history of philosophy, and history at the University of Heidelberg. November: Joins a dueling fraternity, the Allemannia (and resigns in October 1918).
1883	Strasbourg, Alsace	Year-long military training in Alsace. Alsace was placed under direct Prussian military rule following the Franco–Prussian war of 1870. Attends Hermann Baumgarten's (his uncle) seminar at the German University of Strasbourg on Italian political writers of the Reformation.
1884	Berlin	Studies international and German law.
1885	Göttingen, Prussia Strasbourg Verona and Venice	Studies canon law and public, practical, and administrative law. March and April: military exercises as reserve officer. August–September: Travels to Italy with his father.

(Continued)

Year	City	Important Events in Weber's Life
1886	Celle, Lower Saxony Berlin	May: Sits for first state exams in law. Weber moves back into parental home in Charlottenburg and works as trainee lawyer (until 1890). Attends Levin Goldschmidt's seminar on commercial law.
1887	Berlin	Gives seminar paper "Commercial Partnerships According to Medieval Italian and Spanish documents."
1888	Posen, Duchy of Posen, Germany Gnesen, Duchy of Posen	July–September: Officer training and military exercises. August: Visits the Prussian Settlement Commission with the district administrator.
1889	Berlin	October: Awarded doctorate *magna cum laude* with dissertation on medieval trading companies. Weber is commended by leading classical historian Theodor Mommsen in oral public examination. Starts his postdoctoral research into Roman land patterns and tenure, working with the agrarian historian August Meitzen.
1890	Berlin	Weber attends the first Evangelical-Social Congress together with his mother Helene, who supports this new initiative for Christian social action started by socially concerned Protestant pastors. October: Passes main state law examination and is qualified to work as a lawyer.
1891	Berlin	October: Publishes his postdoctoral thesis, *Roman Agrarian History and Its Significance for Public and State Law.*
1892	Berlin	February: Awarded right to lecture (*Venia legendi*) in commercial and Roman law. February–March: Weber starts work on assignment from Association of Social Policy (Verein für Sozialpolitik) to analyze the survey results on the social and economic position of farmworkers east of the Elbe. The 600-page work is published in December. May: Weber meets Friedrich Naumann at the Third Evangelical-Social Congress. Naumann emerges as a political figure as the "poor people's pastor." They share ideas about Germany becoming a democratic power state.
1893	Berlin	March: Weber presents the overall results of the regional surveys of employers into the condition of farmworkers to the general assembly of the Association of Social Policy. He is co-opted into its governing committee.
	Charlottenburg Oerlinghausen, Lippe	May: Weber becomes officially engaged to Marianne Schnitger. September: Max and Marianne marry in Oerlinghausen, where Marianne's grandfather, Carl David Weber, owns and manages a linen business on modern factory lines.
	Berlin	November: Weber is appointed associate professor in commercial and Roman law at Friedrich-Wilhelms-University.

1894	Freiburg im Breisgau, Baden Frankfurt am Main	April: Weber is appointed full professor in economics and finance at the University of Freiburg.
		May: At the Fifth Evangelical-Social Congress, with Paul Göhre, Weber presents results of questionnaire sent out to a national sample of pastors on the condition of farmworkers.
		June and September: Publishes "Developmental Tendencies in the Situation of East Elbian Farm Workers."
		November: Weber publishes "The Börse. The Purpose and Organization of the Börse" in the *Göttingen Workers Library*, edited by Friedrich Naumann.
		November–December: "Results of the Inquiry into the German Börse" published in *Journal for General Commercial Law*
1895	Freiburg i. B.	May: Weber gives inaugural lecture, "The National State and Economic Policy."
	London, England	August–October: Travels in British Isles.
1896	Freiburg i. B.	Weber gives public lecture, "The Social Reasons for the Fall of Classical Civilization," which is published in *The Truth*.
		Gives public lectures across Germany on rural policy and proposals to change law on land inheritance, which would favor German small farmers.
	Berlin	November: Becomes member of government inquiry into the stock and commodity exchanges.
		Winter: Joins the Pan-German League (resigns in 1899).
1897	Heidelberg	January: Appointed professor of economics and finance at the University of Heidelberg. Co-director with Georg Jellinek of the sciences of state seminar and establishes a new seminar and library in economics within the philosophy faculty.
		"The Agrarian Organization of Antiquity" published in the *Handbook of Sciences of the State*.
	Berlin	August: Funeral of Max Weber Sr. He died unreconciled with Max Weber (who had challenged the extent of his patriarchal power over Helene Weber).
	Lourdes; Guernica, Basque Country, Spain	August–September: Vacation and travels in southern France and Spain.
1898	Heidelberg	The theologian Ernst Troeltsch, the philosopher Paul Hensel, the art historian Carl Neumann, and the jurist Georg Jellinek become close Heidelberg colleagues.
		March: Weber consults the psychiatrist Emil Kraepelin for nervous exhaustion and is diagnosed as suffering from "neurasthenia."
		July: Treatment for exhaustion, insomnia, and sexual dysfunction at clinic on Lake Constance.
1899	Heidelberg	Starts book series *The Farm Worker in the Protestant Regions of North Germany*
		Released from lecturing in summer semester due to depression and neurotic symptoms.

(Continued)

Year	City	Important Events in Weber's Life
	Eibsee, Bavaria	August: Travels to spa near Garmisch-Partenkirchen with Marianne.
1900	Heidelberg	January: Given leave of absence by Baden Department of Education.
	Urach, Württemberg	July: Four and half–month stay in clinic in Schwaben Alps. Unable to write simple letters.
	Corsica	Travels to Ajaccio for winter with Marianne and cousin Otto Benecke.
1901	Rome	April: Travels in southern Italy with Marianne for a month. Returns to Rome until beginning of July.
	Switzerland	July–September: Marianne and Max stay in Switzerland, returning to Rome for autumn and winter. Helene Weber and Friedrich Naumann visit. Begins a return to reading academic books.
1902	Heidelberg	April: Returns to Heidelberg and moves into new flat in Hauptstrasse. June: Announces lecture course for winter semester but further inability to work and lecture. December: Travels alone to Nervi near Genoa, returning to Heidelberg mid-January.
1903	Rome	March: Travels to Rome for six weeks.
	Scheveningen, Holland	June: Convalesces on North Sea coast with trips to Amsterdam and the Hague.
	Ostend, Belgium	August: Convalescent trip.
	Hamburg	September: Attends the conference of the Association of Social Policy.
	Heidelberg	October: Weber's resignation as professor is accepted by the Baden Ministry of Education on the grounds of continuing health problems. Weber is given title of honorary professor in the faculty. October: Publishes essay "Roscher's 'Historical Method.'"
1904	Heidelberg	January: Weber becomes member of Eranos Society. April: First issue of the *Archive for Social Science and Social Policy* (hereafter *Archive*). The three editors, Edgar Jaffé, Werner Sombart, and Max Weber, write a joint statement of the journal's approach. The first issue also carries Weber's article, "The 'Objectivity' of Knowledge in Social Science and Social Policy." September: Weber publishes his last article on rural farm policy: "Agrarian-Statistical and Social-Political Considerations of the Prussian Commission on Entailed Estates."
	New York,	30 August: Max and Marianne arrive by steamship in New York and stay five days. Journey onward to Buffalo, Niagara Falls, and North Tonawanda.
	Chicago,	September: Max and Marianne spend a week in Chicago visiting the stockyards, Hull House, the University of Chicago, Northwestern University.

St. Louis,	Mid-September: Weber is member of the German delegation to Congress of Arts and Science and gives lecture on the effect of capitalism on agricultural development in Europe and America. Meets and corresponds with W. E. B. Du Bois.
Oklahoma,	End of September: Max visits Oklahoma and Indian Territories and travels on to New Orleans and Tuskegee.
Knoxville,	October: Max and Marianne stay with relatives (Millers) in Knoxville and Mount Airy. Continue on to Washington, Philadelphia, and Baltimore.
Mount Airy,	End of October–early November: Harvard University library. Meets William James.
Boston,	November: Columbia University library. 19 November departure.
New York Heidelberg	November: Publishes Part One of "The Protestant Ethic and the 'Spirit' of Capitalism" in the *Archive*.
1905 Heidelberg	Weber starts learning Russian to follow the Russian Revolution in the newspapers. June: Part Two of "Protestant Ethic" published in *Archive*. November: Second essay on "Roscher and Knies and the Logical Problems of Historical Economics."
Mannheim	September: Attends Association of Social Policy, which debates "The Situation of Workers in the Private Giant Industries."
1906 Heidelberg	January: Publishes third and final essay on Roscher and Knies. February: "Critical Studies in the Logic of the Cultural Studies" published in the *Archive*. February: "The Situation of Constitutional Democracy in Russia" published in the *Archive* (also translated into Russian). April: Articles on churches and sects in North America published in *Frankfurter Zeitung* and *The Christian World*. August: Publishes "Russia's Transition to Pseudo-democracy" in the *Archive*.
Palermo, Sicily	October–November: Convalescent stay together with Marianne and Helene Weber in Sicily and Capri, Italy.
1907 Heidelberg	February: Publishes "Stammler's 'Overcoming' of the Materialist Conception of History" in the *Archive*.
Lake Como, Italy	March: Convalesces in Italian lakes accompanied by Marianne. Weber is prescribed opiate-derived drugs for continuing insomnia and depression. Weber uses long vacations to detoxify from drug regimen.
Heidelberg	July: First of four replies, published in the *Archive*, to the critical reviews of the *Protestant Ethic* written by the teacher Karl H. Fischer and the historian Felix Rachfahl. Last reply appeared in September 1910.
Oerlinghausen	July: Marianne and Max Weber attend the funeral of Carl David Weber in Oerlinghausen. Marianne inherits a seventh share of the family linen business.

(Continued)

Year	City	Important Events in Weber's Life
	Heidelberg	September: Weber pens long rejection letter of article submitted via Dr. Else Jaffé to the *Archive*. The article was written by Dr. Otto Gross, a proponent of libertarian psychoanalysis and anarchism.
1908	French and Italian Riviera	March and April: Convalescent trip.
	Jena, Thuringia, Germany	September: Weber participates in the Second Conference of German University Lecturers. Weber argues against political and religious discrimination in academic careers and for lecturers to adhere to the standards of academic knowledge.
	Oerlinghausen	September–October: Weber investigates the organization and attitudes of the workforce in linen industry. This research is published in four parts in the *Archive* over 1908–1909 as "The Psychophysics of Industrial Labor."
	Heidelberg	November: Weber attends a political meeting of the National Liberals. He argues for replacement of German imperial dynastic rule by parliamentary government on English and Belgian lines.
		December: Co-founder of the German Society for Sociology. Weber is treasurer until January 1911, and he resigns from society in January 1914.
1909	Heidelberg	January: Weber, after hesitation, finally signs with the publisher Paul Siebeck to become the lead editor in a completely new edition of *Schoenberg's Handbook of Political Economy*, which is renamed *Basic Outline of Social Economics*. The handbook was published in nine volumes from 1914 to 1930 with some forty authors. Weber's own contribution to the handbook was *Economy and Society*, which appeared posthumously in 1921–1922.
	Lake Maggiore, Italy	April: Convalescent trip.
	Heidelberg	June: Weber becomes associate member of the Heidelberg Academy of the Sciences.
		June: Weber criticizes the natural philosophy of the chemist Wilhelm Ostwald in the *Archive*.
	Vienna, Austro-Hungary	September: Attends Association of Social Policy conference, speaks in debates on enterprises and productivity, and mounts an attack with his brother Alfred on the bureaucratic serfdom of state socialism.
	Venice, Italy	October: Short trip with Marianne Weber and Edgar and Else Jaffé.
	Leipzig	October: Weber participates in the Third Conference of German University Lecturers and argues for open selection criteria for appointment of lecturers.

1910	Heidelberg	April: Max and Marianne move to the Fallenstein villa on the north bank of the Neckar. They hold their *jour fixe* on Sunday afternoons, where Karl Jaspers, Georg Lukács, Ernst Bloch, Friedrich Gundolf, and other luminaries attend.
	England	August–September: Convalescent trip.
	Frankfurt am Main	October: First German Society for Sociology conference. Weber outlines research project on the press.
	Heidelberg	December: Weber takes out defamation action against the lecturer Arnold Ruge. Multiple court cases were held over 1911 and 1912; Weber finally won his case, and Dr Ruge was removed from the university. Weber, however, was forced to withdraw from the press research project.
1911	Dresden, Saxony, Germany	October: Weber participates in the Fourth Conference for German University Lecturers. In debate Weber controversially attacks the malign influence of the Ministerial Director at the Prussian Ministry of Education, Friedrich Althoff.
1912	Bayreuth and Munich, Bavaria	August: The Webers attend Wagner concerts accompanied by the musician Mina Tobler. Later that autumn Weber starts his study on the sociology of music, which was posthumously published in 1921.
	Berlin	October: Weber participates in the Second Conference of the German Society for Sociology. The conference debates the sociology of nationality.
1913	Ascona, Tessin, Switzerland	March–April: Recuperation trip to fishing village on Lake Maggiore. Weber acts as legal advisor to Frieda Gross and her companion Ernst Frick, who is under investigation for terrorist offenses.
	Heidelberg	September: Weber publishes "On Some Categories of Interpretive Sociology" in *Logos*. October–November: Following discussion at the Association of Social Policy, Weber outlines his position on the place of value judgments in social science and social policy. This is published in expanded form in 1917 in the journal *Logos*.
1914	Ascona	March–April: Weber supports Frieda Gross in court cases brought by her father-in-law Dr. Hans Gross, the criminologist. Weber debates the limits of ethical goodness and Tolstoy with Ernst Frick.
	Heidelberg	June: First volume of *Outline of Social-Economics* appears. August: Start of World War One. Weber reports to duty as a reserve officer and is appointed captain with responsibilities for Baden military hospitals. Steps down in September 1915.

(Continued)

Year	City	Important Events in Weber's Life
1915	Heidelberg	June: Weber offers his publisher a series of essays, "The Economic Ethics of the World Religions." These appear from October 1915 to January 1920 in the *Archive*. They comprise the famous essays on Confucianism and Taoism, Hinduism and Buddhism, and ancient Judaism. They are accompanied by a crucial introduction and interlinking essay, "Intermediate Reflection."
	Brussels, Belgium	August: Weber sounds out the possibility of a job as an economic advisor with the occupying German government.
	Heidelberg	December: Weber publishes "Bismarck's Foreign Policy and the Present" in the *Frankfurter Zeitung*. It is the first of a series of newspaper articles highly critical of the German high command's conduct of the war and its control of the government.
1916	Heidelberg	February: "Between Two Laws" (those of Christian pacificism and patriotism) appears in the journal *The Woman*. Weber discusses Germany's responsibility before history.
	Berlin	February: Joins committee on economic integration of central European countries. March: Weber sends an opinion to eighteen leading parliamentarians pointing out the unacceptable risks of unrestricted submarine warfare.
	East Prussia	Easter: Weber travels with Lili Schäfer (his sister) to visit the grave of her husband, who was killed on the Eastern Front.
	Vienna and Budapest	May–June: Unofficial information-gathering trip on morale of Germany's wartime allies.
	Munich	October: Invited by the Progressive People's Party to give a lecture, "Germany among the European World Powers."
1917	Heidelberg	April to June: Weber publishes in the *Frankfurter Zeitung* a series of articles entitled "Parliament and Government under a New Political Order. Towards a Political Critique of Officialdom and the Party System."
	Lauenstein, Thuringia, Germany	May and September/October: Weber is a participant in conferences organized by the publisher Eugen Diederichs on the role of culture in the future of Germany.
	Vienna	October: Weber considers offers of professorial chairs. Gives lecture "Problems of the Sociology of the State."
	Munich	November: Gives lecture "Science as a Vocation" at the invitation of the Free Students Society. December: Publishes pamphlet "Suffrage and Democracy in Germany."

1918	Vienna	April to July: Guest professor at the university. Lectures on "Economy and Society. A Positive Critique of the materialist Conception of History."
		June: Gives lecture on socialism to officers of the Austro–Hungarian army.
	Munich	November: Gives a speech on "Germany's New Political Order" shortly before outbreak of German revolutions.
	Frankfurt am Main	November–December: Works with the *Frankfurter Zeitung* on articles on Germany's future state form.
		December: Weber becomes candidate for the Reichstag for the newly formed German Democratic Party. His candidature is unsuccessful.
	Berlin	December: Participant in informal talks on the new German constitution under the leadership of Hugo Preuß, secretary of state for the interior. Weber also participant in the General Economic Parliament.
	Heidelberg	Winter: Makes electoral speeches across the country supporting the German Democratic Party.
1919	Heidelberg	January: Marianne Weber elected representative for the Baden German Democratic Party at the Constitutional Convention.
	Munich	January: Weber gives lecture "Politics as a Vocation" on the invitation of the Free Students Society.
		Weber considers offers of professorial chairs from a number of universities.
	Heidelberg	February: Initial meeting in Weber's house of The Heidelberg Association for a Policy of Justice in respect to war guilt. The one-time Reich chancellor Prince Max von Baden attends.
		April: Weber is named professor for social science, economic history, and economics at the Ludwig-Maximilians-University, Munich.
	Berlin and Versailles	May–June: Advisor to the German peace delegation. Weber accepted the peace treaty but was personally most opposed to the admission of German war guilt.
		Weber tells General Ludendorff, as supreme commander, he should surrender himself to the Allies and carry personal responsibility for the conduct of the war.
	Munich	June: Moves to Munich and gives lecture course, "The Most Universal Categories of the Science of Society."
		August: Becomes a member of the Bavarian Academy of the Sciences.
		October: Helene Weber dies in Charlottenburg.
		Gives lecture course, "Outline of Universal Social and Economic History."

(Continued)

Year City	Important Events in Weber's Life
1920 Munich	January: Weber's lectures disrupted by right-wing, anti-Semitic students. Weber refuses the idea of a judicial pardon for Count Arco, who had assassinated the Bavarian socialist politician and one-time prime minister, Kurt Eisner. February–May: Weber corrects the proofs for volume 1 of the *Collected Essays on the Sociology of Religion* and *Economy and Society*. April: Weber resigns from committee of German Democratic Party because of the extent of its socialization policies. May–June: Lectures on the "General Theory of the State and Politics (Sociology of the State)" and "Socialism." 14 June: Weber dies from pneumonia. Funeral service held in Munich. His ashes are interred in Heidelberg cemetery.

INTRODUCTION

CHAPTER 1

....

MAX WEBER PAST, PRESENT, AND FUTURE

....

EDITH HANKE, LAWRENCE A. SCAFF, AND SAM WHIMSTER

MAX Weber is one of the most important figures in social thought and the human sciences over the past century. Active at the time the social sciences were founded, he contributed significantly to a wide range of academic specialties and disciplines: history and legal studies, social and historical economics, the new science of sociology, the scientific study of religion, political science and the study of complex organizations, methodology, and the philosophy of social science. For the international audience Weber is usually considered a German sociologist, especially because of the way his work was appropriated in the United States and selectively translated into English. However, his leading concepts and his ideas about topics like capitalism, modernity, state formation, bureaucracy, legitimacy, authority, leadership, world religions, academic knowledge, and processes of "rationalization" figure prominently not only in sociology but in a variety of fields of inquiry. In light of such extensive contributions and borrowings, his status as a "classic" has become assured, reinforced by the manifold ways in which his ideas have contributed to understanding our own modern world.

In the human sciences Weber's concepts and modes of explanation showed how comprehensive historical knowledge could be combined with precise structural and economic analysis. His writings demonstrated how individual action could be understood in the context of institutions, organizations, and the imperatives imposed by legal norms. His demand for "intellectual integrity" revealed a singular commitment to the pursuit of truth in scientific investigations and to grasping the difference between factual knowledge and evaluative positions. Intellectual integrity required a thoroughgoing reflexivity of the truth-seeker, a consciousness of the intellectual and cultural presuppositions of knowledge itself. In Weber's concise, self-conscious summation of this principled commitment, "scientific truth is only what *demands* to be true for all those who *want* truth."[1]

But Weber was far more than a founder of a discipline or a representative of scholarship and scientific expertise. The significance of his thought and engagements also extends to the general public discourse about the social and cultural dynamics that we experience today in modern life. As a "public intellectual" *avant la lettre*, Weber was a politically engaged citizen in the era of the Wilhelmine *Kaiserreich*. Beginning at an early age he became passionately involved in the political issues of the day through speeches, newspaper articles, and pamphlets addressed to a popular audience. Hardly any major concern escaped his attention, from competition among the great powers to social conflicts within Germany to the Russian Revolutions of 1905 and 1917. Fundamental issues of constitutional practice—freedom of belief and action, human rights, rule of law, citizenship, the suffrage—run through his commentaries. The cultural and political problems posed by the iron grip of capitalism became a special concern. Indeed, there was no more central theme for Weber than the nature and effects of modern capitalism itself, "the most fateful force in our modern life" in his famous phrase, a harbinger of things to come in our own age of "globalization."[2]

To appreciate the import of Weber's legacy, it is essential to capture his double role as an intellectual committed to both thought and practice, to pursuing scientific truth wherever it led, and to placing one's "hand on the wheel of history" with a responsibility for future generations.[3] So important to Weber himself and expressed forcefully in what may be considered his last testament in "Science as a Vocation" and "Politics as a Vocation," this double aspect has informed much of the subsequent discussion of his work and ideas. It lies at the center of the persistent fascination with the work and the person.

WEBER PAST AND PRESENT

The legacy of Weber's thought has a curious history. Because of the way the work was published, some of it posthumously, then translated into English, and subsequently received and incorporated into various disciplines, there has been a decades-long competition to interpret the work properly and systematically and to recover the elements considered to be its essential core, problematic, or meaning. It is no exaggeration to say that a bibliography of the multifaceted and often contentious literature expounding, analyzing, interpreting, and criticizing Weber's work would fill a massive volume. But this phase of debate may well have run its course, particularly with respect to the textual accuracy and ordering of Weber's writings. The allure of hermeneutics has begun to fade, and in its place a new interest has emerged in the application and extension of the Weberian legacy.

The present handbook investigates this new terrain of the Weberian legacy today. Our aim is to identify the enduring problems and themes associated with Weber's thought. We are less interested in interpreting his work as such, as important as that effort has been, than we are oriented toward posing the questions and exploring the disputes that delineate Weber's contributions to topics having contemporary significance. Such contributions and their underlying problematics comprise the contemporary Weberian project. The handbook should be read as an effort to define the scope and contours of that project, to map the intellectual terrain that scholars continue to explore in the Weberian tradition of inquiry. This terrain has a rich and varied empirical content, and it is global in scope. For this reason, some of the handbook contributions explore not only how Weber's ideas have been used and elaborated in a variety of contexts in different parts of the world but also how the Weberian approach can help illuminate in vastly different societies the kinds of social and political problems that we consider significant in our own time.

There are several considerations that encourage an expansive horizon for investigations inspired by Weber. First of all, among those considered "classics" in the formation of modern social thought, in our present century Weber appears to be the only thinker left standing, having produced a wide-ranging and compelling body of work that continues to inspire and to be appropriated in new contexts and unexpected ways. Standing as a "classic" requires a certain timelessness and sense of general validation in the present. Can Max Weber still say something important to us as an accomplished and timely analyst of modern society and the culture of modernity? What are the topics, problems, or themes in his work that we can learn from, appropriate, and elaborate? What kind of questioning or problematic does his work invite us to consider? In what respects can his thinking seem current and alive to us in the present?

Finding answers to these questions has been given a major assist by the editing and publication of Weber's collected works, the *Max Weber-Gesamtausgabe* (*MWG*), now approaching completion at forty-seven volumes and consisting of his published works, unfinished manuscripts, complete correspondence, and previously unpublished lecture notes. A formidable undertaking begun nearly forty-five years ago, the *MWG* provides for the first time a definitive historical-critical edition of the entire range of his thinking and engagements, not only a basis for a comprehensive account of his life and work but also a resource for moving beyond textual reconstruction and interpretation to new applications and possible extensions of the ideas. Aspects of Weber's thought that were previously hidden can now be explored for their thematic relevance and brought to bear on pressing problems that he may only have anticipated or not perceived at all as urgent and immediate. Finding extensions and applications of Weber's ideas is an important indication of its capacity for renewal, which is always a test for the enduring strength of a body of thought.

As work on this handbook proceeded and manuscripts arrived, we were impressed by the way in which many authors, while exploring new uses and applications, nevertheless returned to Weber's texts as a point of departure. It appeared to many that his work could be approached as an invitation to new readings, a return to original sources, both to confirm previous conceptions and to discover novel possibilities, as befits a true classic having contemporary relevance. With this research practice in mind, we have systematically cited the *MWG* for all references to Weber's work and correspondence in the original German. The texts of the *MWG* must now be considered the standard source, and they should also become the authoritative basis for all new translations of the work.

The *MWG*, in particular the ten volumes of letters, has enabled a more accurate chronology of Weber's life. A handbook is not the place to indulge in biography, but our authoritative chronology will allow the reader to reference the major events in Weber's busy and often turbulent life and the dating of his complex oeuvre.

Existing translations in English that we also reference have their own peculiar compositional history that is worth bearing in mind. There are many examples. Citing only a few, the early well-known translation of "Class, Status, Party" is not a stand-alone essay but a section in *Economy and Society*, which is itself only one part of the multivolume *Grundriss der Sozialökonomik* or *Basic Outline of Social Economics* that Weber coordinated as general editor.[4] The same can be said for the extended essay commonly referred to as Weber's "sociology of law," which is actually another focused investigation in *Economy and Society* of the topic he called *The Developmental Conditions of the Law*.[5] Or the "Author's Preface" (*Vorbemerkung*) is an introduction not to *The Protestant Ethic and the Spirit of Capitalism*, as it appears in translation, but to the three-volume *Collected Essays on the Sociology of Religion* (*Gesammelte Aufsätze zur Religionssoziologie*) that Weber brought together and that was published posthumously in 1920.[6] Similarly, a text like the well-known work on China is not a freestanding book about Chinese civilization but instead a specific part of the comparative studies in the "Economic Ethics of the World Religions," as is the mistitled *The Religion of India*.[7] These are not minor details, but considered as a whole they suggest the importance of reconsidering original sources and reorienting our understanding of Weber's contributions in light of the most current historical-critical scholarship.

Interest in Weber's ideas is only likely to grow because of the situation and emergent conditions of the twenty-first century. Boldly stated, following the end of the short twentieth century, from the outbreak of war in 1914 to the dissolution of the Soviet Union in 1991, many significant problems of Weber's era have begun to re-emerge and dominate public discussion. The most obvious examples are resurgent nationalism and a questioning of capitalism in its current globalized incarnation. But there are many others. What used to be called the "social question" has reappeared in the debate over growing income inequality, the decline of the middle class, and inequalities of class, status, and gender. Global neoliberal economic policy has moved the world away from the post-1945 social consensus and closer to the "gilded age" of Weber's era. Religious conflict, problems posed by migration and immigration, challenges defined by ethnicity and race are as present now as they were then. World politics turns on competition among the great powers, the challenge of a new rising power (China today instead of Germany then), the threat of sleepwalking into a violent confrontation leading to total war, and challenges to nation-state sovereignty and the uncertain prospects for collective security and regional integration.[8] Resonance with the world prior to 1914 has become unmistakable. Astute observers have even noted parallels to the mood of public indifference and denial of threats to social order in an era of relative peace, prosperity, and rapid technological change like that of the previous century.

In such a context it is hardly surprising that Weber's thought has become timely. The thought has many potential uses and applications. Indeed, thinking *with* Weber and his concepts, borrowing the phrasing of one of our authors,[9] can be understood to offer a promising mode of orientation and application to problems *we* face. The handbook is an invitation to explore in the present day the possibilities in such a proposal.

WEBERIAN THEMATICS

In the social sciences it has become commonplace to speak of a "Weberian" or "neo-Weberian" approach, viewpoint, or perspective. But how can we define the field of inquiry set forth in Weber's thought and explored by those who have followed his lead? How should we think about the contours of the Weberian legacy? What exactly is a Weberian perspective?

These questions can be answered in two quite different ways. One suggestive general answer is found in the notion of a distinctive Weberian "paradigm" for inquiry, a view adumbrated by, among others, M. Rainer Lepsius.[10] In his concise appraisal, Weberian analysis is oriented toward the interaction among three dimensions of the social world: the social action of individual actors, the "structural" forms through which action is directed and coordinated, and the configurations of "meaning" produced by social action. The focus on the individual level opens the way for consideration of the conditions under which "rational" action can occur, a central feature of Weberian analysis. Structural forms include the organizations, associations, regulations, social formations, and "rules of the game" that shape all social life. Configurations of meaning refer to the "values," systems of belief, and cultural norms present in all societies.

These three dimensions interact with each other, and for purposes of understanding and explanation, no single dimension has priority or is reducible to any of the others. Their complex interaction provides the "inner dynamic" of the Weberian perspective, which some have also characterized as alert to multiple types of causes and multiple levels of explanation. As Lepsius correctly insists, the analytic interest is always directed toward understanding *processes* and *relations*, as indicated by the attention Weber himself gives to the processes of forming associations or "sociation" (*Vergesellschaftung*) and forming communal and social relationships (*Vergemeinschaftung*). It is these processes and relations of coming together with others, of forming interpersonal, group, and collective relationships, to which Weberian analysis is oriented, rather than to reified abstractions like "society" and "community" or "nation" and "nationalism." This analytic orientation is one of the most fundamental and distinctive aspects of Weberian sociology. Neither society nor the individual is a given; instead, their inherent relationality has to be grasped through the interpretation of complexes of meaning.

With respect to the concept of "rationality" and its specification in a process of "rationalization," Weber always stipulates the context. Rationality is not a singular entity with essential properties. When he writes about "the specific and peculiar 'rationalism' of Western culture [*Kultur*]," Weber immediately notes the ambiguity of the phrase.[11] Rationalism is a "historical concept" referencing many different kinds of configurations, containing a "world of contradictions" within itself. "Rationality" and "irrationality" are contested categories; or, in Weber's words, "what is 'rational' from one point of view may well be 'irrational' from another."[12] The process of rationalization can only be clarified by asking, what is the value-sphere or the order of life in which a particular kind of rationalization occurs, and what direction does it take? In any given social setting, rationalization processes in very different spheres—such as the law, technological know-how, economic life, politics, or religious beliefs—can occur alongside each other, and their directions can contradict each other and vie for dominance. The task of Weberian analysis is to investigate the social and historical determinants, the carriers, outcomes, and consequences of these conflicting processes.

Viewed in this way, the advantage of the Weberian "paradigm" is that its analytic perspectives can be applied to the most varied kinds of problems, situations, and configurations—historical, contemporary, comparative, and cross-cultural. It offers portable tools (such as the methodology of the "ideal type") and "model problems" for thinking (such as the thesis about the relationship between economic action and religious beliefs set forth in *The Protestant Ethic*). These are abstracted from the work and applicable in other contexts, which in the contested field of ideas and interests become relevant and demand investigation. The analysis is configurational, searching for explanations in the "concatenation" or "combination of circumstances" that contributed to a particular outcome.[13] The factors at play might be "material" interests or "ideal" interests or some combination of the two.[14] The point of an investigation is always to analyze and assess circumstances and factors, not to apply a presupposed explanatory schema.

There is a second, alternative approach to answering our questions, one that invites thinking not about analytic tools but about designating the problem areas, questions, and hypotheses identified in the work itself, providing a kind of mapping of the terrain of Weberian inquiry. In his mature writings Weber himself provided the most important signposts. One important exposition is the categories proposed in the "Intermediate Reflection" or "Zwischenbetrachtung," the well-known text placed at the end of the first volume of the *Collected Essays on the Sociology of Religion*. Using the universal ethics of "brotherliness" in salvation religion as a point of departure, the discussion proceeds as a delineation of the life orders or value-spheres characteristic of human experience. Juxtaposed to religion and the moral order are kinship and family, the economy, politics, aesthetics, sexuality and the erotic life, and the sphere of intellectual knowledge and science. Weber emphasizes that these orders and the values associated with them are in conflict with each other. They generate tensions and contradictions that permeate social life. Looking outward from within a single discrete order, the others will likely appear as a threat, a test of resolve, or even a negation of primary values that must never be compromised. Acceptance of a differentiated and fragmented world, one split into life orders and their respective values, is itself a challenge.

The other suggestive statement appears in the thematic framework for *Economy and Society*, where Weber shifts the analytic starting point from religion to the economy. The most comprehensive version of the distinct orders central to his inquiry is the original outline from 1914 for the proposed section of the *Basic Outline of Social Economics*

(*Grundriss der Sozialökonomik*) entitled "The Economy and the Social Orders and Powers," a précis of the text he *intended* to write, which became the unfinished work known as *Economy and Society*. The original outline reads as follows[15]:

1. Categories of the orders of society
    Economy and law in their primary relationship
    The economic relations of associations (*Verbände*) in general
2. Household, *oikos*, and enterprise (*Betrieb*)
3. Neighborhood association, kinship group, local community
4. Ethnic relationships of community (*ethnische Gemeinschaftsbeziehungen*)
5. Religious communities
    Class conditioning of religion
    The world religions and economic attitudes (*Kulturreligionen und Wirtschaftsgesinnung*)
6. Formation of market relationships (*Marktvergemeinschaftung*)
7. The political association
    Developmental conditions of the law
    Status groups (*Stände*), classes, parties
    The nation
8. Rulership, domination, authority (*Herrschaft*)
    a. The three types of legitimate authority
    b. Political and hierocratic authority
    c. Non-legitimate rulership
        Typology of cities
    d. The development of the modern state
    e. Modern political parties

These are substantive topics and themes, building blocks in the architecture of Weber's thinking, always shaped by comparative, historical, and universal perspectives. They underscore the extent to which Weber's approach is oriented toward processes and relational and developmental conditions. The inquiry is not oriented toward complex abstractions or entities, such as "society" as a reality sui generis, but rather toward processes and relations that constitute the formation of social relationships.

In this thematic outline one aspect of the work is omitted, which is crucial for the "Intermediate Reflection," namely Weber's engagement with problems of knowledge and science or *Wissenschaft*—that is, all rational inquiry and the pursuit of knowledge. The basic outline can be completed by adding the methodological principles, topics in the philosophy of social science, and reflections on the scientific vocation that are part of the foundation of knowledge and belong to the order of scientific inquiry itself. Weber was often consumed by such issues, particularly when confronted with questions about education and the conditions of modern science as organized in the modern university and research institute. Taking the themes from the *Zwischenbetrachtung* and combining them with the original outline for *Economy and Society* produces a synthesis of the main categories defining the Weberian field of inquiry: economy, power relations, stratification, community relations (kinship, neighborhood, ethnicity, nation), religion, law, culture (art, music, expression, sensibility, identity), and knowledge (science, technology, communications media).

These two approaches to understanding the Weberian perspective or legacy are completely compatible, for each denotes different ways of thinking about the nature of Weberian analysis and how to proceed. On the one hand, Weber provides us with an array of investigatory tools and modes of analysis; and, on the other, he directs us to specific and substantive areas of social reality which become the focus for study. In this handbook we have aimed for clarity and consistency regarding the paradigmatic features of Weberian thought, and we have then used the main categories of the field of inquiry as an organizing framework for our exposition of major sections and individual chapters.

TOPICS AND PROBLEMS

In Part One, "The Economy: Capitalism in a Globalized World," the authors explore the topic that surely occupied Weber more than any other: the problems of capitalism and its origins, different forms, socioeconomic dynamics, political and cultural consequences, and prospects. The only major competitor to the universal significance of capitalism in his overall thinking is the comparative study of salvation religions. Yet even Weber's studies of the world religions were guided to a great extent by the question of the relationship between different religious ethics and the presence or absence of capitalism. A special German fascination, as Hinnerk Bruhns notes in quoting Weber's friend and colleague Friedrich Naumann, the destiny of capitalism always returned for questioning.

Notwithstanding the emphasis on capitalism, the discussion of Weber's views has suffered a peculiar fate, often distorted by a reading of *The Protestant Ethic and the Spirit of Capitalism* as a "cultural" explanation of the rise of capitalism in the West that is represented as Weber's essential position. In a letter to Heinrich Rickert in 1905, Weber himself understood it as an essay in cultural history, "a kind of 'spiritualistic' construction of the modern economy" and "*modern occupational culture*."[16] The essay was not a historical analysis of the material side of modern capitalism. He promised the readers of the *The Protestant Ethic* he would take up the material origins of modern capitalism—the economic history and class and state formation—at a later date. The promise was fulfilled in the last decade of his life through his engagement with social economics. The overarching purpose of the discussion in this section, then, is to rebalance the received views while using Weber's thinking to investigate different dimensions of the problems of capitalism, such as the complexities in the tripartite division of labor (technical, social, and economic), the neoliberal economic order, money and finance, the development of law, and social and environmental challenges to global capitalism. Especially pertinent in this regard is the retrieval and application of Weber's version of "social economics" as set forth in the overlooked second chapter of *Economy and Society*, "The Basic Sociological Categories of the Economy," an essential text that establishes the basic terminology and outlook of Weberian economic analysis.

The chapters in Part Two, "Society and Social Structure," turn our attention to important aspects of Weberian analysis that investigate problems of social stratification according to class and status, processes of group formation, the nature of civil society and citizenship, and technologically driven forces (such as the new "social media") that affect associational activity. These problems can be addressed comparatively in historical and cross-cultural contexts, as the chapter on the Ottoman Empire and modern Turkey demonstrates. Whatever the particular setting, in this part of his work Weber was always interested not only in the sources of social conflict but also in the social construction of "life chances" and processes of "selection" favoring some groups and personality types over others. Such concerns had to do fundamentally with the distribution of power, with relations of super- and subordination in social life, which are central to the analysis of the structures of corporate power and elites in contemporary globalized capitalism. These relations were important not only for explaining power and the patterns of associative life or *Vergesellschaftung* but because they helped answer the crucial question: what type of individual is favored and produced by a particular type of social structure? Weber placed confidence in the discipline of self, now updated to the "practices of the self." But this important issue becomes increasingly difficult where the contours of civil society and vocational calling are being increasingly redrawn and even destabilized.

Weber's writings on economy and society contained a strong political element, in the specific sense that in his economics and sociology he was unusually alert to struggles for competitive advantage and disparities in power, the means of control or domination, and their sociocultural consequences. Part Three, "Politics and the State," addresses this important dimension of Weberian analysis. At the center of this discussion is Weber's well-known typology of domination or authority (*Herrschaft*) and the subsequent elaboration of his categories of charisma, legality, and tradition, especially in relation to problems of legitimacy and state formation. Much of the development of political sociology and comparative politics has relied upon this fundamental point of departure. With regard to Weber's celebrated definition of the state as the legitimate monopoly of violence within a bounded territory, it is of course the case that many "states" fall far short of this definition. There are territories without states and states which have not yet secured the legitimate control of violence. Nevertheless, Weber's definition stands as a teleological aspiration, and the achievement of full statehood will involve complex and conflictual patterns of association and socialization. Globalization does not detract from statehood, for state sovereignty is the building block of international treaties. Federalism, parliamentary rule, and democratization were central to Weber as a *Homo politicus*; and these processes operate simultaneously within and beyond the territorial state.

For Weber as citizen, free political parties, universal and equal suffrage, and the accountability of the executive to parliament were indispensable to the legitimacy of the state and the destiny of the nation. Crucial for political practice was also the long-standing question of the relationship between politics and ethics, the distinction between an ethic of conviction and an ethic of responsibility which falls so onerously on the mature political leader. Weber was in despair about the Germany of his day where for institutional reasons these attributes had yet to be developed, and he sketched an alternative model of politics in which a direct emotional bond is created by the plebiscitary leader with the masses, an alternative which he regarded as inferior to representative democracy. Demagogy and today's "post-truth" politics characterize a new Caesarism which seeks to create a competing legitimate order.

Part Four, "Ethics and Religion," has the largest number of chapters in the handbook and for good reason: it includes the comparative sociology of religion that Weber initiated with *The Protestant Ethic and the Spirit of Capitalism* and its sections on the Protestant sects and then extended to the religions of China and India (Confucianism, Taoism, Buddhism, Hinduism), ancient Judaism, and commentary along the way on Catholicism, Islam, religion in Japan, and ancient Christianity. This work was left unfinished. Weber wanted to write independent studies of Islam and Christianity as a whole but managed only suggestive, scattered remarks. The Weberian perspective thus generates seemingly open-ended lines of inquiry aiming to fill the gaps in his account or to elaborate and correct his discussion in light of new evidence and recent scholarship. These lines of inquiry are about not only world religions and world civilizations but also ethics in general, belief systems, and the forces of secularization in the modern world. Weber's thesis of "disenchantment," or more literally "de-magic-ation" (*Entzauberung*), and the possibilities for "re-enchantment" in modernity is an essential theme in the many controversies his work has provoked.

One important controversy has to do with the nature of ethics in the modern world. Disenchantment and its discontented world assume the collapse of belief in the possibility of salvation grounded in religion. Today the "Protestant ethic" of Weberian fame is transposed to ethics without the force of religion, and ethical conduct becomes an attribute of ascribed identity or impersonal professional vocation. Modern industrial and finance capitalism can embody an "ethic" by virtue of formal and rational rules, departure from which results in corporate malfeasance. In the sphere of organized religion, a church like the modern Catholic Church, which in Weber's sense is a *Gnadenanstalt* or "compulsory association for the administration of grace,"[17] finds itself forced to adapt papal authority and obligatory morality to secular pluralism and demands for freedom of conscience, as with the reforms of Vatican II. In modern culture as a whole, the hollowing out of public meaning and the erosion of a binding ethic create the conditions for a romanticism of highly individualized and rarified personal expression and asserted meaning.

The Weberian analysis of "culture," the subject of Part Five, has always presented a challenge. One important reason is ambiguity in the term *Kultur*, which can refer to symbolic forms of meaningful expression or "webs of significance," in Clifford Geertz's memorable phrase,[18] as well as to the material accomplishments and practices of civilization and "civilized" living. Culture, as Weber once said, is a "value concept" that can lead us either to inquire into subjective meanings, sometimes associated with a distinctive style of life (*Lebensstil*) and way of conducting one's life (*Lebensführung*), or to investigate the objective contents of cultural expression, such as painting, music, drama, literature, and architecture. In his own work Weber contributed in both ways: *The Protestant Ethic and the Spirit of Capitalism* establishes the direction for any discussion of the fundamental properties of *Lebensführung* and its implications, while Weber's pathbreaking (and unfinished) study of music opens a passage into a cross-cultural history and sociology of art. Weber once even wrote his editor, Paul Siebeck, that he wanted to submit a manuscript on "a sociology of the *contents* of culture (art, literature, world-views [*Weltanschauung*],"[19] a project barely begun and one that Weberian cultural history and sociology continues to pursue in a lineage that runs through Karl Mannheim to Pierre Bourdieu.

Considering music alone, the cultural sphere of Weber's deepest engagement, it is important to note that in his view the "rationalization" of occidental harmony was a specific site of Western cultural uniqueness. The emergence of a distinctive "rational" harmonics provided a window onto his larger thesis about the unique "rationalism" of Western culture announced in the prefatory remarks to the *Collected Essays on the Sociology of Religion*. It is this putative uniqueness of the Occident, explained as a distinctive form of rationalism, that has provoked considerable ongoing debate about similar processes in other civilizations, alleged "multiple modernities," the construction of an existential culture as an antidote to pervasive alienation, or the persistence of tradition itself. The central Weberian problems of *Kultur*—What is the distinguishing characteristic of the Occident? What led to the breakout of ubiquitous traditionalism? What is the fate of modern subjectivist culture?—have remained urgent, open-ended subjects of inquiry.

Part Six, "Science and Knowledge," is a suitable final section as it addresses some of the important features of Weber's personally most cherished sphere of action: *Wissenschaft*, the realm of the intellect, the pursuit of knowledge, and the life of the mind. In "Science as a Vocation," Weber suggested the subject be divided into two parts: the outward institutional features that facilitate but also constrain the pursuit of knowledge and the "inner" meaning of the quest. Weberian inquiry has to some extent followed his lead, investigating the politics of the intellectuals and the modern educational "enterprise," while also confronting the problem of the "value" of science, especially in an age in which to possess knowledge is to possess power and means of control. Weber embraced an unequivocal position about knowledge and science: clear-eyed "realism" about the world, defense of a particular kind of "objectivity" in science, demands for "value-freedom" and "intellectual integrity," and critique of the search for an elusive but present "reality." His position remains provocative and timely in an age, reminiscent of his own, where expert knowledge and science can too often be willfully ignored.

Considering the vicissitudes of publication for a project extending over nearly three years, some topics that we intended to cover unfortunately dropped out of the original outline. No doubt more could be said about the law and legal issues, the professions and professional associations, the idea of *Lebensführung* (conduct of life) as an analytic category, the sources and forms of inequality, ecological perspectives and environmental sociology, the media and modern means of communication, and various aspects of the world's major religions. Such topics are mentioned in the chapters that follow, but in view of the complexities and reach of Weberian inquiry, there will always be space for more comprehensive coverage and new horizons to explore.

THE WEBERIAN FUTURE

Work and thought that have been regarded as "Weberian" in western Europe and North America owe their imprimatur in large part to the English-language translation, reception, and propagation of Weber's texts, concepts, and main ideas, a situation that persisted to the end of the twentieth century. This circumstance concealed a more complex reality, however, because of a parallel contemporaneous history in Japan, where starting in the 1920s Weber was also read, translated, and absorbed in equal measure. Until recently, linguistic barriers and the dominance of English internationally worked against acknowledging and understanding such parallel histories. But this limiting perspective has begun to change with the global reach of intellectual exchange and translations other than English, perhaps symbolized most strikingly by the recent publication of numerous Weber texts in Chinese. No longer confined to intellectual circles with access to the original German or English sources, the Weberian project has taken flight into the arena of international, multilingual discourse. The theme has become "Max Weber worldwide" in an era of crisis and fundamental change.[20]

The vitality of Weberian analysis and its promise for the future is linked to its global appropriation in new settings and its capacity to make sense of the crises provoked by global capitalism and the cultures of modernity. The Weberian method requires the selection of an issue and its framing so as to impute adequate causation to events and processes. At its grandest, the method always produces an answer but one inevitably open to further questioning: Why was the Occident able to break the hold of traditionalism? How were the millennial structures of the provision of wants, of hierarchy, and of belief transformed into the contortions of rules, abstract formalism, calculation, and the shell of modern capitalism—a transition brokered by a nascent finance capitalism? And what happens when the shell cracks and falls apart? Professional life conduct, economic ethics, rational business calculation, citizenship and the accompanying protection of an impartial and efficient civil service, representative democracy, responsible leadership (all of which belong to the Weberian model of civil society and state relations) give way to non-liberal alternatives that are also prefigured in Weber's writings. Productive capitalism succumbs to rentier capitalism, professional ethics to predatory behavior, calculation to recklessness, parliamentary democracy to plebiscitary leader direct democracy and demagogy. State bureaucracy is hollowed out, and citizenship and universal equal suffrage are regressed. We should expect that the rising trend to direct plebiscitary democracy and the cult of the strong leader, along with the weakening of representative democracy, virtually worldwide phenomena, are now attracting the attention of Weberian analysis.

While there is a global diffusion of Weber's ideas, we must still ask whether the conditions of globalization have taken us beyond Weberian models. The question is posed most obviously by information and computer technology and the dominance of social media over older communication technologies, a development Weber with his fascination for modern media of communication could not have envisaged. Yet the growth of these technologies exemplifies the Weberian theory of rationalization, which remains the master explanation of societal process. Indeed, the leading edge of rationalization is the institutionalized embedding of *Zweckrationalität*, the concept of a purposive ends-oriented instrumental rationality that anchors much of Weberian social theory. Can social theory articulate a coherent macro-theory relating the different life orders—economic, political, cultural—in such a way as to master the apparently unstoppable march of technocratic instrumental rationality? Are we destined to be able only to particularize the devastating consequences of human-caused climate change, for example, or to describe a modernity that is expanding its appetite for victims? There could not be a more urgent call to arms for the Weberian public intellectual.

We associate Weber with a "science of reality" and the imperative to give intellectual shape and order to the situation of the day, even though global modernity is a process that started far back in the nineteenth century, to think of the first technologies that interlinked the globe. Imbued with historical consciousness, intellectuals can feel trapped between the traditional and the modern, between a sacred past and a profane present, or between the "magic garden" of a mythic enchanted world and the disenchanting realities brought about by scientific-technological change. But the sense of continuing crisis offers opportunities, such as projecting Weberian modes of thinking into new global settings, from Brazil to China. Innovative cross-national and cross-cultural networks have already begun to form that point to unexpected possibilities for retrieval, renewal, and redefining of the Weberian project.[21] Perhaps, indeed, in the global setting we should resurrect the encyclopedism of Weber's environmentally aware *Grundriss* project.

Reflecting on problems with Weber, the man with a passion for thinking, is itself not new. But thinking with him about current problems, recently revealed, offers interesting and novel possibilities, as does the application of Weberian thought to established fields of scholarship where his ideas find resonance and can offer new perspectives. Consider, for example, the uses of Weberian "realism" in international relations or the exploration of Weberian insights to understand legal aspects of European integration, the nature of central banking and modern finance, or the emerging field of environmental sociology.[22] These kinds of inquiries and similar efforts are in an early stage. We can expect them to develop and expand as Weber's concepts and the Weberian corpus are used to ask different questions and to articulate novel perspectives. "The light shed by the great cultural problems has moved on," citing Weber's imagery; and inquiry finds new standpoints "to contemplate the stream of events from the summits of thought."[23]

We should remember too that it is not only the intellectual advocating "integrity" and a search for "historical truth" but also the passionate engaged Weber who has continued to fascinate and provoke. In Brazil, one of our authors has noted, during the presidency of Fernando Henrique Cardoso, "Weberianism...dominated politics."[24] If asserted only once, this is still a remarkable claim. Can there be a Weberian praxis worthy of public attention, one that comes to terms with the age-old conundrum of the relations between politics and ethics, between humankind and the world? Only by peering with foresight, imagination, and theoretical innovation into a darkening future might we be able to answer the pressing questions of how we shall conduct our lives and understand and control a global modernity.

Notes

1. "Denn wissenschaftliche Wahrheit ist nur, was für alle gelten *will*, die Wahrheit *wollen*." [Translation in text is the editors'.] Max Weber, "The 'Objectivity' of Knowledge in Social Science and Social Policy," in Max Weber, *Collected Methodological Writings*, ed. H. H. Bruun and S. Whimster, trans. H. H. Brunn (London: Routledge, 2012), 121 (hereafter *CMW*); *Zur Logik und Methodik der Sozialwissenschaften. Schriften 1900–1907, Max Weber-Gesamtausgabe* (hereafter *MWG*) I/7, ed. G. Wagner with C. Härpfer et al. (Tübingen, Germany: Mohr [Siebeck], 2018), 193.

2. Max Weber, *The Protestant Ethic and the Spirit of Capitalism*, trans. T. Parsons (New York: Scribner's, 1930), 17 (hereafter *PESC*); "Vorbemerkung," *Die protestantische Ethik und der Geist des Kapitalismus/Die protestantischen Sekten und der Geist des Kapitalismus. Schriften 1904–1920, MWG* I/18, ed. W. Schluchter with U. Bube (Tübingen, Germany: Mohr [Siebeck], 2016), 105.

3. Max Weber, "Politics as a Vocation," in *From Max Weber: Essays in Sociology*, ed. H. H. Gerth and C. W. Mills (New York: Oxford University Press, 1946), 115 (hereafter *FMW*); *Wissenschaft als Beruf 1917/1919—Politik als Beruf 1919, MWG* I/17, ed. W. J. Mommsen and W. Schluchter with B. Morgenbrod (Tübingen, Germany: Mohr [Siebeck], 1992), 227.

4. See "Class, Status, Party" in *FMW*, 180–195; "'Klassen,' 'Stände' und 'Parteien,'" in *Wirtschaft und Gesellschaft. Die Wirtschaft und die gesellschaftlichen Ordnungen und Mächte. Nachlaß. Gemeinschaften, MWG* I/22-1, ed. W. J. Mommsen with M. Meyer (Tübingen, Germany: Mohr [Siebeck], 2001), 252–272.

5. See *Max Weber on Law in Economy and Society*, ed. M. Rheinstein, trans. E. Shils and M. Rheinstein (New York: Simon and Schuster, 1967); *Wirtschaft und Gesellschaft. Nachlaß. Recht, MWG* I/22-3, ed. W. Gephart and S. Hermes (Tübingen, Germany: Mohr [Siebeck], 2010).

6. *PESC*, 13–31; *MWG* I/18, 101–121.

7. See *The Religion of China: Confucianism and Taoism*, trans. and ed. H. H. Gerth (New York: Free Press, 1951); *Die Wirtschaftsethik der Weltreligionen. Konfuzianismus und Taoismus. Schriften 1915–1920, MWG* I/19, ed. H. Schmidt-Glintzer with P. Kolonko (Tübingen, Germany: Mohr [Siebeck], 1989), 128–478 (chapters on China; the volume also contains the "Introduction" and the "Intermediate Reflection"). See also *The Religion of India, The Sociology of Hinduism and Buddhism*, trans. and ed. H. H. Gerth and D. Martindale (Glencoe, IL: Free Press, 1958); *Die Wirtschaftsethik der Weltreligionen. Hinduismus und Buddhismus. 1916–1920, MWG* I/20, ed. H. Schmidt-Glintzer with K.-H. Golzio (Tübingen, Germany: Mohr [Siebeck], 1996).

8. See the chapters in *Alte Begriffe—Neue Probleme*, ed. Thomas Schwinn and Gert Albert (Tübingen, Germany: Mohr Siebeck, 2016).

9. Joshua Derman, *Max Weber in Politics and Social Thought: From Charisma to Canonization* (Cambridge: Cambridge University Press, 2012), 4–9.

10. M. Rainer Lepsius, "Eigenart and Potenzial des Weber-Paradigmas," in *Das Weber-Paradigma. Studien zur Weiterentwicklung von Max Webers Forschungsprogramm*, ed. G. Albert et al. (Tübingen, Germany: Mohr Siebeck, 2003), 32–41.

11. *PESC*, 26; *MWG* I/18, 116 (translation modified according to the original).

12. *PESC*, 26, 78, 194n9; *MWG* I/18, 116, 159n32, 208.

13. The phrase in the "Vorbemerkung," *PESC*, 13; *MWG* I/18, 101.

14. A reference to one of Weber's most quoted passages: "It is interests (material and ideal), and not ideas, which have directly governed the actions of human beings. But the 'world-views' that have been created by ideas have very often, like switches, decided the lines on which the dynamic of interests has propelled behaviour." "Introduction to the Economic Ethics of the World Religions," in *The Essential Weber: A Reader*, ed. S. Whimster (London: Routledge, 2004), 69; *MWG* I/19, 101.

15. *Grundriss der Sozialökonomik. I. Abteilung. Wirtschaft und Wirtschaftswissenschaft* (Tübingen, Germany: Mohr [Siebeck], 1914), x–xi; reprinted in Max Weber, *Wirtschaft und Gesellschaft. Entstehungsgeschichte und Dokumente*, *MWG* I/24, ed. W. Schluchter (Tübingen, Germany: Mohr [Siebeck], 2009), 168–169.

16. Weber to Rickert, April 2, 1905: *Briefe 1903–1905*, *MWG* II/4, ed. G. Hübinger and M. R. Lepsius, with T. Gerhards and S. Oßwald-Bargende (Tübingen, Germany: Mohr [Siebeck], 2015), 448 (editors' emphasis).

17. For Weber's well-known distinction between "church" and "sect," see "The Protestant Sects and the Spirit of Capitalism," in *FMW*, 314; *MWG* I/18, 517.

18. Clifford Geertz, *The Interpretation of Cultures* (New York: Basic Books, 1973), 5.

19. Weber to Paul Siebeck, December 30, 1913, in *Briefe 1913–1914*, *MWG* II/8, ed. M. R. Lepsius and W. J. Mommsen, with B. Rudhard and M. Schön (Tübingen, Germany: Mohr [Siebeck], 2003), 450.

20. See Edith Hanke, "Max Weber weltweit, Zur Bedeutung eines Klassikers in Zeiten des Umbruchs," in *Europäische Wissenschaftskulturen und politische Ordnungen in der Moderne (1870–1970)*, ed. G. Hübinger (Munich: Oldenbourg, 2014), 285–305; "Max Weber in Zeiten des Umbruchs," in *Max Weber in der Welt. Rezeption und Wirkung*, ed. M. Kaiser and H. Rosenbach (Tübingen, Germany: Mohr Siebeck, 2014), 1–21; and "Max Weber Worldwide: The Reception of a Classic in Times of Change," *Max Weber Studies* 16, no. 1 (2016): 70–88.

21. See Victor Strazzeri, "What Comes Next in the Global Max Weber Reception? Call for Participation in the *Young Weber Scholars* Network," *Max Weber Studies* 16, no. 1 (2016): 89–99; also the articles by Stefan Leder (the Arab world), Alexandre Toumarkine (Turkey), Haggag Ali (Egypt), Dittmar Dahlmann (Russia), Marta Bucholc (Poland), and Wolfgang Schwentker (Japan), in *Max Weber in der Welt*, 23–63, 81–143.

22. See *Max Weber and International Relations*, ed. R. N. Lebow (Cambridge: Cambridge University Press, 2017); Andreas Grimmel, *Europäische Integration im Kontext des Rechts* (Wiesbaden, Germany: Springer VS, 2013), esp. chap. 4; Jocelyn Pixley, Sam Whimster, and Shaun Wilson, "Central Bank Independence: A Social Economic and Democratic Critique," *The Economic and Labour Relations Review* 24, no. 1 (2013): 32–50; John B. Foster and Hannah Holleman, "Weber and the Environment: Classical Foundations for a Postexemptionalist Sociology," *American Journal of Sociology* 117, no. 6 (2012): 1625–1673.

23. Weber, "The 'Objectivity' of Knowledge," in *CMW*, 138; *MWG* I/7, 234.

24. Sérgio da Mata, "Modernity as Fate or as Utopia: Max Weber's Reception in Brazil," *Max Weber Studies* 16, no. 1 (2016): 63.

PART I

THE ECONOMY: CAPITALISM IN A GLOBALIZED WORLD

....

CHAPTER 2

ECONOMICS AND SOCIETY AND THE FATE OF LIBERAL CAPITALISM

....

SAM WHIMSTER

WEBER AS A LIBERAL ECONOMIST
....

MAX Weber wrote and taught as an economist throughout his working life. His first post as professor involved teaching theoretical economics and the applied subjects of banking, finance, agrarian economics, and industrial policy. His appointment, at Freiburg in 1894, was as professor of national economy and finance. He took over the syllabus of his predecessor Eugen von Philippovich, which included the texts of the recent marginalist revolution in economics. His lecture course there and later at Heidelberg was entitled "Universal ('Theoretical') National-Economy," and it incorporated leading figures of the Austrian school of economics: Carl Menger, Friedrich von Wieser, and Eugen von Böhm-Bawerk. The way in which those economists had constructed a theoretical economic subject—rational economic man—and proceeded to an abstract theory of market behavior became one element of Weber's thinking about economics.[1]

Another element in his makeup as an economist, and far better known, was his encyclopedic interest in economic history. In his last teaching post, at Munich in 1919–1920, he reluctantly gave in to his students' demand that he lecture on economic history, a subject where his knowledge was legendary. That lecture course was entitled "Outline of Universal Social and Economic History," though given the title "General Economic History" in translation.[2] The Weber scholar and historian Wolfgang J. Mommsen referred to Weber as a "universal historian."[3] When we consider that his teaching career was bookended by two economics courses—theoretical economics and economic history—we could equally describe Weber as a universal economist.

A third element of Weber the economist was his continuous interest in policy questions. Economists in the German-speaking world were, and still are, termed "national economists." This can be translated simply as "economist," but this excludes the national framework within which economic thinking was embedded. Just as today, this generated a large range of applied topics. Throughout the 1890s Weber was part of a large research project investigating the state of the rural economy. This was a fiercely contested policy and political issue with, at one extreme, a farming lobby arguing that Germany should disengage from industrialization if it were not to destroy its rural economy and society. On national security grounds Weber argued against foreign migrant labor on the farms of the eastern border of Germany. On the other hand, he argued against tariffs, with which native farmers sought to protect their produce against the import of cheaper cereals. Was Germany to become a protectionist economy, or would it compete in world markets? Weber argued for the latter option since to withdraw from the international economy meant retarding economic growth and economic strength. The issue had important political consequences, for protectionism would have strengthened the position of a reactionary Prussian elite which sought to control Germany's internal and external development.[4] Weber produced two large research reports in both these areas, one on the position of the farmworker in the east of Germany, the other on the place of futures trading in grain on the German stock exchanges.[5]

A further dimension of Weber's work as an economist was his willingness to engage in discussion and argument with fellow economists. There was considerable polarization between the Austrian "abstract" school and the predominantly historical and institutionalist nature of the German school.[6] Weber spoke to both sides, defining his own position through these debates. Also, to give a more extensive example, Weber was the commissioning editor in a handbook series on social economics. He selected the young Joseph Schumpeter to write the history of economic doctrines and Friedrich von Wieser to write on social economics. Both of these economists injected a new intellectual energy into economics and had a lasting influence on twentieth-century economic thinking: Schumpeter through his quasi-sociological theory of the role of entrepreneur as the driving force behind capitalist innovation, von Wieser for his part in the new theory of marginal utility, which as Schumpeter later noted in his *History of Economic Analysis* "created an analytic tool of general applicability in economic problems."[7]

It is quite legitimate to denote Weber as a professional economist, in the same way as any academic today who lectures on economic theory, economic history, and economic policy would also be recognized as an economist. But this designation requires further explanation since these elements do not form an obvious unity that would identify a distinctively Weberian approach to economic analysis. The recent publication of Weber's economics lectures and the publication of the critical edition of the final version of *Economy and Society*, both by the Max Weber Gesamtausgabe, have revealed his deeper engagement with Austrian economics. This creates a tension between his interest in the Austrian school, on the one side, and his extensive writings that place economic behavior in historical, political, and religious contexts, on the other.[8]

WEBER AND THE AUSTRIAN
SCHOOL OF ECONOMICS

Weber's first lecture course, given at Freiburg in 1895, is now published as "Universal 'Theoretical' Economics." It reveals that Weber was far more closely engaged with the Austrian school of economics than previously realized and that his relegation to economic history, which is where his major contributions and the Protestant ethic studies in particular are placed, is erroneous. Carl Menger, in *Investigations into the Methods of the Social Sciences*,[9] accused the German historical approach to economics of wallowing in facts from which no "exact laws" or "typical statements" could be derived. Menger's own approach was to place the individual economic subject at the center of the economic process, and in doing this it was possible to adduce laws of behavior. Menger's "marginalist revolution" held that market exchanges—in his examples this featured farmers exchanging so many sheep for a cow—are calculated on the marginal value such transactions bring to the economy of each farm.[10] This is termed "subjective value theory," and in the discipline of economics it quickly displaced the classical theory that prices were calculated according to the inputs of the various factors of production. The principal object of Menger's attack in *Investigations* was Gustav Schmoller, who placed economic agency with the state or institutional forms such as guilds or employers' associations.[11]

If Weber is viewed through an exclusively sociological or cultural lens, we would see him siding with Schmoller. After all, what is the Protestant ethic other than argument that religion co-determined, through a new vocational spirit, the rise of capitalism? Weber's own copy of Menger's *Investigations* still exists, and on the page where Menger states that the aim of social science is to trace back "the phenomena of humanity to its most original and most simple factors," Weber has written idiomatically in the margin *alles ganz dunkel*—"the clarity of mud." For Weber, what remains permanently clouded is the complexity of the empirical world. But what has to be applauded—and here Weber publicly backed Menger against Schmoller—is the intellectual ambition to clarify reality through the construction of lawlike statements. Mommsen, as editor of the economics lecture course, comments, "He [Weber] made Menger's fundamental position into his own, which sharply separated between theoretical types and empirical statements. Its methods, namely to develop in purely logical ways theoretical types or lawlike statements, which could then be used to submit empirical reality to rational interpretation, became increasingly important for his own epistemological views."[12]

Weber in referring to the leading Austrian economists in his lecture course—Menger, Wieser, Böhm-Bawerk—sees in their abstract theories a "*constructed* 'economic subject'" that stands in sharp "opposition to empirical persons." Theoretical economics argues with "a non-realistic person, analogous to a mathematical ideal figure," that is, a fictional number.[13] This oppositional duality forms the epistemological basis for his later formulated ideal type. Weber introduced the ideal type in his 1904 essay "The

'Objectivity' of Knowledge in Social Science and Social Policy." On "abstract economic theory" he argued that "It presents us with an *ideal* image of what goes on in a market for goods when society is organized as an exchange economy, competition is free, and action is strictly rational. . . . The substance of this construct has the character of a *utopia* obtained by the *theoretical* accentuation of certain elements of reality." Where we find in empirical reality that these interrelations can be found to some extent, "then we can pragmatically *clarify* the *distinctive character* of that interrelation and make it understandable, by means of an *ideal type*."[14]

In the light of this scholarship, we might conclude that Weber's attraction to the Austrian school was purely methodological in character. The matter is more complicated, however. Melchior Palyi, an economist who knew Weber, attended his lectures, and edited and published Weber's *Universal Social and Economic History* in 1923, penned the following sketch of Max Weber:

> It was my good fortune, in particular, to come in close contact, as their student and assistant, with the two most original thinkers and most brilliant personalities of the period: Lujo Brentano and Max Weber, the foremost social scientists of their age. They were scholars of encyclopedic scope and of statesmanly stature, animated by the ethos of their belief in Liberty and Justice. As true Liberals, they stood in matters of labor policy for trade unionism, the eight hour day, and for factory legislation, as far as compatible with domestic free enterprise and international free trade. They were opposed to dogmatic laissez-faire—which meant paternalism in labor relations— as well as to paternalism in government.[15]

Palyi combines Weber's economic liberalism with his social liberalism. (Weber took over Brentano's chair in economics at the University of Munich in 1919.) Weber's own background and political affiliation were to support the economically liberal party in Germany (the National Liberals) and, as Palyi notes, to oppose governmental paternalism which had been started by Chancellor Bismarck who, in the 1860s, broke with the free-market orientation of the National Liberals. Max Weber's antagonism toward Prussian authoritarianism was both political and economic in nature. His own economic liberalism is *one* part of his makeup as a social scientist.[16]

The Methodological Shortcomings of Neoliberalism

Nicholas Gane has recently drawn attention to the ways in which the Austrian economists Ludwig von Mises and Friedrich Hayek took Weber to be an important antecedent of their own free-market theories.[17] This indicates that today's neoliberalism, which at its core is an attempt to restore the supremacy of the market on a global scale irrespective of national particularities, has a lineage that can be traced through Friedrich Hayek and Ludwig von Mises back to Max Weber. Both Hayek and Mises were impressed by Weber's robust critique (in 1919) of the socialization of production and distribution on the basis of planning and dispensing with money and market prices.[18] Hayek's elevation of the market as the principal mechanism for allocation of resources, production decisions, and economic return to individual agents was shared only in part by Weber, who analyzed markets in terms of unavoidable power inequalities.

In extracting what he saw as Weber's endorsement of an individualist approach to economics, Mises overrode and rewrote Weber's epistemology. Mises's base assumption was as follows: "All action is economizing with the means available for the realization of attainable ends. The fundamental law of action is the economic principle. Every action is under its sway."[19] Like Menger, Mises thought economics was a nomological science capable of formulating laws, which were "valid always and everywhere." An economic rationality underlay all human action, and from this laws of economizing could be inferred. The philosopher of science Hans Albert characterizes Mises' approach as follows: "pure economics is a priori; it is in a way a *'logic of action'* which like logic and mathematics does not stem from experience but from reason."[20] Stephen P. Turner in his chapter in this handbook shows that Weber rejected the possibility of such laws. Against the nomological, Weber asserted his own method, the interpretive understanding of reasons for action. The multiplicity of those reasons could be typified, but they could not be reduced to any one a priori axiom or law.

We are faced with a methodological standoff at this point. Mises claimed nomological validity for economics as a science and moreover used this to justify the normative claims of his version of liberal economics. Weber claimed that social science had to proceed as an interpretive science, able to discern patterns of social behavior and to uncover causal explanation of occurrences. This did not justify normative demands—for example, the creation of free markets in the name of economic liberty—on the basis of science. Weber was emphatic that science cannot determine value or normative choices. Those belong in the realm of belief, opinion, and politics. As Hans Henrik Bruun shows in his chapter in this handbook, it is in the nature of ethical choice to separate our scientific knowledge of the world from how we choose to act. During a conference on science and technology, Weber observed that productivity is a concept of economic science but that its pursuit has to be justified on political and ethical grounds. For example, robotics greatly increases the productivity of the worker, to the point of eliminating her from the factory. Misean economizing justifies this; Weber says the productivity gain has to be argued out in terms of the overall sociological consequences and policy implications for citizens. Failure to maintain the separation will end badly: "To mix up prescriptive demands with scientific questions is the work of the Devil," as Weber castigated his fellow economists.[21]

The Misean tendency in contemporary economics has flourished under the banner of neoliberalism over the last decades. On the basis of the primacy of the market over state regulation and opposition to an interventionist and redistributive state, Hayek first launched neoliberalism as an explicit political program at the inauguration of the Mont Pèlerin Society in 1947.[22] The *new* liberalism was a call for a return to neoclassical economics in the face of the distortions of communism, fascism, and the welfare state. While they claimed to co-opt Wieser and Weber, both of the latter were foremost in understanding *social* economics and where the market ended and the institutions and spheres of society began. Wieser, who is credited with placing the idea of marginal utility on the intellectual map, drew out the social consequences of this theory in his *Social Economics*. The rejection of classical theory and its derivation of value from land, labor, and capital meant that property (land and capital) had no preemptive claim over economic policy and neither did labor as a class.[23] On this line of thinking there is considerable reciprocal influence between Wieser and Weber.

"Neoliberalism," as it has come to be used since the 1980s, immediately fails the Weberian test of clarity of concept and definition. In the name of free markets, it has licensed large corporations, bank oligopolies, and a deregulated financial industry to insert freedom of access over hitherto non-market institutions and value spheres. For example, politics gives way to governance and technocratic administration, and all public governmental decisions have to be assigned a private market value. The sociologist William Davies defines contemporary neoliberalism as the disenchantment of politics by economics.[24] Weber invoked the disenchantment of the "iron cage," whereas today the power of markets displaces all other value standards.

Since the great financial crisis of 2008 "neoliberalism" is now subject to extensive critical onslaught—precisely because of the sociological consequences. It is a large subject and requires a much fuller treatment than space allows here. But many of the critical responses, such as the excellent *Nobel Factor* by Offer and Söderberg,[25] are in line with Weber's methodological position that social science does not deal with axiomatic assertions that justify all policy decisions. To give one very consequential example, the theory of rational expectations, which had come to dominate economics and economic policy by the 1990s, held that economic agents were rational and reacted to future events and trends, such as inflation or government spending. From Weber's standpoint this would be an interesting heuristic that might yield some interesting patterns of behavior, despite being based on the unrealistic assumption that all economic agents are able to anticipate the future. But within the Misean conceptual framework, rational expectations theory was held to be axiomatically true. The policy decisions that were derived from it declared that all governments' attempts to stabilize an economy were self-defeating, even in a financial crisis, because they had already been factored into economic agents' decisions.[26] Austerity economics, as it has afflicted Europe, is one consequence of this erroneous theory.

THE ECONOMICS OF MODERN CAPITALISM

In this section I turn to how we should place Weber the economist within the wider frame of the social and historical sciences. Weber sets out his overall approach to economics in an essay published in 1904 in the *Archiv für Sozialwissenschaft und Sozialpolitik (Journal for Social Science and Social Policy)*. The *Archiv* had been relaunched in 1904 with a new owner, Edgar Jaffé, and a new editorial team, of Edgar Jaffé, Werner Sombart, and Max Weber. Jaffé was a businessman turned academic, and his expertise was banking. Sombart was one of the most famous economists in Germany, though with a certain Marxist notoriety. Together they penned a joint article (*Geleitwort*) explaining the new approach of the journal, which under its previous editor had concentrated on empirical studies on the dire state of labor and working conditions as well as the required social legislation.

> Today, our journal has to consider the historical and theoretical investigation into the *general cultural significance of the development of capitalism* as the scientific problem that is dedicated to [dealing with it].[27]

This, their statement continues, will involve the neighboring disciplines of "the general theory of the state, legal philosophy, social ethics, with studies in social psychology and with those inquiries usually categorized under the name of sociology." The statement signs off on a methodological note that "the specific significance of social phenomena of culture" demands the formulation of "clear and unambiguous concepts."[28]

The Transition from Traditional to Acquisitive Capitalism

Weber systematically elaborates the nature of this transformation in Chapter 2 of *Economy and Society*, which is entitled "The Basic Sociological Categories of the Economy." At its heart the chapter pursues the idea of "economizing." How do different individuals and groups seek profit opportunities, and what are the sociological boundaries through which this activity is allowed and enabled? The Misean axiom of economizing is shown to be dependent on specific sociological structures. Only in the West has a configuration of features come about in which the free use of labor has become determinative. Weber refers to these interlinked features as "peculiarities" (*Eigenschaften*) of the West (or the "Occident" as he terms it). It is only in the West that a cold-eyed pursuit of profit has been enabled as in no other civilization. The *Protestant Ethic* provided the motivational grounds for this turnaround, and his historical comparative studies in religion and economy came up with a range of answers as to how Occidental civilization came to be configured so as to enable the free development of these "peculiarities."[29] (See the chapter by Joshua Derman in the handbook.)

The Occident, therefore, has cleared all sociological obstacles in the domain of the economy for an acquisitive capitalism to pursue profit unimpeded. This is behavior "oriented to opportunities for seeking new powers of control (*Verfügungsgewalt*) over goods."[30] Goods and services, exchange of goods, and business credit are all elements, or means, for gaining advantage in making a profit. "'Profitability' ('*Rentabilität*'), means, in the rational case, one of two things: (1) the profit estimated as possible by ex-ante calculations the attainment of which is made an objective of the entrepreneurs' activity; or (2) that which the ex-post calculation shows actually to have been earned in a given period, and which is available for the consumption uses of the entrepreneur without prejudice to his chances of future profitability."[31] The use of capital, the use of labor, the sale of goods, and the estimation of market opportunities all have to be considered, and a power of disposal exercised, in order to assure profitability. Paramount in this is "the highest possible degree of calculability as the basis for efficient capital accounting." Weber says of this economic/business calculus, "It is far from the case that only economic factors are important to it. On the contrary, it will be shown that the most varied sorts of external and subjective barriers account for the fact that capital accounting has arisen as a basic form of economic calculation in the Western World (*Okzident*)."[32]

Weber's economic sociology shows us how this was achieved, and this takes us to the ruthless core of modern capitalism, which as he lamented at the end of the *Protestant Ethic* now imprisons us like an "iron cage." Making a world free for capital accounting requires the exercise of power, applied to existing social and political structures. The theme of power is threaded through Weber's economic sociology.

Processes of Appropriation and Expropriation

"Capital accounting in its formally most rational shape thus presupposes the battle of man with man." Weber follows up this startling statement with another: "No economic system can directly translate 'subjective feelings of need' into effective demand, that is, into demand which needs to be taken into account and satisfied through the production of goods."[33] Where capital accounting is most advanced, it has already altered the balance of powers within a society. As Weber notes, "In an economy which makes use of capital accounting and which is thus characterized by the appropriation of the means of production by individual units, that is by 'property', profitability depends on the prices which the 'consumers' ... can and will pay." "For purposes of economic theory, it is the marginal *consumer* who determines the direction of production. In actual fact, given the actual distribution of power, this is only true in a limited sense for the modern situation."[34]

How does "property" appropriate the "means of production"? Such a statement could be taken directly from Karl Marx's *Capital*. In fact, the current English translation exaggerates the similarity, and a more correct translation of the German *Beschaffungsmittel* is "means of procurement," which has the wider sense of assembling all the inputs required for production, the organization of labor in relation to the production process, and, finally, marketing, distribution, and retailing.[35] Weber himself occasionally uses the term "means of production" (*Produktionsmittel*), and there is a degree of interchangeability between the concepts. So, which economic groups are being appropriated by property?

Weber outlines a prior situation in § 20 of Chapter 2 of *Economy and Society*. There, the means of procurement are complementary to labor. Quite simply, the means of procurement are appropriated by workers (individually or in association) or by owners or by regulating associations of third parties. In premodern capitalist societies, individuals as settlers, as farmers, or as craftspeople had control of their own means of procurement or means of their own livelihood. This can also exist within modern capitalism, as is the case with cooperative associations. Owners, to think of feudal lords, have also laid claim to means of procurement by rights to property (for example, the manor and related labor services) in feudal law, as did the church in medieval Europe.

Section 21 ("Appropriation of Disposing [Human] Accomplishments") outlines the role of managers, as determined by the type of appropriation. Today, we are very much familiarized with the distinction between "labor" and "management." Weber holds to the overriding concept that the performance of human labor (*menschliche Leistungen*)—that is best translated as human accomplishments—is the production of outputs (products or services). Historically, across many societies, persons or groups of persons have themselves disposed over those outputs. That a manager disposes over other people's labor is a feature of that peculiarity of modern capitalism. The endowment of managers with the power of disposal of other people's labor is conferred by the owners of property, in this case the means of production/means of procurement. Management is another form of propertyless free labor, except in this case it is a form of bureaucratic or clerical labor. The way in which the occupation of a manager is designated is an aspect of the social division of labor.

Commentators have usually contrasted Weber to Marx by saying that Weber's argument is about calculability whereas Marx's is about the prior expropriation of the means of production by capitalists and the subsequent exploitation of the working class by the bourgeois class.[36] It is certainly the case that Weber starts from the necessity of capital accounting (while Marx holds to the impersonal dynamic forces of capital itself). But Weber is just as insistent as Marx that this involves a wholesale rearrangement of the use of capital (means of procurement) and so of changes to the class and status structure. Expropriation of preexisting forms of appropriation has to take place in order to render society, any society, susceptible to the unique peculiarity of modern industrial capitalism. The peasant is thrown off his land, as in the enclosure movements; the craftsperson or cottage industry is forced into wage labor in factories.

The starkness of this argument has been forgotten and overlooked ever since sociology gave up its interests in political economy (or social economics, as Weber terms it). This occurred after 1945 when in advanced countries a different form of capitalism—social welfare capitalism or the social market—was ushered in as central to the postwar settlement imposed by the Pax Americana. A new form of citizenship was conferred on the propertyless worker. Workers were accorded not just political and legal rights but rights to welfare, and an efficient and effective fiscal state interposed itself between labor (as mere calculable inputs) and capital. Governments regulated markets, especially financial markets and the free flow of capital across national borders.

In the 1950s and 1960s a whole school of sociology developed that sought to explain how stratification, class, capitalism, and politics operated in ways that maintained society as a coherent entity. This is encapsulated in T. H. Marshall's classic book *Citizenship and Social Class*.[37] This explained how the ineradicable conflict between capital and labor was managed by the post-1945 nation-state. This process goes into reverse under the neoliberal regime whose political phase is triggered by the new conservatism of the Reagan presidency in the 1980s and Prime Minister Thatcher in the United Kingdom. The neoliberal regime of our age has returned us to the contours of capitalism that were familiar to Weber in his day. Through a re-engagement with Weber's economic sociology we can analyze and explain how social–liberal capitalism was returned to market capitalism, through a process of re-expropriation of labor and citizen rights.

The Triadic Division of Labor

The ways in which economic needs are met in a mass production/mass consumption capitalist economy is through a complex and specialist division of labor. Weber uses the term the "technical" division of labor, and this analysis is very much in the tradition of Adam Smith's classic description of breaking down the manufacture of pins into its component parts and allocating a different worker to each task and, likewise, Henry Ford's reorganization of car assembly through the slow-moving production line.[38] Most of economic and business discourse concentrates on the technical division of labor, and it is very much concerned with the productivity of labor and managerial prerogatives. (See the chapter by John Scott in this handbook.) In the management literature there is a general fascination, probably not shared by most workers, with how far the division of tasks can be taken and with the social psychological effects on workers. Weber himself was coauthor of such a study.[39] However, in the larger scheme of economic sociology, the *social* division of labor takes precedence for Weber. This is an issue of power, of who has the power of control over resources, the stages of production, and marketing. Weber analyzes this through the concepts of appropriation and expropriation. The issue of the calculability of capital demands total control and complete expropriation of previous forms of appropriation.

Weber is quite aware of the empirical complexity that inheres in the social division of labor. On one side, owners of firms may well join in the performance of human labor and may themselves handle management functions. On the other extreme, managers appointed and employed by the shareholders (the owners) of joint stock companies may arrogate to themselves a large amount of autonomy. Weber handles this spectrum through the well-known principal-agency distinction, which has generated a whole genre of management literature.[40] The latest variation on the place of the manager in the social division of labor is the inclusion of the manager in the ownership of the company, through remuneration with stock options. This was introduced under the (very contentious) assumption that giving managers an ownership stake would align the interests of managers with those of shareholders.[41]

How production in firms is organized, the technical organization, comes down to who has the power of disposal over *menschliche Leistungen*, or human performance; and this in turn depends on the social division of labor. Another important and pervasive illustration of this conceptualization is the fairly recent phenomenon of value chains. Factories are no longer closed establishments where most of the production process occurs within the factory walls, issuing a range of finished products for the market. Transport technology and information technology have allowed the production of components at local sites across the world. An automobile or mobile phone is the outcome of complex production and labor processes, each adding, through the production of a component, a value to the final product. In the literature this is termed "post-Fordist production,"[42] though Weber's term, the "means of procurement," is open to these developments.

In a Weberian analysis it is a mistake to attribute the complexity of modern production to the visible technical division of labor. The complexity resides in the insufficiently explored social division of labor. A Californian mobile telephone and computer company, to think of Apple Inc., can own plants in a number of different countries; and within those plants the disposing powers of managers extend to the dictatorial. Within the People's Republic of China, half a billion propertyless wage laborers were created when released from collectively owned farms and manufacturing units. The latter disposed over their labor and the managerial function was part of the collective enterprise. Once the Chinese Communist Party had decided it would pursue capitalism with Chinese characteristics, it was decreeing a fundamental change in the social division of labor.

The *economic* division of labor completes the triad. The move from a traditional capitalism or capitalism regulated by convention to that of aggressive profit-seeking acquisitive capitalism represents the economic division of labor. Weber defines it as follows: "Finally 3. in every manner of combination of [human] accomplishments with the material means of procurement and by the manner of their allocation (*Verteilung*) to economic entities (*Wirtschaften*) and [mode of] appropriation, the *economic* question has to be asked: is this a householding (*haushaltsmäßige*) or a profit-making acquisitive (*erwerbsmäßige*) operation?"[43] A householding economy is a very large category in Weber's economic sociology. A royal household, a manorial economy, the *oikos* of Roman antiquity all fall into this category, where production is oriented according to sociologically and politically determined need. Its economy may be intermittent or continuous and surpluses sold on the market, but it is not predominantly oriented to profit-making on a capitalistic market. As in the traditional "putting out" system of home-based production,[44] it can be capitalistic without being profit-obsessed. Weber overlaps this distinction with that between productive capital and wealth (*Vermögen*). Until comparatively recently, in Western economies, the assumption has been that productive capital is employed and driven by profit-making acquisition, an *Erwerbswirtschaft*. Explaining the transition from traditional capitalism to the acquisitive economy is the basic theme of the *Protestant Ethic* (and it becomes very clear in Weber's disputing of Sombart's use of acquisitiveness).[45] Today, capitalist wealth-accumulating strategies, the major thesis of Piketty's book *Capital in the Twenty-First Century*, in Weberian terms come under the heading of a householding and *Vermögen* strategy. The rise of rentier finance capitalism, expanded in the section below—"From Acquisitive to Rentier Capitalism", concerns the *economic* division of labor.

Specifying the Preconditions for Neoliberalism

In Chapter 2, § 30 of *ES*, "The Conditions (*Voraussetzungen*) of Maximum Formal Rationality of Capital Accounting," we can find a complete specification of the aims of today's neoliberalism. We have already outlined the first precondition (on the appropriation of the means of production/procurement). Following on, we have (2) the "complete autonomy in the selection of management by the owners" and (3) free labor, freedom of the labor market, and freedom in selection of workers. Weber frames "free labor" in terms of appropriation: "complete absence of appropriation of jobs and of opportunities for earning by workers and, conversely, the absence of appropriation of workers by owners." In the former, workers have control over their own labor; and in the latter, ownership of labor is foregone, as in slavery and serfdom. The remaining preconditions are (4) the freedom of parties in any economic transaction to freedom of contract and the absence of regulation on consumption, production, and prices; (5) (we have already encountered) the complete calculability of technical conditions of the production process plus rational technology; (6) the predictable functioning of public administration and a rational legal order; (7) the complete separation of a household economy from an enterprise economy or firm and (8), which takes us into the realm of today's financial capitalism, "a monetary system with the highest possible degree of formal rationality."[46]

What for Weber is an ideal type, against which empirical reality can be assessed, turns out to be a more or less exact specification of neoliberalism. If we take the European Single Market, which has been laid down by a series of treaties starting in 1986 (and therefore has the status of international law), the free movement of goods, services, labor, and capital is the foundation of the European Union's free market. National governments are not allowed to intervene to subsidize or regulate the movement of labor, to regulate prices, or to obstruct the movement of capital. Weber does not quite capture this last requirement since he worked in the framework of national economies. But it is fully consistent with the freedom of capital to maximize its profit opportunities, by moving capital where the technical division of labor returns the greatest profit on capital and labor deployed. European Union law decrees that governments will uphold this framework, so satisfying precondition 6. In addition, the European Court of Justice upholds contractual freedom. The European Union also has a common currency and a European Central Bank, whose operations are based on enhancing the Single Market. This is in complete contrast to the role of a central bank, which is to assist the national state in its foreign policy goals and domestic development of a banking system. For Weber, capitalism flourished from the competition between nation-states, and he actually doubted whether capitalism would survive the demise of the national state: "as long as the national state does not give place to a world empire capitalism also will endure."[47]

From the outset this regime has been criticized as a charter for free-market capitalism, and at the present time its operation threatens the very existence of the European Union as a political association. The reasons for its shortcomings and possible failure as a political and economic project are too complex to enter into at this point. But the complexity can be rendered in Weberian terms as a problem of translating what seemingly works in theory (formal rationality) into substantive rationality. They belong to two different realms: one of thought, the other empirical reality. The ideal type belongs to the intellectual realm, and formal rationality cannot be replicated or realized in empirical reality.

Without going into the many critiques of the Single Market, what is to be learned from Weber's analysis of how formally rational capitalism generates substantive irrationalities? These, as will be seen, are sufficient for formal conditions to be transmogrified into the undermining and dissolution of modern capitalism, as understood according to the liberal tenets of rationality.

"The fact that the maximum of *formal* rationality in capital accounting is possible only where the workers are subjected to domination by entrepreneurs, is a further specific element of *substantive* irrationality in the modern economic order."[48] This is the existential irrationality of life, or life conduct, under conditions of "pure" capitalism, which assumes the domination of the worker by the entrepreneur, or through his managerial employee who is able to enforce discipline on the workforce. The presence of trade unions and political parties founded to protect the interests of the majority of the labor force will, of course, ameliorate the absolute control of managers and entrepreneurs in enforcing that work discipline—as was the intention of the Cohesion Fund in the European Union as well as directives on working hours by the European Commission. This has been the trend in Organisation for Economic Co-operation and Development countries since 1945 but is now in reverse with the reassertion of managerial and entrepreneurial power under neoliberal regimes. As the technical division of labor has opened up value chains across the world, the conditions of workers have tended to precarious employment, the loss of rights, the impossibility of forming effective trade unions, and labor law and courts antipathetic to the rights of employees.

From Acquisitive to Rentier Capitalism

Aside from this existential and material irrationality, Weber also notes the irrational tendencies of finance. The two aspects are mutually reinforcing. "In a market economy a management which is not hampered by any established rights of the workers, and which enjoys unrestricted control over the goods and equipment which underlie its borrowing, is of superior credit-worthiness."[49] The de-unionization of firms and the withdrawal of government protections, which have been explicit goals of US conservatives, have reduced the risk of lending to such firms.[50] Weber was writing in an era of shortage of capital and far stricter rules on how much credit a bank could advance in relation to its cash reserves and liabilities.

That noted, Weber is also clear that wherever credit notes, in the form of bills, bonds, or promissory notes, can be freely exchanged between parties, there will come into existence financial speculation and the subsequent risk of bank collapses. Weber appends the following sentence after his enumeration of the preconditions for the modern capitalist enterprise: "A further motif is speculation, which becomes important from the moment when property can be represented by freely negotiable paper. Its early development [in the seventeenth century] is marked by the great economic crises which it called forth."[51] "In modern economic life the issue of credit instruments is a means for the rational assembly of capital."[52] As Geoffrey Ingham (in his chapter in the handbook) demonstrates, bank credit and credit instruments are intrinsic to the rise of modern capitalism, its maintenance, and its further development. These aspects also belong to the social division of labor.

The process of appropriation—and Weber's main focus is the appropriation of the means of production and labor and the imposition of managerial control—does not stop there. The possibility cannot be excluded "that a wide degree of control over the policies of management may rest in hands outside the enterprise (*betriebsfremde Erwerbsinteressenten*), by virtue of their powers over credit or financing—for instance, the bankers or financiers who finance the enterprise." The position and role of the manager "may come, through appropriation, into the hands of 'outside interests' representing the resources of shareholder wealth interests (*Vermögensinteressenten: Anteilsbesitzer*)."[53] At this point, Weber notes, a number of things may happen. If a wealth fund controls a firm, through its stake in the shares of a company, it can demand a high rate of income. In other words, it can demand high dividend payments rather than reinvestment in the firm itself, for instance, in new technology. Another possibility is "through temporary stock acquisitions, into the hands of speculative 'outside interests' seeking gains only through the resale of their share." Or the management of a firm falls into "the hands of outside business interests, by virtue of power over markets or over credit (such as banks which provide credit or 'financers')."[54] In the current neoliberal regime huge privileges have been accorded to banking and finance, which in Weberian language have appropriated the producer-owners and the management of companies. Hedge funds, private equity, investment trusts, and investment banks have all acted in the ways described by Weber but on a scale he would not have comprehended. These financial powers "may pursue their own business interests, often foreign to those of the organization as such."[55] Weber could have included in the list of possibilities the role of investment banks in driving relentless mergers and acquisitions of companies, from the motive not of superior performance and economies of scale but of short-term profits. This is the raison d'être of large pools of private wealth, such as hedge funds and private equity.

The usual situation in profit-making firms in modern capitalism is to borrow so long as the profit opportunities exceed the rate of interest, and this in turn is determined by the power situation between the firm making goods and the income of those buying them. Classically, this was achieved by Henry Ford, who ensured that workers could afford to buy his cars; and, more generally, a high-wage economy is good for the profits of large producers of consumption goods. This situation is theorized by economists, continues Weber, in terms of the marginal utility of producers and consumers. But then he writes, "Economic *theory*—which could, however, also be developed along very different lines."[56] It just happens that the power distribution favors those who own the means of procurement to proceed in the Fordist way. Another form of ownership, what Weber terms "wealth" (*Vermögen*), would organize capitalism differently; and this would require another economic theory. The type of ownership—borrowed capital for purposes of investment in production versus accumulated wealth—overrides orthodox economic theory and ushers in another form of capitalistic practice. [57]

"The management of wealth (*Vermögensverwaltung*) and the acquisitive enterprise (*Erwerbsbetrieb*) may be outwardly so similar as to appear identical. The former can in fact only be distinguished from the latter according to actual final *meaning* of the economic activity: On the one side, increasing and maintaining the profitability and the position of market power of the enterprise, and on the other side, the security and increase of wealth and income."[58] On the surface both cases are capitalistic and seek to make a profit, but underneath very different strategies are being pursued.

This can be illustrated in terms of economic power. Edsel Ford in the 1920s created banking trusts to supply cheap and available credit to customers, thus maintaining the primacy of the car factory. General Motors from the 1990s onward became increasingly oriented to making money from financial products rather than from its production plants. It was pursuing a wealth strategy for its shareholders. Again, whole national economies are structured according to the interests that determine the capitalistic economic division of labor. Ingham's classic book on the City of London and industry in the United Kingdom demonstrates how a strategy of maximization of financial capital operated to the detriment of the acquisitive profit-making capitalism preferred by industry.[59]

STRATIFICATION

The theme of stratification has its own chapter in *Economy and Society*, Chapter 4 "Classes and Status Groups." Weber did not complete the chapter, and his presentation is schematic. We do have an earlier version (written c. 1912), which was translated and published by Gerth and Mills as a free-standing essay.[60] These circumstances have led to a situation where stratification is not adequately related to economic sociology. When Weber composed the first version, entitled "Classes, Status Groups, Parties," he had yet to write his economic sociology; and when he had written his comprehensive economic sociology in 1919, he only provided the schematic version of "Classes and Status Groups," and this lacked the usual extended handbook exemplification in smaller font. Sociological discourse subsequently has developed themes such as occupational and class structure and how status modifies class determination. However, the larger themes of appropriation and the triadic division of labor remain unexplored, and it is these sections of Chapter 2 that need further development if the true potential of the *Economy and Society* project is to be realized. Now that Piketty and colleagues have foregrounded the issue of rentier financial capitalism and inequality, the Weberian contribution to the economic division of labor requires further attention.

Weber first defines "class situation," which means "the typical probability of: 1) the provision of goods, 2) gaining a position in life, 3) a sense of destiny in life, a probability which derives from the relative control over goods and skills and from their income-producing uses within a given economic order."[61] The first part of this definition almost equates to saying that class situation is lifestyle broadly understood. The second part of the definition makes clear that any lifestyle is dependent on the economic order and where one is positioned within that order to receive income and goods.

This connects to the economic sociology of Chapter 2 of *Economy and Society* and is most clearly seen in the section on occupation (*Beruf*). What one derives from one's occupation—whether this is a professional occupation, a skilled trade, or a manual occupation—is closely related to the triadic division of labor. Going back to the example of the manager, his or her position ultimately rests on what kind of social division of labor predominates. Chief executive officers of contemporary corporations (joint stock companies with limited legal liability) can be said to have attained the highest class position of managers in history. They are given ownership rights (as in share bonuses), they are given managerial powers approaching dictatorial proportions weakly controlled by the company board or shareholders, and they operate in a system that accords them unheard of remuneration. This has come about through the weakening of shareholders' power as well as employee power. It is the changing configuration of the social division of labor that has allowed the emergence of the chief executive as a new elite. And their power of disposal over the technical division of labor and the occupation and skilled needs of the workforce in turn determines the class position of company employees. In the present era ordinary workers are being declassed and reduced to a "precariat," and professional occupations, forming the middle class, are facing reduced career opportunities.

To give another example, universities are staffed by highly trained and educated lecturers, and on that basis they can claim educational *status*. (Educational qualification and training, for Weber, is the major marker of status difference in the modern world.[62]) But, as most lecturers come to realize, universities are now more important as an economic sector rather than in their role of learning and education. Their economic importance has overridden their position as self-governing academic communities whose economy stood on a relatively unconsidered householding basis. The economic division of labor has changed their relatively privileged class and status situation into a university employee with declining career and income opportunities. And in the technical division of labor within the university, self-governing councils have been suborned to a new managerial stratum. Status has given way to class position, and this has resulted from changes in the economic division of labor within a wider capitalistic knowledge economy.

With Chapter 4 of *Economy and Society* unfinished, there are some general remarks at the end of Chapter 2 offering a brief analysis of the sources of income, wages, and profits as they are received in various class and status situations of different societies. Weber refers the reader to another economist (Robert Liefmann) who had published at some length "Return and Income" (*Ertrag und Einkommen*). In regard to the occupational structure and the opportunities for income, Weber merely directs the reader to "problems of 'class' and 'status.'"[63] So, the linkages between the two chapters are flagged up but not adequately developed by Weber.

Nevertheless, what we have there can be reworked for present times. In outline Weber offers the components of class according to (1) property classes, (2) commercial classes, and (3) social classes. Commercial classes is a rough translation of *Erwerbsklasse*, a word whose difficulty we have already noted. Each class is positively or negatively privileged, and it is the entrepreneur and manager who heads up the positive class situation in the acquisitive (*erwerbsmäßige*) order of modern capitalism, with the negatively privileged being the laborers, whether skilled or unskilled.

Weber's property classes range far and wide, and this is because they include premodern societies like feudal and slave regimes. The list of the negatively privileged gives us the flavor in this regard: first, the unfree (which is also a status distinction); second, the declassed, and Weber supplies the example of the Roman *proletarii* (the non-property-owning sons of Roman citizens); and third, the "paupers" (Weber's quotation marks). Sociologists usually talk of the changing class structure in order to explain the re-emergence of the poor and the declassed in the contemporary world. A stricter Weberian approach examines changes in the division of labor.

Rentiers are prominent in the list of positively privileged holders of property. Rentiers receive income from a list that includes men (as in owning slaves), land, mines, factories and equipment, ships, creditors (of livestock, grain, or money), and securities. Rentiers do not appear in the list of the positively privileged *Erwerbsklasse*. Piketty has handled the issue of rentiers extensively and elegantly in his *Capital in the Twenty-First Century*. There, they make their appearance as a well-established nineteenth-century social class living off securities (e.g., consols), whose value and return remained constant.[64] (They would also count as a status group since their lifestyle would be ruled by convention-seeking refinement and antimaterialist outlook.)

Dynamic profit-seeking capitalists displace the rentier. This occurred in the rapidly expanding industrial capitalism of the late nineteenth century, which is accompanied by the thrusting entrepreneur, acquisitive in his attitude and capable of deploying capital for the greatest return. A new class of industrialists appears, often seen as supermen or heroic figures, as depicted by Veblen and others.[65] In Piketty's terms, such is the rate of capital formation—industrial equipment, factories, transport infrastructure, urban development—that the return to property owners of this new capital stock is much higher than the low but dependable rate of return on modest amounts of savings. In Weber's terminology, living off wealth (*Vermögen*) is replaced by the return on the investment in capital, and the driver of an expanded deployment of capital and consequent transformation in the division of labor is the acquisitive attitude of the industrial capitalist.

By around 1900 capitalism had reached the stage characterized by Sombart and Weber as "high capitalism" (*Hochkapitalismus*). Technology and science, in particular electromagnetism and chemicals, were making the production process far more sophisticated; and a new middle class of scientists, technologists, and clerical workers and retail personnel, including of course accountants, was interposed between the brute relations of capitalist factory owner and dragooned workers. The new middle class derives its sense of class and lifestyle through education and skill as a technician, bureaucrat (or white-collar worker), and manager. Achieving rentier status through lifetime savings was no longer the prime objective; rather, consumption, career, and rising income from work were the goals. And in a literary sense the new middle class explored the modernist dilemmas of the various emancipations on offer compared to the staid rentier and patriarchal bourgeoisie, as, for instance, dramatized in the plays of Henrik Ibsen.

Over the twentieth century the return to capital (in the form of profits and dividends) has been around 30 percent and 70 percent to labor. The new rentier capitalism that has been emerging from the 1980s onward, for Piketty, is caused by a disproportionate accumulation of capital and property in general by the capital-owning class. This tendency, inherent in an acquisitive capitalist order, is severely disrupted at points in the twentieth century through the destruction of capital and savings because of wars, financial crashes, and economic depression. This, Piketty argues, restores an advantage to all employees because their share of overall income increases relative to the return from a depleted capital stock. The increase in capital and property and its concentration in the hands of the top 5 percent of the population, since the 1980s, have created the new inequality of today. This has severely impacted both the working and middle classes since, with reduced wages and incomes both in purchasing power and relative to the wealthy, the sense of being a skilled manual worker or professional middle-class person has deteriorated.

Piketty is echoing Weber in showing that rentier capitalists do not want to reinvest and apply new technologies to their businesses, to the extent that this was the case in the productive phase of capitalism. Instead, rentier capitalists want to extract greater profits for themselves, to reduce the wage costs of their businesses, and to engage in financial engineering such as tax avoidance and share buy-backs. This altered trajectory has consequences not only for the lifestyle and class situation of employees but for political attitudes as well. Changes, originating in the *economic* division of labor, have effects not only on class and status but also on *politics*.

Class, Status, and Rentier Politics

"If we lay the causal chain before us, one moment it moves from technological to economic and political matters, and the next moment, from political to religious and then to economic and other matters. At no point do we have any resting place."[66] Weber made this point in a discussion on the relation of technology and culture, and it recalls the project of the *Archiv* that would consider the relation of the economic in relation to culture. *Economy and Society* is the encyclopedic working out of these propositions. The main underlying argument of "Classes and Status Groups" is that a common class situation will have a projection into politics. Under a Marxist formulation a class acts for itself as a revolutionary force in the political arena. Weber qualifies this assumption by specifying preconditions for this to occur. Workers have to be able to face the class enemy (as in workers and bosses), there needs to be a sufficient mass of workers in the same class situation, the workplace (factory) has to be conducive to collective action, and an intelligentsia needs to be in place to provide a roadmap for political goals.[67] For these reasons Weber adjudged the revolutionary movement to have passed in Germany around 1900, and the main schools of political sociology in the twentieth century have concurred with this judgment.

However, the matter of the reciprocal actions of class and status on politics is not laid to rest. Throughout the twentieth century class-based labor reforms have successfully introduced welfare, labor laws, and social reform into the political arena, most frequently against conservative parties representing the interests of capital.

Neoliberalism has operated with an ideology that its superior delivery of economic welfare renders all class-influenced politics obsolete. Class conflict within national political arenas is to be replaced by "governance," where economically enlightened experts would administer the course of economic affairs. The hollowing out of the industrial working class was ignored on the calculation that economic welfare according to a global measurement was increasing. The imposition of austerity following the great financial crisis of 2008 has exacerbated inequality and loss of economic opportunity for large sections of the labor force.

How would a Weberian analysis conceptualize and explain the rise of populism and the politics of "economic nationalism"? In an ideal-typical spirit I suggest a *Vermögenspolitik*, or rentier politics. This follows an economic strategy that seeks to confine personal wealth exclusively to an increasingly closed elite (already discussed) and to appropriate political powers. And to follow Weber's suggestion, such a process would lead to the formation of a status group. The ownership of property, the basis of class determination, is transformed into a status group that is signified not simply by conspicuous consumption and unaffordable luxury for the many but by the closing of opportunity for others by economic and political means. "The development of hereditary status groups is generally a form of the (hereditary) appropriation of privileges by an organization or qualified individuals. Every definite appropriation of political powers and the corresponding economic opportunities tends to result in the rise of status groups, and vice versa."[68] As the quote indicates, Weber did not envisage this occurring in the modern world; rather, he was thinking of medieval societies with feudal lords, guilds, and other closed associations. The argument now has to be considered that extraordinary class advantage is being translated into status group privilege, and all political means are being used to secure both class and status advantage.

Weber considered that there was an elective affinity or natural fit between acquisitive capitalism and bourgeois representative democracy. The rise of the middle-class entrepreneur occurred in the face of the resistance of the old regime of the landed, semi-feudal, property-owning class who ruled through a legislative chamber where entry was determined by privileged (entailed) landed estates. Weber identified himself as a self-avowed bourgeois in the fight to sweep away the reactionary landed class of the Prussian Junkers and their dominance of German politics through the Prussian upper house.[69] England had won the battle against landed interests in 1846 with the repeal of protectionist corn laws, and England par excellence was the country of parliamentary, middle-class democracy and admired by Weber.[70]

Weber handles this topic in Chapter 3 of *Economy and Society*, "The Sociology of Rulership" (*Herrschaftssoziologie*) in § 21, entitled "Representation." "One factor in the development of free representation was the undermining of the economic basis of the older status groups (*Stände*). This made it possible for persons with demagogic gifts to pursue their career regardless of their social position. The source of this undermining process was modern capitalism."[71] Modern, acquisitive capitalism, as Weber noted in the *Protestant Ethic*, was a revolutionary movement. In pushing aside the old order of landed privilege, it transformed politics into free representation, parliaments, and political parties. For Weber, the role of the demagogue and orator was always important in the development of new political forms, whether in ancient Athens or republican Rome and, in the modern age, liberal as well as socialist politics. The main point, though, is that the "formal rationalization of the economic order and the state which was favorable to capitalistic development, could be strongly promoted by parliaments."[72]

Weber then qualifies this argument by saying that parliament works most successfully when the free representatives are drawn from the classes of "education and property" (*Bildung und Besitz*). Property qualifications are used to hinder the extension of the electoral franchise, postponing as long as feasible the entry of the proletarian class into parliament. But when this occurs, which Weber himself came to support around 1917, the nature of parliament is itself radically transformed in the direction of class politics.[73] Weber died in 1920 and did not have the opportunity to comment on the progress of class-based politics in the Weimar Republic. Ever since the 1920s to the present, the representation of class and the collective interests of the working class in parliamentary politics have been much debated.[74] There is an inherent antagonistic relation between working-class representation in parliaments and acquisitive capitalism, on the grounds that capital accounting wants predictability and functionality from politics and the state, whereas proletarian politics, at the extreme, abolish parliament and institute soviets or, in retaining bourgeois forms, insist on variations of social democracy. Turning back to Chapter 2, Weber makes it very clear that contemporary capitalism is committed to mass consumption and mass production, and at some level this has to be consistent with mass society including mass franchise. His political sociology does not examine the feasibility of this and how it might function.

What we do have in his writings is the basis for an analysis of how a *Vermögens-* capitalism might operate in the political arena, specifically § 22 of Chapter 3 of *Economy and Society*, "Representation by the Agents of Interest Groups" (*Repräsentation durch Interessenvertreter*). To some degree this is to be expected under contemporary capitalism. Industrial and agricultural sectors, professional occupational groups, as well as trade unions will appoint people to represent their interests. However, Weber notes, the variations in this kind of representation can have "very different significance." A representative chosen on the basis of occupation or class can have extreme consequences, either "radically revolutionary or extremely conservative in character." In the former case, Weber instances soviet revolution where property owners are excluded from political rights. In the case of conservatism the aim is to "disenfranchise the numerically superior masses."[75] This approximates to the situation of conservatives in the US Republican Party who have made significant inroads in disenfranchising segments of the population that are regarded as debilitating to the property interests of the wealthy.

This is achieved by various means: lobbying of the US Congress to reduce welfare benefits to the propertyless, making voter registration onerous, and the gerrymandering of electoral districts for state legislatures and the US House of Representatives. This is enabled by the financing of political parties where the normal allowances for party financing and electoral financing are biased to the wealthy contributors. In the United States this has greatly accelerated with the Supreme Court's 2010 ruling *Citizens United*, which opened the way to unlimited contributions from corporations, wealthy individuals, and unions for political candidates.

Weber discusses agent representation in terms of occupational groupings. This concerns fighting for political influence between occupations, where occupational difference has become pronounced within a broader capitalist economic order of an acquisitive kind. The property interests of the wealthy become the basis for instructing their agents, their representatives in the political assemblies, not to vote freely according to conscience or within a wider political manifesto but according to the interests of narrowly drawn electoral districts or franchises. In the United States associations of the very wealthy, such as the libertarian Cato Institute, have organized electoral candidates to ensure that they adhere to a narrow conservative agenda.[76] More generally, this would be termed simply plutocracy. What Weber's theory allows is how the representation operates in parliamentary-type assemblies.

A *Vermögenspolitik* is reactionary and very much against the grain of normal political economy in advanced societies. "Genuine parliamentary representation with the voluntaristic play of interests in the political sphere, the resulting plebiscitary party organization with its consequences, and the modern idea of rational representation by interest groups, are all peculiar to the Western World."[77] Weber thought that this destiny or outcome was inscribed in the unique way in which status groups and classes had developed historically. Acquisitive capitalism produced formally free classes and occupational status groups, and these formed the basis of removing the political privileges of the monarchically led patrimonial states in favor of the rational state and legal constitutional order. However, the logic of a capitalism of a wealthy rentier class reverses this historic destiny in favor of privileged access to power, by the political disenfranchisement of the propertyless and their immiseration.

CONCLUSION

This last sentence in tone is a value judgment on my part. Weber, according to his own methodological standards, offers an impassive analysis of the two forms of capitalism, acquisitive and wealth-accumulating. Both of these are possible within modern capitalism, just as the birth of modern capitalism itself was an outcome of a number of contingencies, most of which involved a degree of ruthlessness. Within the public sphere, however, as citizens we are required to express our views and judgment. Writing in a political capacity on the need for Germany to move quickly to universal suffrage with no privileged groups of voters, he criticized the rentiers of his own time. He railed against those who wanted a more "easy-going way of life": "These are the parasitic ideals of a stratum of prebendaries and *rentiers* who have the impertinence to judge the hard daily struggle of their fellow citizens who are engaged in physical and mental work against the standards dreamed up at their writing-desks." The context is different, but the sentiment still applies. The rentier class today takes as its standard the glossy consumerist standards of "How to Spend It."

The economic cosmos of mass production and mass consumption will, said Weber, contain an economic power imbalance that decides just what needs will be met and at just what level effective demand is set. In his capacity as a political opinion former, he wrote, "*equal* voting rights corresponds to the essential nature of today's state. The modern state is the first to have the concept of the 'citizen of the state' (*Staatbürger*)."[78] The political sociologist Alan Scott comments on this: "Universal suffrage is not an expression of natural equality, but a momentary political counterbalance to otherwise ubiquitous *social* inequality. It represents a brilliant institutional resolution of one of the central paradoxes of modern societies: they are founded on egalitarian political principles but nonetheless run through with economic and social inequalities." In the voting booth "the promise of modern democracy is made good."[79]

Today's neoliberals in claiming Weber as part of the liberal heritage have failed to recognize that Weber's specification of modern capitalism is rigorous and that its attainment was to pass through a very narrow historical-civilizational gate. As a liberal, his specification did not involve privileging the economic and the market over the political, the social, the cultural, or economic science itself, for these were counterbalancing forces to the power of capitalism that once unleashed was, for Weber, monstrous.

NOTES

1. Max Weber, *Allgemeine ("theoretische") Nationalökonomie. Vorlesungen 1894–1898*, Max Weber-Gesamtausgabe (hereafter *MWG*), III/1, ed. Wolfgang J. Mommsen with C. Judenau, H. H. Nau, K. Scharfen, and M. Tiefel (Tübingen, Germany: J. C. B. Mohr [Paul Siebeck], 2009), 26–29. For an outline of the syllabus see Sam Whimster, *Understanding Weber* (London: Routledge, 2007), 23–28.
2. Max Weber, *Abriss der universalen Sozial- und Wirtschaftsgeschichte. Mit- und Nachschriften 1919/20. Mit- und Nachschriften, MWG*, III/6, ed. Wolfgang Schluchter with Joachim Schröder (Tübingen, Germany: J. C. B. Mohr [Paul Siebeck], 2011); *General Economic History*, trans. Frank H. Knight (London: George Allen & Unwin, 1927). Hereafter *GEH*.
3. Wolfgang J. Mommsen, "The Universal Historian," in *The Age of Bureaucracy* (Oxford: Blackwell, 1974), chap. 1.
4. See Keith Tribe, "Prussian Agriculture–German Politics. Max Weber 1892–7," in *Reading Weber*, ed. K. Tribe (London: Routledge, 1989), 85–130.
5. Max Weber, *Die Lage der Landarbeiter im ostelbischen Deutschland. 1892, MWG*, I/3, ed. Martin Riesebrodt (Tübingen, Germany: J. C. B. Mohr [Paul Siebeck], 1984); *Börsenwesen, Schriften und Reden 1893–1898, MWG*, I/5, ed. Knut Borchardt with C. Meyer-Stoll (Tübingen, Germany: J. C. B. Mohr [Paul Siebeck], 1999).

6. Fiona Maclachlan, "Max Weber within the *Methodenstreit*," *Cambridge Journal of Economics* (2016): 1–15; "Battle of the Methods," in *The Max Weber Dictionary*, ed. R. Swedberg and O. Agevall (Stanford, CA: Stanford Social Sciences, 2016), 15–16.

7. Joseph Schumpeter, *Economic Doctrine and Method. An Historical Sketch* (London: George Allen & Unwin, 1954 [1912]), 912; Friedrich von Wieser, *Theorie der gesellschaftlichen Sozialökonomie* (Tübingen, Germany: J. C. B. Mohr [Paul Siebeck], 1914), trans. A. Hinrichs as *Social Economics* (New York: Greenberg, 1927).

8. On the latter contextualizing approach, see Richard Swedberg, *Max Weber and the Idea of Economic Sociology* (Princeton, NJ: Princeton University Press, 1998); on Weber as part of the universe of economists, see Keith Tribe, "A Lost Connection: Max Weber and the Economic Sciences," in *Das Faszinosum Max Webers. Die Geschichte seiner Geltung* (Constance, Germany: UVK, 2006), 313–330.

9. Carl Menger, *Untersuchungen über die Methode der Socialwissenschaften, und der politischen Ökonomie insbesondere* (Leipzig, Germany: Duncker & Humblot, 1883).

10. Carl Menger, *Principles of Economics* (New York: New York University Press, 1981 [1871]).

11. Weber disagreed with Schmoller's periodization of economies; see Weber, *Economy and Society* (hereafter *E&S*), ed. G. Roth and C. Wittich (Berkeley: University of California Press, 1978), 118; *Wirtschaft und Gesellschaft. Soziologie. Unvollendet 1919–1920*, MWG, I/23, ed. K. Borchardt, E. Hanke, and W. Schluchter (Tübingen, Germany: Mohr [Siebeck], 2013), 302.

12. Weber, *Allgemeine ("theoretische") Nationalökonomie*, MWG, III/1, 26.

13. Ibid., 122–123; Whimster, *Understanding Weber*, 25–26.

14. Max Weber, "The 'Objectivity' of Knowledge in Social Science and Social Policy," in *Collected Methodological Writings* (hereafter *CMW*), ed. H. H. Bruun and S. Whimster, trans. Hans Henrik Bruun (London and New York: Routledge, 2012), 124–125.

15. Melchior Palyi, *Compulsory Medical Care and the Welfare State* (Chicago: National Institute for Professional Services, 1949), 15.

16. On the historical and family background, see Guenther Roth, *Max Webers deutsch-englische Familiengeschichte 1800–1950* (Tübingen, Germany: Mohr Siebeck, 2001). Roth places Weber as a "cosmopolitan nationalist."

17. Nicholas Gane, "Sociology and Neoliberalism: A Missing History," *Sociology* 48, no. 6 (2014): 1092–1106; see also *Max Weber and Contemporary Capitalism* (New York: Palgrave Macmillan, 2012), chap. 5.

18. *E&S*, 104–107. Weber references Mises' own critique of socialist calculation, *E&S*, 107; MWG, I/23, 280–285.

19. Ludwig von Mises, *Epistemological Problems of Economics* (Princeton, NJ: Van Nostrand, 1960 [1933]), 80. Hayek wrote approvingly of Weber who had made clear "the impossibility of a rational calculation in a centrally directed economy from which prices are necessarily absent" in F. A. Hayek, *Individualism and the Economic Order* (London: Routledge & Kegan Paul, 1949), 144. See Swedberg's research in *Max Weber and the Idea of Economic Sociology*, 301–303.

20. Hans Albert, "Hermeneutics and Economics. A Criticism of Hermeneutical Thinking in the Social Sciences," *Kyklos*, 41 (1988): 589.

21. *CMW*, 358–360, quotation at 358.

22. Gane points out that Hayek and Mises are quite different at an epistemological level. Hayek agreed with Weber's refusal to accept a "positivist" view of social science. And Mises adopted part of Weber's theory of social action, in what he called "praxeology." Gane, "Sociology and Neoliberalism," 1094ff.

23. For both Weber and Wieser the line between the social and economic is permeable, and relations of exchange constitute an early form of sociality, which Weber termed *Vergesellschaftung*—the formation of the social. Wieser explained this as follows: "Acquisitive enterprises are instruments of a great social productive and acquisitive process following a division of labour. This social productive and acquisitive process, and with it, the inseparable process of exchange together comprise the social economy." *Social Economics*, 151.

24. See, for example, William Davies, *The Limits of Neoliberalism. Authority, Sovereignty and the Logic of Competition* (London: Sage, 2016).

25. Avner Offer and Gabriel Söderberg, *The Nobel Factor* (Princeton, NJ: Princeton University Press, 2016).

26. Ibid., 25–33.

27. Edgar Jaffé, Weber Sombart, and Max Weber, "Accompanying Remarks," in *CMW*, 95–99, 97; "Geleitwort," in Weber, *Zur Logik und Methodik der Sozialwissenschaften. Schriften 1900-1907, Max Weber-Gesamtausgabe, MWG*, I/7, ed. G. Wagner with C. Härpfer et al. (Tübingen, Germany: Mohr [Siebeck], 2018), 125–134, 130.

28. Jaffé, Sombart, and Weber, "Accompanying Remarks," *CMW*, 97, 98; *MWG*, I/7, 131, 133.

29. Weber, "Prefatory Remarks to the Collected Essays in the Sociology of Religion" in *The Essential Weber: A Reader* (hereafter *Essential*), ed. S. Whimster (London: Routledge, 2004), 101–112, 103; Weber, "Vorbemerkung," in *Die protestantische Ethik und der Geist des Kapitalismus/Die protestantischen Sekten und der Geist des Kapitalismus. Schriften 1904-1920, MWG*, I/18, ed. W. Schluchter with U. Bube (Tübingen, Germany: Mohr [Siebeck], 2016), 101–121, 105.

30. *E&S*, 90; *MWG*, I/23, 258.

31. *E&S*, 91; *MWG*, I/23, 260.

32. *E&S*, 92; *MWG*, I/23, 261.

33. *E&S*, 93; *MWG*, I/23, 262.

34. *E&S*, 92–93; *MWG*, I/23, 262–263.

35. S. Whimster, "Issues in Translating Weber's Writings on Economics," *Max Weber Studies*, 16, no. 2 (2016): 189–210.

36. See Simon Clarke, *Marx, Marginalism and Modern Sociology. From Adam Smith to Max Weber* (Basingstoke, UK: Palgrave, 1982).

37. T. H. Marshall, *Citizenship and Social Class* (Cambridge: Cambridge University Press, 1950). For a parallel analysis see M. Rainer Lepsius, *Soziale Schichtung in der industriellen Gesellschaft* (Tübingen, Germany: Mohr Siebeck, 2015). For the American situation, see R. Bendix and S. Lipset, eds., *Class, Status and Power* (Glencoe, IL: Free Press, 1953).

38. In fact, Weber's acknowledged source is Karl Bücher.

39. Max Weber, *Zur Psychophysik der industriellen Arbeit. 1908-1912, MWG* I/11, ed. W. Schluchter with Sabine Frommer (Tübingen, Germany: Mohr [Siebeck], 1995).

40. See A. Berle and G. Means, *The Modern Corporation and Private Property* (New York: Harcourt, Brace & World, 1968 [1932]); Oliver E. Williamson, *Economics of Discretionary Behaviour: Managerial Objectives in a Theory of the Firm* (Englewood Cliffs, NJ: Prentice Hall, 1965).

41. William Lazonick and Mary O'Sullivan, "Maximizing Shareholder Value: A New Ideology for Corporate Governance," *Economy and Society* 29, no. 1 (2000): 13–35.

42. A. Amin, ed., *Post-Fordism: A Reader* (Oxford: Blackwell, 1994).

43. *E&S*, 114 (translation changed); *MWG*, I/23, 297.

44. Weber outlines the traditional putting out system in the mid-nineteenth-century German textile industry and its transformation into a modern acquisitive undertaking in *The Protestant Ethic and the Spirit of Capitalism*, trans. Talcott Parsons (London: George Allen & Unwin, 1948), 76.

45. Whimster, *Understanding Weber*, 33–40.

46. *E&S*, 161–162; *MWG*, I/23, 375–376.

47. *GEH*, 337; *MWG*, III/6, 368.

48. *E&S*, 138; *MWG*, I/23, 336.

49. *E&S*, 138; *MWG*, I/23, 335.

50. Nancy Maclean, *Democracy in Chains. The Deep History of the Radical Right's Stealth Plan for America* (Melbourne, Australia, and London: Scribe, 2017); Greta R. Krippner, *Capitalizing on Crisis* (Cambridge, MA, and London: Harvard University Press, 2011).

51. *GEH*, 286; *MWG*, III/6, 326.

52. *GEH*, 279; *MWG*, III/6, 320.

53. *E&S*, 139 (translation changed); *MWG*, I/23, 337–338.

54. By "financer" and not "financiers" Weber is referring to those who buy companies from the banks. See *MWG*, I/23, 337n56. Today we would refer to private equity firms specializing in buyouts.

55. *E&S*, 139; *MWG*, I/23, 338.

56. *E&S*, 97; *MWG*, I/23, 270.

57. *E&S*, 97–98; *MWG*, I/23, 270.

58. *E&S*, 98 (translation changed); *MWG*, I/23, 270.

59. Geoffrey Ingham, *Capitalism Divided? The City and Industry in Britain's Social Development* (London: Macmillan, 1984).

60. *From Max Weber*, ed. and trans. Hans Gerth and C. Wright Mills (London: Routledge & Kegan Paul, 1948), 180–195.

61. *E&S*, 302; *MWG*, I/23, 592.

62. Max Weber, "Status Groups and Classes," in *Essential*, 176, 181, cf. 180–181; *MWG*, I/23, 592–600, cf. 598–600.

63. *E&S*, 140; *MWG*, I/23, 339.

64. Thomas Piketty, *Capital in the Twenty-First Century* (Cambridge, MA, and London: Harvard, Belknap Press, 2014).

65. Thorstein Veblen, *Theory of Business Enterprise* (New York: Scribner, 1904).

66. Max Weber, "Technik und Kultur. Diskussionsbeitrag zum Vortrag von Werner Sombart auf dem Ersten Deutschen Soziologentag am 20. Oktober 1910 in Frankfurt am Main," in *Verstehende Soziologie und Werturteilsfreiheit. Schriften und Reden 1908–1917, MWG I/12*, ed. J. Weiß with S. Frommer (Tübingen, Germany: Mohr [Siebeck], 2018), 226–236, 236; "Remarks on 'Technology and Culture,'" trans. Beatrix Zumsteg and Thomas Kemple, *Theory, Culture & Society* 22, no. 4 (2005): 23–38.

67. Weber, "Status Groups and Classes," 179; *MWG*, I/23, 596–597.

68. Weber, "Status Groups and Classes," 180; *MWG*, I/23, 599.

69. Wolfgang J. Mommsen, *Max Weber and German Politics. 1890–1920* (Chicago: Chicago University Press, 1984).

70. Wolfgang J. Mommsen, "A Liberal in Despair," *Age of Bureaucracy*.

71. *E&S*, 296; *MWG*, I/23, 586.

72. *E&S*, 296–297; *MWG*, I/23, 587.

73. *E&S*, 297; *MWG*, I/23, 587.

74. Seymour Martin Lipset, *Political Man. The Social Bases of Politics* (Garden City, NY: Doubleday, 1960).

75. *E&S*, 297–298; *MWG*, I/23, 587–588.

76. MacLean, *Democracy in Chains*, 209–210.

77. *E&S*, 299; *MWG*, I/23, 591.

78. Weber, "Suffrage and Democracy in Germany" in *Weber: Political Writings*, ed. P. Lassman and R. Speirs (Cambridge: Cambridge University Press, 1994 [1917]), 103; *Zur Politik im Weltkrieg*, *MWG*, I/15, ed. W. J. Mommsen and G. Hübinger (Tübingen, Germany: Mohr[Siebeck], 1984), 369.

79. Alan Scott, "Capitalism, Weber and Democracy," *Max Weber Studies* 1, no. 1 (2000): 40.

CHAPTER 3

MAX WEBER'S ANALYSIS OF CAPITALISM

HINNERK BRUHNS

CAPITALISM AS AN ECONOMIC AND AS A SOCIAL ORDER

"JUST as the French have their theme—what is the great revolution?—so for a long time we [Germans] have as our theme: what is capitalism?"[1] So wrote Friedrich Naumann who was closely associated with Max Weber through evangelical theology and social policy and as a publicist. Capitalism in France, where the word originated, remained in its first period: there was indeed much capital and many capitalists but actually little in the way of capitalism; also, capitalism was still very individualistic: what one sees, says Naumann, are "capitalists working separated from each other." In contrast, Germany had entered its second period of capitalism, which was characterized by "the organization of capitalists"; that is, capitalism was a "social structure, it is a social order."

Capitalism is the large theme that runs through the whole of Max Weber's work. It is not primarily, as is often assumed, a part phenomenon of Weber's occidental rationalization process on which he had already cast doubt in his study *The Protestant Ethic and the "Spirit" of Capitalism*[2] but was instead a social, economic, and political phenomenon of the present time, particularly so in the German Empire. In the east of Germany Weber studied the penetration of capitalist ways of production into agriculture[3] and agrarian capitalism and in the West the development of industrial capitalism. In combining his socioeconomic observations and analysis with his universal-historical comparative studies on the specific nature of the modern bourgeois enterprise capitalism, the picture emerged of contemporary capitalism as the "most fateful force of our modern life."[4] It is an immense cosmos that imposes the norms of economic action upon human beings to the extent that they are caught up in the totality of the market.[5]

It was not just capitalism that preoccupied Weber as the formative element in the life of human beings and the societal order. As an economist and an economic sociologist Weber analyzed economic action, the economic order, and systems of different epochs and regions from the most different points of view and in their relationships, dependencies, and reciprocal interactions along with political, social, geographical, mental, and other factors. Weber's analysis of capitalism should not be considered in isolation since his analyses and posing of questions and conceptual structures are always—and often primed by—reactions to expositions and conceptualizations of colleagues or interlocutors, above all Werner Sombart and Lujo Brentano but also Eberhard Gothein, Georg Simmel, Karl Bücher, Eduard Meyer, Ettore Ciccotti, and many others.[6] The different historical expressions of capitalism including the contemporary capitalist economic order are for Weber fundamental themes of the discipline to which he felt throughout his life he belonged; that is, economics within whose discourse he debated, including the years in which he did not hold a chair in economics—from the time he gave up his professorship in Heidelberg in 1903 until his re-entry into academic teaching in Vienna (in the summer semester of 1918) and Munich (1919–1920). When in 1904 he took over Heinrich Braun's *Archive for Social Legislation and Social Statistics*, together with Edgar Jaffé and Werner Sombart, he described the journal's field of inquiry as "the historical and theoretical investigation into the *general cultural significance of the development of capitalism*," indeed from the specific viewpoint of "the economically conditioned nature of cultural phenomena."[7] A few pages further on, in his article "The 'Objectivity' of Knowledge in Social Science and Social Policy," Weber himself defined once more the field of inquiry of the (renamed) *Archive for Social Science and Social Policy* as "the scientific investigation of the *general cultural significance and importance of the social-economic structure of human communities* and their historical forms of organization."[8] The archive remained until Weber's death and beyond, until its closure in 1933, the German-speaking social science journal in which the most important contributions on capitalism were published.

In those same years when Naumann had declared capitalism the national theme of the Germans, when Werner Sombart after his *Modern Capitalism* of 1902 extended his analysis of capitalism to Judaism (1911) and the "bourgeoisie" (1913),[9] and when Ernst Troeltsch saw an equivalence of the economic development of the modern world with capitalism and demarcated the nineteenth century from previous history on the basis of the capitalist system,[10] Max Weber in a "Planned Contents" conceives the structure and content of the work that, had his plans been fully realized (to be published in 1912), would have been his most important contribution to the analysis of contemporary capitalist economic order: *The Handbook of the Political Economy*.[11] The modern capitalist economy is the central subject of the handbook conceived by Weber, which later is renamed *The Outline of Social Economics*. The first volume of the *Outline* appeared in 1914, with the war interrupting the work that Weber was coordinating. Further volumes were published after Weber's death, among them *Economy and Society*—Weber's own fragmentary contribution. *Economy and Society* was actually only one part of what Weber had intended to be additional contributions by himself to the *Outline*.

In the "Division of the Complete Work" which was published in the first volume of the *Outline* in 1914, Weber had placed his own contribution, *Economy and Society*, as part of the planned first book, the "Foundations of the Economy." The following four books covered (II) "Specific Elements of the Modern Capitalist Economy," (III) "The Individual Sectors of the Capitalist Economy and the Economic Domestic Policy of the Modern State," (IV) "Capitalist International Relations and the Foreign Economic and Social Policy of the Modern State," and (V) "The Social Relationships of Capitalism and the Social Domestic Politics of the Modern State." The formulations used by Weber exactly mirror what Friedrich Naumann was indicating in the opening quotation of the present chapter.

The names of the authors did not appear in the "Division of the Complete Work," other than in the "Planned Contents" of 1910. We need to note this if we are going to comprehend what Weber was considering as his own domain in the subject area of the analysis of the capitalist economy. Weber had reserved the following themes for himself at this point. In the first book ("Economy and Economic Science") it was not just the complex of "Economy and Society" with its accompanying subtitles of "Economy and Law," "Economy and Social Groups," and "Economy and Culture (Critique of Historical Materialism)" but also the interrelationship "Economy and Race" and then the episte-mological dimension: "Object and Logical Nature of the Formulation of Questions in the Economic Sciences." In the second book, in which the specific elements of the modern capitalist economy were to be treated, Weber had reserved for himself the topic of the legal foundations of the relationships between the modern state and capitalism as well as, referring to the technological foundations of capitalism, the investigation of the "Universal Significance of Modern Market Conditions and of the Modern News Media." In the third book ("The Individual Production Sectors etc.") Weber wanted to handle the "Limits of Capitalism in the Rural Economy"; in the fifth book ("The Social Relationships of Capitalism etc.") Weber had reserved for himself, firstly, the questions of the "Types and Consequences of the Restrictions, Reflex Effects and Reverses on Capitalist Development," then the interrelationship between "Agrarian Capitalism and Population Groupings" as well as, shared with the Viennese economist Eugen Schwiedland, almost the whole complex of "Capitalism and the Middle Class" from the manufacturing and the peasant trade union policy to "The Politics of Internal Colonization" and, finally, the "So-called New Middle Class." Weber also wanted to research the effects of capitalism on the working class: "Nature and Social Position of the Working Class (a. Concept of the 'Worker,' material class position and material class interest, b. the social position of the proletariat)." Together with his brother, Alfred, he planned the final chapter: "The Tendency of the Inner Transformation of Capitalism (monopolistic, communal economy and bureaucratizing developmental tendencies and their social consequences; the rentiers, the tendencies of social transformation)."

Weber's own contributions were naturally only a small segment of the analysis of the capitalist economy, as it was envisioned by him as editor of the *Handbook of Political Economy/Outline of Social Economics*. Enterprise management, capital formation and appropriation, capital markets, price formation, production, conjunctures and crises, circulation of goods, nature of credit banks, theory of location, business theory in capitalist heavy industry, nature of insurance, overseas capital investment, consumption, determination of wages, worker protection, social policy, anti-capitalist mass movements, and many other themes were to be included in this work on the basis of the most recent research in the German-speaking economic sciences.

Weber's handbook project revealed an economic and social order in the phase of large-scale capitalism which, on the one side, had to share the field in parts of Germany with the still powerful agrarian capitalism and capitalist farming and, on the other side, was threatened, restricted, or transformed from within by forces from several directions: social-revolutionary movements, communal economy, and bureaucratic and monopolistic developmental tendencies, on the one side, and, on the other, tensions between entrepreneurs and tendencies toward rentier capitalism. In addition, Weber perceived twin dangers: on the one flank, the degeneration in the quality of the population due to capitalist farming and capitalist large-scale industry and, on the other, the emergence of an "economic and social aristocracy" in this capitalistic era.

So far we have been only using keywords to describe Weber's overall picture of capitalism in its socioeconomic perspective, one that always relates the economic and social order to the state and so to politics. The connections between "the forms of the economy and rulership"[12] are one of the most important questions posed by Weber. Next to it, and for Weber no less important, stands another complex of questions: What is the core of modern capitalism? How is it to be distinguished from other forms of capitalism, and which factors are responsible for its origins? Why has the economy in other epochs and regions of seeming comparability, in sometimes even more favorable circumstances, failed to develop "modern" capitalism as it occurred in the Occident?

MAX WEBER'S CONCEPT OF CAPITALISM

All of Weber's researches and statements on "modern capitalism" reflect a certain tension with Werner Sombart's major work *Modern Capitalism*, which appeared in 1902 and was greatly extended in its second edition of 1916, as well as with other works by Sombart. Sombart distinguished precapitalist economies, early capitalism, modern (or high) capitalism, and late capitalism. Weber disputed Sombart's analysis on a number of central points—so, in relation to the "spirit" of capitalism and the role of religion—but on many points he was in complete agreement with him. Weber would only accept in part Sombart's developmental-historical approach. Nevertheless, he scarcely disputed Sombart's dictum that there is "only a history of modern capitalism and not a history simply of capitalism."[13]

This leads to the question of conceptually defining, on the one side, modern capitalism and, on the other, other types of capitalism. In some places of his work Weber was very precise in which sense he was using the concept of capitalism. As a starting point we can select three different definitions of capitalism from the years 1919–1920, the last year of his life.

Example 1

In the winter semester of 1919–1920 Weber gave a lecture course at the University of Munich to economics students, "Universal Social and Economic History," which was published after his death on the basis of his notes and other transcripts of the lectures. From the transcripts, at the start of the chapter "The Origins of Modern Capitalism," Weber provides the following technical conceptual definition:

> Capitalism is present wherever the industrial provision for the needs of a human group is carried out by the method of *enterprise*, irrespective of what need is involved. More specifically, a *rational* capitalistic establishment is one with capital accounting, that is, an establishment which determines its income yielding power by calculation according to the methods of modern bookkeeping and the striking of a balance. The device of the balance was first insisted upon by the Dutch theorist Simon Stevin in the year 1608. It goes without saying that an individual economy may be conducted along capitalistic lines to the most widely varying extent.[14]

This definition applies to modern capitalism without Weber at this point adding a definition of non- or premodern capitalism. In a later section, § 7 "Citizenship" (*Bürgertum*), of the same chapter he speaks of "different species of capitalism," characterizing them briefly as, on the one side, "various types of 'non-rational capitalism,'" and, on the other side, "speculative trader capitalism." These sorts of capitalism are oriented to booty, taxes, office fees, official usury, tributes, and exploitation of real emergency situations. These are economically irrational phenomena, which can never lead to a "rational system for the organization of labour." The organization of work, orientation to market opportunities, and selling on a mass scale are, by contrast, features of capitalism as a system, as it has developed in the Occident since the end of the Middle Ages.[15]

The general conceptual definition of modern capitalism places the enterprise at the center, and more specifically it adds the criterion of capital accounting as a presupposition of modern capitalism. Capital accounting in its turn presupposes a whole series of elements: the appropriation of the material means of production by private entrepreneurs, the freedom of the market from limitations of a feudal or other nature, rational technology and rational law, a free labor market, as well as the general use of share certificates for shareholding in a business and for rights to property; the "commercialization of the economy" is for Weber a prerequisite of speculation. In the course of his lectures Weber expanded on the definition of elements, going beyond a purely technical definition; for example, "meeting the everyday needs in a capitalist way has succeeded only in the Occident and only since the second half of the nineteenth century."[16]

Example 2

At the same time as Weber was giving this definition of capitalism to his students, he was editing the major chapter, "Basic Sociological Categories of the Economy," of *Economy and Society* as his contribution to the *Outline of Social Economy*. In no place there does he give a definition of capitalism. The reader finds instead a listing of five stages and defined realizations on the path to the "development of capitalism." From the sum of these stages and realizations modern capitalism reveals itself.[17]

The first stage is the factual "monopolization of commercial money" by the entrepreneur, thereby obtaining disposal over the product, even though formally, as in manufacture and mining, the means of acquisition are still in the hands of the worker. The second stage is the "appropriation of the *rights* of sale over products." It is based on the monopolization of the knowledge of the market and so of market opportunities and commercial money, whether by authoritarian monopolistic guilds and associations or whether by the conferral of privileges by the political powers. Only these two stages of capitalist development in respect to trade and industry are universal, occur as a universal phenomenon outside the Occident, and in fact are "not exclusively" based on economic factors. There follows, thirdly, the "domestic discipline of the skilled craftsmen," for whom the raw materials and work tools are supplied by the entrepreneur. The next step is the creation of "workshops without a rational specialization of labour in operation." The whole of the material means of production are now appropriated by the entrepreneur, or put differently, the worker is expropriated from the means of production. As a final step to the capitalist transformation of the production enterprise, Weber designates the mechanization of production and of transport as well as the introduction of capital accounting. All material means of production are now "standing" or productive capital, all labor power is run as "hands"—as figures in capital accounting. The enterprises are transformed into associations of stockholders. In this way the manager of the business is also expropriated and formally becomes a clerical worker, while the "owner becomes substantively the trustee of the provider of credit (the banks)." This exposition of the stages of the emergence of the capitalist economic system in manufacturing enlarges Weber's exposition of the "unfolding of the modern form of capitalism" to be found in the "Sociology of Rulership" of some years earlier, where Weber had analyzed the relationship of patrimonial and feudal structural forms of rulership in their relation to the economy.[18]

Example 3

Weber a broader perspective in the same period, when in early 1920 in the famous "Prefatory Remarks" to the "Collected Essays on the Sociology of Religion," he draws the conclusions from his comparative researches into the economic ethics of the world religions. Only in the Occident has modern capitalism developed itself, "the most fateful power of our modern life."[19] This emphatic generalization follows a definition which extends about several pages. Weber begins with a central idea: capitalism, and not least its "spirit," is in no way the equivalent of "unconstrained lust for acquisition" but could "simply be identical with *constraint*, at least with rational tempering, of this irrational drive." Capitalism, in contrast, is identical with the striving after ever renewed profit, after profitability in continuous, rational capitalistic business. Also in the "Prefatory

Remarks" Weber takes the perspective of the economist, insisting "more precisely" that "a 'capitalist' economic act is to be defined as one such that is based on the expectation of profit through the exploitation of exchange possibilities: thus on (formally) peaceful commercial possibilities." He adds further criteria: the orientation to capital *accounting* in money, the separation of the household from the business, rational bookkeeping, and, as a decisive criterion, the rational-capitalist organization of (formally) *free labor as a business*. At this point Weber emphasizes that in a universal history of civilization the central problem is "purely economically…the emergence of the *middle class business* capitalism with its rational organization of *free labour*" or, put differently, "the emergence of western *citizenship* [*Bürgertum*]." Weber contrast this middle-class business capitalism with other forms of capitalism and capitalistic enterprises, which have existed in all the civilized countries in the world: a capitalism oriented to war, politics, administration, and their possibilities for gain, the "adventurer- and speculative trader capitalism and all possible forms of politically determined capitalism." Weber includes in this settler capitalism and large-scale speculative capitalism, colonial capitalism, modern finance capitalism, as well as, and above all, "capitalism specifically oriented to war." The decisive differentiating criterion is the actual manner of acquisition, thus, on one side, rational, peaceful economy on the basis of formally free labor and, on the other side, acquisition through means of violence (war booty, fiscal exploitation, the plundering of helpless subjects, etc.)

An Inventory of Differences: Ancient and Modern Capitalism, Occident and Orient

Weber agreed with his contemporary economists and economic historians that capitalism also existed in other epochs and regions and not just in Europe and North America from the end of the eighteenth century. In this context Weber drew on the developmental stages of capitalism introduced by Werner Sombart—early, high, and late capitalism, though admittedly only on occasions and on the margins. He favored another perspective. It was not simply a concession to the terminological usage of the times when Weber understood capitalism as a universal phenomenon. The application of modern concepts to earlier periods of history is for him legitimate since every epoch must work with its own conceptual vocabulary, with the fundamental limitation that social science is a continuous construction, deconstruction, and reconstruction of concepts.[20] The concept "capitalism" applied to earlier epochs thus for Weber is perfectly legitimate and so demands a clarity of concepts.

The definitions of capitalism outlined in the previous section belong to Weber's last creative period, but his engagement with the concept of capitalism is much older. In the two decades before the First World War the German debate over the universality of capitalism concentrated with a particular sharpness on capitalism in antiquity. In this regard, in the winter of 1907–1908, Weber undertook a penetrating conceptual clarification. This was occasioned by a heated dispute, started in the 1890s, between the ancient historian Eduard Meyer and the economist Karl Bücher (and their partisan followers) over the nature of the ancient economy.[21] Another important reason for Weber was the numerous critical objections to his 1904–1905 essay *The Protestant Ethic and the "Spirit" of Capitalism*, in particular the accusation that he misread both the context of origins as well as the nature of capitalism. Against this twin background Weber, in 1907–1908, first turned to the issue of capitalism in the ancient world in his long article "Agrarverhältnisse im Altertum,"[22] which appeared in the *Handwörterbuch der Staatswissenschaften* (3rd ed. 1909). In the years 1911–1914 he pursued the question of the determinative conditions for the emergence of modern capitalism in a study of the "the city" in the European Middle Ages and in antiquity. This was only published after his death in 1921, and in it Weber had included the city in the Orient in his comparative analysis. This then is the starting point for his studies "Economic Ethics of the World Religions," which were published during the war and which, together with the revised *Protestant Ethic and the Spirit of Capitalism*, were republished (and revised) as "The Collected Essays in the Sociology of Religion." A central question, albeit not the only question, of all these investigations is the reasons that have prevented the development of modern capitalism in these epochs and regions. Antiquity and China are both cases that Weber investigated intensively.

The contemporary debates over capitalism in antiquity relate to epochs in which the following phenomena are to be found: (1) the emergence of urban export industries with a high labor intensity and quality of labor; (2) the permanent dependence on cereal imports (from the Black Sea, Egypt); and (3) a market for slaves and the dominance of specific trade interests in politics. Weber posed the question whether "in these intermittently swelling and receding 'chrematistic' epochs" there was in fact "'capitalist' structure."[23] Here he introduced a minimal definition of the concept "capitalist": "by 'capital' has to be understood continuous 'productive-capital' on a private economic basis if the terminology is to have any classificatory value." Capital in this sense is thus goods "which serve the goal of 'profit' in the *market exchange* of goods." Capitalism necessarily involves an economy with market exchange as the basis for business: "On the one side therefore: that the *products* (at least in part) *become* objects for exchange. On the other side, however: that the *means of production were* objects of exchange." This definition provides Weber with a basic distinction between funds providing a rent and a capitalist enterprise and in an agrarian context in relation both to the ownership of property and to the exploitation of the subordinated as labor power on the large estates.

Capitalism as a "structural principle of the economy," according to Weber, can take different forms of the organization of labor and different forms of enterprise: As a "capitalist slave-enterprise" in antiquity,[24] as large-scale industrial enterprise or rationalized rural-economic enterprise in modernity. Weber engages, as he concedes, with the not unmotivated tendency to restrict the concept of the "capitalist economy" to a definite form of capital *valorization*, namely the exploitation of alien labor through contract with the formally free worker. By this, however, says Weber, social aspects are introduced in the concept of capitalist economy. If one limits oneself to the purely economic definition— capitalism exists wherever "property objects, which are the matter of exchange, are used by private persons for the purpose of acquisitive value through market exchange"—then there exists "nothing more firmly than a wide-ranging 'capitalist' imprint on whole epochs, and certainly the 'greatest' of ancient history."[25] Following on from the research of an "important single point," namely the "determinateness of the origins of an 'economic ethic': of the 'ethos' of an economic form, by certain religious beliefs,"[26] as he formulated it looking back in 1920, his research into the determinants for the emergence of the modern economy expanded enormously from 1907 on: thematically, chronologically, and geographically.

The abstraction of the social features of formally free work and its exploitation is not Weber's aim, indeed quite the opposite. He needs this methodological device in order to highlight further specifics of modern capitalism in comparison to antiquity. This comparison is conducted as an inventory of differences. The most important of these, and so the unique characteristics of antiquity that have prevented its development toward modern capitalism, were for Weber, in the first instance, the *political* specificity of the ancient political community (its social structure, finance, tax farming, slavery, war, etc.) and, in the second instance, its *economic* uniqueness.

He outlines the latter as follows: production for the market was restricted in consequence of limits on the transport capacity of goods from and into domestic territory. In addition, there was an economically determined liability in capital stock and capital formation, as well as the technical limitations of the exploitation of slave labor in large enterprises. Also, the possibility of rational calculation was restricted, especially the use of slave labor. To this has to be added the (politically and socially) precarious position of the *entrepreneur* in ancient capitalism, and this precariousness contrasts with those who use capital as a source of *rent*. The anti-chrematic character of ancient political philosophy was another factor, and antiquity lacked every ethical transfiguration of gainful acquisition.[27] With reference to the economic ethos, ancient capitalism presented, according to Weber's categories, a traditional economy.

These itemized economic characteristics are a mirror reflection of those of the modern capitalist economy. The contrast of the two in terms of purely economic specifics is by itself insufficient. Weber saw ancient capitalism essentially as a politically oriented capitalism, and here his argumentation refers exclusively to the autonomy of the *polis* and Rome. This prevented the highly developed capitalist economy of antiquity developing in the direction of modern (middle-class enterprise) capitalism. The political and social structures did not direct the energies of citizens into peaceful, rational acquisition through the market, as was the case for the citizenry of a defined type of the autonomous medieval city.

The highly developed capitalism of antiquity and modern capitalism are distinguished, firstly, economically and, secondly, by their embedding in different political structures, which in their turn partly determine those economic differences. Weber considered ancient capitalism essentially to be a politically oriented capitalism.[28] In contrast, modern economically oriented capitalism requires "political, legal, cultural, educational institutions that are adequate to it."[29] Wolfgang Schluchter has demonstrated that the four major processes elaborated by Weber (i.e., market socialization, bureaucratization and democratization, disenchantment, individuation) have produced a configuration of the social order which is radically different from the social order in which ancient capitalism was embedded.

Weber's efforts to bring out the particularity of modern occidental acquisitive capitalism by comparing it with other forms of capitalism is neatly illustrated by the example of China, which for Weber was an especially interesting case. Working from the assumption that capitalism has existed in all epochs, two questions presented themselves to him: firstly, the variety of different forms of capitalism and the structural grounds for them; secondly, the much more important issue of the factors and structural conditions that favored the emergence of modern middle-class enterprise capitalism—"rational profit-making capitalism"[30] and conversely what prevented this. Some "highly paradoxical interrelations" appear at this point. The prerequisites for the modern economy are not just a rational (i.e., a predictable and calculable) state but also rational technology and science, including a certain form of rational conduct of life. Why, asks Weber, "did not modern capitalism originate in China? It had several millennia to do so!"[31] In arguing in this way Weber was going against the normal interpretation of economic historians that the rise of capitalism was based on the large increase in population, the supply of precious metal, an enhanced money economy, intensive trade, a widely spread acquisitive instinct, etc.—factors which characterized the Chinese economy more so than the European.

At the level of the structure of the state, China had no middle-class industrial capitalism that was capable of developing from small-capitalist beginnings.[32] Instead of this, "the usual politically determined capitalism of the patrimonial states of money lenders and suppliers to the princes ... was very important and [has] operated with a high rate of profit." The capitalism of suppliers to the state and tax farmers ("i.e., political capitalism") flourished and sometimes enjoyed "true orgies." Also, a purely economic form, that is capitalism living from the "market," had emerged in China. Trade and "domestic booty-capitalism" had determined the accumulation of wealth and land.[33] It was not just that industrial rational capitalism did not originate in China. Weber also spelled out the structural conditions that in China were an obstacle "for the unfolding also of all those types of capitalism which in occidental Antiquity and Middle Ages were common with modernity: those varieties of booty capitalism as they appear in the overseas trade (and piracy) and colonial capitalism of middle-sized countries."[34]

TYPES OF CAPITALISM

"Rational construction of concepts, types and systems" are for Weber the essential instruments of social scientific theory building, and this also includes the cultural sciences.[35] Variants or types of capitalism are numerous in Weber's writings, but he did not build a system from them. As a rational conceptualization in the sense just mentioned, one can consider only his concept of modern (rational, economically oriented) capitalism, opposed to politically oriented and irrational capitalism. The concept of modern rational acquisitive capitalism was constructed by Weber as an ideal type. This means that united in this concept is a series of elements in a one-sided overemphasis, which one would not find, or at least seldom find, in reality. Johannes Berger had shown "that the profitability-capitalism of modernity based on exact calculation—which is the basis of everything else!—has nothing 'natural', about it but is a highly improbable form of economy" and that Weber searched out the determinants that made such a type of economy possible.[36] What was very much in the foreground for Weber, as we have seen the element of "capital accounting,"[37] was at the time of 1900 only sporadic in business and firms. Weber states, "What is decisive is not the empirical facts, but the principle possibility of capital accounting."[38] In the construction of the ideal type of "modern rational acquisitive capitalism" Weber blanked out those dimensions of contemporary capitalism from his model which were "common with [the capitalism] of Antiquity and the Middle Ages as well as the modern Orient." Weber repeatedly emphasizes that "a capitalism that feeds itself on usury or from the credit and supply needs of the state, or from the robber capitalism of colonialism, is nothing specifically modern, but quite the reverse: this is what modern capitalism of the Occident has in common with that of Antiquity and the Middle Ages as well as with the modern Orient. What is characteristic of modern capitalism in contrast to Antiquity (and the Far and Near East) is the capitalistic organization of production."[39] It is therefore clear how the ideal-typical definition consciously blanks out definite elements of empirical reality.

Weber's ideal types are frequently presented as dichotomies, as in the contrast of ancient and medieval cities or in that of oriental and European cities.[40] This is not the case with capitalism, with the exception of the opposition of a market-oriented with a politically oriented capitalism. There is no ideal-type construction or definition of other capitalisms other than the modern. The diverse types and kinds of capitalism, which one encounters in his writings,[41] are distinguished from each other by a whole series of criteria, which partially overlap:

- according to epochs: ancient/modern capitalism
- according to epochs in combinations with different forms of rulership or economic policy: patrimonial capitalism, early mercantilist capitalism
- geographical: Western-American capitalism/extra-European capitalism
- related to religious confession and religiously motivated economic ethos: Jewish capitalism, speculative pariah capitalism, puritan capitalism
- according to the degree of rationality: irrational, prerational, rational capitalism
- according to the carriers of capitalism: traders, suppliers to the state, adventurers, founders/settlers, large speculative capitalism, and the occidental middle-class carriers of capitalism
- according to the developmental stage: highly developed capitalism (antiquity), early modern capitalism, small-scale capitalism, modern capitalism, large-scale capitalism

- according to economic sectors: agrarian and farming capitalism, slave capitalism, trader capitalism, manufacturing and industrial capitalism, finance capitalism, industrial private capitalism
- according to orientation and profit opportunities: market-oriented capitalism, war-oriented capitalism, tax farming capitalism, rentier capitalism, political capitalism, finance capitalism, purely economically oriented capitalism, acquisitive capitalism

This listing is in no way complete. Weber is an enthusiastic fabricator of concepts, and this involves both precision and clarity. These distinctions and the resultant types of capitalism serve as descriptive and classifying categories for the analysis of reality, of historical and actual empirical reality. The diversity of conceptual variants should not detract from the fact that Weber operated with two main types of capitalism: market-oriented capitalism, on the one side, and, on the other, politically oriented capitalism. This conceptualization is not completely unified: market-oriented capitalism is also termed "rational capitalism" and the political as "prerational." As noted, Weber never forced the many variants of capitalism into a classificatory schema. Some of these variants correspond very well with the schema of the kinds of capitalistic orientation of gainful acquisition, and these are deployed by Weber in the chapter "Basic Sociological Categories of Economy."

In this chapter he distinguishes six different orientations to acquisition. Four of them are encountered where exchange, the money economy, and credit money are present: orientation to gainful acquisition in money and credit companies, orientation to opportunities for acquisition through booty by politically or politically oriented associations (war financing, financing revolutions, etc.), orientation to the possibilities of continuous acquisition through the guarantee of political violence by authorities (colonial, fiscal), orientation to the opportunities of acquisition through extraordinary supplies to political associations.[42]

Two orientations are unique to the Occident: on the one side, the orientation to profitability opportunities of continuous trade (buying and selling through the market) and the industrial production of goods using capital accounting; on the other side, the orientation to acquisitive opportunities. This is split up by Weber as follows: opportunities for acquisition (a) through purely speculative transactions in goods or company shares, (b) through the processing of continuous payment transactions of public associations, (c) through the financing of business start-ups through the sale of equity to subscribers, (d) through the speculative financing of capitalist enterprises with the aim of profitable regulation of enterprise or of power.[43] These two orientations correspond, respectively, to rational industrial capitalism and to finance capitalism ("modern financialization-capitalism"[44]).

The next step concerns the orientation of capitalism itself. Weber distinguishes, as mentioned, the (autonomous) market-oriented capitalism and the politically oriented (or rather determined) capitalism. The terminology varies a little. For example, pure market capitalism of free exchange versus the politically and monopolistically oriented capitalism.

The "orientation" of capitalism—to the market or to politics or to both or further motives—comprises a whole series of variations which Weber distinguishes according to the manner of profit opportunities; this division overlaps in certain ways with the different kinds of acquisition or acquisition possibilities. Adventurer capitalism belongs to political orientation in the widest sense and is usually designated as adventurer or robber capitalism—also the capitalism of tax farming, the leasing of offices and sale of offices, the capitalism of state supply and war financing, plantation and colonial capitalism, as well as of course imperialist capitalism. Political and non-political criteria can occur together, as when Weber speaks of capitalism which feeds itself from usury or from the state and its supply and credit needs and of the colonial robber economy. Weber elucidates this as the opposite of the politically oriented variants of capitalism and trader capitalism.

These and other variants of capitalism, as Weber makes clear in his sociology of rule, in the section "Feudalism, the Estates and Patrimonialism," can thrive under all possible forms of the organization of the state; this is similar to trader capitalism since wholesale trade can easily adapt itself to changing conditions. For "a capitalist system of the economy" other political conditions are a prerequisite. Weber elucidates this as the opposite to the politically oriented variants of capitalism and of trader capitalism:

> Industrial capitalism is different. It means, where it takes the form of industrial enterprise, an organization of work with the aim of selling on a mass scale and depends on the possibility of more reliable calculations, and even more so the more intensive capital becomes and the more saturated with standing capital. It must be able to rely on the continuity, security and practicality of the functioning of the legal order, on the rational in principle predictable character of legal judgements and administration. Otherwise those guarantees of calculability fail, which are indispensable for the large capitalist industrial concerns.[45]

GENESIS AND DEVELOPMENTAL
TENDENCIES OF CAPITALISM

If capitalism in its many variants is a universal phenomenon, then the existence of a non-universal type—like occidental, rational industrial capitalism—throws up the question of its genesis and developmental tendencies. From the point of view of the biography of Weber's writings, he proceeds in several steps. At the start of *The Protestant Ethic and the "Spirit" of Capitalism* (1904–1905) is the issue of the "spirit" of capitalism and the possible influence of certain religious factors, and this is not simply concerned with refuting Sombart's handling of these issues in the first edition of *Modern Capitalism* (1902). At the end result of Weber's investigation into the genesis of modern capitalism stand a whole bundle of factors, among which the religious is essential but only one of many: the factor that has contributed to the rationalization of the conduct of life and so to the formation of the capitalistic form of economy. For Weber, in the present time, religion is only a *caput mortuum*.[46] In the modern factory labor force, as Weber writes four years after the publication of the *Protestant Ethic*, differences are no longer due to the confession (Catholic or Protestant) of the workers but are the result of the intensity with which the one or the other confession influences the conduct of life in the particular case. Present-day Catholicism for the entrepreneur could equally be a useful means of domestication "just as much as any Protestant asceticism."[47] In a similar manner Weber relativized the importance of cultural factors for present and future in the comparison of Europe with Asia. His fundamental distinction between Confucian and Puritan rationalism ("rational adaptation to the world vs. rational mastery of the world")[48] has a historical importance for Weber, namely in relation to the explanation why modern capitalism, despite externally more favorable circumstances, did not develop in China. For the future, however, Weber prognosticated that the Chinese "would probably be more capable than the Japanese of adopting economically and technically fully developed capitalism in the modern cultural era."[49] Behind this statement lies Weber's conviction in the universal dispersion of capitalism and its closely connected form of life, namely "bureaucratic organization on the basis of rationality, division of labour and expertise of all human power structures, from the factory, to the army, and to the state."[50]

This prognostication signifies for Weber not that market-oriented capitalism will completely suppress the politically oriented. In his diagnosis of the present, Weber saw alongside modern, middle-class acquisitive capitalism, political and imperial capitalism, especially in his form of colonial booty capitalism.[51] Booty and acquisition are two polar opposites. Weber labels as "grandiose booty capitalism"[52] what today takes the form of speculative takeovers and acquisitions by entrepreneurs (today's financial market capitalism) and comparable to the whole large "finance and colonial booty enterprises"[53] of older times.[54] These variants of capitalism, including war-supply capitalism, are placed by Weber in their historical and contemporary context but not analyzed in their particulars.

Weber's analysis changes when he considers with concern developments at the heart of modern capitalism itself. Weber distinguishes in his contemporary Germany industrial capitalism, on the one hand, and agrarian capitalism, on the other. "Agrarian capitalism" is not just a concept, which denotes a definite type of capitalism. It is at the same time a cipher for the socioeconomic development of the German east, which up to the time of the First World War was a source of worry. In this period he coined the concept "land-capitalist."[55] The concepts of "industry-capitalism" or "industrial capitalism" in contrast appear less often in his writings.[56] But this should not be interpreted as a sign of less interest in industrial capitalism. Weber's methodological instructions for empirical inquiries in great industrial factories and his work on the "psychophysics" of industrial labor show his concern with the future development of the working class and the new class of employees. Modern industry and modern capitalism are for Weber closely bound together. For Weber, industry capitalism is of urban origin: it characterizes development in west and south Germany, France, and Italy; and it is impossible "to understand its genesis and course without that very distinctive political competition and 'equilibrium' situation of the European state powers of the last half century."[57] The course of development was entirely different "in our un-urbanized cereal exporting East, where capitalism has made its home on the flat countryside."[58] The "capitalistic character of the large estates of the German East" has grown continuously since the fifteenth century. By "capitalistic character" Weber means the development of rational capitalist enterprise. And that is a common core characteristic of modern industrial capitalism and of modern agrarian capitalism. What warranted Weber to introduce a sharp distinction between the two variants of contemporary capitalism? Alongside their structural, economic, and organizational similarities there are large differences on account of their completely different embedding in the actual social and political environment. This produces as an end result a different economic form in agrarian capitalism in contrast to industrial capitalism. Weber undertook an analysis of agrarian capitalism against the background of the rural constitution of the German east, and he compared this with the rural constitution of west and south Germany, Italy, and France and then with the United States of America. In his analysis of the interrelation of the rural constitution and agrarian capitalism Weber emphasized the effects of the credit and rural policies of the Prussian institute of the so-called *Landschaften*. In the eighteenth and nineteenth centuries this policy had supported the development of rational, capitalistic businesses on the land with the following measures: (1) through enhanced capital investment in the form of privileged provision of credit, (2) through the classification of the estates receiving credit according to their economic return, (3) through the resultant enhanced incentive to lay off the labor force and in their place to raise the price of leases held by peasants, (4) through the concentration of ownership of property— made possible through credit provision—in the hands of the "lords of the estates."[59] "In the capitalism that required enhanced capital for the agrarian economy, it leads to the growth of the idle rentier on the land."[60]

The danger that agrarian capitalism would turn ever more firmly into a capitalism of the rentier (instead of the entrepreneur) in Weber's view was acute and was strengthened at the start of the twentieth century by the planned "Fidei Commission" legislation for Prussia. The accumulation of land by the landowner did not lead in the direction of the "entrepreneur of the farm economy," but "he wants rents, rents according to his lifestyle status, more rents for status, and so he needs even more land."[61] "The possibility of creating a middle class and recently ennobled aristocratic Fidei Commission steers "the middle class German capital away from the economic conquest in the wide world more towards the path of creating a rentier existence, which anyway lies within the ambit of our protectionist politics."[62] Agrarian capitalism in this form, firstly, was a negative form of conflict since it offended against the national interest[63] and, secondly, represented a tendency that was diametrically opposed to the orientation of modern middle-class acquisitive capitalism.[64] In this regard English capitalism was the exemplary model because it had served "to extend the power and the people across the globe."

PROSPECT

Weber was neither a defender of capitalism nor a friend of capitalists. Certainly, he saw in "private capitalism" an element of freedom in the sense of checks and balances in relation to the danger of the damaging power of a bureaucratic state. His indignation over "the stupid literary critics antagonistic to 'capitalism' "[65] was based on the conviction that an incompetent anti-capitalism strengthened the rentier mentality and in combination with protectionism would turn Germany into an economically stagnant country. In the political debates over the economy during the war years, which turned on the transition of the capitalist economy to a war economy and then to a " 'communal economy', 'solidarity economy', 'cooperative economy' (or whatever the phrase is)," Weber poured scorn on the naive idea that the way of life of the office clerk and the worker in nationalized, socialized enterprises would in a way be noticeably different from that in large capitalist firms.[66] Already before the war Weber had relativized the significance of the issue of the capitalist or socialist organization of production in relation to the effects of "the organization of industrial production," whose existence is independent of the alternatives of capitalism versus socialism.[67] Against the contemporary striving for socialism he advocated the market economy but not that of the capitalist economy. The concept of the "market economy" is indifferent to "whether it [the economy] is 'capitalist', i.e. oriented to capital accounting and its extent."[68] Weber's sociology of social action designated the market economy as "by far the most important form of all typical and universal social action oriented to the 'interest situation'." In what ways the market economy fulfills the meeting of needs is for Weber the subject of economic theory.[69] Capitalism and all its variants aside, what interested Weber were the interconnections between the economic dynamic and the social order.[70] This perspective goes back to his first contact at the beginning of the 1890s with the social and political effects of agrarian capitalism in the German east. In his inquiries on the position of the farmworker east of the Elbe, the issue is also one concerning the effects of the economic order on humanity. He poses this question not only in *The Protestant Ethic and the "Spirit" of Capitalism* from the viewpoint of the modern specialist human person in general but also a little later in an empirical investigation into the industrial workforce.[71]

The importance of rationalization of the conduct of life for modern capitalism and its origins Weber took up in relation to the discussion started by Werner Sombart on the spirit of capitalism. It leads him later, most clearly in his study of China, to the recognition that conduct of life can be rationalized in different directions, with contradictory effect on the economic form.

Weber's analysis of capitalism is closely tied to his time. He sees the relation of the state and capitalism under three principal aspects: (1) the guarantee of legal certainty as one of the prerequisites for calculability, (2) the endangering of capitalism by bureaucratization, and (3) the mobilization of the resources of the state for the enforcement of particular capitalist interests. In his analysis of economic bodies there is potential for a more exact understanding of the relationship between the state, politics, and the economy. (His categories of economically oriented bodies distinguish between the economizing association, the economic association, the regulating economic body, and the regulatory association.[72]) The beginnings of "organized capitalism" during the war, under the sign of the war economy, Weber analyzed from the viewpoint of the large producer-enterprises, on the one side, and bureaucratization, on the other. In contrast to the debates on the war economy in Germany at the time, also pursued by colleagues close to him—debates, on one side, over war socialism, state socialism, social economy, and the death of capitalism and, on the other, complete capitalization of the state[73]— Weber interpreted the social and economic transformation in war and revolution as the acceleration of a process long since underway, and he observed with concern the concrete social consequences. It would be anachronistic to expect that Weber could make available concepts with whose help we could analyze the relationship of state, party, and capitalism in China in the twenty-first century without those concepts undergoing possible modification or even creating new concepts. The same applies to the actual helplessness of even large states in the face of large capitalist enterprises operating worldwide.

Weber has made available a series of concepts and categories which could still prove useful today, under the assumption that they are used flexibly and possibly altered and reconstructed. His ideal-typical construction of modern enterprise capitalism, which forms the foundation for the "specialist humanity" (*Berufsmenschentum*),[74] can be interesting for the understanding of today's forms of capitalism, especially with regard to methodology. This limitation is not based on the fact that those elements and dimensions of modern capitalism illuminated by Weber no longer exist but rather that for us today problems and "value-ideas," to use Weber's term, are in large part different from those of his epoch—since "the light of the great civilizational problems" moves on, as Weber himself formulated it in 1904.

It was scarcely conceivable around 1900 that the cardinal problem of the future order of economy and society was less the "burning up" of the last hundredweight of fossil fuel[75] as the rapidly progressing destruction of the natural basis of life. Analogues also apply to a definition of capitalism which foregrounded the meeting of the everyday needs of the people through capitalist enterprise but could not anticipate the irrational dynamic of the consumer society that not only supplies those needs but actually generates them.

Despite these limitations Max Weber's analyses are fruitful and stimulating for the understanding of contemporary capitalism. Three examples suffice. (1) Weber named things by their names. Thus, his concept of booty capitalism is a suitable naming of today's happenings in computer-driven finance capital. As important as a keyword is in clarifying the nature of profit opportunities, it does not replace a precise analysis on the footing of empirical investigation. (2) Weber's question on the cultural significance of capitalism remains today even more strongly than in 1900 in the light of globalization and growing social inequality. (3) Weber had already exposed in the 1890s a principal problematic of capitalist economy, and this also applies to a socialist economy: the assertion of those committed to politics, science, and economy that productivity (we could also say gross national product and economic growth) contains an unquestioned background value standard, the "final value" of economics and economic policy.[76] In the context of the uncompleted nation-building following the era of Bismarck, Weber opposes such value-ideas with a concern for the future of the nation and the quality of its people. The problematic remains the same, even though we would not formulate and answer it in the same way in today's world. Weber stood against all harmonizing ideas of neoclassical economic theory; for him competition on the market was market struggle, market prices are "products of conflict and compromise," "desire" does not rule the production of goods but rather the "buying power of desire," and the rationality (calculation) of capitalist economy is bound to the existence of "power relationships."[77] This is just as valid for today's capitalism.

Translated from the German by Sam Whimster

Notes

1. Friedrich Naumann, "Das Suchen nach dem Wesen des Kapitalismus," *Die Hilfe* 178, no. 37 (1911): 579.
2. Max Weber, *The Protestant Ethic and the Spirit of Capitalism*, trans. T. Parsons (New York: Scribner's, 1958), 78 (hereafter *PESC*); "Die protestantische Ethik und der 'Geist' des Kapitalismus," in *Gesammelte Aufsätze zur Religionssoziologie*, 9th ed. (hereafter *GARS*) (1904; Tübingen, Germany: J. C. B Mohr, 1988), 1:62. Max Weber, *Asketischer Protestantismus und Kapitalismus. Schriften und Reden 1904–1911*, ed. Wolfgang Schluchter, with Ursula Bube, *Max Weber-Gesamtausgabe* (hereafter *MWG*) I/9 (Tübingen, Germany: J. C. B. Mohr [Paul Siebeck], 2014), 176. Cf. Johannes Berger, "Kapitalismus," in *Max Weber-Handbuch. Leben–Werk–Wirkung*, ed. Hans-Peter Müller and Steffen Sigmund (Stuttgart/Weimar, Germany: J. B. Metzler, 2014), 71–74.
3. Cf. Martin Riesebrodt, "Vom Patriarchalismus zum Kapitalismus. Max Webers Analyse der Transformation der ostelbischen Agrarverhältnisse im Kontext zeitgenössischer Theorien," *Kölner Zeitschrift für Soziologie und Sozialpsychologie* 37 (1985): 546–567, and Wolfgang Schluchter, "Der autoritär verfaßte Kapitalismus. Max Webers Kritik am Kaiserreich," in *Rationalismus der Weltbeherrschung. Studien zu Max Weber* (Frankfurt, Germany: Suhrkamp, 1980), 134–169.
4. Weber, "Vorbemerkung," *PESC*, 17; *GARS*, 1:4. Max Weber, *Die protestantische Ethik und der Geist des Kapitalismus/Die protestantischen Sekten und der Geist des Kapitalismus. Schriften 1904–1920*, *MWG* I/18, ed. Wolfgang Schluchter, with Ursula Bube (Tübingen, Germany: J. C. B. Mohr [Paul Siebeck], 2016), 105.
5. Weber, *PESC*, 54; *GARS* 1:37; *MWG* I/9, 151.
6. For the contemporary German debate on capitalism, see Richard Passow, *"Kapitalismus." Eine begrifflich-terminologische Studie* (Jena, Germany: Fischer, 1918, 2nd. ed. 1927) and Talcott Parsons, "'Capitalism' in recent German Literature: Sombart and Weber," *Journal of Political Economy* 36 (1928): 641–61, and 37 (1929): 31–51.
7. The Editors (Werner Sombart, Max Weber und Edgar Jaffé), "Geleitwort," *Archiv für Sozialwissenschuft und Sozialpolitik* 19 (1904): V. *Zur Logik und Methodik der Sozialwissenschaften. Schriften 1900–1907*, Max Weber-Gesamtausgabe (hereafter *MWG*) I/7, ed. G. Wagner, with C. Härpfer et al. (Tübingen, Germany: Mohr [Siebeck], 2018), 130

English translation: "Accompanying Remarks," in Max Weber, *Collected Methodological Writings* (hereafter *CMW*), ed. Hans Henrik Bruun and Sam Whimster, trans. Hans Henrik Bruun (London and New York: Routledge, 2012), 97.

8. Weber, "The 'objectivity' of knowledge in social science and social policy," *CMW*, 110; "Die 'Objektivität' sozialwissenschaftlicher und sozialpolitischer Erkenntnis," *MWG* I/7, 166.

9. Werner Sombart, *Die Juden und das Wirtschaftsleben* (Leipzig, Germany: Duncker & Humblot, 1911); *Der Bourgeois. Zur Geistesgeschichte des modernen Wirtschaftsmenschen* (Munich: Duncker & Humblot, 1913).

10. Ernst Troeltsch, "Das Wesen des modernen Geistes" [1907] and "Das Neunzehnte Jahrhundert" [1913], in *Deutscher Geist und Westeuropa. Gesammelte kulturphilosophische Aufsätze und Reden*, ed. Hans Baron (Tübingen, Germany: Mohr, 1925, reprint Aalen, Germany: Scientia Verlag, 1966), 309 and 635.

11. Cf. "Stoffverteilungsplan" and "Einteilung des Gesamtwerkes," in Max Weber, *Briefe 1913–1914, MWG* II/8, ed. M. Rainer Lepsius and Wolfgang J. Mommsen, with Birgit Rudhard and Manfred Schön (Tübingen, Germany: J. C. B. Mohr [Paul Siebeck], 2003): 808–823.

12. Max Weber, *Economy and Society*, ed. and trans. Guenther Roth and Claus Wittich (Berkeley: University of California Press, 1978), 942 (hereafter *E&S*); *Wirtschaft und Gesellschaft. Die Wirtschaft und die gesellschaftlichen Ordnungen und Mächte. Nachlaß. Teilband 4: Herrschaft, MWG* I/22-4 ed. Edith Hanke with Thomas Kroll (Tübingen, Germany: J. C. B. Mohr [Paul Siebeck], 2005), 128.

13. Werner Sombart, "Geleitwort zur zweiten Auflage," in *Der moderne Kapitalismus. Historisch-systematische Darstellung des gesamteuropäischen Wirtschaftslebens von den Anfängen bis zur Gegenwart*, 2nd ed., vol. 1 (1916; Munich and Leipzig: Duncker & Humblot, 1987).

14. Max Weber, *General Economic History* (hereafter *GEH*), trans. Frank H. Knight (London: George Allen & Unwin, n.d.), 275. Max Weber, *Wirtschaftsgeschichte. Abriß der universalen Sozial- und Wirtschaftsgeschichte. Mit- und Nachschriften 1919/20, MWG* III/6, ed. Wolfgang Schluchter, with Joachim Schröder (Tübingen, Germany: J. C. B. Mohr, 2011), 318. Cf. Randall Collins, "Weber's Last Theory of Capitalism. A Systematization," *American Sociological Review* 45 (1980): 925–945.

15. Weber, *GEH*, 334; *MWG* III/6, 366.

16. Weber, *GEH*, 276 (translation modified); *MWG* III/6, 318, cf. 346–47.

17. Weber, *E&S*, 147–48; *Wirtschaft und Gesellschaft. Soziologie. Unvollendet 1919–1920*, ed. Knut Borchardt, Edith Hanke, and Wolfgang Schluchter (Tübingen, Germany: J. C. B. Mohr, 2013), *MWG* I/23, 352 sq. Cf. Weber, *GEH*, 186; *MWG* III/6, 248 sq.

18. Weber, *Herrschaft, MWG* I/22-4, 418 sqq., 436 sqq., *E&S*, 1070–1110.

19. Weber, "Vorbemerkung," *PESC*, 17–26; *GARS*, I, 4–11; *MWG* I/18, 105–116.

20. Max Weber, "Objektivität," *MWG* I/7, 225: Das "Ergebnis [der kulturwissenschaftlichen Arbeit] ist ein steter Umbildungsprozeß jener Begriffe, in denen wir die Wirklichkeit zu erfassen suchen." Weber, "Objectivity," *CMW*, 134: "The outcome [of the advances of the cultural sciences] is a constant process of reshaping of those concepts by means of which we seek to grasp reality."

21. Cf. Moses I. Finley, ed., *The Bücher-Meyer Controversy* (New York: Arno Press, 1979).

22. Max Weber, *The Agrarian Sociology of Ancient Civilizations*, trans. R. I. Frank (London: New Left Books, 1976); hereafter *ASAC*.

23. Max Weber, "Agrarverhältnisse im Altertum," in *Zur Sozial- und Wirtschaftsgeschichte des Altertums. Schriften und Reden 1893–1908, MWG* I/6, ed. Jürgen Deininger (1909; Tübingen, Germany: J. C. B. Mohr [Paul Siebeck], 2006), 335; *ASAC*, 48 (new translation).

24. Weber, *ASAC*, 53; *MWG* I/6, 340.

25. *ASAC*, 50–51; *MWG* I/6, 338.

26. Weber, "Vorbemerkung," *PESC*, 27; *GARS*, 1:13; *MWG* I/18, 117.

27. Weber, "Agrarverhältnisse," *ASAC*, 66–67; *MWG* I/6, 359. Cf. Weber's explications in *Economy and Society*, especially concerning slave labor: *E&S*, 162–63; *MWG* I/23, 376–78.

28. Max Weber, *Wirtschaft und Gesellschaft. Die Stadt*, ed. Wilfried Nippel (Tübingen, Germany: J. C. B. Mohr, 1999); *MWG* I/22–5, 263; *E&S*, 1346–47.

29. Schluchter, "Der autoritär verfaßte Kapitalismus," 156.

30. Letter to Robert Liefmann, March 9, 1920, in Max Weber, *Briefe 1918–1920*, ed. Gerd Krumeich and M. Rainer Lepsius, with Uta Hinz, Sybille Oßwald-Bargende, and Manfred Schön, *MWG* II/10 (Tübingen, Germany: Mohr Siebeck 2012), 949.

31. Ibid., 949.

32. Max Weber, *Die Wirtschaftsethik der Weltreligionen. Konfuzianismus und Taoismus. Schriften 1915–1920, MWG* I/19, ed. Helwig Schmidt-Glintzer, with Petra Kolenko (Tübingen, Germany: J. C. B. Mohr, 1989), 279; *The Religion of China: Confucianism and Taoism,* trans. Hans H. Gerth (New York: Free Press, 1951), 84 (hereafter *RC*).

33. Weber, *RC*, 86; *MWG* I/19, 257 sq.

34. *RC*, 104; *MWG* I/19, 282.

35. Werner Sombart and Max Weber, "Erklärung," *Archiv für Sozialwissenschaft und Sozialpolitik* 44 (1917): 348; *Verstehende Soziologie und Werturteilsfreiheit. Schriften und Reden 1908–1917, MWG* I/12, ed. J. Weiß with S. Frommer (Tübingen, Germany: Mohr [Siebeck], 2018), 515. English translation: "Declaration," *CMW*, 302.

36. Berger, "Kapitalismus," 73.

37. Cf. Knut Borchardt's explications concerning the utilization of this concept by Max Weber, Friedrich von Wieser, and Robert Liefmann in *MWG* I/23, 259n29.

38. Weber, *E&S*, 156; *MWG* I/23, 365.

39. Weber, *E&S*, 1203; *MWG* I/22–4, 667. Cf. Weber, *RS,* 248–49; *MWG* I/19, 476 sqq.

40. Cf. Hinnerk Bruhns, "Ein Sozialökonom blickt auf die Stadt," in Hinnerk Bruhns, *Max Webers historische Sozialökonomie. L'économie de Max Weber entre histoire et sociologie* (Wiesbaden, Germany: Harrassowitz, 2014), 1–16.

41. See also Weber, *GEH*, 334–337; *MWG* III/6, 366–369.

42. Weber, *Soziologie, MWG* I/23, 379; *E&S*, 164–65.

43. Ibid.

44. Weber, "Vorbemerkung," *PESC*, 21; *GARS* 1:7; *MWG* I/18, 110.

45. Weber, *E&S*, 164–65; *MWG* I/22–4, 427.

46. Weber, *Wirtschaft und Gesellschaft. Religiöse Gemeinschaften*, ed. Hans G. Kippenberg, with Petra Schilm and Jutta Niemeier (Tübingen, Germany: J. C. B. Mohr, 2001), *MWG* I/22–2, 366; *E&S*, 575; "The religious root of modern economic humanity is dead; today the concept of the calling is a *caput mortuum* in the world." *GEH*, 368–369; *MWG* III/6, 395.

47. Max Weber, *Zur Psychophysik der industriellen Arbeit. Schriften und Reden 1908–1912, MWG* I/11, ed. Wolfgang Schluchter, with Sabine Frommer (Tübingen, Germany: J. C. B. Mohr [Paul Siebeck], 1995), 362n95.

48. Weber, *RC*, 248; *MWG* I/19, 476.

49. Ibid.

50. Max Weber, "Parlament und Regierung im neugeordneten Deutschland," in *Political Writings*, ed. Peter Lassman and Ronald Speirs (Cambridge: Cambridge University Press,

1994), 155 (hereafter *PolW*); *Zur Politik im Weltkrieg. Schriften und Reden 1914–1918*, *MWG* I/15, ed. Wolfgang J. Mommsen, with Gangolf Hübinger (Tübingen, Germany: J. C. B. Mohr, 1984), 461.

51. Weber, *Wirtschaft und Gesellschaft. Gemeinschaften*, ed. Wolfgang J. Mommsen with Michael Meyer (Tübingen, Germany: J. C. B. Mohr, 2001), *MWG* I/22–1, 236; *E&S*, 918.

52. Weber, *E&S*, 1118; *MWG* I/22–4, 485.

53. Paul Windolf, "Was ist Finanzmarktkapitalismus?" Special issue, *Kölner Zeitschrift für Soziologie und Sozialpsychologie* 45 (2005)L 20–57. French translation: *Trivium. Revue franco-allemande en sciences humaines et sociales*, no. 28 (2018): http://journals.openedition.org/trivium/.

54. Weber, *E&S*, 1118; *MWG* I/22–4, 485.

55. Weber, "Die Nobilitierung der Kriegsgewinne," *MWG* I/15, 209.

56. For example, *E&S*, 354; *MWG* I/22–1, 106.

57. *E&S*, 354; *MWG* I/22–1, 107.

58. Max Weber, "Die Kredit- und Agrarpolitik der preußischen Landschaften," *Wirtschaft, Staat und Sozialpolitik. Schriften und Reden 1900–1912*, *MWG* I/8, ed. Wolfgang Schluchter, with Peter Kurth and Birgitt Morgenbrod (1908; Tübingen, Germany: J. C. B. Mohr [Paul Siebeck], 1998), 338.

59. Weber, "Kredit- und Agrarpolitik," *MWG* I/8, 340 f. Cf. Weber's speech in St. Louis: "Thus capitalism causes the increase of the number of idle renters of land by the increase of capital for agricultural óperation," "Capitalism and Rural Society in Germany," in *From Max Weber: Essays in Sociology*, ed. Hans H. Gerth and C. Wright Mills (New York: Oxford, 1958), 366–67 (translation modified); *MWG* I/8, 217.

60. Weber, "Kapitalismus und Agrarverfassung," *Zeitschrift für die gesamte Staatswissenschaft* 108 (1952): 434 sq. (i.e., Weber's St. Louis speech retranslated by Hans Gerth).

61. Weber, "Fideikommißfrage in Preußen," *MWG* I/8, 153. See Wolfgang Schluchter's introduction to this text, 164 sq.

62. Max Weber, "Agrarstatistische und sozialpolitische Betrachtungen zur Fideikommißfrage in Preußen" (1904), *MWG* I/8, 185.

63. See Weber, "Fideikommißfrage," *MWG* I/8, 170.

64. Weber, "Wahlrecht und Demokratie in Deutschland," *MWG* I/15, 351 sqq; *PolW*, 100–101.

65. Weber, "Die Nobilitierung der Kriegsgewinne," *MWG* I/15, 212.

66. Cf. Weber, *PolW*, 105, 157–58; *MWG* I/15, 356, 464.

67. Max Weber, "Methodologische Einleitung für die Erhebungen des Vereins für Sozialpolitik über Auslese und Anpassung (Berufswahlen und Berufsschicksal) der Arbeiterschaft der geschlossenen Großindustrie," in *Zur Psychophysik der industriellen Arbeit. Schriften und Reden 1908–1912*, *MWG* I/11, ed. Wolfgang Schluchter, with Sabine Frommer (Tübingen, Germany: J. C. B. Mohr [Paul Siebeck], 1995), *MWG* I/11, 148 sq.

68. Weber, *E&S*, 113; *MWG* I/23, 295.

69. *E&S*, 111; *MWG* I/23, 290.

70. *E&S*, 206; *MWG* I/23, 448.

71. Cf. Wilhelm Hennis, *Max Weber's Central Question*, 2nd ed., trans. Keith Tribe (Newbury, UK: Threshold Press 2000); Wilhelm Hennis, *Max Weber's Science of Man. New Studies for a Biography of the Work*, trans. Keith Tribe (Newbury, UK: Threshold Press, 2000).

72. Cf. Hinnerk Bruhns, "Wirtschaft und Ordnung. Zur Begrifflichkeit Max Weber," in *Recht als Kultur. Beiträge zu Max Webers Soziologie des Rechts*, ed. Werner Gephart and Daniel Witte (Frankfurt am Main, Germany: Vittorio Klosterman, 2017), 457–470. See also Bruhns "Max

Weber's 'Basic Concepts' in the Context of His Studies in Economic History" (trans. Keith Tribe), in "Max Weber's Economics," Special issue, *Max Weber Studies* (2006): 39–69.

73. Cf. Hinnerk Bruhns, *Max Weber und der Erste Weltkrieg* (Tübingen, Germany: Mohr Siebeck), 117.

74. Max Weber, "Erste Diskussionsrede zu E. Troeltschs Vortrag über «Das stoisch-christliche Naturrecht» auf dem ersten Deutschen Soziologentage in Frankfurt 1910," *MWG* I/9, 760.

75. Weber, *PESC*, 181; *MWG* I/18, 487.

76. This is a central idea of Weber's inaugural lesson at Freiburg University in 1895: "Der Nationalstaat und die Volkswirtschaftspolitik. Akademische Antrittsrede," in Max Weber, *Landarbeiterfrage, Nationalstaat und Volkswirtschaftspolitik. Schriften und Reden 1892–1899*, ed. Wolfgang J. Mommsen, with Rita Aldenhoff (Tübingen, Germany: J. C. B. Mohr [Paul Siebeck], 1993), *MWG* I/4; "The Nation State and Economic Policy (Inaugural Lecture)," *PolW*, 1–28.

77. Weber, *E&S*, 107–109; *MWG* I/23, 285 sqq.

CHAPTER 4

···

MONEY, CREDIT, AND FINANCE IN CAPITALISM

···

GEOFFREY INGHAM

THE analysis of money was an unfortunate and ironic casualty of the intellectual balkanization of the social sciences that followed the *Methodenstreit* between historians and theorists in late nineteenth- and early twentieth-century social science.[1] The disciplinary separation of economics and sociology led to the neglect of arguably the core institution in modern capitalism—the monetary system. On the one hand, mainstream economics settled on a theory of money as an analytically unimportant "neutral veil" over the operation of the "real" economy, as concisely summarized by Schumpeter:

> Real analysis proceeds from the principle that all the essential phenomena of economic life are capable of being described in term of goods and services, of decisions about them, and of relations between them. Money enters the picture only in the modest role of a technical device... it does not affect the economic process, which behaves in the same way as it would in a barter economy: this is essentially what the concept of Neutral Money implies. Thus, money has been called a "garb" or "veil" over the things that really matter.... Not only can it be discarded whenever we are analysing the fundamental features of the economic process but it must be discarded.... Accordingly, money prices must give way to the exchange ratios between commodities that are the really important thing "behind" money prices.[2]

These foundational assumptions, minimizing the role of money,[3] have had quite astonishing consequences for the theoretical frameworks that have informed monetary policy.[4] For example, macroeconomic models used by governments and central banks immediately before the 2008 financial crisis did not include money and finance. In his evidence to an investigation of the causes, Larry Summers—doyen of American economics, former chief economist at the World Bank, and former director of President Obama's National Economic Council—confessed that economic models did not include money as a dynamic independent force; consequently, the "vast edifice of economic theory constructed since the Second World War had been virtually useless."[5]

On the other hand, the sociological analysis of the creation of money as a social institution, as opposed to its cultural and social meanings and effects, became a marginal pursuit.[6] Money was deemed to be in the "economic" realm and left to the economists whom it was assumed were better qualified to deal with it. It was, Randall Collins perceptively observed, as if money "were not sociological enough" to warrant attention.[7] Consequently, money was left in limbo.

As Weber had labored so vigorously to resist the developing methodological antinomies in the social sciences, it is ironic that his analysis of money and banking and their crucially important role in the development of modern capitalism subsequently received so little attention within his own discipline. With very few exceptions, most notably Randall Collins,[8] generations of sociologists have focused on the role of religion and have consequently conveyed a distorted and incomplete appreciation of Weber's analysis of the development of capitalism.[9]

MONEY IN THE *METHODENSTREIT*

The analysis of money was one of the main battlegrounds between the proponents of deductive economic theory—such as Menger and von Mises—in their clash with representatives of the Older and Younger Historical School, notably Roscher, Knies, Schmoller, and Knapp.[10] Menger's "On the Origins of Money" remains a canonical text for orthodox "real" economic analysis, as depicted by Schumpeter.[11] In this praxeological (deductive) theory of human action, rational agents seek to maximize their exchange opportunities in barter, which leads to the spontaneous emergence of the most tradable commodity—that is, the one that "buys" all others.[12] Money's existence as a *medium of exchange* is unintentionally produced, facilitating efficient transactions by avoiding the "inconveniences of barter."[13]

Menger was adamant that money is *nothing* more than a *medium of exchange*—that is, a commodity that emerges as the one that is *exchangeable* for all others. His vehement insistence was directed against those in the Historical School who contended that money originated outside the market as a *means of payment* for settling debts that were denominated in a unit, or money, of account—taxes, bride price, compensatory damages, etc.[14] As a result of the dispute between the theorists and historians, the significance of this distinction between *medium of exchange* and *means of payment* has been lost to social science and, indeed, common sense. However, it is important for an understanding of the theory of money and especially for Weber's contribution.

Obviously, tradable goods can be media of exchange—for example, drugs in prisons and commodities to pay taxes where monetary systems break down, for example, in Russia after the collapse of communism.[15] However, commodities used in this way will typically have varying and fluctuating exchange ratios, based on individual preferences in bilateral trades. One hundred goods could yield 4,950 exchange ratios.[16] Consequently, mere tradable goods are an inadequate basis for denominating debt and price contracts, which require a nominal unit (money of account) that is stable over time. Empirically, some commodities are more tradable than others; but without the addition of further conditions to the model of otherwise unrelated individuals engaged in barter, the purely logical derivation of the emergence of a *single* medium of exchange with a stable nominal value for denominating contracts is not only historically unknown but also implausible.[17] In barter exchange, "there are as many valuations as there are goods and circumstances of exchange, with no possibility of being able to deduce anything whatever from them."[18]

Knapp's *State Theory of Money* contains the most comprehensive statement of the Historical School's alternative account of money's origins and of the central importance of money of account for monetary theory. Historical evidence supported the contention that the unit of value for the denomination of debts and the means of their payment ("Nominality of the Unit of Value") had been established by legal authority or agreed convention; it had not emerged spontaneously from market exchange.[19]

In typical fashion, Weber did not explicitly align himself exclusively with either side; but, ultimately, he followed Knapp's lead. On the one hand, Weber found the economist von Mises' monetary theory to be "most acceptable"[20]; but he also believed that "the explanatory methods of pure economics are as tempting as they are misleading."[21] Therefore, this may have been the qualified endorsement that von Mises had merely advanced the most acceptable of the various formulations of a strictly economic theory of money. Weber also appears to imply the legitimacy of distinct spheres of inquiry for economics and sociology by suggesting that the formation of prices might not belong "to the field of economic sociology at all."[22] Nonetheless, as we shall see, Weber clearly believes that economics' recently developed "marginal utility" theory cannot grasp the specific nature of economic action in the formation of prices, consumption, and the profit-making enterprise.[23]

Knapp was the major influence on his analysis of money. Despite a critique of its treatment of inflation in a lengthy "excursus," the *State Theory of Money* is acclaimed as "otherwise absolutely correct and brilliantly executed" and "solves the formal problem brilliantly."[24] Although there is no further clarification, it is possible that Weber is referring to the way in which Knapp's conceptual framework resolves the problem of the contentious distinction between economic theory's *media of exchange* and state theory's *means of payment*. Both could be referred to as forms of money, but they were different phenomena. While it is not spelled out in quite the same way as I have outlined, Weber unerringly sees that the differences had significant consequences for one of his major concerns—Western capitalism's rational economic calculation.

On the one hand, as economic theory maintained, "a material object will be called a *'medium of exchange'* so far as it is typically accepted by virtue of the fact that the recipients estimate that they will...be able to utilize it in another exchange to procure other goods...regardless of whether it is exchangeable for all other goods or only certain specific goods."[25]

On the other hand, following Knapp, Weber continues, "an object will be called a *means of payment* so far as its acceptance in payment of specific agreed or imposed obligations is guaranteed by convention or by law... [these] will be called chartal when they…enjoy a definite quantum…of formal validity…within a territorial area…[and] are divisible in such a way that they represent a *particular unit of nominal value* or a multiple or a fraction of it, so that it is possible to use them in arithmetical calculations."[26]

Weber agrees with Knapp that the modern state, in the pursuit of fiscal considerations, had secured a control of money's "formal validity"—that is, it had established money of account as the denomination of the legal means of payment within the state territory. In this regard, "the *continuity* of the *nominal* unit of money, even though the monetary material may have changed" is essential for establishing debt contracts acceptable to both parties—especially tax debts to the state and its interest debts on loans.[27]

The early seventeenth-century English state's sovereign control of money of account in defining the means of payment is exemplified by the legal judgement on *Gilbert v. Brett* (1604), known as the "Case of Mixt Money."[28] For political and fiscal reasons, Elizabeth I had reduced the silver content of Irish currency in 1601. An Irish merchant, Brett, proffered payment of a £100 debt, in the debased coinage, owed to his London supplier Gilbert. As their silver content was less than £100 of coins would have contained at the time of the contract, these were duly rejected by Gilbert. His challenge was summarily dismissed by the chief judges of the Queen's Privy Council, confirming that the money of account decreed by the sovereign determined the measure and mode of payment regardless of the latter's metallic content. (As we shall see, it is argued that this nominal monetary stability was an important factor in England's capitalist development.)

Although not explicitly stated, Weber sees the forging of sovereign monetary space, defined by the unit of account, in conjunction with the monopoly of physical force within a given territory as primary attributes of the modern state. Russia in the 1990s after the fall of communism and Argentina after the default and devaluation in 2001 show how the weakening of state monopoly control of the money of account is followed by a proliferation of media of exchange and means of payment, creating monetary instability and a deterioration of state finance.[29]

Weber's formulation subtly reverses the economic theory's logic that money's nominal value derives from the mere exchangeability of goods: "money we call a chartal means of payment which is also a means of exchange"[30]; "historically the function of a prescribed means of payment is the older of the two."[31] In other words, means of payment become media of exchange; but it cannot be expected that merely exchangeable commodities will be accepted as payment of debts that are denominated in a money of account.[32]

Although the state can establish "formal validity" of money—that is, what will be accepted as payment of taxes, Weber is at pains to make clear that this is to be distinguished from its "substantive validity"—that is, its actual valuation in relation to marketable goods. As economic theory explains, he agrees that this is determined by the relative scarcity of money and commodities. However, as the largest maker and receiver of payments in the economy, the modern state has a considerable indirect impact on— but cannot establish—the substantive value of money.[33]

After listing the consequences of the use of money— indirect exchange of goods separated by time and space, deferring of payment, storage of value, and the transformation of economic power into the control of money—Weber concludes that these are all "dependent on what is in principle the most important fact of all—the possibility of *calculation*; that is the possibility of assigning monetary values to all goods and services."[34] A "definite quantum of formal validity," money is an essential precondition in the development of the two other core institutions that define the modern economy: the *market* and *capital*. Weber's analysis implies that these core components of modern capitalism were to a significant extent the unintended consequence of the state's pursuit of its fiscal interests which required a stable money of account for budgetary calculation. Capitalism was not merely the spontaneous result of rational agents maximizing their utility, as economic theory contended.

Money and the Market

"Indirect exchange," by which it is possible to obtain goods, separated in time, space, and persons involved, from those offered, permits a "tremendous extension of the area of possible exchange relationships."[35] In other words, a genuine market of multilateral transactions between anonymous agents separated by time and space, as opposed to direct bilateral barter exchange, is made possible by money. Weber again contrasts his analytical framework with economic theory's restricted focus on subjective want satisfaction by the exchange of utilities: "monetary calculation means that goods are not evaluated merely in terms of their immediate importance as utilities at the given time and place and for the given person only. Rather, goods are more or less systematically compared whether for consumption or for production with all potential future opportunities of utilization or of gaining a return."[36] Monetary calculation is essential for comparing alternative courses of economic action in the pursuit of maximum profit which characterizes the historical specificity of modern rational capitalism, as opposed to economic theory's ahistorical model of the individual's search for utility.

Capital and Calculation

"There is a form of monetary accounting which is peculiar to rational economic profit-making; namely capital accounting."[37] In contrast to economic theory's conception of capital in terms of the physical properties of "stocks" of productive resources in the "real" economy, Weber sees capital as "the *money value* of the means of profit-making available to enterprise at the balancing of the books."[38] An economic enterprise (*Unternehmen*) is defined in terms of its ability to perform capital accounting—that is, the ex-ante calculation of the probable risks and chances of profit[39] ... "[which] has arisen as a basic form of economic calculation only in the Western World."[40]

Again, Weber explicitly contrasts his analysis of the profit-making capitalist enterprise with economics' concept of "marginal utility," introducing further considerations which clearly show his departure from pure economic theory. Money is not merely a "neutral" measure for pricing the value of commodities and capital which is determined by their utility in want satisfaction or functional contribution to the production process. Rather, money plays an essential and active role in determining capitalist enterprise production.[41]

The pursuit of money profit by means of enterprise using capital accounting presupposes a particular—that is to say, historically specific—power constellation: "the formal rationality of money calculation is dependent on certain quite specific substantive conditions."[42] In other words, Weber specifies the institutional and social structural conditions which make monetary calculation possible. First, there must be market freedom in a struggle between autonomous economic agents—that is, economic activity is not determined by norms governing production and consumption as it is in "patrimonial" and "traditional" society. The market is "the battle of man against man" and money is a "weapon in this struggle."[43] Second, capital accounting can only occur under certain substantive conditions: (1) competition enabled by "thorough market freedom," that is, in the absence of monopolies, and (2) the complete appropriation of the means of production and the imposition of "shop discipline." In other words, capital accounting presupposes the power to control the means of profit-making.[44] Third, it is not demand for goods in the sense merely of subjective wants that determines production based on calculations of money accounting but purchasing power, which is determined by the distribution of wealth and income.[45]

This formulation resembles Keynes' characterization of modern capitalism as a "monetary production economy" in contrast to economic theory's model of exchange in a "cooperative" or "natural" economy.[46] In the latter, money is merely the medium which enables utility-seeking agents to exchange commodities without the inconveniences of barter, as depicted, for example, in Marx's C[ommodity]–M[oney]–C[ommodity] formula. In contrast, capitalist production is driven by the pursuit of money profit (M–C–M), which is ultimately dependent, as Keynes emphasized, on "effective demand"—that is, adequate purchasing power.[47]

In effect, Weber's analysis of the consequences of the use of money implies a "social theory of value" in contrast to "substance" or "utility" theories advanced in classical and neoclassical economic theory and Marxism.[48] Economic theories of value "attempt to explain the exchangeability of commodities by assuming the existence of a quality that endows goods with intrinsic value."[49] Two "substances" have been held to possess this intrinsic value—labor and utility. For Marx and some classical economics, the value of a commodity was endowed by the socially necessary labor time involved in its production, including money itself, which consisted of mined and minted gold.[50] Weber flatly rejected such "substance" theories: "any attempt to reduce all means to ultimate expenditures of labor is erroneous."[51] In later neoclassical economic theory, value was determined by the interaction of myriad supply and demand schedules representing an individual's final increment of satisfaction, or "marginal utility," afforded by a scarce commodity.

However, as Weber avers, "economic theory...could, however, also be developed along very different lines."[52] In his analysis, the supply and demand of utility-seeking individuals takes on the radically different character of a power struggle between different interests in which money is both the "weapon" and object of struggle which produce the prices that enable "effective" calculation—that is, externally generated prices that have to be taken as given in any calculation.[53] For example, following this approach in his theory of profit, Smithin contends that "the profit share of GDP is...determined by (a) Keynesian considerations of effective demand and (b) the bargaining power of the other main players in the struggle over income distribution, namely labour and the rentier class, represented, in practice, primarily by the setting of interest rates by the central bank on behalf of the financial constituency."[54, 55]

Money and the Critique of the Possibility of Socialism

The question of the viability of a socialist economy became more widely considered after the Russian Revolution in 1917 and the prospect of large-scale non-capitalist organization of production. What became known as the "socialist calculation debate" was triggered by von Mises' article "Economic Calculation in the Socialist Commonwealth" (1920), later supported by von Hayek and challenged by Marxist and left-wing neoclassical economists, most notably, Lange, Lerner, and Dobb.[56]

In an early contribution to the debate, Weber uses his analysis of money in a critique of Otto Neurath's contention that money led to unproductive speculation and should be eliminated in a completely socialized economy.[57] Calculation based on money prices could be replaced, Neurath argued, by accounting "in kind," based on the functional contribution (use value) of physical magnitudes to production, which the organization of the economy in the First World War had shown to be viable. For example, from a strictly technical standpoint by arbitrarily assigning a numerical value to factors of production, it might be possible to show that a greater quantity of labor could increase output more than, say, increased use of electricity. However, Weber contended that unless the numerical values assigned to factors of production were money "prices"—that is, established in a market struggle between autonomous agents—the cost effectiveness and efficiency of the substitution of labor for electricity could not be determined.

The calculation of *profitability* was a superior method for enabling the efficient use of resources which could only be pursued rationally by the ex post calculation of costs and revenues represented by "effective"—that is, externally given—money prices. Calculation "in kind" was only technically possible "in one of two ways: by adherence to tradition or by an arbitrary dictatorial regulation" which prescribes "the pattern of consumption *and* enforces obedience" (emphasis in original).[58] Weber agreed that the organization of the war economy was effective but also exceptional in that it was oriented to a single goal and under the control of the authorities who could use a level of power not tolerated in peacetime except "where the subjects are slaves of an authoritarian state."[59] Weber emphasizes that his critique is based on the objective possibility of effective calculation and not on an ethical consideration of the "absolute value" of socialist society, which is beyond the scope of any science.[60]

For Weber, the identification of capital accounting with modern capitalism is the focal point of its contrast with non-Western and pre-capitalist economies. *Money accounting* for budgeting in bureaucratic pre-capitalist systems in ancient Egypt and Mesopotamia is distinguished from rational *capital accounting* of *profit and loss*, which "presupposes the existence of effective prices and not merely fictitious prices conventionally employed for technical accounting purposes."[61] Arbitrarily assigned nominal values, or "fictitious prices," can be used for the budgetary management of resources. But as Weber explained in his critique of the "complete socialization" of the economy, this form of accounting could only be employed for the entire economy by a bureaucratic—but not necessarily efficient—authoritarian state.

The ex ante calculation of profit and loss in capital accounting requires that "effective prices" are established independently by the competitive "struggle for economic existence" between free agents and enterprises. Consequently, "money can *never* be merely a harmless "voucher" or a purely nominal unit of accounting so long as it is money" (original emphasis).[62] In the same way that bread tokens were used in Ptolemaic Egypt, the purchase of goods with vouchers given in payment for a quantity of "socially useful labor [in a socialist economy] would follow the rules of barter exchange, not of money."[63]

Although Weber does not pursue the question much further, it strongly implied that any socialist or communist system would lack dynamism and efficiency in a way comparable to the patrimonial bureaucratic empires of Ptolemaic Egypt, ancient Babylon, and China.[64] For Weber, capital accounting, as *the* definitive feature of rational capitalism, "has arisen as a basic form of economic calculation only in the Western World."[65] This theme will be pursued shortly in an examination of Weber's analysis of the role of money in China's economic backwardness. However, we must first examine a less thoroughly explored, but nonetheless equally important, element in Weber's thesis of the uniqueness of the West—capitalist banking.

CAPITALIST BANKING, FINANCE, SPECULATION, CRISES

In his posthumous *History of Economic Analysis*, Joseph Schumpeter outlines two different conceptions of how banks operate in the modern capitalist economy. These correspond to the two opposed conceptions of money, which in turn derive from the two conceptions of the economy—economics' analytical "real" model and historically located capitalism. On the one hand, it was widely held in orthodox economics that "bankers remain middlemen who collect 'liquid capital' from innumerable small pools.... They add *nothing* to the existing mass of liquid means, though they make it do more work" (emphasis added).[66] On the other hand, in the heterodox view, expounded—at times with some ambivalence—by Schumpeter, banks are seen to create *new* money "in their act of lending."[67] In the first view, deposits create loans and, in the second, loans create deposits. In other words, capitalist banks do not use depositors' money to make loans in the same way that a traditional moneylender would do by taking coins from a hoard. Banks lend by creating with the stroke of a pen, or tap on a keyboard, a deposit in the borrower's account. Then banks borrow from each other and, most importantly in the modern system, from a central bank to balance their books. Unless there is a run on a bank in which all depositors wish to withdraw their money simultaneously, banks can continue to produce money by lending.

Creation of money in this way was the result of the gradual development of banking networks (giros) trading in acknowledgments of debt (bills, promissory notes, etc.), which eventually came to be orchestrated and underwritten by "public," later "central," banks that financed and held state debt as assets. Indeed, Schumpeter believed that "the development of the law and practice of negotiable paper and of 'created' deposits afford the best indication we have for dating the rise of capitalism."[68] The *differentia specifica* of capitalism is to be found in its distinctive monetary institutions, in which privately contracted credit relations are routinely "monetized" by the linkages between the state and its creditors, the central bank and the banking system.[69]

In a developed capitalist banking system loans are *private debts* which are transformed into *public money* when they enter the economy by being spent by the borrower.[70] These institutional arrangements enabled an unprecedented expansion of the supply of money, which became at one and the same time a source of capitalism's dynamism and instability.[71]

Weber devoted very little attention to banking in *Economy and Society*[72] and produced no more than a sketch in *General Economic History*.[73] However, this is entirely consistent with Schumpeter's analysis and the subsequent heterodox economic and sociological analyses of money.[74] The two distinctive and novel elements in capitalist banking referred to by Schumpeter—"negotiable paper" and "created deposits"—are dealt with briefly but concisely by Weber. Although banks existed in the ancient and classical economies, he notes that they did not create circulating credit money in the manner of capitalist banks. Pre-capitalist banking activity involved money changing, where domestic and foreign coins circulated together; making payments at a distance; and intermediation between depositors. This developed further in Rome, where current account deposits became the means for clearing debts between depositors to avoid cumbersome cash transactions. In a comment, which was surely addressed to the economic theorists, Weber warns that we should guard against thinking of these banks "in terms too modern." Regarding the "notes" used for settling transactions between customers, "one must not think in this connection of bank notes in our sense, for the modern bank note circulates independently of any deposit by a particular individual."[75] In other words, pre-capitalist banks did not make loans by advancing "credit" in new deposits of transferable notes and, thereby, increase the supply money in the manner of the modern capitalist banking system.

Weber accurately pinpoints the distinctive element in capitalist banking by tracing the development of assignable (transferable) debt from the use of bills of exchange, which led to a vast increase in "liquidity" and the supply of money.[76] As subsequent research has shown, the bill of exchange was a key element in these developments.[77] Exchange by bill probably originated in Islamic trade and entered Europe through the Italian maritime city states in the thirteenth century. Bills facilitated trade without the risk of transporting precious metal means of payment across unsafe territory in the Near East and late medieval Europe. Exchange by bill required two networks—one of merchants and one of bankers. Trader A would draw a bill from a local banker B to use as payment for imported goods from a seller C, who would then present the bill to a banker D in the same network as banker A for exchanging into C's local currency. Originally, the bills represented the value of the goods in transit; but over a long period, the credit bills gradually developed into "negotiable"—that is, "transferable"—means of payment to any "bearer" of the bill quite independently of any particular goods. Eventually, by the sixteenth century transferability had been legally established by the maxim *chi accetta paghi* ("the acceptor must pay"). "This unconditional assurance of payment made it possible for the bill of exchange to become the bank paper of today."[78]

In a section of *Economy and Society*, "Institutions Auxiliary to Actionable Contract: Agency; Assignment; Negotiable Instruments," Weber further discusses the institutional changes in traditional society that eventually enabled the legal transferability of debt as an "indispensable [element] for a modern capitalistic society."[79] However, "as a result of the highly personal character of the debt-relationship...instruments payable to order of the payee or to the bearer, which served for the transfer both of claims, especially monetary claims, and of powers of disposition over commercial goods and membership rights in the commercial enterprises...had been utterly unknown in Roman law."[80]

However, the use of negotiable debt as a means of payment in the relatively small-scale private mercantile networks was constantly dislocated by bank failures and subsequent liquidity crises.[81] Consequently, "the pressure of events was in the direction of monopolistic banking," which was furthered by mutually advantageous financial agreements between banks and states. States granted monopolies to privately owned banks in return for finance provided by the merchant owners and depositors, which "made banking a public enterprise."[82] These first appeared in Italian city states during the fifteenth century and reached their apogee with the Bank of England in 1694.

Weber accords great significance to the Bank of England's role in the development of an integrated monetary system, based on freely produced credit money, which had important consequences for the growth of capitalism. In 1672, the financial arrangement between the English monarchy and the mercantile bourgeoisie broke down when Charles II defaulted, creating pressure for the establishment of a public bank to rationalize government finance. In exchange for lending its entire original share capital to the monarch, the Bank of England was granted, among other things, the right to deal in bills of exchange (transferable debts). Using its privileged position as the state's banker, the Bank of England was able to exchange the country banks' lower-quality bills, at a profitable discount, for its own more acceptable ones, which were backed by "sovereign" promises to pay. The unintended consequence was to expand the money supply by securing and shortening credit lines for producers and merchants. This critical institutional change did not occur in China; and, as we shall see, Weber strongly implies that this had at least as important an impact as religious ethics on its economic development.[83] In short, the creation of national debts and an effective taxation system with which to service the interest on loans from private investors was a result of a "memorable alliance between the rising states and the sought-after and privileged capitalist powers that was a *major factor* in creating modern capitalism."[84]

Despite the attention given to the distinctive institutional development of capitalist credit money, it does not appear as a separate element in Weber's ideal type of capitalism presented in Chapter 22 ("The Meaning and Presuppositions of Modern Capitalism") of *General Economic History*. Rather, at the end of the chapter, Weber refers to "another factor not yet mentioned, namely speculation... [which] reaches its full significance from the moment when property takes on the form of *negotiable paper*."[85]

Twenty pages or so later, Weber picks up the theme in Chapter 24 ("The First Great Speculative Crises"), which clearly demonstrates the importance that he attached to capitalism's monetary and financial structure. Negotiable debt gives rise to speculation, debt default, and inevitable liquidity crises, which present a subtly different emphasis in the explanation of the "great economic crises" that "Karl Marx had in view when in the Communist Manifesto he prophesised the downfall of capitalism."[86] Superficially, the crises which had become "an imminent factor of the economic order" appeared as the result of the overproduction of goods beyond the capacity for their consumption. More fundamentally, however, this could only occur as a consequence of the speculative overproduction of the means of production; and "speculation... becomes important from the moment when property can be represented by freely negotiable paper."[87] In other words, crises of capitalism were generated fundamentally by its monetary and financial structure, as, for example, Schumpeter and his student Minsky argued.[88]

Money and banking form only a small part of Weber's work, but subsequent research in history, sociology, and heterodox economics has confirmed its accuracy and analytical force. He identified the distinctive and interdependent characteristics of Western capitalist money and banking: how negotiable debt forms the basis for the elastic creation of credit money and how these arrangements were eventually consolidated by the public banks' holding state debts as assets.[89] The latter development was the result of the "memorable alliance" between the merchant bourgeoisie and states in early modern Europe, which Weber considered to be of critical importance in shaping the trajectory of Western capitalism. States and merchant capital developed a mutually advantageous relationship which contrasted sharply with the antagonism and mutual suspicion displayed in the economically stagnant oriental states such as China.

THE "GREAT DIVERGENCE" AND
CHINA'S "MISSING LINK"

Some time ago, I was astonished to discover that Weber's *Religion of China* opens with an analysis of Chinese money, which finds that it "was, until modern times, scarcely as well developed as it was in Ptolemaic Egypt."[90] The underdevelopment is evident in precisely those two elements in western European money that Weber considered to be so important in the development of capitalism. First, as a major consequence of the establishing of stable moneys of account, "the occidental world alone became the abode of money computation while in the orient computation in kind has remained the rule."[91] Second, the institutions in European medieval cities which led to the use of depersonalized, transferable credit as a means of payment either were absent or followed a different path of development in China.[92]

Although Weber did not pursue these themes in depth, this does not warrant their almost complete subsequent neglect. Following Weber's lead, I examined the long-standing question of China' stagnation after the sixteenth century and its "great divergence" from the West's developmental path.[93] I argued that the Chinese state's failure to establish a stable money of account throughout its territory and the absence of a state–bourgeois coalition that led to a stable banking network in some Western states might be the "missing links" in China's capitalist development.[94]

For the very same reasons that I have adduced, a consideration of these factors was also "missing" from the analyses of capitalist development in the two dominant traditions in the social sciences. On the one hand, historians, influenced by orthodox economic theories of growth, focused on material and technological factors of production and until very recently minimized the autonomous role of money and finance.[95] On the other hand, social scientists, influenced—at least indirectly—by Weberian sociology, concentrated on the impact of religion. Sociology completely ignored Weber's comments on money and the way in which calculation and taxation in kind had impeded capitalist development in China and elsewhere.

Weber's conclusion that the Chinese state had "not only failed in its currency policy but also in its attempt to establish the money economy" was echoed by the president of its Currency Board set up in the early twentieth century to remedy the situation.[96] Liang Qichao lamented, "Alas our nation has been established for thousands of years, yet is still known as a nation with no money."[97] This was not intended to mean that China didn't have media of exchange and payment. On the contrary, China had too many different money things that the state had not been able to subsume under a single uniform unit of account. In addition to the persistence of payment in kind and precious metal by weight, there were myriad moneys of account restricted in their applicability to different commercial sectors and regions. Other commentators agreed with Liang Qichao's conviction that monetary anarchy, in contrast to the West, had impeded economic development.[98]

Subsequent research has supported Weber's conclusion that Chinese "money shops" contained the potential to become a prototype for capitalist banking but that ultimately they did not "offer a parallel to that of Europe."[99] The monetary anarchy inhibited the development of Chinese mercantile credit networks into widely circulating transferable means of payment, denominated in a common money of account, as had occurred in the West.[100] Furthermore, unresolved conflict between the Chinese mandarin bureaucracy and the merchants was a major barrier to the creation of a capitalist banking system based on a "memorable alliance."

Three types of merchant capital–state relation are to be found in the early modern period: (1) isomorphism in which the state is itself a mercantile trading company, most notably in the Italian city state republics such as Venice in the sixteenth century[101]; (2) mutual interdependence, as in Holland and England[102]; and (3) antagonistic mutual exclusion, which persisted in China until the twentieth century.[103] In China, the patrimonial state in which "a thin stratum of so-called officials, the mandarins, existed above the unbroken power of the clans and commercial and industrial guilds" was a barrier to the paths followed in the West.[104]

CONCLUSION

As I have outlined, the way in which the social sciences evolved during the twentieth century has meant that Weber's analysis of money has had almost no direct influence. However, it is a significant measure of his intellectual acumen that his work is entirely consistent with later important contributions to our understanding of money and the critique of the "creation myth" of its emergence from barter. These have been produced in the broadly heterodox tradition in economics which has followed the path laid down by Schumpeter and Keynes.[105] In this regard, as we have seen, three aspects of Weber's analysis of money are noteworthy: (1) the emphasis on money's definitive property as a measure for economic calculation (money of account), (2) the understanding of the nature of modern capitalist banking as the creation of negotiable debt as a means of payment and its link to distinctively capitalist crises, and (3) the fundamental importance of the state in the production of money.

Modern "neo-chartalist" economists have employed Knapp's "state theory of money," which had such a marked influence on Weber and Keynes, in a critique of the orthodox monetary policy that is informed by conventional economic theory.[106] "Neo-chartalist" modern monetary theory emphasizes the autonomy and discretion that the modern state has at its disposal in the creation of money. It contends that modern states "spend money into existence" and consequently that the prior collection of taxes is not a necessary precondition of expenditure. The state does not need its citizens' taxes before it spends; rather, citizens need the state's money to be able to pay the taxes. Any constraint on government spending is self-imposed—for example, by fixing the value and supply of currency to a stock of gold or by principles of "sound" fiscal policy and arbitrary limits on government expenditure and debt.

However, modern money theory's focus on the narrowly "economic" or "account-ancy" question of whose money really pays for government spending overlooks the sociological significance of the struggles between debtors, creditors, taxpayers, and government bondholders. In Weberian terms, the question of "sound" and "unsound" budget finance, like the question of the value of money itself, cannot be separated from the economic "battle of man with man" in which money is a "weapon."[107] Concepts of "sound finance" and "fiscal norms" are not derived from economic "laws" but are deter-mined by the struggles between the state, economic classes, and other interests. There are encouraging signs that this Weberian approach, which I have used in my own work, might be developed further—for example, in the analysis of the euro as a "weapon" in European politics.[108]

NOTES

1. Geoffrey Ingham, "On the 'Underdevelopment' of the Sociology of Money," *Acta Sociologica* 41, no. 10 (1998): 3–15; André Orléan, *The Empire of Value* (Cambridge, MA: MIT Press, 2014).
2. Joseph A. Schumpeter, *History of Economic Analysis* (1954; London: Allen & Unwin, 1994), 277.
3. Orléan, *Empire of Value.*
4. C. A. E. Goodhart, "The Continuing Muddles of Monetary Theory: A Steadfast Refusal to Face Facts," *Economica* 76 (2009): 821–830.
5. Cited in Felix Martin, *Money: The Unauthorised Biography* (London: Vintage, 2014), 190.
6. Ingham, "On the 'Underdevelopment' of the Sociology of Money"; Geoffrey Ingham, *The Nature of Money* (Cambridge: Polity, 2004).
7. Randall Collins, "Review of Mayer, *The Bankers,*" *American Journal of Sociology* 85 (1979): 196.
8. Randall Collins, "Weber's Last Theory of Capitalism: A Systematization," *American Sociological Review* 45 (1980): 925–942.
9. Geoffrey Ingham, "Schumpeter and Weber on the Institutions of Capitalism: Solving Swedberg's 'Puzzle,'" *Journal of Classical Sociology* 3, no. 3 (2003): 297–309; Geoffrey Ingham, *Capitalism* (Cambridge: Polity, 2011).
10. Haim Barkai, "The Old Historical School: Roscher on Money and Monetary Issues," *History of Political Economy* 21, no. 2 (1989): 181–200; H. Ellis, *German Monetary Theory: 1905–1933* (Cambridge, MA: Harvard University Press, 1934); Mark Peacock, *Introducing Money* (London: Routledge, 2013); Fiona Maclachlan, "Max Weber Within the *Method-enstreit*," *Cambridge Journal of Economics* 41, no. 4 (2017): 1161–1175; H. Peukert, "Max Weber: Precursor of Economic Sociology and Heterodox Economics," *American Journal of Economics and Sociology* 63, no. 5 (2004): 987–1020.
11. C. Menger, "On the Origins of Money," *Economic Journal* 2, no. 6 (1892): 239–255.
12. R. Clower, "A Reconsideration of the Microfoundations of Money," in *Money and Markets,* ed. D. Walker (1967; Cambridge: Cambridge University Press, 1984), 81–89.
13. W. S. Jevons, *Money and the Mechanism of Exchange* (London: Appleton, 1875).

14. G. F. Knapp, *The State Theory of Money* (1924; New York: Augustus Kelly, 1973).

15. D. Woodruff, *Money Unmade* (Ithaca, NY: Cornell University Press, 1999).

16. Ingham, *Nature of Money*, 22–25; G. Davies, *A History of Money* (Cardiff, UK: University of Wales Press, 1996), 15.

17. Geoffrey Ingham, "Revisting the Credit Theory of Money," in *New Perspectives on Emotions in Finance*, ed. Jocelyn Pixley (London: Routledge, 2012), 121–139.

18. Orléan, *Empire of Value*, 127.

19. Knapp, *State Theory of Money*, chap. 1. Following Knapp, Keynes opened his *A Treatise on Money* with the statement that money of account, "in which Debts Prices and General Purchasing Power is expressed, is the primary concept of a Theory of money" and that this description of money "is claimed by all modern states" (J. M. Keynes, *A Treatise on Money* [London: Macmillan, 1930], 3–4).

20. Max Weber, *Economy and Society* (hereafter *E&S*), ed. Guenther Roth and Claus Wittich (Berkeley and Los Angeles: University of California Press, 1978), 78–79; Weber, *Wirtschaft und Gesellschaft. Soziologie. Max Weber-Gesamtausgabe* (hereafter *MWG*) I/23, ed. K. Borchardt, E. Hanke, and W. Schluchter (Tübingen, Germany: Mohr [Siebeck], 2013), 239–240.

21. *E&S*, 115; *MWG* I/23, 298.

22. *E&S*, 79; *MWG* I/23, 243.

23. *E&S*, 97; *MWG* I/23, 269.

24. *E&S*, 78, 169, 184–193; *MWG* I/23, 239–240, 388, 415–427.

25. *E&S*, 75–76; *MWG* I/23, 235.

26. *E&S*, 76 (emphasis added); *MWG* I/23, 235–236.

27. *E&S*, 168; *MWG* I/23, 387.

28. D. Fox, "The Case of Mixt Monies," *Cambridge Law Journal* 70, no. 1 (2011): 144–174.

29. Woodruff, *Money Unmade*; Ingham, *Nature of Money*.

30. *E&S*, 76; *MWG* I/23, 236.

31. Max Weber, *General Economic History* (hereafter *GEH*), trans. F. H. Knight (1927; New Brunswick, NJ: Transaction, 1981), 236; Weber, *Abriß der universalen Sozial- und Wirtschafts- geschichte. Mit- und Nachschriften 1919/20*, *MWG* III/6, ed. W. Schluchter, with J. Schröder (Tübingen, Germany: Mohr [Siebeck], 2011), 288.

32. A creditor may agree to accept goods in payment of a debt that is denominated in money of account of say £100; but this is essentially a monetary transaction as the goods are priced in money of account and thereby become a temporary surrogate for money that is specific to the transaction. The creditor cannot expect that the goods he accepted would be accepted as payment of a £100 that he owes, which would be the case with means of payment denominated in money of account.

33. *E&S*, 178–184; *MWG* I/23, 404–415.

34. *E&S*, 80–81; *MWG* I/23, 244–245.

35. *E&S*, 80; *MWG* I/23, 244.

36. *E&S*, 81; *MWG* I/23, 245. Transactions based on the evaluation of the "immediate impor- tance" of the utilities of goods for "given" persons at a "given" time and "given" place are *barter* exchange.

37. *E&S*, 91; *MWG* I/23, 259.

38. *E&S*, 91; *MWG* I/23, 259.

39. *E&S*, 91; *MWG* I/23, 260.

40. *E&S*, 92; *MWG* I/23, 261.

41. Hodgson has argued for the reintroduction into economics of the concept of "capital" as "money-capital" and not merely material means of production. See Geoffrey Hodgson, *Conceptualizing Capitalism* (Chicago: University of Chicago Press, 2015).

42. *E&S*, 107; *MWG* I/23, 285.

43. *E&S*, 93, 108; *MWG* I/23, 263, 286.

44. "Conditions of Maximum Formal Rationality of Capital Accounting" (*E&S*, 161; *MWG* I/23, 375). (1) Complete appropriation of all material means of production by owners and complete market freedom. (2) Complete autonomy in selection of management by owners—that is, complete absence of appropriation of rights to managerial functions. (3) Complete absence of appropriation of jobs by workers and of workers by owners—that is, formally free labor. (4) Complete absence of substantive regulation of consumption, production, and contract. (5) Complete calculability of technical conditions of production—that is, mechanically rational technology. (6) Complete calculability of public administration and legal order and their guarantee by the political authority. (7) The most complete separation possible between the enterprise and the household budget. (8) Monetary system with the highest possible degree of formal rationality. See also Weber, *GEH*, 254–266; *MWG* III/6, 302–317 (= 3. Kapitel, § 7).

45. *E&S*, 92–94; *MWG* I/23, 261–264.

46. J. M. Keynes, "A Monetary Theory of Production," reprinted in *Collected Writings*, vol. 21, ed. D. Moggridge (1933; London: Macmillan, 1973); "The Distinction Between a Co-operative Economy and an Entrepreneur Economy," reprinted in *Collected Writings*, vol. 29, ed. D. Moggridge (1933; London: Macmillan, 1979).

47. J. M. Keynes, *The General Theory of Employment Interest and Money*, reprinted in *Collected Writings*, vol. 21, ed. D. Moggridge (1936; London: Macmillan, 1973), chap. 3.

48. Ingham, *Nature of Money*; J. Smithin, *Money, Enterprise and Income Distribution* (London: Routledge, 2009); Orléan, *Empire of Value*.

49. Orléan, *Empire of Value*, 13.

50. Ingham, *Nature of Money*, 61–63.

51. *E&S*, 66; *MWG* I/23, 221.

52. *E&S*, 97; *MWG* I/23, 270.

53. *E&S*, 92–94; *MWG* I/23, 261–264.

54. Smithin, *Money, Enterprise and Income Distribution*, 91, 103.

55. On the conflict theory of inflation, see R. E. Rowthorn, "Conflict, Inflation and Money," *Cambridge Journal of Economics* 1, no. 3 (1977): 215–239; Scott Aquanno and Jordan Brennan, "Some Inflationary Aspects of Distributional Conflict," *Journal of Economic Issues* 50, no. 1 (2016): 217–244.

56. For a survey of the debate, see David Levy and Sandra Peart, "Socialist Calculation Debate," in *The New Palgrave Dictionary of Economics*, ed. Stephen Durlauf and Laurence Blume (London: Palgrave Macmillan, 2008). http://www.dictionaryofeconomicsarticle?id=pde2008_5000535; and Stephen Parsons, "Max Weber, Socialism and the Space for Time," *Political Studies* 49 (2001): 495, 512.

57. *E&S*, 104–107; *MWG* I/23, 280–285.

58. *E&S*, 104 (emphasis in original); *MWG* I/23, 279.

59. *E&S*, 106; *MWG* I/23, 283: "bei 'Staatssklaverei' der 'Untertanen.'"

60. *E&S*, 104; *MWG* I/23, 280.

61. *E&S*, 93; *MWG* I/23, 263.

62. *E&S*, 79 (emphasis in original); *MWG* I/23, 243.

63. *E&S*, 79–80; *MWG* I/23, 244.

64. See, for example, *E&S*, 1094–1097; Weber, *Wirtschaft und Gesellschaft. Nachlaß. Herrschaft. MWG* I/22-4, ed. E. Hanke with Th. Kroll (Tübingen, Germany: Mohr [Siebeck], 2005), 418–431.

65. *E&S*, 92; *MWG* I/23, 261.

66. Schumpeter, *History of Economic Analysis*, 1113.

67. Ibid., 1114.

68. Ibid., 78.

69. Ingham, *Nature of Money*; Charles W. Calomiris and Stephen H. Haber, *Fragile by Design: The Political Origins of Banking Crises and Scarce Credit* (Princeton, NJ: Princeton University Press, 2014).

70. In conventional monetary economics this is referred to as "endogenous" money as opposed to the "exogenous" money that emits from the state and central banks. See John Smithin, *Controversies in Monetary Economics* (Cheltenham, UK: Edward Elgar, 2003) for a comprehensive account. As "endogenous" money points to a limit on their control, monetary authorities have been reluctant publicly to recognize how the banking system creates money in this relatively autonomous way. However, this has recently been acknowledged by the Bank of England (McLeay et al., "Money Creation in the Modern Economy," *Bank of England Quarterly Bulletin* Q1 [2014]). Betraying the persistent implicit influence of the old commodity theory of money, orthodox economics continues to refer to this as money creation ex nihilo. However, these deposits of money are created out of "nothing" only in the sense that they do not represent the material existence of money "things." Rather, the deposit of new money is created by the borrower's *promise* to repay.

71. Hyman Minsky, "The Financial Instability Hypothesis," in *Financial Crises*, ed. C. P. Kindleberger and J.-P. Laffarge (Cambridge: Cambridge University Press, 1982).

72. *E&S*, 159–161; *MWG* I/23, 370–375.

73. Weber, *GEH*, 254–266, chap. XX "Banking and Dealings in Money in the Pre-Capitalistic Age"; *MWG* III/6, 302–317 (= chap. 3, § 7).

74. See, for example, Ingham, *Nature of Money*; Smithin, *Controversies in Monetary Economics*; L. Randall Wray, *Modern Money Theory* (London: Palgrave Macmillan, 2012).

75. Weber, *GEH*, 255; *MWG* III/6, 303.

76. Weber, *GEH*, 260–262; *MWG* III/6, 307–310.

77. John H. Munro, "The Medieval Origins of the Financial Revolution: Usury, *Rentes*, and Negotiability," *International History Review* 25, no. 3 (2003): 505–562; Ingham, *Nature of Money*, chap. 6.

78. Weber, *GEH*, 263; *MWG* III/6, 310.

79. *E&S*, 681–682; Weber, *Wirtschaft und Gesellschaft. Nachlaß. Recht, MWG* I/22-3, ed. W. Gephart and S. Hermes (Tübingen, Germany: Mohr [Siebeck], 2010), 333: "für den modernen Kapitalisten."

80. *E&S*, 681–682; *MWG* I/22-3, 334–335. The view that Roman money was restricted to coinage has recently been challenged: W. V. Harris, "A Revisionist View of Roman Money," *Journal of Roman Studies* 96 (2006): 1–24; W. V. Harris, "The Nature of Roman Money," in *The Monetary Systems of the Greeks and Romans*, ed. W. V. Harris (Oxford: Oxford University Press, 2008), 174–207. Harris argues that credit relations were widespread in Rome and consequently that economic growth was not impeded by a shortage of money. A comprehensive assessment cannot be made here, but Harris does not show how far credit in the form of acknowledgments of debt contracts between individuals was anonymously

transferable—that is, could be used to settled third-party debts. For a clear understanding of the gradual development of negotiability, see Munro, "Medieval Origins of the Financial Revolution." Weber holds that there was a speculative market in land centered on Rome: "Rome [was] the real estate exchange of the world"; "The subsignatio [signature] could be used to authorize a mortgage [on land], and it had the advantage that the mortgage could be sold, generally to speculators in risky loans." See Weber, *Roman Agrarian History*, trans. Richard I. Frank (1891; Claremont, CA: Regina, 2008), 68–69.

81. *GEH*, 260; *MWG* III/6, 308.

82. *GEH*, 260; *MWG* III/6, 308: "verstaatlichte…das Bankwesen."

83. *GEH*, 265–266; *MWG* III/6, 312–313.

84. *E&S*, 353 (emphasis added); Weber, *Wirtschaft und Gesellschaft. Nachlaß. Gemeinschaften. MWG* I/22-1, ed. W. J. Mommsen with M. Meyer (Tübingen, Germany: Mohr [Siebeck], 2001), 106.

85. *GEH*, 278 (emphasis added); *MWG* III/6, 320. This slight treatment is presumably why credit and money are not discussed in Collins's excellent gloss on *General Economic History*. (Collins, "Weber's Last Theory of Capitalism").

86. *GEH*, 290; *MWG* III/6, 330.

87. *GEH*, 286; *MWG* III/6, 326.

88. Minsky, "Financial Instability Hypothesis"; for an overview of these terms of the "great financial crisis" of 2008, see Ingham, *Capitalism*, 227–264.

89. See Munro "Medieval Origins of the Financial Revolution"; for a survey of the subsequent historical evidence, see Ingham, *Nature of Money*, and Calomiris and Haber, *Fragile by Design*.

90. Max Weber. *The Religion of China. Confucianism and Taoism* (hereafter *RC*), trans. and ed. H. H. Gerth (New York: Free Press, 1951), 3; Weber, *Die Wirtschaftsethik der Weltreligionen. Konfuzianismus und Taoismus, MWG* I/19, ed. H. Schmidt-Glintzer, with P. Kolonko (Tübingen, Germany: Mohr [Siebeck], 1989), 132 ("Neuzeit").

91. *GEH*, 224; *MWG* III/6, 278.

92. *RC*, 3; *MWG* I/19, 132; *GEH*, 265–266; *MWG* III/6, 312–313.

93. Kenneth Pomeranz, *The Great Divergence* (Princeton, NJ: Princeton University Press, 2000).

94. Geoffrey Ingham, "The 'Great Divergence': Max Weber and China's 'Missing Links,'" *Max Weber Studies* 15, no. 2 (2015): 1–32.

95. Richard Sylla, "Financial Systems and Economic Modernization," *Journal of Economic History* 62, no. 2 (2002): 227–291; Ingham, "'Great Divergence.'"

96. Weber, *RC*, 13; *MWG* I/19, 148.

97. Quoted in Ingham, "'Great Divergence,'" 17.

98. See Ingham "'Great Divergence.'" Ray Huang (collaborator on Joseph Needham's monumental study *Science and Civilization in China* [Cambridge: Cambridge University Press, 1954–2008]) has argued that from the eighteenth century, in contrast to England, China's economy and tax system never became "mathematically manageable": R. Huang, *Broadening the Horizons of Chinese History* (New York: M. E. Sharpe, 1999), 94.

99. Weber, *GEH*, 265; *MWG* III/6, 312; see Peng Xinwei, *A Monetary History of China*, 2 vols., trans. E. H. Kaplan (1954; Bellingham: Western Washington University, 1994), 633–634.

100. David Faure, *China and Capitalism: A History of Business Enterprise in Modern China* (Hong Kong: Hong Kong University Press, 2006), 21.

101. On Venice, see S. Whimster, "Lagoon Immobility. The Exceptional Case of Imperial Venice," in *Critical Junctures in Mobile Capital*, ed. J. Pixley and H. Flam (Cambridge: Cambridge University Press, 2018), 182–188.

102. Ingham, *Nature of Money*; Calomiris and Haber, *Fragile by Design*.

103. Wenkai He, *Paths Towards the Modern Fiscal State: England, Japan and China* (Cambridge, MA: Harvard University Press, 2013); Faure, *China and Capitalism*.

104. *GEH*, 338; *MWG* III/6, 369.

105. Ingham, *Nature of Money*; Smithin, *Controversies in Monetary Economics*; Wray, *Modern Money Theory*.

106. Wray, *Modern Money Theory*.

107. *E&S*, 93, 108; *MWG* I/23, 263, 286.

108. Wolfgang Streeck, *How Will Capitalism End?* (London: Verso, 2016), esp. chap. 7.

CHAPTER 5

···

LAW AND THE DEVELOPMENT OF CAPITALISM

···

LAURA R. FORD

JURISPRUDENTIAL FORMATION
···

MAX Weber's initial training was in law and legal history, a fact of great importance in understanding his intellectual development and the fruits of his scholarly projects. Weber was educated under leading figures in legal and socioeconomic history, whose influence is still felt today. One very central theme in Weber's work, developed particularly under the tutelage of Theodor Mommsen and Levin Goldschmidt, concerned the social and legal bases for claims to property.[1]

Weber's approach to law was heavily influenced by a particular philosophical "school" of jurisprudence, the historical school, which is closely identified with the scholarship of Friedrich Carl von Savigny. The historical school had sharpened a debate about Roman "reception" in German law: a wide-ranging influence of Roman law, which was perceived by some as displacing local strands of law that were more flexibly adapted to "Germanic" ways of life. The issues at stake concerned both legal history and legal interpretation, particularly the relative significance of customary law and Roman law for contemporary law. Thus, it was no accident that Weber's enduring interest in the relationship between law and modern capitalism focused, very centrally, on early historical developments, including the impacts of Roman law.[2]

Modern Market Finance
Capitalism and the Law

Unlike many social theorists and historians today, Max Weber did not regard capitalism as uniquely modern. One of his most general definitions of capitalism, in fact, is given in the introduction to a book-length essay on agrarian economies in antiquity, first published in 1909. In this essay, translated as *The Agrarian Sociology of Ancient Civilizations*, Weber proposed a strictly economic definition of capitalism, characterizing it as existing wherever "we find that property is an object of trade and is utilized by individuals for profit-making enterprise in a market economy."[3] In offering this generic definition of capitalism, Weber was seeking to provide a ground upon which to compare the various forms of capitalism that have appeared throughout history and particularly to enable systematic distinction between ancient and modern forms of capitalism. Capitalism did indeed exist in the ancient world, Weber argued, and it was most emphatically not unique to the West. What was unique to the modern period of Western dominance, Weber believed, was a very specific type of capitalism, what is often called "rational" capitalism.[4]

This specific type of capitalism, Weber argued, involves a combination of legal, religious, political, and economic conditions, which, in his mature sociology, may be analyzed as social patterns resulting from orientation to different orders (*Ordnungen*). Modern Western capitalism involves a characteristic orientation in intentionality (purposiveness), one that is focused on acquisition (*Erwerben*) in markets and through financial transactions. Modern Western capitalism is thus market finance capitalism.[5]

From a legal perspective, modern market finance capitalism may be seen as resting on a tripartite foundation: (1) private laws delineating the framework of property, contract, and redress of social wrongs (tort/delict); (2) laws establishing a framework for the activity of institutional organizations (corporations, banks, municipalities), which act as the primary issuers and holders of financial instruments; and (3) public laws establishing the institutional environment in which business is conducted (international, constitutional, and administrative law). This tripartite foundation both depends upon and has developed together with the modern nation-state system and the modern law of financial instruments, such as stocks, bonds, and paper money.[6]

This elaborate legal framework for market finance capitalism depends on a combination of sociolegal conditions, which is analytically identified and historically traced in Weber's extended essay, *The Developmental Conditions of the Law*, formerly known as the "Sociology of Law" in *Economy and Society*. Of primary importance is the very idea of public law, as distinct from private law, and the legal framework of the modern nation-state as a unitary, quasi-corporate actor. Additional important factors include early modern freedom of contract, medieval developments in property law, and negotiability of financial instruments. Most fundamental, however, is an underlying process of rationalization, which is carried by a very particular set of social actors: *jurists*.[7]

Law contributes to market finance capitalism, from a Weberian perspective, by contributing semantic (meaningful) content to the conceptual orders (*Ordnungen*) that inform social activity and intentionality. In other words, law provides conceptual meanings, *legal semantics*, that guide the intentional social behavior of market actors, corporate managers, and governmental officers. The latter in particular play an important role for Weber because they constitute a "staff" whose official duty and personal interest are bound up with the enforcement of the law.[8]

In fact, for Weber, where an enforcing staff does not exist, there is no law; rather, there is convention, which may nevertheless be quite powerful in virtue of its enforcement through social disapproval. Even where a law-enforcing staff exists, however, this is not enough to produce the legal meanings themselves. For conceptual legal meanings—*legal semantics*—to exist we need a set of social actors who purposively develop these meanings, in their effort to work out what, precisely, the legal semantics (e.g., property) mean. A set of social actors like this are for law what other distinctive social strata, like Brahmins, are for religion: they are culture-carriers. Drawing on a concept from Roman law, Weber often called the legal culture-carriers *jurists*, a set of social actors whom he viewed as distinguishing Western law.[9]

In his essays on law in *Economy and Society*, Weber was, among other things, working through the historical and social processes by which legal frameworks and legal semantics were developed in the post-Roman West by jurists and have contributed to the modern economy. His answer focused on a set of legal concepts, together with a style of law-finding and law-giving, that Weber viewed as distinctive to Western jurisprudence. The style of law-finding and law-giving that the jurists ultimately worked out involved *formal rationality*, a mode of interpreting, articulating, and applying law that involves generality, abstraction, and the strictest possible logical and/or empirical conformity. The set of conceptual legal semantics distinctive to Western jurisprudence, as Weber saw it, included the concept of the corporation, the public–private binary, the legal freedom to bind oneself through contractual promises, and an idealization of written documents, conceived formalistically (even religiously) as binding legal instruments. Inextricably tied to each of these distinctive legal concepts was a post-Roman idealization of property, one that was both conceptually looser than classical Roman law and, if possible, more pervasive.

PROPERTY, CALCULABILITY, AND MONEY

Max Weber had a very realistic theory of property that remained remarkably stable across the body of his scholarly work, particularly as seen in both the older and newer "parts" of *Economy and Society*. In common with theories of property endorsed by legal scholars today, Weber emphasized "exclusivity" as an essential criterion of property, while also working out systematically the social conditions upon which such exclusivity depends.[10]

Property, for Weber, involves an exclusivity in powers of control and disposal exercised over objects, which may be either tangible or intangible. Such powers come to be "monopolized" by social groups in the foundational processes by which communities coalesce, closing themselves against unlimited entry by arbitrarily defined "outsiders." Such monopolistic appropriation processes are a necessary counterpart to processes of community-formation, but they may not go all the way toward the development of private ownership (*Eigentum*). Where such private ownership does emerge, it is characterized by fully appropriated "rights," which are permanently allocated to particular members of a community, to the degree that they are passed through inheritance, rather than returning to the community upon the death of the owner.[11]

Weber placed considerable emphasis on property in his fully developed economic sociology, articulated in a concentrated form in Chapter 2 of *Economy and Society*. In his foundational definition of "economic action"—social activity involving non-violent exercise of control over resources, which is consciously oriented toward economic ends—Weber emphasized the extent to which this type of social activity depends on the existence of appropriated "powers of control and disposal" (*Verfügungsgewalten*). Any organization of economic activity will involve these, whether they are formally recognized as legal rights or simply exercised as de facto powers, as might be seen in a socialist economy. In modern capitalistic economies, however, these dispositional powers are "the principal source of the relation of economic action to the law." Talcott Parsons noted that this "is another way of saying that concretely economic action depends on a system of property relations."[12]

In theory, the range of objects that might be defined as economic resources is perhaps infinite. However, Weber emphasized the extent to which such resources tend always to become standardized and routinized, whether through custom, "constellation of interest," formally enforced law, or informally enforced convention. Nevertheless, consistent with the economic theory of property rights recently developed by Yoram Barzel, Weber also emphasized the extent to which the perception of economic "return" from resources depends on the useful qualities that these are *perceived* to afford. It is the delivery or performance of these useful qualities (*Nutzleistungen*) that is the primary target of economic action, and this may or may not be legally recognized as a legitimate object of dispositional powers. This points to a role for culture, meaning, and social processes of communication in the perception of economic objects and to an important role for law in giving formally enforced legitimacy to such perceptions.[13]

Weber considered instrumental rationality (*Zweckrationalität*) to be paradigmatic for modern capitalism, and he delineated four canonical or "typical measures" as possibilities for instrumental rationality in economic action. In the first, characteristic of *saving*, present dispositional powers over useful qualities of resources are systematically traded against those of the future. In the second, a range of possibilities for dispositional powers over such useful qualities are weighed against one another, and systematic allocation is based on relative urgency. Although Weber did not use anything like this term, we could label the second possibility as *spending*. He considered both saving and spending to primarily involve allocation of money incomes in the modern world and did not see them as responsible for economic growth.[14]

Weber evidently considered the third and fourth "measures" as those that are primarily responsible for economic growth in modern rational capitalism. In the third, characteristic of *production*, dispositional powers over useful qualities of resources are acquired through an instrumental, generative process: the objects responsible for the desired useful qualities are first made and then acquired by the owner of the instrumental means by which they are made. The essential social conditions enabling this process involve ownership of the means of production. In the fourth, dispositional powers over useful qualities of resources are acquired by associative agreement (*Vergesellschaftung*), either an agreement that involves an ongoing association, such as a regulative or administrative organization, or a one-off compromise of interests in transactional exchange. In these third and fourth instances, in other words, we have social foundations for the organization of productive economic activity, capital investment, and market exchange.[15]

Modern market finance capitalism depends fundamentally on calculability. The scale and complexity of ongoing market transactions, together with intense competition, mean that highly refined techniques of calculation are essential to survival. Money is "the most 'perfect' means of economic calculation."[16] In modern market finance capitalism, a specific type of monetary accounting is deployed, namely "capital accounting," which facilitates the acquisitive activity that is distinctive to capitalism: seeking new opportunities for powers of control and disposal over objects (i.e., new property). It does so through a temporally defined process of valuation, in which the capacity for acquiring new property is precisely calculated. Total assets at the end are compared to those at the beginning, with the goal of precisely measuring the acquisitive potential of the enterprise. "Profit," in the precise Weberian sense, means enhanced acquisitive *potential*, precisely measured, which may characterize either a growing business or a growing national economy.[17]

Weber saw a developmental tendency in modern capitalism, namely to press ever further toward increasing "formal rationality" in capital accounting and profit-seeking. A social "system" is, in effect, established in which the final goal structuring the pattern of interacting components is one of increasing acquisitive potential (i.e., profit). Because certain patterns of property ownership serve this goal better than others, these patterns come to be characteristic of modern market finance capitalism. With an eye on modern European conditions, Weber works with a basic distinction between labor and capitalistic owners in delineating these patterns of property ownership.[18]

In modern market finance capitalism, the means of production have been expropriated from workers and are owned by a business organization separated from the household. The bodies of the workers, however, are not owned by the enterprise but are left within the dispositional control of the workers themselves. Workers are not physically compelled to work, although they very typically work "under duress," in the sense that they will not survive if they do not earn a wage. In modern market finance capitalism, labor is "formally free." The legal system, in other words, does not recognize legitimate ownership interests of one human being over another human being.[19]

Political communities, such as nation-states, contribute in essential ways to the overall system by (1) supplying money and overseeing its integrity; (2) transacting business, collecting taxes in money, and issuing securities; and (3) constituting and regulating the legal institutions.[20] Political communities for Weber are social structures of authority (*Herrschaft*), and they act as regulators and coordinators of social activities for the individual persons, households, and business organizations that compose their membership. At the same time, however, political communities are closed social relationship structures (*Verbände*) which enable property to exist in the first instance. A social "system" organized around ever-increasing acquisitive potential depends on the existence of property, both to sustain households and business organizations and to be an object for further acquisition. Political communities are thus organizational structures that underpin and coordinate the patterns of appropriation and exchange upon which modern market finance capitalism depends.

Public and Private Law in a Nation-State System: Legal Conditions of Modern Market Finance Capitalism

In his essay, *The Developmental Conditions of the Law*," prepared as part of his contributions to the *Outline* (*Grundriß*) *of Social Economics*, Weber elaborated a number of "decisive legal [juristic] conceptions" that had contributed to the developmental processes of emerging modern market finance capitalism. Weber thought natural law was crucially important as, together with the Roman concept of the corporation and French legal doctrine, it created the intellectual conditions of possibility for the idea of the "state" and a rationally developed public law.[21]

The "state," as Weber posits it, is a social–political organization and institutional unit, comprised of legally privileged persons, which is conceived as a kind of public, quasi-corporate entity (*Anstalt*). Its laws, and pre-eminently its constitutional laws, are conceived as "public laws," applicable to all individuals comprising the organization, while at the same time it issues laws facilitating a "private" realm of voluntaristic ordering. The public/private distinction is fundamental to the legal framework of modern market finance capitalism, as Weber saw it. At the same time, he emphasized the difficulty in drawing a precise distinction between public and private law, particularly under modern conditions involving powerful state actors.[22]

From a contemporary legal perspective, the realm of "private" law is comprised of contracts and property, together with protections against social harms known as "torts" (in common law systems) or "delicts" (in civil law systems). These form points of contact with economic activity, yet at the same time they depend on "the frame of a 'statal' legal order" (*staatliche Ordnung*).[23] Both the market form of association and the rapid tempo of business transactions require a predictable and calculable legal system, one that monopolizes and regulates the "legitimate" exercise of overwhelming coercive power, in the form of a unitary and universalist institution.[24]

The crucial step in differentiating public law from private law came, Weber argued, with the rise of *imperium*, the power to issue commands and to take violent action in enforcing those commands. With imperium it became important to set boundaries and define differentiated competencies for the exercise of power. Weber largely agreed with Montesquieu that the concept of public law became possible through the separation of governmental powers. However, he qualified this by asserting that a genuine public law is only possible where separation-of-powers doctrine contributes rationally differentiated competencies and administrative units to a political organization (*Verband*) that takes the form of a compulsory institution (*Anstalt*). Weber thought this development had only occurred in the modern West, and he was careful to differentiate older notions of functionally differentiated imperia, such as were found in ancient Rome or medieval England.[25]

As the compulsory, institutionalized state organization with limited and differentiated powers comes into existence, "rights" can be increasingly recognized and deliberately created through private law. Weber was especially interested in the way that modern "freedom of contract," which has been so important to modern financial instruments and modern capitalism, had developed historically. Adopting an evolutionary, anthropological perspective in which modern law emerges out of animistic religious beliefs and magical practices, Weber traced a development leading from contracts rooted in ascribed legal status to "purposive contracts," corresponding to modern notions of "freedom of contract." He was firm in reiterating, however, that formal freedom of contract does not mean substantive freedom for all contracting parties. To the contrary, formal freedom of contract means that wealth-based inequalities in bargaining power can operate all the more inexorably in favor of the stronger or wealthier party.[26]

An essential step toward private law, as we know it today, takes place when the non-performance of an agreement by one party vis-à-vis another party becomes a harm that is legally perceived to affect the political community as a whole and therefore one to be remedied through state action, rather than through kinship-based vengeance. Private law, in other words, develops in a relationship of dependence on public law, even while public law also depends on the differentiating sphere of private law transactions, which pre-eminently include contracts and property but also include marriages, wills, and an increasing array of legally remediable social harms (torts/delicts).[27]

With the rise of state-enforced private law, and especially of purposive contracts, possibilities come to the fore that hindsight shows to be essential to modern market finance capitalism: agency, negotiable financial instruments, and legal forms of business organization, particularly partnerships and corporations. Each of these may be thought of as a legal enablement for the creation and transfer of obligations, the archetype of which is debt. With the legal institution of agency, a business organization can incur obligations through a range of persons acting as agents, and thus can operate on a much wider geographic and temporal scale. With assignability and negotiability of financial instruments, obligations can be transferred from one person to another, creating a wider set of possibilities for making and meeting obligations. Legal forms of business organization enable enduring social structures to be created, in which obligations can be jointly and/or collectively incurred, with payment insured through the pooling of assets, vastly increasing the scale and scope of business activity.[28]

In late antiquity and the early medieval period, such legal institutions were missing in Roman law, which in many other respects continued to influence legal systems surrounding the Mediterranean. With respect to the emergence of modern financial instruments, in particular, Weber pointed to important influences from the eastern Mediterranean: Byzantine developments in notarial practices, together with Syrian and Arabic developments of written contractual instruments, known later as "commercial paper." Weber also considered the "irrational" religious beliefs of "Germanic" peoples in western Europe, involving semi-sacralizing attitudes to written documents, as being of decisive importance. Wherever written instruments were treated as *constituting* an obligation, rather than merely *evidencing* an obligation, Weber saw the influence of such religious ideas. In Italian coastal cities like Venice, Pisa, and Genoa, these combined influences came together and spread to the north and west, even reaching the British Isles, albeit in attenuated form.[29]

Weber's interest in the historically changing legal forms of business organization had persisted from the time of his dissertation, in which he focused on the forms of business association that had been most important in Europe's "commercial revolution" that began circa 1000 CE and extended to the Black Death in the fourteenth century. By the thirteenth century, ubiquitous legal sources testify to the importance of commercial legal forms, including forms of business organization, in this economic transformation. Weber had access to many of these sources through the library of his teacher, Levin Goldschmidt, and he was interested in identifying the developments in legal doctrine that had contributed to the transformation. What were the legal sources for the new forms of commercial organization: were they adaptations of ancient Roman forms, or did they originate through revived juristic reflection on medieval commercial practice? Weber concluded that it was the latter.[30]

Both his dissertation and *The Developmental Conditions of the Law* include extended reflections on the implications of differing structural forms of business organization for liability and debt. Unlike the business corporations that we know today, medieval forms of business organization did not involve limited liability. Partners holding a share in the enterprise were personally "on the hook" for liabilities and obligations incurred by the partnership. However, there was nonetheless a variability in the way these liabilities and obligations were legally structured. Weber was particularly interested in the ways that jurists brought their Roman law–based legal doctrines to bear on customary medieval commercial practices and in the modern forms of business organization that ultimately emerged from the meeting of doctrine and practice.[31]

Weber was not familiar with the gigantic business corporations that we know today— corporations like Google and Facebook, for example, which operate on a financial scale and with a social pervasiveness that challenges national policy for even the largest nation-states. However, he was familiar with historical cases of gigantic corporate organization which challenged older forms of political organization. Examples that he discussed included the Hanseatic League of northwest European cities and the colonial companies, like the British and Dutch East India Companies. The rise of gigantic corporations exercising quasi-political powers would not have surprised him.[32]

As a good lawyer, however, Weber would remind us that, from a formal legal perspective, even the largest of private corporations is dependent for its very existence on a charter from a nation-state or from a subunit of a national state, like the state of New York. The chartering system may seem nominal and formalistic, but it still exists and still means a degree of oversight and control from the national state and its legal system. The chartering process of legal recognition is what gives the modern business corporation its legal personality: its capacity to act as a unitary bearer of legal rights and obligations. In the US legal system, such corporate legal personality extends beyond business corporations like Google and includes local government organizations, like the City of New York and the Port Authority of New York & New Jersey. These are also "bodies corporate," dependent on a charter from the state which grants them the legal capacity to incur rights and obligations as a unitary entity.[33]

Weber considered the modern nation-state itself as constituting, from a legal perspective, a kind of quasi-corporate entity. In the realm of international law, nation-states enter into contracts with one another ("treaties"), and they exert claims over property. The modern territorial state is a property-owning entity, which historically was envisioned by legal architects of the international system very much along the lines of an ancient Roman property owner (*dominus*). We can see echoes of this in our archaic English word for sovereignty, *dominion*, which is derived from the Latin word for ownership and mastery in Roman law: *dominium*.[34]

In modern market finance capitalism, the "public realm" of national states is inextricably linked with the "private realm" of market transactions. This is a fundamental conviction of the Weberian perspective. We have seen the extent to which this is implicit in Weber's developmental scheme for legal history, in which the very categories of possibility for public and private law develop differently together. We can see this much more concretely in his writings about financial markets, or *Bourse*.[35]

In his *Bourse* writings, Weber addressed a number of legal and political issues arising out of new developments in financial exchanges and financial instruments, developments that seemed especially threatening to the East Prussian landed aristocracy, the *Junkers*. Weber argued in favor of the new exchanges in commodities futures, both because he saw their potential to level regional and seasonal fluctuations in commodity prices and because he was committed to embracing public policy initiatives that would strengthen the emerging German nation-state. As Wolfgang Mommsen and others have shown, when it came to the realm of public policy, Weber was firmly on the side of *Realpolitik*.[36]

From a legal perspective, it has always been difficult to draw a firm line between "legitimate" financial instruments and legalized gambling. In the late nineteenth and early twentieth centuries, the debate was carried out in relation to early forms of "derivative" instruments in the United States and in Germany. As was seen recently in the efforts to discern the contribution of speculation in "derivatives" to the 2008 financial crisis, the problem has not disappeared. Weber argued firmly against those who would condemn early forms of derivatives (i.e., futures contracts) as illegal (and immoral) speculation. To turn against the new forms of financial instruments and financial exchanges would be fatal to German national economic growth, Weber thought, and would pander to the backward-looking forces of protectionism (like the Junkers) and reactionary socialism.[37]

Weber saw Germany entering into an economic arena of competition and struggle between quasi-corporate powerhouses, in the form of nation-states. Any policy position that did not orient itself to this basic reality was either naive or, worse, a form of self-destructive protectionism. Germany's national leaders should embrace the economic and political realities, accept the legality of financial exchanges, and address risks to the public by establishing limitations on participation. Value freedom, for Weber, did not mean political neutrality; rather, it meant that when he engaged in political debate, he spoke openly of the means he judged to be best suited for achieving political ends, not of scientific certainties.[38]

In the world of competing nation-states that Weber saw in the early 1900s, law had become a rationalistic instrument in the pursuit of national goals, which are cast in an acquisitive light. Economic growth for the nation, very much like that of the private corporation, means growth in acquisitive capacity and is typically evaluated in relation to the comparable capacities of other nation-states. Developments in legal thought and practice had contributed to this legalistic, capitalistic world. In much the same way that Brahmins have shaped the thought-world of Hinduism, a particular social stratum—jurists—have shaped a formalist, "legal–rational," sociopolitical structure of rulership (*Herrschaft*) for the modern West.[39]

JURISTS, RATIONALIZATION, AND RELIGION

The heart of Weber's extended essay *The Developmental Conditions of the Law* is a complex series of reflections on rationalization processes in different types of law and on the differing types of legal actors who contribute to these rationalization processes. Weber added nuance to his developmental perspective by differentiating a variety of possible lines the process could take. In law, Weber essentially identified two differentiating factors: (1) sources and (2) training. The sources to which they look in seeking the law and the ways in which they are trained to articulate the law fundamentally distinguish different types of legal actors. At the same time, the positions that they typically occupy in social structures of political power impact their outlooks on the world and channel their broader impact on their societies.[40]

Weber was probably writing his essay *The Developmental Conditions of the Law* while he was undertaking his ambitious comparative studies of world religion, *The Economic*

Ethics of the World Religions. The impact of this scholarly overlap between Weber's sociology of law and his sociology of religion is particularly apparent in his studies of jurists—whom he sometimes calls *honoratiores*—and the legal rationalization processes to which they contribute.[41]

Part of what made Western law distinctive, Weber argued, involved peculiarities in the ways religion and law were at first combined, then pulled apart, in the course of rationalization processes led by clerics and jurists. During the "long morning" of Europe, legal practices were carried forward from late antiquity primarily by clerics who received their training in literacy from church-affiliated organizations, such as monasteries or local schools run by bishops. Secularizing tendencies inherited from Roman law, however, together with unique aspects of the Western church's organizational structure, enabled a characteristically Western dualism in the relationship between Christianity and law. With the rise of university-based legal study, law became a relatively secularized discipline, which could move in rational and formal directions with less interference from the idealistic and ethical commitments of the clergy. In the West, idealistic and ethical commitments in law derived ultimately from clerical adherence to a revelatory religious *and legal* text, the Latin Christian Bible, and from apostolic-patristic traditions, which are pervaded with legal language and ideas.[42]

Although clerics may have been the primary literate bearers of early medieval legal practices, Weber also recognized the extent to which such practices made sense to a wide range of social actors in early medieval Europe. The common appeal of "customary" legal practices inherited from late antiquity is especially seen in scholarly compilations of medieval charters and *placita*, or records from legal assemblies. Less popular but no less significant are the records of royal and church assemblies, which are only partially differentiated from one another and from other more local legal assemblies. Weber periodically refers to these records, albeit obliquely, when he discusses "cautelary jurisprudence," "custumals" (*Weistümer*), and "moot communities," together with "barbarian" *leges* (e.g., *Lex Salica*), in the early Middle Ages.[43]

The overall trajectory of rationalization in Western law, as Weber presents it, involves movement from this popular and accessible law, a law in which morality, religion, and law are inseparable, to a type of law ("formally rational law") that is clearly separated from ethics and religion and that is far removed from popular consciousness. Formally rational law in its finally developed form is highly systematized, both in its substantive concepts and principles and in the procedural rules governing utilization of the system. The high level of systematization flows from careful delineation of legal concepts and principles and rigorous logic in relating these concepts and principles to each other. A strict and uncompromising commitment to protecting the semantic and logical coherence of the system contributes to its popular inaccessibility, in terms of both understanding and cost. This same commitment, however, makes for the highest possible level of consistency and predictability of legal outcomes.[44]

Formally rational law, as Weber outlines it, represents the pinnacle of consistency and predictability in law; and this is what makes it so conducive to modern market finance capitalism. Modern market finance capitalism involves long-term, socioeconomic structures of investment and debt (e.g., bonds typically issued with thirty-year [sometimes even fifty-year or hundred-year] terms for repayment). Such structures would be impossible, particularly for large organizations employing capital accounting methods, without some degree of consistency and predictability in law, which for Weber comes with formal rationality. But, Weber warned, formal rationality in law is unpopular, and the pressures of the age are ever-increasingly toward substantive commitments to ethics and justice in law, which place systemic coherence in a lower priority. As Weber looked toward the future of Western law, he saw a future in which formal rationality would likely be sacrificed in favor of substantive rationality, that is, the rationality of ethical, moral, or political commitments, including utilitarian commitments like efficiency.[45]

One important complication for Weber's famous contrast between formal and substantive rationality in law comes in his comparisons between continental European and English law, a complication explored through a relatively extensive literature on "the England problem."[46] The problem derives from apparent inconsistencies in Weber's treatment of English law: at times he presented English law as being quite low on the scale of formal rationality, while at the same time he called England the "first and most highly developed capitalist country."[47] The so-called England problem is at least partially resolved by Weber, however, through his view of early modern English law as involving two levels of legal access: for wealthy proto-capitalists English law was formally rational, but for ordinary folks the law of the justices of the peace operated as a kind of "qadi-justice," which sought particular justice in each case and ignored broader questions of systematic coherence. For modern capitalism, Weber argued, this kind of dualism is actually ideal as it reserves consistency and predictability for those who most need it, while also preventing discontent through wide popular perception of fairness in the law.[48]

Leaving aside the peculiarities of English law, there was one type of legal actor that Weber considered a vital bearer of formal rationality in law, with crucial importance for early developments in commercial law and market finance capitalism: the notary. The Western notary constituted a cultural carrier of a "developed commercial law" during the crucial period of transition from late antiquity into the high Middle Ages, when commercial legal practices again become visible, as seen particularly in the notarial records of north Italian cities as well as in Mediterranean cities linked to them through trade, such as Marseilles. Receiving Roman law as "the very law of commerce," notaries were a vitally important carrier of legal rationality, especially because of their emphasis on documentary evidence, in contrast to older, irrational, and popular procedural methods.[49]

Notaries, as carriers of Western commercial law and legal rationality, were at the same time an important part of the associational structures of the Western city. They played an intervening role in legal study and political administration, and their importance was partly displaced once university-based study of law was revived, beginning in Bologna. This development would not have occurred without the notaries, however, and in the political administration of the northern Italian cities it bore their indelible imprint.

In Mediterranean-based practices of commercial law, moreover, their importance would continue long after the scholarly methods of legal study had spread across Europe, touching even England. "Thus the Italian notaries were not only the oldest but also one of the most important of the strata of legal honoratiores who were interested and practically involved in the establishment of the *usus modernus* of Roman law."[50]

The *usus modernus* was a methodology for the interpretation of Roman law involving generalization and harmonization of Roman law principles, rendering them more applicable to contemporary social conditions. It was developed through study of Roman law texts and was strongly influenced by the new humanistic methods of critical engagement with ancient texts, which had been developed especially for biblical interpretation. As a forerunner to modern legal concepts and principles, the *usus modernus* was particularly influential in the development of international law. It also helped lay the foundation for modern commercial law and human rights law.[51]

The notion of universal human rights, protected by the rule of law, is today a cornerstone of ethics-based interventions in international, national, and local arenas. It can be seen, for example, in the debates over pharmaceutical patents on life-saving medications in developing countries. The identifying feature is typically a reference to a higher, universal law, which works critically against any contradictory forms of positive law, particularly those that undermine fundamental human rights.[52]

Historically speaking, the notion of universal human rights was built partly on the foundation of natural law, which Weber saw as a culmination of Western legal rationalization processes in which the logical coherence of formal rationality is powerfully but unstably joined to the ethical commitments of substantive rationality. Pre-eminently in the English, American, and French Revolutions and echoed (after Weber's death) in the Universal Declaration of Human Rights, Western natural law has carried the force of an immanent *and* transcendent legal truth, which is nonetheless also capable of a formalistic logical elaboration.[53]

When Weber discussed natural law in its formalistic, logical elaboration, he referred particularly to English law, to developments of the seventeenth and eighteenth centuries, and to conceptualizations of contractual freedom. "Powerful religious, particularly Anabaptist influences" were at work in the origins of this modern, formalistic version of natural law. The religious influences were combined, however, with "indigenous" elements in English law, including the notion that Magna Carta rights were the "birthrights" of all freeborn Englishmen, together with pan-European revivals of a teleological conception of nature's "will," rooted in the Renaissance. Under additional influences from rationalistic, sectarian Christianity, these elements were combined in a formalistic doctrine of natural law, which could provide a legitimizing background for positive law. References to the US Supreme Court make it quite clear that Weber is thinking particularly of American developments.[54]

The economic implications of a religiously inflected yet formalistic notion of "freedom of contract," as seen, for example, in nineteenth-century US Supreme Court decisions, can be very powerful, Weber notes. The result is a logically coherent and principled position opposed to any public interference in market forces. In the relationship between commercial law and modern market finance capitalism, there is, in other words, a kind of quasi-religious support for "free competition":

> The price which was to be rejected as "unnatural" was now one which did not rest on the competition of the free market, i.e., the price which was influenced by monopolies or other arbitrary human intervention. Throughout the whole puritanically influenced Anglo-Saxon world this principle has had a great influence up to the very present. Because of the fact that the principle derived its dignity from natural law, it remained a far stronger support for the ideal of "free competition" than those purely utilitarian theories which were produced on the Continent.[55]

Even in this formalistic natural law, Weber saw ever-present tendencies toward an ethically rooted, substantive rationality. This was partly because the English notion of "reason"—equated in certain formalistic, Anglo-American natural law doctrines with nature itself—often focused on the outcomes of action. This meant an ever-present tendency to consequentialism in defining natural "reasonability" and often to utilitarianism. Critical developments in the academic study of law were also working to undermine any remaining notions of transcendence in the realm of law. The appeal of formal rationality in law has a kind of aesthetic quality that perhaps can only be felt by legal scholars, who carry with them a normative commitment to the systemic coherence of law. Today, when faced with a choice between substantive justice and systematic coherence, the latter can hardly win. In the future, Weber saw substantive ethical and/or political commitments overtaking formal rationality in law.[56]

I want to emphasize the religious element that Weber saw in modern manifestations of formal rationality in law, particularly in formalistic natural law and its commitment to freedom of contract. As US legal history has illustrated, the formalistic commitment to freedom of contract can mean a substantive unwillingness to sanction legal reforms premised on notions of public welfare and a social safety net. We will fail to fully understand this unless we realize that a religiously inflected notion of law lies behind it, one that is intimately connected to the very same notion of law that stands behind a commitment to fundamental human rights and social welfare.[57]

Max Weber was fascinated by paradoxes, and there is perhaps no greater paradox than the American attachment to a natural law tradition that feeds both capitalism and claims to social justice. There is a religious quality to this attachment that Weber recognized, and this is one among many points of enduring value in his sociology of law.[58]

CONCLUSION

Max Weber famously diagnosed a uniquely Western propensity to build bureaucratic and capitalistic systems that mutually reinforce one another, "elective affinities" in law, politics, and the economy that have become a "steel-hard casing" (or "iron cage," in

Talcott Parson's words) for Western modernity and for the world it has impacted. As Weber presents them, jurists are a type of social actor—a cultural carrier or propagating stratum—that has contributed in important ways to this modern cage. They have done so by offering a unique promise of salvation, one that Weber recognized is fading in its appeal: the promise of formal rationality in law. If modern, "rational" capitalism was ushered into the Western world with help from a radically reformed theology of predestined grace, it has been sustained in this-worldly, "secular" forms with help from another theologically inflected salvation-good: the "rule of law," with its intimate connections to the universalizing promise of innate, human rights.

Religion, as Weber conceptualized it, is an ideational and social force that works, fundamentally, by promising a solution to the problem of human suffering. Such promises are "salvation goods" that ideationally inform meaningful social action. Not all religion is transcendent and "other-worldly" or premised on belief in divine beings. Salvation could take the form of a promise to solve harmful social injustices, to ensure adequate economic provisioning for all, or quite simply to provide social peace and harmony. Looked at in this way, modern law, as we relate to it today, often works for our societies very much like a religion, as a "this-worldly" solution to the problem of human suffering, the one in which we place our trust and hope, failing all other options. This is true even if we ignore the overtly theocratic—Jewish, Christian, and Platonic—elements that remain in Western systems of law.[59]

The Weberian tradition of sociology is distinctive especially for the way in which it traces a bidirectional link between ideational and socioeconomic forces, between worldviews and socioeconomic structures, like capitalism. What remains to be fully appreciated, I think, is the extent to which this distinctive quality also infuses Weber's legal sociology. Law, for Weber, is unquestionably a coercive force in modern society; but it is also an ideational, idealistic, and even religious force. Placing trust and hope in the formal rationality of law and seeking a promise of social peace, Western jurists have contributed to the sociolegal structures of a globalized, nation-state system that is fundamentally committed to "liberal" structures of free contracts and individual rights. In contributing to this system, however, jurists have also nourished a capitalist system, one with inherent instabilities from risk-taking in financial markets and economic inequality. There is an irony and a pathos in this story, too, which share something of Weber's artistry in *The Protestant Ethic and the Spirit of Capitalism*.[60]

In this essay, I have traced elements of this story in focusing on Weber's own juristic formation, his theory of property, and his theory of the developmental process by which religious and legal systems were rationalistically differentiated. In this developmental process as it took place in the West, public and private law became mutually dependent parts of a modern nation-state system. Commercial law, in particular, developed from private law ingredients, especially property, contracts, and legal forms for the social organization of business. Consumerist households were severed from productive firms, and an ever-increasing scale of economic activity was facilitated by an array of doctrinal legal structures: corporate personality, limited liability, bankruptcy, and securities law.

The common element in all of this is a very particular sociolegal structure of obligation, one that Weber saw as being distinctive to the West.

Law has contributed to modern capitalism by giving semantic form to the ways that we think about our obligations to one another and social form to the structures within which we act on those obligations. Trained as a jurist himself, in a time and place where the historical sources of Western legal systems were being critically assembled and interpreted by the founding generation for a new nation-state, Max Weber was very well placed to see (and to help us see) the relationship between law and modern, "rational" capitalism.

NOTES

1. Timothy J. Cornell, *The Beginnings of Rome: Italy and Rome from the Bronze Age to the Punic Wars (c. 1000–264 B.C.)* (London: Routledge, 1995 [Kindle]), references to Mommsen, e.g., ll. 2770 and n78; Jürgen Deininger, "Einleitung," in Max Weber, *Die Römische Agrargeschichte in ihrer Bedeutung für das Staats- und Privatrecht. 1891, Max Weber-Gesamtausgabe* (hereafter *MWG*) I/2, ed. Jürgen Deininger (Tübingen, Germany: Mohr [Siebeck], 1986), 1–24; Gerhard Dilcher, "From the History of Law to Sociology: Max Weber's Engagement with the Historical School of Law," trans. Lutz Kaelber, *Max Weber Studies* 8, no. 2 (2008), 163–186; Gerhard Dilcher, "Einleitung," in Max Weber, *Zur Geschichte der Handelsgesellschaften im Mittelalter. Schriften 1889–1894, MWG* I/1, ed. G. Dilcher and S. Lepsius (Tübingen, Germany: Mohr [Siebeck], 2008), 1–41, 57–89, 91–95; Laura R. Ford, "Max Weber on Property: An Effort in Interpretive Understanding," *Socio-Legal Review* 6 (2010): 31–33; Werner Gephart, *Law, Culture, and Society: Max Weber's Comparative Cultural Sociology of Law* (Frankfurt am Main, Germany: Klostermann, 2015), 15–38; Werner Gephart, "Einleitung," in Max Weber, *Wirtschaft und Gesellschaft. Die Wirtschaft und die gesellschaftlichen Ordnungen und Mächte. Nachlaß. 3: Recht, MWG* I/22-3, ed. W. Gephart and S. Hermes (Tübingen, Germany: Mohr [Siebeck], 2010), 1–29; Lutz Kaelber, "Max Weber's Dissertation in the Context of His Early Career and Life," in *Max Weber, The History of Commercial Partnerships in the Middle Ages*, trans. Lutz Kaelber (Lanham, MD: Rowman & Littlefield, 2003), 1–47; Lutz Kaelber, "Weber's Dissertation and Habilitation," in *The Anthem Companion to Max Weber* (London: Anthem, 2016), 27–44; Lutz Kaelber, "Max Weber's Dissertation," in *The Foundation of the Juridico-Political: Concept Formation in Hans Kelsen and Max Weber*, ed. I. Bryan, P. Langford, and J. McGarry (Oxford: Routledge, 2016), 207–224; Dirk Käsler, *Max Weber: An Introduction to His Life and Work*, trans. P. Hurd (Chicago: University of Chicago Press, 1988), 3–7; Anthony T. Kronman, *Max Weber* (Stanford, CA: Stanford University Press, 1983), 1; Alan Sica, "Max Weber Invents Himself," in *The Anthem Companion to Max Weber*, 1–25; Richard Swedberg, *Max Weber and the Idea of Economic Sociology* (Princeton, NJ: Princeton University Press, 1998), 82–84; Stephen P. Turner and Regis A. Factor, *Max Weber: The Lawyer as Social Thinker* (London: Routledge, 1994), 2–7; Marianne Weber, *Max Weber: A Biography*, trans. and ed. Harry Zohn (New Brunswick, NJ: Transaction, 1988), 65, 95–96, 105–106, 112–115, 162–166; Franz Wieacker, *A History of Private Law in Europe*, trans. T. Weir (Oxford: Clarendon Press, 1995), 330–334; Sam Whimster, "Max Weber's Roman Agrarian History: Jurisprudence, Property, Civilization," in *Recht als Kultur? Beiträge zu Max Webers Soziologie des Rechts*,

ed. Werner Gephart and Daniel Witte (Frankfurt am Main, Germany: Klostermann, 2017), 229–278; James Whitman, "Commercial Law and the American *Volk*: A Note on Llewellyn's German Sources for the Uniform Commercial Code, *Yale Law Journal* 97 (1987): 156–175.

2. Gephart, *Law, Culture, and Society*, 33–38; Wieacker, *History of Private Law*, 300–346.

3. Max Weber, *The Agrarian Sociology of Ancient Civilizations* (hereafter *AS*), trans. R. I. Frank (London: Verso, 1988), 51; *Agrarverhältnisse im Altertum*, in *Zur Sozial- und Wirtschaftsgeschichte des Altertums. Schriften und Reden 1893–1909, MWG* I/6, ed. J. Deininger (Tübingen, Germany: Mohr [Siebeck], 2006), 338; see Richard Swedberg and Ola Agevall, *The Max Weber Dictionary: Key Words and Central Concepts*, 2nd ed. (Stanford, CA: Stanford University Press, 2016), 27.

4. *AS*, 48–67; *MWG* I/6, 335–360; Randall Collins, "Weber's Last Theory of Capitalism: A Systematization," *American Sociological Review* 45, no. 6 (1980): 925–942, 927, 938.

5. Max Weber, *Economy and Society: An Outline of Interpretive Sociology* (hereafter *E&S*), ed. G. Roth and C. Wittich (Berkeley: University of California Press, 2013), esp. 22–43, 63–100, 164–166; *Wirtschaft und Gesellschaft: Soziologie. Unvollendet. 1919–1920, MWG* I/23, ed. K. Borchardt, E. Hanke, and W. Schluchter (Tübingen, Germany: Mohr [Siebeck], 2013), 172–198, 216–272, 379–382.

6. A good way to see how these legal foundations come together in relation to modern market finance capitalism is to review the introductory chapters to a securities law textbook, such as the casebook authored by John C. Coffee, Jr., together with coauthors who have varied over the years: see *Securities Regulation*, ed. J. Coffee, Jr., H. Sale, and M. Henderson, 13th ed. (New York: Foundation Press, 2015).

7. See *Max Weber on Law in Economy and Society*, ed. M. Rheinstein, trans. E. Shils and M. Rheinstein (New York: Simon and Schuster, 1967); Weber, *Wirtschaft und Gesellschaft. Nachlaß. Recht, MWG* I/22-3, ed. W. Gephart and S. Hermes (Tübingen, Germany: Mohr [Siebeck], 2010); Hubert Treiber, "On Max Weber's *Sociology of Law*, Now Known as *The Developmental Conditions of the Law*. A Review Essay on MWG 1/22-3: *Recht*," *Max Weber Studies* 12, no. 1 (2012): 121–138.

8. Laura R. Ford, "Semantic Ordering as an Organizing Force: An Interpretation of Max Weber's Sociological Theory of Property," *Max Weber Studies* 11, no. 1 (2011): 69–97; *E&S*, 33–36; *MWG* I/23, 185–191.

9. Hubert Treiber, "'Elective Affinities' between Weber's Sociology of Religion and Sociology of Law," *Theory and Society* 14, no. 6 (1985): 809–861; Laura R. Ford, "Dharma and Natural Law: Max Weber's Comparison of Hindu and (Occidental) Christian Traditions," *Max Weber Studies* 17, no. 2 (2017): 160–195.

10. *E&S*, 43–46, 341–348; *MWG* I/23, 198–202; *Wirtschaft und Gesellschaft. Nachlaß. Gemeinschaften, MWG* I/22-1, ed. W. J. Mommsen with M. Meyer (Tübingen, Germany: Mohr [Siebeck], 2001), 82–95; Larissa Katz, "Exclusion and Exclusivity in Property Law," *University of Toronto Law Journal* 58 (2008): 275–315.

11. *E&S*, 43–46, 341–348; *MWG* I/23, 198–202; *MWG* I/22-1, 82–95; Weber, *General Economic History* (hereafter *GEH*), trans. F. Knight (New York: Greenberg, 1927), 26–73, 136–143; *Abriß der universalen Sozial- und Wirtschaftsgeschichte. Mit- und Nachschriften 1919/20, MWG* III/6, ed. W. Schluchter with J. Schröder (Tübingen, Germany: Mohr [Siebeck], 2011), 119–157, 206–212.

12. *E&S*, 63–68, 206 editors' n5; *MWG* I/23, 216–223.

13. *E&S*, 67–69, 72, 201–202, 339–355; *MWG* I/23, 222–225, 230, 440–441, *MWG* I/22-1, 75–107; Yoram Barzel, *Economic Analysis of Property Rights*, 2nd ed. (Cambridge: Cambridge University Press, 1997); Ford, "Semantic Ordering," 71–74.

14. *E&S*, 69–74; *MWG* I/23, 225–232.

15. *E&S*, 71–74; *MWG* I/23, 227–232; Weber does not use the language of "investment" here; I am simplifying and imposing this language in order to highlight the extent to which Weber is discussing the type of economic activities that contemporary economists associate with production, exchange, and economic growth.

16. *E&S*, 86; *MWG* I/23, 242.

17. *E&S*, 74–113, esp. 85–100; *MWG* I/23, 232–295, esp. 251–272.

18. *E&S*, 114–118, 125–166; *MWG* I/23, 295–303, 314–382.

19. *E&S*, 107–113, 125–153, 161–166; *MWG* I/23, 285–295, 314–360, 375–382; see also *Weber on Law*, 188–191; *MWG* I/22-3, 424–429.

20. *E&S*, 164–166, 193–202; *MWG* I/23, 379–382, 427–441; see also Weber, *GEH*, 178–191; *MWG* III/6, 241–252.

21. *Weber on Law*, 58–59; *MWG* I/22-3, 297–298.

22. *Weber on Law*, 41–60, 145–191, esp. 57–59; *MWG* I/22-3, 274–300, 367–429; see also *E&S*, 48–56; *MWG* I/23, 204–215; Hubert Treiber, "Max Weber's Conception of the State: The State as Anstalt and as Validated Conception with Special Reference to Kelsen's Critique of Weber," in *The Reconstruction of the Juridico-Political: Affinity and Divergence in Hans Kelsen and Max Weber*, ed. I. Bryan, P. Langford, and J. McGarry (Oxford: Routledge, 2016), 61–96.

23. *Weber on Law*, 39; *MWG* I/22-3, 247.

24. *Weber on Law*, 39–40; *MWG* I/22-3, 245–247; see also *E&S*, 48–56, 375–380, 635–640; *MWG* I/23, 204–215, *MWG* I/22-1, 145–154, 193–199.

25. *Weber on Law*, 56–60, 82, 256; *MWG* I/22-3, 294–300, 453, 552.

26. *Weber on Law*, 98–191; *MWG* I/22-3, 306–429.

27. *Weber on Law*, 99–122; *MWG* I/22-3, 307–333.

28. *Weber on Law*, 105, 122–125; *MWG* I/22-3, 315, 333–339.

29. *Weber on Law*, 122–125, 131–132, 209–212, 247–250; *MWG* I/22-3, 333–339, 347–348, 491–495, 541–543. See also Susan Kelly, "Anglo-Saxon Lay Society and the Written Word," in *The Uses of Literacy in Early Medieval Europe*, ed. R. McKitterick (Cambridge: Cambridge University Press, 1990), 36–62; John H. Pryor, *Business Contracts of Medieval Provence: Selected Notulae from the Cartulary of Giraud Amalric of Marseilles, 1248* (Toronto: Pontifical Institute of Mediaeval Studies, 1981).

30. For discussion and references with respect to Weber's dissertation, see note 1. On the "long economic boom," see Chris Wickham, *Medieval Europe* (New Haven, CT: Yale University Press, 2016 [Kindle]), ll. 2726–3129. Weber does indicate that increasing commercial complexity was a factor in the increased need for legal specialists: *Weber on Law*, 96; *MWG* I/22-3, 474–475.

31. *Weber on Law*, 154–191; *MWG* I/22-3, 379–429; *GEH*, 202–215, 223–229; *MWG* III/6, 259–270, 276–282; Pryor, "Historical Introduction," in *Business Contracts of Medieval Provence*, 1–52.

32. *GEH*, 230–235, 281–282; *MWG* III/6, 282–287, 322–323.

33. *Weber on Law*, 140–141, 154–191; *MWG* I/22-3, 359–361, 379–429; The Port Authority of New York & New Jersey, Official Statement dated July 12, 2017, Consolidated Bonds, 205th and 206th Series, available at The Municipal Securities Rulemaking Board, Electronic

Municipal Market Access, https://emma.msrb.org (accessed August 31, 2017), 1–1 ("The Port Authority is a municipal corporate instrumentality and political subdivision of the States of New York and New Jersey..."); Hendrik Hartog, *Public Property and Private Power: The Corporation of the City of New York in American Law, 1730–1870* (Ithaca, NY: Cornell University Press, 1989).

34. *Weber on Law*, 102–103, 145–146, 154–191, 221; *MWG* I/22-3, 312–313, 367–368, 379–429, 507; see also *GEH*, 337; *MWG* III/6, 369: "[I]t is the closed national state which afforded to capitalism its chance for development—and as long as the national state does not give place to a world empire capitalism will also endure."

35. Weber, *Börsenwesen. Schriften und Reden 1893–1898*, *MWG* I/5, ed. K. Borchardt with C. Meyer-Stoll (Tübingen, Germany: Mohr [Siebeck], 1999/2000); Max Weber, "Stock and Commodity Exchanges ['Die Börse' (1894)]," trans. S. Lestition, *Theory and Society* 29 (2000): 305–338; Max Weber, "Commerce on the Stock and Commodity Exchanges [Der Börsenverkehr]," trans. S. Lestition, *Theory and Society* 29 (2000): 339–371; Knut Borchardt, "Max Weber's Writings on the Bourse: Puzzling Out a Forgotten Corpus," trans. K. Tribe, *Max Weber Studies* 2, no. 2 (2002): 139–162.

36. Weber, "Commerce on the Stock and Commodity Exchanges," 366–369; *MWG* I/5, 619–657; Borchardt, "Weber's Writings on the Bourse," 144, 152–153; Ford, "Max Weber on Property," 69–73; Wolfgang J. Mommsen, *Max Weber and German Politics, 1890–1920*, trans. M. S. Steinberg, 2nd ed. (Chicago: University of Chicago Press, 1984), 73–76; see also Lawrence A. Scaff, *Max Weber in America* (Princeton, NJ: Princeton University Press, 2011), 27; Sam Whimster, *Understanding Weber* (New York: Routledge, 2007), 20–21.

37. Lynn A. Stout, "Derivatives and the Legal Origin of the 2008 Credit Crisis," *Harvard Business Law Review* 1 (2011): 1–38; Weber, "Commerce on the Stock and Commodity Exchanges," 359–370; "Stock and Commodity Exchanges," 305; *MWG* I/5, 641–657; 135.

38. Weber, "Commerce on the Stock and Commodity Exchanges," 369; *MWG* I/5, 655.

39. Max Weber, "The Social Psychology of the World Religions," in *From Max Weber: Essays in Sociology*, trans. and ed. H. H. Gerth and C. W. Mills (New York: Oxford University Press, 1946), 298–299; "Einleitung," in *Die Wirtschaftsethik der Weltreligionen. Konfuzianismus und Taoismus. Schriften 1915–1920*, *MWG* I/19, ed. H. Schmidt-Glintzer with P. Kolonko (Tübingen, Germany: Mohr [Siebeck], 1989), 124–125; see also Max Weber, "Introduction to the Economic Ethics of the World Religions," trans. Sam Whimster, in *The Essential Weber*, ed. Sam Whimster (Oxford: Routledge, 2004), 55–80; *MWG* I/19, 83–127.

40. *Weber on Law*, 61–64, 130–132, 65–97, 198–223, 224–255, 274–279; *MWG* I/22-3, 301–305, 345–348, 430–475, 476–509, 510–550, 578–585; Gephart, *Law, Culture, and Society*, 85, 95–104.

41. *Weber on Law*, 61–64, 130–132, 65–97, 198–223, 224–255; *MWG* I/22-3, 301–305, 345–348, 430–475, 476–509, 510–550; Gephart, *Law, Culture, and Society*, 95–104, 108.

42. *Weber on Law*, 199–200, 205–223, 224–234, 250–255, 274–279; *MWG* I/22-3, 478–479, 486–509, 544–550, 578–585. On the "long morning" of Europe, see Jennifer R. Davis and Michael McCormick, "The Early Middle Ages: Europe's Long Morning," in *The Long Morning of Medieval Europe: New Directions in Medieval Studies* (Oxford: Routledge, 2016); for discussion of the rise of a secularizing, lay intelligentsia in law, contrasting the legal culture in northern Italy and northern France, see Ronald G. Witt, *The Two Latin Cultures and the Foundation of Renaissance Humanism in Medieval Italy* (Cambridge: Cambridge University Press, 2012). For discussion of law in early Christianity, see John Witte, Jr., "Introduction," and Luke Timothy Johnson, "Law in Early Christianity," in

Christianity and Law: An Introduction, ed. J. Witte, Jr., and F. S. Alexander (Cambridge: Cambridge University Press, 2008), 5–9, 53–69.

43. *Weber on Law*, 103, 111–114, 186–187, 65–97, 212–223, 224–229; *MWG* I/22-3, 313–314, 322–324, 422–424, 430–475, 495–509, 510–517. See *The Settlement of Disputes in Early Medieval Europe*, ed. W. Davis and P. Fouracre (Cambridge: Cambridge University Press, 1986); Rosamond McKitterick, *The Carolingians and the Written Word* (Cambridge: Cambridge University Press, 1989).

44. *Weber on Law*, 103, 111–114, 186–187, 65–97, 212–223, 224–229, 250–283; *MWG* I/22-3, 313–314, 322–324, 422–424, 430–475, 495–509, 510–517, 544–591.

45. *GEH*, 277, 313–314, 338–343; *MWG* III/6, 319, 349–350, 369–374; *Weber on Law*, 301–332; *MWG* I/22-3, 615–639.

46. David M. Trubek, "Max Weber on Law and the Rise of Capitalism," *Wisconsin Law Review* 1972, no. 3 (1972): 720–753, esp. 746–748; Trubek's interpretation of Weber on English law is today generally considered to be flawed. See Swedberg, *Weber and the Idea of Economic Sociology*, 105–107; also Sally Ewing, "Formal Justice and the Spirit of Capitalism: Max Weber's Sociology of Law," *Law & Society Review* 21, no. 3 (1987): 487–512; Hubert Treiber, "'Elective Affinities,'" 839–843.

47. *E&S*, 977; *Wirtschaft und Gesellschaft. Nachlaß. Herrschaft, MWG* I/22-4, ed. E. Hanke with Th. Kroll (Tübingen, Germany: Mohr [Siebeck], 2005),192.

48. *Weber on Law*, 61–64, 130–132, 77–86, 198–202, 220–223, 228–231, 315–318; *MWG* I/22-3, 301–305, 345–348, 447–459, 476–484, 506–509, 516–519, 631–636. As Richard Swedberg has emphasized, Weber's analysis focuses attention on calculability as the factor that matters most for modern capitalism: see *Weber and the Idea of Economic Sociology*, 99–107; also Treiber, "'Elective Affinities,'" 839–843.

49. *Weber on Law*, 122–125, 131–132, 209–212; *MWG* I/22-3, 333–339, 347–348, 491–495.

50. *Weber on Law*, 209–212, 219–220; *MWG* I/22-3, 491–495, 505–506. In emphasizing the vital importance of notarial practice for later, secular-rational developments in the *jus commune* of modern Europe and in drawing a sharp contrast between developments in northern Italy and northern France, Weber's argument is strongly echoed in Witt, *Two Latin Cultures*.

51. *Weber on Law*, 281–282; *MWG* I/22-3, 589–590; Henry J. Steiner and Philip Alston, *International Human Rights in Context: Law, Politics, Morals* (Oxford: Clarendon Press, 1996); Brian Tierney, *The Idea of Natural Rights* (Grand Rapids, MI: Eerdmans, 1997); Richard Tuck, *Natural Rights Theories: Their Origin and Development* (Cambridge: Cambridge University Press, 1979); Wieacker, *History of Private Law*, 159–195, 199–221.

52. United Nations, Office of the High Commissioner for Human Rights, "Intellectual Property Rights and Human Rights," Sub-Commission on Human Rights resolution 2000/7 (August 17, 2000), http://www.ohchr.org/EN/pages/home.aspx (accessed September 1, 2017); Laurence R. Helfer, "Human Rights and Intellectual Property: Conflict or Coexistence?" *Minnesota Intellectual Property Review* 5, no. 1 (2003): 47–61.

53. *Weber on Law*, 284–300; *MWG* I/22-3, 592–614.

54. *Weber on Law*, 289–292; *MWG* I/22-3, 598–602.

55. *Weber on Law*, 296; *MWG* I/22-3, 608.

56. *Weber on Law*, 292–321; *MWG* I/22-3, 602–639.

57. See also Gephart, *Law, Culture, and Society*, 125–127.

58. See also Gephart, *Law, Culture, and Society*, 136–140. For Weber as a diagnostician of fundamental paradoxes in modernity, see Wolfgang Schluchter, "The Paradox of

Rationalization: On the Relation of Ethics and World," in Guenther Roth and Wolfgang Schluchter, *Max Weber's Vision of History: Ethics and Methods* (Berkeley: University of California Press, 1979), 13.

59. Weber, "Introduction," in *The Essential Weber*, 60–64; *MWG* I/19, 89–95.

60. *Weber on Law*, 188–191, 284–321; *MWG* I/22-3, 424–429, 593–639; Gephart, *Law, Culture, and Society*, 79, 146; Whimster, *Understanding Weber*, 49.

CHAPTER 6

··

IS THERE A FUTURE FOR
BOURGEOIS LIBERALISM?

··

ROBERT J. ANTONIO

"The 'free' market, that is the market which is not bound by ethical norms,
with its exploitation of constellations of interests and monopoly positions,
and its dickering, is an abomination to every system of fraternal ethics."[1]

THE ethos of bourgeois culture, Max Weber held, is an extreme, systematized iteration
of the West's "specific and peculiar rationalism."[2] In a classic essay, however, Karl Löwith
argued that Weber believed that "every instance of radical rationalization is inevitably
fated to engender irrationality." In Weber's view, he contended, capitalism's clockwork
efficiency does not insure equitable provision for needs and autonomy—rather the more
rationalized, secularized, and intellectualized, the more antinomy and meaninglessness
riddle bourgeois culture and the more it moves toward an "irrational way of life."[3]
Contra Marx, Löwith explained, Weber had no hope for emancipation, and he warned
that such romantic notions fuel fanatic ethics of conviction in mass-democratic politics,
pathways to the authoritarian state. Löwith composed this essay when Weber's worst
fears about bourgeois culture's contradictions were becoming reality—Hitler was coming to power, and a total state was on the near horizon.[4]

In this chapter I analyze Weber's views about irrational consequences of rationalization manifested in "free-market" capitalism, which he held is aimed to maximize formal
rationality oriented to capital accounting and profitability.[5] Employing free-market
ideas and methods to reshape society accordingly today, "neoliberals'" unremitting
effort to accelerate accumulation has generated major substantive irrationalities and a
nascent legitimacy crisis of their regime. Weber contrasted bourgeois era, rationalized
economic practices to premodern "'adventurers' capitalism," stressing political extraction
and irrational speculation. He argued, however, that speculators, promoters, hucksters,
exploiters of political position exist in all monetary economies.[6] These paradoxical coun-
tertendencies plague neoliberalism's leading finance sector, mass politics, and overall

money culture, which combine irrational modes of speculation with exceptionally sophisticated calculative systems. This essay will explore the relevance of deeply pessimistic threads of Weber's thought about bourgeois culture for contemporary capitalism.

Weber's Vision of Bourgeois Culture on the Edge

"Behold! I show you *the last human being*."[7]

Weber's reformed Protestant carriers of early bourgeois culture were purposive, effective folk who prevailed against enormously powerful institutions and people (e.g., state churches, aristocrats, monarchs) who detested Puritan, rationally calculative, workaday ways. Weber admired the Puritan "reserve," "cool" and "temperate self-control," frugality, and reliability that gave rise to secularized bourgeois culture and the "best type of English or American gentleman today."[8] He explained how the fire of exceptionally demanding, all-encompassing control, extreme suppression of bodily and social pleasures, and profound "spiritual isolation" helped forge these character traits. Steely, prudent, devoted Puritan carriers of the Protestant ethic, Weber held, were *the* decisive force in overcoming economic "traditionalism," the impenetrable barrier everywhere to economic rationalism and distinctly modern capitalism. He argued that Puritan economic ethics and ways of life (e.g., beliefs in specialized work, tireless labor, and disciplined enterprise and "pharisaically good conscience" about unlimited legal acquisition and inequality) gave rise to "rational bourgeois economic life" and "stood at the cradle of modern economic man."[9] Their asceticism, dispassionate self-control, and dedication to vocation were infused with meaning and motivated by beliefs that their efforts served God's will and provided evidence that they were in "His" grace and among the elect.

As the "religious roots" gradually withered away and the Protestant ethic transformed into the "spirit of capitalism," Weber asserted that moneymaking became "an end in itself" and the "ultimate purpose" of bourgeois existence. This shift reduced "duty in a calling"—*the* "social ethic of capitalistic culture"—to inexhaustible earthly striving for maximum gain and success. Weber held that market-liberal "rationality" does not subordinate "economic acquisition" to need satisfaction and therefore appears to noncapitalist peoples as "irrational," "foreign," heedless "avarice." The mundane, strictly inner-worldly rewards of bourgeois professions, he implied, no longer infused life with ultimate meaning as Puritan vocations did.[10] Moreover, he contended that economic compulsion rules in modern capitalism; Puritans "wanted to work in a calling," but "we are forced to do so," he said.[11] Weber understood that capitalists in competitive struggle must maximize profits via formally rational work processes and accounting to survive, but consequent stringent domination of wageworkers and starkly unequal economic outcomes manifest the bourgeois order's "substantive irrationality."[12] Formally "free labor" is an all-important, unique feature of modern capitalism said Weber, but, lacking independent means of subsistence and freely fired, he said, wageworkers are compelled by "the whip of hunger."[13] He saw "economic survival of the fittest" and the techno-economic order to determine individual fate with "irresistible force." Famously, Weber declared that "material goods" exert historically unparalleled, "inexorable power" over our lives—insatiable hunger for economic acquisition has become an "iron cage" that may persist "until the last ton of fossilized coal is burnt."[14]

Weber implied that the animate core of bourgeois culture is its steel-hard shell—the cultural beliefs and institutional, organizational, and technical complex that serve the operation and reproduction of its expansionary economic machinery. He held that secularization and rationalization savaged the structures of meaning that motivated Puritan carriers of bourgeois economic ethics and justified and emotionally sustained intense work, enterprise, and overall "progress" in the dawning bourgeois era. Weber contended that Enlightenment ideals, which enshrined rationality and liberal rights, are "irretrievably fading" and that the idea of vocation is now a "ghost of dead religious beliefs" or "*caput mortuum*" (worthless residue).[15] He argued that entrepreneurs have difficulty explaining the purpose of their restless acquisitive practices. They exist for their businesses rather than the obverse, "irrational" from the substantively rational vision of cultivating a "good life."[16] In bourgeois culture's American heartland, Weber said, people often abandon efforts to justify compulsive moneymaking and simply treat it as competitive "sport." He provided a vivid example of a wealthy Ohio entrepreneur so single-mindedly obsessed with growing his business that he could not keep his eyes off the clock or engage with his family on Sunday, as reported by the old man's German-born son-in-law who declared "what a futile life!" Weber cautioned that bourgeois culture's ultimate fate is contingent, but he portrayed its exhaustion in emphatic, color-ful evaluative terms—he decried its "mechanized petrification" and "convulsive self-importance" and called it a "nullity." Employing Nietzsche's reference to late moder-nity's failing "last humans" (self-satisfied, clueless, mediocre, directionless, conformist, reactive), Weber mourned the passing of the early bourgeois era's self-directed, steady, temperate, focused, active character type of men and women he so admired.[17]

Weber said that modern capitalism is "identical with the pursuit of profit and forever *renewed* profit, by means of continuous, rational, capitalistic enterprise"; and it commands the same precise, unambiguous, continuous, fast operations from its bureaucratic infra-structure. He saw "calculability of results" to be a distinguishing "peculiarity" of bourgeois culture.[18] Weber contrasted this "formally rational" ethos with the uninhibited greed found in nearly all cultures (albeit usually exercised outside one's own community in non-capitalist orders). "Adventure capitalists" (e.g., financiers, promoters, speculators, kleptocrats) pursue gain outside prescribed paths in "irrational," unconventional, politi-cal, amoral, illegal ways, often with risky, incalculable outcomes.[19] Although contrary in style to conventional businesspersons, he held, adventure capitalists operate in the inter-stices and center of modern capitalism (e.g., banks, finance). He said that credit vehicles and stock markets provide a "rational assembly of capital" and that "big capitalists," on the London exchange grasp its commercial purposes and act prudently. By contrast, "small speculators" who "play the exchange," he argued, undercut its rational features.[20] Weber held that speculation increases with the importance of "negotiable paper."[21] He saw finance as an arena for arbitrage and speculation and thus modern adventure capitalists. Entwining rational forces with irrational forces, the "capitalist spirit" has a "double nature," he said.[22] Weber called purely income-seeking investors in the enterprise "outside interests" oriented to "short-run speculative" gain or a "purely gambling interest" oblivious to its long-term success and drivers of economic crises. That "outside interests" can exert control over managers selected according to the "highest degree of *formal* rationality," Weber asserted, manifests the "*substantive* irrationality specific to the modern economic order."[23]

Weber thought that modern capitalism favors a class society with plutocratic tendencies and that its substantively irrational features bear heavily on lower classes, especially where free-market justifications and policies rule.[24] Contending that secularization destroyed heavenly compensation for "working-class" miseries and economic crises, he argued that wageworkers blame the "social order" and that "inevitable" class tensions inspire visions of "rational socialism."[25] Arguing that socialism would only intensify capitalism's substantively irrational features, however, he held that a planned economy would "nationalize or socialize top management," centralize power maximally, and leave workers propertyless, disempowered, and tethered to their niche in the division of labor. In his view, socialism would harden capitalism's "steel frame" or "shell of bondage"; party elites and their staffs would have unchecked power, eliminate market-based provisioning, and undercut the formal rationality needed for abundance and human flourishing. Weber believed that the total state, whether socialist or fascist, would reinstitute a new version of antiquity's authoritarian "liturgical state" armed with a formally rationalized bureaucratic machine and panoptical methods of control.[26] At the end of "Politics as a Vocation," Weber warned that "sterile excitation" and revolutionary politics in the wake of Germany's lost war, no matter which side won, would lead to a "period of reaction" or "polar night of icy darkness and hardness" in which the total state would erase everyone's rights.[27]

Weber's argument about the "spirit of capitalism" suggests a narrowing and hollowing out of bourgeois culture, which undercuts the meaning of individual lives and community. He suggested that relentless capitalist rationalization, severed from its religious roots, produces substantively irrational impacts that disrupt the orderly bourgeois way of life and erode its legitimacy. He warned that "material interests and calculations of advantage" alone do not insure loyalty in unstable situations.[28] By contrast to religious rationalization, he explained, the modern process rationalizes each of the numerous, differentiated sociocultural spheres in accord with its own distinct characteristics, sharpening boundaries between them and diminishing overall cultural coherence and meaning. Weber described those occupying scientific vocations (in the broad, inclusive sense of systematic intellectual practices) as an "unbrotherly aristocracy" whose each step forward in rationalizing, intellectualizing, disenchanting, and differentiating the natural and social worlds leads increasingly to "devastating senselessness" that robs the life course and death of meaning. He saw modern culture's normative complex to be a hodgepodge of "irreconcilably antagonistic values."[29] Weber warned that demagogic, Caesarist tendencies of plebiscitary mass-democratic politics endanger formal democracy and liberal institutions, especially when inflamed by economic and sociopolitical inequality and crises. In his view, deliberative democracy is a pipe dream.

Weber emphasized plural causal forces, contingent futures, and divergent historical paths and therefore did *not* see modernity through a monistic pessimistic lens. He also pointed to civilizing resources worthy of defending, cultivating, and strengthening (e.g., parliamentary democracy, liberal rights, ethically responsible leadership, pluralistic culture, competitive politics, and free spaces for individual expression).[30] Even his portrayal of the "bureaucratic machine" identifies indispensable instrumental benefits, as long as countervailing powers are preserved and a total state is avoided. And he considered science to be among modernity's most valuable resources, which in addition to mediating humanity's relation to nature, fosters truth-seeking practices that can cultivate an ethic of consequences, sober realism, and "matter-of-factness" (*Sachlichkeit*) in sociopolitical decision-making. However, Weber saw capitalism as modernity's "most fateful force." Its elites amass enormous power and deploy it to resist substantively rational economic regulation, planning, and redistribution and formally irrational reductions of capitalist control, calculability, and profit.[31] Weber did not mesh his pessimistic assessments of capitalism's substantive irrationalities with his views about democratic associational life, civic culture, and politics or entertain possible social democratic regimes capable of mediating contradictory substantive and formal rationalities and irrationalities.[32] Considering market exchange to be the "archetype of all rational social action," he contended that the more powerful bourgeois elites grow, the greater their effectiveness at acquiring productive forces, exerting ever more control over wageworkers "without limitations" and achieving "continuous extension of the free market." He held that the more bourgeois culture approximates a free-market regime, the more it stresses exclusive concern with "the commodity" over "obligations of brotherliness and reverence."[33] Consequently, he would hardly be surprised that today's brazen "free-market" regimes suffer major substantive irrationalities and legitimacy crises.

"FREE-MARKET" REDUX: HEGEMONIC FINANCE AND ADVENTURE CAPITALISTS

> "The triumph of the West ... is evident ... in the total exhaustion of viable systematic alternatives to Western liberalism."[34]

At the end of the 1980s, after the Thatcher–Reagan break with Keynesianism and when the Soviet bloc was in tatters, Francis Fukuyama declared famously that US-style market liberalism is *the* unsurpassable, "optimal route to prosperity" for all nations.[35] After a decade-long stock market boom, Thomas L. Friedman said that "free-market capitalism" ruled nearly worldwide and "blew away all the major ideological alternatives." Readily shifting investments from "bloated," "overregulated" welfare states to the most market-friendly locations, he held, the "Electronic Herd" of global investors grow the economy and limit political choice to "Pepsi or Coke." The consequent highly unequal "winners take all society" is the only alternative to backwardness, he added.[36] *New Left Review* editor Marxist Perry Anderson bitterly disagreed with Friedman's gushing praise for "neoliberalism" or market fundamentalism but concurred about its "universal diffusion" and "uncontested consolidation" and absence of any effective "collective agency" or even "systematic rival outlooks" that could challenge its hegemony.[37] Politically diverse pundits and critics celebrated, decried, or simply reported "the end of left and right" and repeated variously the Thatcherite mantra "there is no alternative."[38] The scenario parallels Weber's vision of a powerful "free-market" regime unchecked by substantial countervailing power and with unchallenged control over workers, minimal social regulation and redistribution, and severe substantive irrationalities.[39] Neoliberalism's global reach and worker quiescence in its English-speaking heartland might have surprised Weber.

A variety of historical conditions, some of which Weber discussed, have precluded strong socialist and social democratic traditions in the United States. Rather, market liberals, stressing unregulated capitalism, strong property rights, and minimal social welfare, have battled social liberals, embracing modest versions of regulation, redistribution, and social welfare. Both traditions have supported capitalism and liberal democratic rights (e.g., freedom of speech, assembly, religion), albeit colored by different ideologies, constellations of interest, and historical contexts.[40] During the Great Depression, social liberals came to power promising to address market failure, steep economic inequality, and other substantive irrationalities of extreme capitalism. Market liberals framed their latest version to deal with a profit squeeze, inflation, and slow growth, which they blamed on the post–World War II "Great Society's" burdensome regulation and redistribution. Neoliberals privatized, deregulated, deunionized, cut taxes, and overall shrunk the state's social and regulatory arms. Championing "flexible" work and free flow of capital, commodities, and workers across national borders, they greatly enhanced the power of capital (especially its wealthiest fractions) over labor. Both major American political parties helped forge the neoliberal regime domestically and exported it globally via US power in international governance institutions (e.g., International Monetary Fund, World Bank, World Economic Forum, G20). Embracing neoliberal policies, states, finance ministers, and wealthy global financial and technical elites converged in the "Washington Consensus." Neoliberals celebrated "market freedom" but captured and deployed state power for their ends.[41]

Neoliberal-era[42] tax cuts reduced the top marginal US federal income tax rate to 39.6 percent; it averaged 81 percent from 1932 to 1980.[43] Of thirty-five Organisation for Economic Co-operation and Development nations, only three have lower tax rates than the United States, yet the Trump administration and Republican Party passed an enormous tax cut that reduced the top marginal rate to 37 percent and the corporate rate from 35 percent to 21 percent. The massive 2017 Trump tax cut will widen this gap and accelerate the plutocratic trend.[44] Neoliberals hold that upper-bracket tax reductions increase investment capital and grow the "real economy" (goods and nonfinancial services) and middle-class jobs, but they have mostly sharply increased financial profits and concentrated wealth at the top. Neoliberals also intend to "starve the beast" or shrink the social state by maximally commodifying public goods, especially reducing health, education, and welfare. Lacking political support to institute a full free-market, "enterprise society" and unwilling to take responsibility for draconian cuts of public goods, neoliberal legislators made major tax cuts without sufficient entitlement reductions to pay for them with the expectation that "market discipline," enforced by investors and lenders, would eventually necessitate program cuts.[45] Neoliberal financial deregulation and much increased debt have grown the finance sector and helped increase its independence from the real economy. The US finance sector peaked at 8 percent of gross domestic product (GDP) and 40 percent of all profits in the early 2000s (1950s and 1960s profits ranged 10–15 percent). In the neoliberal era, finance has had much higher profits than manufacture and other services, and such profits have remained high despite sector growth and increased competition.[46] Official figures understate financial profits because they do not include "nonfinancial firms," which have sharply increased their portfolio income and sale of financial services. In addition, tax loopholes permit companies to shelter profits offshore.[47] The top 1 percent households own 38 percent of stock shares, and the top 10 percent own 82 percent of shares, while the bottom 80 percent own only 8 percent. Financialization breeds plutocracy.[48]

Arguably neoliberalism's central theoretical doctrine, the "efficient market hypothesis" holds that financial prices in the regime's deregulated, supposedly transparent financial markets reflect all public information available and always trade at their fair value, eliminating asset price bubbles, insuring short-term share-price maximization, long-term vitality of firms, and robust shareholder returns.[49] Efficient market theorists treat stock market prices as the best guide for the value of all assets and health of the overall economy. They put a halo around financialization. Executives receive stock options supposedly to motivate pursuit of "shareholder value maximization," but they have often stressed "financial engineering" to maximize their short-term gains at the expense of the firm's long-term vitality and other shareholders. Finance has the highest executive incomes of any sector, but financialization of the corporate economy caused overall executive pay to skyrocket. Average annual chief executive officer (CEO) compensation at the 350 largest US firms was $15.6 million in 2016; it soared from 20 times the average worker in 1965 to 271–1 today (before the financial crisis it peaked at about 383–1). From 1978 to 2015, CEO inflation-adjusted compensation increased over 937 percent, 70 percent faster than the stock market.[50] Corporate executives led neoliberal restructuring by outsourcing manufacturing, fighting unions, and expanding part-time and contingent low-wage service jobs at the cost of full-time, higher-wage industrial jobs. They lobbied for deregulation and tax cuts.[51] Political contributions, campaign costs, and lobbying organizations all grew enormously in the 1990s and early 2000s along with concentrated finance capital and a political, legal, and cultural climate that endorsed political money as free speech.[52]

Friedman declared US financial markets to be the most transparent, with the highest accounting standards in the world. He employed Enron and its CEO Kenneth Lay as models of "Americanization-globalization's" hyperefficient, revolutionary "fast world."[53] The wave of corporate scandals that followed proved Friedman wrong. Enron shut down after its shameless fraudulent practices were exposed, Ken Lay went to prison for his lead role in the corruption, and top accounting firm Arthur Anderson had to shut down for its complicity. The same issues on a much more massive scale occurred with the housing bubble and banking and accounting scandals of the 2008–2009 financial crisis. Weber understood that corporate power could distort normal capital accounting and business practices, but the fusion of formally rational technique with corrupt practices and normalization of the latter in the largest, supposedly most reliable financial institutions might have surprised him. This ascent of imprudent neoliberal financial wizards is the reverse of Weber's description of rational, prudent Puritans and their allies taking control of the Bank of England from adventure capitalist Will Paterson and his crew.[54] From the start, critics warned that neoliberal financialization was giving rise to a "casino society," where Keynes held that financial maneuvering replaces effective production of goods and services.[55]

Nobel laureate, economist Joseph Stiglitz argues that neoliberal-era finance has operated largely as a "market in speculation" and "rent-seeking sector" instead of a driver of "true economic productivity." Speculative management has stressed short-term returns, endless transaction fees, and predatory loan and credit card practices. Big banks developed risky financial instruments and acted in reckless, unscrupulous ways. Finance embraced neoclassical economics and its exceptionally rational view of economic actors and employed mathematicized theory and elegant mathematical models. Quantitative financial "geniuses" appeared to create enormous wealth in magical ways. Employing models of its founders Nobel winners Robert Merton and Myron Scholes, long-term capital management's supposedly low-risk, high-return hedge fund collapsed in 1998. The Federal Reserve had to bail out the highly leveraged fund to avert a banking crisis. In 1999, the US Congress repealed provisions of the Glass-Steagall Act that separated commercial banks (which accept deposits and loan money) and investment banks (which specialize in large, riskier transactions). The big banks created complex derivatives of mortgage-based assets overloaded with subprime loans; rating agencies contracted by the banks rated the derivatives AAA; mortgage originators sold to unqualified homebuyers; and the Federal Reserve reduced interest rates to historically low levels, which fueled the bubble and culminated in a global financial crisis and the largest government bailout ever. Sophisticated accounting schemes and mathematical models created an illusion of certainty and formally rational cover for deeply misaligned interests, obvious moral hazards, gross regulatory failure, rampant irresponsibility and corruption, and inexcusable "too big to fail banks." Finance sector political contributions and power helped big banks convince the state to socialize the costs of their malfeasance and avert the usual executive terminations and restructuring, which are supposed to fix responsibility for gross mismanagement and business failure and prevent their recurrence.[56]

Helping globalize the financial economy, a network of trained, certified "trust and estate practitioners" (lawyers and accountants) "protect" the wealth of "ultrahigh net worth" people, enriched mostly through financial investment and bloated executive compensation. They help the richest investors find high-yield, low-risk investments open only to them and employ sophisticated financial and legal knowledge to create strategies for systematic tax avoidance and creation of complex trust arrangements outside public scrutiny and often hidden in multiple offshore tax havens, designed to be hard to trace. The Society for Trust and Estate Planners lobbies states worldwide to reduce super-rich taxation and shrink social states.[57] Well represented at the national and state levels especially among conservative legislators and supported by some of the largest US corporations, the American Legislative Council (ALEC) provides model free-market legislation, often adopted word for word by legislative supporters. In the wake of the 2008–2009 financial crisis, ALEC championed austerity legislation at all levels of government and "partnered" with the State Policy Network of state-level think tanks to lobby for ALEC-sponsored legislation and provide supportive informa-tion and spin.[58] Neoliberal financialization increased corporate profits and concen-trated wealth. Productivity gains helped grow corporate profits, but worker shares have lagged. Regime critics contend that "growth" of financial wealth has been driven largely by politically organized "accumulation by dispossession" or upward redistribution from lower and middle classes via corporate suppression of union power, tax cuts, commodi-fication of public goods, predatory financial practices, and employment of debt to impose austerity.[59]

Financiers and CEOs played a major role in corporate restructuring, namely mergers, acquisitions, and hostile takeovers, as well as use of leveraged buyouts, high-yield junk bonds, greenmail, asset stripping, and other speculative strategies aimed at short-term gains. Bold-acting, risk-taking financiers and developers, often operating imprudently and sometimes illegally, have been major, highly publicized figures in the neoliberal era. Corporate raiders such as Carl Icahn, T. Boone Pickens, and Victor Posner and enabler investment bankers such as convicted racketeer Michael Milken accumulated windfall wealth by hollowing out firms. Ponzi schemes and corporate fraud brought enormous wealth and then prison to CEOs like Kenneth Lay (Enron), Bernie Ebbers (World Com), and Dennis Kozlowski (Tyco). Operator of the largest Ponzi scheme ever, Bernie Madoff was a former NASDAQ chair and subject of an HBO movie. Prime time TV show *American Greed* has covered the rise and demise of such figures for eleven years and has yet to run out of stories. However, many or even most "scam artists" have not been exposed or brought to trial—executives complicit in the 2008–2009 financial crash kept their positions, bonuses, and reputations. Neoliberal-era, speculative financial practices blurred boundaries between legitimate business practice, imprudence, and illegality.[60]

The movie *Wall Street* (1987), especially its main character, financier Gordon Gekko, iconically represents the ruthlessness, unlimited greed, and willingness to deploy almost any means at whatever cost to satisfy outsized ambitions.[61] Yet many Americans embrace the celebrity culture that glorifies such "success" as evidenced by long runs of *Lifestyles of the Rich and Famous* and *The Apprentice*. Neoliberalism is a cultural habitus as well as a policy regime in these sectors of society. Weber was brutally realistic about the less than stellar figures that often ascend the heights in academe, the papacy, and politics; but given his hopes about democratic facets of American life, he surely would have found befuddling the election of real estate developer, financial operator, and reality show host Donald Trump to the presidency. Knowing today's neoliberal context, Weber might have seen the election of this latter-day adventure capitalist, who played "hard-ball" with workers, contractors, and creditors and experienced multiple bankruptcies and scandals, to culminate a voracious money culture and sociocultural breakdown paralleling that described so graphically in the last pages of his most famous text. Weber's concepts of charismatic and patrimonial domination pertain, respectively, to Trump's enthusiastic "base" who believe unshakably that he serves their needs, hopes, and beliefs and to his tendency to favor loyalty and personal and familial ties over competence in administrative appointments. Notably, from a Weberian perspective, both are opposed to rational-legal forms of authority. The toxic mix of Caesarism with class resentment and racial antipathy toward immigrants and African Americans (which Weber presciently warned is the most fractious US divide) contributing to the electoral outcome would have deeply troubled but not surprised Weber.[62]

Twilight Time of Bourgeois Culture: Plutocracy and the Ecological Wall

"The egalitarian pioneer ideal has faded into oblivion, and the New World may be on the verge of becoming the Old Europe of the twenty-first century's globalized economy."[63]

Unplanned, exponential economic growth is a sine qua non of liberalism per se. GDP, or the monetary value of US finished goods and services, is the standard measure of growth and overall economic health. That GDP does not take account of economic inequality, social well-being, or ecological sustainability manifests Weber's central point about market-liberal maximization of formal rationality. Productive powers and profits must grow continuously, liberals argue, to increase the quantity, quality, and diversity of goods and services; meet consumer demand; and drive socioeconomic progress. Growth is a presupposition of American consumer culture and capitalism; investments, job security, debt repayment, retirement, healthcare, lifestyle, and public goods all depend on it. Differential diligence and merit require unequal proportional rewards, but everyone benefits from growth, liberals contend. By contrast, prolonged slow growth or contraction and the consequent socioeconomic squeeze inflict pain and generate legitimacy crises and political shifts.

Weber argued that formal rationality says nothing about "want satisfaction" unless coupled with knowledge of income distribution. Thomas Piketty criticizes neoclassical economics for ignoring distribution, relying too heavily on elegant mathematical abstractions, and conflating them with "highly ideological speculation."[64] Piketty elaborates the neoliberal reversal of postwar egalitarianism and consequent "drift toward oligarchy." From 1979 to 2014, the lower 90 percent of US real wages rose from $28,500 to $33,300 while the top 1 percent wages soared from $269,100 to $671,100 and the top 0.1 percent from $599,200 to $2,543,000. The higher the centile fraction, the greater the income gain. Annual post-tax income for the top 0.01 percent was $20,300.000 and for the top 0.001 percent $88,700,000 in 2014 (up 617 percent since 1980). The inflation-adjusted federal minimum wage peaked in 1968 at $9.90 per hour and was $7.25 in 2017.[65] Stratospheric corporate executive pay, Piketty explains, produced "record level" US labor income inequality, likely higher than any society ever.[66] He contends that the enormous, rising income gap is ossifying and transforming the United States into an oligarchic "rentier society," similar to hierarchical orders of the past where kinship and marriage determined social status and place in society. Piketty calls rentiers the "enemy of democracy." Only "radical shock," he argues, can alter the course toward rentier society.[67] Weber called investors with strictly income interests "rentiers" and said that US democracy does not preclude the rise of "raw plutocracy" or an "'aristocratic' prestige group," but he did not imagine a capitalist pathway back to a static society.[68]

Former World Bank economist Branko Milanovic portrays the United States as a "'perfect storm' of inequality" that remains formally democratic but increasingly resembles "plutocracy." The United States has the highest percentage of global 1 percenters of any nation and the smallest middle class among wealthy Western democracies, he notes. Milanovic says polarization will increase in rich nations and produce a sharper divide between the very rich and the rest who service them. He holds that robotics will substantially reduce demand for labor, an oversupply of highly educated people will diminish education's role in mobility, and success will increasingly depend on being "born well" and "lucky." Economist Robert J. Gordon holds that future prospects for the "bottom 99 percent" are poor and "fundamental causes" of growing inequality will be exceptionally hard to reverse. Most workers' wages have substantially lagged productivity gains, and many older workers lack sufficient retirement savings. Younger workers face tough labor markets, more 25- to 35-year-olds live with their parents than ever before, and student debt is at record levels. Low-income workers have lost ground; suffer authoritarian, insecure work places; and have wages stolen. The black–white income gap has grown with inequality, and poor, young African Americans suffer from terrible schools, high unemployment, and repressive policing and incarceration. The lower three-quintiles overall suffer from an income squeeze, lost benefits, and erosion of well-being. Sociologist Wolfgang Streeck argues that the plutocratic trend has eviscerated "democratic capitalism" and opens the way for "authoritarian liberalism." Milanovic sees increased inequality, insecurity, and immigration, all driven by neoliberal globalization, as fueling a rising transnational tide of right-wing populism and nativism.[69] These reactionary currents suggest an emergent legitimation crisis of neoliberalism.

The post–World War II expansion followed by neoliberal-era global consolidation of capitalism greatly accelerated the speed and volume of natural resource throughput and waste production and intensified the contradiction between unplanned, exponential growth and the Earth's biophysical carrying capacity.[70] We have altered ecosystems much faster and much more extensively in this period than ever before, degraded more than 60 percent of ecosystem services, and impeded United Nations' human development goals. Biodiversity loss has increased so sharply that scientists argue "the sixth great extinction" is underway. Exceeding the biosphere's carrying capacity at increasing rates, we now consume ecological resources equal to 1.7 Earths, and globalized US-style consumption would take five Earths. Poor nations have already suffered serious ecologically driven human development setbacks (e.g., floods, famine, disease, forced migrations) and rich ones increased ecological problems and risks. Scientists warn that we have exceeded planetary boundaries and may be approaching tipping points for major Earth processes, which could cause sudden state changes. Global environmental problems (e.g., climate change, biodiversity loss, ocean acidification, chemical pollution, ozone depletion, deforestation, atmospheric aerosol pollution, disturbed nitrogen and phosphorus cycles) constitute enormous risks especially for poor, young, and future generations and other species with which we share the planet. Environmental impacts have accelerated so greatly that scientists contend that a new "Anthropocene" geologic epoch has dawned in which humans are the primary drivers of overall ecological change and possible catastrophe looms.[71]

Climate change's global reach, complex feedbacks, speed, and threat to end the unusually stable Holocene climate, which has sustained complex civilizations and large populations, make it the greatest ecological threat. The Intergovernmental Panel on Climate Change targeted a maximum 2°C increase over the preindustrial average to reduce chances for catastrophe. The current 1°C rise has already generated irreversible instabilities of Arctic sea ice and Greenland and Antarctic ice sheets, worldwide retreat of glaciers, higher seas and storm surges, and severe drought and floods. Top climate scientists warn that even a 2°C rise would be disastrous. They argue that the impact of greenhouse gas (GHG) already emitted, augmented by release of heat stored in seas and in permafrost and likely reduced aerosol pollution in newly industrialized nations (especially China), will drive temperatures well beyond 2°C.[72] The most long-lasting GHG, carbon dioxide, has already breached the planetary boundary. Neoliberal "business as usual" and consequent increased GHG emissions could produce a 4–6°C increase and radically degrade the planet for human habitation. Other leading climate scientists warn that societal "core values" unadjusted to "external conditions" open the society to ecological "shock," as is the case, they say, for today's "growth-oriented economy based on neoliberal economic principles and assumptions."[73] Climate change mitigation and adaptation require huge public investment and extensive transnational regulation and planning, which conflict with neoliberalism's growth imperative, possessive individualism, consumerism, and antiregulatory, antitax, antiredistributive, "starve the beast" politics.

Climatologists Kevin Anderson and Alice Bows contend that climate scientists self-censor reportage about likely climate change impacts to avoid political attack. Neoclassical economists and neoliberal policymakers have shaped climate policy and tenaciously defend the growth imperative and ignore "the elephant in the room" (i.e., "business as usual" will generate ecological damages that preclude economic growth).[74]

The 1992 Rio Declaration committed its more than 170 signatory nations to curtail climate change and other global environmental problems. However, this and other nonbinding agreements have produced little progress. The international trading regime forged by neoliberal governance organizations, whose members signed the climate treaties, officially support sustainable development; but their trade rules do not. Prioritizing market liberalization and exponential unplanned growth, they reject binding regulation needed to enforce targeted changes. Leader of the global neoliberal regime and top historical GHG emitter, the United States usually has opposed or has tepidly supported global environmental regulation. President Trump's withdrawal from the Paris Agreement, aggressive support of the fossil fuel industry, appointment of Scott Pruitt (who rejects climate science and ecological regulation) to head the Environmental Protection Agency, and overall "free-market" agenda is designed to reverse modest, insufficient efforts to cope with climate change.[75]

The World Economic Forum global risk assessment reports income and wealth inequality and climate change as the top global threats. It also warns about other serious environmental problems, underemployment, post-truth politics, populist parties, eroded social protection systems, and a crisis of Western democracy.[76] This neoliberal organization maps the problems quite well but does not address their roots in the free-market regime and its formally rational shell. Rentier wealth concentrated at the very top combined with erosion of well-being in the lower- and middle-income quintiles generate major tensions that weaken democracy in neoliberal heartland nations and beyond. Massive growth of workers dependent on wage labor along with relentless mechanization and automation in core capitalist and newly industrialized nations are increasing underemployment and casual labor and precluding absorption of the rapidly growing global reserve army into the full-time labor force. Neoliberal policies have not recovered postwar-style growth, which produced full employment, grew incomes of all quintiles, and advanced abundance, opportunity, and autonomy.[77]

Do Bourgeois Liberalism and the Planet Have a Future?

"Someone once said that it is easier to imagine the end of the world than to imagine the end of capitalism."[78]

Neoliberal regimes could morph, as Piketty warns, into a new ancien régime; right-wing populism could erupt into barbarism, as it did last century; or oppositional politics to Brexit, Trump, and populism could ignite a new progressive movement. Yet revived progressivism would face the uncharted task of reviving socioeconomic justice while designing a new regime absent the growth imperative. Coping with plutocracy and climate change demands massive redistribution and comprehensive planning. Climate change denial and gross underestimation of its imminence and gravity are common, in part, because even well-informed people have trouble fathoming the enormous public investment and the fundamental change in everyday life that mitigation and adaptation require, especially in wealthy, high-consuming nations. Weber's prophetic assertion "until the last ton of fossilized coal is burnt" points to the absolute limit of bourgeois culture—ecological overshoot threatening life on the planet and necessitating radical reconstruction or transcendence of the neoliberal regime and even capitalism per se, as we have known them. Prioritizing calculability in service of capital accumulation ad infinitum at this moment imperils the biophysical and sociopolitical foundations of capitalism and democracy.

In a Weberian moment, Piketty warns against equating "democratic rationality" and "economic and technological rationality," an insight propaedeutic to reconstructing democracy. He acknowledges climate change as the "world's principal long-term worry," but he implies that democracy must first "regain control over globalized financial capitalism." While fearing only "shock" will stir collective action sufficient to this task, he asserts we must imagine and invent "new forms of participation and governance."[79] Although underestimating the speed of climate change, Piketty understands that a continued slide into plutocracy means eventual sociopolitical and ecological catastrophe. President Trump and certain other right-wing "populist" leaders manifest an emerging legitimacy crisis of neoliberalism, and their authoritarian liberalism generates opposition that provides opportunity for wider, more inspired political vision and a sharper change of course than return to the status quo ante. Our collective fate and that of the biosphere depend on envisioning and creating a democratic culture and institutions capable of securing the social and biophysical commons that hegemonic bourgeois culture devalues, undercuts, and threatens to destroy. Concluding a famous meditation on "objectivity" in social science with a comment on rupture, Weber said eloquently when "the way forward fades away in the twilight. The light shed by the great cultural problems has moved on. Then science, too, prepares to find a new standpoint and a new conceptual apparatus, and to contemplate the stream of events from the summits of thought."[80] Such a moment is upon us.

NOTES

1. Weber put quotation marks around "free" to problematize the view that markets can be independent of substantial sociopolitical embeddedness: *Economy and Society* (hereafter *E&S*), ed. G. Roth and C. Wittich (Berkeley: University of California Press, 1978), 637; *Wirtschaft und Gesellschaft. Die Wirtschaft und die gesellschaftlichen Ordnungen und Mächte. Nachlaß. Gemeinschaften, Max Weber-Gesamtausgabe* (hereafter *MWG*) I/22-1, ed. W. J. Mommsen with M. Meyer (Tübingen, Germany: Mohr [Siebeck], 2001), 195.
2. Max Weber, *The Protestant Ethic and the Spirit of Capitalism* (hereafter *PESC*) (New York: Scribner's, 1958), 26; *Die protestantische Ethik und der Geist des Kapitalismus/Die protestantischen Sekten und der Geist des Kapitalismus. Schriften 1904–1920, MWG* I/18, ed. W. Schluchter with U. Bube (Tübingen, Germany: Mohr [Siebeck], 2016), 116.
3. Karl Löwith, *Max Weber and Karl Marx*, trans. H. Fantel (London: Allen & Unwin, 1982), 41.

4. Shortly after publication of *Max Weber and Karl Marx*, Löwith had to resign his position because of Jewish ancestry. See Karl Löwith, *My Life in Germany before and after 1933* (Urbana: University of Illinois Press, 1986). For more on Weber and cultural pessimism, see Lawrence A. Scaff, *Fleeing the Iron Cage* (Berkeley: University of California Press, 1989).

5. *E&S*, 161–164; *Wirtschaft und Gesellschaft. Soziologie, MWG* I/23, ed. K. Borchardt, E. Hanke, and W. Schluchter (Tübingen, Germany: Mohr [Siebeck], 2013), 375–378.

6. *PESC*, 56–58; *MWG* I/18, 163–175.

7. Friedrich Nietzsche, *Thus Spoke Zarathustra*, trans. Adrian Del Caro (Cambridge: Cambridge University Press, 2006), 9.

8. *PESC*, 63, 69, 71, 119; *MWG* I/18, 182, 191, 193, 327.

9. *PESC*, 174, 176; *MWG* I/18, 471, 476.

10. *PESC*, 53–56, 69–70; *MWG* I/18, 159–172, 191–192.

11. *PESC*, 181; *MWG* I/18, 486.

12. *E&S*, 138; *MWG* I/23, 336.

13. *PESC*, 20–21; *MWG* I/18, 110; Max Weber, *General Economic History* (hereafter *GEH*), trans. Frank Knight (New York: Dover, 2003) 277; *Abriß der universalen Sozial- und Wirtschaftsgeschichte. Mit- und Nachschriften 1919/20, MWG* III/6, ed. W. Schluchter with J. Schröder (Tübingen, Germany: Mohr [Siebeck], 2011), 319–320.

14. *PESC*, 53–57, 180–181; *MWG* I/18, 159–173, 486–487. On Parsons' translation of this section and *stahlhartes Gehäuse* as "iron cage," see Lawrence A. Scaff, *Max Weber in America* (Princeton, NJ: Princeton University Press, 2011), 223–224. Stephen Kalberg translates the phrase as "steel-hard casing": Max Weber, *The Protestant Ethic and the Spirit of Capitalism. The Revised 1920 Edition*, trans. S. Kalberg (New York: Oxford University Press, 2011), 177, 397n133.

15. *E&S*, 1209; *Wirtschaft und Gesellschaft. Nachlaß. Herrschaft, MWG* I/22-4, ed. E. Hanke with Th. Kroll (Tübingen, Germany: Mohr [Siebeck], 2005), 679; *GEH*, 368–369; *MWG* III/6, 394–396.

16. *PESC*, 70; *MWG* I/18, 191–192.

17. *PESC*, 182, 283n115; *MWG* I/18, 488. Weber wrote "Specialists without spirit, sensualists without heart; this nullity imagines that it has attained a level of civilization never before achieved." Here he referred to Nietzsche's *letzte Menschen*, which Kalberg translated as "last humans" and Parsons omitted. Weber also mentions Nietzsche and "last men" in "Science as a Vocation," in *From Max Weber: Essays in Sociology* (hereafter *FMW*), ed. H. H. Gerth and C. W. Mills (New York: Oxford University Press, 1946), 143; *Wissenschaft als Beruf 1917/1919—Politik als Beruf 1919, MWG* I/17, ed. W. Schluchter and W. J. Mommsen with B. Morgenbrod (Tübingen, Germany: Mohr [Siebeck], 1992), 92. In *Thus Spoke Zarathustra* Nietzsche saw markets to be "last humans'" prime habitat. Francis Fukuyama suggests the same in his *The End of History and the Last Man* (London: Penguin, 1992), 336–339.

18. *PESC*, 17; *MWG* I/18, 106; Weber saw modern market exchange to be the driver of bureaucracy's "'objective' discharge of business" in accord with "*calculable rules* and 'without regard for persons'": *FMW*, 215; also *E&S*, 635–636; *MWG* I/22-1, 194–195.

19. *PESC*, 20, 24, 56–58, 69, 76, 166, 174; 186n6; 199–200n22; *MWG* I/18, 109–110, 114, 168–176, 191, 207, 445, 470.

20. *GEH*, 279; *MWG* III/6, 320. Max Weber, "Stock and Commodity Exchanges (*Die Börse* [1894])," trans. Steven Lestition, *Theory and Society* 29 (2000), 330–335; *Bösenwesen. Schriften und Reden 1893–1898, MWG* I/5, ed. K. Borchardt with C. Meyer-Stoll (Tübingen, Germany: Mohr [Siebeck], 1999), 135–174; Richard Swedberg, *Max Weber and the Idea of*

Economic Sociology (Princeton, NJ: Princeton University Press, 1998), 48–52; Reinhard Bendix, *Max Weber: An Intellectual Portrait* (New York: Anchor, 1962), 23–30, 42. Sandro Segre, *A Weberian Analysis of Business Groups and Financial Markets*, trans. N. Stern (Burlington, VT: Ashgate, 2008), 85–97.

21. *GEH*, 278, 279–291 passim; *MWG* III/6, 320–331. See Swedberg, *Max Weber*, 50, 231n144; Dirk Käsler, *Max Weber: An Introduction to his Life and Work*, trans. P. Hurd (Chicago: University Chicago Press, 1988), 65.

22. Weber said the borders of "rational calculation" and "speculative calculation" blur (*E&S*, 159); *MWG* I/23, 370. Weber treated charismatic financier, journalist, "robber capitalist" Henry Villard as an exemplary modern adventure capitalist: *E&S*, 1118; *MWG* I/22-4, 484; Swedberg, *Max Weber*, 51, 231–232n147; Scaff, *Max Weber in America*, 234.

23. *E&S*, 139–140; *MWG* I/23, 338.

24. *FMW*, 215, 230–232, 224–225, 240–244; *MWG* I/22-4, 186–187, 201–202, 211–213, 228–234.

25. *GEH*, 291, 369; *MWG* III/6, 331, 395–396.

26. On socialism, see *E&S* 110–111, 138–139, 1401–1403, 1453; *MWG* I/23, 289–290, 336–337; *Zur Politik im Weltkrieg. Schriften und Reden 1914–1918*, *MWG* I/15, ed. W. J. Mommsen with G. Hübinger (Tübingen, Germany: Mohr [Siebeck], 1984), 462–465, 541; on planning, *E&S*, 103–104, 109–111; *MWG* I/23, 278–280, 288–290.

27. *FMW*, 127–128; *MWG* I/17, 249–251.

28. *PESC*, 53–54n9, 193–194; *MWG* I/18, 159–161; *E&S*, 213; *MWG* I/23, 450.

29. *FMW*, 355–357; *Die Wirtschaftsethik der Weltreligionen. Konfuzianismus und Taoismus. Schriften 1915–1920*, *MWG* I/19, ed. H. Schmidt-Glintzer with P. Kolonko (Tübingen, Germany: Mohr [Siebeck], 1989), 517–522; *FMW*, 129–136 passim; *MWG* I/17, 71–83; Max Weber, *Collected Methodological Writings* (hereafter *CMW*), trans. H. H. Bruun, ed. H. H. Bruun and S. Whimster (London: Routledge, 2012), 314–315; *Verstehende Soziologie und Werturteilsfreiheit. Schriften und Reden 1908–1917*, *MWG* I/12, ed. J. Weiß with S. Frommer (Tübingen, Germany: Mohr [Siebeck], 2018), 469–470.

30. For Weber's ideas on American democracy pitched against totalizing views of his iron cage theme, see Stephen Kalberg, *Searching for the Spirit of American Democracy* (Boulder, CO: Paradigm, 2014), 68–82 and passim. On Weber and politics, see David Beetham, *Max Weber and the Theory of Modern Politics* (New York: Polity, 1985), and Peter Breiner, *Max Weber and Democratic Politics* (Ithaca, NY: Cornell University Press, 1996).

31. *PESC*, 17; *MWG* I/18, 105–106.

32. On Weber's iron cage thesis and views about democratic associative facets of American culture, see Claus Offe, *Reflections on America*, trans. P. Camiller (Cambridge: Polity, 2004), 43–68, 93–105; Scaff, *Max Weber in America*, 90–97, 133–136, 185–193.

33. *E&S*, 635–640; *MWG* I/22-1, 193–199; Weber (*E&S*, 638; *MWG* I/22-1, 195) cautioned that advancing "free markets" does not preclude their supporters buying political influence or seeking monopolies limiting market freedom.

34. Francis Fukuyama, "The End of History?" *National Interest* 16 (Summer 1989): 3.

35. Fukuyama, *The End of History and the Last Man*, 234.

36. Thomas L. Friedman, *The Lexus and the Olive Tree* (New York: Anchor, 2000), 9, 103–106, 308–309, 355.

37. Perry Anderson, "Renewals," *New Left Review* 1 (2000): 10, 17.

38. Robert J. Antonio, "Immanent Critique and the Exhaustion Thesis: Neoliberalism and History's Vicissitudes," in *The Palgrave Handbook of Critical Theory*, ed. M. J. Thompson (New York: Palgrave Macmillan, 2017), 655–676.

39. *E&S*, 107–111, 137–140; *MWG* I/23, 285–290, 334–339.

40. In the United States, the Republican Party has been the primary carrier of market liberalism and the Democratic Party the primary carrier of social liberalism. Market liberalism has had the upper hand, but the balance between "market justice" and "social justice" has varied in space and time. See Wolfgang Streeck, *Buying Time*, trans. P. Camiller (London: Verso, 2014), 58–63.

41. On neoliberalism, see David Harvey, *A Brief History of Neoliberalism* (Oxford: Oxford University Press, 2005); Philip Mirowski and Dieter Plehwe, *The Road from Mont Pelerin* (Cambridge, MA: Harvard University Press, 2009); Miguel A. Centano and Joseph N. Cohen, "The Arc of Neoliberalism," *Annual Review of Sociology* 38 (2012): 317–340; Fred Block and Margaret R. Summers, *The Power of Market Fundamentalism* (Cambridge, MA: Harvard University Press, 2014); Alessandro Bonanno, *The Legitimation Crisis of Neoliberalism* (New York: Palgrave Macmillan, 2017). For comprehensive mapping of neoliberal globalization, see Peter Dicken, *Global Shift* (New York: Guilford, 2015).

42. Framing neoliberalism in the 1970s, economists and policy-oriented pundits in conservative think tanks drew heavily on Friedrich Hayek and the Austrian school and Milton Friedman and the Chicago school. The "neoliberal era" began by the early 1980s after the elections of Thatcher and Reagan and implementation of "free-market" policies.

43. Thomas Piketty, *Capital in the Twenty-First Century*, trans. A. Goldhammer (Cambridge, MA: Harvard University Press, 2014), 507.

44. Ian Salisbury, "This Chart Shows How Much Americans Pay in Taxes vs. the Rest of the World," *Money* (July 19, 2017), http://time.com/money/4862673/us-tax-burden-vs-oecd-countries/ (accessed July 30 2017).

45. Streeck, *Buying Time*; Greta R. Krippner, *Capitalizing on Crisis* (Cambridge, MA: Harvard University Press, 2011), 138–150; James K. Galbraith, *The Predator State* (New York: Free Press, 2008), 25–37.

46. FIRE sector (finance, insurance, real estate) profits have been substantially higher than manufacture and nonfinancial services: Krippner, *Capitalizing*, 28–57; Dicken, *Global Shift*, 510–538; Noah Smith, "How Finance Took Over the Economy," *Bloomberg View*, April 20, 2016, https://www.bloomberg.com/view/articles/2016-04-20/how-finance-came-to-dominate-the-u-s-economy (accessed July 17, 2017).

47. Gabriel Zucman, *The Hidden Wealth of Nations*, trans. Teresa L. Fagan (Chicago: University of Chicago Press, 2015).

48. The figures are for 2013. Danielle Kurtzleben, "While Trump Touts Stock Market, Many Americans Are Left Out of the Conversation," *NPR* (March 1, 2017), http://www.npr.org/2017/03/01/517975766/while-trump-touts-stock-market-many-americans-left-out-of-the-conversation (accessed July 30, 2017).

49. The theory argued that current share price is the best indicator of future share prices. John Quiggin, *Zombie Economics* (Princeton, NJ: Princeton University Press, 2010), 48–49.

50. Ibid., 36–79; Robert J. Shiller, *Irrational Exuberance* (New York: Broadway Books, 2001); Joseph Montier and Phillip Pilkington, "GMO: The Deep Causes of Secular Stagnation and Rise of Populism" (white paper, March 22, 2017), https://www.gurufocus.com/news/494452/gmo-the-deep-causes-of-secular-stagnation-and-the-rise-of-populism (accessed July 17 2017); Lawrence Mishel and Jessica Schieder, "CEO Pay Remains High Relative to Pay of Typical Workers and High-Wage Earners," Economic Policy Institute (July 20, 2017), http://www.epi.org/publication/ceo-pay-remains-high-relative-to-the-pay-of-typical-workers-and-high-wage-earners/ (accessed July 23, 2017).

51. Bennett Harrison and Barry Bluestone, *The Great U-Turn* (New York: Basic Books, 1988); David Harvey, *The Condition of Postmodernity* (Malden, MA, and Oxford: Blackwell, 1989), 121–189; David M. Gordon, *Fat and Mean* (New York: Free Press, 1996).

52. Robert B. Reich, *Supercapitalism* (New York: Alfred A. Knopf, 2007), 131–225.

53. Friedman, *Lexus*, 167–193, 387–388.

54. *GEH*, 350–351; *MWG* III/6, 379–380.

55. Harrison and Bluestone, *Great U-Turn*, 53–75.

56. Dan Krier, *Speculative Management* (Albany: State University of New York Press, 2005); Charles R. Morris, *The Two Trillion Dollar Meltdown* (New York: Public Affairs, 2008); Simon Johnson, "The Quiet Coup," *Atlantic* (May 2009), https://www.theatlantic.com /magazine/archive/2009/05/the-quiet-coup/307364/ (accessed August 7, 2017); Joseph E. Stiglitz, *Freefall* (New York: W. W. Norton, 2010).

57. Brooke Harrington, *Capital without Borders* (Cambridge, MA: Harvard University Press, 2016); "Trusts and Financialization," *Socioeconomic Review* 15, no. 1 (2017), 31–63.

58. Quiggin, *Zombie Economics*, 209–239; Jamie Peck, "Pushing Austerity: State Failure, Municipal Bankruptcy and the Crisis of Fiscal Federalism in the USA," *Cambridge Journal of Regions, Economy and Society* 7 (2014): 17–44.

59. Harvey, *Brief History*, 152–182; Joseph E. Stiglitz, *The Price of Inequality* (New York: W. W. Norton, 2012); Larry M. Bartels, *Unequal Democracy* (Princeton, NJ: Princeton University Press, 2008).

60. Kaushik Basu, "The Whole Economy Is Rife with Ponzi Schemes," *Scientific American* (June 2014): 70–75: Stiglitz, *Freefall*, 274–297.

61. Other movies stressing the money culture: *Margin Call* (2000), *The Wolf of Wall Street* (2013), and *Beatriz at Dinner* (2017).

62. Weber referred to problems of race and immigration as "big black clouds" over American life: Marianne Weber, *Max Weber: A Biography*, trans. H. Zohn (New York: John Wiley & Sons, 1975), 302; Scaff, *Weber in America*, 98–116; David A. Graham, "The Many Scandals of Donald Trump: A Cheat Sheet," *Atlantic* (January 23, 2017), https://www.theatlantic .com/politics/archive/2017/01/donald-trump-scandals/474726/ (accessed July 28, 2017).

63. Piketty, *Capital*, 514.

64. *E&S*, 107–109; *MWG* I/23, 285–287; Piketty, *Capital*, 31–33, 424, 573–575.

65. Lawrence Mishel and Will Kimball, "Wages for Top Earners Soared in 2014: Fly Top 0.1 Percent Fly," http://www.epi.org/blog/wages-for-top-earners-soared-in-2014-fly-top-0-1 -percent-fly/ (accessed July 25, 2017); Thomas Piketty, Emanuel Saez, and Gabriel Zucman, *Distributional National Accounts: Methods and Estimates for the United States*, NBER Working Paper Series, http://www.nber.org/papers/w22945.pdf, 40–41 (accessed July 25, 2017); Piketty, *Capital*, 514.

66. Piketty, *Capital*, 265.

67. Ibid., 264, 422–424; 514. In past rentier societies, the upper decile owned about 90 percent of the wealth and the top 1 percent half of it. The US top decile held 77.2 percent of the wealth, and the top 0.1 percent share increased from 7 percent in the late 1970s to 22 percent in 2012. The bottom 90 percent share declined from 36 percent in the 1980s to 23 percent in 2012: Gabriel Zucman, "Wealth Inequality," *Pathways: The Poverty and Income Report 2016*, (2016): 40–42, http://inequality.stanford.edu/sites/default/files /Pathways-SOTU-2016.pdf (accessed July 21, 2017).

68. *E&S*, 140; *MWG* I/23, 338; Weber, "Suffrage and Democracy in Germany," in *Political Writings*, ed. P. Lassman and R. Speirs (Cambridge: Cambridge University Press, 1994), 121–122; *MWG* I/15, 388–389.

69. Branko Milanovic, *Global Inequality* (Cambridge, MA: Harvard University Press, 2016), 38, 180–217; Robert J. Gordon, *The Rise and Fall of American Growth* (Princeton, NJ: Princeton University Press, 2016), 528–531, 652; Wolfgang Streeck, *How Will Capitalism End?* (London: Verso, 2016), 71–94, 151–163; Nancy Maclean, *Democracy in Chains* (New York: Viking, 2017).

70. Herman E. Daly, "Economics in a Full World," *Scientific American* (September 2005): 100–107.

71. Millennium Ecosystem Assessment, *Ecosystems and Human Well-being, Synthesis* (Washington, DC: Island Press, 2005), http://www.millenniumassessment.org/documents/document.356.aspx.pdf (accessed August 2, 2017); Gerardo Ceballos, Paul A. Ehrlich, and Rodolfo Dirzo, "Biological Annihilation via the Ongoing Sixth Great Extinction Signaled by Vertebrate Population Losses and Declines," *Proceedings of the National Academy of Sciences USA* 114, no. 30 (2017): E6089–E6096, doi: 10.1073/pnas.1704949114.

72. James Hansen, et al., "Assessing Dangerous Climate Change, Required Reduction of Carbon Emissions to Protect Young People, Future Generations and Nature," *PLoS One* 8, no. 12 (2013): e81648, https://doi.org/10.1371/journal.pone.0081648.

73. Will Steffen, et al., "The Anthropocene, from Global Change to Planetary Change," *Ambio* 40, no. 7 (2011): 751–752. The planetary boundary is estimated to be about 350 parts per million (ppm), and levels are now (June 14, 2018) about 411 ppm (see https://www.co2.earth/).

74. Kevin Anderson and Alice Bows, "A New Paradigm for Climate Change," *Nature Climate Science* 2 (202): 639–640.

75. Peter Christoff and Robyn Eckersley, *Globalization and the Environment* (Lanham, MD: Rowman & Littlefield, 2013), 171, 161–207.

76. World Economic Forum, *The Global Risks Report 2017*, http://www3.weforum.org/docs/GRR17_Report_web.pdf (accessed July 27, 2017).

77. Tony Judt, *Ill Fares the Land* (New York: Penguin, 2010); Piketty, *Capital*.

78. Fredric Jameson, "Future City," *New Left Review* 21 (2003): 76.

79. Piketty, *Capital*, 424, 567–569, 570.

80. *CMW*, 138; *Zur Logik und Methodik der Sozialwissenschaften. Schriften 1900–1907, MWG* I/7, ed. G. Wagner with C. Härpfer et al. (Tübingen, Germany: Mohr [Siebeck], 2018), 234.

PART II

SOCIETY AND SOCIAL STRUCTURE

CHAPTER 7

CONTEMPORARY CAPITALISM AND THE DISTRIBUTION OF POWER IN SOCIETY

JOHN SCOTT

MAX Weber's views on power must count as one of the most frequently cited sets of discussions in the whole of the social sciences, his arguments providing a constant source of inspiration and contention. These discussions, however, have generally treated "power" in isolation from his other work and have, in consequence, involved many misunderstandings and misinterpretations of his arguments and their significance. This problem has been exacerbated by the fragmentary and incomplete character of much of Weber's work, not least his writings on power.

Despite this, Weber's arguments underpin much of the empirical work on economic and political power in contemporary capitalist societies. This has sometimes been intentional when researchers explicitly draw on Weberian concepts. More often than not, however, Weberian ideas have been implicit and unrecognized. Weber's carefully argued views provide a clear basis for understanding economic and political tendencies, and those researching in the area have been impelled to rediscover and restate views that Weber first set out.

My aim in this chapter is to provide a clear elucidation of Weber's conceptual framework. I do not claim that this is a definitive interpretation, but I hope to show that a logically coherent view of power can be uncovered from Weber's corpus of work and that its analytical underpinnings can be made clear. I will show how this Weberian view can inform recent theoretical discussions of power, and I will then briefly illustrate the relevance of this framework for studies of contemporary capitalism through a consideration of some of the key studies of economic and political power. In doing so, I hope to show that Weber provides a conceptual scheme that will continue to prove fruitful in future research.

Weber's explicit remarks on power were left unfinished when he died and were published only posthumously as distinct fragments on power and stratification that are now most familiar as parts of the text known, in its English translation, as *Economy and Society*.[1] In these fragments, Weber discussed the conceptualization of power in relation to issues of social stratification through "class" (*Klasse*) and "status" (*Stand*), seeing these social phenomena as being closely associated with each other. His earliest and longest set of notes on the distribution of power, most probably written between 1910 and 1914, first appeared in an English-language translation in C. Wright Mills and Hans Gerth's *From Max Weber*, with the title "Class, Status, Party"; and this was subsequently changed to "The Distribution of Power Within the Political Community: Class, Status, and Party" in the Roth and Wittich edition of *Economy and Society*.[2] Weber returned to this text, some years after first drafting it, when he began to draw out the elements of a more analytical framework that could serve as part of the introduction to his more concrete comparative and historical investigations. This second version, written between 1919 and 1920 and published as the first part of *Wirtschaft und Gesellschaft*, was divided into two separate discussions, "Power and Domination" (as a part of Chapter 1)[3] and "Status Groups and Classes" (as Chapter 4).[4] While the first is relatively comprehensive, the section on social stratification is very brief and incomplete and is the most unsatisfactory part of the whole text. The latter fragment appeared as "Estates and Classes" in the English translation by Henderson and Parsons in 1947.[5]

It is striking that, like Marx whose manuscript for the third volume of *Capital* broke off in the midst of a brief discussion of classes, Weber's work breaks off in the midst of each of his separate discussions of power and stratification. I will examine these fragments in order to reconstruct the view of power and its various forms that I believe Weber was trying to draw out. My discussion will be, in part, a textual exegesis, in so far as I seek to identify and clarify Weber's particular linguistic usages. My main aim, however, is a reconstruction and extension that goes beyond the text to outline a viable approach to power but remains true to Weber's ideas. I shall then illustrate the ways in which these ideas can and have been used, whether intentionally or not, by theorists and researchers interested in structures of economic and political power in modern capitalism.

POWER AND DOMINATION

Weber started by distinguishing between the general idea of *Macht* and the more specific idea of *Herrschaft* as a systematically structured form of *Macht*. The nearest equivalent distinction in English words is perhaps that between "might" and "mastery," though these words have come to have a more specific and restricted meaning in English. The English words "power" and "domination" are now the more widely used terms for designating these phenomena. Power (*Macht*), Weber held, consists simply in the chances that the will of an agent, whether individual or collective, can be imposed on that of others, even against their resistance.[6] It is any actual imposition and is realized in action through the opportunities and capacities available to an agent, whatever the basis of these may be. Power becomes domination (*Herrschaft*), when it is formed into stable and enduring relationships of social control. Power is structured into distinctive forms of domination through processes that underpin more conscious and deliberate social acts. Domination, then, is "canalized" power,[7] working through institutions to produce regular and persistent patterns of action.

Weber suggested that there are "two diametrically contrasting types of domination" rooted, respectively, in expediency and legitimacy.[8] In the first case, social order is sustained by calculations of self-interest, while in the latter it is sustained by commitments to ultimate values.[9] I have argued elsewhere that Weber was here highlighting two distinct forms of influence in social relations that I called "corrective influence" and "persuasive influence."[10] Corrective influence is a mechanism that operates in and through relational structures, while persuasive influence operates through institutional structures, a distinction drawn by López and Scott.[11] Corrective influence is a form of strategic or instrumental action that involves the use of resources as punitive or remunerative sanctions to shape the actions of others by affecting their assessment of their own interests. It involves causing others to act or preventing them from acting by direct restraint or by altering the conditions under which they calculate their actions. Persuasive influence is a form of committed or communicative action in which a discursive signification offers reasons for acting in one way rather than another that are accepted as valid or plausible by others. Persuasiveness depends on shared cognitive and evaluative symbols that allow an agent to offer intrinsically appropriate reasons for action to others and for these to be regarded as acceptable by them. A particular course of action thereby comes to be seen as morally or emotionally appropriate. Wrong has called this mode of power simply "persuasion," but he notes that it has to be distinguished from forms of persuasion in which no element of power exists.[12] Wartenberg calls it "influence," and he, too, notes the need to distinguish influential persuasion from "rational persuasion" in which no power arises.[13] To make this point clear and explicit, I prefer to combine Wrong's and Wartenberg's views into the single term "persuasive influence." The attempt to develop a satisfactory distinction between persuasive influence and persuasion that operates through free, rational discussion is central to Habermas' idea of the ideal speech situation.[14]

In a relationship of corrective influence all the participants act rationally in accordance with their interests, so the subordinate agents perceive it as in their interest to contribute to the realization of the competing interests of the dominant agent. Organized as domination, such power is exercised "by virtue of a constellation of interests" and has been termed "allocative control" by Giddens.[15] Weber saw this occurring in its clearest form in situations where an agent has possession of a monopolistic control over goods and skills in the market.[16] The principal example that Weber gave was that of the domination that a large credit bank can exercise over the client companies that depend on it for finance. I have elaborated on this idea elsewhere.[17] In another example, Weber discussed the economies of cities as exemplifying non-legitimate domination.[18]

Such a structure of domination may exist between a monopoly retailer and a small producer or between a bank and a company seeking investment capital. In each case, the structure of domination arises from a rational adjustment of the economic interests of the participants.

Relationships of persuasive influence are organized into forms of domination rooted in value commitments and legitimation and that Weber termed domination "by virtue of authority." Giddens called this "authoritative domination."[19] This involves processes of discursive signification that organize cultural ideas into complex structures that define what can be accepted as right, correct, justified, or valid in some way.[20] This legitimation involves the internalization of significant cultural meanings and identification with those who are seen as their guardians or guarantors through their election, appointment, or recruitment to positions by some accepted procedure. In relations of persuasive influence, agents convince others of the need to follow a particular course of action by building emotional commitments that limit their willingness to consider alternative courses of action instrumentally. This may involve commitment to or recognition of ideas or values that are accepted as beyond question, as providing intrinsically appropriate reasons for acting.

The two polar forms of corrective influence can be termed "force" and "manipulation." In a relation of force, negative physical sanctions such as weapons, imprisonment, the denial of food, or the destruction of property are used to block or prevent the actions of others. In a force relationship a person is restrained from pursuing a course of action that he or she would prefer to pursue or behaves in a way that he or she would avoid if it was at all possible.[21] In its most extreme form, as violence, it comprises direct force against the body or mind of another person. Non-violent force, on the other hand, involves placing physical restraints on a person's freedom of action. Canalized into domination, force becomes a structure of coercion through repressive means of control. Thus, the conformity of a person subject to repressive military coercion is a forced conformity.

In a relation of manipulation, on the other hand, both positive and negative sanctions are used to influence the rational, interest-oriented calculations of others. Manipulation involves the use of such resources as money, credit, and access to employment, which allow an agent to alter the basis on which others must calculate among the action alternatives available to them and so can ensure that their rational choices lead them to act in desired ways.[22] Examples of manipulation include advertising and price adjustment, where information and prices are adjusted in order to secure particular outcomes. Organized as domination, manipulation is expressed in structures of inducement that comprise forms of control through "free" exchange relationships. The labor performance of an employee is a mere "dull compulsion" that results from a manipulated calculus of self-interest. The actions of subordinates, or subalterns, in a structure of domination by virtue of a constellation of interests are shaped by the tessellating interests determined by the resources available to the dominant, or principal, agents. (I use the terms "principal" and "subaltern" from Antonio Gramsci and Partha Chatterjee.[23])

In his work on the sociology of organizations, Etzioni described the two forms of domination—coercion and inducement—as "coercive" and "utilitarian" power and has seen them as likely to generate, respectively, an alienative and a calculative involvement on the part of the subordinates in a power relationship.[24]

There are similarly two forms of persuasive influence: mastery and advocacy. Mastery operates through evaluative signification and the building of value commitments toward particular ideas or states of being.[25] Evaluative signification gives a normative character to proposed actions. An emotional attraction to a particular individual may be sustained by rhetoric and demagoguery that reinforce this attraction. Organized as domination, mastery is expressed as command, resting on the idea of the right to give orders and a corresponding obligation to obey. There is willing compliance on the part of a subaltern because of an evaluative commitment to the legitimacy of the source of the command, not because of an independent and autonomous evaluation of its content. Principal and subaltern agents orientate themselves to norms that define the various institutionalized social positions to which rights and obligations are attached. In an organizational context, Gouldner has described the classic form of bureaucratic author-ity as involving a "punishment-centred" control by line managers who combine the right to command with the rightful capacity to sanction disobedience.[26] What is crucial here is the culturally justified issuing of orders and commands and the corresponding expectation that others will feel an obligation to obey.

"Advocacy" operates through cognitive signification, the use of symbols and repre-sentations that lead people to define situations in certain ways by drawing them into a shared interpretative frame of reference. Organized as domination, advocacy is expressed in structures of expertise. This occurs when cognitive symbols are structured into organized bodies of knowledge in relation to which some agents can claim superior knowledge or skills. In this type of domination, those who defer to this superiority place their trust in the other's competence to propose a particular course of action. Expertise depends on the successful assertion of a monopoly of specialist knowledge within a particular sphere and so rests upon specific knowledge or wisdom accepted on trust. It is the typical authority of the priest or the scientific expert. The authority of a doctor over a patient, for example, is based on his or her possession of a specialized technical competence in medical matters to which the patient defers. Wrong refers to this form of power as "competence" rather than "expertise," but the point is the same.[27] Expertise is a form of persuasive influence that rests on a substantive *trust* in the competence of the person proposing a course of action and a corresponding acceptance of one's own lack of competence.[28]

Weber outlined a view of expertise in his lengthy discussion of bureaucracy,[29] and Gouldner formalized this by contrasting the positional authority of command with the "representative" authority of technical staff managers who rely on a possession of supe-rior knowledge that allows them to influence those who recognize this superiority.[30]

Weber was particularly interested in the case of authority and stated that he would use the word *Herrschaft*, unless otherwise specified, to refer to authoritative structures of command.[31] Understandable as this may be for reasons of brevity, it has led to some

Table 7.1. Modes of Domination

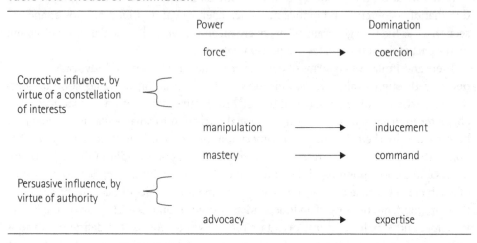

	Power		Domination
	force	$\longrightarrow$	coercion
Corrective influence, by virtue of a constellation of interests			
	manipulation	$\longrightarrow$	inducement
	mastery	$\longrightarrow$	command
Persuasive influence, by virtue of authority			
	advocacy	$\longrightarrow$	expertise

confusion among commentators. For the sake of clarity and consistency I will always refer in full to domination by virtue of authority, or simply authority. These distinctions can be clarified in Table 7.1.

Coercion, inducement, command, and expertise are idealized modes of domination that rarely appear in their pure forms. In most concrete structures of domination, these forms will operate in combination, and they generally depend upon each other in complex ways. An authoritative relationship in business, Weber argued, might comprise the legal right of a bank director to issue commands to the board of an industrial company, of which he is a director, because of specific conditions that are attached to a loan. Where a bank can use its control over investment funds to set rates of interest and make decisions on the purchase of share capital, it is also able to induce other companies to act in particular ways because of the particular constellation of financial interests in which they are involved. Similarly, persuasion may occur alongside in isolation from or in conjunction with force or manipulation, as in the advertising industry's reliance on "hidden persuaders" where persuasion is combined with manipulation.[32] States, business enterprises, universities, churches, families, and gangs, for example, combine the different forms of power to form the concrete patterns of power that give them their specific characteristics. It is important, nevertheless, to understand their specific and distinctive features if we are to understand their concrete combinations.

THREE FORMS OF POWER

There is a widely held view—one that I share—that Weber set out the basis for a three-dimensional approach to power, holding that there are three principal forms in which power appears in concrete historical societies. This interpretation of Weber has, however, been presented in misleading ways that have hampered theoretical and empirical advances in the study of power and stratification. The somewhat misleading titles given to his various discussions of stratification and power have compounded the problem of interpretation. While Weber has correctly been seen as recognizing three forms or dimensions of social stratification, he has often been seen as holding that "power" is one of the three dimensions alongside "class" and "status." Despite the fragmentary form of his discussion, Weber's work gives no textual warrant for this interpretation. In fact, he says quite clearly that the trilogy of terms with which he is concerned—"class," "status," and "party"—are *all* to be seen as aspects of the social distribution of power.

More sophisticated commentators have seen him as slavishly following the title invented by his editors and as proposing that the three dimensions are to be seen as class, status, and party. This view, again, completely misunderstands what Weber was seeking to do. He stated quite clearly—as is recognized in the title—that he was concerned with the distribution of power within a "political community" or "political association." He limited his attention in that fragment to two aspects or dimensions of power: "class" and "status" (a preferable translation of *Stand* to either "estate" or the narrower "status group"). These underpin the formation of the various politically organized "parties" that compete for power within such political associations as the modern nation-state.

The third dimension or aspect of power that Weber identified cannot be reduced to the relations of "parties" alone.[33] A clear understanding of this third form must go beyond the fragmentary texts to consider Weber's extensive analyses of states, forms of authority, and systems of bureaucratic administration. It is here that he outlined an analysis of politically organized power into what he called "leadership" groups and "ruling minorities" and so provides an insight into the elements missing from his fragments. This analysis of political association complements his arguments on class and status and effectively completes the conceptual discussion of social stratification. The three dimensions of power, then, are economically organized power (formed into classes), symbolically organized power (formed into statuses), and politically organized power (formed into what might be termed "echelons"). Each of these dimensions is aligned with particular forms of influence, and each is most clearly apparent when Weber turned from analytical definition to comparative and historical sociology.

Weber saw politically organized power as arising from the institutionalized regulation of a territory or sphere of activity through coercion and command. This may occur in a national territory, a transnational agency, or a subnational association or organization. A nation-state is a sovereign organization of command within a particular territory, organized through a specialized structure of coercive agencies and mechanisms or "repressive apparatuses."[34] State coercion is integrally linked with forms of command to structure its control over a territory. A state exercises its authority on the basis of a monopolization of the legitimate use of force, while other political associations exercise authority within a national territory and within a framework of legitimate regulation backed up by the power of the state. The hierarchical structuring of politically organized power produces command and coercive structures that exist as distinct echelons of power: ruling minorities or power elites, subjects, citizens, servants, and so on.

It is important to consider the argument of Michael Mann, who sees coercive military power as distinguishable from the political power of command. Military power, according to Mann, comprises the organized use of physical force as a means for defense, aggression, or internal control: it involves "coerced controls" over the actions of others.[35] It is socially organized as "concentrated lethal violence."[36] However, this analytical separation of military and political power is rarely apparent in real situations, a fact that led Gianfranco Poggi to reject Mann's position and to support the view that concrete forms of political power rest on a combination of coercion and command.[37] The assertion of a monopoly over the use of violence requires an organizational structure that claims and has recognized, however minimally, the legitimacy of its monopoly.

This fusion of coercion and command was also recognized by Parsons, who noted the precarious instability of the "Hobbesian" situation of sheer coercion and military repression in pre-state societies. To be stable and effective in securing social order, the coercion that underpins state domination must be grounded in a normative structure of institutionalized authority.[38] This view was further developed in Parsons' later work, where he argued that political power involves the "activation" of value commitments that are "latent"—Giddens would say "virtual"—and that underpin the periodic exercise of coercion and render it as the foundation for authoritative commands.[39] Thus, politically organized power can be seen as collective goal attainment through command backed by coercion.

Economic power involves inducement rooted in the mobilization of resources but embedded in institutional relations of property and labor regulation that secure "utility." It exists most particularly where institutional rights of access, use, exclusion, and disposal organize processes of production, distribution, and consumption into networks of market exchange that are structured by the use of money as the symbolic representation of the value of objects in exchange.[40] A market is a system of spatially extended acquisitive relations, comprising the dispersed and localized transactions that occur in factories, offices, banks, and shops; and economic action in the market creates a constantly shifting pattern of rewards and costs. Business enterprises operate in a market through command and inducement. They nevertheless depend upon a framework of law that is established and supported by a particular state that maintains public support for the laws of property and contract on which they depend. Economic power, like military power, requires an underpinning of legitimacy.

Actions within the market create "market situations" for individuals and enterprises and comprise both the specific life chances available to particular "classes" of agents and the constellations of interests through which an enterprise or the members of a class are able to induce others to act in particular ways. Thus, owners and controllers of property are able to shape the behavior of those they employ, banks can influence the investment patterns of industrial enterprises, and producer firms can influence the behavior of individual consumers.

The third dimension of power—symbolically organized power—is most clearly discussed by Weber as religious power. This involves the expertise through which a "clergy" of qualified persons can shape the attitudes and actions of "faithful" believers through the system of meanings that they monopolize. The clergy exercise power over their adherents, devotees, and disciples through myths, scriptures, and theologies that present constructions of reality as authoritative for the definitions of the situations accepted by the actors involved. This power is especially apparent in Weber's conception of "charismatic" authority and his discussion of churches in his sociology of religion.[41]

This conception of religious power has been generalized by Mann and Poggi into what they both call "ideological power" but that might better be called "symbolic power."[42] Symbolic power rests on "the extent to which certain constructions of reality affect the individual's capacity to locate mentally his or her own existence within an encompassing reality endowed with some moral purpose."[43] Symbolic power refers to domination through cultural distinction relative to established values. It rests on the ability of an individual or organization to elaborate and to monopolize the elaboration of a system of concepts and norms that they are able to disseminate to others and so to ensure that those others will act upon it. Weber explored such ideas in his discussion of Hindu rule in India.[44]

Religious power develops in a secular direction with the disenchantment of the world. Symbolic power is then exercised by a "literati" of cultured and learned experts—scholars, scientists, lawyers, etc.—each claiming expertise within a particular sphere of "professional" competence and so exercising power over laypersons who recognize their expertise and who listen to or consult them. These laypersons are their followers, clients, patients, and audiences. The literati monopolize "the *supply* of cognitive meanings, of moral regulation, of compelling aesthetic expression" and so can exclude alternatives from serious consideration by denying or disparaging them as heretical, unorthodox, or otherwise unfounded.[45] Literati are able to build the trust, loyalty, and solidarity that underpin cooperation. Certain forms of activity are seen as appropriate or compelling because they symbolize significant sentiments and values.[46] They may claim competence not only within their specialist sphere but also to contribute to discussion within the public sphere and the state.[47]

Expertise and command are closely associated in many contexts as the symbolic constructions of experts are typically drawn on to legitimate command. Thus, Catholicism in medieval Europe was sustained through a network of churches, monasteries, and courts that defined the rights of bishops and abbots to command the obedience of the lower clergy, monks, and friars and the ability of priests to influence laypeople through the interpretation of a Latin text that the latter were unable to read.

Symbolically organized power may also involve the definition of estates or social orders that are distinguished by their standing relative to established beliefs. A person's "status situation" consists of the effects on their life chances of the various cultural distinctions they experience. Where a culture is differentiated and pluralistic, there is likely to be a fragmentation of estates and a plurality of specialized, perhaps conflicting, statuses and status situations.

As will be apparent, the three dimensions of power are often associated with each other in particular concrete situations. However, an awareness of the three dimensions and the ways in which the analytical elements of power and domination enter into their constitution provides a way of exploring the complex dynamics of power relations in actual societies. For example, in modern societies state agencies have relied, to an ever greater extent, on technical expertise. The provision of health, education, and welfare services by the state depends upon the employment of experts for their delivery. Such experts may be recruited to positions of command, exercising authority through a combination of command with expertise. Thus, a doctor is an expert in relation to her or his patients but may be both an expert and a holder of a position of command in relation to the nurses and technicians who work alongside her or him in a hospital or clinic.

Large business enterprises operate principally through command and inducement, controlling their members and relating to other enterprises through managerial hierarchies of command, through wage or salary payments, and through loans and other forms of finance. Many business enterprises, however, rely on experts to undertake some of their activities: they employ accountants, lawyers, industrial chemists, engineers, and so on. Not only may these experts play a key role in the provision of services to business customers but they may also undertake command roles within enterprises and so participate in the wider structure of managerial command. Dalton explored this in terms of a complex relationship between "line" and "staff" management,[48] while Gouldner wrote of the relationship between "punishment-centred" and "representative" bureaucracy.[49]

Having reconstructed Weber's approach to power and amplified some of the key themes, it is now possible to outline some of the ways in which these ideas have been used in empirical work or can be used to reinterpret empirical findings on a consistent conceptual basis. This was, perhaps, the kind of task for which Weber thought it worthwhile to engage in his encyclopedic conceptual exposition.

POWER IN THE ECONOMY

There has been a long tradition of work investigating the exercise of power within capitalist economies, much of this inspired by critical commentary on Marxist views. Explicit use of Weberian concepts has not been at all widespread, though the Weberian concepts that I have elucidated in this chapter can be used to organize and reinterpret much of this work. In this section I will briefly indicate the principal ways in which Weber's work has been used in research on the organization and exercise of economic power and on the specifically political forms of power exercised within and between economic organizations.

Economic power through manipulation and inducement has been a central theme in studies of property regulation and the relationship between ownership and control. Explored initially in Marxist theory by Karl Renner, this was classically formulated by Adolf Berle and Gardner Means.[50] The argument of the latter was that the growing scale of industrial production posed capital requirements that are beyond the means of the individual entrepreneur or the individual capitalist family. Joint stock companies that had been formed to limit the financial liability of the capitalist allowed the mobilization of large amounts of capital through the flotation of shares on the stock exchange. As a result, Berle and Means argued, share capital came to be dispersed ever more widely and the original owners found their control declining. At first, they could exercise "minority control" or ally themselves with other substantial shareholders, but eventually the scale of the undertaking was such that no individual or group of shareholders was able to exercise any significant degree of control. This "separation" of ownership from control, Berle and Means held, was well advanced in the United States by the 1930s, and later research suggested that it was all but complete by the 1960s.[51]

This argument did not go unchallenged. Marxist writers, in particular, had pointed to the ability of banks and financial intermediaries to affect business decision-making through the power inherent in the making of loans. Allied with their ability to collate and control the shares owned by the large numbers of small shareholders and savers, banks could be seen as building a system of "finance capital," as in Hilferding.[52] Writers such as Anna Rochester and Ferdinand Lundberg in the United States and Sam Aaronovitch in Britain held that this was, in fact, the true situation,[53] and powerful variants of this argument were formulated by David Kotz and Maurice Zeitlin.[54]

The counterargument held that it was not the financiers who now held economic power but the "managers." Their argument was that the separation of ownership and control meant that shareholders had lost all power of financial inducement and so no longer had a basis for any voice in business affairs. This created a power vacuum into which the "technically indispensable" salaried experts could rise. In addition to their power of technical advocacy, the key experts were able to occupy executive positions at the top of the business hierarchy and so could shape business strategy without having to face any shareholder influence. This argument echoed that of former Marxist James Burnham, who depicted a "managerial revolution" that pointed to the demise of capitalism and capitalist property.[55] This was taken up politically in Roosevelt's New Deal and in Crosland's revisionist policy that laid the basis for "New Labour."[56]

This issue of whether financiers with economic power or managers with expertise were the new controllers of business enterprises and whether shareholders had any continuing economic power began to be addressed in the 1970s when researchers began to directly investigate the distribution of shareholdings. It was found that the dispersal of shareholdings had not gone so far as Berle and Means had anticipated and that banks and financial enterprises were themselves the holders of large blocks of shares. Edward Herman argued that the commanding power of top managerial executives was "constrained" by the economic power inherent in large shareholder blocks.[57] In my own research I showed that the distribution of shareholdings was such that a constellation of shareholding financial institutions surrounded the internal management of each company and could exercise what Weber had defined as control through a constellation of interests.[58] This dominance of financial interests was advanced through the liberalization of financial markets that became the basis of neoliberalism.

The rise of managers, albeit within a structure of continuing financial power, highlighted the question of the internal and external power relations of large corporations:

who is able to occupy the top positions in the corporate hierarchy that carry the politically organized powers of command over subordinate managers and workers and that give them wider powers over economic activities? C. Wright Mills was not the first to raise this question, but he did so in a particularly clear way in his critique of the managerialist thesis that initiated a tradition of research into the social background and recruitment of a corporate "elite." He showed that directors were still recruited from property-owning backgrounds, even when they had some technical expertise and qualifications and could be seen as drawn from a "managerially reorganised" capitalist class.[59]

Mills further explored the "interlocking directorships" that tie together leading enterprises whenever a person holds a directorship in two or more companies. Subsequent studies have shown that interlocking directorships are formed into extensive networks in which loose bank-centered groupings can be identified and that stand in a clear relationship to the corporate constellations that dominate in shareholding.[60] The corporate elite within this network exercise economic power across whole sections of the economy and, through their involvement in business organizations and advisory bodies, hold positions with a degree of expert advocacy.

The increasing globalization of business activity since the 1970s has led to a number of studies that have explored the implications of what Manuel Castells called the "network society."[61] Transnational circuits of credit have resulted in a financialization of national economies and a growing interconnection of businesses into transnational corporate elites.[62] Alongside the financiers within national and transnational corporate elites are now found a growing number of legal and financial experts who serve as consultants and advisers and exercise power over corporate strategies.[63]

POWER IN THE STATE

Weberian concepts can also be successfully used to understand the organization and exercise of political power through command and coercion. Theories of state power, their leadership groups, and ruling minorities have a long history in sociology. Gaetano Mosca and Vilfredo Pareto introduced the idea of the "elite" as an alternative idea to that of the ruling class, and a long line of state theorists have also explored the relationship between political and military forces within state structures and the ways in which states are able to exercise sovereignty over territories and to invade or conquer others.[64] Clearly formulated by Weber's contemporary Franz Oppenheimer (1914), this approach has been investigated empirically in powerful studies by Theda Skocpol and Michael Mann.[65]

The involvement of economic and other elites within state structures has been most influentially investigated by C. Wright Mills.[66] Mills held that the concept of a power elite, as the echelon at the head of the political, military, and economic hierarchies, could be used as an empirical category without prejudging the question of whether all members of the power elite were drawn from a particular class or shared a similar status: these characteristics were empirical matters and were not to be determined by definitional fiat. The power elite and its role within the state is to be investigated, Mills argued, by exploring the degree of structural cohesion through interlocking relationships among the various elite groups and the recruitment patterns to these elite positions.

Mills' argument was most influentially developed by Ralph Miliband and associated with numerous other empirical studies of other politically organized elites (for example, Guttsam).[67] This approach allowed investigators to explore the wider aspects of Burnham's managerial revolution thesis as Burnham had seen bureaucratic managers within the state—the civil servants—as also rising in power and supplanting elected politicians. This argument on the rise of the expert was especially strong in critical studies of power in socialist Eastern Europe and the Soviet Union.[68] In the United States and Western Europe, the approach led to debates on the growth of technocracy and corporatism.[69]

Nicos Poulantzas agreed that there was a class basis to state power but rejected what he saw as the Weberian approach through elite recruitment. He held, instead, that the state had to be seen as embedded in a structure of propertied class relations that constrained and limited the capacity of a state, however its leaders were recruited, to exercise autonomous power.[70] His argument can be seen, however, as demonstrating the continuing importance of economic power and class relations alongside politically organized power. The mainstream of empirical research continued to see elite recruitment and integration as a crucial element in state power. Typical of this work are the many studies of William Domhoff, who showed the importance of exploring the lobbying and pressure exercised within and against elites by organized associations or "parties."[71] Of particular importance was his linkage of political and economic power with the symbolic power relations that lead to ideological domination.[72]

Political globalization has involved the formation of transnational political blocs and organizations that now exist alongside the continuing nation-states.[73] Such organizations are increasingly involved in the networks through which state policies are shaped.[74] Martin Smith traced the ways in which such policy networks have created opportunities for pressure and protest groups to push their interests and concerns, and the relative fragility of transnational networks enhances the opportunities for radical protest groups.[75] Margaret Keck and Kathryn Sikkink have highlighted the importance of expertise in the formation of transnational "advocacy networks" in which knowledge and arguments can be mobilized to shape global agendas.[76]

CONCLUSION

Weber's fragmentary discussions of power and stratification have been frequent sources of discussion but have typically been interpreted in overly simple and misleading ways. I have shown that a more adequate interpretation can be gained by placing the fragments in the context of Weber's wider work—where he intended them to be read—and so completing his brief remarks. By utilizing more recent discussions of power and its bases, I have shown that Weber's remarks can be unpacked and amplified to produce the kind of coherent conceptual exposition at which he was aiming. In the final part of the chapter I briefly indicated how this conceptual framework can help to bring a degree of order to the many empirical discussions of economic and political power in contemporary capitalism. I hope that others will be inspired to make more explicit use of these Weberian ideas in studies of the further development of contemporary societies.

Notes

1. Max Weber, *Economy and Society: An Outline of Interpretive Sociology* (hereafter *E&S*), ed. Guenther Roth and Claus Wittich (Berkeley: University of California Press, 1978).
2. Max Weber, "Class, Status, Party," in *From Max Weber: Essays in Sociology*, trans. H. H. Gerth and C. Wright Mills (New York: Oxford University Press, 1946), 180–195; corresponding passage in Weber, *E&S*, 926–939. The *Max Weber-Gesamtausgabe* (hereafter *MWG*) uses the title, unconfirmed by Max Weber, " 'Klassen', 'Stände' und 'Parteien' ": *Wirtschaft und Gesellschaft. Die Wirtschaft und die gesellschaftlichen Ordnungen und Mächte. Nachlaß. Teilband 1: Gemeinschaften*, *MWG* I/22-1, ed. W. J. Mommsen, with M. Meyer (Tübingen, Germany: Mohr [Siebeck], 2001), 252–272.
3. *E&S*, 53–54. The first part now forms a separate volume of the *MWG*, I/23: *Wirtschaft und Gesellschaft. Soziologie. Unvollendet. 1919-1920*, ed. K. Borchardt, E. Hanke, and W. Schluchter (Tübingen, Germany: Mohr [Siebeck], 2013).
4. *E&S*, 302–307; *MWG* I/23, 592–600.
5. Max Weber, *Theory of Social and Economic Organization*, trans. A. M. Henderson and T. Parsons (New York: Oxford University Press, 1947).
6. *E&S*, 926, 942, 53; *MWG* I/22-1, 252; *Wirtschaft und Gesellschaft. Die Wirtschaft und die gesellschaftlichen Ordnungen und Mächte. Nachlaß, Teilband 4: Herrschaft*, *MWG* I/22-4, ed. E. Hanke, with Th. Kroll (Tübingen, Germany: Mohr [Siebeck], 2005), 128; *MWG* I/23, 210–211.
7. Karl Mannheim, *Freedom, Power and Democratic Planning* (London: Routledge and Kegan Paul, 1951), 48–49.
8. *E&S*, 943; Weber, *Wirtschaft und Gesellschaft. Die Wirtschaft und die gesellschaftlichen Ordnungen und Mächte. Nachlaß, Teilband 2: Religiöse Gemeinschaften. MWG* I/22-2, ed. H. G. Kippenberg, with P. Schilm (Tübingen, Germany: Mohr [Siebeck], 2001), 129.
9. *E&S*, 30; *MWG* I/23, 181.
10. John Scott, *Power* (Cambridge: Polity Press, 2001).
11. John Scott and José López, *Social Structure* (Maidenhead, UK: Open University Press, 2000).
12. D. Wrong, *Power: Its Forms, Bases, and Uses* (New Brunswick, NJ: Transaction, 1979).
13. T. Wartenberg, *The Forms of Power: From Domination to Transformation* (Philadelphia: Temple University Press, 1990).
14. Jürgen Habermas, "On Systematically Distorted Communication," *Inquiry* 13 (1970): 205–218; "Towards a Theory of Communicative Competence," in *Recent Sociology, Number 2*, ed. H. P. Dreitzel (New York: Macmillan, 1970), 360–375.

15. Anthony Giddens, *Central Problems in Social Theory* (London: Macmillan, 1979); *A Contemporary Critique of Historical Materialism*, vol. 1, *Power, Property and the State* (London: Macmillan, 1981).

16. *E&S*, 943; *MWG* I/22-2, 129.

17. John Scott, *Corporate Business and Capitalist Classes* (Oxford: Oxford University Press, 1997), 48–49.

18. *E&S*, 1212; *Wirtschaft und Gesellschaft. Die Wirtschaft und die gesellschaftlichen Ordnungen und Mächte. Nachlaß. Teilband 5: Die Stadt, MWG* I/22-5, ed. W. Nippel (Tübingen, Germany: Mohr [Siebeck], 1999), 59.

19. Giddens, *Central Problems*, 100–101.

20. David Held, *Political Theory and the Modern State* (Cambridge: Polity Press, 1989), 102; David Beetham, *The Legitimation of Power* (Houndmills, UK: Macmillan, 1991), 1–12.

21. Wrong, *Power*, 24–28; Wartenberg, *Forms of Power*, 93.

22. Wrong, *Power*, 28–32.

23. Antonio Gramsci, *The Prison Notebooks [Selections From]* (London: Lawrence and Wishart, 1971); Partha Chatterjee, *Nationalist Thought and the Colonial World* (London: Zed Books, 1986).

24. Amitai Etzioni, *Modern Organizations* (Englewood Cliffs, NJ: Prentice-Hall, 1964).

25. Anthony Giddens, *The Constitution of Society* (Cambridge: Polity Press, 1984), 29ff.

26. Alvin W. Gouldner, *Patterns of Industrial Bureaucracy* (New York: Free Press, 1954), 207.

27. Wrong, *Power*, 52–60.

28. Wartenberg, *Forms of Power*, 54.

29. *E&S*, 1914: 956ff.; *MWG* I/22-4, 157ff.

30. Gouldner, *Patterns of Industrial Bureaucracy*, 187–189.

31. *E&S*, 1914: 946; *MWG* I/22-4, 135.

32. Vance Packard, *Hidden Persuaders* (Harmondsworth, UK: Penguin, 1960); Wrong, *Power*, 32–34.

33. John Scott, *Stratification and Power: Structures of Class, Status and Command* (Cambridge: Polity Press, 1996).

34. Louis Althusser, *Lenin and Philosophy and Other Essays* (London: New Left Books, 1971).

35. Michael Mann, *The Sources of Social Power*, vol. 1, *A History of Power from the Beginning to AD 1760* (Cambridge: Cambridge University Press, 1986), 26.

36. Michael Mann, "The Sources of Social Power Revisited: A Response to Criticism," in *An Anatomy of Power. The Social Theory of Michael Mann*, ed. J. A. Hall and R. Schroeder (Cambridge: Cambridge University Press, 2006), 351.

37. Gianfranco Poggi, *Forms of Power* (Cambridge: Polity Press, 2001), 180.

38. Talcott Parsons, *The Structure of Social Action* (New York: McGraw-Hill, 1937).

39. Talcott Parsons, "On the Concept of Value Commitments," in *Politics and Social Structure*, ed. T. Parsons (1968; New York: Free Press, 1969), 448; "On the Concept of Political Power" [1963], in *Politics and Social Structure*.

40. Talcott Parsons and Neil J. Smelser, *Economy and Society* (New York: Free Press, 1956).

41. *E&S*, 1914, 399ff.; *MWG* I/22-2, 121ff.

42. See also John B. Thompson, *The Media and Modernity* (Cambridge: Polity Press, 1995), 16–17; Michael Mann, *The Sources of Social Power*, vol. 2, *The Rise of Classes and Nation States, 1760–1914* (Cambridge: Cambridge University Press, 1993), 7; Mann, "Sources of Social Power Revisited," 345; Robert D. Jessop, *Social Order, Reform and Revolution*

(London: Macmillan, 1972), 58; W. Garrison Runciman, *A Treatise on Social Theory*, vol. 2 (Cambridge: Cambridge University Press, 1989), 12.

43. Poggi, *Forms of Power*, 63.
44. Max Weber, *The Religion of India*, trans. and ed. H. H. Gerth and D. Martindale (New York: Macmillan, 1958); Weber, *Die Wirtschaftsethik der Weltreligionen. Hinduismus und Buddhismus. MWG I/20*, ed. H. Schmidt-Glintzer, with K.-H. Golzio (Tübingen, Germany: Mohr [Siebeck], 1996).
45. Poggi, *Forms of Power*, 66.
46. Ibid.
47. Talcott Parsons, "On the Concept of Influence" [1963], in *Politics and Social Structure*.
48. Melville Dalton, *Men Who Manage* (New York: John Wiley and Sons, 1959).
49. Gouldner, *Patterns of Industrial Bureaucracy*.
50. Karl Renner, *The Institutions of Private Law and their Social Function* (London: Routledge and Kegan Paul, 1904); Alfred A. Berle and Gardiner C. Means, *The Modern Corporation and Private Property* (London: Macmillan, 1932).
51. Robert Larner, *Management Control and the Large Corporation* (New York: Dunellen Press, 1970).
52. Rudolf Hilferding, *Finance Capital* (1910; London: Routledge and Kegan Paul, 1981).
53. Anna Rochester, *Rulers of America* (London: Lawrence and Wishart, 1936); Ferdinand Lundberg, *America's Sixty Families* (New York: Halcyon House, 1939); Sam Aaronovitch, *Monopoly. A Study of British Monopoly Capitalism* (London: Lawrence and Wishart, 1955).
54. David Kotz, *Bank Control in Large Corporations* (Berkeley: University of California Press, 1978); Maurice R. Zeitlin, *The Large Corporation and the Capitalist Class* (Cambridge: Polity Press, 1989).
55. James Burnham, *The Managerial Revolution* (New York: John Day, 1941).
56. Arthur M. Schlesinger, *The Coming of the New Deal 1933–35*, vol. 2, *The Age of Roosevelt* (Boston: Houghton Mifflin, 1958); Anthony Crosland, *The Future of Socialism* (London: Jonathan Cape, 1956).
57. Edward O. Herman, *Corporate Control, Corporate Power* (New York: Oxford University Press, 1981).
58. John Scott, *Corporations, Classes and Capitalism* (London: Hutchinson, 1985); *Capitalist Property and Financial Power* (Brighton, UK: Wheatsheaf, 1986); *Corporate Business and Capitalist Classes* (Oxford: Oxford University Press, 1997).
59. Charles Wright Mills, *The Power Elite* (New York: Oxford University Press, 1956).
60. Beth Mintz and Michael Schwartz, *The Power Structure of American Business* (Chicago: Chicago University Press. 1985); John Scott and Catherine Griff, *Directors of Industry* (Cambridge: Polity Press, 1984); Frans Stokman, Rolf Ziegler, and John Scott, eds., *Networks of Corporate Power* (Cambridge: Polity Press, 1985).
61. Manuel Castells, *The Information Age: Economy, Society and Culture*, vol. 1, *The Rise of the Network Society* (Oxford: Blackwell, 1996).
62. Kies van der Pijl, *Transnational Classes and International Relations* (London: Routledge and Kegan Paul, 1989); Leslie Sklair, *The Transnational Capitalist Class* (Oxford: Blackwell, 2001); William K. Carroll, with Colin Carson et al., *The Making of a Transnational Capitalist Class* (London: Zed Books, 2010).
63. William K. Carroll, *Corporate Power in a Globalizing World. A Study in Elite Social Organization* (Toronto: Oxford University Press, 2004); Olivier Godehot, "What Do Heads of Dealing Rooms Do?," in *Remembering Elites*, Sociological Review Monographs, ed. M. Savage and K. Williams (Oxford: Blackwell, 2008).

64. Gaetano Mosca, "Elementi di Scienza Politica Volume One," in *The Ruling Class*, ed. G. Mosca (1896; New York: McGraw Hill, 1939), chap. 1–11; Vilfredo Pareto, *The Rise and Fall of Elites* (1901; New York: Bedminster Press, 1968); John Scott, "Pareto and the Elite," in *Vilfredo Pareto: Beyond Disciplinary Boundaries*, ed. J. V. Femia and A. J. Marshall (Farnham, UK: Ashgate, 2012).

65. Franz Oppenheimer, *The State* (1914; Montreal: Black Rose Books, 1975); Theda Skocpol, *States and Social Revolutions* (Cambridge: Cambridge University Press, 1979); Michael Mann, *The Sources of Social Power*, vol. 3, *Global Empires and Revolutions, 1890-1945* (Cambridge: Cambridge University Press, 2012); Michael Mann, *The Sources of Social Power*, vol. 4, *Globalizations, 1945-2011* (Cambridge: Cambridge University Press, 2013).

66. Mills, *Power Elite*.

67. Ralph Miliband, *The State in Capitalist Society* (London: Weidenfeld and Nicolson, 1969); William L. Guttsman, *The British Political Elite* (London: MacGibbon and Kee, 1963).

68. Bruno Rizzi, *The Bureaucratisation of the World* (1939; London: Tavistock, 1985); Mikhail Voslensky, *Nomenklatura* (London: Bodley Head, 1984).

69. Jacques Meynaud, *Technocracy* (London: Faber and Faber, 1964); Philippe Schmitter, "Still the Century of Corporatism," in *Trends Towards Corporatist Intermediation*, ed. P. Schmitter and G. Lehmbruch (London: Sage, 1979).

70. N. Poulantzas, "The Problem of the Capitalist State," *New Left Review* 58 (1969): 67–78.

71. G. William Domhoff, *Who Rules America?* (Englewood Cliffs, NJ: Prentice Hall, 1967); *The Higher Circles: The Governing Class in America* (New York: Vintage Books, 1971).

72. John Scott, "Modes of Power and the Conceptualisation of Elites," in *Remembering Elites*, Sociological Review Monographs, ed. M. Savage and K. Williams (Oxford: Blackwell, 2008); "Class, Elites and Power. A Contemporary Perspective," in *C. Wright Mills and the Sociological Imagination. Contemporary Perspectives*, ed. J. Scott and A. Nilsen (Cheltenham, UK: Edward Elgar, 2013).

73. Zeev Maoz, *Networks of Nations* (New York: Cambridge University Press, 2011).

74. Edward O. Laumann and D. Knoke, "Policy Networks of the Organisational State," in *Networks of Power*, ed. Robert Perrucci and Harry R. Potter (New York: de Gruyter, 1989).

75. Martin J. Smith, *Pressure, Power and Policy: State Autonomy and Policy Networks in Britain and the United States* (Hemel Hempstead, UK: Harvester Wheatsheaf, 1993).

76. Margaret E. Keck and Kathryn Sikkink, *Activists Beyond Borders: Advocacy Networks in International Politics* (Ithaca, NY: Cornell University Press, 1998); Robert O'Brien et al., *Contesting Global Governance* (Cambridge: Cambridge University Press, 2000); Derrick L. Cogburn, *Transnational Advocacy Networks in the Information Society* (New York: Palgrave Macmillan, 2017).

CHAPTER 8

WEBERIAN SOCIAL THEORY

Rationalization in a Globalized World

RALPH SCHROEDER

WEBER is still thought to provide one of the most penetrating sociological accounts of our current condition—this despite the fact that his oeuvre does not contain a systematic theory but rather analyses of many separate topics in a number of disciplines. This chapter reconstructs some of his main arguments about the patterns of modern societies, centered on the concept of rationalization, and how his insights have been taken further by some contemporary theorists. The chapter will review Weber's conceptual apparatus, assess a number of thinkers who have taken his ideas forward, and evaluate the continued relevance of his ideas.

The chapter is organized as follows: after briefly arguing that rationalization should be seen as a master process in Weber's thought, the chapter examines rationalization in the societal orders of politics, the economy, and culture in turn (and culture, as we shall see, can encompass science and technology as well as the media). Weber's thought sometimes differentiated between several additional societal orders or spheres of life, but I have simplified his schema in accordance with a more standard way of separating them. In the case of each of these orders, after summarizing Weber's position, the chapter analyzes some key thinkers who have built on or extended his ideas. In the concluding section the chapter examines Weber's ideas in relation to contemporary debates about globalization and geopolitics. This macro level is where the societal orders and Weber's ideas about rationalization come together—or fail to do so—even if there is also an overarching or "umbrella" sense of rationalization. The chapter ends with an outlook on Weberian sociological thinking.

We can begin, however, by noting the difficulty of understanding Weber's thought as a unified or systematic whole. Weber has been seen as a theorist of social action and as offering a multidimensional account of social change.[1] Yet these two interpretations do not by themselves show how his writings contain a substantive account of contemporary society and whether he assigns primacy to any particular social forces. One way to overcome this problem is indicated by the title of an early version of *Economy and Society*, which was titled "The Economy and the Societal Orders and Powers" (*Die Wirtschaft und die gesellschaftlichen Ordnungen und Mächte*). The notion of "societal orders" (*Ordnungen*) or "value spheres" (*Wertsphären*) and their logics also appears elsewhere in his work.[2] One theme of this chapter is how exactly these orders or spheres relate to each other.

I will refer here to "societal orders" and "spheres" interchangeably (and come back to the terminology used by those who build on his work). There are, however, certain processes that Weber saw as central to modern social change—"rationalization" foremost among them. To appreciate its centrality, we can turn briefly to one of his key texts. Discussion of "rationality" and "rationalization" can be found throughout Weber's writings, but the most systematic statement of his position can be found in the "Author's Introduction" to the *Collected Essays in the Sociology of Religion*, which is worth recapitulating (in my own translation, emphases in the original): Weber says that in his "universal history of culture the central problem is...the emergence of *middle class* [*bürgerlich*] enterprise capitalism with its rational organization of *free labour*...this uniquely occidental capitalism is shaped...by its *technological* conditions. Its rationality is today mainly determined by the *calculability* of its technically crucial components: the foundation of which is exact calculation. In truth, this means: through the uniqueness of Western science, and in particular its mathematical and experimentally exact natural sciences."[3] He goes on to list the calculability of work and rational law and administration as part of this uniqueness and asks why China and India did not take this path of "rationalization" or toward the "unique 'rationalism' of Western culture."[4] He points out that there can be different kinds of rationalization in different spheres of life, which could, from a different vantage point, also be seen as irrational.

At that point, he turns to the topic of the *Protestant Ethic*, to explain the emergence of "economic rationalism" with particular reference to its emergence via "practical-rational ways of *life-conduct*."[5] He adds that his explanation in no way makes a value judgment about this development[6]; his only interest is in a causal explanation of this phenomenon. Weber's aim is thus to explain the pattern of history or the shaping of modern society. Rationality (a way of life), rationalism (the distinctive shape of culture and society), and rationalization (the process) are all aspects of this single object of explanation. One key to understanding how Weber presents a coherent account of the patterns of modern society is therefore to see how rationalization works differently and similarly across the various societal orders.

Before we do this, we can note that "rationalization" also has several meanings: most common is the growth of instrumental "rationality."[7] Yet Weber also saw rationalization, secondly, in terms of "calculability," or an intensification or extension of applying scientific knowledge (and "applying" scientific knowledge includes technology, so henceforth I will use "technoscience" when they are combined). Thirdly, rationalization means the routinization of charisma. Mastery over the environment—broadly conceived as both the social and natural environment—is part of all three, as is impersonality and organizational control. There is an additional meaning of "rationalization" in Weber's thought which is how there are certain "inner logics" to worldviews and religions themselves whereby they develop greater internal consistency. These different senses of rationalization will need to be borne in mind in the present discussion.

Weber thought that the process of rationalization is pervasive throughout the various societal orders. Rationalization for Weber produces increasingly impersonal relations, structures that become frozen and inescapable, leading to an "iron cage." In the realm of culture, science and technology increasingly dominate, disenchanting the world and displacing religious and other worldviews with "cold" but effective knowledge and displacing the management of social relations on a smaller intimate scale with managing them via large impersonal technological systems. In the economy, the personal ties of household and patrimonial relations are being displaced by impersonal market relationships and economic organizations as firms become more and more bureaucratic (and, as Weber noted, these impersonal relations govern both capitalist and socialist economies). Finally, politics too, in the modern world, is becoming dominated by bureaucracies and party apparatuses, both impersonal forms of rule which also extend the formal rule-boundedness (and so instrumental-rational nature) of social relations.

We will return to detail further manifestations of this process. Before we do so, it can be pointed out that his theory of rationalization has, with few exceptions,[8] not been systematically developed by social theorists. Weber counterposed the force of charisma against the process of an almost inescapable bureaucratization, a view of history which set the dynamic or creative role of individuals and their ideas against impersonal and stagnant structures. This suggests a pessimistic view of history, though this is also misleading since Weber was well aware of the positive side of a greater mastery over the world. He recognized the power and effectiveness of techniques that could extend the scale, scope, and penetrative capabilities of political and economic organizations and of science or knowledge. Yet, at best, Weber's idea of rationalization is double-edged, and Mommsen has aptly called him a "liberal in despair."[9]

RATIONALIZATION AND MODERN CULTURE

Weber's ideas about rationality and rationalization in the cultural sphere have been largely overlooked. One exception is Ernest Gellner, who argues, like Weber, that modern culture is characterized by the dominance of a particular type of rationality, instrumental rationality.[10] This type of rationality aims at the most efficient means to achieve given ends and operates without regard to persons and is therefore "cold" and "disenchanted." Yet Gellner rejected Weber's pessimism about this force, arguing instead that the benefits of increased technological and productive powers free up our lifeworld for an enchanted consumerism—a "rubber" rather than an "iron cage."[11] Again, we will come back to this point, but we can already register that Gellner in this way takes Weber's thought further in recognizing that science is the exclusively legitimate mode of thought in modern culture: for serious matters, Gellner argues, we rely on science. It may well be that in other matters, the cozy worlds of everyday life and of popular culture, relativism can reign.[12] Yet when culture needs to be effective—powerful—only scientific knowledge will do.

Gellner was mainly concerned with epistemology and the validity and legitimacy of modes of thought. A different direction of Weberian thought, which moves us somewhat away from the sphere of culture and into the economic sphere, is how Collins used Weber's ideas about technology to develop a Schumpeterian account of innovation.[13] Collins develops arguments about how innovations take place and become diffused with market and geopolitical competition. He has also argued that technological advances, especially in information and communication technology, are increasingly squeezing especially middle classes out of their jobs.[14] The core of Collins' argument is that Marx and Engels focused on the crisis which would be brought about by the economic conditions of the working class, but "they did not foresee the rise of the massive middle class of white-collar employees" which saved capitalism.[15] Yet it is precisely this middle class that, in his view, is now in danger of being displaced by the mechanization of information and communication technologies, and he asks, "can capitalism survive this second wave of technological displacement?" And while he goes through a number of scenarios which might avert this danger, including the creation of new jobs in the realm of information and communication technologies and further credential inflation (more university education), he is pessimistic about these "escapes" and foresees major social upheaval.

The key point in the context of rationalization is that Weber's ideas, drawing on Gellner and Collins, can be developed into a fully fledged account of how scientific knowledge moves out of the laboratory and into consumer markets.[16] Sometimes this diffusion takes the form of stand-alone technologies, but the more permanent "cages" are large technological systems or infrastructures such as transportation, energy, and communication.[17] In this way instrumental rationality suffuses into everyday life both in lasting infrastructures as well as via a stream of new consumer devices. So even if technoscientific rationalization displaces certain types of work or professions on the side of production, it also leads to the transformation of leisure on the side of consumption.

There is another aspect to this form of rationalization which spills from the sphere of culture into the sphere of politics, where it leads to the use of new technologies for mass persuasion and surveillance.[18] Recently these technologies have become more powerful due to innovations in how digital networks enable ever more extensive and fine-grained control. The intensification of rationalization in this case, as elsewhere, has taken place via "calculability." Thus, the public's and consumers' preferences are being measured, now online, and products and services tailored and targeted toward them. The main current examples are social media, search engines, and online entertainment services, which maximize engagement for the sake of increasing attention to advertising and subscriber fees. Napoli has described this process of audience measurement as an ongoing "rationalization."[19] And although media have always sought information about their readership, viewership, and listenership, digital technologies extend and deepen the calculability of audiences and consumers.[20]

The reason the sphere of culture partly overlaps with the sphere of politics is that audiences are also citizens consuming news. Weber sketched a sociology of journalism where he was mainly concerned with the media of his day—newspapers—and their role in politics.[21] His plans for analyzing media fit with his notion that the tools of persuasion were becoming increasingly important in a mass society. The tradition of mass media effects or media as propaganda has waxed and waned in communication research.[22] But it is also apt to see Weber's ideas as foreshadowing the "mediatization"[23] of the world, whereby media increasingly become an apparatus that interposes itself between publics or consumers and elites. As Bastin has pointed out, "Weber is not so much interested in how the press affects the ideas of individuals but more their everyday life through the rationalization and universalization of the tools through which individual life worlds are interpreted."[24] In other words, Weber's sociology of journalism is part of a broader process whereby culture is ever more technologically mediated.

Mediatization furthermore highlights an important element that has been missing in the sociology of media, namely, as indicated earlier, that media are large technological systems with "logics" of their own and which impose particular formats on news professionals and their audiences.[25] One aspect of rationalization is therefore how publics and audiences are increasingly subject to measurement. Media have become barometers of policy preferences and of cultural tastes, and these measurements are, in turn, used by elites to enhance their legitimacy and as tools for marketing.

Media have become by far the largest component of culture, whether this is measured by time spent, proportion of the population reached, or influence. But the focus in media and communications research has until recently been on the content of media messages rather than on audiences. This focus has started to shift in recent decades and now, with social media, has reached the point where the more effective targeting of audiences and tailoring messages to particular groups, as well as seeking to engage audiences in more powerful ways, has become paramount. Thus, a more balanced picture has come into view whereby there is an interaction between how elites shape and respond to the worldviews of audiences via media. Weber could not have foreseen these developments, but a Weberian perspective of rationalization, and a comparative historical perspective—since media had a much more limited reach and were confined to elites before the onset of modernity[26]—sheds important light on them. Yet we should remember that there are also limits to this process: the world is not, as some media theories would have it, entirely constructed by mediated worldviews[27]; instead, social development shapes how media represent the world, including new social forces and how these forces are able to use digital technologies, sometimes circumventing traditional media.

Most of media is consumer culture, so before we leave the realm of culture, it is worth noting that Weber's most widely known work is, of course, his analysis of how religion fostered modern capitalism. Here, too, his ideas about rationalization have been taken further: Weber's *Protestant Ethic* thesis continues to be debated, and so much is written on this topic that it can be left to one side here (though it can be mentioned that the focus on understanding the origins of modern capitalism has shifted away from cultural explanations). Yet one aspect of culture that still needs explanation is consumerism, which can be seen as the dominant cultural orientation in contemporary societies.[28] In this case, however, a convincing Weberian account of the rise of modern consumerism has been put forward by Campbell, whereby the restless drive for fulfillment has become an inescapable "cage" of constantly seeking novel experiences.[29] Like the *Protestant Ethic*, this transformation of a "romantic ethic" into the "spirit of consumerism" is a case of rationalization in the sense of development via an inner logic of worldviews. Combining the perpetual seeking of novel experiences with a Weberian understanding of the pervasiveness of new media technologies therefore provides, in this author's view, a penetrating account of modern consumer culture: after all, again, the vast bulk of leisure time in contemporary societies is spent with media.

RATIONALIZATION AND MODERN POLITICS

In political sociology, Weber's definition of the state, as the monopoly of legitimate violence, is still widely used. The problem is not his conception of the state but that the types of legitimacy are limited to charismatic, legal-rational, and traditional: Weber did not have a systematic account of democracy. Breuer[30] tried to make up for this shortcoming, and Collins has developed a Weberian account of democratization, based on a combination of decentralized power plus the reach or breadth of suffrage.[31] But the main Weberian tradition in political sociology that has been carried forward revolves around state capacity.[32] Bureaucratization, on this view, was largely driven by war, with states creating centralized apparatuses for military competition. But the state's penetration of society also gave rise to social movements. As Collins describes it, the effect of the second late nineteenth-century wave of bureaucratization "was to expand formal political participation, to make every individual a citizen of the state, and hence subject to state regulation"; but this also meant that "political and social movements now had a target for their actions."[33] Thus, Weber's ideas can be indirectly linked to democracy via the struggle to incorporate ever wider groups within the—growing—state, though arguably this movement toward democratization from below has recently stalled.[34]

Weber was closer to the "mass society" tradition which has regarded "the people" as providing legitimation for dominant leaders and parties. The tradition in political sociology just sketched, in contrast, is one whereby pressure from below, by different classes and citizen groups or social movements, democratizes the state (though it can also lead to authoritarian regimes of the left and the right). In this tradition, the forces of civil society progressively—though not unilinearly—gain rights from the state over the course of time. The most systematic account of this arc of development can be found in the work of Michael Mann,[35] though here again it is useful to remind ourselves that this process is double-edged: in addition to democratization from below, the state, as Dandeker points out, has to develop large-scale bureaucracies in order to capture, quantify, and serve its citizens within modern welfare states.[36]

Beyond rationalization, Weber did not ignore the continuing role of conflict in society, both in domestic politics and in geopolitics. Weber's ideas about geopolitics have been developed by Collins, who proposed a theory of how great powers gain advantage by means of expanding territorial control and superior military technology.[37] Weber's ideas about geopolitics focused on the struggle among great powers for pre-eminence. This idea of a continuing struggle among nation-states sets Weber apart from world-society theorists who claim that states increasingly follow similar scripts or models, converging in a functionalist manner on a harmonious world order.[38] It also sets him apart from world-systems theorists like Wallerstein, who argue that there are economic contradictions in the world system of capitalism.[39] For Weber, instead, there continues to be a political struggle for pre-eminence among nations. The main reason for mentioning geopolitical conflict in this context, however, is that on this macro level, social change escapes rationalization so that the reach of rationalization does not extend to this level but in politics remains contained within nation-states, unlike in the cultural and economic spheres (though it can be mentioned that some, like Slaughter, have argued, that an increasingly dense web of bureaucratic rule-making also pervades international politics).[40]

RATIONALIZATION AND THE MODERN ECONOMY

Weber thought that modern capitalism operates quite differently from traditional forms of capitalism. Personalistic relations governed premodern household economies and predatory political capitalism, whereas modern rational capitalism has excluded all criteria apart from exchange for the sake of profit-making: "the production of goods was emancipated from all the bonds of inherited tradition, and came under the dominance of the freely roving intelligence."[41] Modern market exchange is open-ended, and firms ceaselessly seek to extend their control. Capitalist economies have become characterized by formally free (contractual) labor, exchange via money, and above all calculability. And calculability, as already mentioned, is at the core of rationalization. Mau has recently argued in a Weberian vein that "digitalization and economization of society...are two main driving forces of the quantification of the social."[42] These are extensions and intensifications of existing processes of applying scientific knowledge. Yet, as Mau notes, the quantification of social life, with its rankings and ratings, is also a way of promoting competition: when phenomena become measured, there are winners and losers, and there is always room for improvement. And quantification is a means of seeking objectivity in the service of mechanisms for steering social processes: in this sense, rationalization can be seen as the logic of control under the condition of seeking profits in a competitive market economy.

The story of how top-down rationalization has grown, organizing capitalist enterprises and extending their scale and scope, has been told in a Weberian vein on a number of occasions.[43] As we saw with media, the most recent intensification of this process is data-driven. Large digital media companies in particular are increasingly able to measure consumers and tailor messages to audiences and target them.[44] There are limits to the global spread of these companies: the Chinese Internet, for example, has been until now largely separate so that, although social media companies like Google, Facebook, and Amazon can measure and tailor their offerings to billions of users across large parts of the globe, in the People's Republic their Chinese equivalents (Baidu, Tencent, and Alibaba) are dominant. And China is not the only territory that has boundaries around its social media users; Russia, Iran, and other countries to some extent do so too.

DiMaggio and Powell have described how Weberian organizations spread, via institutional isomorphism.[45] Economic power, in this case the diffuse and extensive power characteristic of modern capitalism,[46] entails that more effective—rationalized—firms increasingly dominate. Yet again, there are limits to the globalization of this process, which returns us to technologies: even the spread of technologies has taken different directions. India, for example, has a tradition of "small technologies," such as the spinning wheel, bicycles, and now mobile phones, whereas China (like the Soviet Union) has had a tradition of carrying out large infrastructural projects.[47] And these traditions continue to be partly reflected in the distinct economic organizations of the two countries. In any event, once established and embedded in everyday life, bureaucracies—economic and political—become invisible, as do large technological systems or infrastructures; and they mainly come into focus when there are controversies, such as over privacy or how the algorithms of government or private sector information systems shape people's lives, or if there are breakdowns, such as when energy systems fail or administrative errors occur on a large scale. We can remember here, finally, that Weber lived at a time when the dangers of large-scale organizational failures, such as nuclear energy disasters or massive data breaches, were not yet on the horizon.

RATIONALIZATION AND GLOBALIZATION

In Weber's time, instead of a debate about globalization, global change was seen from a longer-term perspective in terms of the rise and dominance of the West, on the one hand, and through the lens of great power rivalry, on the other hand. This is still the world in which we live, although the debate about the West has been subsumed in a wider debate about China's failure to "take off" during the nineteenth century and how the constellation of great powers has shifted toward the East in the twenty-first century. The most Weberian-scale attempt in regard to understanding globalization has been the work of Michael Mann, who positions himself halfway between Marx and Weber: unlike Weber (and similar to Marx), he wants to make generalizations about social transformations. Yet unlike Marx, he wants not to assign ultimate primacy to any one form of power in history but to chart their interplay.[48] But Mann is also closer to Weber in seeing people as increasingly "caged" by the sources of power and in arguing that the nation-state is still the main bounded unit that "cages" citizens. The question that can be addressed in this final section of the chapter is therefore whether the "cages" or rationalization are one or many; in other words, in what sense they are global.

Before we turn to this question, it can be noted that Weber's thought has been a strong influence in social theory but mainly among thinkers who have not been part of a school. In the 1960s and into the 1980s, social thought could be divided between followers of Marx and followers of Weber; but Marxism has been in retreat in the social sciences in the twenty-first century, and nothing has come to replace it in terms of macro social theory. But if there is no Weberian tradition in social science or social theory, there has also been no dominant alternative theoretical tradition: poststructuralism and its construc-tivist successors and rational choice theory have never provided coherent macro social theories, and the current turn to computational social science is atheoretical. However we answer the question of whether Weber and Weberianism provide a global or system-atic social theory then, it should be borne in mind that little currently exists by way of a mainstream or dominant alternative to such a theory.

So far I have argued that Weberian thought still provides persuasive insights into sev-eral modern processes—technoscientific advance (which includes media), bureaucracy and struggles over democratization, and the ongoing disembedding or impersonaliza-tion of markets. What ties these together is rationalization—a globalizing process at a minimum in the sense that it spreads modernity. But rationalization, as we have seen, can be disambiguated into different forms in the cultural, political, and economic orders or powers. And apart from globalizing processes, we have found no single global system or single process except perhaps the (non-systemic) and non-rationalized conflict between the great powers, themselves shifting. Ultimately, the lack of the several spheres or orders forming a whole in which all of the parts come together neatly therefore leaves Weber's thinking open-ended (recall the point made at the outset that many regard Weber's thinking as "multidimensional"). In this respect his successors have followed him in developing open-ended theories. This approach—a combination of ongoing globalizing processes on the macro level and several spheres intersecting orthogonally, plus geopo-litical conflict—again, is still an accurate representation of a complex social world.

But there is a tension here: it may seem that an open-ended or multidimensional account of modern or contemporary society would be in keeping with a Weberian approach. Yet this is misleading since, as Gellner notes, social scientists and others inev-itably have an implicit view of history.[49] It is also misleading since social science must have an overall framework for explaining societal development that includes the catego-ries for analyzing macro social processes; methodological precepts alone cannot pro-vide the concepts and relationships for analyzing these processes. So the picture just presented—different processes of rationalization in several orders that also intersect, plus an open-ended struggle and shift among global powers—should also be regarded as a coherent framework, even if not a systemic one, that must be improved upon. The way forward in a Weberian spirit should therefore be to continue to refine and sharpen the concepts pertaining to macro social processes, fitting them into an overall picture of their interrelationships insofar as this is possible. This idea is in keeping with Weber's idea of science, whereby the world—in this case, the social world—becomes increasingly disenchanted. Unlike more limited phenomena, particularly in the physical environment, however, macro societal development is not subject to mastery by means of disenchanted scientific knowledge (the exception here, tellingly, is climate change, where it may be necessary to achieve enhanced mastery of the whole of this planet's—physical—environment or even to curtail this mastery). Hence, unlike in other areas of (physical) science, there remains a disconnect between our social scientific representation of a phenomenon and our ability to control it. Still, it is useful to have a clearer and more useful picture of the options ahead, including an understanding of the limitations in shaping the forces that shape us.

Weber saw the greatest challenges for modern societies as laying in the political order, and we can follow him in this regard. Perhaps there are now other challenges, such as growing economic inequalities, that were not central to Weber's thought or environmental issues that came after his time. Weber's prescience about politics, on the other hand, is still with us. Politics is the arena where Weber personally intervened most closely in current affairs, also via his writings, and where he saw the rationalization process shaping mass opinion and making the public subject to the followership of elites or leaders. Unlike most political science, however, his analysis of politics is grounded in a wider account of social change.

Weber could not have foreseen the current rise of (especially right-wing) populism, though there are eerie echoes of Weber's conception of plebiscitary leader democracy legitimated by mass followings of "the people."[50] The current rise of populisms in many parts of the world can be seen as exemplifying Weber's idea of leadership in the face of mass politics, though it has been noted that populism is not always leader-centric but can be party-centric or movement-centric.[51] These new politics are also enabled by changes in communication, especially digital media, which disintermediate between leaders and "the people" (though they also add new forms of mediation). And although populism is not necessarily leader-centric, it does aim at more direct or non-mediated decision-making, either in the direct acclaim of populist leaders and parties by their followers or via referenda. It remains to be seen how right-wing populism strengthens economic and political borders and sentiment against cosmopolitan elites in the face of the force of increased globalization. In any event, populism can also be regarded not just in Weber's terms of leaders and mass followings but also in Weberian terms (as discussed in the section on Rationalization and Modern Politics above) as the latest instantiation of social movements seeking to change the direction of a state with growing bureaucratic and infrastructural capacities, especially seeking to keep "others" out of the cages of national welfare states.

Against this backdrop of a Weberian analysis of contemporary politics, we can return to Weber's followers. In a globalizing world, the rationalization process that Weber saw as the central dynamic of modern society takes several different forms and yet also provides some unity to a Weberian analysis. In this way, the thinkers that Weber has influenced, on the one hand, and the social reality they try to capture, on the other hand, mirror each other: there are only limited intersections between the ongoing bureaucratization of the state and the extension of disenchantment by technoscience and the growing depersonalization of markets, three processes that can be combined with open-ended competition at the level of geopolitics. The most Weberian element in the thought of contemporary social theorists is therefore not the tripartite schema of class, status, and power or the types of social action or the types of rationality. Instead, it is perhaps the separation between economic, political, and cultural power. There is some variation here: for example, Mann and Collins want to add geopolitics (or military power) as a fourth arena, so they follow Weber's "realism" in international relations, although Mann goes beyond "realism" in recognizing the force of regulatory and diplomatic "regimes." And Gellner (and Schroeder)[52] want to distinguish between culture and science, or between where Weber saw the force of value-rationality (or what he sometimes called the "intellectual sphere" or the "aesthetic sphere")[53] as against the "instrumental rationality" and "disenchantment" of science (again, going beyond three spheres by dividing one sphere into two distinct parts). The weakness here is that there is only limited agreement on these concepts or ways of delimiting different "orders" or "spheres"—or "the sources of social power." In other words, there is no uniform explanatory apparatus that could allow social science in the case of these concepts to cumulate as do some areas in the natural sciences and within the social sciences. The strength of this position, on the other hand, is that it allows for a non-reductionist but still powerful synthetic analysis. And perhaps the persuasiveness should rest here not just on theory but on accurately capturing a complex reality.[54]

All of this can be put differently if we reframe the problem of "spheres" in terms of power or domination in Weber's work (see also John Scott's chapter in this handbook): domination is clearest for politics where rule over others must be legitimated within nation-states and between states where there is a (non-rationalized) "realist" struggle between great powers. But domination is different in markets inasmuch as domination is based on resources and power is diffuse and fleeting except where monopolies can be established. The domination of science and technology over the environment is different again since it is not zero-sum, as with political power, but takes the form of greater control (with conflict where this control leads, for example, to resource problems) over the social and especially over the physical environment. These forms of power and domination were not elaborated systematically in Weber's work, but they fit closely with his substantive analyses and have been systematized in the writings of others.[55]

Weber has thus left a multifaceted legacy of long-term historical and comparative analyses of social transformations. Yet his ideas do not add up to a unified picture of modern or contemporary social change since the rationalization of the world operates differently in different domains. I have argued that we should nevertheless forge a Weberian account of social change as best we can. Weber saw rationalization overall as a unidirectional process, disenchanting the modern world. This process is not all-encompassing, nor does it work in one way—for example, in relation to states and their bureaucracies as against how scientific knowledge displaces "enchanted" cultural understandings and in contrast with how markets are becoming increasingly disembedded. Note too that these three processes have a different reach; bureaucracies are tied to nation-states, while scientific knowledge is global and the reach and depth of markets are globalizing (markets seek to become global but face barriers in practice).

Weber did not systematize or align these processes since he did not attempt a comprehensive macro sociology. And his successors have solved the problem of the relation between the different orders or powers operating differently. Mann, for example, in addition to his four intersecting and overlapping networks and sources of power, sometimes uses "orthogonality."[56] Gellner sought to put the relation between the different orders or powers into comparative-historical perspective, charting their interdependence or the lack thereof.[57] In a similar vein, Collins has analyzed individual long-term trajectories without imposing the claim that they provide an overarching key to societal development.[58]

Weber's pronouncements about rationalization were rather pessimistic. These negative views can be partly attributed to the influence of Nietzsche. But on this point Weber is not just misleading because, as mentioned, he failed to see the re-enchanting side of a "rubber cage" of consumer culture. He also misleads because rationalization, as we saw, is a precondition for the provision of welfare and the comforts of new technologies as well as for continued economic growth. The main limits of rationalization in this regard are the limits of technoscience which strain physical—environmental—resources.[59] Otherwise, rationalization and depersonalization and how they promote the capacity of welfare states and market growth and how they may need to adapt to inflexible structures can be seen as trade-offs rather than limits. In the context of Weber's pessimism it should also be remembered that he was writing at the time of the emergence of a mass society when the costs of industrialization were more strongly in the foreground. Today, in contrast, it has become evident that societies have come much further in providing the means for the development of individual capacities, enabled by rationalization, on a large scale.

This brings us back, finally, to rationalization and globalization. As we have seen, rationalization can be seen as consisting of one pervasive or "umbrella" process that occurs throughout society or as taking different forms in the realms or "orders" of culture, politics, and economy. Weber did not make explicit whether he meant one or the other of these: a possible exception is his "Religious Rejections" essay, but this essay does not clear up confusion on this point since he also has an "intellectual" and "erotic" "sphere," for example, in addition to a "political" and "economic" one.[60] Hence, it is not clear how many "spheres" there were or whether the list is exhaustive. A brief comparison can be made here with those who promote Bourdieu's ideas of "fields"[61]; the problem with theories like this is that it is important to specify at any given point in history how many "fields" there are, which Bourdieusians fail to do.[62] Weber too fails on this score, except that he also uses the widely accepted tripartite schema of economy, culture, and politics, for example, in the chapter "Class, Status and Party."[63] Those who build on Weber's thinking, apart from those mentioned,[64] also distinguish only three (or four, in Mann's case) spheres or powers—for example, Luhmann and Habermas.[65]

One way to understand the "umbrella" process then could be via the notion of "instrumental rational action" which displaces the other types of action, but this is of course an idea that applies to the individual level rather than a structural one or one which allows charting macro social change. The lack of consistency between the "umbrella" process and its different forms in the three spheres or orders can only be resolved by tracing and detailing the unity and differences (or overlaps or interrelations between) the forms of rationalization as closely as possible, on the one hand. And, on the other, a Weberian approach would specify the limits of these processes in each case. Specifying the limits of rationalization processes prevents us from regarding this process as some kind of master key to understanding the whole of history or of social change rather than as one among several other such main processes. Consider, for example, that disenchantment is limited by the fact that much of the social world is still "enchanted," as illustrated by the persistence of religion.[66] Or again, rationalization in the sense of the growth of state bureaucracies is limited as measured, for instance, by the plateauing number of staff or state employees in advanced societies.[67] Or finally we can think of how economic organizations have tried to become less "top-down" or hierarchical and more "networked" or horizontal by decentralization.[68] Finally, the limits of the "umbrella" process of rationalization are the limits of calculability across the three domains—though, as we have seen, even if there is one process, the limits of this overall globalization confine its reach and depth in different ways.

Limits, both geographically and for each of the rationalization processes substantively, thus leave room for identifying other more central processes apart from or outside of rationalization, such as geopolitical competition or cultural, political, and economic processes untouched or less affected by rationalization. Once the limits of the umbrella process and its three component processes have been thus specified, which goes beyond the scope of this essay, we would be able to intone, with Weber, his pessimistic pronouncement on a rationalizing and modernizing, now globalizing and disenchanted, modernity: "culture's every step forward seems condemned to lead to an ever more devastating senselessness."[69] Doing so in the light of subsequent Weberian thought, however, and recognizing the limits of his ideas and without sharing his pessimism, leaves space for the other or remaining main globalizing and non-global processes and for social life outside the cages of rationalization.

NOTES

1. See Lawrence A. Scaff, *Weber and the Weberians* (Basingstoke, UK: Palgrave Macmillan, 2014).
2. Max Weber, "Religious Rejections of the World and Their Directions," in *From Max Weber: Essays in Sociology* (hereafter *FMW*) (London: Routledge and Kegan Paul, 1948), 323–362; "Zwischenbetrachtung: Theorie der Stufen und Richtungen religiöser Weltablehnung," in Max Weber, *Die Wirtschaftsethik der Weltreligionen. Konfuzianismus und Taoismus. Schriften 1915–1920, Max Weber-Gesamtausgabe* (hereafter *MWG*) I/19, ed. H. Schmidt-Glintzer with P. Kolonko (Tübingen, Germany: Mohr [Siebeck], 1989), 479–522.

3. Max Weber, "Vorbemerkung," in *Die protestantische Ethik und der Geist des Kapitalismus/ Die protestantischen Sekten und der Geist des Kapitalismus. Schriften 1904–1920, MWG* I/19, ed. W. Schluchter with U. Bube (Tübingen, Germany: Mohr [Siebeck], 2016), 101–121, 114; *The Protestant Ethic and the Spirit of Capitalism* (hereafter *PESC*), trans. T. Parsons (London: Unwin, 1967), 13–31, 23–24.

4. Weber, "Vorbemerkung," *MWG* I/18, 115–116; *PESC*, 24–26 (translation modified).

5. Weber, "Vorbemerkung," *MWG* I/18, 116–117; *PESC*, 26 (translation modified).

6. Weber, "Vorbemerkung," *MWG* I/18, 120–121; *PESC*, 30–31.

7. See Rogers Brubaker, *The Limits of Rationality: An Essay on the Social and Moral Thought of Max Weber* (London: George Allen and Unwin, 1984), for a discussion of "rationality," and Ralph Schroeder, *Max Weber and the Sociology of Culture* (London: Sage, 1992), for the different senses of "rationalization."

8. Jürgen Habermas, *Theorie des kommunikativen Handelns* (Frankfurt am Main, Germany: Suhrkamp, 1982).

9. Wolfgang J. Mommsen, *The Age of Bureaucracy: Perspectives on the Political Sociology of Max Weber* (Oxford: Blackwell, 1984).

10. For example, Ernest Gellner, *Reason and Culture: The Historic Role of Rationality and Rationalism* (Oxford: Blackwell, 1992).

11. Ernest Gellner, *Culture, Identity and Politics* (Cambridge: Cambridge University Press, 1987), 152–165.

12. Ernest Gellner, *Postmodernism, Reason and Religion* (London: Routledge, 1992).

13. Randall Collins, *Weberian Sociological Theory* (Cambridge: Cambridge University Press, 1986).

14. Randall Collins, "The End of Middle Class Work: No More Escapes?" in *Does Capitalism Have a Future?* ed. Immanuel Wallerstein et al. (Oxford: Oxford University Press, 2013), 37–70.

15. Ibid., 39.

16. Ralph Schroeder, *Rethinking Science, Technology and Social Change* (Stanford, CA: Stanford University Press, 2007).

17. Thomas Hughes, "The Evolution of Large Technological Systems," in *The Social Construction of Technological Systems*, ed. Wiebe Bijker, Thomas Hughes, and Trevor Pinch (Cambridge, MA: MIT Press, 1987), 51–82.

18. Christopher Dandeker, *Surveillance, Power and Modernity* (Cambridge: Polity Press, 1990).

19. Philip Napoli, *Audience Evolution* (New York: Columbia University Press, 2012).

20. See also Joseph Turow, *The Aisles Have Eyes: How Retailers Track Your Shopping, Strip Your Privacy, and Define Your Power* (New Haven, CT: Yale University Press, 2017).

21. Max Weber, "Towards a Sociology of the Press," *Journal of Communication* 26, no. 3 (1976): 96–101; "Vorbericht über eine vorgeschlagene Erhebung über die Soziologie des Zeitungswesens," in *Hochschulwesen und Wissenschaftspolitik. Schriften und Reden 1895–1920, MWG* I/13, ed. M. R. Lepsius and W. Schluchter with H.-M. Lauterer and A. Munding (Tübingen, Germany: Mohr [Siebeck], 2016), 211–228.

22. Russell Neumann, *The Digital Difference: Media Technology and the Theory of Communication Effects* (Cambridge, MA: Harvard University Press, 2016).

23. Stig Hjarvard, "The Mediatization of Society: A Theory of the Media as Agents of Social and Cultural Change," *Nordicom Review* 29, no. 2 (2008): 105–134.

24. Gilles Bastin, "The Press in the Light of Modern Capitalism: A Planned Survey by Max Weber on Newspapers and Journalism," *Max Weber Studies* 13, no. 2 (2013): 151–175, 165.

25. Ralph Schroeder, *Social Theory after the Internet: Media, Technology and Globalization* (London: UCL Press, 2018).

26. Elizabeth Eisenstein, *The Printing Revolution in Early Modern Europe*, 2nd ed. (Cambridge: Cambridge University Press, 2005).

27. Niklas Luhmann, *The Reality of the Mass Media* (Cambridge: Polity Press, 2000).

28. Frank Trentmann, *Empire of Things: How We Became a World of Consumers, from the Fifteenth Century to the Twenty-First* (London: Allen Lane, 2016).

29. Colin Campbell, *The Romantic Ethic and the Spirit of Consumerism* (Oxford: Basil Blackwell, 1987).

30. Stefan Breuer, "The Concept of Democracy in Weber's Political Sociology," in *Max Weber, Democracy and Modernization*, ed. Ralph Schroeder (Basingstoke, UK: Macmillan, 1998), 1–13.

31. Randall Collins, "Democratization in World-Historical Perspective," in *Max Weber, Democracy and Modernization*, ed. Ralph Schroeder (Basingstoke, UK: Macmillan, 1998), 14–31.

32. Randall Collins, "Maturation of the State-Centred Theory of Revolution and Ideology," in *Macro-Sociology: Essays in Sociology of the Long Run* (Stanford, CA: Stanford University Press, 1999), 19–36.

33. Randall Collins, "Rationalization and Globalization in Neo-Weberian Perspective," in *Frontiers of Globalization Research*, ed. Ino Rossi (New York: Springer 2007), 383–395, 386.

34. Colin Crouch, *Post-Democracy* (Cambridge: Polity Press, 2004).

35. Michael Mann, *The Sources of Social Power*, vol. 4, *Globalizations, 1945–2011* (Cambridge: Cambridge University Press, 2013).

36. Dandeker, *Surveillance, Power and Modernity* (Cambridge: Polity Press, 1990).

37. Collins, *Weberian Sociological Theory*.

38. John Meyer, John Boli, George Thomas, and Francisco Ramirez, "World Society and the Nation-State," *American Journal of Sociology* 103, no. 1 (1997): 144–181; Volker Schmidt, *Global Modernity: A Conceptual Sketch* (Basingstoke, UK: Palgrave, 2014).

39. Immanuel Wallerstein, "Structural Crisis, or Why Capitalists May no Longer Find Capitalism Rewarding," in *Does Capitalism Have a Future?* ed. Immanuel Wallerstein et al. (Oxford: Oxford University Press, 2013), 9–36.

40. Ann-Marie Slaughter, *A New World Order* (Princeton, NJ: Princeton University Press, 2004).

41. Max Weber, *General Economic History*, trans. Frank H. Knight (New Brunswick, NJ: Transaction Books, 1981), 306; *Abriß der universalen Sozial- und Wirtschaftsgeschichte. Mit- und Nachschriften 1919/20, MWG* III/6, ed. W. Schluchter with J. Schröder (Tübingen, Germany: Mohr [Siebeck], 2011), 343.

42. Steffen Mau, *Das metrische Wir: Über die Quantifizierung des Sozialen* (Frankfurt am Main, Germany: Suhrkamp, 2017), 18.

43. Alfred D. Chandler, *Scale and Scope: The Dynamics of Industrial Capitalism* (Cambridge, MA: Belknap Press of Harvard University Press, 1990); Dandeker, *Surveillance, Power and Modernity*.

44. Schroeder, *Social Theory after the Internet*.

45. Paul DiMaggio and Walter Powell, "The Iron Cage Revisited: Institutional Isomorphism and Collective Rationality in Organizational Fields," *American Sociological Review* 48, no. 2 (1983): 147–160.

46. Michael Mann, *The Sources of Social Power*, vol. 1, *A History of Power from the Beginning to 1760 AD* (Cambridge: Cambridge University Press, 1986).

47. For India, see David Arnold, *Everyday Technology: Machines and the Making of India's Modernity* (Chicago: University of Chicago Press, 2013); for China, see Paul Josephson, *Resources under Regimes: Technology, Environment and the State* (Cambridge, MA: Harvard University Press, 2004).

48. Mann, *Sources of Social Power*, 4:423–432.

49. Ernest Gellner, *Plough, Sword and Book: The Structure of Human History* (London: Collins Harvill, 1988).

50. Jeffrey Green, *The Eyes of the People: Democracy in an Age of Spectatorship* (Oxford: Oxford University Press, 2010).

51. Benjamin Moffitt, *The Global Rise of Populism: Performance, Political Style, and Representation* (Stanford, CA: Stanford University Press, 2017); Cas Mudde and Cristobal Rivera Kaltwasser, *Populism: A Very Short Introduction* (Oxford: Oxford University Press, 2017).

52. Ralph Schroeder, *An Age of Limits: Social Theory for the 21st Century* (Basingstoke, UK: Palgrave Macmillan, 2013).

53. Weber, "Religious Rejections of the World and Their Directions," *FMW*, 340–343, 350–359; "Zwischenbetrachtung," *MWG* I/19, 499–502, 512–522.

54. Dinxin Zhao, *The Confucian-Legalist State: A New Theory of Chinese History* (Oxford: Oxford University Press, 2015).

55. By Michael Mann, Randall Collins, and Ernest Gellner; see also Schroeder, *An Age of Limits*.

56. Mann, *The Sources of Social Power*, vol. 4.

57. Gellner, *Plough, Sword and Book*.

58. Collins, *Weberian Sociological Theory*.

59. Schroeder, *An Age of Limits*.

60. Weber, "Religious Rejections of the World and Their Directions," *FMW*, 323–359; "Zwischenbetrachtung," *MWG* I/19, 479–522.

61. Neil Fligstein and Doug McAdam, *A Theory of Fields* (Oxford: Oxford University Press, 2012).

62. Philip Gorski, "Bourdieusian Theory and Historical Analysis: Maps, Mechanisms, and Methods," in *Bourdieu and Historical Analysis*, ed. Philip Gorski (Durham, NC: Duke University Press, 2013), 327–366.

63. Weber, "Class, Status and Party," *FMW*, 180–185; "'Klassen,' 'Stände' und 'Parteien,'" in Weber, *Wirtschaft und Gesellschaft. Nachlaß. Gemeinschaften*, *MWG* I/22-1, ed. W. J. Mommsen with M. Meyer (Tübingen, Germany: Mohr [Siebeck], 2011), 252–272.

64. Mann, Collins, Gellner, and Schroeder, see note 55.

65. Niklas Luhmann, *Social Systems* (Stanford, CA: Stanford University Press, 1995); Habermas, *Theorie des kommunikativen Handelns*.

66. Philip Gorski, *American Covenant: A History of Civil Religion from the Puritans to the Present* (Princeton, NJ: Princeton University Press, 2017).

67. Vito Tanzi and Ludger Schuhknecht, *Public Spending in the Twentieth Century: A Global Perspective* (Cambridge: Cambridge University Press, 2000).

68. Walter Powell, "Neither Market nor Hierarchy. Network Forms of Organizations," *Research in Organizational Behavior* 12 (1992): 295–336; Viktor Mayer-Schonberger and Thomas Ramge, *Reinventing Capitalism in the Age of Big Data* (London: John Murray, 2018).

69. Weber, "Religious Rejections of the World and Their Directions," *FMW*, 357; "Zwischenbetrachtung," *MWG* I/19, 519.

CHAPTER 9

··

DEMOCRACY, PARTISANSHIP, AND CIVIL SOCIETY

··

SUNG HO KIM

"But with the member of a Nonconforming or self-made religious community, how different! The sectary's *eigene große Erfindungen*, as Goethe calls them...cannot but, as he has voluntarily chosen them, and is personally responsible for them, fill his whole mind. He is zealous to do battle for them and affirm them, for in affirming them he affirms himself, and that is what we all like."

Matthew Arnold[1]

CIVIL society is a nebulous concept. History does not demonstrate clearly what this concept refers to. Even today, all sorts of politics and policies are advocated in the name of civil society; and yet it is hard to identify what they have in common while sharing this edifice. Compare and contrast this semantic situation with that surrounding its notional counterpart—the state. Max Weber famously defined the state as a "human community that successfully claims the *monopoly of the legitimate use of physical force* within a given territory."[2] Notable in Weber's definition is the fact that, despite its parsimony, it is so evocative of symbols, institutions, and performances—recall parading soldiers in full regalia or chaotic passport control lines—that are rooted in our quotidian experience. In respect of vividness and tangibility, civil society pales in comparison. Michael Walzer's oft-quoted definition reads, "civil society is the sphere of *uncoerced* human association between the individual and the state, in which people undertake collective action for normative and substantive purposes, relatively *independent* of government and the market."[3] Eloquent as it is, this definition leaves unspecified everything from the levels of coercion to the degrees of independence involved in conceptualizing civil society. If the state is written in prose using nouns, defining civil society seems more akin to a work of poetry peppered with adjectives.

This elusiveness may be a matter of logic since civil society can only be defined in negative spatial terms, that is, as a set of complements to the state.[4] It may also have to do with the tendency that this conceptual antinomy comes often with moral presumptuousness in favor of righteous civil society rising up against the repressive state. For one reason or another, most endeavors to give a generic outlook to the concept of civil society seem unable to avoid overly detached generalizations as they try to encompass a vast spectrum of meaning, aspirations, and usage in actual practice. Unsurprisingly, its definitions abound, and not all of them get along with one another by any logical and/or practical necessity. For instance, Michael Edwards (the editor of *The Oxford Handbook of Civil Society*) identifies three very different clusters of normative and analytic perspectives from which civil society is approached. Those distinct visions see civil society as a *part* of society (the world of voluntary associations), as a *kind* of society (embodying certain social norms), and as a *space* for civic deliberation and engagement (often described as a public sphere).[5]

The first approach focuses on different sociological *forms* of associations, and, drawing from (a partial reading of) Tocqueville, the one deemed most suitable for a wholesome civil society is that which is based on voluntary membership principles. Evidently this definition puts civil society in stark contrast not only to the state based on compulsory, territorial membership but also to all forms of allegedly non-voluntary associations, such as familial or ethnic communities, while potentially encompassing market institutions. By contrast, the second approach excludes market institutions from the definition of civil society as it is built on certain normative aspirations in addition to voluntary membership. Here, the expectation is that a dense and robust voluntary associational life would naturally inculcate in those living that experience positive social *norms* such as trust, tolerance, and cooperation—a grass-roots accumulation of "social capital" that would bring about macro-level achievements in coping with poverty, discrimination, inequality, and other large-scale social ills. The third approach highlights civil society as a kind of space in which citizens are engaged in a public deliberation process for collective self-rule. It is a *public* space in that it is open equally to all as long as they are willing to present their reasoned opinions about common affairs considered from an impartial perspective. It is also a space for *deliberation* in that those public opinions are bound to exist in plural, and the final conclusion would be determined as a result of mutual persuasion via public justification.

While at times overlapping, these approaches may come into tension with each other in crucial respects both normative and analytic. For instance, it remains unclear as to whether the "market" is a constituent part of civil society; disseminating impartiality necessary for a public sphere may not be conducive to building up social capital that feeds on shared partialities. It may well be that, despite the profusion of its currency as a "conception," there is no single, basic "concept" of civil society after all.[6] In short, debates in, about, and around civil society are fueled by the difficulty of casting it in generic-notional relief and different, even conflicting, approaches to its analytic and normative underpinnings. Civil society is less a fact, entity, process, or phenomenon that readily presses on our naked eyes than an ideal type that can be constructed only with the help of theoretical imagination. In part because of this robust "theory-ladenness," the concept of civil society has become a magnet for so many debates. And it is against the background of these rich theoretical debates that I will place Weber's vision of civil society and assess its contemporary relevance.

Naturally, the very first issue to be addressed is whether Weber had a *theory* of civil society as such and, if so, what kind of basic contours and outlooks it exhibited. These two questions will constitute the main task of the following two sections of this contribution, respectively. They will be followed by a section 4 in which I will return to (some of the) theoretical debates surrounding civil society against which to compare Weber's theory and locate its place in the contemporary discursive context. The final section will zoom in on one latest strand of democratic theories (i.e., the partisanship theory) and reread Weber's politics of civil society in its light so as to foreground its contemporary relevance with more clarity.

Sect, America, and Civil Society

Weber's abiding interest in America from his early childhood is now generally recognized.[7] Unlike many of his German colleagues, who viewed all things American with Old World condescension, Weber maintained a more nuanced interest in the New World throughout his life as well as during his extensive American trip in 1904. This interest was expressed in numerous articles and lectures, finding its most theoretically elaborated version in the "Die protestantischen Sekten" chapter of the *Gesammelte Aufsätze zur Religionssoziologie*, which he was editing at the time of his death in 1920. Several discussions of these texts exist,[8] and, for the present purpose, it suffices to note that his interest centered on two points. Religion fascinated him most, although the emerging secular modernism in America did not elude his attention either; and, among those religious phenomena, it was what he called the "*organizational* strength of religious spirit"[9] that caught his interest in America above all. Applying the sect–church dichotomy, Weber attributed this "eminent power to form communities"[10] to the sect mode of organizing American society.

> It is according to the schema of the "sect" [*nach dem Schema der Sekte*] that the great deluge of associations [*sozialer Gebilde*], which have penetrated every corner of American life, is constituted. Whoever imagines, as our romantics love to do, "democracy" to be a mass of humanity ground down to atoms, is profoundly mistaken at least when it comes to American democracy.... The old "sect spirit" [*Sektengeist*] holds sway with relentless force in the intrinsic nature of such [voluntary and exclusive] associations.[11]

America as a sect-like society occupied an enduring corner in Weber's political imagination. As late as November 1918, for instance, upon being asked his opinion of the political tasks facing defeated Germany, Weber replied as follows:

> Foremost among these, too, is the restoration of that moral "decency" [*Anständigkeit*] which, on the whole, we had and which we lost in the war—our most grievous loss. Massive problems of education, then. The method: only the "club" in the American sense [*das amerikanische Klubwesen*] (and associations of every kind based on selective choice of members), starting with childhood and youth, no matter for what purpose.[12]

Two themes stand out in this terse, yet unambiguous, template for the postwar political rehabilitation of Germany. One is his insistence on the pressing need for associational pluralism and its critical role for civic–moral education and the other, America as the model for such an educational project. Here we can detect the trace of a coherent agenda that has long informed the liberal political imagination. Linking civic education, civil society, and America is hardly a novel idea, in other words; Tocqueville's fame rests upon it. More puzzling is the fact that it was Weber who so expressed it and that not merely in passing—as we see in his persistent interest in America as a sect-like society.

Despite this enduring fascination with civil society, however, Weber chose not to use the German equivalent, *bürgerliche Gesellschaft*, in his writings on sect or America. When this German term is introduced in different contexts, it is frequently paired in opposition to a "socialist or proletariat" (*sozialistische oder proletarische*) society, making its meaning more or less equivalent to a "bourgeois society" or even capitalism itself.[13] Such a usage was common in the Germany of his time, a semantic practice that owes its conceptualization to Hegel's and Marx's permutation thereof. Hegel maintained that civil society, located between the private family and the public state, contained two heteronymous instances in addition to basic legal institutions—a "system of needs," a purely economic sphere of market activities, and a "system of integration," a social sphere of associations and corporations. While the former was driven by the immanent conflicts between private interests, Hegel considered the latter responsible for social harmony through the socialization of otherwise self-interested individuals. The conceptual tension between these two instances of civil society was resolved by Hegel through the invocation of the bureaucratic state as a higher third.[14] The state for Marx was, however, merely an executive apparatus of civil society under bourgeois class hegemony, and this tension knew no easy resolution. He took over from Hegel the concept of civil society with an emphasis on its economic aspect and an added twist—it was now seen as a depository of false class ideologies and a site of their indoctrination via socialization, which is dictated in the last instance by the economic logic of market and the bourgeois class hegemony. The "system of integration" was now subordinated to the "system of needs" as a thinly guised veil for class exploitation, making the mediating function of the state hopeless and total revolution all but inevitable.[15]

Evidently, Weber could not have used the term in this Marxian sense lest his own vision of civil society be imbued with an unduly economic tone, for he was interested in the social, that which could not be reduced simply to economic factors and which, inversely, determined the economic in some instances. This can be seen, for instance, in his frequent use of an anecdote about the social regulation of credit-worthiness in America.[16] In this overwhelming emphasis on the social, Weber could have allowed his vision of civil society to be framed in Hegelian terms, yet the problem there was no less. The social aspect of Hegel's civil society (i.e., guild-like associations and semi-feudal corporations) was concerned primarily with socialization toward an organic and harmonious integration, and yet it was precisely this Hegelian function of civil society that Weber found most troubling in Germany. Instead, as we will see in the section on civility and partisanship, Weber's civil society was to be a site of political competition, contestation, and struggle. After all, the bureaucratic state that Hegel suggested as a superior remedy for the shortcomings of civil society's integrative function was not at all a solution to Weber. It was *the* problem against which he would hone and deploy his politics of civil society. It is little wonder that Weber could not have used *bürgerliche Gesellschaft* and resorted instead to a church–sect dichotomy to elaborate his contrasting vision of civil society.

DISCIPLINE, CONTESTATION, AND THE POLITICAL

For Weber, sect-like society is a purposefully (trans)formative site in which certain moral characters and civic virtues are cultivated through social *discipline*. In the methodological writings, Weber describes the moral character he deems ideal as "personality" (*Persönlichkeit*), "charismatic individual" in *Wirtschaft und Gesellschaft*, and "person of vocation" (*Berufsmensch*) in *Die protestantische Ethik*.[17] Whatever their label, this ideal moral character is built upon a sober confrontation with reality which makes possible a clear understanding of the responsibility of one's action and an unflinching value conviction despite full knowledge of its lack of absolute certainty. For instance, Weber demands that scientists accept the reality that their achievements are necessarily subjective value–laden but still urges them to take responsibility personally and strive toward that unattainable goal—objective value freedom. As such, this moral character refuses to turn away from the world despite the recognition of uncertain grounds of one's faith, still participating in such a hermeneutically chaotic world via principled and responsible actions. Weber found the archetype of this kind of life conduct (*Lebensführung*) in the Puritan inner-worldly asceticism (*innerweltliche Askese*) in which somber self-knowledge, passionate conviction, and methodical self-discipline were willfully combined to form a total personality (*Gesamtpersönlichkeit*). In other words, against a plethora of subjective inner values and the objective outer life caught in a cage as hard as steel (*stahlhartes Gehäuse*), a Janus-faced predicament that defines the modern condition, Weber proposes a unique "practice of the self" by which to foster a moral character that can (re)couple principled idealism and pragmatic realism—or conviction (*Gesinnung*) and responsibility (*Verantwortung*), in his own words.[18]

Given this Augustinian shade in Weber's moral anthropology, one would suspect a Nietzschean individual of solipsistic defiance in his concept of the person of vocation. As an astute sociologist, however, Weber does not fail to notice its social dimension either—"that connection of the internal isolation of the individual…with his ability to form social groups having the most stable cohesion and maximum impact at first was realized most fully in the climate of the formation of the sects."[19] Indeed, Weber's social imagination reveals its keenest sense of irony when he traces the root of the intense socialization and communal discipline of the sect-like society to the isolated and intro-spective subjectivity of the Puritan person of vocation. The irony is that this kind of self-absorbed individual and his or her recalcitrant and non-conformist outlook can only be fostered within a tightly organized, small-scale voluntary associational life governed by ethical conformism. For this social mechanism to play such a disciplinary function, Weber believes that the sectarian principles of rigorous selection of members and their supervision of daily activities coupled with a constant threat of expulsion have to be maintained by voluntary associations. Such "gatekeeping" is possible only when an association maintains not only voluntary but also exclusive membership principles, thereby overcoming the (ascriptive and exclusive) *Gemeinschaft* and (voluntary and inclusive) *Gesellschaft* dichotomy.[20]

A psychological effect of this syncretic mode of "associative practice" (*Vergesellschaftung*) must be the unyielding social anxiety which cannot but drive the members to conform and devote themselves to the goals and principles of their chosen associations. "The old 'sect spirit' holds sway with relentless effect in the intrinsic nature of such associations," Weber thus observes, for the sect is the first mass organization to combine individual agency and social discipline in such a systematic way. Membership in exclusive voluntary associational life is open, and it is such membership, or "achieved quality," that guarantees the ethical qualities of the individuals with whom one interacts. Weber thus claims that "the ascetic conventicles and sects…formed one of the most important foundations of modern individualism."[21] A charismatic individual he calls the person of vocation is forged in the sect-like society, in short, that angst-ridden cru-cible of surveillance, discipline, and conformism.

It is from this ironical perspective that Weber finds the German civil society of his time wanting despite its apparent vigor. In his *Vereinswesen* speech of 1910, for instance, the various aesthetic sects, traditional choral societies, and even Freud's German disci-ples are lumped together and given varying degrees of critical examination. Weber sus-pects that they all contribute to the formation of personalities likely to renounce this world and withdraw into a purely private world of mystic contemplation (as in the Stefan George circle) or into conformism bred by congenial sociability (as in neighborhood choral societies) or into a quietism coming from the preoccupation with mental hygiene and emotional sublimation (as in Freudian sects). These voluntary associations merely produced a " 'good citizen' in the passive sense of the word" by failing to discipline and nurture personalities who can readily adopt a principled, and even defiant, moral stance characterized by passionate conviction and a sober sense of responsibility—the virtues, in short, that constitute the charismatic person of vocation.[22] Lacking in German civil society is less a sufficient number of institutions of socialization than the kind of civic education they provide. Thus, he laments, "the quantitative distribution of associations does not go hand in hand with qualitative significance."[23]

For a sect-like civil society to be reinvigorated, Weber suggests in his later political writings that the elements of struggle need to be amplified both "within" and "without." In other words, associations should combine constant internal competition among members for the leadership position with an active external contestation against the associations of differing worldviews. Especially, Weber calls attention to the manner in which leadership is formed inside the voluntary associations and what competition between associations, including political parties, does to their individual members.[24] Political parties count indeed among the most salient components of Weber's civil society[25]; he defines "the essence of all politics" as "conflict, the recruitment of allies and a voluntary following," and political parties as associations "directed at free recruitment."[26] Political parties, especially ideological parties (*Weltanschauungsparteien*), are important for Weber since they present a selection process for leaders under whose direction the associations in turn become a medium for group dynamism in modern political society. The alternative in Weber's view is the triumph of a monolithic bureaucracy in both public and private spheres. Although even these voluntary associations, especially mass political parties, are also susceptible to bureaucratization, Weber still endorses a vigorous civil society so long as associational pluralism and the consequent elements of struggle can ameliorate the social petrification brought about by a bureaucratic leviathan.

Thus articulated, we recognize in Weber's civil society a singularly *political* vision. In its preoccupation with group struggle and competition, his vision is sharply opposed to a *communitarian-social* model which emphasizes socialization toward organic harmony and integration. It is no less opposed to a *liberal-judicial* model in which identity is safely assumed (and set aside) and what matters is a fair arbitration of different ideas and manifest interests through rational communication and public deliberation. Rather, Weber's civil society is meant to be a site in which certain moral characters and civic virtues are reproduced and charismatic leadership tested, proved, and selected, through intense politicization. The final goal of these political agitations is to arrest the otherwise inevitable bureaucratization of politics and society, thereby imbuing the late modern "iron cage" once again with vibrancy, enterprise, and dynamism.

STATECRAFT, SOULCRAFT, AND CITIZENSHIP

Now re-enter civil society. Recall that it is a nebulous concept that had no corresponding reality in the "short twentieth century." This was a time in which the economy of gigantic scale, whether capitalist or not, was welcomed with little questioning, while the immense pervasive bureaucracy, whether the totalitarian or welfare-state variant, dominated public life. Merely a pale reflection of an "idealized nineteenth-century," civil society was nowhere to be found but in a romantic lament for its erosion.[27]

Against this historical background, it comes as a surprise that the twentieth century in its last decade witnessed the sudden resurgence of civil society all over the world. The unanticipated collapse of the communist bloc and the Third World democratization— or the "third wave of democratization" à la Samuel Huntington—were all lumped together and seen as evidence that civil society, long thought dormant, had finally reasserted itself over the overbearing states.[28] Civil society in this context was understood mostly as a zone of overt and/or covert resistance against the authoritarian state, often equated with the oppositional social movement as such. In more established democracies, too, it was widely believed that civil society was the answer to the governance and legitimacy crises of the welfare state since it would make the government bureaucracy less intrusive while more responsive to the everyday needs and concerns of the people. For this purpose, the reinvigorated civil society was expected to play a check-and-balancing role by monitoring and holding accountable the government actions while channeling grass roots–level inputs into the policy decisions. It was also in the same vein that Britain's New Labour advocated the "Third Way," expecting non-government sector actors to form partnerships with the state to enhance the quality of governance without increasing the size of the government.[29] In all, the putative triumph of civil society was greeted with much hubris—most notably, the Hegelian celebration of the "end of history" that ironically came with the end of the Hegelian state.[30]

Underwriting these various expectations and aspirations was (and still is) a *liberal-juridical* understanding of civil society as a set of determinate institutions that stand apart from, independent of, or even in opposition to the state. In this view, civil society is a sphere of institutionalized self-regulation buttressed by the formal rule of law (e.g., the constitutional freedom of association) and formed through spontaneous interaction among rights-bearing individuals pursuing their own ends religiously. Its inspiration comes from, along with a Lockean liberalism, the social imagination of "commercial society" articulated originally by the Scottish Enlightenment thinkers and its model, a laissez-faire market where ideas and opinions would circulate throughout society as freely as money. Further, the state is to be an institutional agent that faithfully services and implements the mandates given by civil society, one that confers legitimacy on the state and sometimes withdraws it. The actions and policies of the state should be ultimately accountable to "we the people," who could check and balance, even topple, the state by organizing themselves into a civil society. The alleged Hegelian end of history, then, was to inaugurate a profoundly anti-Hegelian age in a dual sense: one, the relationship between the state and civil society was to be completely reversed from the way Hegel posited it and, two, formal-juridical institutionalism of civil society was to trump the *ethical-formative* principle (*Sittlichkeit*) of the state as Hegel saw it.

This reversal, however, does not mean that the reinvigorated civil society would remain indifferent to the Hegelian question of *good* citizenship. Civil society was expected to be the harbinger of the engaged citizenship without which neither a wholesome democratic self-rule nor the individual liberty and rights could be realized meaningfully. In this liberal view, in short, civil society nurtures and sustains the "conditions of liberty."[31] The difference from Hegel's project, then, lies less in a principled indifference to the moral matters than in the institutional framework advocated for the empowerment of public citizenship. This ultimate ethical stage is reachable through the institutionalization of voluntary associational life free of paternalistic interference of even the benevolent state. This liberal project of civil society, one might say, rejects a Platonic politics of the soul only to embrace a laissez-faire politics of the soul—"it is an invisible hand argument applied to associational life."[32] Tocqueville (in this libertarian guise) was to replace Hegel as *the* political theorist of our allegedly post-historical era.

As the initial euphoria subsided, however, there emerged a different understanding of civil society that was conceived more explicitly in terms of human *capabilities*, both moral and political, than of social, economic, and legal *institutions*. This conceptual reorientation was predicated upon the realization that many of the optimistic outcomes that were to ensue from a (re)invigorated civil society, gauged in terms of density and proliferation of voluntary associational life, did not come as promised. The simple presence of voluntary associational life, no matter how autonomously instituted and operated, and a laissez-faire politics of the soul, for all its implicit concern with good citizenship, did not seem to do enough to ameliorate political dysfunction, social disintegration, and economic anxiety. According to Amy Gutman, "We cannot assume that the more secondary associations that exist, the better off liberal democracy will be. More of civic importance probably depends on the nature of associations in America than on their numbers."[33] Quantity did not go hand in hand with quality, as Weber criticized the German civil society of his time.

Further, it became increasingly apparent that civil society sometimes did more harm than good. Organized special interests were only deepening the general public's sense of alienation from the democratic processes; the neighborhood groups organized for gated communities were hardly an assurance for the reinstatement of civic solidarity. A one-sided liberal-juridical or institutional approach did not seem able to make this critical distinction between good and bad forms of civil society, and that was one of the main reasons why democratic theorists of largely communitarian persuasions began to pay closer attention to the more substantive side of what civil society could and should do. In other words, the question to be raised about civil society became less about the density, profusion, and autonomy of voluntary associational life per se than about the variegated civic educational effects that voluntary associations exerted on their members' civic-moral makeup. Thus, Nancy Rosenblum observed the following:

> The orthodox preoccupation with associations as buffers against government and avenues to political participation, and with freedom of association as an aspect of personal liberty has been eclipsed. Today, the dominant perspective is *moral*: civil society is seen as a school of virtue where men and women develop the disposition essential to liberal democracy.[34]

Theoretically at stake in this *civic-moral turn* is a more profound and troubling question about the self-sustainability of value-neutral "procedural liberalism" on its own terms. Can a liberal democratic regime sustain itself while remaining indifferent to the moral disposition and civic virtues of its citizens? What is the role of civil society with regard to the continuing viability of a liberal democratic regime (statecraft) and the self-constitution of its citizens (soulcraft)? Cutting across a vast array of left- and right-wing positions, a large number of political theorists of Tocquevillean persuasions converged on the following points. First, a liberal democratic regime cannot be sustained in a robust form without certain kinds of virtues and characters in its general citizenry that can capacitate and motivate their active and responsible public engagement. Second, these types of agency are cultivated, (re)produced, and constantly reinforced through a local voluntary associational life in a pluralistically organized civil society. Third, therefore, the liberal doctrine of value neutrality needs to be softened, if not totally abandoned, to allow and encourage a stronger form of political and civic education of democratic citizenship via a formative intervention in the organization and structure of civil society. Criticizing the liberal dogma of the separation of statecraft and soulcraft, in short, this communitarian position suggests a politics of civil society in which state-craft and soulcraft are combined to sustain a more robust liberal democracy.

Against this background, Weber's views on civil society, as outlined in the previous two sections, can be surmised in two ways: one pertains to its affinity with the commu-nitarian politics of civil society and the other, to its crucial distance. On the one hand, Weber agrees with the communitarians that cultivating a certain type of moral character he called the person of vocation is critical for the continuing vitality of the modern liberal-democratic regime, that its virtues and dispositions can be fostered in an idio-syncratic social environment he found in America and its sect-like society, and that the decline of civil society and the concomitant degeneration of democratic citizenship must be restored as one of the central agendas for liberal democratic politics. Statecraft and soulcraft are not separated in Weber's politics of civil society, nor can or should they be separated.

On the other hand, Weber cautions that not just any revivification of civil society would conduce to the empowerment of the good citizenship, for he is far more sensitive than many communitarians, not to mention liberals, to the fact that the simple presence of a vibrant associational life cannot be immune, in and of itself, to the problem of "uncivil" or "bad civil society."[35] Further, the kind of "habits of the heart" acquired through voluntary associational life is not necessarily compatible with the political skills required of vigilant citizenship since those social habits may produce merely obedient and pusillanimous "good citizens" in the passive sense of the term. Not all forms of civil society are conducive to robust liberal democracy—some are in fact detrimental toward it. Through a genealogical reconstruction, instead, Weber seeks to resuscitate a peculiar form of civil society as the site where his politics of voluntary associational life and a unique civic educational project intersect and interact. It is this historically reconstructed ideal type, crisscrossing his larger reflections on modernity and modernization, that stabilizes the theoretical vista from which is issued Weber's emphatic call for an intense politicization of civil society.

CIVILITY, IMPARTIALITY, AND PARTISANSHIP

On this extraordinary emphasis on the "primacy of the political," a growing number of contemporary democratic theorists seem inclined to agree with Weber, for it is due to a similar skepticism about the liberal celebration of civil society for its own sake that they are refocusing on voluntary associational life in its most politicized form—namely, political parties and partisanship.[36] These latest advocates of partisanship also share the broadly communitarian proposition about civil society and recognize the practical need to revitalize voluntary associational life for some kind of civic education. However, they are far less sanguine than most communitarians, let alone liberals, about its practical possibilities, hence paying much closer attention to the political and social conditions under which the celebrated cycle between associational life and civic virtues may be obtained. Their point of parting comes when they find it hard to endorse a key assumption that underwrites the communitarian proposition. This is an assumption that the social skills and habits learned in civil society shall spill over into political society and prove to be useful civic virtues there as well.[37]

For the theorists of partisanship, this kind of automatic transmission cannot be taken for granted barring the articulated social dynamics and connecting mechanisms. In the absence of those sociological accounts, they find it hard to dispel the suspicion that "tensions between civicness and civility" are, if not inevitable, "real tendencies" still.[38] That is to say, the temperate social virtues of *civility* (that regulates relationships within a face-to-face group) do not necessarily go together with the aggressive political virtues of *civicness* (that pertain to members of a democratic community who remain mostly anonymous to one another). The former is necessary to sustain common grounds and opinions, or pretense thereof, even at the expense of shushing and covering up the differences between the known faces; the latter presupposes those material differences, urging mutual strangers to confront each other openly, even rudely, before finding a way of mediating and reconciling them. That is why "democracy may require withdrawal from civility itself"[39] and introducing divisive partisan politics is often seen as corroding civil relationships as such. To say the least, "the civility of good manners and *public* civility have very different objects" in Edward Shils' classic terms.[40]

Instead of the liberal and communitarian optimism about the compatibility between civility and civicness, the theorists of partisanship believe that contemporary civil society is in need of not less but more politics, or "not less partisanship but better partisanship."[41] In order to make this seemingly counterintuitive proposition, they submit that political parties are crucial components of civil society indeed and that partisan identity and practice should be encouraged for the benefit of civic education. Political parties are groups "people identify with, actively join, contribute to, work within, become officers of, and participate in setting agendas, goals, and strategies."[42] In other words, they are like any other voluntary associations formed for civic purposes. They have, however, a distinct advantage over other civic advocacy groups thanks to their *creative* and *pluralistic* (read anti-foundational) nature which together comprise the core of the partisan "associative practice"—or what Weber would call *Vergesellschaftung*.

To be a partisan is to stand *for* something, both standing *with* others and *against* others. Here what matters is that this kind of us–them distinction is not merely reflective of the fault lines embedded in society already, nor can it be reduced to them in the final analysis. Rather, partisanship reproduces, amplifies, and sustains the divisiveness *of its own creation*. This means that political parties do not exit the scene once a certain cause, say Prohibition, ceases to generate social divisions but would graft themselves onto another set of issues that will continue to fuel the differences of opinions and interests—or "pluralism *without foundations*."[43] This creative and pluralistic nature of partisanship, precisely the reason it is so often reviled and loathed in the name of civility, is seen as its virtue by its advocates, for political parties give a sturdy form to citizens' transient and wayward political preferences so that principled and responsible commitments to generalizable civic projects may be practiced with efficacy and over a long duration of time.

As such, the partisan *Vergesellschaftung* has a clear benefit. Among others, it helps partisans maintain their civic commitments in a far more articulate, practical, sustained, disciplined, and responsible manner than do those without a clear partisan identity or the apathetic, disengaged citizenry. *Responsible*: The partisan commitment is more responsible because partisans are no free-riders, and they actively bear out the financial and other costs for promoting their shared civic project. *Sustained and disciplined*: Established political parties provide an enduring organizational structure by which to keep their members in line not just at sporadic points in time, such as general or presidential elections, but from one generation to the next. *Practical and articulate*: Partisans are constantly engaged in the business of winning enemies, not to mention uninitiated strangers, over to their vision of generalizable public good by appealing to the masses regardless of their political and other differences. It is a work of "public justification" that cannot but compel the partisans to articulate their political ideas more sharply and participate in the practical implementation of those ideas with stronger motivation and enthusiasm. In short, the partisan *Vergesellschaftung* (re)produces *epistemic*, *motivational*, and *executive* capabilities and resources that help its practitioners "sustain and enhance political commitment" and thereby become more informed and engaged citizenry.[44]

On account of this last emphasis on public justification, the latest theories of partisanship might look as though they were a variant of deliberative-democratic theories and their vision of partisan civil society, a genus of "public sphere" à la Jürgen Habermas. It is not to be so conflated. Partisan persuasion, no matter how much attention is paid to the need of public justification, does not aspire to the deliberative-democratic ideal of calm and *impartial* reason; and it is better that way for democracy in the eyes of the partisan theorists. That is to say, what happens in a partisan civil society is *not* primarily the open exchange and fair deliberation of disinterested opinions until reasonable consensus emerges. Instead, it is to be an arena of organized rivalry, competition, and struggle on behalf of the irreducibly *partial* claims to truth between which consensus—be that reasonable, overlapping, or bipartisan—may not always be found. Some deep disagreements are reasonable *and* permanent, and it is not necessarily a bad thing for democracy as long as those *permanent* disagreements remain peaceful.[45] From this perspective, the best that can be expected is some kind of mixture of those partial claims—a *compromise* wherein lies the true meaning of *political* virtue.[46] It is in this sense that restoring the "primacy of the political" would help overcome apathetic citizenship and improve participatory democracy in both quantity and quality. Politics do for democratic deliberations the "work that philosophy cannot,"[47] for they hone conflict so that it is politically pertinent and cast it in an oppositional frame so as to compel citizens' informed choices and principled compromises.

In summary, the partisan civil society is a public sphere only to the extent that it is conceptually distinguishable from the realm of voluntary associational life per se. Partisan theorists believe that social capital cannot be automatically converted into political capital. Civicness is not primarily about good manners and well-tempered arguments but about firm convictions and commitments to join struggles on their behalf despite their partiality. A *good* partisan civil society is, then, an agnostic site of rival claims based on partial truths, and the "*high* partisanship" relies on those citizens who understand the virtue and necessity of making a statesmanly compromise precisely because they know they do not know the whole truth despite their passionate convictions. It is in the politicized form of civil society that citizens will learn to stand *for* their convictions by standing *with* fellow partisans and *against* others *without* losing sight of the political compromise that can be made at the end of the fighting.

How do Weber's politics of civil society compare to this latest democratic theory of partisanship? At the outset, for sure, it must be granted that even this rough outline discloses a considerable gulf between them. For one, cultivation of leadership and selection of genuine leaders, the most important function of civil society for Weber, hardly concern the partisan theorists who reject elitist democratic theories (of Michels, Mosca, Schumpeter, and their ilk) to which Weber's entrenched skepticism about democracy is often likened as a kin or precursor.[48] For another, the partisan democratic theorists tend to show little interest in nationalism or patriotism as a way of counterbalancing the centrifugal pluralism ("without foundation") intensified by partisan politics, whereas Weber expected liberal nationalism to work exactly as such a countering, centripetal force.[49] Be that as it may and their differences notwithstanding, it cannot be overlooked that both visions of civil society still have remarkably a lot in common.

Weber and the contemporary advocates of partisanship are both critical of the orthodox liberal view that simply equates civil society with voluntary associational life itself and the underwriting legal-institutional infrastructures. Instead, their abiding interest in civil society begins with the question of the *civic-moral* effects that those "associative practice," or *Vergesellschaftung*, have on the members living that experience. This shared interest comes from the fact that Weber and the contemporary partisanship theorists are both keenly aware of the possibility of "bad civil society." No less an important reason and, at the same time, that which also makes both of them different from the conventional communitarians is their shared suspicion that political-civic virtues to be inculcated in civil society are very different from the social-civil virtues that regulate our private lives. That is why they both refuse to endorse the proposition that the kind of social capital gained by investing in voluntary associational lives shall be automatically transmitted to the political realm as a useful set of skills and virtues for democratic politics. Political capital can be acquired by living *political* experiences daily. This realization leads Weber and a growing number of contemporary democratic theorists to converge on an insistent call for the politicization of civil society with a renewed appreciation of the political parties' contribution to democracy.

Last but not least, it should be noted that their intensely political vision of civil society is different from a Habermasian "public sphere," a putatively democratic haven for calm, rational, and impartial deliberation for consensus-building. In sharp contrast, for Weber as well as the partisan democratic theorists, civil society is to be a passion-ridden arena of contention, competition, and struggle between organized claims that cannot but be partial, where finding a consensus, let alone agreement, is increasingly unlikely given the incommensurable value fragmentation of our time. Ironically, however, it is precisely because all partisan claims are so partial that a political compromise can be made at least between *good* partisans. Neither too unprincipled (as in vainglorious power-seekers) nor too principled (as in moral purists), good partisan citizens welcome a political compromise, albeit their passionate value convictions, because they know that some reasonable disagreements are permanent. Then, the kind of political capital expected to be accumulated in a good partisan civil society is a mixture of "principle and pragmatism"[50]—a political virtue much akin to Weber's syncretic ethics of conviction (*Gesinnungsethik*) and responsibility (*Verantwortungsethik*).

Together, Weber's ethics also demand that political leaders and public citizens combine unflinching faiths in higher causes (which make them different from mere bureaucratic careerists) with sober realism that no political claim, including their own, can represent the whole truth (which makes them different from moral zealots). This syncretic ethic is the ultimate hallmark of the political agents with a sense of vocation (*Berufspolitiker*) who would fight for their convictions with fierce determination yet not without a "sense of pragmatic judgment" (*Augenmaß*)[51] that a compromise is unavoidable between incommensurable value positions, and all they can do in the end is to take robust responsibility for the consequences, either intended or unintended, of what *they* thought was a principled compromise. This is why Weber said the following in 1920: "The politician must make compromises...the scholar may not cover them [*Der Politiker muß Kompromisse machen...der Gelehrte darf sie nicht decken*]."[52] It is this type of political virtue that Weber wants to instill at the citizenship as well as leadership level, and the site of this political education is a dynamic civil society in which leaders and citizens can experience the creative divisiveness perpetually (re)produced by the partisan politics.

CONCLUSION

Sheldon Wolin, the doyen of the democratic theorists in postwar America, once issued a warning that "in the age of vast concentrations of corporate and governmental power, the desperate problem of democracy is not to develop better ways of cooperation, but to develop a fairer *system* of contestation over time, especially hard times."[53] Ours is indeed one of those perilous times for democracy. The "concentrations of corporate and governmental power" are still hanging over democracy as ominously as ever. This perennial problem has been exacerbated lately by the alarming way in which the "contestation" against those "concentrations" has been staged, that is, populism. One need not go further than Brexit and Trump to see what populist politics, once coupled with utterly irresponsible and demagogic leadership, can do to undo democracy.

Against this latest background, Weber's politics of civil society may be located somewhere in between the perceived democratic deficit of the remote technocracies or the "deep state" and the largely misguided and undisciplined oppositions to those detached powers in Brussels or inside the Beltway. Weber refuses to endorse a civil society which merely breeds civility and solidarity among citizens sharing a certain kind of voluntary associational life. What matters to him is an active citizenry who can make a firm and informed commitment and participate in the sustained and responsible struggles on its behalf, and this singularly political virtue can be cultivated only in a *political* associational life. This is why we find in Wolin's counsel for partisans of democracy a strong resonance of Weber's politics of civil society, for the problem of democracy in our time is not about staging oppositions per se, much less about nurturing cooperation, but about designing a *system* of contestation. That system might well look like a civil society in Max Weber's sense.

NOTES

1. Matthew Arnold, *Culture and Anarchy*, ed. S. Collini (Cambridge: Cambridge University Press, 1993), 195–196.
2. Max Weber, "The Profession and Vocation of Politics," in *Political Writings* (hereafter *PolW*), ed. P. Lassman and R. Speirs (Cambridge: Cambridge University Press, 1994), 309–369, 310–311; "Politik als Beruf" in *Wissenschaft als Beruf 1917/1919—Politik als Beruf 1919*, *Max Weber-Gesamtausgabe* (hereafter *MWG*) I/17, ed. W. J. Mommsen and W. Schluchter, with B. Morgenbrod (Tübingen, Germany: Mohr [Siebeck], 1992), 113–254, 158–159.
3. Michael Walzer, "The Idea of Civil Society: A Path to Social Reconstruction," in *Community Works: The Revival of Civil Society in America*, ed. E. J. Dionne (Washington, DC: Brookings Institution Press, 1998), 123–144, 123–124 (italics added).

4. Simone Chambers and Jeffrey Kopstein, "Civil Society and the State," in *The Oxford Handbook of Political Theory*, ed. John S. Dryzek, Bonnie Honig, and Anne Phillips (Oxford: Oxford University Press, 2006), 363–381, 365.

5. Michael Edwards, "Introduction: Civil Society and the Geometry of Human Relations," in *The Oxford Handbook of Civil Society*, ed. M. Edwards (Oxford: Oxford University Press, 2011), 3–14, 7.

6. Mark Jensen, *Civil Society in Liberal Democracy* (New York: Routledge, 2011), 35–39.

7. Lawrence A. Scaff, *Max Weber in America* (Princeton, NJ: Princeton University Press, 2014).

8. Among others, see Jan Rehmann, *Max Weber: Modernisation as Passive Revolution, A Gramscian Analysis*, trans. M. Henniger (Leiden, the Netherlands: Brill, 2013), 17–47; Sung Ho Kim, *Max Weber's Politics of Civil Society* (Cambridge: Cambridge University Press, 2007), 59–94; and Stephen Kalberg, "Tocqueville and Weber on the Sociological Origin of Citizenship: The Political Culture of American Democracy," *Citizenship Studies* 1, no. 2 (1997): 199–222.

9. Marianne Weber, *Max Weber: A Biography*, trans. H. Zorn (New Brunswick, NJ: Transaction, 1988), 288; *Max Weber: Ein Lebensbild* (Tübingen, Germany: Mohr [Siebeck], 1926), 301 (italics added).

10. Max Weber, "'Kirchen' und 'Sekten' in Nordamerika: Eine kirchen- und sozialpolitische Skizze," *Die Christliche Welt* 20 (1906): 558–562 and 577–583, 579; edited in Weber, *Asketischer Protestantismus und Kapitalismus. Schriften und Reden 1904–1911*, MWG I/9, ed. W. Schluchter, with U. Bube (Tübingen, Germany: Mohr [Siebeck], 2014), 426–462, 451–452.

11. Ibid., 580–581; *MWG* I/9, 453.

12. Weber's letter to Otto Crusius, November 24, 1918, in Weber, *Briefe 1918–1920. MWG* II/10, ed. G. Krumeich and M. R. Lepsius, with U. Hinz, S. Oßwald-Bargende and M. Schön (Tübingen, Germany: Mohr [Siebeck], 2012), 318. Cf. Marianne Weber, *Biography*, 635–636; *Lebensbild*, 647 (translation altered).

13. For example, Weber, "Socialism," in *PolW*, 272–303, 294; *Zur Politik im Weltkrieg. Schriften und Reden 1914–1918, MWG* I/15, ed. W. J. Mommsen, with G. Hübinger (Tübingen, Germany: Mohr [Siebeck], 1984), 597–633, 630–631.

14. G. W. F. Hegel, *Elements of the Philosophy of Right*, ed. Allen W. Wood, trans. H. B. Nisbet (Cambridge: Cambridge University Press, 1991), 220–274.

15. Karl Marx and Friedrich Engels, *The German Ideology: Part One with Selections from Parts Two and Three and Supplementary Texts*, ed. C. J. Arthur (New York: International Publishers, 1981), 57–68.

16. For example, Weber, *Economy and Society* (hereafter *E&S*), ed. G. Roth and C. Wittich (Berkeley: University of California Press, 1978), 1206; Weber, *Wirtschaft und Gesellschaft. Nachlaß. Herrschaft. MWG* I/22-24, ed. E. Hanke with Th. Kroll (Tübingen, Germany: Mohr [Siebeck], 2005), 672.

17. Harvey Goldman, *Politics, Death, and the Devil: Self and Power in Max Weber and Thomas Mann* (Berkeley: University of California Press, 1992).

18. See, generally, Wilhelm Hennis, *Max Weber: Essays in Reconstruction*, trans. K. Tribe (London: George Allen & Unwin, 1988).

19. Weber, "'Kirchen' und 'Sekten' in Nordamerika," 581; *MWG* I/9, 457.

20. Kim, *Max Weber's Politics of Civil Society*, 65–67.

21. Weber, "The Protestant Sects and the Spirit of Capitalism," in *From Max Weber: Essays in Sociology* (hereafter *FMW*), ed. and trans. H. H. Gerth and C. Wright Mills (Oxford:

Oxford University Press, 1946), 302–322, 321; *Die protestantische Ethik und der Geist des Kapitalismus/Die protestantischen Sekten und der Geist des Kapitalismus. Schriften 1904–1920*, MWG I/18, ed. W. Schluchter, with U. Bube (Tübingen, Germany: Mohr [Siebeck], 2016), 493–548, 543–544.

22. Weber, "Voluntary Associational Life (*Vereinswesen*)," ed. and trans. Sung Ho Kim, *Max Weber Studies* 2, no. 2 (2002): 199–209, 205; "Geschäftsbericht der Deutschen Gesellschaft für Soziologie," in Weber, *Hochschulwesen und Wissenschaftspolitik. Schriften und Reden 1895–1920. MWG I/13*, ed. M. R. Lepsius and W. Schluchter, with H.-M. Lauterer and A. Munding (Tübingen, Germany: Mohr [Siebeck], 2016), 274–284, 280.

23. Weber, "Voluntary Associational Life," 200; *MWG* I/13, 275.

24. Weber, "Voluntary Associational Life," 202–203; *MWG* I/13, 277–278.

25. Weber, "Voluntary Associational Life," 207; *MWG* I/13, 282–283.

26. Weber, "Parliament and Government in Germany Under a New Political Order," in *PolW*, 130–271, 173 (original italics), 149; *MWG* I/15, 421–596, 482, 455.

27. Eric Hobsbawm, *The Age of Extremes: A History of the World, 1914–1991* (New York: Vintage Books, 1996), 13.

28. Padraic Kenney, *A Carnival of Revolution: Central Europe 1989* (Princeton, NJ: Princeton University Press, 2002).

29. Anthony Giddens, *The Third Way: The Renewal of Social Democracy* (Cambridge: Polity Press, 1999).

30. Francis Fukuyama, *The End of History and the Last Man* (New York: Free Press, 1992).

31. Ernest Gellner, *Conditions of Liberty: Civil Society and Its Renewals* (London: Penguin Books, 1994).

32. Chambers and Kopstein, "Civil Society and the State," 372.

33. Amy Gutman, "Freedom of Association: An Introductory Essay," in *Freedom of Association*, ed. A. Gutman (Princeton, NJ: Princeton University Press, 1998), 3–32, 31.

34. Nancy Rosenblum, *Membership and Morals: The Personal Use of Pluralism in America* (Princeton, NJ: Princeton University Press, 1998), 26 (italics added).

35. Bob Clifford, "Civil and Uncivil Society," in *The Oxford Handbook of Civil Society*, 206–219; Sheri Berman, "Civil Society and the Collapse of the Weimar Republic," *World Politics* 49, no. 3 (1997): 401–429; Simone Chambers and Jeffrey Kopstein, "Bad Civil Society," *Political Theory* 29, no. 6 (2001): 837–865.

36. Jonathan White and Lea Ypi, *The Meaning of Partisanship* (Oxford: Oxford University Press, 2016); Russel Muirhead, *The Promise of Party in a Polarized Age* (Cambridge, MA: Harvard University Press, 2014); Nancy Rosenblum, *On the Side of the Angels: An Appreciation of Parties and Partisanship* (Princeton, NJ: Princeton University Press, 2008).

37. The most notable example would be Michael Walzer, "Equality and Civil Society," in *Alternative Conceptions of Civil Society*, ed. S. Chambers and W. Kymlica (Princeton, NJ: Princeton University Press, 2002), 34–49. Also sharing this assumption is Benjamin Barber, *A Place for Us: How to Make Society Civil and Democracy Strong* (New York: Hill & Wang, 1998).

38. Nina Eliasoph, "Civil Society and Civility," in *Oxford Handbook of Civil Society*, 220–231, 226.

39. Michael Shudson, "Why Conversation Is Not the Soul of Democracy," *Critical Studies in Mass Communication* 14 (1997): 297–309, 308.

40. Edward Shils, *The Virtue of Civility: Selected Essays on Liberalism, Tradition, and Civil Society*, ed. S. Grosby (Indianapolis, IN: Liberty Fund, 1997), 80 (italics added).

41. Muirhead, *Promise of Party*, 110.

42. Nancy Rosenblum, "Political Parties as Membership Groups," *Columbia Law Review* 100, no. 3 (2000): 813–844, 817.
43. Rosenblum, *On the Side of the Angels*, 365 (italics added).
44. White and Ypi, *Meaning of Partisanship*, 23.
45. For example, Jeremy Waldron, "Precommitment and Disagreement," in *Constitutionalism: Philosophical Foundations*, ed. L. Alexander (Cambridge: Cambridge University Press, 1998), 271–300.
46. Muirhead, *Promise of Party*, 54.
47. Rosenblum, *On the Side of the Angels*, 307.
48. Peter Breiner, *Max Weber and Democratic Politics* (Ithaca, NY: Cornell University Press, 1996).
49. Kim, *Max Weber's Politics of Civil Society*, 133–168.
50. Muirhead, *Promise of Party*, 41–42.
51. Weber, "The Profession and Vocation of Politics," *PolW*, 369; "Politik als Beruf," *MWG* I/17, 251–252.
52. Weber's letter to Clara Mommsen, April 14, 1920, in *MWG* II/10, 983, and as quoted in Hans Henrik Bruun, *Science, Values and Politics in Max Weber's Methodology*, new exp. ed. (Burlington, VT: Ashgate, 2007), 244.
53. Sheldon Wolin, "The Liberal/Democratic Divide: On Rawls's Political Liberalism," *Political Theory* 24, no. 1 (1996): 97–119, 115.

CHAPTER 10

··

NATION, NATION-STATE, AND NATIONALISM

··

JOHN BREUILLY

POLITICS AND SCIENCE

··

IN *Politics as a Vocation* and *Science as a Vocation* Weber insisted on a clear distinction between these two practices.[1] The scientist should not preach politics nor the politician justify actions scientifically. However, the distinction is complex as Weber did not believe science was based on "pure fact" or politics on "pure value." Scientists must select research questions according to nonscientific judgments as to their significance; responsible politicians must take account of relevant scientific analysis. Politics is a legitimate object of science; values determine the investment of resources into scientific research.

The distinction was especially difficult for Weber with respect to nation, nation-state, and nationalism. He has justifiably been called an "instinctive nationalist."[2] Much of his political writing promoted German interests at home and abroad. As a scientist he wrote about ethnic community, national community, and state (though rather less about nationalism and nation-state). What is noteworthy is the striking discrepancy between his clear, extensive, and definite political and his unclear, brief, and indeterminate scientific writing on these subjects, something which I will address.

Weber is not alone in encountering such difficulties. There is an almost irresistible temptation to treat nation as a "given," a "thing in the world," rather than as a concept. Yielding to this temptation makes difficult scientific analysis of the nation and goes along with a tendency to treat nation-state and nationalism as secondary phenomena in relation to nation.

Yet Weber's ideas concerning "worldviews," the modern state, political parties, voluntary associations, the press, and power and prestige in international relations can help us understand the emergence and spread of nationalism. His distinctive approach to sociology can illuminate these subjects in ways he himself did not explore and which remain underutilized. I will propose such a Weberian interpretation.

Although something must be said about Weber's writing on nation, nation-state, and nationalism, that is not my primary purpose.[3] There are many such studies. Some claim to discover what Weber "really" meant.[4] Others note changes, even contradictions, sometimes explaining these in biographical terms.[5] Some focus on the politics–science tension and the problems with his scientific treatment of nation.[6] However, to the best of my knowledge, no one explores better alternatives which Weber's own concepts make available. One reason is that the relevant literature is by Weber scholars interested in his ideas about nationalism, not scholars of nationalism interested in how Weber might help them.[7] I note the injunction of the editors to explore the ongoing significance, development and present-day application of Weber's lines of thought in social, political and historical inquiry.

Accordingly, I begin not with Weber but with nationalism studies. After a brief historical background, I outline the central concepts, questions, and interpretations which I take to constitute this field. I then turn to Weber, briefly with biographical detail but principally to relate these concepts, questions, and interpretations to his political and scientific writing. Having argued that his scientific writings fall short of his own conceptual and empirical standards, I seek to explain why this was and suggest a way forward.

The literature on Weber is large, and I am not a Weber scholar. I focus on key texts. I refer to Weber scholarship only when relevant. I use the *Max Weber-Gesamtausgabe* unless the text concerned has not yet been published in that edition. I refer to English translations when these are reliable and available.

NATIONALISM STUDIES: THE HISTORICAL BACKGROUND

"Nation" and "state" are words with a long history in English and other languages. "Nation-state" is more recent and less investigated etymologically. France and England were referred to as "national" in the sixteenth century but not as nation-states. "Nationalism" has been more intensively studied and seems only to have entered common usage in the late nineteenth century.[8] Etymological sequence is often taken to reflect historical sequence, with nation regarded as the necessary condition of nation-state and nationalism. There is less consensus on the relationship between nation-state and nationalism.

Frequently nation-state formation is seen to precede nationalism for "old" nations (e.g., England, France, Spain), with the sequence reversed for "new" ones (e.g., United States, Indonesia, Ghana).[9] This implies that nation was a European creation exported to the rest of the world, requiring two different ways of understanding the "original" and the "derivative" forms.[10] Before mid-eighteenth century those few states regarded as "national" were also empires, "national" referring to their European core. The American and French Revolutions transformed "national" into "nation-state" by defining the state in terms of the democratic participation of its citizenry: the nation or people.[11] In the nineteenth century nation-state formation became a repeatable act, beginning with Spanish colonies in America and "small nations" (Greece, Serbia, Belgium) in Europe. It extended to "large nations" (Germany, Italy, Japan) after mid-century. Movements aiming to form such states, both successful and failed, were dubbed "nationalist." When Weber died in 1920, most of the world remained subject to "alien" rule; there was no standard diplomatic formula for forming and recognizing nation-states, and the League of Nations was just being established. Generalizing the nation-state model across the world came in three waves: after two world wars and the collapse of the Soviet Union.[12]

Nation-state has been the least theorized of the three concepts, so in order to focus on nation and nationalism, I will define it pragmatically as a state which claims to be national, is not strongly challenged from within by oppositional nationalism, and is recognized as a nation-state by the international community.[13] Even by these criteria there has been constant change in the legitimations used to obtain international recognition. The problem is to legitimize the connection between nation as people and nation as homeland. An ethnonational emphasis dominated after 1918 (the new central European states), a territorial one (the former colonial states) after 1945, an ethno-territorial one (non-Russian republics, republics of the former Yugoslavia) after 1990.[14]

These differences demonstrate that "nation" is a contested concept. Attempts at definition range from nation as an objective reality to nation as fragile and volatile state of mind. As the nation-state became the global norm, involving recognition of regimes with little prior trace of national identity, the credibility of the assumption that nation was a necessary condition for nation-state and nationalism weakened. Yet even when the nation concept is rejected as foundational and coherent, it remains difficult to find alternative ones by which to understand nation-state and nationalism. Many historians continue the practice of making the nation the unit for long-run accounts of nationalism and nation-state, an approach known as "methodological nationalism."[15]

Weber lived at a time of "unification nationalism," including the formation of the German nation-state.[16] Unification nationalism and/or pan-nationalism, successful and failed, were integral components of the era of imperialist competition between the world's most powerful nation-states. Weber died as those empires were being challenged by the first wave of nation-state formation. Only then were contemporaries confronted with the problem of understanding nation-state and nationalism as global phenomena rather than cases confined to the powerful national cores of imperial states. Understandably, Weber had little to say about the nationalism of "small" nation-states and "stateless nations." Most of his writing focused on nation in terms of its orientation to the prestige, honor, and interest of powerful states (*Machtstaat*), especially Germany.

Nation remains the foundational concept in public and political discourse. This has practical consequences, as when US president Clinton described the violence in former Yugoslavia as the flaring up of ancient ethnic hatreds. Reconciling such deep-seated animosities will appear more difficult than if such conflicts are understood as recent, based on interests and ideologies, not stubborn identities. To challenge Clinton's "common sense," one must detach the concepts of nationalism, nation, and nation-state from each other and only then connect them in contingent ways.

THE INTELLECTUAL FIELD
OF NATIONALISM STUDIES

The early critics of the nation-centered view were often marginal figures from new disciplines. Robert Michels, a close colleague of Weber's, was such a person. In 1912 he delivered a paper to the second meeting of the German Sociological Association (*Deutsche Gesellschaft für Soziologie* [DGS]), arguing that nation was a modern idea and not one shared by many of "its" members.[17] He cited those many "Germans" who supported Napoleon against his "German" opponents. However, Michels took this little beyond insisting that national identity was more complex and less strong than commonly assumed. Tellingly there was little discussion recorded of this paper. One can find hints of this view in Weber's writings, but they are not systematically explored.[18]

Alternative approaches were pioneered between 1920 and 1980 but remained isolated works rather than establishing a framework for sustained debate.[19] Only around 1980 did such a debate begin, one which questioned assumptions about the foundational status of nation. This shaped an increasingly abundant literature after 1990 as "nationalism" again came to dominate international affairs.

One approach was to make nationalism foundational instead. This was cogently expressed in the opening of the pioneering work *Nationalism* (1960) by Elie Kedourie: "Nationalism is a doctrine invented in Europe at the beginning of the 19th century."[20] Kedourie argued that it was nationalism which endowed "nation" with its modern meaning, both justifying and motivating nation-state formation. Kedourie treated nationalism as a doctrine which spread like a virus and which had largely been "cured" with the defeat of the Axis powers in 1945.[21]

Some five years later Ernest Gellner adumbrated a broader sociological theory of nationalism which connected it to modernization but only in one chapter of a general work which was largely ignored.[22] This was not the case with his full-length book *Nations and Nationalism* (1983).[23] In that same year appeared *Imagined Communities: Reflections on the Origins and Spread of Nationalism* by Benedict Anderson,[24] the single most cited text on the subject. Along with a cluster of other publications around that time, these developed ideas which came to constitute the field I will call "nationalism studies."[25]

An intellectual field is one of contestation made possible by the sharing of basic assumptions. The assumption was that nationalism was not just modern but an aspect of modernity and something more than an expression of national identity. Scholars have focused on different aspects of nationalism: ideology, political movement, popular sentiment. They have linked these to different features of modernity: industrialism, capitalism, state, popular politics, mass communications, mass culture.

The key disagreements concern how nationalism relates to nation-state and nation, especially nation. Is nationalism a distinctively modern expression of a longer-enduring nation or the principal creator of national identity, or are they two separate concepts only contingently related? What role does nationalism play in nation-state formation? Is it more a way of legitimating and rationalizing nation-state formation than an essential contribution to it? Is the nation-state itself the major force promoting nationalism and turning national identity into mass sentiment? These are a rich set of questions which have enabled nationalism studies to flourish for some two decades.

Intellectual fields are not so much discredited as exhausted or abandoned.[26] There has been waning interest in such questions as "when was the nation?" and "how has nationalism shaped ideas of nation?" and "what role has nationalism played in the formation of nation-states?"—questions which constituted the field of nationalism studies. Instead, other questions arise such as "will globalization undermine the nation-state?" and "can we equate nationalism with populism—both left-wing and right-wing?" and "is multiculturalism a form of nationalism?" Such questions reflect new problems. The interest in globalization as something which threatens or at least reshapes national identity and nationalism has stimulated efforts to move away from the national framework which hitherto underpinned even comparative research. However, these new questions have not yet been organized within an intellectual field but tend to be raised as discrete issues. Could Max Weber help us organize current questions about nationalism, nation, and nation-state more effectively?

WEBER AND GERMANY

Max Weber hardly knew any Germany other than the Second Empire. He was imbued with sentiments of pride in the new nation-state from his childhood. However, along with pride in German power and high culture went a harsh critique of German political culture. Weber regarded this as a poisonous legacy bequeathed by Bismarck and the Junker class from which Bismarck sprang. It had produced a deferential middle class unfit to transform Germany so as to enable it to meet the challenges of the modern world.

Weber's critique took the new nation-state as given, both as fact and as norm. As fact, the major European states, along with the United States and latterly Japan, were nation-states and the most important "power containers" in the world. As norm, these nation-states, by virtue of their power, had the obligation to defend and promote national and "civilized" (occidental, Western) values. On that cultural basis they could legitimately claim the loyalty of their citizens.

However, this was a recent state of affairs, with those few powerful nation-states both competing and cooperating while subjecting the rest of the world to their power and culture. It also turned out to be a short-lived, violent, and disruptive condition, especially for Germany, the only one of these states with no significant imperial hinterland.[27] Weber's own experiences of and thinking about nation, nationalism, and nation-state were shaped by this condition.

WEBER THE NATIONALIST

Weber's nationalism as well as his scientific interest in national questions became clear in his involvement in a research project concerning agrarian problems in East Elbian Germany, especially his inaugural lecture in May 1895 as professor of national economy at Freiburg University.[28] Briefly, Weber claimed that ethnic German workers and small farmers were culturally distinct from ethnic Poles, placing a higher value on freedom, and that this helped explain their higher rate of outmigration even when they had a higher standard of living. Weber went on to advocate state measures to combat this undermining of Germandom, extended his arguments to the need for Germany to assert itself in the wider world, and asserted that it was the proper task of the discipline of national economics to promote the national interest.[29]

Following his nervous breakdown and retirement from academic employment, Weber published little as a nationalist until after the outbreak of the First World War.[30] In those later writings Weber insisted on a sharp separation of science and politics. This even shaped his prose style. Weber's academic writing continued to be tortuous and unclear, almost as if his language had to reflect the immense complexity of what he was trying to understand. By contrast his political writing was terse and energetic, informed by his aim to persuade readers. That in turn was linked to a further distinction between a political ethic of responsibility and one of conviction. Applying this distinction, Weber was increasingly disgusted at political irresponsibility. He was somewhat tolerant of socialists and anarchists, partly because they were practicing the ethic of conviction and partly because they lacked power. He reserved his fiercest vituperation for the irresponsibility of right-wing nationalists who advocated policies which would lead Germany into defeat and disaster. This included politicians, such as those who founded the Fatherland Party, and intellectuals for whom Weber reserved the term *Literaten*, meaning dilettantes who lacked political skill or experience. (One could say the same about Weber, although he had been raised in a political household.)

There are many examples of Weber the responsible nationalist, indeed claiming his own views to be "national" and reserving the word "nationalist" for those he regarded as irresponsible.[31] These include opposing the decision to commence unrestricted submarine warfare not on moral grounds but because it would bring the United States into the war against Germany with devastating consequences. He opposed annexationist aims as making it more difficult to come to terms with the Western Allies and threatening the essence of a nation-state. After the war Weber advocated parliamentary democracy and a powerful elected president not as a liberal democrat but as ways to produce strong government able to pursue national recovery after defeat.[32]

These clear, energetic, definite nationalist writings implied that one could have clear knowledge of what "nation" and "national interest" meant. However, in turning to Weber's academic writing on the concept of the nation, one gains a very different impression.

WEBER'S SCIENTIFIC
TREATMENT OF NATION

Around 1910 Weber turned to scientific writing about nation and allied concepts such as ethnic community. Some of these manuscripts were incorporated by Marianne Weber into the posthumous edition of *Economy and Society* (1922) and constitute Weber's best-known pronouncements on the subject. These are closely related to contributions Weber made to the first two meetings of the DGS in 1910 and 1912. Other participants presented papers on the themes of nation, race, and ethnic community. Weber had pressed for such subjects to be discussed at the 1912 meeting.[33]

From these sources one can see what Weber considered *not* to be appropriate for the concept of nation. Biological concepts of race were rejected as having no sociological meaning. Nation could not be equated with practices like language, religion, ethnicity, or state membership. This was because national identity could and did draw upon any or all such practices and because common or similar actions/sentiments alone do not suffice to constitute social practices. It is the meanings individuals attribute to such practices and how they orient themselves to one other in performing those practices which matter. Thus, in his writing on ethnic community, Weber defined this as *belief in common ethnic origins*. It was that belief and how it informed social action which mattered. Weber speculated that such beliefs originated with conquest and assimilation—events predating reliable historical records—and had nothing to do with "objective" ethnic lineage.[34]

These negative arguments led Weber to a positive one. The nation must be understood as the attribution of national meaning to certain kinds of communal relations. Such attribution varied in character, strength, extent, and duration within any given population. In his 1895 lecture Weber claimed that Germans lacked the "everyday" sense of nationality of the English because they lacked the experience of and instinct for power of the English.[35] Only a crisis like war could induce the social meanings among Germans which would contribute to a sense of national community.

Those national meanings varied across social strata. They were strongest and most enduring among national power elites and to a national intelligentsia, to whom fell the task of cultivating national values.[36] Weber thought the sense of national community diminished as one descended the social scale. He referred to national feeling as being able occasionally to penetrate petty bourgeois strata, implying that such groups usually did not consider themselves to be members of the nation and that German workers were indifferent or hostile. Weber was concerned about how workers could be brought into the nation.[37] He thought the crisis of war had achieved this, especially through mass conscription which radically expanded, transformed, and intensified the sense of national community.

Yet throughout these scattered observations in correspondence, reported conversations, and talks it is the tentative, vague, changeable nature of national community which is most striking. Nation is *feeling*. In one passage Weber suggested that ethnic community was an intangible idea which *evaporates* as one approaches it.[38] The nation is real and vague, unlike an ideal type which is ideal and clear. Given that Weber considered ideal types as essential for scientific analysis, his concept of nation was not fit for purpose.

The only definite way forward was his argument that what gives national feeling substance and focus—in short, social meaning—is its orientation to the state. Apart from that we are left with little more than a wide range of volatile feelings. Weber implicitly rejects alternative arguments which understand nation in terms of social practices independent of orientation to the state. At the 1912 DGS meeting there was reference to the ideas of the Austro-German socialist Otto Bauer. Bauer, along with his comrade Karl Renner, had constructed a theory of nation as a "community of fate," building on the idea of a common language enabling a shared national culture which penetrates into lower social strata with growing literacy and cultural participation.[39] These ideas influenced later theorists including Karl Deutsch, Hans Kohn, Ernest Gellner, and Benedict Anderson. Yet the only reference in Weber's writings to Bauer is about a completely different matter. Weber was "shy" about acknowledging intellectual debts and destroyed most of his notes and prepublication drafts. However, Weber does not merely fail to cite Bauer but does not engage with Bauer's ideas except in the form of a blunt negative: shared language or culture is not the basis of national community. Weber almost certainly knew of Bauer's arguments—he echoes Bauer's language in using the term "pathos" and the phrase "community of fate (*Schicksalsgemeinschaft*)"[40] when writing about ethnic community—but that is all.

Thus, we are left with the concept of nation as a community based on shared feelings of national belonging. These feelings cannot be connected to specific social practices and vary in strength, character, duration, extent, and social penetration. The principal agents cultivating such national feelings are intellectuals. Such feelings only acquire social significance when oriented toward the nation-state, something primarily enabled by its political and intellectual elites.

A Weberian Analysis of the Concept of Nation: Weber's Connecting of Nation to Nationalism

What are the major problems with Weber's ideas about the concept of nation? How can Weber's fundamental sociological concepts be used to address these problems?

Weber's scientific arguments outlined various routes to and expressions of national community understood as feeling. He contracted this variety by arguing that such feelings only acquire social meaning when oriented to the state, especially the powerful nation-state. His political arguments then presented his own nationalism as the best expression of national values and interests, criticizing others for political irresponsibility. Each connection is an arbitrary jump.

Occasionally Weber went further. His account of non-Russian national sentiment in the 1905 revolution and his concern to harness Polish nationalism during the First World War acknowledged that a coherent sense of national identity can form among individuals who have no nation-state to which to orient themselves. He also recognized in cases such as Belgium that a sense of national community can be oriented to the small nation-state.

However, when moving beyond nation as feeling Weber confined himself to the concept of nation as oriented to the powerful nation-state, above all Germany. This orientation can be called "nationalism," although Weber rarely used that word. So the connections were nation as feeling means nationalism as orientation of this feeling toward the powerful nation-state, which means responsible nationalism versus irresponsible nationalism.

By contrast, modernist views of nationalism treat it not as an expression of widespread feelings of national community but as the making of claims which are justified on the grounds of being such an expression. "Nation" is a necessary term deployed in nationalist discourse, not an independent variable shaping that discourse. Furthermore, it is nationalism as political ideology and movement which orients nation to state, not a shared sense of national identity.

WEBER'S JOURNEY TO SOCIOLOGY

Weber's writing on nation as community is brief and fragmentary compared to writings on other kinds of community such as family, market, and even ethnic community.[41] Furthermore, it does not relate its sketchy assertions to Weber's basic concepts, especially those concerned with community formation (*Vergemeinschaftung*). One reason might be that his writing about the concept of nation precedes his major 1913 and 1920 texts on sociological concepts.

There was no established discipline of sociology in Weber's academic world. Weber studied law and economics, held professorships in national economics and social sciences more generally, and co-edited a journal on social science and social policy. By 1909 Weber was moving toward self-definition as a sociologist (though disliking the word), as evidenced by his role in founding and managing the DGS. However, he was distancing himself from the DGS by 1912. Still, this was when he engaged systematically with what he considered should be the basic concepts for this discipline. The main outcomes were *Categories* in 1913 and *Basic Concepts* in 1920, the texts on which I focus.[42]

In these writings one can trace links to two close colleagues: Ferdinand Tönnies and Georg Simmel. In 1887 Tönnies published *Gemeinschaft und Gesellschaft*. Weber treated as basic the distinction between *Gemeinschaft* (community) and *Gesellschaft* (society) as ways of conceptualizing two different socialization processes and types of social relationship. However, Weber rejected the way Tönnies used these concepts, namely to characterize two *types of society*. Even if "type" meant ideal type, and not some real "thing" in the world, the notion of "type of society" was not one Weber considered usable.

This was because Weber rejected the holist notion of "society" along with the entire nineteenth-century intellectual tradition seeking to establish a "science of society." Simmel had outlined an alternative approach in the 1890s. Humans were social animals, but that entailed the concept of "socialization," not of "society." Simmel went on to make "exchange" the fundamental concept of formal sociology, using this to analyze many social relationships, from flirtation to money, with a particular interest in how socialization processes were formative of different kinds of individuals.

This was not Weber's principal concern. Weber insisted that the irreducible and *sole* unit for the social sciences was the individual human being. This was a methodological insistence; the individual was the formal unit necessary for sociology, not a "real" or "unique" individual. It was the necessary formal unit because sociology could not use either supraindividual concepts like society or subindividual concepts like organism.[43]

This approach made Weber careful to define social relationships in terms of the expectations that individuals held about how other individuals would respond to their actions. Social relationships existed to the extent of the probability that those expectations were realized. Thus, Weber once defined law as the expectations individuals held about the decisions courts would make. Weber deployed the notion of socialization in conjunction with the distinction between community and society. Instead of "community" and "society" as types of society, Weber focused on "communal socialization" (*Vergemeinschaftung*) and "societal socialization" (*Vergesellschaftung*) as different kinds of social exchanges. However, it is confusing that he developed these ideas in different ways in *Categories* and *Basic Concepts*.[44]

To complicate matters further, most of what was published as Part Two of *Wirtschaft und Gesellschaft* after Weber's death was a set of manuscripts he had written before *Basic Concepts*, which itself was published as a section of Part One of that work. There has been some debate as to how far his detailed application of his sociological concepts in Part Two was shaped by the thinking which led to *Categories* rather than *Basic Concepts*. I will not explore these questions as I lack the necessary expertise and consider that the inadequacy of Weber's writing on the concept of nation does not merit such exploration. Instead, I focus on the problems and opportunities which ideas worked out in these two texts present to someone today trying to understand the concept of nation.[45]

In *Categories* Weber makes the community/society distinction in terms of the source of those expectations individuals hold about the response of others to their actions. The communal source is other individuals. The societal source is what Weber calls "instituted or social orders."[46] Examples of communal socialization are household and family. One learns to play social roles in relation to particular individuals such as mother, father, and siblings. The state provides many orders of societal socialization. For example, the legal codes of the state specify how individuals should behave toward one another, along with sanctions if these expectations are not fulfilled.

Weber, as was his wont, complicated the distinction. He realized that market exchanges involve impersonal relationships which appear to follow rules (e.g., recognition by third parties of property rights and acceptance of money as a medium of exchange) but do not necessarily exist as a prior social order. He wrote of tacit agreements or consensus. He stressed the fluidity between mass similar action which is not social (e.g., a panic stampede in a burning building), implicit consensual action, communal action, and societal action. He insisted that we cannot directly read off motives from social behavior but rather should analyze such behavior "as if" certain motives were at work.

Such complications may account for changes Weber introduced in *Basic Concepts*. Here, Weber linked the two modes of socialization to his four categories of action which he had outlined earlier in this text. Proceeding in this way, Weber did not need to distinguish between whether expectations have their source in particular individuals or a social order but could focus on the categories of action involved. These categories were affect (or emotion), tradition, instrumental rationality, and substantive rationality.

Communal relations engaged the categories of affect and tradition and societal relations, those of instrumental and substantive rationality. What this shares with his distinctions in *Categories* is the implication that societal relationships come late in historical development, are central to modernity and the process of rationalization which Weber identified as the hallmark of modernization, and enable large-scale social relationships.

Having surveyed Weber's basic concepts, one can see why the concept of nation posed a problem. The nation is a large-scale group which becomes central in modern times and acquires definition and focus in its orientation to the powerful nation-state, itself understood either as a social order (*Categories*) or as a set of relationships in which instrumental and substantive rationality are the central categories of action (*Basic Concepts*). Yet Weber writes about nation in communal terms. However, relations between "particular" individuals can hardly transpose to a large group, nor the category of tradition transpose to social relationships oriented to the modern state. This leaves Weber with little option but to reduce the communal character of nation to affect, with all the consequent vagueness and volatility.

Modern nationalism studies has a similar problem. "Nation" denotes large-scale social relations comprehending millions, even billions, of strangers; but it is described in a language more appropriate to friendships or families, tribes or villages. Such a language is suggestive, a matter of analogies, metaphors, images—hardly the language of social science.

Furthermore, affect does not intrinsically involve social meaning. People act out of love or anger or envy, but unless these emotions are given social definition, we cannot frame this in terms of expectations individuals have of how others will respond to their actions. Even if people act simultaneously in similar ways on the basis of similar emotions, Weber had insisted that mass similar action did not itself have social meaning.

We might associate a social relationship, such as a feud or revenge killing, with anger; but we cannot define feuds and revenge killings in terms of anger. As sociologists we must start with the feud or revenge killing. Typically, certain social relationships can then be associated with certain emotions, such as feud with anger.

The question then is how to retain the insight that nation only exists as a significant social form under conditions of modernity and involves large-scale social interactions, when these are framed not in terms of substantive and instrumental rationality but as affect and tradition, concepts which are inadequate for understanding modern, large-scale societal relationships?

Sketch of a Weberian
Theory of Nation

I will outline one possible way to answer this question using Weber's basic sociological concepts. I start with Weber's observation that societal socialization can set in train communal socialization.[47] He gives the example of a formal association such as a bowling club. Weber notes that such associations have what later sociologists call "latent functions,"[48] for example, signaling credit-worthy economic status or establishing one's social and cultural capital.

Weber further noted that such associations are products of a social order, in which ends are clearly specified (substantive rationality) and the means of achieving those ends set out as rules for members (instrumental rationality). Over time, as people come to know each other personally, they invest those formal roles with affect and routines (traditions?), thereby creating expectations of action extending well beyond those specified by the association's rationality. Might national communities arise in a similar way?

The obvious objection is that a small-scale association easily permits this transition to communal relations. In scale it is more like a family, household, or village community than a territorial state bureaucracy or extensive market exchanges.

There are ways of countering this objection. One is that large-scale modern rational institutions are composed of smaller-scale relationships. A modern army, for example, is organized around progressively smaller units. Military sociologists have stressed the importance of the army platoon for promoting precisely those emotional bonds which elicit solidarity and mutual sacrifice, perhaps greater than any commitment to the "official" cause for which the army is fighting. Indeed, this is a key reason why military leaders organize armies in such a way and develop a particular "socialization" process ("basic training") for new recruits.

Edward Shils applied the notion of primordial identity to such small groups. By this he did not mean identity as something enduring with deep historical roots, which is how those arguing for the key role of national identity frequently present it. Instead, it was the emotional context of identity that mattered; it felt to those it embraced to be something *given*, not *chosen*. Yet such identity might be brief, a set of relationships lasting no longer than a single campaign.[49]

We can extend this line of reasoning. We can build on Weber's insight that nation is a community feeling that acquires definition and focus in its orientation to the state. However, the modern state is a complex of institutions, and one must expect a plurality of orientations.

Take Weber's own Germany. As a newly formed state overarching existing states, it had a multitude of federal and imperial state institutions, such as parliaments and bureaucracies. Over the lifetime of the Second Empire its population was transformed from predominantly rural and agricultural to urban and industrial. Consequently, the imperial state and its federal units touched upon the lives of an increasing number of subjects in many different ways. Children were compelled to attend elementary school. Welfare measures bound people into networks concerned with such matters as income supplements, health provision, and workplace accidents. The state intruded into everyone's lives through its fiscal and military exactions. Regulations ("social orders") such as contract and employment law, health and safety measures, and tariffs created networks of interest groups ("orientations to the state").

As the franchise for elections to the national lower house of parliament—the *Reichstag*—was that of universal manhood suffrage based on direct and secret elections on a constituency basis, and historians generally agree that the state effectively sanctioned electoral fraud, *and, more to the point, was believed to do so by many* voters, so electoral participation increased. (The "rationality" involved can be discerned by noting that electoral participation for elections to the Prussian lower house, which had a deeply undemocratic franchise, lagged far behind that for the *Reichstag*.) Voters could "orientate" themselves toward the state through the medium of professionally led and mass-based political parties.[50] The moves toward universal literacy—a combined product of universal elementary education, urbanization, and industrialization—meant that these many interests—economic, political, cultural—were articulated in print and other media. Thus, "orientation to the state" covered many social relationships, framed as much in terms of conflict and opposition as consensus and support.

We can relate this to Weber's own socialization as member of the nation and nationalist. Try a thought experiment in which Weber was born in 1844, not 1864. He would not have grown up with a father who was a leading figure in the National Liberal Party. He would not have been schooled in the achievements of national unification. As a child he would not have witnessed parades and other events symbolizing this achievement.[51] He would probably not have performed military service as effective universal conscription which included the sons of bourgeois families only came into effect in Prussia in the early 1860s. Given the absence of all these institutions, networks, and socialization processes, it seems unlikely that this imaginary Max Weber would have felt the same kind of Germanness that the real Max Weber did. This is not to deny that national feeling and nationalism existed before unification, but it took different forms and cannot be understood as "orientation to the powerful nation-state."[52]

Some orientations to "social orders" extended beyond the state. Markets begin as impersonal and tacit relationships. They become rationalized and formalized through associations such as employer cartels and trade unions and the elaboration of contract and other law. They may acquire primordial identities through the way smaller subunits develop, rather like platoons in the army. For example, emotions aroused during a strike can generate forms of solidarity framed in local, occupational, and class terms. In such cases the state acts not as a direct pole of orientation but instead as the ultimate frame within which such collective actions operate. It is as much the increasingly defined territoriality of the Second Empire in relation to its subjects which matters as the state as the focus for political action.

There is another source of extensive social relationships which can take on a national quality but which Weber had treated dismissively: language. Let us leave aside that Weber framed his view of language within the behavioralist assumptions of his time, assumptions which have been discredited ever since Chomsky demolished the arguments of Skinner concerning language acquisition.[53]

One might still argue that languages continue to be highly diverse, differentiating into many dialects which inhibit any extended set of social relations, although large-scale modernization reduces such difference. However, this is not true of *written languages*. When Benedict Anderson wrote of the nation as an imagined community, he made "print capitalism" the key mechanism for enabling mass imagining. A mass print media requires mass literacy, and the foundation of that is the explicit formulation and standardization of rules and their sustained and disciplined teaching and learning. This surely is a social order of central importance in modern society. As Gellner argued, modern society might not deliver on promises of democracy, freedom, and rights; but it always delivers on that of mass literacy.

One may reasonably object that Anderson's concept of imagining, rather like Weber's of affect, does not in itself constitute social relationships; that even an imagined social relationship does not constitute socialization in terms of *action by individuals oriented to expectations about how other individuals will act in response*.

In a manner akin to Anderson, Weber writes of how the press can help shape "objective, supra-individual cultural values."[54] It is not clear if this is itself a social relationship or a non-social mass similarity. However, even if regarded as not yet a social relationship, such mass similar values provide the basis for a swift transition to such relationships and possible forms of collective action. The many different networks, state and non-state, which accompany modernity, as in the German Second Empire, provide many orientations which enable that transition.[55]

Not all of these orientations are national. Modernity enables many large-scale social imaginings and the transition to social relationships. One criticism of Anderson is the question of why national imagining should be privileged by mass print media. The latter could and did do the same for imaginings of class, religion, gender, race, ethnicity, and even humanity.

What explains, therefore, the way in which national identity seems to prevail as a political force over these other identities from Weber's time to our own? Gellner offered the most comprehensive sociological explanation by connecting the changed relationship between culture and identity in industrial societies to the role of the state in equating that culture with standardized written language. I cannot engage with this and related arguments here but suggest that such accounts must be complemented by others.

When Anderson writes of "imagining," Gellner of the transformed role of culture as identity in industrial society, and Weber of "orientation to the state," one problem is identifying the agency involved. All in their different ways focus on the "intellectual" or the "intelligentsia." This emphasis is also to the fore in Kedourie's account.

I suggest that one must introduce the distinct role of nationalism as political ideology and movement. The orientation of nation to state, or more generally to organized political action, involves a two-way interaction between leaders and followers. That in turn is framed by the various networks of nationally framed affiliations that modernity has created.

Weber himself understood this. In the "Objectivity" essay he wrote that

> the "state", to whose "interest" we are wont to relate such individual interests [Weber had earlier mentioned the "agricultural interest"]…is often nothing more than the cover address for an extremely complicated tangle of value ideas to which we relate "the state" in each individual case. [Weber then enumerates many such cases.][56]

This fits with Weber's refusal to define the state in terms of purpose or function but instead defines it in terms of how it works.[57] Nationalism represents one ideological attempt to project a central purpose upon the state.

To relate nation and nationalism to the various networks of the modern state, I find useful Dieter Langewiesche's concept of the nation as "resource community."[58] Within the national framework, networks can be focused on military capacity, tariff protection, welfare provision, and much else. This helps explain why "nationalism," understood as claims justified by the overriding priority of national values over others, can take on many different and conflicting forms. Often, the national identity claim is hidden through the focus on the particular values and interests involved. This in turn is obscured by the tendency to narrow the term "nationalist" to those who stress the identity claim and abstract it from these "entangling" interests and values.

For example, in France around 1900 Charles Maurras is regarded as a "nationalist" because his highly artificial framing of nation in terms of Catholicism, monarchy, and hierarchy abstracts from the increasingly secular, republican, and egalitarian habits of everyday behavior. By contrast, Jean Jaurès is defined as a socialist because he relates these habits to a particular ideal of social justice and solidarity. Yet Jaurès and his fellow socialists were as concerned to defend "France" as were members of *Action Française*. Furthermore, in terms of their capacity to mobilize mass support for that defense, they were far more important. In relation to the "nationalist" response to August 1914, which "nationalism" is the more significant?[59]

These variants on nationalism must be framed as political ideology and organized as political movement in order to make claims in the public sphere. Those claims will only command a following if they can connect to the various national networks we can call "resource communities." Weber stressed the importance of "worldviews" in shaping political values and actions, and we can see how this informed his own behavior as a nationalist. Ideology can be regarded as one kind of worldview, the primary function of which is not to engage emotion or to specify ends and means (though eventually it does these things) but to provide a cognitive map to enable large numbers of people to act together in a complex modern world. Having done that, they can go on to pursue certain ends, use certain means, and invest such action with certain emotions.

We can now see how, in Weberian terms, this leads to the formation of national communities which extend beyond affect. Modernity is associated with many extended networks which give rise to social expectations and images. Especially within the powerful nation-state many of these will be framed in national terms, not just because of the state as focus of loyalty but because the state provides many of the social orders such as the school teaching of literacy which engage national concerns. It also holds many of these together within a strong territorial frame.

However, it can—if more weakly—also shape national networks in multinational states and non-national settings. It is no accident that Bauer and Renner, who theorized nationality in terms of language and culture and distinguished this from state membership, were citizens of the Habsburg Empire. This, more than any other multiethnic empire before 1914, modernized and carved out institutional frameworks within which nationally oriented networks were formed, such as by instituting language censuses and recognizing various nationality rights.[60]

At the same time, the small units of which such networks were composed and the passions aroused by conflicts within such networks enabled the framing of these social relationships in an emotional language based on notions of primordial identity. One area where more historical research is needed is to look at the chains of relationships which can take one from such small units as the village community or the factory branch of a trade union up to the level of the nation-state.[61] Another is the ways in which particular cultural traditions focusing on national community are formed and diffused both within and across different state societies in nineteenth-century Europe.[62]

Finally, when the nation-state itself is apparently threatened existentially (which itself must be framed in terms of social beliefs and expectations in part managed by governments and nationalist elites), the primordial identity claim at the heart of nationalist ideology trumps the claims of the different and divided networks which had hitherto masked their national orientation through attention to specific interests and values.

CONCLUSION

Weber was a strong German nationalist with a vigorous view of the national interest which he sought to develop in terms of the "ethic of responsibility." By contrast, in social science writing about the nation he never managed to develop an extensive and coherent account of the "nation" which could provide the ground toward which such a view might be oriented.

However, in *Categories* and *Basic Concepts* Weber developed intellectual instruments which can be used to develop a powerful theory of nation and nationalism. In that theory nationalist intellectuals like Weber are key agents in grafting "community" values and images upon the many large-scale social relationships and networks which are formed within the modernizing state, especially in powerful nation-states such as the German Second Empire.

Ironically, Weber's determination to pursue "value-free" science, to distinguish between politics and science as two separate vocations, may have led him to neglect the possibility that it is precisely the politics of nationalist intellectuals like himself that constitutes a key component of an adequate theory of the nation and nationalism.

Acknowledgment

My thanks to Dieter Langewiesche, Keith Tribe, and Sam Whimster for comments on drafts of this chapter.

Notes

1. Max Weber, *Wissenschaft als Beruf 1917/1919—Politik als Beruf 1919*, *Max Weber-Gesamtausgabe* (hereafter *MWG*) I/17, ed. W. J. Mommsen and W. Schluchter, with B. Morgenbrod (Tübingen, Germany: Mohr [Siebeck], 1992). From many English translations I suggest that in *The Essential Weber: A Reader*, ed. Sam Whimster (London: Routledge, 2004), 257–287.
2. Theodor Heuss, quoted in Wolfgang J. Mommsen, *Max Weber and German Politics, 1890–1920*, trans. Michael S. Steinberg (Chicago: University Chicago Press, 1984), 38.
3. Mommsen, ibid., is the seminal work which challenged the view of Weber the liberal democrat, though without falling into the opposite interpretation of him as an authoritarian elitist.
4. Fritz Ringer, *Max Weber: An Intellectual Biography* (Chicago: University Chicago Press, 2004); and Karl Palonen, *A Political Style of Thinking: Essays on Max Weber* (Colchester, UK: ECPR Press, 2017).
5. Jakob Lehne, "Max Weber and Nationalism—Chaos or Consistency?," *Max Weber Studies* 10, no. 2 (2010): 209–234.
6. Outstanding is Dieter Langewiesche, "Nation bei Max Weber: soziologische Kategorie und politisches Bekenntnis. Zum Verstummen des Soziologen als *homo politicus* vor seinem Wertgott," in *Max Weber 1864–1920: Politik—Theorie—Weggefährten*, ed. Detlev Lehnert (Cologne, Germany: Böhlau Verlag, 2016), 39–65.
7. There are exceptions, notably some essays in two collections by M. Rainer Lepsius, *Interessen, Ideen und Institutionen* (Opladen, Germany: Westdeutscher Verlag, 1990); *Demokratie in Deutschland: soziologisch-historische Konstellationsanalyse* (Göttingen, Germany: Vandenhoeck & Ruprecht, 1993); and Langewiesche, "Nation."

8. See the book-length entry "Volk, Nation, Nationalismus, Masse" in *Geschichtliche Grundbegriffe: Historisches Lexikon zur politisch-sozialen Sprache in Deutschland*, ed. Otto Brunner, et al. (Stuttgart, Germany: Klett-Cotta, 1972); and Aïra Kemilainen, *"Nationalism": Problems Concerning the Word, the Concept and Classification* (Yvaskyla, Finland: Kustantajat Publishers, 1964).

9. Hugh Seton-Watson, *Nations and States: An Inquiry into the Origins of Nations and the Politics of Nationalism* (London: Methuen, 1977).

10. This dual idea is central in different ways in Benedict Anderson, *Imagined Communities: Reflections on the Origins and Spread of Nationalism*, 2nd ed. (London: Verso, 1991) (nationalism as "pirated"); Elie Kedourie, *Nationalism* (New York: Praeger, 1960) (intellectual imitation); Ernest Gellner, *Nations and Nationalism*, 2nd ed. (London: Blackwell, 2006) (resentful periphery intellectuals).

11. The Declaration of Independence of 1776 refers to the "People of these Colonies." The 1789 French Declaration of the Rights of Man and Citizen asserted that sovereignty resided in the "Nation."

12. Andreas Wimmer, *Waves of War: Nationalism, State Formation, and Ethnic Exclusion in the Modern World* (Cambridge: Cambridge University Press, 2013).

13. See John Breuilly, "Nationalism, Self-Determination and International Relations," in *The Globalization of World Politics: An Introduction to International Relations*, ed. John Bayliss, et al. (Oxford: Oxford University Press, 2017), 434–449, 437.

14. I am indebted to the arguments in a forthcoming book by James Kennedy and Liliana Riga on US diplomacy in Europe following the world wars and the collapse of Yugoslavia.

15. Daniel Chernilo, "Methodological Nationalism and Its Critics," in *The Sage Handbook of Nations and Nationalism*, ed. Gerard Delanty and Krishan Kumar (London: Sage, 2006), 126–140.

16. See my chapter on unification nationalism and that by Cemil Aydin on pan-nationalism in John Breuilly, ed., *The Oxford Handbook of the History of Nationalism* (Oxford: Oxford University Press, 2013).

17. Robert Michels, "Die historische Entwicklung des Vaterlandgedankens," in *Verhandlungen des Zweiten Deutschen Soziologentages vom 20.-22. Oktober 1912 in Berlin* (Tübingen, Germany: Mohr [Siebeck], 1913), 140–184.

18. The record of Weber's own comments on papers delivered at this meeting does not include any discussion of the paper from Michels, although he does engage with other papers on related subjects. See Max Weber, *Verstehende Soziologie und Werturteilsfreiheit. Schriften und Reden 1908–1917, MWG I/12*, ed. Johannes Weiß, with Sabine Frommer (Tübingen, Germany: Mohr [Siebeck], 2018), 319–328.

19. See John Breuilly, "Modernism and Writing the History of Nationalism," in *Writing the History of Nationalism*, ed. Stefan Berger and Eric Storm (London: Bloomsbury Academic, forthcoming).

20. Kedourie, *Nationalism*.

21. For an analysis of Kedourie's argument, see John Breuilly, "Nationalism and the History of Ideas," *Proceedings of the British Academy* 105 (2000): 187–223.

22. Ernest Gellner, *Thought and Change* (London: Weidenfeld & Nicolson, 1964).

23. The second edition (2006) has a long introduction by myself outlining and critiquing Gellner's arguments.

24. (London: Verso 1983).

25. John Breuilly et al., "Benedict Anderson's Imagined Communities: A Symposium," *Nations and Nationalism* 22, no. 4 (2016): 625–659.

26. Thomas Kuhn's notion of "paradigm shift" applies more to natural science fields such as physics and biology than to the humanities and social sciences.

27. France and Britain had extensive non-European empires, Russia a massive non-Russian empire within Europe, the United States its own continental hinterland, and Japan an initial imperial expansion following military victories over China and Russia.

28. Max Weber, "Der Nationalstaat und die Volkswirtschaftspolitik," in *Landarbeiterfrage, Nationalstaat und Volkswirtschaftspolitik. Schriften und Reden 1892–1899, MWG* I/4, ed. W. J. Mommsen, with R. Aldenhoff (Tübingen, Germany: Mohr [Siebeck], 1993), 535–574; trans. Ben Fowkes, in *Economy and Society* 9 (1980): 428–449.

29. There is much more to say about Weber's writings and actions as a nationalist in the late 1890s, but I leave that for another occasion as my focus here is on Weber's scientific writings and concepts.

30. I omit his writing on the Russian Revolution of 1905, for which see Lehne, "Weber and Nationalism." Although Weber addressed national questions here, notably autonomy for non-Russian nationalities in the Romanov Empire and the prospect for liberal nationalism in Russia, arguably he did so as a nationalist because non-Russian autonomy and liberalization would reduce the threat Russia posed to Germany.

31. See *Weber: Political Writings*, trans. and ed. Peter Lassman and Ronald Speirs (Cambridge: Cambridge University Press, 1994).

32. Again, my comments on Weber the nationalist are necessarily brief and assertive.

33. My thanks to Jakob Lehne for providing me with a copy of the record of the 1912 DGS meeting. For Weber's suggestions, see letter of March 4, 1912, to Michels and one written after March 21, 1912, to the DGS Vorstand: in Max Weber, *Briefe 1911–1912, MWG* II/7, ed. M. R. Lepsius and W. J. Mommsen, with B. Rudhard and M. Schön (Tübingen, Germany: Mohr [Siebeck], 1998), 448–449, 483–484.

34. His comments on ethnic communities are published in Max Weber, *Wirtschaft und Gesellschaft. Nachlaß. Gemeinschaften, MWG* I/22-1, ed. W. J. Mommsen, with M. Meyer (Tübingen, Germany: Mohr [Siebeck], 2001), 162–190, and on ethnicity as belief translated in *The Essential Weber*, 50–55. Weber anticipated recent historical work on "ethnogenesis" and ethnic lineages as nation-building myths. Of course, Weber did not have DNA evidence which modern researchers can also use.

35. Weber, "Nationalstaat," *MWG* I/4, 571; trans. Fowkes, 446.

36. It is not clear whether Weber regarded this as something intellectuals *should* do or as a social function integral to the very constitution of a national community, that is, a sociological claim. Many intellectuals not only did not cultivate national values but actively opposed other values to nationalism.

37. On his concerns about integrating workers and turning the Socialist Party into a reformist one, see John Breuilly, "Eduard Bernstein and Max Weber," in *Max Weber and His Contemporaries*, ed. Wolfgang J. Mommsen and Jürgen Osterhammel (London: Allen & Unwin, 1987), 345–354.

38. Weber, "Ethnische Gemeinschaften," *MWG* I/22-1, 185. Quoted in Langewiesche, "Nation," 47.

39. Bauer published his major work on the subject in 1907. For an English translation of the second edition of 1924, see Otto Bauer, *A Question of Nationalities and Social Democracy* (Minneapolis and London: University of Minnesota Press, 2000).

40. Weber, "Ethnische Gemeinschaften," *MWG* I/22-1, 190; "eine spezifische Art von Pathos, welches sich in einer durch Sprach-, Konfessions-, Sitten- oder Schicksalsgemeinschaft verbundenen Menschengruppe...verbindet" ("a specific kind of pathos which binds people together in groups through a community of language, religion, custom or fate").

41. In the most cited passage in *MWG*, even the title "Power, Prestige and National Feeling" is an editorial decision, replacing others used by Marianne Weber, other earlier German editors, and the English edition by Roth and Wittich. The section breaks off abruptly (*MWG* I/22-1, 247). Internal evidence points to this being composed around 1910. For a translation see *The Essential Weber*, 146–149.

42. These are the short titles I will use for "On Some Categories of Interpretive Sociology" (1913) and "Basic Sociological Concepts" (1920). "Categories" is yet to be published in *MWG* I/12, 383–440, but there is a good English translation in *Max Weber: Collected Methodological Writings* (*CMW*), ed. Hans Henrik Bruun and Sam Whimster (London: Routledge, 2012), 273–301. *Basic Concepts* is in Part One of *Economy and Society*, *Wirtschaft und Gesellschaft. Soziologie*, *MWG* I/23, ed. K. Borchardt, E. Hanke, and W. Schluchter (Tübingen, Germany: Mohr [Siebeck], 2013), 147–215. For an English translation of the relevant section, see *The Essential Weber*, 311–358.

43. Sam Whimster has suggested that "methodological nominalism" is less likely to cause confusion than "individualism." Keith Tribe argues that the basic concepts of Weber are those such as *Verband, Herrschaft, Legitimation, Stab*, and *Verwaltung*; but I regard these as a subset of all the possible frames within which people are socialized.

44. In what follows I am deeply indebted to Klaus Lichtblau, "Vergemeinschaftung und Vergesellschaftung in Max Weber: A Reconstruction of His Linguistic Usage," *History of European Ideas* 37 (2011): 454–465.

45. I am grateful to Keith Tribe for showing me the introduction to be published with his new translation of Part One of *Economy and Society*.

46. Weber, "Categories," *MWG* I/12, 408 ("gesatzte Ordnung"); cf. *CMW*, 282–283, esp. translator's explication, 491.

47. I draw on Weber's sketches of two possible sociological research projects—on journalism and associations—in a paper given to the 1910 DGS. For the German original, see Max Weber, "Geschäftsbericht" (1910), in *Hochschulwesen und Wissenschaftspolitik. Schriften und Reden 1895–1920*, *MWG* I/13, ed. M. R. Lepsius and W. Schluchter, with H.-M. Lauterer and A. Munding (Tübingen, Germany: Mohr [Siebeck], 2016), 256–286. For an English version see Christopher Adair-Toteff, *Sociological Beginnings: The First Conference of the German Society for Sociology* (Liverpool, UK: Liverpool University Press, 2005).

48. I believe the term was coined by Robert Merton. It has subsequently become a standard concept, contrasted with that of "manifest function."

49. See various essays in Shils, *Center and Periphery: Essays in Macrosociology* (Chicago: University of Chicago Press, 1975), especially Part IV: "Expansion and Dependence of the Center: Privacy and Primary Groups." The introduction to this book is illuminating about both the influence of Weber on Shils and his "central question" concerning how modern individuals come to conceive of themselves as living in "a society" which they call a "nation."

50. A subject Weber analyses acutely in "Politics as a Vocation."

51. For the parades he *did* see, Sam Whimster, "Weber in the World of Empire," in *Max Weber in der Welt: Rezeption und Wirkung*, ed. Michael Kaiser and Harald Rosenbach (Tübingen, Germany: Mohr Siebeck, 2014), 65–79, 71–72. Whimster also notes the celebration of Sedan Day in Weber's school.

52. For a recent study addressing change of this kind, see Jasper Heinzen, *Making Prussians, Raising Germans: A Cultural History of Prussian State-Building After Civil War, 1866–1935* (Cambridge: Cambridge University Press, 2017).

53. Keith Tribe has pointed out to me that there are problems with Chomsky's approach. My key point is the negative one: the demolition of behavioralist theories of language acquisition.

54. Adair-Torteff, *Sociological Beginnings*, 84.

55. Keith Tribe commented that the approach I outline to the modernization of the German Second Empire is similar to that taken toward France in Eugen Weber's seminal book *Peasants into Frenchmen: The Modernisation of France* (Stanford, CA: Standford University Press, 1976). I agree: modernization is a general process with different patterns in various places. It would not be relevant to explore that here, but I have argued that Weber (Eugen, not Max!) laid too much stress on modernization as an elite-driven project and not as a set of general socialization processes. Breuilly, in *Writing the History of Nationalism* (forthcoming).

56. Weber, "The 'Objectivity' of Knowledge in Social Science and Social Policy," in *CMW*, 136; *Zur Logik und Methodik der Sozialwissenschaften. Schriften 1900–1907, MWG* I/7, ed. G. Wagner, with C. Härpfer et al. (Tübingen, Germany: Mohr [Siebeck], 2018), 230.

57. For how Weber understood the state, for which he never produced an extended sociological theory, see Andreas Anter, *Max Weber's Theory of the Modern State: Origins, Structure and Significance* (Basingstoke, UK: Palgrave Macmillan, 2014).

58. Dieter Langewiesche, "The Nation as a Developing Resource Community: A Generalizing Comparison," in *Comparative and Transnational History. Central European Approaches and New Perspectives*, ed. H.-G. Haupt and J. Kocka (New York and Oxford: Oxford University Press, 2009), 133–148.

59. I elaborate this argument in John Breuilly, "What Does It Mean to Say That Nationalism Is Popular?," in *Nationhood from Below: Continental Europe in the Long Nineteenth Century*, ed. Maarten Van Ginderachter and Marnix Beyen (Basingstoke, UK: Palgrave Macmillan, 2012), 23–43.

60. I develop this argument comparatively in "Popular Nationalism, State Forms and Modernity in the Era of the First World War," in *Nations, Identities and the First World War: Shifting Loyalties to the Fatherland*, ed. Nico Wouters and Laurence van Ypersele (London: Bloomsbury, 2018), 97–114.

61. One study of peasant nationalism in Habsburg Galicia shows both how modernization creates a peasant "public sphere" which can intersect with elite nationalist ideology and how this was not available to Polish-speaking peasants in Prussian and Russian Polish regions up to 1914. Kelly Stauter-Halsted, *The Nation in the Village: The Genesis of Peasant National Identity in Austrian Poland 1848–1914* (Ithaca, NY: Cornell University Press, 2001).

62. For example, romanticism on which we now have the invaluable and massive *Encyclopaedia of Romantic Nationalism in Europe*, ed. Joep Leerssen, 2 vols. (Amsterdam: Amsterdam University Press, 2018).

CHAPTER 11

THE WEBERIAN CITY, CIVIL SOCIETY, AND TURKISH SOCIAL THOUGHT

LUTFI SUNAR

THE SOCIOLOGICAL FRAMEWORK: CITY AND CIVIL SOCIETY

THE origin and development of cities have always been issues central to sociology. This is because one of the primary factors that caused sociology to emerge as a discipline was the changing rate and pace of urbanization in conjunction with modernization. Therefore, issues related to modern urbanization have been of primary interest to sociology. As Anthony Giddens states, "'urban sociology' is more than just one branch of sociology among others—it stands at the heart of some of the most fundamental problems of general sociological interest."[1]

It is not only due to its larger size and population compared to the village that the city illustrates historical development. It is also because the social organization that the city requires is more complex, comprehensive, and differentiated. Above all, the city represents a social structure in which individuals depend on each other. This interdependence creates a unique type of interpersonal relationship and therefore a unique social structure. The distinction between "civil" (citizen) and "barbarian" (rural) has been a principal element of Western social and political analysis since ancient Greece. People living in the city, which was the center of law, religion, commerce, and craft production, were assigned attributes of civility, courtesy, and temperance and considered civilized. The Enlightenment especially enshrined this distinction as a peculiar characteristic of modern society.

There is a close link between the birth of sociology and the description of modern society among or against other societies in the world. In this regard, the city has been subjected to special attention in the developmental history of society because it is a primary indicator of the level of development of a social structure. Based on the belief that modern society is the most developed, complex, and advanced social formation, the history of cities has been interpreted and written in a manner to support this preconception. In modern social theory the nature of the city, citizenship, and civil society has then been juxtaposed to the problem of despotism.[2] According to the dominant view, as Western society developed, a commercial and educated middle stratum or bourgeoisie (Weber's *Bürgertum*) arose between the nobility, gentry, and higher clergy, on the one hand, and the lower classes of artisans, craftsmen, and peasants on the other. The existence of an urban middle class encouraged the growth of civil society and a political struggle over the rights of citizens and the nature of the state, affecting all social classes. The celebrated "rise of the middle class" represented the crucial step on the path to modernity.

If this pattern of development is typical of Western societies, then what of the East, the Orient? According to one prominent view, no such middle stratum existed in the Orient. Due to the absence of cities in the sense of autonomous urban communities having self-governing institutions and a distinctive legal–political status, societies in the East tended to be characterized by despotic forms of rule, repression of civil society, and an absence of "citizenship" in the Western sense. This difference could encourage the view that while "civilization" emerged in the West, other societies remained in this regard "uncivilized."[3]

In this chapter I consider Weber's reasoning and arguments concerning the occidental city, its definition and development. The social, political, and economic relations characteristic of the city are important for understanding the formation of modern civil society. Weber's views about the occidental city can then be contrasted with his less extensive and comparative comments on oriental cities. Finally, the Weberian interpretations regarding the city and civil society in Turkish social thought are critically examined.

THE OCCIDENTAL CITY: THE HISTORICAL DEVELOPMENT AND THE EMERGENCE OF CIVIL SOCIETY

The main subject of Weber's studies is the interpretation of the birth and future of modern society around the concept of rationalization. Weber associates the development of rationalism specifically with the simultaneous occurrence of the consequences of the urban revolution, to which we can add the Gregorian reform, and the feudal revolution. "Only the occident knows rational law," Weber claims, "and only in the occident is found the concept of citizen (*civis Romanus, citoyen, bourgeois*) because only in the occident again are there cities in the specific sense."[4] The political foundation of the *urban revolution* is formed by the emergence of citizenship-based medieval cities as commercial centers. *Gregorian reform* represents the independence of the church from secular rulers, and *feudal revolution* represents the division of power and establishment of contract-based rights. According to Weber,[5] there are also economic criteria: a city's economy should not depend on agriculture but on commerce and production for an extensive market. Thus, the urban city is contrasted to the agrarian countryside. Economically, Weber differentiates four types of cities: *consumer cities, agricultural cities, production cities, commercial cities.*[6]

Weber explains the development of cities in various studies. Most concisely, his ideas may be found in his study on the city, which was posthumously published as the last chapter[7] of his encyclopaedic masterpiece *Economy and Society*, under the title of "City: Non-Legitimate Domination."[8] The expression "non-legitimate" refers to what Weber sees as the basic characteristic of the occidental city since antiquity: the governed delegitimize the autocratic ruler of the city and replace his authority with a new authority they create themselves as they find new ways to come together.[9] A number of studies investigating Weber's ideas on the city have been written based on this work. Though the text of *Economy and Society* plays an important role in understanding his approach to the city, complementary and detailed information can be obtained through careful examination of other works, such as his study of the economic ethics of world religions in *The Religion of China, The Religion of India,* and *Ancient Judaism*; his lengthy essay on agrarian relations in antiquity, translated as *The Agrarian Sociology of Ancient Civilizations*; and his last lectures compiled from student notes as *General Economic History*. With publication of Weber's early university lectures, we also know that his interest in the economy and politics of the occidental city was a lifelong preoccupation.[10]

Weber sees the development of cities in the West as a step within the whole of the universal-historical development of humanity. According to him,[11] the development of cities, as it was later and more neatly theorized by Gordon Childe,[12] corresponds to a leap in the social organization of agricultural societies. Weber states that there are seven stages comprising the birth and rise of cities from ancient Greece to modernity.[13]

Weber attributes a central position to ancient Greek city states in the history of the development of cities. According to him, in antiquity "in the city states there always remained the possibility of accumulating and investing capital."[14] On the other hand, that was not the case for monarchies of the Near East, whose cities remained underdeveloped.[15] The establishment of city states (*poleis*) started a change in social relationships that reflected the characteristics of Greek civilization. Coastal city states began to participate in overseas trade. With the growth of shipping and Mediterranean commerce, Greek colonization also increased. In this regard, in ancient Greece at a very early stage, "the city was also given staple privileges and other laws regulating commerce were enacted, for the *polis* was not only a political but also an economic center—a market."[16]

In the classical epoch, military self-sufficiency and independence of the *polis* was the primary factor that made it possible to sustain other characteristics. Not having a central bureaucratic management system, each city state could develop its own military power, often based on the self-equipped hoplite army of free male citizens. Political relationships with other cities took the form not of a bureaucratically administered empire, as in the Near East, but a system of alliances or a loosely bounded confederation. The emergence of the hoplite *polis* paved the way for the democratic citizen *polis*, with the rights of citizens "no longer dependent on ownership of land," a radical break with previous institutions.[17] Having transcended the liturgical state with its dominating priesthood, the democratized and secular city state—a "purely secular civilization" in Weber's words—established the conditions for a kind of "capitalism" in Greek antiquity: that is, the city having a market economy, with profit-oriented economic action, and citizens using property as a commodity.[18] This pattern of the development of cities continued into the Hellenistic and Roman eras. But with the fall of the Roman Empire, the political and economic foundation that sustained cities disappeared in the West. In the Middle Ages, which were characterized by a politically inward orientation and detachment from the Mediterranean, the coastal cities of antiquity were replaced by castle-based inland cities and so-called ruralization, including the survival of self-sufficient latifundia. However, according to Weber, the developments conducive to the appearance of modern capitalism should be sought not in civilization's shift to the interior but rather in the emergent medieval cities themselves.[19] In this context, the fundamental differences between medieval and ancient cities arose from the differences regarding the power position and residential location of the aristocracy and princes. The development of the ancient city started as a "fortress kingdom," using Weber's term; but when kings were banished by the civic aristocracy, their base of authority in rural areas could threaten the independence of the city, a recurring pattern of conflict for the Italian city states. Beyond the city walls, medieval society and its political structure were characterized by feudal relations binding the peasantry to a hegemonic landholding rural aristocracy. With these relations in mind, medieval city developments should be characterized by the independence of civic citizens from these feudal and juridical authorities.[20] In Weber's concise formulation, "during all of the Early and High Middle Ages, towns had political space in which to develop their characteristic features, and in this period cities were not only centers of a money economy but also of administration, because of their official responsibilities. They were surrounded by the hierarchy of authorities based on feudal and service relationships, but in general their own citizens did not participate in these relationships."[21] In sum, for Weber the occidental city is the product of multiple and complex developments which can be characterized ideal typically by the pursuit of autonomy in social, economic, political, administrative, military, and juridical affairs.

Weber especially emphasizes the city's identity as a political community. The fact that the city became an autocephalic and autonomous structure with its own law is related to the development of an independent civic community. It had to gain its independence from the central authority that imposed its power and control on feudal lords, and it had to create a powerful economic structure that was able to surpass the dependence on the rural areas around the city. Weber's emphasis on the civic communities in medieval cities provides a powerful foundation for his thesis of the bourgeoisie's role in the development of modern capitalism. In German the terms "Bürger" and "Bürgertum" imply the civil status, the social standing, and (especially since Marx) the economic position of the middle class. In this regard, the bourgeoisie emerged from the organization of craftsmen, merchants, and traders. The guilds in cities played an important role in the creation of the core of the bourgeoisie. According to Weber, "As a rule, the fraternization of the citizenry was carried through by the fraternization of the guilds, just as the ancient *polis* in its innermost being rested upon the fraternization of military associations and sibs."[22] Independently from its legal form, the late medieval city depended on the fraternity of its productive citizens. Therefore, guilds and associations seized political power legally or even illegally, which is meant by the title "non-legitimate domination" of the "City" chapter.

Though this development based on the craft guilds and early industrial transformation was important, Weber essentially seeks the origins of the modern city not in the intra-continental industrial cities but in Italian cities that continued to flourish in the post-Roman ruralized economy. Thanks to benefitting from a revived Mediterranean trade, late medieval Italian cities were able to create impressive economic power. "It is in Italy, therefore," Weber adds, "that in spite of the ambiguity of many sources the sociological meaning of the burgher association can best be determined."[23] In this regard, *coniurationes* in Italy and confraternities in Germany played important roles in establishing the bourgeoisie's superiority in cities, seizing the authority and establishing a rule of law by declaring the autonomy of the city.

Weber's explanation of the occidental city establishes the basis for his bourgeois liberalism. According to this view, the medieval burgher was the fundamental actor for the emergence of the city in the West. "Even in the Middle Ages," Weber maintained, "the seeds of these phenomena were present in the Western World, and *only* there. It is only in the Western World that 'cities' and 'estates' (*rex et regnum*), 'bourgeois' and 'proletarians' have existed."[24] These burghers, who constituted the city community, demanded political rights, insisted on the active participation in political life that is shaped within the framework of contract theory, and created a specific form of democratic legitimacy which Weber briefly described as the fourth type of legitimate domination.[25] Through such civic engagement the authentic structure of the city and the essential features of "civil society" were formed.

The existence of civic communities, which Weber considered the fundamental condition of the city, has two consequences: political and military autonomy and the administration of the city's own law. The reason the development of the city was obstructed in Asia, while it flourished in Europe starting from Mediterranean civilization, is the development of *solidarity associations* and civic *communities*. In order to have political autonomy, it is important that citizens of the city come together as a society that shares common interests and is able to create an armed force to defend these interests when necessary. The presence of a citizen militia is also useful for cities to unite against the centralized royal or feudal forces. Within this framework, Weber places great importance on the way the army is formed. According to him, Western medieval soldiery depends on chivalry. In chivalry, the individual who takes on the military service provides his own equipment. This is an important indicator of the military *autonomy* of the individual. In the early cities this autonomy turned into an army fundamentally composed of citizens in the city.[26] In this manner the city was able to close its gates and fight for its interest when it was necessary and to build a political unity and social solidarity. Such considerations minimized the decisive control of princes, kings, and feudal lords over the city, thereby allowing the city to develop by itself and create its own social and political structure. Although "the medieval urban commune gained political independence and, in some cases, conducted an expansionist foreign policy, maintaining a permanent military force, concluding alliances, conducting long wars, holding large land areas and occasionally other cities in complete subjection and acquiring overseas colonies," these cities generally continued to exist as singular cities with a very small field effect.[27] In Italy, only Venice and Genoa succeeded in maintaining overseas colonies.

The emergence of an autonomous civic bourgeois community with a militia composed of citizens was an important factor in the emergence of the city in the West. This is because, according to Weber, the absence of a political authority intervening from the top helped to develop competition and a flourishing of economic and commercial life. Military and political autonomy played an important role in the creation of legal and political institutions within the city, as seen especially in Italian cities. Cities had their own councils, legal systems, and forms of adjudication that were administered by representatives chosen from among the bourgeoisie. There was an economic balance of power between the bourgeoisie and the political or manorial lord of the city, determined by the city's financial strength and the lord's need for money. This need made it possible for the city to gain its rights and to have the financial power to protect these rights.[28] Therefore, the city became a place where the bourgeoisie managed its own law and administration. This autonomy that became identified with the minimization of external powers' influence on the economic life of the city was demonstrated through taxation, construction of markets, and formation of monopolies. According to Weber, "The market was part of every medieval city, and the supervision over the market had everywhere in a considerable measure been taken out of the hands of the city lord by the council. In later periods, the regulation of trade and production was concentrated either in the hands of the municipal authorities or in those of the craft associations, depending upon the local power structure; the city lord continued to be largely excluded."[29]

Complementing this administrative autonomy, cities had the right and power to develop their own law. City councils were the basis for self-administration and autonomous lawmaking.[30] The city councils played a significant role in the rationalization and codification of law.[31] In the civic judicial systems we find the origins of legal institutions adaptable to capitalism.[32] Guaranteeing individual rights and the existence of legal institutions warranted and stabilized by rights supported the development of cities, helping them become gradually more influential and central to the socioeconomic order. According to Weber, the emergence of capitalism depended on the existence of established legal procedures and a standard judicial system whose outcomes would be predictable. Such a system was provided by the bourgeoisie, who created a juridical structure that could protect them against autocratic and arbitrary political authority.[33]

THE ORIENTAL CITY AND
ORIENTAL SOCIETIES

We have to go back to ancient history to understand the common roots but also the development of different types of cities and civil societies in occidental and oriental cultures. According to Weber, the urbanization experience in ancient Greece spread to the Near East with the expedition of Alexander, as can be seen by cities that Alexander established in various parts of the Near East. Hellenistic states emerged after Alexander encouraged urbanization "energetically" and became "agents of Hellenization."[34]

> Under the Roman Empire the *polis* continued its triumphant expansion throughout the ancient world. Just as the Macedonians brought the *polis* to the Far East with the founding of Alexandreschata on the borders of Turkestan, so the Romans reached the Far West with their unification of the Lusitanians; with their colonies and policies of urbanization they extended the sway of the *polis* throughout Britain, Gaul, Mauretania, and the lands bordering on the Rhine and Danube.[35]

However, according to Weber, the spread of cities through the political conquest of Alexander and the Roman Empire was not permanent, and Hellenistic cities in the Orient disappeared after the fall of the Roman Empire. In addition to ancient Greece, the Hebrew community constituted the origin of the West. According to Weber, the role of Judaism in the rationalization of religious doctrine made it one of the fundamental sources of disenchantment. Weber established similarities and connections between the ancient Jewish community and Hellenistic Greeks in order to link ancient Palestine to ancient Greece and Europe through the Phoenicians.[36] He conserves this perspective in his efforts to explain the origin of occidental cities. In *Ancient Judaism* Weber examined the relationship between geographical conditions and urbanization in detail.

Weber considered the civilized society of ancient Palestine as a form of ancient Mediterranean urbanism. Ruling families dwelled in a city surrounded by walls under the management of a sovereign oligarch, and as a result, a ruling class composed of prosperous civic families and city patriarchs emerged. Revenues from the middle class, commerce, taxes on caravan trading, and land rent established the basis for the formation of a civic population that was able to spare time for politics and warfare. Weber states, "While the early Israelite city at its height was an association of hereditary, charismatic sibs economically qualified to·bear arms, quite similar to the early Hellenic and early medieval city, the composition of this association was as unstable in Israel as in the West."[37] As is the case for Greece and the Roman Empire, this city's hegemony based on the monopoly of weapons led to a class struggle between the city patriarchs and villagers whose power decreased continuously. Weber argued that the social evils which prophets in sacred books had to struggle against were shaped by this tension. And this tension was one of the fundamental motives of rationalization in Judaism.

According to Weber, there was a parallelism between the rising sovereignty of cities and "oriental despotism". Weber argued that oriental despotism was not due to a powerful person (tyrant) but was instead a social phenomenon; therefore, there must have been a social basis maintaining this despotism. The conditions that gave rise to despotism and sustained it stemmed from the problem of the control of water and its usage in agriculture in large river valley civilizations, like the Yellow River (Hwang Ho), the Long River (Chang Jiang), the Ganges, the Euphrates, the Tigris, and the Nile. In all large river valley civilizations, barrages, dams, and canals had to be built to overcome these problems. This was only possible with the construction of a patrimonial system and a corresponding bureaucratic political structure. With the emergence of centralized bureaucratic domination, the feudal aristocracy was repressed and social activities became a part of state affairs. At this point, according to Weber, the Hebrew people did not form such a despotic political system, even though it was in the middle of large hydraulic civilizations, because of the geographical and climatic conditions of ancient Palestine and the historical character of the Jewish people.[38] Thus, cities flourished in Palestinian lands which were quite open to economic development in major cultural areas from the beginning.[39] As Weber noted, "The almost universal transition to urbanism appears complete in the political geography of Palestine as given in the Book of Joshua."[40]

The existence of a civic community based on citizenship differentiates the medieval city from both the ancient polis and oriental cities.[41] According to Weber, the most crucial disadvantage of oriental cities is the absence of a political community similar to the bourgeoisie:

> It [urban burgher community] can be found neither in China nor in Japan or India, and only in abortive beginnings in the Near East....
>
> In China the city was a fortress and official seat of the imperial agencies; in Japan the "city" in this sense was completely unknown. In India the cities were royal seats or official centers of the royal administration as well as fortresses and market centers....
>
> In Near Eastern and Egyptian Antiquity the cities were fortresses or official administrative centers with royal market privileges....
>
> Later, neither politically autonomous cities and a burgher stratum of the Occidental type nor a special urban law alongside the royal law can be found in Mesopotamia.[42]

For these reasons occidental cities are different from oriental cities. For example, in the East and ancient Egypt, where warrior princes preceded cities, judicially independent cities could not emerge. Weber attributes this to early centralization due to artificial irrigation. In addition to this, religious taboos prevented a military alliance with foreigners and therefore prevented the emergence of formally independent cities. Ritual ostracization of classes in India created the same effect. More generally, whereas the cities in the ancient West practiced their own rituals, in Asia and the Middle East, traditional clergy exercised a monopoly on communication with gods. Internal development of a rich and autonomous guide and community life in the city was closely related to the legal and political liberalization of the city from the intervention of patrimonial or feudal officers. Whereas occidental cities were able to make contracts and build alliances, Asian irrigation societies were characterized by the centralized bureaucratic control over warfare and commerce. Patrimonial governance in the Orient separated the soldier and the military equipment from each other. Military equipment was the property of the state, and keeping soldiers available and fed was realized through the manorial system by the landholders' centralized bureaucracy.[43] Therefore, the master could exercise his authority over his subjects who had no political unity or military autonomy directly. According to Weber, as a direct consequence of this system, cities could not emerge.[44]

Weber's analysis of the relationship between the emergence of a modern form of society and the birth and rise of cities can only be understood when considered in relation to his general sociological perspective. As discussed in another study, the primary objective of Weber's sociology is proving the uniqueness of the West generally and the modern form of society specifically.[45] In order to realize this objective, Weber frequently resorts to comparisons between occidental and oriental societies and tries to show that the rationalization that paved the way for this development took place fully only in the West. Weber's historical analyses on cities are related to the development of oriental cities in association with this general objective.[46]

While discussing city formation in the West and non-formation in the Orient, he speaks of two social structures opposite to each other. Whereas in the West magic was eliminated through a process shaped by various factors and rationalization was realized, the oriental perspective continued to be magical due to developments in the opposite direction and rationalization was not realized. When we go through this in detail we see that Weber resorts to geographical and climatic explanations that most of the Enlightenment thinkers in the eighteenth century and orientalists in the nineteenth century resorted to. According to him, geographical conditions and the need for a power and structure to organize the irrigation systems were the most determinative factors in the oriental world. For this reason, patrimonialism with a centralized state has emerged. However, there was no such need in the West, and that resulted in the non-emergence of such a centralized state structure.

The fundamental distinction that Weber makes can be seen in his analysis of the differentiation of ancient Greek and Hebrew societies from the oriental societies surrounding them. As he discussed in a detailed and distinctive manner, we can consider his analysis of the difference between Hebrew social structure and the strong structures in Egypt and Mesopotamia. As mentioned previously, ancient Hebrew society's geographical conditions did not require artificial irrigation; hence, the Hebrew people started to differentiate from the irrigation-based societies surrounding them. This was followed by the unification of outcast ancient Hebrew society around charismatic prophets in order to survive against their powerful enemies. Due to the special relationship that the Hebrew people had with their Jahwe, their religious thought was purified from magic. Therefore, ancient Hebrew society constituted the foundation of a social structure that would spring to life only in the West. Weber used a similar line of thought to explain the differentiation of ancient Greek social structure from the social structure of Egypt and Mesopotamia. According to this view, differing foundations created by differing geographical conditions let democracy flourish in Greece and led to some forms of political rationalization. Obstacles in the way of the rationalization of religious belief in the East due to the position of bureaucracy did not occur in Greek society thanks to the special position of religious thinking and the clergy. Therefore, in contrast with the despotic system of the East, democratic ideals were determinative in Greece.

Weber answered the question of why the city emerged in the Mediterranean basin and in the West but not in Asia in relation to patrimonial political structure and non-rationalized social life.[47] The need for regulation of the rivers and access to water led to the formation of royal bureaucracies in the East and created an opportunity for them to build and sustain large armies that constituted the foundation of a centralized power. In such an environment, political burgher communities could not gain their independence from the royal powers. According to Weber, military units composed of farmers, knights, or burgher militias had to provide their equipment themselves as a principle in the West. The final outcome was the separation of status-like powers and the development of burgher communities.[48]

Demonstration of this differentiation through the development of cities is quite important for Weber. He gives a central place to cities in the context of differentiating between the West and the East.[49] Considering the historical process, the development of cities in practice is as important as the concept of rationalization in theory. In other words, Weber thinks that in the realization of ultimate rationalization made possible with the assembling of distinctive characteristics of the West, the development of cities occupies a fundamental place. Cities were determined by the fundamental social differentiation and witnessed rationalization in various areas. The development of a rational law, a rational political system, the rationalization of economic production, and transactions were able to take place in the environment created by cities. More importantly, cities let the developments in these areas occur in an interrelated and mutually reinforcing manner.

In order to explain the differentiation between the East and the West, oriental and occidental cities could be comparatively examined. Understanding why the developments observed in the West did not take place in the East is essential. This is clearly indicated in the letter Weber sent to conservative historian Georg von Below about the composition of *Economy and Society* and the concept of patrimonialism. Weber stated that he would address the topic of political associations "*comparatively* and systematically." The obligation of the historian should be to explain a phenomenon comparatively through the analysis of differences with other phenomena. Weber argued that it was only possible to understand the *specific* characteristics of the medieval city by determining "what was *missing* in *other* cities (ancient, Chinese, Islamic)." In his view such comparative analysis gave the historian the means "to *explain* causally that which is *specific*" to the phenomenon under investigation, just as it provided the essential preparatory work for the sociologist's explanations.[50] In another writing, Weber similarly stated that a "striking contrast to the Asian conditions is presented by the city of the medieval Occident, in particular by the city of the lands North of the Alps wherever it developed in a form approximating the ideal type."[51] It is apparent that Weber attached importance to comparative examinations with the East to explain the social structure of the West, and within this context he attributed a central place to the city.[52]

CIVIL SOCIETY IN TURKEY: A WEBERIAN BASIS FOR DISCUSSION

The explanation of the origin of the modern Western political formation in relation to the conflict between feudal elements at the center and cities, burghers, and later industrial labor at the periphery is one of the topics that Western political science literature insistently emphasizes. This approach has been adapted to Ottoman society within the framework of theses employing the concepts of oriental despotism and especially Weberian patrimonialism. According to these interpretations, historically the primary factor determining Ottoman-Turkish sociocultural and political-economic life has been the state itself. Civil society has been overshadowed by the overwhelming power of the state and could not evolve effectively. According to this approach, the state has controlled everything bureaucratically but has been disconnected from the people. This disconnection rendered it almost a transcendental power.

The relation between the state and the society, the assertion that a civil society has not developed, and the claim that a middle class has not formed have been some of the hot topics since the 1960s. The list of those who contributed to this discussion is quite impressive. Halil İnalcık, Şerif Mardin, Kemal Karpat, and İdris Küçükömer were among those who brought the subject up for discussion. Among the next generation of political scientists and sociologists, authors like Metin Heper, Ersin Kalaycıoğlu, Çağlar Keyder, Fuat Keyman, İlkay Sunar, İlter Turan, Ömer Çaha, and Ahmet İnsel contributed to the subject substantially. Almost all of them tried to explain the model of Ottoman society within the framework of Weberian patrimonialism, and in this context, they traced the roots of centralization in the modernization period and today's state-centered political system back to quite old times.

Mardin led the way of those who brought up the analysis of patrimonialism and the absence of civil society in Turkey. With reference to explanations on civil society in political theory, Mardin stated that the conflict between the social powers in the West resulted in various forms of compromise and reconciliation. However, there was not such a transitivity between the center and periphery in Ottoman society.[53] This was because of the absence of a civil element in Ottoman society that could provide such a balance. According to Mardin,[54] who widely used the classical Weberian theses, it was patrimonial oriental despotism that had historically been prevalent in Turkish society. According to him, the "Ottoman Empire seems to approximate the optimum equilibrium of an 'Oriental Despotism'... under which there are ideally only two 'social sets': the ruler and his executive servants on the one hand and the ruled on the other."[55] Though he is criticized often, Mardin's explanations have frequently been used as a reference in regard to the interpretation of the relations between the state and the society in Turkey.

Another author who contributed to the discussion on civil society in Ottoman history is Kemal Karpat. According to him, the primary reason for the lack of dynamism in the structure of Ottoman society was the absence of a middle class.[56] Karpat states that throughout Ottoman history, merchants and craftsmen were not allowed to attain high positions.[57] The *ayan* class, a stratum of local Muslim notables, was a candidate to form a middle class but was oppressed by the central bureaucracy.[58] The space left by *ayans* was filled by small merchants and artisans. According to Karpat, *ayans* played an important role during the social transformations of the nineteenth century, though it also blocked the way to capitalism.[59] This middle class developed a nationalist secular character and established the sociopolitical structure that modern Turkey is built upon. Ultimately, in the early nineteenth century, with "the removal of the *ayans*,"[60] centralization of bureaucracy and power was completed. Under Mahmut II, Weber's definition of "sultanism" became the practical principle of government and its personalized absolutism.[61]

Another contributor to the debate is Idris Küçükömer, who examines the reasons for the underdevelopment of civil society in Turkey. He points out as a reason that industrialization and embourgeoisement did not take place at a higher level in Turkey.[62] According to this interpretation, the fact that modernization in the Ottoman Empire was realized by secular-statist bureaucrats resulted in the oppression of the society and led the way to a strict and centralizing understanding of the path to modernization. Hence, neither could a middle class to construct civil society form nor could the fundamental social and economic agents of modernization evolve. In this respect, Küçükömer states that civil society could not develop in Turkey because of the bureaucracy that maintained the highly centralized Ottoman state.[63]

Metin Heper is also one of those who developed these theses. In his work *The State Tradition in Turkey*, he examines Ottoman socioeconomic structure in comparison with European feudalism. According to him, whereas the central authority was balanced by opposing social and political forces in the Western feudal system, the center of Ottoman patrimonialism did not have any opposing force against it. Hence, society was under the strong control of the state apparatus.[64] This system became so established that there was no one left to protect the society except for the state. Therefore, even the revolts that took place in Ottoman society only aimed at changing the rulers but never targeted the system itself. Heper argues that the idea of the circle of justice (*daire-i ʿadliye*)[65] in Ottoman society can be basically interpreted as the protection of the state.

All of these approaches are based upon the thesis that the state and the society were disconnected in the Ottoman Empire. Moreover, they constitute a sort of sociology of absences as they tend to describe the social structure and relations in Ottoman society with Western patterns. Nevertheless, in the Ottoman model of society, there was a unique relationship between the state and the society molded by a political thought that is distinct from its Western counterparts, and it is necessary to understand and analyze this relationship in order to discuss the issue of civil society beyond the theses of oriental despotism and Weberian patrimonialism.

Nevertheless, the validity of these Weberian analyses should be questioned. In a seminal article Halil Inalcik, who carried out significant research on Ottoman economics and social history, criticized the Weberian patrimonialism and sultanism theses. Inalcik emphasizes the inaccuracy of the Weberian approach, which claims that "the Islamic city in general was unorganized, unstructured, and completely dependent on the state."[66] With a vast web of trade and crafts, Ottoman cities not only functioned as headquarters for the sultan but also had a complex structure of production and management within themselves. In addition, Inalcik opposed the depictions of Ottoman bureaucracy as solely comprising the servants of the sultan.[67] According to him, Ottoman bureaucrats cannot be depicted as servants of the patrimonial master, without any sort of specialization. These bureaucrats did not always obey the sultan without question; rather, they tried to restrict the personal and arbitrary practices through regulations (*nizamname*) and the rulers' edicts (*ferman*) or rescripts of justice (*adaletname*) that they issued to solve urgent problems.[68] Inalcik states that at least the sultans had no other choice but to protect the financial bureaucracy, which operated a very complex calculation system and thus tried to protect the balance of income and expenditures. For him, Ottoman bureaucracy preserved and symbolized the sultan's high position intentionally for using it as a basis for its own management and regulations. In fact, there is this kind of bureaucracy behind the reforms in the Ottoman state after the eighteenth century.[69]

However, the most significant claims of the patrimonialism thesis relate to the premise that there is no mid-level rank between the state (palace) and the society. Inalcik states that this premise comes with a lot of problems and false suppositions. He states that it was "the civil and military bureaucrats and the *ulema*, evolving into increasingly autonomous groups that finally replaced the sultans' patrimonial rule."[70] The *ulema*, who were perceived as the strongest observers of customs and traditions, restricted the sultan's personal authority in the name of sharia and tradition. Other groups that wished to preserve their status before the sultan also found refuge in the protection of the *ulema* from time to time. Inalcik talks about various social groups that had their own autonomy and were in balance and harmony with one another at the same time: guilds (*lonca*), *ulema*, and bureaucracy are some examples of this.[71] Consequently, he believes that the Weberian scheme which divides the East and the West, and which was borne out of the Asiatic despotic empires theory, is reductionist and fails to recognize the unique features of the Ottoman system.[72] Having pointed out Inalcik's set of criticisms, it is still possible to state that he himself did not fully break away from the Weberian scheme, and he suggested a novel and restructured model of patrimonialism. Nevertheless, Inalcik's earlier study of rescripts of justice (*adaletnames*) presented some hints leading us to the alternative theories about the management of the Ottoman societal model.[73]

In the Ottoman political model, the primary mechanism connecting the state and the society was the administration of justice. The idea of justice here implies a long-term balance in the social structure. There were two main components of this balance: the first was the social mobility that represented and constituted vertical movements in the society and prevented the concentration of political power; and the second component was the mechanism of redistribution, which prevented the concentration of wealth.

Social mobility was mostly realized through madrasahs, which were autonomous civil educational institutions that raised qualified people for state affairs, whereas redistribution was realized through the autonomous institution of *vaqf*, a nonprofit foundation which Weber compared with the institution of Prussian *Fideikommiß*.[74] It provided solutions to social problems and various benefits to the society. These two institutions complemented and empowered each other. Hence, the Ottoman model of political balance was based on the operations of these two civil elements. This system allowed even the poorest of the society to climb up the political and economic hierarchy in accordance with their talents and efforts and helped to organize the distribution and redistribution of the wealth produced in the society among its members. Hence, nongovernmental civil structures became an indispensable part of the Ottoman social model.

The disconnection between the center and periphery in the Ottoman political model is the product of centralization that took place in the modernization period. Toward the end of the eighteenth century, when the Ottoman Empire confronted the Western central bureaucratic nation-states and their central armies, it quickly realized that its own system could not survive against these huge power machines. After that, starting from the early nineteenth century, a rapid modernization and centralization took place. During this transformation, Ottoman civil elements were eliminated, but a bourgeois middle class could not be formed to replace them. This was because while centralization took place, democratic institutions to balance the process were not yet completely formed. Therefore, the history of modern Turkey is characterized by the manifestations of a weak civil society and a strong state. However, the primary reason for this outcome lies in modernization policies rather than in the Ottoman sociopolitical model. In this context, efforts to assess Ottoman history within the framework of Weberian patrimonialism and classical oriental despotism not only have prevented a correct interpretation of classical Ottoman social structure but also have hampered the development of an understanding of the oriental modernization process.

Notes

1. Anthony Giddens, *A Contemporary Critique of Historical Materialism* (Berkeley: University of California Press, 1981), 140.
2. For the development of the term "despot" for defining non-European societies, see Richard Koebner, "Despot and Despotism: Vicissitudes of a Political Term," *Journal of the Warburg and Courtauld Institutes* 14 (1951): 275; and Joan-Pau Rubiés, "Oriental Despotism and European Orientalism: Botero to Montesquieu," *Journal of Early Modern History* 9 (2005): 109–180. For a discussion of the usage of despotism for Muslim societies, see Michael Curtis, *Orientalism and Islam: European Thinkers on Oriental Despotism in the Middle East and India* (Cambridge: Cambridge University Press, 2009).
3. See my essay for a broader discussion on the constitution of Eurocentric modernity and the changing position of the other in modern social theory: "The Constitution of Eurocentric Modernity and the Changing Position of the Other," in *Eurocentrism at the Margins: Encounters, Critics and Going Beyond*, ed. Lutfi Sunar (London: Routledge, 2016), 21–40.

4. Max Weber, *General Economic History* (hereafter *GEH*), trans. F. H. Knight (Mineola, NY: Dover, 2003), 313–314; *Abriß der universalen Sozial- und Wirtschaftsgeschichte. Mit- und Nachschriften 1919/20, Max Weber-Gesamtausgabe* (hereafter *MWG*) III/6, ed. W. Schluchter with J. Schröder (Tübingen, Germany: Mohr [Siebeck], 2011), 349–350.

5. Max Weber, *Economy and Society* (hereafter *E&S*), ed. G. Roth and C. Wittich (Berkeley: University of California Press, 1978), 1212–1214; *Wirtschaft und Gesellschaft. Nachlaß. Die Stadt, MWG* I/22-5, ed. W. Nippel (Tübingen, Germany: Mohr [Siebeck], 1999), 59–63.

6. For the discussion of Weber on the types of cities, see *E&S*, 1215–1217; *MWG* I/22-5, 63–67.

7. As stated by Wolfgang J. Mommsen, "Max Weber's 'Grand Sociology': The Origins and Composition of *Wirtschaft und Gesellschaft. Soziologie*," in *Max Weber's Economy and Society: A Critical Companion*, ed. C. Camic, P. S. Gorski, and D. M. Trubek (Stanford, CA: Stanford University Press, 2005), 70–100. Though "City" is the last chapter of the book, it is one of the first chapters that Weber wrote.

8. *E&S*, 1212–1372; *MWG* I/22-5, 59–299 (with the title "Die Stadt"). Johannes Winckelmann, who was the editor of the fourth edition in German, titled this chapter "Die nichtlegitime Herrschaft" ("Typologie der Städte") in reference to the title that Weber used in the first draft of the book. Therefore, editors of the English edition of *Economy and Society* preferred to use a title including both.

9. *E&S*, 1234n1.

10. See "Die Stadtwirtschaft und die Entstehung der geldwirtschaftlichen Unternehmungsformen," in Max Weber, *Allgemeine ("theoretische") Nationalökonomie. Vorlesungen 1894–1898, MWG* III/1, ed. W. J. Mommsen with C. Judenau et al. (Tübingen, Germany: Mohr [Siebeck], 2009), 456–499.

11. Max Weber, *The Agrarian Sociology of Ancient Civilizations* (hereafter *ASAC*), trans. R. I. Frank (London: Verso, 1988), 69; *Zur Sozial- und Wirtschaftsgeschichte des Altertums. Schriften und Reden 1893–1908, MWG* I/6, ed. J. Deininger (Tübingen, Germany: Mohr [Siebeck], 2006), 362.

12. V. Gordon Childe, *What Happened in History* (New York: Penguin, 1942).

13. *ASAC*, 69–75; *MWG* I/6, 362–368.

14. *ASAC*, 64; *MWG* I/6, 355–356.

15. *ASAC*, 64–65; *MWG* I/6, 355–357.

16. *ASAC*, 163; *MWG* I/6, 477.

17. *ASAC*, 74; *MWG* I/6, 368.

18. *ASAC*, 50–51, 76, 158; *MWG* I/6, 337–339, 370–371, 470–471.

19. *ASAC*, 340–341; *MWG* I/6, 695–697.

20. *ASAC*, 343–344; *MWG* I/6, 698–700.

21. *ASAC*, 346; *MWG* I/6, 702.

22. Max Weber, *The Religion of India*, trans. H. Gerth and D. Martindale (New York: Free Press, 1958), 36; *Die Wirtschaftsethik der Weltreligionen. Hinduismus und Buddhismus, MWG* I/20, ed. H. Schmidt-Glintzer with K.-H. Golzio (Tübingen, Germany: Mohr [Siebeck], 1996), 94.

23. *E&S*, 1251; *MWG* I/22-5, 127.

24. *E&S*, 299; *Wirtschaft und Gesellschaft. Soziologie, MWG* I/23, ed. K. Borchardt, E. Hanke, and W. Schluchter (Tübingen, Germany: Mohr [Siebeck], 2013), 591.

25. Max Weber, *Wirtschaft und Gesellschaft. Nachlaß. Herrschaft, MWG* I/22-4, ed. E. Hanke with Th. Kroll (Tübingen, Germany: Mohr [Siebeck], 2005), 755.

26. *E&S*, 1324; *MWG* I/22-5, 234.

27. *E&S*, 1323; *MWG* I/22-5, 234.

28. *E&S*, 1326–1327; *MWG* I/22-5, 237–240.

29. *E&S*, 1328; *MWG* I/22-5, 241.

30. *E&S*, 1259; *MWG* I/22-5, 140–141.

31. *E&S*, 1254; *MWG* I/22-5, 131.

32. *E&S*, 1325; *MWG* I/22-5, 236–237.

33. Max Weber, *The Religion of China: Confucianism and Taoism*, trans. H. Gerth (New York: Free Press, 1951), 100–101; *Die Wirtschaftsethik der Weltreligionen. Konfuzianismus und Taoismus*, *MWG* I/19, ed. H. Schmidt-Glintzer with P. Kolonko (Tübingen, Germany: Mohr [Siebeck], 1989), 279.

34. *ASAC*, 228; *MWG* I/6, 556.

35. *ASAC*, 336; *MWG* I/6, 690.

36. Max Weber, *Ancient Judaism* (hereafter *AJ*), trans. and ed. H. Gerth and D. Martindale (New York: Free Press, 1952), 22; *Die Wirtschaftsethik der Weltreligionen. Das antike Judentum*, *MWG* I/21, ed. E. Otto with J. Offermann (Tübingen, Germany: Mohr [Siebeck], 2005), 270.

37. *AJ*, 20; *MWG* I/21, 268.

38. *AJ*, 5–10; *MWG* I/21, 244–250.

39. *AJ*, 61; *MWG* I/21, 322.

40. *AJ*, 43; *MWG* I/21, 300–301.

41. *E&S*, 1240, 1249–1250; *MWG* I/22-5, 107–108, 121–125.

42. *E&S*, 1229–1230; *MWG* I/22-5, 88–93.

43. Weber, *Religion of China*, 16; *MWG* I/19, 153–154; *ASAC*, 72; *MWG* I/6, 365.

44. *E&S*, 1260–1262; *MWG* I/22-5, 143–145. For discussions on the opinions of Weber regarding the differentiation between the East and the West, see Reinhard Bendix, *Max Weber: An Intellectual Portrait* (Garden City, NY: Doubleday, 1960), 93; J. M. Blaut, *The Colonizer's Model of the World: Geographical Diffusionism and Eurocentric History* (New York: Guilford, 1993), 83; Randall Collins, *Max Weber: A Skeleton Key* (Beverly Hills, CA: Sage, 1986), 92; and Bryan S. Turner, *Weber and Islam: A Critical Study* (London: Routledge, 1974), 97–98.

45. See Sunar, "Constitution of Eurocentric Modernity."

46. For a detailed discussion, see Sunar, *Marx and Weber on Oriental Societies: In the Shadow of Western Modernity* (New York: Routledge, 2016), 135–141.

47. *GEH*, 320–322; *MWG* III/6, 355–357.

48. Fritz K. Ringer, *Max Weber: An Intellectual Biography* (Chicago: University of Chicago Press), 208.

49. Reinhard Bendix, *Max Weber: An Intellectual Portrait* (Garden City, NY: Doubleday, 1960), 118–123.

50. Weber to Georg von Below, June 21, 1914, in *Max Weber Briefe 1913–1914*, *MWG* II/9, ed. M. R. Lepsius and W. J. Mommsen with B. Rudhard and M. Schön (Tübingen, Germany: Mohr [Siebeck], 2003), 724.

51. *E&S*, 1236; *MWG* I/22-5, 100.

52. Ringer, *Max Weber*, 204.

53. Şerif Mardin, "Center–Periphery Relations: A Key to Turkish Politics?" *Daedalus* 102 (1973): 169–190.

54. Şerif Mardin, *Religion, Society and Modernity in Turkey* (Syracuse, NY: Syracuse University Press, 2006), 85. According to Mardin, "The type of power wielded by the Ottoman's elite fits easily into" Weberian categories (p. 25).

55. Şerif Mardin, "Historical Determinants of Stratification: Social Class and Class Consciousness in Turkey," *Siyasal Bilgiler Fakültesi Dergisi* 22 (1967): 111–142, 119–120.

56. Kemal H. Karpat, *Studies on Ottoman Social and Political History: Selected Articles and Essays* (Leiden, the Netherlands: Brill, 2002), 29–30.

57. Kemal H. Karpat, *Osmanli Modernleşmesi: Toplum, Kurumsal Değişim ve Nüfus* (Ankara, Turkey: Imge Kitabevi, 2008), 31.

58. Kemal H. Karpat, "The Transformation of the Ottoman State, 1789–1908," *International Journal of Middle East Studies* 3 (1972): 243–281, 254.

59. Karpat, *Studies on Ottoman Social and Political History*, 35–45.

60. Ibid., 39.

61. Kemal H. Karpat, *The Politicization of Islam: Reconstructing Identity, State, Faith, and Community in the Late Ottoman State* (New York: Oxford University Press, 2001), 224.

62. İdris Küçükömer, *Düzenin Yabancilaşmasi* (Istanbul, Turkey: Bağlam Yayincilik, 1994).

63. İdris Küçükömer, *Sivil Toplum Yazilari* (Istanbul, Turkey: Bağlam Yayincilik, 1994).

64. Metin Heper, *The State Tradition in Turkey* (Beverley, UK: Eothen Press, 1985), 14.

65. "Circle of Justice" (*daire-i ʿadliye*) is the name of a political aphorism often written in a circle starting and ending with the notion of justice. It is the basic principle of oriental political systems since ancient Persia. It has often been used when describing state–societal relationships in the premodern era of the Ottoman Empire. The nineteenth-century Tanzimat reforms led to dramatic shifts in these relations.

66. Halil Inalcik, "Comments on 'Sultanism': Max Weber's Typification of the Ottoman Polity," *Princeton Papers in Near Eastern Studies* 1 (1992): 49–73, 62.

67. Ibid.

68. Ibid., 64.

69. Ibid., 63–65.

70. Ibid., 65.

71. Ibid., 50.

72. Ibid., 66–67.

73. Halil Inalcik, *Adaletnameler* (Ankara, Turkey: Turk Tarih Kurumu Basimevi, 1967).

74. *MWG* I/22-4, 429.

PART III

POLITICS AND THE STATE

CHAPTER 12

THE MODERN STATE AND ITS MONOPOLY ON VIOLENCE

ANDREAS ANTER

THERE is hardly any study in contemporary international state theory that would not relate to Max Weber. Since his concept of the state has prevailed, it is "quite simply the most commonly used working definition found in contemporary historical and political writing."[1] In between, a "Weberian approach" has been established in state theory,[2] and even the state itself is sometimes referred to as a "modern Weberian state."[3] A theorist whose research object is labeled with his own name has comprehensively imposed himself. In methodological respect, Weber's theory marks a turning point in the history of political and legal science, which was dominated by doyens like Georg Jellinek at that time, while *angry young men* like Hans Kelsen were already challenging the prevailing opinion. This upheaval is somehow personified in Weber, for he was influenced by sociological ideas, while remaining largely committed to a legal mode of thinking.[4]

In various parts of his writing, it becomes evident how much his political thought is dominated by the state. This goes particularly for his political writings but also for his early agrarian studies, his methodological essays, his sociology of law, and his sociology of domination. Time and again, he refers to the state as "the most important constitutive element of all cultural life."[5] As different as the work contexts are the images and metaphors he uses for the state: as a "complex of human action," as a "machine," as a "tangle of value ideas," as a "relation of domination," and as a "bureaucratic apparatus."

These varieties of state experience, to be sure, rely primarily on the various manifestations of the object itself, which causes one of the central problems of state theory, that is, to reduce the varieties to a single concept. It was not without reason that Weber described the notion of the state as "the most complex and interesting case" of the problem of concept formation.[6] Every definition of the state faces the problem of how this abstract, diverse, and constantly changing phenomenon can be distilled to a clear concept. It is Weber who identifies this problem of complexity. He provides a conception of the state which marks a key solution to a problem that can be traced back in modern political and legal thought over more than one hundred years.

Despite all of his rich theoretical reflections on statehood, Weber never developed a systematic theory of the state. He always deals with the state only in passing. The fragments are scattered throughout his work and can be found in the most various contexts. In his later years, he planned to develop a "sociology of the state," which was intended to be the keystone of his sociology of domination; but he did not carry out this intention.[7] Wilhelm Hennis is certainly right in discounting the declarations Weber made on his proposed "sociology of the state," objecting that nothing in this line was to be expected.[8] Hennis' thesis becomes particularly evident when regarding the syllabus to Weber's Munich lecture on the sociology of the state.[9] Since the syllabus largely overlaps with his sociology of domination, it is very unlikely that his planned "sociology of the state" would have broken new ground. Whoever wants to gain an overview of Weber's ideas has to reconstruct the relevant fragments scattered throughout his work.[10]

THE MODERN STATE AND ITS MONOPOLY OF FORCE

In his "Basic Sociological Concepts" Weber defines the state as a political institution that claims successfully the "*monopoly of legitimate* physical force."[11] He explicitly underlines that the monopoly of physical force is not the only defining feature. The "manner in which the state lays claim to the monopoly of rule by force is as essential a current feature as is its character as a rational 'institution' and continuous 'organisation'"; formally characteristic of the modern state is not only the monopoly of physical force but "an administrative and a legal order subject to change by statute, to which the organized group activity of the administrative staff...is oriented."[12]

Since the rise of the modern occidental state went hand in hand with the formation of modern bureaucracy, Weber regards the bureaucracy as the nucleus of the state.[13] Due to the increasing demands on the administration, mainly with respect to social policy, the contemporary state becomes more and more "technically dependent upon a bureaucratic foundation."[14] Like the prevailing legal positivist theorists of his time, Weber thought domination to be an essential criterion of the state[15]; but unlike the positivist theorists, he tied the existence of domination to the criterion of legitimacy. The category of legitimacy is the Archimedean point of his sociology of domination. In his view, domination cannot last if it lacks a legitimate basis. Accordingly, every state requires a legitimating foundation that provides validity for its orders. The legitimacy of the modern state, to be precise, rests primarily on the belief in the *legality* of its orders.[16]

Despite such specifications, the monopoly of physical force nevertheless is the key element of Weber's theory. The definition is a result of his historical studies revealing the monopoly as the decisive criterion which distinguishes the modern state from all other historical forms of domination. He makes many further specifications which make clear that physical force is neither the only nor the normal instrument of state acting and that the application of force is only the last resort when other means have failed.[17]

Thus, Weber is not an apologist of violence. He came upon his findings of its constitutive role by his historical studies. This historical perspective is clearly evident particularly in his treatment of "political communities" in *Economy and Society*. Using examples from European history, he illustrates that all political communities are based on force: every community has resorted to physical force to protect its interests.[18] The monopolization of force by the state was the result of a long-term and violent process in which the local holders of powers were gradually expropriated by a central force. Today's historians date the enforcement of the monopoly from the early modern age.[19] However, this dating could easily be postponed for some centuries. State authority and jurisdiction in the East Elbian territories of Prussia, for example, were exercised by the landlords until the late nineteenth century. As late as 1837, a quarter of the Prussian population was under patrimonial jurisdiction, which was abolished in 1848 but reintroduced only five years later.[20] As a young agrarian statistician, Weber himself came into contact with this atavistic structure in his survey of the East Elbian rural workers.[21]

It is not easy to come to an exact historical dating in this case since the monopoly of force didn't come overnight but during a long, protracted process. This is why the monopoly of violence is actually not an absolute term. The fact that Weber does not even make an approximate dating depends not least on the fact that his sociology of domination is not based on a precise concept of the state: the later definition of the state in his "Basic Sociological Concepts" is only a result of his historical studies. Furthermore, Weber was not particularly interested in the question of origin. Even after Weber's death, sociologists were not interested in this question for many decades.[22] Weber refrains from commenting on the birth of the monopoly of force, but he emphasizes that the Middle Ages lacked access to it: "The things we are now accustomed to regard as the content of the unified 'supreme authority' ('*Staatsgewalt*') fell apart under that system into a bundle of individual entitlements in various hands. There was as yet no question of a 'state' in the modern sense of the word."[23]

The process of monopolization occurs not only in the exercise of force but also in administration, legislation, judicial decision-making, and other spheres. For Weber, the emergence of the modern state was a comprehensive process of centralization of powers. On the tracks of Weber, Heinrich Popitz perceives the contemporary result of this as a "routinization of centralized domination" that is

> accompanied by the centralized provision of the goods required for the conduct of a civilized existence. In the morning with a look at the clock, we ascertain the centrally set time, we avail ourselves of centrally provided water, light, and heat at (it is hoped) centrally controlled prices, we grimly meet at the breakfast table (within the framework of the laws of marriage and family), we in leaving our house slip into the channels of the traffic code, and we are not allowed to take the law into our hands even if someone parks in front of our garage.[24]

Regarding the process of centralization and monopolization, Weber follows the historical research of Rudolph Sohm, his academic teacher, who also inspired his concept of charisma.[25] In his essays on state theory, the canonist Sohm pointed out how the emerging modern state gradually dominated the local forces, eliminating all of the other instances of domination.[26] Even the concept of the monopoly of force was coined by Sohm, who formulated legal coercion as a "monopoly of the state" since "all use of force within the state can only be based on behalf and in representation of the state authority."[27] Quite similar, Rudolf von Jhering defined coercive force as the "absolute monopoly of the State."[28] Subsequently, this formula became a commonplace in later nineteenth-century theories of the state. Hence, Weber's notion is borrowed almost literally from German canonists and legal theorists of his time.

Evidently, Weber's theory of the state is historically based.[29] If the state is characterized by the monopoly of violence and the monopoly emerged first in early modern Europe, the state is a located phenomenon. According to Weber, only the modern, occidental, and rational state is really a state. This clear understanding is entirely contradicted by the casual way he refers to the "state" of the ancient Romans, Greeks, Egyptians, or Chinese.[30] This casual usage of the word is in sharp contrast to his otherwise nominalist meticulousness. Therefore, it is hardly comprehensible how a Weber expert like Carl Schmitt could praise the "conceptual restraint" in "distancing himself from a generalising use of the term 'state'" which he did not project "on to the ruling organisations of other cultures and epochs."[31] There can be no question of such abstinence.

Today's political and legal theorists are convinced that the notion of the state cannot be used arbitrarily,[32] but in practice, everyone does it the way it has been done for a hundred years: first, one emphasizes the historicity of the concept but only to ignore it afterward. Weber occupies nevertheless an important position in the development of modern state theory since he formulated more clearly than anyone else the monopoly of violence as the elementary criterion of the state. It is not by chance that he is known worldwide as *the* theorist of the monopoly of force. Whenever this monopoly is mentioned in contemporary social and legal science, he is constantly referred to. Having already been confirmed by classical sociologists like Norbert Elias,[33] Niklas Luhmann,[34] and Heinrich Popitz,[35] Weber's concept of the state seems to be established more than ever before in present-day social and legal sciences.[36]

THE CONTEMPORARY DEBATE ON THE MODERN STATE AND ITS MONOPOLY

Regarding the current debate on the state and its monopoly of violence, Weber's theory seems to be more relevant than ever. The debate turns particularly to the question of the role of the monopoly in the process of state-building, its function in securing the legal process and domestic peace, and the fact that the monopoly is constantly endangered in the European states—and does not even exist in many parts of the world. Until now, hardly any country in Africa[37] or Latin or South America[38] could establish a monopoly of violence—and therefore no state. Not least the global threat of Islamic terrorism has rendered the monopoly of violence in many states as highly tenuous.[39]

As many states have troubles in fulfilling their primary protective duties, the number of private security companies is worldwide increasing.[40] Does this create new power instances that are no longer subject to democratic control? Do they potentially undermine the monopoly of violence? From a Weberian perspective, an expansion of privatization of security would certainly invoke a reversal of the previous historical development, and, moreover, it would undermine at least the legitimacy of the modern state.[41] Private security companies, after all, are not doing their job on behalf of public interests but on behalf of the commercial interests of their customers. Hence, security would turn into a commodity that could only be acquired by those with the appropriate financial resources. But the legitimacy of the modern state rests on the supposition that all citizens obtain security and protection without distinction, at least in principle.

Regarding the fact that there is no universal enforcement of the monopoly of violence, already decades ago critics like Sheldon Wolin maintained that Weber's theory has become obsolete: "whatever the 'uniqueness' of the modern state may be, it does not consist in a monopoly of the means of violence."[42] For a long time, it was fashionable to speak of the state only in the past tense. The state was said to no longer exist.[43] This thesis is evidently wrong because the state is still very alive. Furthermore, modern history reveals its tremendous changeability and dynamism, which is part of its nature and is to be seen as one of its characteristics.

However, Stefan Breuer is right in observing a "modified distribution of force" in the Western world.[44] Violence is not threatening the state's existence as long as the vast majority of citizens agree with its legal order. But things are different when growing parts of the population reject the existing order. In many European societies, the current immigration flow from Islamic cultures has created parallel societies that are alien to the majority society and have even developed their own parallel justice.[45] Since they are mostly shaped by cultures of violence,[46] new violent potential emerges in European societies. The states therefore face the difficult task of confronting the potential of violence as well as the parallel justice if they don't want to jeopardize their stability and legitimacy.

If we want to ask for the relevance of Weber's theory, we first have to look at the concept of monopoly. In the context of violence, it means something different from what it means in economics. While an economic monopoly is relatively easy to enforce, a monopoly of violence never can be absolute. Not even a total or dictatorial state would be capable of preventing all competing sources of violence. The monopolization always remains incomplete since violence is a form of human action that is—weather latent or manifest— always present.[47] This incompleteness of the monopoly of violence drives us to respecify the meaning of this notion. Its conceptual as well as its practical problems derive from the fact that a "real" monopoly can only be partially realized. Therefore, the monopoly has to be understood not in absolute terms but in a teleological sense, for it is a claim that has to be constantly asserted and enforced. This enforcement depends, first, on the institutionalization of the means of force by the state and, second, on a basis of legitimacy that ensures the compliance of such a claim. In this sense, the state can always only *aim* at prohibiting non-state violence.

Maintaining the monopoly of force is of fundamental importance for present-day democratic states based upon the rule of law since it guarantees that democratically legitimate decisions have the chance to be enforced. Thus, the "rule of law" and the monopoly of violence are very closely linked to each other. The fact that violence in the outlined sense is monopolized by the state does not mean that the problem of violence is solved once and for all. It appears again and again, for it is not abolished by monopolization; and, moreover, it is shifting to a new level: the state itself must make use of violence to maintain its monopoly claim. Hence, every state faces a double bind: the promise of putting an end to non-domesticated and uncontrolled violence is only realized at the cost of being itself potentially violent. Following Weber, Heinrich Popitz concludes that violence is a "necessary condition" of the preservation of order. An order that does not surrender its existence must protect itself forcefully when threatened with violence.[48]

To be sure, many European states have gaps in their monopoly of violence, but gaps like this have persecuted the modern state from the beginning and occur in every historical epoch. Weber himself was a witness of violent attacks that shook the state's monopoly, and it is unlikely that he was not aware of its fragile nature.

THE WEBERIAN STATE AND THE INTERNATIONAL ORDER

Many observers also believe that the state suffers increasing losses of power in the international sphere due to transfer of sovereign rights to supranational communities and organizations so that its sovereignty is threatened at large. Weber's state, to be sure, is far from the "anarchical society" Hedley Bull observed as an organizational form of the international community.[49] It is also far from the *multilevel system*, the *global governance*, or the *global society* with its global media communication, dehierarchification, and globalization.[50] In political and legal science, the current metamorphosis is reflected by permanent attempts to grasp this process, rapidly and constantly changing descriptions and images of the state,[51] whose adjectives are often out of date at the time of their invention.[52]

To ensure their functioning, many states form supranational communities to which they assign parts of their sovereign rights. They are actively pursuing this process, and, moreover, they remain the key actors in it. As Josef Isensee points out, "the international organisations did not absorb the state and did not make it superfluous. The international community is still essentially a community of states. The states are still the bearers of the international order, and they are the actual creators and guarantors of international law."[53] Thus, the widespread talk about the "end of the state" is even in the international sphere simply to be considered as counterfactual. The fact that the state continues to be irreplaceable is not least demonstrated by its security policy since the beginning of the twenty-first century. As Catherine Colliot-Thélène notes, "the principle of sovereignty has remained a cornerstone of international law up to now."[54] The number of states has even increased since the late twentieth century. The fall of the Soviet Union as well as the disintegrated multinational Yugoslavia gave rise to a multitude of new nation-states.

However, the idea that the state as an occidental model of political order may be transferred to other regions of the world has turned out to be illusory. Comparing the worldwide situation of political communities, we can observe a very heterogeneous tableau. Disintegrated orders and state-free territories are facing stable political communities with a high degree of statehood. In global comparison, the Weberian state is rather the exception than the rule of political organization. Only 16 percent of the world population live under the conditions of modern statehood, while nearly three quarters live in areas of low statehood and 10 percent live in completely state-free and disordered territories.[55] An intelligent policy of global governance therefore would have to promote the emergence of solid statehood since without state structure a legitimate political system cannot emerge. For this reason, an active state-building is required for many areas.[56]

One of the essential tasks of international community and global governance actually is to promote the formation of state structures in territories shaped by uncontrolled violence. The realization of such state-building[57] requires not only the provision of the necessary resources and instruments[58] but also an in-depth reform of the way of thinking in Western political communities, which pursued the policy of denationalization for decades. The ubiquitous violence in the unregulated territories and failed states of Africa, Latin America, and Asia can make clear a *differentia specifica*. It shows that all civilization rests on "functioning state structures and an enforced monopoly of violence."[59] It is certainly no coincidence that today's theorists of state-building rely on Max Weber,[60] the sober analyst of the significance of the modern state.

NOTES

1. Duncan Kelly, *The State of the Political: Conceptions of Politics and the State in the Thought of Max Weber, Carl Schmitt and Franz Neumann*, 2nd ed. (Oxford: Oxford University Press, 2008), 4.

2. Matthias vom Hau, "State Theory," in *The Oxford Handbook of Transformations of the State*, ed. Stephan Leibfried et al. (Oxford: Oxford University Press, 2015), 131–151, 135ff.

3. Nicolas Lemay-Hébert, Nicholas Onuf, and Vojin Rakić, "Introduction: Disputing Weberian Semantics," in *Semantics of Statebuilding: Language, Meanings and Sovereignty*, ed. Nicolas Lemay-Hébert, Nicholas Onuf, Vojin Rakić, and Petar Bojanić (New York: Routledge, 2014), 1–18, 7.

4. Cf. Andreas Anter, *Max Weber und die Staatsrechtslehre* (Tübingen, Germany: Mohr Siebeck, 2016), 3ff.

5. Max Weber, "The 'Objectivity' of Knowledge in Social Science and Social Policy," in *The Essential Weber (hereafter Essential)*, ed. Sam Whimster (London: Routledge, 2004), 359–404, 371; *Zur Logik und Methodik der Sozialwissenschaften. Schriften 1900–1907, Max*

Weber-Gesamtausgabe (hereafter *MWG*) I/7, ed. G. Wagner with C. Härpfer et al. (Tübingen, Germany: Mohr [Siebeck], 2018), 142–234.

6. Weber, "The 'Objectivity' of Knowledge," 394; *MWG* I/7, 216.

7. See Gangolf Hübinger, "Einleitung," in Weber, *Allgemeine Staatslehre und Politik (Staatssoziologie)*, *MWG* III/7, ed. G. Hübinger with A. Terwey (Tübingen, Germany: Mohr [Siebeck], 2009), 1–39; Stefan Breuer, "Max Webers Staatssoziologie," *Kölner Zeitschrift für Soziologie und Sozialpsychologie* 45 (1993): 119–219, 215ff.

8. Wilhelm Hennis, *Max Weber's Central Question*, trans. Keith Tribe, 2nd ed. (Newbury, UK: Threshold Press, 2000), 98.

9. Cf. Weber, *Allgemeine Staatslehre und Politik*, 66.

10. For this attempt, see Andreas Anter, *Max Weber's Theory of the Modern State: Origins, Structure and Significance*, trans. Keith Tribe (Basingstoke, UK: Palgrave Macmillan, 2014).

11. Weber, "Basic Sociological Concepts," in *Essential*, 311–358, 356; *Wirtschaft und Gesellschaft. Soziologie*, *MWG* I/23, ed. K. Borchardt, E. Hanke, and W. Schluchter (Tübingen, Germany: Mohr [Siebeck], 2013), 147–215, 212.

12. Weber, "Basic Sociological Concepts," 357; *MWG* I/23, 214.

13. Weber, *Economy and Society. An Outline of Interpretive Sociology* (hereafter *E&S*), ed. G. Roth and C. Wittich (New York: Bedminster Press, 1968), 212–301, cf. 223; *MWG* I/23, 449–591, cf. 463.

14. *E&S*, 971 (translation modified); *Wirtschaft und Gesellschaft. Nachlaß. Herrschaft*, *MWG* I/22-4, ed. E. Hanke with Th. Kroll (Tübingen, Germany: Mohr [Siebeck], 2005), 181.

15. For this, see Anter, *Max Weber's Theory of the Modern State*, 46ff.; Stefan Breuer, *"Herrschaft" in der Soziologie Max Webers* (Wiesbaden, Germany: Harrassowitz, 2011); Edith Hanke and Wolfgang J. Mommsen, eds., *Max Webers Herrschaftssoziologie* (Tübingen, Germany: Mohr Siebeck, 2001).

16. *E&S*, 215; *MWG* I/23, 453.

17. Weber, "Basic Sociological Concepts," 356; *MWG* I/23, 212.

18. *E&S*, 904–905; *Wirtschaft und Gesellschaft. Nachlaß. Gemeinschaften*, *MWG* I/22-1, ed. W. J. Mommsen with M. Meyer (Tübingen, Germany: Mohr [Siebeck], 2001), 208–209.

19. See Thomas Ertman, *Birth of the Leviathan: Building States and Regimes in Medieval and Early Modern Europe*, 2nd ed. (Cambridge: Cambridge University Press, 2008); Philip S. Gorski, *The Disciplinary Revolution: Calvinism and the Birth of the State in Early Modern Europe* (Chicago: University of Chicago Press, 2003), 79ff.

20. Cf. Reinhart Koselleck, *Preußen zwischen Reform und Revolution* (Stuttgart, Germany: Klett-Cotta, 2001), 674, 547.

21. Weber, *Die Lage der Landarbeiter im ostelbischen Deutschland 1892*, *MWG* I/3, ed. M. Riesebrodt (Tübingen, Germany: Mohr [Siebeck], 1984), 914.

22. However, important exceptions are the works of Charles Tilly, Stefan Breuer, Philip S. Gorski, and Thomas Ertman.

23. Weber, "Suffrage and Democracy in Germany," in his *Political Writings*, ed. Peter Lassman and Ronald Speirs, 6th ed. (Cambridge: Cambridge University Press, 2008), 80–129, 101; *Zur Politik im Weltkrieg. Schriften und Reden 1914–1918*, *MWG* I/15, ed. W. J. Mommsen with G. Hübinger (Tübingen, Germany: Mohr [Siebeck], 1984), 347–396, 367.

24. Heinrich Popitz, *Phenomena of Power: Authority, Domination, and Violence*, trans. Gianfranco Poggi (New York: Columbia University Press, 2017), 185.

25. For this, see "Max Weber und Rudolph Sohm," in Anter, *Max Weber und die Staatsrechtslehre*, 47–68; Stephen P. Turner and Regis A. Factor, *Max Weber: The Lawyer as Social Thinker* (London and New York: Routledge, 1994), 110ff.

26. Cf. Rudolph Sohm, "Die Entwicklungsgeschichte des modernen Staates," *Cosmopolis* 5 (1897): 853–872, 861.

27. Rudolph Sohm, *Die Fränkische Reichs- und Gerichtsverfassung* (1871), 2nd ed. (Leipzig, Germany: Duncker & Humblot, 1911), XIV.

28. Rudolf von Jhering, *Law as a Means to an End* (1877), trans. Isaac Husic (Boston: Boston Book, 1913), 238.

29. For historical aspects, see Anter, *Max Weber's Theory of the Modern State*, 149ff.

30. Cf. *E&S*, 970–971, 990, 1089–1090, 1097, 1102–1103; *MWG* I/22-4, 180–181, 212–213, 416ff., 431–432, 441–442.

31. Carl Schmitt, "Staat als ein konkreter, an eine geschichtliche Epoche gebundener Begriff" (1941), in his *Verfassungsrechtliche Aufsätze aus den Jahren 1924–1954* (Berlin: Duncker & Humblot, 1958), 375–385, 384.

32. See Thomas Vesting, "Absolutismus und materiale Rationalisierung. Zur Entstehung des preußischen Patrimonialstaates," *Archiv des öffentlichen Rechts* 119 (1994): 369–399; Helmut Quaritsch, *Staat und Souveränität*, vol. 1 (Frankfurt am Main, Germany: Athenäum, 1970), 32ff.; Ernst-Wolfgang Böckenförde, "Die Entstehung des Staates als Vorgang der Säkularisation" (1967), in his *Recht, Staat, Freiheit* (Frankfurt am Main, Germany: Suhrkamp, 1991), 92–114.

33. Norbert Elias, *The Civilizing Process: Sociogenetic and Psychogenetic Investigations*, vol. 2, trans. Edmund Jephcott, rev. ed. (Oxford: Blackwell, 2000).

34. Niklas Luhmann, *Political Theory in the Welfare State*, trans. John Bednarz (Berlin and New York: de Gruyter, 1990), 74.

35. Popitz, *Phenomena of Power*, 184–185.

36. See Paul du Gay and Alan Scott, "State Transformation or Regime Shift? Addressing Some Confusions in the Theory and Sociology of the State," *Sociologica* 2 (2010): 1–23; Colin Hay and Michael Lister, "Theories of the State," in *The State: Theories and Issues*, ed. Colin Hay, Michael Lister, and David Marsh (Basingstoke, UK: Palgrave Macmillan, 2006), 1–20, 7ff.; Francis Fukuyama, *State-Building: Governance and World Order in the 21st Century* (New York: Cornell University Press, 2005), 19f.; Josef Isensee, "Staat und Verfassung," in *Handbuch des Staatsrechts der Bundesrepublik Deutschland*, ed. Josef Isensee and Paul Kirchhof, vol. 2, 3rd ed. (Heidelberg, Germany: C. F. Müller, 2004), 3–106, 40–41; Gianfranco Poggi, *Forms of Power* (Cambridge: Polity Press, 2001), 12ff.

37. See David Andersen et al., "State Capacity and Political Regime Stability," *Democratization* 21 (2014): 1305–1325; Keith Krause, "Hybrid Violence: Locating the Use of Force in Postconflict Settings," *Global Governance* 28 (2012): 39–56; Bruce Baker, "Beyond the State Police in Urban Uganda and Sierra Leone," in *Afrika Spectrum* 41 (2006): 55–76.

38. Cf. Daron Acemoglu, James A. Robinson, and Rafael J. Santos, "The Monopoly of Violence: Evidence from Colombia," *Journal of the European Economic Association* 11 (2013): 5–44; Dennis Rodgers and Robert Muggah, "Gangs as Non-State Armed Groups: The Central American Case," *Contemporary Security Policy* 30 (2009): 301–317.

39. See Walter Laqueur, *A History of Terrorism*, exp. ed. (New York: Routledge, 2017), 175 ff.; Bruce Hoffman, *Inside Terrorism*, 2nd ed. (New York: Columbia University Press, 2006).

40. See Molly Dunigan and Ulrich Petersohn, eds., *The Markets for Force: Privatization of Security across World Regions* (Philadelphia: University of Pennsylvania Press, 2015); Elke Krahmann, *States, Citizens and the Privatization of Security* (Cambridge: Cambridge University Press, 2010).

41. In this sense Stefan Breuer, *Der Staat* (Reinbek b. Hamburg: Rowohlt, 1998), 296.

42. Sheldon Wolin, "Postmodern Politics and the Absence of Myth," *Social Research* 52 (1985): 217–239, 226.

43. See, for example, Wolfgang Reinhard, *Geschichte der Staatsgewalt*, 3rd ed. (Munich, Germany: C. H. Beck, 2003), 535.

44. Breuer, *Der Staat*, 298.

45. Cf. Joachim Wagner, *Richter ohne Gesetz. Islamische Paralleljustiz gefährdet unseren Rechtsstaat* (Berlin: Ullstein, 2012). Cf. further Josef Isensee, "Integration mit Migrationshintergrund. Verfassungsrechtliche Daten," *Juristenzeitung* 65 (2010): 317–327; Wolfgang Bock, "Islam, Islamisches Recht und Demokratie," *Juristenzeitung* 67 (2012): 60–68.

46. Cf. Gudrun Krämer, "Gewaltpotentiale im Islam," in *Religionen und Gewalt. Konflikt- und Friedenspotentiale in den Weltreligionen*, ed. Reinhard Hempelmann and Johannes Kandel (Göttingen, Germany: Vandenhoeck & Ruprecht, 2006), 239–248.

47. See Popitz, *Phenomena of Power*, 31ff.

48. Ibid., 40.

49. Hedley Bull, *The Anarchical Society: A Study of Order in World Politics*, 4th ed. (New York: Columbia University Press), 2012.

50. Cf. Saskia Sassen, *A Sociology of Globalization* (London and New York: W. W. Norton, 2007).

51. See, for example, Andreas Voßkuhle, "Der 'Dienstleistungsstaat.' Über Nutzen und Gefahren von Staatsbildern," *Der Staat* 40 (2001): 495–523.

52. See the critical remarks by Paul du Gay and Alan Scott, "Against the 'Adjectival State,'" *Sociologica* 2 (2010): 1–14.

53. Josef Isensee, "Die vielen Staaten in der einen Welt—eine Apologie," *Zeitschrift für Staats- und Europawissenschaft* 1 (2003): 7–31, 12.

54. Catherine Colliot-Thélène, *Demokratie ohne Volk* (Hamburg, Germany: Hamburger Edition, 2011), 214.

55. Dieter Senghaas, "Der Leviathan in diesen Zeiten," *Leviathan* 36 (2008): 175–190, 176–177.

56. Ibid., 190.

57. For this, see David Chandler and Timothy D. Sisk, eds., *The Routledge Handbook of International Statebuilding* (London and New York: Routledge, 2013; Aidan Hehir and Neil Robinson, eds., *State-Building: Theory and Practice* (New York: Routledge, 2007).

58. Cf. Fukuyama, *State-Building*.

59. Wolfgang Knöbl, "Zivilgesellschaft und staatliches Gewaltmonopol. Zur Verschränkung von Gewalt und Zivilität," *Mittelweg* 36, 15 (2006): 61–84, 81.

60. Cf. Lemay-Hébert et al., "Introduction," 1–18; Nicolas Lemay-Hébert, "Rethinking Weberian Approaches to Statebuilding," in Chandler and Sisk, *The Routledge Handbook of International Statebuilding*, 3–14; Fukuyama, *State-Building*.

....

CHAPTER 13

THE RELEVANCE OF WEBER'S CONCEPTION AND TYPOLOGY OF *HERRSCHAFT*

....

STEFAN BREUER

THE SOCIOLOGY OF DOMINATION: GENESIS AND CONCEPTION

....

AMONG the classics of sociology, Max Weber stands out as the scholar who was concerned most intensively and fruitfully with the phenomenon of *Herrschaft*, or domination. In understanding Weber we are well advised not to trace his ideas back to the influence of other authors but instead to consider his training in legal and economic history and his resultant research focus. Even if "domination" was not always front and center in Weber's thought, he encountered it at every turn, whether it was a matter of the condition of agrarian labor in East Elbian Prussia, agrarian relations in antiquity, the Italian city of the Middle Ages, bureaucracy in China, or the caste system in India.

Weber presented the systematization of his views only within the framework of his contributions to the *Grundriß der Sozialökonomik* after 1909–1910. Numerous manuscripts on the theme originated before the outbreak of the First World War—on bureaucracy, patrimonialism, feudalism, and charisma, for example—although at first Weber withheld them from publication. Only after the war did he set about including them in his plan of work, from which emerged the significantly shorter Chapter 3, "Types of Domination," in *Economy and Society*, Part One. Until publication of this chapter in the first edition of *Economy and Society* only a few sketches on the theme were available to the public.[1] In addition, in 1922 the *Preußischen Jahrbücher* published "The Three Pure Types of Legitimate Domination" ("Die drei reinen Typen der legitimen Herrschaft"), whose origin cannot be dated with certainty.[2]

It comes as no surprise that a working process stretching over decades would lead to changes and deferrals. This is true of terminology, such as the vacillation between "traditional" and "traditionalistic authority" (*traditional, traditionell, traditionalistisch*). It also affects semantics: for example, the meaning of "patriarchalism" and "patrimonialism," which oscillates between narrower and broader senses of the terms. And it even affects the number of types of legitimacy: thus, in a Vienna lecture in 1917, the otherwise rigorously maintained triad was expanded to include a fourth type: domination "that at least officially derives its own legitimacy from the will of those who are ruled."[3] To be sure, because in this case the sentence came from a newspaper report, it is not clear whether the statement was Weber's or instead the reporter's interpretation. At least in the final version of his text, Weber did not repeat the thought and reaffirmed his threefold distinction. "Democratic legitimacy" does indeed appear again but under the heading "Die herrschaftsfremde Umdeutung des Charisma" or the transformation of charisma in an antiauthoritarian direction alien to domination.[4]

Power, Domination, Legitimacy

According to Weber, domination is a "special case of power (*Macht*)."[5] The line of demarcation between *genus proximum* and *differentia specifica* coincides with that between history and sociology. Whereas the former is oriented toward "causal analysis and explanation of individual actions, structures and personalities possessing cultural significance," the latter is oriented toward "type concepts and generalized uniformities of empirical process."[6] For Weber power relationships are "sociologically amorphous" and thus the subject matter of history, whether or not it is a matter of unproblematic compliance, actual or constraining force, or coercion. Power becomes sociologically relevant precisely when the "probability (Chance)" occurs that "a command with a given specific content will be obeyed by a given group of persons."[7] Commands may contain very simple or very complex instructions, as is evident in the difference between the command "stand at attention!" and operational directives delivered by the general staff of an army command. In any case it is not simply the presence of mechanical stimuli but rather "a specific meaningful connection between two actions," namely, on the side of the commander particular instructions and information combined with an appeal or imperative and on the side of the obedient party a corresponding understanding and willingness to comply. Once again, this is only possible within the framework of a relational structure that does not have to renew itself with every situation, as do pure power relationships, but instead is determined by a clear allocation of roles between the ruler and the ruled, thus creating an "order."[8]

In the "Basic Sociological Concepts" section of *Economy and Society* Weber couples order so closely with legitimacy that a non-legitimate order does not appear within the field of vision. This has favored readings like that of Talcott Parsons which view any order of domination as legitimate per se and the concept of non-legitimate domination as a contradiction in terms.[9] In the first place, however, in the "division of the complete work" he prepared for the *Grundriß der Sozialökonomik* Weber explicitly proposed writing a chapter on "non-legitimate domination." Secondly, the condition of the text is unambiguous, as became apparent early in opposition to the Parsonian reading.[10] The probability of a command resulting in obedience clearly depends on obedience occurring as a result of the fear of sanctions or the calculation of interests, thus in no way implying consent to the grounds of validity claimed by the dominant party. Belief in legitimacy is present as such because of the actual power of the relations of domination and their impact. Such belief is, as Weber clearly stated, a "superadditum"[11] that does not bring about domination as such but simply supports and stabilizes it. If this belief is missing, then we are dealing with simpler, that is to say, non-legitimate domination based on "the appeal to material or affectual or ideal motives as a basis for its continuance."[12] Such domination may be more unstable when compared with legitimate domination. But empirically there are ample examples of dictatorships and despotisms that have demonstrated a degree of coercive force sufficient to maintain themselves over a long period of time.

The Three Pure Types of Legitimate Domination

An order of domination achieves much greater stability when it emerges with a claim to legitimacy that produces a willingness to comply. This claim can be based on three principles or "grounds of validity": the "belief in the legality of enacted rules and the right of those elevated to authority under such rules to issue commands"—legal domination; the "established belief in the sanctity of immemorial traditions and the legitimacy of those exercising authority under them"—traditional domination; and the belief in "an extraordinary quality of a person"—charismatic domination.[13]

Weber worked with three dualities in the more detailed exposition of these types. In light of the distinction between "everyday" and "extraordinary" patterns, legal and traditional domination stand together on one side, whereas they are distinguished from each other on the basis of the difference between "personal" and "impersonal" or "objective" motives. From the standpoint of the latter distinction, traditional and charismatic domination are close to each other, for their validity rests on "the exceptional sanctity, heroism or exemplary character of an individual person, and of the normative patters or order revealed or ordained by him."[14] Moreover, the attribute "sanctity" or "sacredness" that appears repeatedly in all versions of the typology pulls traditional and charismatic domination into close proximity and at the same time pushes them into opposition with legal domination. This excludes the possibility of identifying legitimacy with charisma and the sacred and in doing so moving Weber closer to Durkheim, as Parsons had proposed.[15] Traditional domination can be sacred, for instance, when it is due to the routinization of charisma. But it need not be sacred, as is indicated by Weber's frequent equating of tradition with habit or custom. Legal domination is really defined conceptually by its diametrical opposition to sacredness or charisma. Furthermore, Weber always spoke only of *belief* in the sanctity of a tradition or a person, whereas Durkheim claimed to derive the sacred from collective actions, rites, and the emotional states they produce. Belief is something other than action, however. For Weber the opposite of the sacred was not the profane but another belief, namely the notion "that any law (*Recht*) can be created and any existing law can be changed by enactment that is decided by formally correct procedure."[16] The issue of "arbitrariness" also emerged in the context of charismatic and traditional domination, though within certain limits. Those norms considered binding for the actor "were at first not conceived as the products, or as even the possible subject matter, of human enactment," for "legal decisions did not originally have any normative element at all," even though today "we take it for granted that legal decisions constitute the 'application' of fixed and stable rules."[17]

The Validity of the Claims to Legitimacy and the Organizational Structure

The three pure types of domination are not generic concepts. They define an appropriate range of possibilities that allows different combinations and gradations both in view of the reasons for legitimacy and in terms of organizational structure. As to the former, legal domination rests primarily on positive statutes, although it can also contain value-rational norms or customary rights. Traditional domination is based on the validity of that which has always existed. But this excludes neither the affective belief in the validity of that which is newly revealed or exemplary, nor the value-rational convictions or belief in the legality of statutory orders. Charismatic domination is based primarily on affectively mediated belief in that which is revealed through a specifically qualified person. But such a belief can acquire intrinsic value over the charisma of a specific person, and consequently it can be value-rational and through its routinization contribute to the legitimation of traditional as well as legal orders of domination.

Weber sketched the following possibilities for organizational structure: legal domination is equated with the approval of any kind of action, limited only by commitment to a rational system, that could be characterized best as domination by means of a bureaucratic administrative staff. Such a bureaucracy is distinguished, on the one hand, by modification of rules and positions and changes in personnel according to principles and, on the other, by precise and predictable handling of official business based on rules.[18] Under particular conditions other organizational forms are also possible, such as "Officialdom through rotation, lots and election, parliamentary and cabinet government, and all kinds of collegial rule and governing bodies."[19]

Traditional domination includes domination by *honoratiores*, or notables based on social honor and prestige, but also alongside it household authority sanctified by filial and domestic piety. Structurally, these types of domination are accompanied by political forms, such as "patrimonial" administration, in which the ruler's capriciousness and the bonds of tradition are in a precarious equilibrium, thus implying a kind of decentralization and giving the members of the staff a certain veto power. "Sultanism" is another political form characterized by a strong bond tying the administrative apparatus to the ruler and affirming the ruler's power and right to intervene and take decisive action. Finally, there is "estate-type domination" in which the administrative staff appropriates extensive powers to itself, as well as the material means of administration.

Charismatic domination ranges across a spectrum of possibilities, from relatively unstructured face-to-face relationships in communal associations, such as a warrior brotherhood or a community of disciples, to more stringent forms of organization that lead to a "transformation of the meaning of charisma itself."[20] Orders based upon "hereditary charisma" belong to the latter category, as represented in the "dynastic state," for example. In addition, there is the enduring structure of "charisma of office," resting on "an objectification (*Versachlichung*) of charisma through ritual," that Weber observed above all in hierocratic associations like the Catholic Church, though not just there alone.[21]

Genuine Charisma

For Weber the manifestation and attribution of genuine charisma is primarily a phenomenon of crises and emergencies and thus not limited to a specific epoch or a particular place. Hence, there is a correspondingly enormous range of studies dealing with charisma. They stretch from status rivalries in acephalous groups—the social order of "regulated anarchy" or "anarchy moderated by compliance with customs"[22]—to the plebiscitary presidency in modern mass democracies. The preferred mode of inquiry is biographical case studies that often take little more from Weber than a few key words, while also confusing charisma with media-inspired celebrity status, thus often leading to debatable revaluations.[23] The use of the concept of charisma in political leadership research is far removed from Weber. So is the literature on corporate governance and management, as well as the by now endless self-help literature promoting "30 minutes of charisma training" or the bromide that "everyone possesses charisma." These directions reflect a growing interest in the mediated "production" or "staging of charisma," though this interest is not easy to reconcile with Weber's thesis.[24] With routinization of the powers that be, perhaps it is charisma's fate to give way either to tradition or to rational forms of association.

Weber himself had introduced an escape route with the qualification that under these conditions charisma "recedes as a creative force and erupts only in short-lived mass emotions with unpredictable effect, during elections and similar occasions."[25] As examples he introduced, among others, Gladstone's election campaign in Great Britain and Theodore Roosevelt's in the United States, the rise of Kurt Eisner after the collapse of the monarchy in Bavaria, and Bonapartism in France. Weber's comments about Bonapartism have mainly attracted attention in the literature.[26] Yet it remains an open question as to what changes exactly in this process whereby the charismatic acclamation of the ruler shifts to the election of the ruler by the community of the ruled: is it only the legitimacy at the top reinterpreted as "antiauthoritarian," or is it the structure of the organized group subject to charismatic authority (*Herrschaftsverband*) as a whole? Weber's model of "plebiscitary democracy" points more in the first direction, though he did not explicitly exclude other alternatives. Today such alternatives are discussed above all in investigations of fascist movements, which not only are concerned with charismatic leadership of a party but also analyze fascist parties as a whole from the standpoint of the "emotional form of communal relationship," a point of view typically used when studying charismatic organized groups.[27] There are informative studies of individual leaders, as well as studies of the paramilitary groups that support them.[28] The analyses of Germany, Italy, and Spain show how differentiated the routinization of charisma can become.[29] The interpretation of the Nazi regime in Hans-Ulrich Wehler's *Deutscher Gesellschaftsgeschichte* has a strong connection to Weber, although instead of working with a conception of the antiauthoritarian transformation of charisma and its legitimate variants, he draws upon a concept of "political religion" that cannot be found in Weber.[30] Moreover, in the study of fascism, charismatic domination is often dealt with simply by notions about a "sacralization of politics" that tilt toward Durkheim, Gustave Le Bon, or Mircea Eliade and are only contingently compatible with Weber's sociology.[31]

THE INSTITUTIONALIZATION OF CHARISMA

The "institutional expression of charisma" became an additional focal point for the reception of Weber's ideas. Following Parsons' interpretation of Weber, his comrade-in-arms, Edward Shils, emphasized that charisma did not simply apply to prominent individual personalities. Sociologically, "institutional charisma" had much greater significance, manifesting itself in two ways: as an expression of institutionally concentrated power as such that evokes "the sense of *tremendum mysteriosum*" in all those who come into contact with it, "which Rudolf Otto designated as the central property of the 'idea of the holy,'" and as the link connecting this power with the "central value system of the society."[32] In this double configuration charisma would contribute to the legitimacy of traditional as well as rational-legal orders so that Weber's claim of a disjunction between modern and premodern orders cold be dismissed as "too historicist."[33] S. N. Eisenstadt put forward the same argument when issuing a selection of texts in 1968 under the title *Max Weber on Charisma and Institution Building*.[34]

No doubt the dedication of Parsons and his school can be thanked for the worldwide acclaim awarded Weber's sociology. Yet there was a considerable price to pay, especially for the sociology of domination. *Herrschaft* was converted to "authority" and "leadership" instead of domination, thus losing the imperative character that Weber considered so central to its meaning. Charisma in turn became more or less identical with the normative order, which for its part was assimilated to the sacred in the sense used by Rudolf Otto. But presumably it was these "creative misinterpretations," in Guenther Roth's phrase, that paved the way for Weber's typology to be used in other disciplines, such as anthropology, ethnology, archeology, or theology. Even so, from this perspective the boundary between charisma and the sacred became blurred, as was the case with scholars like Durkheim and Eliade; and a concept like charismatic kingship could be seamlessly transposed into "divine kingship" or "sacred kingship," well-known concepts since James Frazer and Arthur Hocart.

Clifford Geertz's work can be read as exemplary for this development: in 1977 he published an essay, "Center, Kings, and Charisma," in a commemorative volume for Edward Shils and subsequently developed his thinking further in a book about the Balinese theater state of the nineteenth century. While the essay addressed the ceremonial forms "by which kings take symbolic possession of the realm," the book described the charismatic significance of ceremonial regalia and priestly rituals, highlighting in contrast to Weber's concept the idea of charisma (*sekti*) as a supernatural power "which grows out of imagining the truth, not out of believing, obeying, possessing, organizing, utilizing, or even understanding it."[35] Furthermore, Geertz downplayed the issue of proving oneself or testing (*Bewährung*) that was so important for Weber, not least because it could be reflected in the material well-being of the ruled, as perspicacious critiques have shown, even though mostly written from other than a Weberian point of view.[36]

Geertz's thesis that the relationships of the king to the priesthood and to the material world, as well as each one to the other, are all simultaneously constructed in the cult of the divine king has been taken up by Stanley Tambiah and notably expanded by him. Tambiah maintained that the rituals possessed organizational and coordinating importance not only for the center (*negara*) but also for the village and rural periphery (*desa*). In place of the more static theater state he introduced the ideal type of the "galactic polity," which lacks stable hereditary charisma and whose claim to domination is based much more on the pure personal charisma of pretenders to authority, with the result of continuous palace rebellions, struggles over succession, and secessions.[37] While its origins have become obscured, this ideal type that for Tambiah clearly referred back to Weber has by now had a successful career in different fields and has been used in investigations of the Mayans, the southern Amazon, and Tibet.[38]

Whereas interpretive anthropology was inclined to concentrate on the expressive and more spectacular features of charismatic domination, ignoring the aspect of proving oneself, the exact opposite was true of neo-evolutionary approaches. For example, in a comparison of segmented African lineages with Polynesian ramages, Marshall Sahlins advanced the thesis that the transition from the tribal stage, with its purely personal charismatic leadership, to the stage of chiefdom, with its reliance on hereditary and office charisma, could not be separated from the development of permanent economic and political functions. These functions could be combined in the concept of redistribution.[39]

Though Sahlins failed to mention Weber, Elman Service invoked him all the more in his representation of the same process, admittedly in a framework derived primarily from Durkheim. For Service the institutional deployment of charisma was the result of a conversion of mechanical solidarity into organic solidarity.[40] This book strongly influenced the new archeology, though in the meantime this field had also produced work having to do more with Weber than with Durkheim.[41] Various studies of the rise of kingship in Japan or the institutionalization of Shi'ite Islam have also referred to less common types of charisma, such as military or religious charisma.[42]

TRADITIONAL AUTHORITY:
PATRIMONIALISM

Traditional domination or authority includes a spectrum ranging from the most common household form of rule (patriarchalism) and gerontocracy to the most varied forms of patrimonialism and feudalism. With respect to patriarchalism and gerontocracy, if anything it was the casual nature of Weber's exposition that inhibited a more in-depth look at the relationship. But with feudalism it was the complexity involved in the construction of the concept, especially the relationship between prebendal, fiefdom (*Pfründe*) and benefice (*Lehen*) feudalism, as well as urban or *polis* feudalism. Few authors have engaged with these finer conceptual distinctions.[43] Thus, the history of the reception of the concept has been confined to patrimonialism, which appeared in the older version of *Economy and Society* as "arbitrary" and "stereotypical" patrimonialism and in the newer version as "pure" or "estate-type" patrimonialism. In a careful textual analysis Siegfried Hermes has disaggregated these concepts.[44] Various studies of S. N. Eisenstadt have demonstrated how the concepts can be utilized for improving theories of modernization. He has also addressed the use of patrimonialism to account for the form assumed by a traditional world empire, a novel use only implied by Weber's ideal type.[45]

Weber probably first encountered patrimonialism in his investigations of agrarian relations in antiquity: the ideal types of the "bureaucratic city kingdom," the "bureaucratic river kingdom," or the "authoritarian liturgical state" already contained essential features of patrimonial domination. But his insights found little resonance in either Egyptology or studies of the ancient Orient. Exceptions are a minor study, "The Early State in Egypt," and a major work on the city of Ugarit.[46] Similarly, in studies of the anthropology of the Americas, a field well beyond Weber's horizon, it remained an isolated suggestion to understand the states of the Andean world as patrimonial states without a bureaucratic administrative staff.[47]

By contrast, investigations of China and India obviously reveal a much more profound reception of the work, conditioned by Weber's studies in the sociology of religion. In the case of China one nevertheless comes across highly contradictory judgments.

Such a knowledgeable expert on early Chinese history as David Keightley has seen the essential features of a "patrimonial theocracy" already developing in the Shang dynasty (c. 1600–1046 BCE), while at the same time conceding "that the Shang polity still shared some of the features of complex chiefdoms."[48] Wolfram Eberhard described the development of the succeeding state of the Zhou (1046–221 BCE) as one from patrimonialism to feudalism, whereas Cho-yun Hsu maintained that the dynasty's late phase marked a change from traditional to rational-legal domination.[49] On the other hand, Li Feng conceived of the Zhou dynasty as a hybrid of characteristics drawn from rational bureaucracy in Weber's sense and the more archaic structures of a "delegatory kin-ordered settlement state."[50] Gary Hamilton reproached Weber for having constructed his ideal type of patrimonialism too narrowly on the Roman idea of *patria potestas*, while also considering the type mutatis mutandis meaningful for China.[51] But Karl Bünger strongly opposed this view.[52] In this regard the work of Arnold Zingerle still provides an indispensable corrective, for many of these judgments are derived from only one type of legitimacy that is misunderstood as "a summary of an underlying reality."[53]

The state of the discussion is less controversial with respect to the aspects of the sociology of domination related to Hinduism and Buddhism. In 1966 Louis Dumont confirmed Weber's diagnosis of a clear separation between political and hierocratic powers, although without engaging with the concept of patrimonialism.[54] But that engagement did occur with Tambiah's work on the Mauryan Empire and in the work of Blake, Hardy, and Pernau on the Mughals and their followers.[55] Divergent views that started with Hocart or Aidan Southall were put forward for the medieval kingdoms of southern India. One of the most prominent representatives of this interpretation was Burton Stein. A few years after publication of his book *Peasant and State in Medieval South India*, he saw a development of patrimonialism in the "segmented state" of Chola (ninth to thirteenth centuries), which only achieved full expression in the state of Vijayanagara (fourteenth to sixteenth centuries) and then finally assumed the form of "sultanism" in the eighteenth-century kingdom of Mysore.[56] Hermann Kulke and Jakob Rösel arrived at similar results, along with Georg Berkemer, who referred to Weber extensively.[57] The "theater state" in Indonesia, under strong Indian influence, was also conceived by J. J. Bakker as a variant of patrimonialism.[58]

Pre-revolutionary Russia is another outstanding representative of patrimonialism in Weber's writings, even with the qualification that around 1800 its system of domination still "showed strong similarities to the monarchy of Diocletian," while since then outgrowing such traditions and "finally entering the path of specifically European development."[59] Weber believed that tradition could still be attributed only to the orthodox church and the agrarian peasant commune and even here only with qualification in view of caesaropapism and advancing agrarian capitalism. Richard Pipes saw matters the same way, even after a mostly negative discussion of Weber's writings on Russia. In his version of patrimonialism (seen from the standpoint of its partial breakdown in the eighteenth and early nineteenth centuries), the concept and practice were narrowed so much to mean the arbitrary exercise of domination that the czarist empire already appeared to prefigure modern totalitarianism. Patrimonialism in this sense was distinguished from totalitarianism only by lack of technical efficiency and half-hearted concessions to Western models.[60] Without embracing the thesis of a buildup into totalitarianism, Vatro Murvar also advanced this interpretation and postulated a continuity of patrimonial domination from the empire of the czars to Brezhnev.[61] Others have confined themselves to the Stalinist regime.[62] And still others locate the Bolsheviks in the vicinity of charismatic domination but differ on the question of whether the routinization of charisma is to be understood as a traditionalist revival, a kind of neo-traditionalism, or a functionally incompatible combination of rational and traditional elements.[63] Weber's view that we are dealing with forms of non-legitimate domination in Russia since the late nineteenth century is a compelling assessment, especially in view of the difficulties of making something of "tradition" in a regime, like that in the Soviet Union, which experienced rapid economic and social change. The non-legitimate forms were introduced with the czarist police state and henceforth oscillated between the poles of pure terrorism and "naked bureaucratic domination."[64]

Beyond these observations, Weber provided only scattered references about the relevance of patrimonialism in Europe, with the result that the reception of his concept has remained limited and isolated. This holds true for the late Roman Empire, in which Peter Eich has located elements of a "personal bureaucracy."[65] It is also the case for the post-Carolingian middle ages, where Thomas Bisson has found signs of patrimonial domination.[66] And it applies above all to the absolutist states of the early modern period, a few of which, such as Prussia, tended more toward "arbitrary patrimonialism," whereas others like the *ancien régime* in France were caught in the struggle between arbitrary and "stereotypical patrimonialism."[67] With sights set on France, Prussia, and Russia, John Armstrong has produced a comparative study of the restrictive effects of patrimonialism with regard to the development of modern bureaucracy.[68] Some authors have also identified patrimonial structures in the colonial empires of the European powers, as well as in their successor states, a view that has gained a lot of attention especially in Latin America.[69]

Patrimonialism has probably been amplified most in connection with an essay of Guenther Roth's in which he proposed to elaborate and extend Weber's typology. Roth's starting point was the observation that in the new states tradition has in many cases lost its legitimating force, though without having been replaced by "legal-rational modernity." Thus, a situation has arisen in which forms of personal domination assert themselves that do not require any type of legitimation like that found in Weber's typology but are instead based overwhelmingly on "material incentives and rewards" or, more clearly stated, on clientelism and corruption.[70] The term "neo-patrimonialism" soon emerged for this new "de-traditionalized, personalized patrimonialism." Since then, the term has emerged in numerous investigations, especially those dealing with postcolonial regimes and successor states of the Soviet Union, more or less replacing the expression "authoritarian regime" that had been in common use previously. There are undoubtedly such relations of domination, and they can persist for excessively long periods. However, corruption depends on the availability of material resources, which must be sufficiently large to outbid potential competitors. Clientelism then becomes a strategy of social exchange that can perhaps generate support but never legitimacy.[71] In short, in these cases it is a matter of forms of non-legitimate domination that are precarious, and one should identify them as such, instead of confusing them terminologically with the types of legitimate domination.

LEGAL AUTHORITY WITH A BUREAUCRATIC ADMINISTRATIVE STAFF

If concepts like charisma and patrimonialism have been widely accepted and used, then the same cannot be said about legal domination or authority with a bureaucratic administrative staff. On the contrary, in this regard an opposition developed early to both aspects of this ideal type. From neo-Aristotelians like Leo Strauss and Eric Voegelin to neo-Marxists like Herbert Marcuse and Theodor Adorno, a phalanx formed of those who saw Weber's type as an expression of the subjectivizing and formalizing of reason and then equated it with a capitulation to positivism and a collapse into nihilism, decisionism, and irrationalism. Nothing was altered by more differentiated interpretations as they either denied that Weber had shied away from the ultimate consequences of Nietzsche's thought, and thus had followed his transition to a kind of practical nihilism, or they limited their critique to the charge that Weber had renounced the application of his comprehensive concept of rationality at the level of institutions. This criticism in turn meant that he had arrived at a completely implausible notion of legality as an independent, stand-alone type of legitimate authority or domination.[72] Opposing such a view and given their conception of the "positivity of law," systems theorists like Niklas Luhmann fully accepted Weber's understanding of legality but then rejected as outdated the model of command so central to his theory of bureaucracy and to his conception of *Herrschaft*. Indeed, the model of command was just as obsolete as the ends/means scheme. Considering legality, narrowing organizations to a single type of communication and taking as a basis "the rationalization of the standpoint of an individual participant, such as a founder, an entrepreneur or a sovereign," the latter criticism of the model of command gave priority to the insight "that the ends/means scheme as a model of rational action does not describe in the same vein the structuring of rationality in rational systems."[73]

Weyma Lübbe has maintained in a convincing argument that Weber's sociology is not a kind of legal positivism, a position that also corrects the interpretations of Habermas and Luhmann.[74] We only note that the expressed tendency found among critics as well as many defenders of Weber to identify the mode of functioning in modern bureaucracies with purposive or instrumental rationality only partially captures Weber's perspective. To be sure, in the essay "On Some Categories of Interpretive Sociology," Weber wrote about "an ever wider-ranging purposively rational ordering [*zweckrationale Ordnung*] of consensual action through ordinance[s] and, in particular, the increasingly frequent transformation of associative groupings into institutions ordered in a purposively rational manner."[75] Yet modern bureaucracies are not fully characterized in this way. On the one hand, this obscures the basic structural framework that is essential and, on the other, this type of bureaucracy (in contrast to traditional institutions) does not simply embody purposive rationality but instead carries out "formal rationalized purposive action, according to which every undertaking is predictable, certain and machine-like."[76] But formal rationality—Weber's often invoked notion of a "calculative spirit" (*Rechenhaftigkeit*)—is analytically independent from purposive or instrumental rationality (*Zweckrationalität*). As the result of rationalization through science and scientifically oriented technology described in "Science as a Vocation," purposive or instrumental rationality is on a higher level than the four types of social action presented in the "Basic Sociological Concepts" in *Economy and Society*. It makes possible above all "that all the elements of the scene of action can be organized and made reversible."[77]

By contrast with political philosophy and sociological macro-theory, empirically oriented research has to this day found useful instruments in Weber's toolkit for making sense of the vicissitudes of action and the highly conflictual way in which action occurs.[78] Consider a few examples: in his previously cited comparison of nineteenth-century French and Russian higher administration, John Armstrong has illuminated the modalities and causes of "bureaucratic regression." Or, using the example of Prussia, Joachim Renn has described the combination of formal-rational bureaucracy and habitual certitude resting on membership in a particular cultural milieu, while Eugenie Samier has pursued "the transformation of senior administration from a mandarinate to the new managerialism" on the basis of different states in the Commonwealth.[79] Scholars have justifiably criticized the way in which Weber's ideal types have been trimmed, pruned, and decontextualized and complained about ignoring his warning that it is rare for organized groups to be characterized by only one of the three pure types of domination. Samier herself has demonstrated that an investigation oriented toward the recognition of mixed forms of domination has much to offer by way of a more differentiated analysis. The administrative systems she has studied display a peculiar mixture of personal rule and impersonal rationality, which has less to do with rational-legal domination than with an efficiency-oriented economy.[80] Mixed types of legitimate domination also play an important role in an investigation of the German Democratic Republic, as well as in an instructive comparison on administrative rationalization in England, France, the United States, and Japan, which concludes that "at least two varieties of role systems govern the form and structure of the rationalized administrative organization": namely, the "organizational orientation" emphasized by Weber, and the "professional orientation" that can be observed especially in England.[81]

DEVELOPMENTAL TRENDS OF
LEGAL AUTHORITY

As for the situation at the beginning of the twenty-first century, some authors have insisted that we concentrate on the persistence of the hierarchical patterns of control that Weber described.[82] Or they have insisted at the very least on speaking of a "neo-Weberian state" in which the conventional constitutional and regulatory culture of the state should be bound together with new "managerial" elements.[83] The latter view may have a certain justification in view of different developmental paths for the nation-state, but it does not take fully into account the changes affecting the administrative staff responsible for enforcing bureaucratic norms, as well as the challenges to faith in legality and the rule of law. Regarding the former, Weber could not have imagined the extent to which central public responsibilities could be privatized either entirely or partially—basic tasks like safeguarding public safety with the police and the military. Nor could he have anticipated that health services and social security could be administered primarily from the point of view of economic efficiency, rather than according to juridical principles.[84] Weber did see that in terms of specialized technical and factual knowledge only the private entrepreneur, within his or her own sphere, could as a general rule be superior to the state bureaucracy. But he did not appreciate the extent to which bureaucracy would become dependent on outside expert scientific knowledge, especially natural scientific and technical knowledge.[85] Nor did he foresee that in the real world, for instance, in planning or fiscal administration, success could only be achieved if officials renounced a total commitment to the instrumentalities of sovereign authority and instead relied on bargaining strategies and informal consensus formation, even in the criminal law, as the phenomenon of "plea-bargaining" demonstrates.[86]

These discussions do not leave faith in the law and legality unaffected. When belief in the rule of law is grounded not in particular norms but instead in a "mode of producing norms whose results should be independent from the will of those concerned and regardless of their consent,"[87] this way of establishing norms surely does imply the compatibility of the new norms with those already in existence; that is, it implies respect for the system of existing law. Weber himself thought this assumption was no longer self-evident. In the concluding passages of his sociology of law, he postulated a "weakening" or indeed a "dissolution of legal formalism" and, even more than that, an increasing "particularization" of the law revealed in a progressive differentiation into more and more specialized legal domains. Sociological, economic, and ethical reasoning became superimposed on purely legalistic constructions. Instead of being an autonomous system, law increasingly became a heteronomous structure, for "In the great majority of its most important provisions, it has been unmasked all too visibly, indeed, as the product or the technical means of a compromise between conflicting interests."[88] This statement by Weber reads like an anticipation of new concepts, with the development of the law determined by methods of "policy analysis."[89] Moreover, it also suggests a description of legislative and implementation processes that are typical not only for sovereign individual states but also for a confederation of states like the European Union, where decisions are arrived at through compromise by political trade-offs and the reconciliation of competing interests.[90] The impracticality of revising such decisions because of high transaction and decision-making costs can even contribute to undermining the foundational belief for rational-legal domination "that any law can be created and any existing law can be changed by enactment that is decided by formally correct procedure."[91] It is especially the analyses oriented toward Weber that have opened our eyes to such possibilities.[92]

Translated from the German by Lawrence A. Scaff

Notes

1. See Max Weber, "On Some Categories of Interpretive Sociology," in *Collected Methodological Writings* (hereafter *CMW*), ed. H. H. Bruun and S. Whimster, trans. H. H. Bruun (London: Routledge, 2012), 299–301; *Zur Logik und Methodik der Sozialwissenschaften. Schriften 1900–1907, Max Weber-Gesamtausgabe* (hereafter *MWG*) I/7, ed. G. Wagner, with C. Härpfer et al. (Tübingen, Germany: Mohr [Siebeck], 2018), 436–440; "The Social Psychology of the World Religions" (= "Introduction to the Economic Ethics of the World Religions"), in *From Max Weber: Essays in Sociology* (hereafter *FMW*), ed. H. H. Gerth and C. W. Mills (New York: Oxford University Press, 1946), 295–300; *Die Wirtschaftsethik der Weltreligionen. Hinduismus und Buddhismus, MWG* I/20, ed. H. Schmidt-Glintzer, with K.-H. Golzio (Tübingen, Germany: Mohr [Siebeck], 1996), 119–127; "Probleme der Staatssoziologie" in *Wirtschaft und Gesellschaft. Nachlaß. Herrschaft, MWG* I/22-4, ed. E. Hanke, with Th. Kroll (Tübingen, Germany: Mohr [Siebeck], 2005), 745–756; "Politics as a Vocation," in *FMW*, 78–80, *Wissenschaft als Beruf 1917/1919—Politik als Beruf 1919, MWG* I/17, ed. W. J. Mommsen and W. Schluchter, with B. Morgenbrod (Tübingen, Germany: Mohr [Siebeck], 1992), 160–163.
2. "The Three Pure Types of Legitimate Rule," in *The Essential Weber* (hereafter *Essential*), ed. S. Whimster (London: Routledge, 2004), 133–145; *MWG* I/22-4, 726–742.
3. *MWG* I/22-4, 755.
4. Weber, *Economy and Society* (hereafter *E&S*) ed. G. Roth and C. Wittich (Berkeley: University of California Press, 1978), 266–271; *Wirtschaft und Gesellschaft. Soziologie, MWG* I/23, ed. K. Borchardt, E. Hanke, and W. Schluchter (Tübingen, Germany: Mohr [Siebeck], 2013), 533 ff.; Roth and Wittich translated this section heading as "The Transformation of Charisma in a Democratic Direction."
5. *E&S*, 941; *MWG* I/22-4, 127.
6. *E&S*, 19; *MWG* I/23, 169.
7. *E&S*, 53; Parsons translated *die Chance* ("opportunity," "chance") as "probability;" *MWG* I/23, 210–211.
8. Hartmann Tyrell, "Gewalt, Zwang und die Institutionalisierung von Herrschaft: Versuch einer Neuinterpretation von Max Webers Herrschaftsbegriff," in *Person und Institution*, ed. R. Pohlmann (Würzburg, Germany: Königshausen und Neumann, 1980), 59–92, 73–74, 76–77, 80–81.

9. Talcott Parsons, *The Structure of Social Action*, 2nd ed. (Glencoe, IL: Free Press, 1949), 658 ff.; Klaus Schreiner, "Die mittelalterliche Stadt in Max Webers Analyse und die Deutung des okzidentalen Rationalismus," in *Max Weber, der Historiker*, ed. J. Kocka (Göttingen, Germany: Vandenhoeck & Ruprecht, 1986), 119–150, 126.

10. Jere Cohen, Lawrence E. Hazelrigg, and Whitney Pope, "De-Parsonizing Weber: A Critique of Parsons' Interpretation of Weber's Sociology," *American Sociological Review* 40 (1975): 229–241, 237 ff.

11. *E&S*, 327; *Wirtschaft und Gesellschaft. Nachlaß. Recht*, MWG I/22-3, ed. W. Gephart and S. Hermes (Tübingen, Germany: Mohr [Siebeck], 2010), 227.

12. *E&S*, 213; *MWG* I/23, 450.

13. *E&S*, 215; *FMW*, 295; *MWG* I/23, 453; *Die Wirtschaftsethik der Weltreligionen. Konfuzianismus und Taoismus. Schriften 1915–1920*, MWG I/19, ed. H. Schmidt-Glintzer, with P. Kolonko (Tübingen, Germany: Mohr [Siebeck], 1989), 122; in the passages in *Economy and Society* Roth and Wittich translate *Herrschaft* not as "domination" but as "authority."

14. *E&S*, 214; *MWG* I/23, 453.

15. Parsons, *Structure*, 662 ff., and the criticism in Whitney Pope, Jere Cohen, and Lawrence E. Hazelrigg, "On the Divergence of Weber and Durkheim: A Critique of Parsons' Convergence Thesis," *American Sociological Review* 40 (1975): 417–427.

16. *Essential*, 133; *MWG* I/22-4, 726.

17. *E&S*, 760; *MWG* I/22-3, 445–446.

18. Hartmann Tyrell, "Ist der Webersche Bürokratietypus ein objektiver Richtigkeitstypus?" *Zeitschrift für Soziologie* 10 (1981): 38–49, 46, 48.

19. *Essential*, 135; *MWG* I/22-4, 728–729.

20. *Essential*, 142; *MWG* I/22-4, 739.

21. *Essential*, 143; *E&S*, 248, 1139–1141; *MWG* I/23, 501ff.; *MWG* I/22-4, 519, 741.

22. *E&S*, 1134; *MWG* I/22-4, 514.

23. *Virtuosen der Macht. Herrschaft und Charisma von Perikles bis Mao*, ed. Wilfried Nippel (Munich: C. H. Beck, 2000); *Caribbean Charisma. Reflections on Leadership, Legitimacy and Populist Politics*, ed. Anton L. Allahar (Kingston, Jamaica: Randle, 2001); *Charismatische Führer der deutschen Nation*, ed. Frank Möller (Munich: Oldenbourg, 2004); Franz Walter, *Charismatiker und Effizienzen. Porträts aus 60 Jahren Bundesrepublik* (Frankfurt am Main, Germany: Suhrkamp, 2009); *Charisma und Herrschaft. Führung und Verführung in der Politik*, ed. Berit Bliesemann de Guevara and Tatjana Reiber (Frankfurt am Main, Germany: Campus, 2011); *Political Leadership, Nations and Charisma*, ed. Vivian Ibrahim and Magit Wunsch (London: Routledge, 2012); Andrew D. McCulloch, *Charisma and Patronage. A Dialogue with Max Weber* (Farnham, UK: Ashgate, 2014); *Das Charisma des Herrschers*, ed. Dietrich Boschung and Jürgen Hammerstaedt (Paderborn, Germany: Fink, 2015).

24. Jay A. Conger and Rabindra Nath Kanungo, *Charismatic Leadership in Organizations* (Thousand Oaks, CA: Sage, 1998); Johannes Steyrer, *Charisma in Organisationen* (Frankfurt am Main, Germany: Campus, 1995); Ronald M. Glassman, "Manufactured Charisma and Legitimacy," in *Max Weber's Political Sociology. A Pessimistic Vision of a Rationalized World*, ed. R. Glassman and V. Murvar (Westport, CT: Greenwood Press, 1984), 217–235; Jürg Häusermann, ed., *Inszeniertes Charisma. Medien und Persönlichkeit* (Berlin: De Gruyter, 2001); Malte Lenze, *Postmodernes Charisma. Marken und Stars statt Religion und Vernunft* (Wiesbaden, Germany: Deutscher Universitätsverlag, 2002).

25. *E&S*, 1146; *MWG* I/22-4, 558.

26. Hans-Ulrich Thamer, "Napoleon—der Retter der revolutionären Nation," in Nippel, *Virtuosen der Macht*, 121–136; Jörn Leonhard, "Das Präsens der Revolution. Der Bonapartismus in der europäischen Geschichte des 19. und 20. Jahrhunderts," in *Kommunikation und Konfliktaustragung*, ed. Werner Daum et al. (Berlin: Berliner Wissenschafts-Verlag, 2010), 293–317.

27. *E&S*, 243; *MWG* I/23, 493; Stefan Breuer, "Towards an Ideal Type of Fascism," *Max Weber Studies* 8, no. 1 (2008): 11–47.

28. Ian Kershaw, *Hitler* (Harlow, UK: Longman, 1991); Bettina Vogel-Walter, *D'Annunzio – Abenteurer und charismatischer Führer* (Frankfurt am Main, Germany: Lang, 2004); *Charisma and Fascism in Interwar Europe*, ed. António Costa Pinto (London: Routledge, 2007); Oliver Jens Schmitt, *Căpitan Codreanu. Aufstieg und Fall des rumänischen Faschistenführers* (Vienna: Paul Zsolnay Verlag, 2016); Sven Reichardt, *Faschistische Kampfbünde. Gewalt und Gemeinschaft im italienischen Squadrismus und in der deutschen SA* (Köln, Germany: Böhlau, 2000); Constantin Iordachi, *Charisma, Politics and Violence. The Legion of the "Archangel Michael" in Interwar Romania*, Trondheim Studies on East European Cultures and Societies (Trondheim, Norway: Program on East European Cultures and Societies, Norwegian University of Science and Technology, 2004).

29. M. Rainer Lepsius, "Charismatic Leadership: Max Weber's Model and Its Applicability to the Rule of Hitler," in *Conceptions of Leadership*, ed. C. Graumann and S. Moscovici (New York: Springer, 1981), 53–66; Maurizio Bach, *Die charismatischen Führerdiktaturen. Drittes Reich und italienischer Faschismus im Vergleich ihrer Herrschaftsstrukturen* (Baden-Baden, Germany: Nomos, 1990); Steffen Bruendel, "Caudillaje und Charisma 1936 bis 1947. Eine herrschaftssoziologische Annäherung an den frühen Franquismus," in *Rechtsstaat statt Revolution, Verrechtlichung statt Demokratie? Transdisziplinäre Analysen zum deutschen und spanischen Weg in die Moderne*, ed. D. Schulze et al. (Münster, Germany: Westfälisches Dampfboot, 2010), 746–767.

30. Hans-Ulrich Wehler, *Deutsche Gesellschaftsgeschichte*, vol. 4 (Munich: C. H. Beck, 2003).

31. Emilio Gentile, "The Sacralisation of Politics: Definitions, Interpretations and Reflections on the Question of Secular Religion and Totalitarianism," *Totalitarian Movements and Political Religions* 1 (2000): 18–55.

32. Edward Shils, "Charisma, Order, and Status," *American Sociological Review* 30 (1965): 199–213, 205, 209.

33. Ibid., 203.

34. Shmuel N. Eisenstadt, *Max Weber on Charisma and Institution Building* (Chicago: University of Chicago Press, 1968).

35. Clifford Geertz, "Center, Kings, and Charisma: Reflections on the Symbolics of Power" (1977), in *Local Knowledge. Further Essays in Interpretive Anthropology* (London: Fontana Press, 1993), 121–146, 125; *Negara. The Theatre-State in Nineteenth Century Bali* (Princeton, NJ: Princeton University Press, 1980), 106.

36. Martin Ramstedt, *Weltbild, Heilspragmatik und Herrschaftslegitimation im vorkolonialen Bali* (Frankfurt am Main, Germany: Lang, 1998); Brigitta Hauser-Schäublin, "The Precolonial Balinese State Reconsidered," *Current Anthropology* 44 (2003): 153–170.

37. Stanley Jeyaraja Tambiah, *Culture, Thought, and Social Action. An Anthropological Perspective* (Cambridge, MA: Harvard University Press, 1985), 317–318, 325.

38. Arthur A. Demarest, "Ideology in Ancient Maya Cultural Evolution: The Dynamics of Galactic Politics," in *Ideology and Pre-Columbian Civilizations*, ed. A. Demarest and G. Conrad (Santa Fe, NM: School of American Research Press, 1991), 135–158; Michael

Heckenberger, *The Ecology of Power. Culture, Place, and Personhood in the Southern Amazon, A.D. 1000–2000* (New York: Routledge, 2005), 124 ff.; Geoffrey Samuel, *Civilized Shamans. Buddhism in Tibetan Societies* (Washington, DC: Smithsonian Institution Press, 1993), 62–63.

39. Marshall D. Sahlins, *Tribesmen* (Englewood Cliffs, NJ: Prentice Hall, 1968), 91ff.

40. Elman R. Service, *Origins of the State and Civilization: The Process of Cultural Evolution* (New York: Norton, 1975), chap. 4.

41. Werner Leuthäusser, *Die Entwicklung staatlich organisierter Herrschaft in frühen Hochkulturen am Beispiel des Vorderen Orients* (Frankfurt am Main, Germany: Suhrkamp, 1998); Stefan Breuer, *Der charismatische Staat* (Darmstadt, Germany: Wissenschaftliche Buchgesellschaft, 2014); Julia Linke, *Das Charisma der Könige. Zur Konzeption des altorientalischen Königtums im Hinblick auf Urartu* (Wiesbaden, Germany: Harrassowitz, 2015).

42. Joan R. Piggott, *The Emergence of Japanese Kingship* (Stanford, CA: Stanford University Press, 1997); Liyakatali Takim, *The Heirs of the Prophet. Charisma and Religious Authority in Shi'ite Islam* (Albany: State University of New York Press, 2006).

43. Luigi Capogrossi Colognesi, "Il 'feudalesimo cittadino' nella interpretazione weberiana delle società antiche," *Dialogues d'histoire ancienne* 27 (2001): 7–32; Siegfried Hermes, *Soziales Handeln und Struktur der Herrschaft. Max Webers verstehende historische Soziologie am Beispiel des Patrimonialismus* (Berlin: Duncker & Humblot, 2003), 123 ff.; Stefan Breuer, *"Herrschaft" in der Soziologie Max Webers* (Wiesbaden, Germany: Harrassowitz, 2011), 160ff.

44. Hermes, *Soziales Handeln*.

45. S. N. Eisenstadt, *Traditional Patrimonialism and Modern Neopatrimonialism* (Beverly Hills, CA: Sage, 1973); *Tradition, Change and Modernity* (New York: John Wiley & Sons, 1973); *The Political Systems of Empires* (1963; New Brunswick, NJ: Transaction, 1993).

46. Jac J. Janssen, "The Early State in Egypt," in *The Early State*, ed. H. Claessen and P. Skalník (The Hague, The Netherlands: Mouton, 1978), 213–234; J. David Schloen, *The House of the Father as Fact and Symbol: Patrimonialism in Ugarit and the Ancient Near East* (Winona Lake, IN: Eisenbrauns, 2001).

47. Alan L. Kolata, "Of Kings and Capitals. On the Nature of the Andean State," in *The Archaeology of City-States: Cross-Cultural Approaches*, ed. D. Nichols and T. Charlton (Washington, DC: Smithsonian Institution Press, 1997), 245–254.

48. David N. Keightley, "The Shang: China's First Historical Dynasty," in *The Cambridge History of Ancient China. From the Origins of Civilization to 221 B.C.*, ed. M. Loewe und E. Shaughnessy (Cambridge: Cambridge University Press, 1999), 232–291, 290.

49. Wolfram Eberhard, "Die institutionelle Analyse des vormodernen China. Eine Einschätzung von Max Webers Ansatz," in *Max Webers Studie über Konfuzianismus und Taoismus. Interpretation und Kritik*, ed. Wolfgang Schluchter (Frankfurt am Main, Germany: Suhrkamp, 1983), 55–90, 60 ff.; Cho-yun Hsu, *Ancient China in Transition. An Analysis of Social Mobility, 722–222 B.C.* (Stanford, CA: Stanford University Press, 1965), 1, 92, 96; Herrlee G. Creel, "The Beginnings of Bureaucracy in China: The Origin of the Hsien," *Journal of Asian Studies* 23 (1964): 155–183.

50. Li Feng, *Bureaucracy and the State in Early China: Governing the Western Zhou* (Cambridge: Cambridge University Press, 2008), 294.

51. Gary G. Hamilton, "Patriarchalism in Imperial China and Western Europe: A Revision of Weber's Sociology of Domination," *Theory and Society* 13 (1984): 393–425.

52. Karl Bünger, "War China ein patrimonialer Staat?" *Oriens Extremus* 24 (1977): 167–178.

53. Hamilton, "Patriarchalism," 419; Arnold Zingerle, *Max Weber und China. Herrschafts- und religionssoziologische Grundlagen zum Wandel der chinesischen Gesellschaft* (Berlin: Duncker & Humblot, 1972).

54. Louis Dumont, *Homo Hierarchicus: The Caste System and Its Implications* (Chicago: University of Chicago Press, 1980), 71–72, 213ff., 287ff.

55. Stanley Jeyaraja Tambiah, *World Conqueror and World Renouncer* (Cambridge: Cambridge University Press, 1976), 54ff., 63; Stephen P. Blake, "The Patrimonial-Bureaucratic Empire of the Mughals," *Journal of Asian Studies* 39 (1979): 77–94; Peter Hardy, "Islamischer Patrimonialismus: Die Mogulherrschaft," in *Max Webers Sicht des Islams. Interpretation und Kritik*, ed. Wolfgang Schluchter (Frankfurt am Main: Suhrkamp, 1987), 190–216; Margrit Pernau, *The Passing of Patrimonialism. Politics and Political Culture in Hyderabad, 1911–1948* (New Delhi, India: Manohar, 2000).

56. Burton Stein, *Peasant State and Society in Medieval South India* (Delhi, India: Oxford University Press, 1980); "Vijayanagara and the Transition to Patrimonial Systems," in *Vijayanagara: City and Empire*, ed. A. Dallapiccola and S. Lallemont (Stuttgart, Germany: Steiner, 1985), 1:73–87; "State Formation and Economy Reconsidered: Part One," *Modern Asian Studies* 19 (1985): 387–413.

57. Hermann Kulke, "The Study of the State in Pre-Modern India," in *The State in India 1000–1700*, ed. H. Kulke (Delhi, India: Oxford University Press, 1997), 23ff.; Jakob Rösel, "Max Weber, India, and the Patrimonial State," in *Recent Research on Max Weber's Studies of Hinduism*, ed. D. Kantowsky (Munich: Weltforum Verlag, 1986), 117–152; Georg Berkemer, *Max Weber und Indien. Eine Einführung*, ed. Michael Mann (Heidelberg, Germany: Draupadi Verlag, 2012), 117ff.

58. J. I. Bakker, "Patrimonialism, Involution, and the Agrarian Question in Java: A Weberian Analysis of Class Relations and Servile Labor," in *State and Society*, ed. J. Gledhill et al. (London: Unwin Hyman, 1988), 279–301.

59. Max Weber, *The Russian Revolutions*, trans. and ed. G. Wells and P. Baehr (Ithaca, NY: Cornell University Press, 1995), 46, 110; *Zur Russischen Revolution 1905. Schriften und Reden 1905–1912, MWG* I/10, ed. W. J. Mommsen, with D. Dahlmann (Tübingen, Germany: Mohr [Siebeck], 1989), 110, 272.

60. Richard Pipes, "Max Weber and Russia," in *World Politics* 7 (1955): 3711–3741; *Russia Under the Old Regime* (London: Weidenfeld & Nicolson, 1974).

61. Vatro Murvar, "Max Weber and the Two Nonrevolutionary Events in Russia 1917: Scientific Achievements or Prophetic Failures?" in *Max Weber's Political Sociology*, 237–272.

62. Graeme Gill, "Ideology, Organization and the Patrimonial Regime," *Journal of Communist Studies* 5 (1989): 285–302; Mikhail Maslovski, "Max Weber's Concept of Patrimonialism and the Soviet System," *Sociological Review* 37 (1996): 294–308.

63. Robert C. Tucker, "The Theory of Charismatic Leadership," *Daedalus* 97 (1968): 731–756; Hélène Carrère d'Encausse, *Le pouvoir confisqué. Gouvernants et gouvernés en U.R.S.S.* (Paris: Flammarion, 1980), 238–239; Kenneth Jowitt, "Soviet Neotraditionalism: The Political Corruption of a Leninist Regime," *Soviet Studies* 35 (1983): 275–297; *New World Disorder. The Leninist Extinction* (Berkeley: University of California Press, 1992), 192ff.; Thomas H. Rigby, "Political Legitimacy, Weber, and Communist Mono-Organisational Systems," in *Political Legitimation in Communist States*, ed. T. Rigby and F. Feher (London: Macmillan, 1982), 1–26.

64. Max Weber, "Parlament und Regierung im neugeordneten Deutschland," in *Zur Politik im Weltkrieg. Schriften und Reden 1914–1918, MWG I/15*, ed. W. J. Mommsen, with G. Hübinger (Tübingen, Germany: Mohr [Siebeck], 1984), 469; *MWG I/10*, 155, 210, 213, 333; Felix Schnell, *Ordnungshüter auf Abwegen? Herrschaft und illegitime polizeiliche Gewalt in Moskau 1905–1914* (Wiesbaden, Germany: Harrassowitz, 2006); Mikhail Maslosvski, "Max Weber's Concept of Patrimonialism and the Soviet System," *Sociological Review* 44, no. 2 (1996): 294–308.

65. Peter Eich, *Zur Metamorphose des politischen Systems in der römischen Kaiserzeit. Die Entstehung einer "personalen Bürokratie" im langen dritten Jahrhundert* (Berlin: Akademie Verlag, 2005).

66. Thomas N. Bisson, *The Crisis of the Twelfth Century. Power, Lordship, and the Origins of European Government* (Princeton, NJ: Princeton University Press, 2009), 494.

67. Thomas Vesting, "Absolutismus und materiale Rationalisierung. Zur Entstehung des preußischen Patrimonialstaates," *Archiv des öffentlichen Rechts* 119 (1994): 369–399; Ernst Hinrichs, *Ancien Régime und Revolution. Studien zur Verfassungsgeschichte Frankreichs zwischen 1589 und 1789* (Frankfurt am Main, Germany: Suhrkamp, 1989), 87ff., 123ff.

68. John A. Armstrong, "Old-Regime Governors: Bureaucratic and Patrimonial Attributes," *Comparative Studies in Society and History* 14 (1972): 2–29; "Old-Regime Administrative Elites: Prelude to Modernization in France, Prussia and Russia," *International Review of Administrative Sciences* 38 (1972): 21–40.

69. Gina Zabludowsky, "The Reception and Utility of Max Weber's Concept of Patrimonialism in Latin America," *International Sociology* 4 (1989): 51–66.

70. Guenther Roth, "Personal Rulership, Patrimonialism, and Empire-Building in the New States," *World Politics* 20 (1968): 194–206.

71. Luigi Graziano, "Center-Periphery Relations and the Italian Crisis: The Problem of Clientelism," in *Territorial Politics in Industrial Nations*, ed. Sidney Tarrow et al. (New York: Praeger, 1978), 294.

72. Robert Eden, "Weber and Nietzsche: Questioning the Liberation of Social Science from Historicism," in *Max Weber and His Contemporaries*, ed. W. J. Mommsen and J. Osterhammel (London: Allen and Unwin, 1987), 405–421; Jürgen Habermas, *The Theory of Communicative Action*, vol. 1, *Reason and the Rationalization of Society*, trans. T. McCarthy (Boston: Beacon Press, 1984), 264–267.

73. Niklas Luhmann, *Politische Planung*, 3rd ed. (Opladen, Germany: Westdeutscher Verlag, 1983), 92.

74. Weyma Lübbe, *Legitimität kraft Legalität. Sinnverstehen und Institutionenanalyse bei Max Weber und seinen Kritikern* (Tübingen, Germany: Mohr Siebeck, 1991).

75. Weber, "On Some Categories of Interpretive Sociology," in *CMW*, 273–391, 299; *Verstehende Soziologie und Werturteilsfreiheit, MWG I/12*, ed. J. Weiß, with S. Frommer (Tübingen, Germany: Mohr [Siebeck], 2018), 389–440, 437.

76. Tyrell, "Weberscher Bürokratietypus," 40; Rainer Döbert, "Max Webers Handlungstheorie und die Ebenen des Rationalitätskomplexes," in *Max Weber heute*, ed. J. Weiß (Frankfurt am Main, Germany: Suhrkamp, 1989), 210–249, 221.

77. Döbert, "Handlungstheorie," 246.

78. Günther Schmid and Hubert Treiber, *Bürokratie und Politik. Zur Struktur und Funktion der Ministerialbürokratie in der Bundesrepublik Deutschland* (Munich: Fink, 1975);

Hubert Treiber, "Moderner Staat und moderne Bürokratie bei Max Weber," in *Max Webers Staatssoziologie*, ed. A. Anter and S. Breuer, 2nd ed. (Baden-Baden, Germany: Nomos, 2016), 121–157.

79. Joachim Renn, "Bürokratie zwischen 'traditioneller Rationalität' und 'rationaler Traditionalität': Max Weber, Preußen und die Rationalität soziologischer Rationalitätstypen," in *Der Sinn der Institutionen. Mehr-Ebenen- und Mehr-Seiten-Analyse*, ed. M. Stachura et al. (Wiesbaden, Germany: Verlag für Sozialwissenschaften, 2009), 255–286; Eugenie Samier, "Demandarinisation in the New Public Management: Examining Changing Administrative Authority from a Weberian Perspective," in *Max Webers Herrschafts-soziologie*, ed. E. Hanke and W. J. Mommsen (Tübingen, Germany: Mohr Siebeck, 2001), 235–263, 258.

80. Samier, "Demandarinisation," 248.

81. Sigrid Meuschel, *Legitimation und Parteiherrschaft in der DDR* (Frankfurt am Main, Germany: Suhrkamp, 1992); Bernard S. Silberman, *Cages of Reason: The Rise of the Rational State in France, Japan, the United States and Great Britain* (Chicago: University of Chicago Press, 1993), 10.

82. Hans-Ulrich Derlien, "German Public Administration: Weberian Despite 'Modernization,'" in *Comparative Bureaucratic Systems*, ed. K. Tummala (Lanham, MD: Lexington Books, 2003), 97–122; Jörg Bogumil and Werner Jann, *Verwaltung und Verwaltungswissenschaft in Deutschland. Einführung in die Verwaltungswissenschaft*, 2nd ed. (Wiesbaden, Germany: VS Verlag für Sozialwissenschaften, 2009), 249.

83. Christopher Pollitt and Geert Bouckaert, *Public Management Reform: A Comparative Analysis*, 4th ed. (Oxford: Oxford University Press, 2017), 121–124.

84. Keith Krause, ed., *Challenging the Weberian State: Armed Groups and Contemporary Conflicts*, special issue, *Contemporary Security Policy* 30, no. 2 (2009); Patrick Le Galès and Alan Scott, "A British Bureaucratic Revolution? Autonomy Without Control, or 'Freer Markets, More Rules,'" *Revue française de sociologie* 51 (2010): 117–143.

85. Rainer Wolf, "Zur Antiquiertheit des Rechts in der Risikogesellschaft," in *Politik in der Risikogesellschaft*, ed. U. Beck (Frankfurt am Main, Germany: Suhrkamp, 1991), 378–423.

86. Hubert Treiber, *Vollzugskosten des Rechtsstaates und andere Studien zum Recht* (Baden-Baden, Germany: Nomos, 1989), 245ff.; Polly Sprenger, *Deferred Prosecution Agreements. The Law and Practice of Negotiated Corporate Criminal Penalties* (London: Sweet & Maxwell, 2015).

87. Weyma Lübbe, "Wie ist Legitimität durch Legalität möglich? Rekonstruktion der Antwort Max Webers," *Archiv für Rechts- und Sozialphilosophie* 79 (1993): 80–90, 86.

88. *E&S*, 875, 882, 884; *MWG* I/22-3, 612, 617, 620; Hubert Treiber, *Max Webers Rechtssoziologie—eine Einladung zur Lektüre* (Wiesbaden, Germany: Harrassowitz, 2017), 161ff.

89. Duncan Kennedy, "The Disenchantment of Logically Formal Legal Rationality," *Hastings Law Journal* 55 (2003-2004): 1031–1076.

90. Maurizio Bach, "Jenseits der Souveränitätsfiktion: Der Nationalstaat in der Europäischen Union," Special issue, *Zeitschrift für Politik* (2013): 105–124.

91. Weber, "The Three Pure Types of Legitimate Rule," in *Essential*, 133; *MWG* I/22-4, 726; Bach, "Jenseits der Souveränitätsfiktion," 118.

92. M. Rainer Lepsius, *Demokratie in Deutschland* (Göttingen, Germany: Vandenhoeck & Ruprecht, 1993); Rainer Wolf, "Herrschaft in Zeiten der Entgrenzungen. Die Europäische Union als Herrschaftsverbund," in *Herrschaftstheorien und Herrschaftsphänomene*, ed. H. Aden (Wiesbaden, Germany: VS Verlag für Sozialwissenschaften, 2004), 177–200; Maurizio Bach, *Europa ohne Gesellschaft. Politische Soziologie der europäischen Integration* (Wiesbaden, Germany: VS Verlag für Sozialwissenschaften, 2008); Andreas Anter, "Max Webers Herrschaftskonzept, die EU-Superbürokratie und die Staatenwelt der Gegenwart," in *Alte Begriffe—neue Probleme. Max Webers Soziologie im Lichte aktueller Problemstellungen*, ed. T. Schwinn and G. Albert (Tübingen, Germany: Mohr Siebeck, 2016), 117–131; Ute Mager, "Zur Aktualität des Idealtypus der legalen Herrschaft aus rechtswissenschaftlicher Sicht," in *Alte Begriffe*, 133–148.

CHAPTER 14

THE SUPRANATIONAL DIMENSION IN MAX WEBER'S VISION OF POLITICS

KARI PALONEN

A lifelong *Homo politicus*, Max Weber was from his youth a keen follower of world events. In his academic as well as his journalistic writings, a certain vision of world politics can be detected, which is somewhat bound to the time period but also visible in the nuances to his distinct way of thinking about politics.

Max Weber's discussion of world politics is shaped by his style of thinking about both politics and scholarship. He regards the human world as inherently contingent. Weber's key analytic concept is *chance*, a horizon of possibilities in a situation to which the ends, means, and unintended consequences of human actions should be related.[1] For Weber, chance is a formal concept, including the chance of catastrophe. The entire setting of the narrative of "orders and powers" (*Ordnungen und Mächte*) in *Wirtschaft und Gesellschaft* operates with chances. All constitutive concepts, such as *Macht*, *Herrschaft*, and *Staat*, are, indeed, formed on the basis of their specific profiles with respect to chance. When, for example, politics are conducted by the medium of "the state," certain types of chances are excluded, others are possible, and others may even be advisable.[2]

From this perspective, furthermore, he questioned the strong divide between international and domestic politics and analyzed their interplay in both directions.

Like many of his contemporaries, Weber assumed that European politics was still shaped by a balance of powers, called the "European concert" or the "Westphalian order." The latter term, which I shall use here, refers, of course, to the treaty signed in Osnabrück and Münster in 1648, although as an analytical concept it was coined by scholars much later. Below the level of the allegedly sovereign states there existed an international polity and international law consisting of "peace, security and justice as agreed between the members of the system," to quote Martti Koskenniemi.[3] For Weber, the great powers

(*Weltmächte*) were the main actors in the international polity. They cannot violate the rules and conventions of the polity without damaging themselves, and they must learn to use the polity in order to maintain or strengthen their status within it.

Nonetheless, President Woodrow Wilson's idea of a League of Nations challenged the Westphalian order during World War I. Max Weber took this idea seriously, in particular in his early 1919 essay "Zum Thema der 'Kriegsschuld'" ("On the Question of 'War Guilt'"),[4] although he interpreted it in his own way. The essay calls attention to chances to transcend the Westphalian type of international polity, which previously had been an inherent part of Weber's way of thinking politically, as I shall discuss in this chapter.

Wolfgang J. Mommsen's dissertation *Max Weber und die Deutsche Politik (1890–1920)* from 1959 has canonized the view of Weber as a German nationalist. Later scholars, in particular Wilhelm Hennis, have disputed or relativized this thesis; but Mommsen's view still seems to dominate, at least outside of Weberian scholarship.[5] In accordance with a rhetorical view of conceptual change, I apply the Weberian principle of speculating with unrealized possibilities to world politics beyond his lifetime.[6] I want to think what Weber could have said in relation to particularly the United Nations and the European Union.

WEBER AND *WELTPOLITIK* FROM THE 1890S TO WORLD WAR I

In his Freiburg inaugural lecture, Max Weber included himself among the "economic nationalists."[7] Earlier he had discussed the situation of the East Elbian agricultural workers from the perspective of the reason of state.[8] In the 1890s *Weltpolitik* did not mean simply world politics but the extension of the policy of the great European powers to the colonization of countries and regions outside Europe. Weber also spoke of *deutsche Weltmachtpolitik*,[9] situating German politics in the European and global contexts.

In his polemic against the Prussian Junkers' hiring of agricultural workers from Russian Poland, Weber claimed that the hiring of this cheap labor would lower the cultural level of human beings and weaken the position of the German culture (*Deutschtum*) in the eastern areas of the *Reich*.[10] In his biography, Dirk Kaesler speaks of Weber's *rassistischen Polenbeschimpfungen* (that is, his racist abuse of the Poles) during this period.[11] Still, Weber denied that he practiced *Chauvinismus* and emphasized the "level" of humanity as the main point.[12] This implies for Weber a characteristic normative dimension to the international polity of great powers.

In the inaugural address Weber speaks of Germany as a nation-state or, in his words, the "circumstance that our state [*Staatswesen*] is a *nation state*."[13] He presents this as a fact, neither excluding the possibility of other types of states nor elevating the nation-state as a model for all states. His appeal to *Staatsraison* similarly supports Germany's foreign political interests, not as having inherent value but as a regular part of doing politics among the great powers. Weber blames Germans for Germany's late and timid engagement in power politics overseas (*überseeische "Machtpolitik"*).[14] Without participating in the competition for colonies, Germany could not maintain its status as one of the great powers. In line with his principle, Weber also justified his support for creating a strong German navy.[15]

Revolutionary events shattered the Russian Empire in 1905, obliging the tsar to undertake reforms, including the creation of the State Duma. Although the new regime was far from parliamentary government, it inaugurated a new beginning for Russian politics. Max Weber followed the events with enthusiasm, mediated by Russian academics in Heidelberg. Starting as a remark in the *Archiv* to S. J. Giwago's book review on the constitutional project,[16] Weber himself wrote two extensive articles, "Bourgeois Democracy in Russia" ("Zur Lage der bürgerlichen Demokratie in Rußland") and "Russia's Transition to Pseudo-constitutionalism" ("Rußlands Übergang zum Scheinkonstitutionalismus"), which he characterized as "journalistic," indicating a shift away from his earlier, nationalistic tone.[17]

Inspired by the ideas of Ukrainian scholar Mikhail Dragomanov, Weber now took a stand in favor of cultural autonomy for Russian Poland and other western parts of the empire.[18] More importantly, he saw in the revolutionary events a chance for west European ideas of individualism, human rights, and parliamentary democracy to gain support in Russia. They were advocated in the zemstvos of local self-government and by the Constitutional Democratic Party,[19] though Weber saw strong obstacles to such a program, both in the ruling bureaucracy and in the collectivist ideas concerning the agrarian question on both the right and the left of Russian politics.

Against evolutionist ideologists, such as the Russian liberal Struwe, Weber argued that the contemporary advancement of capitalism provided no guarantee of the rise of freedom, democracy, and individualism. On the contrary, everywhere the housing is ready for the new serfdom (*das Gehäuse für die neue Hörigkeit*).[20] Against the emphasis on the material conditions, Weber declared himself an " 'individualist' and partisan of 'democratic' institutions."[21]

In the essay on pseudo-constitutionalism, Weber first discusses how the constitutional reforms of 1905–1906 fall far short of the ideal types in matters of human rights, universal suffrage, and parliamentary government. The ruling bureaucracy did its best to marginalize them, creating a semiappointed second chamber and measures to bypass the Duma's budgetary powers.[22] In the Duma elections, however, the constitutional democrats and other regime-critical parties gained a majority, and Weber appreciated the legislative efforts of the Duma, though the Duma was dissolved by the tsar in July 1906.[23] Nevertheless, the electoral results and parliamentary practices gave Weber some hope for Russia.

Weber detected in the revolution of 1905 a chance that, by westernizing its political institutions and values, Russia would become accepted as a full player in the European polity. Weber's expectation in this situation was that the German Empire would take a clear stand in favor of a west European type of politics. However, he became disappointed by the interventions of the kaiser in world politics, juxtaposing to that the British parliamentary culture as a model for German foreign policy.[24]

WELTPOLITIK VERSUS EXPANSIONIST POLICY

At the outbreak of the war, Weber volunteered to become head administrator of a military hospital in Heidelberg. He strongly opposed the counter-revolutionary "ideas of 1914" of Rudolf Kjellén and Johann Plenge as well as other war apologists.[25] After resigning from the hospital in autumn 1915, Weber wrote several journalistic articles in support of moderate war aims. The articles also contain sketches of his vision of world politics, including a discussion of various actions and what consequences they might have after the war.

The first of the articles, written in the late autumn of 1915, was published only posthumously by Marianne Weber in 1921, with the title "Zur Frage des Friedenschließens." It begins with a remarkable declaration of Weber's view on *Weltpolitik*:

> The peace agreement of a European power in our geographical position, with an intention to practise *Weltpolitik* also in the future, must take as its point of departure the fact that besides us there are also six other powers, which want to pursue their own *Weltpolitik* and of which some of the strongest, next to our borders, are able to do so. The consequence of this constellation is that such intentions are for us not realisable, even in the case of a nearly complete victory. It is impossible for us to conduct *Weltpolitik*, even if we otherwise have the chance, and also if in the future we are at every step always to be confronted with the same coalition as the one currently formed against us. The possibility must be kept open to reach a durable conciliation in the long perspective with at least one of the strongest among them. This will not happen immediately, but the conditions of peace shall not be such as would permanently exclude that possibility.[26]

In his journalism Weber speaks of Germany as a "we" that is opposed to his nominalistic view in "Basic Sociological Concepts," which explicitly denies the understanding of the state as an "'acting' collective personality."[27] In his characteristic way of neutralizing concepts, such as *Herrschaft*,[28] Weber now strips *Weltpolitik* of its imperialist connotations and makes it a formal concept, dealing with a worldwide polity consisting of a limited number of great powers (*Mächte*). None of the powers is fully allowed to realize its aims. Weber assumes that, whatever the outcome of the war, the "winners" cannot alone dictate the conditions of peace; but, on the contrary, they must keep open the possibility of forming an alliance with their former enemies.

To this extent, he accuses German expansionists of ignoring the basic realities at the time in European and world politics. A continuation of the coalition against Germany after the war would have permanently paralyzed the possibility for a German *Weltpolitik*.[29] For Weber, the alternative was either for Germany to practice a *Weltpolitik* in competition with the other great powers or to pursue an expansionist policy in western Europe against the other world powers (*Weltmächte*). An annexationist policy in Belgium would prove to be Germany's key failure in its relationships with Britain and France.[30]

This perspective on world politics also shaped Weber's next wartime articles, which were more focused on the actually existing political constellations in the world and in Europe. With "Bismarck's Foreign Policy and the Present" ("Bismarcks Außenpolitik und die Gegenwart"), Weber reminds readers of the triple alliance between Britain, Germany, and Russia. Weber recognized that the alliance no longer had a chance and blamed Germany's political leadership for causing this by its disregard for the country's international position. In colonial policy, the other powers had simply ignored Germany; but according to Weber, no great power can repeatedly be put into a formal decision-making situation, only to be presented with a fait accompli and then continue with its politics-as-usual.[31]

With Bismarck, Weber maintained a detached view over judging what is possible and permanently desirable[32] and contrasted this view to national vainglory (*Eitelkeit*). Culture is bound to nationality; but states are not necessarily nation-states, and even such states can serve the cultural interests of several nationalities.[33] Weber no longer classified Germany as a nation-state but as a great power that must play the game of *Weltpolitik*. The European polity is not just any balance-of-power system of great powers but contains also the aspect of "civilizing" this polity. Therefore, Russia remained a threat for the *Weltpolitik* as such, as did the German expansionists.

The entry of the United States into the war against Germany, due to the latter's decision to use unrestricted submarine warfare, would bring a different danger to Germany as a world power. Weber predicted the consequences of this before it actually happened in his essay warning against a policy of intensified and unlimited submarine warfare, "Der verschärfte U-Boot-Krieg." He judged that a shift of the center of financial power from the City of London to New York City would have grave consequences for the international polity. Germany would have played out its foreseeable future as world power.[34]

In "Between Two Laws" ("Zwischen zwei Gesetzen") Weber detected a further danger for Germany in the pacifist tendencies to refuse to make a distinction between great powers and other states. Within the European polity, the great powers serve also as "an obstacle in the path of other *Machtstaaten*," which also protect the civilization, in particular against the Russian peasants, who lack *Kultur*.[35] The great powers are for Weber major participants in the struggle between values, and he situates Germany—despite its military duties as a *Machtstaat*—among the west European powers in defending the higher cultural level of the polity.[36]

GERMANY AMONG THE WORLD POWERS

In "Germany Among the European World Powers" ("Deutschland unter den europäischen Weltmächten"), as in part in "Between Two Laws," Weber moves from actual issues in wartime politics to the general situation of world powers during the "Great War."[37] Being surrounded by three great land powers and one great sea power, Weber perceived Germany's situation as more precarious than that of any other country. Therefore, it was particularly important for its political leaders to avoid vanity (*Eitelkeit*) and to practice a sober-minded (*sachlich*) foreign policy in line with its position among the world powers. Weber thus appeals to a political judgment that respects the basic realities of the European polity and which, unlike the pan-Germanists (*Alldeutsche*), would not put the polity at risk. An anglophile, Weber was particularly disturbed by the pan-Germanists' dreams of destroying Britain as a sea power.[38]

In his analysis of the political constellation of World War I, Weber situates himself in part within the Bismarckian tradition, however militantly he criticized the Bismarckian heritage in domestic politics.[39] Due to Bismarck's politics, an alliance with France was, however, politically impossible after 1871; and this shaped the entire German situation in world politics. Weber's view on maintaining freedom of choice, or what he termed *Erhaltung der Wahlfreiheit*,[40] in possible partnerships in world politics is opposed to having any archenemies. He does not share the view, later made famous by Carl Schmitt, that the political should be marked by decisions based on perceived friends and enemies; instead, Weber believes that within the order of powers there should also be intermediate levels of agreement or understanding (*Verständigung*), which is something he strives for in relation to France and Russia.[41]

Weber supports freedom of choice in the politics of the great powers for the same reason that he supports parliamentary debate on alternative courses of action. Within the European polity, the situation of being a great power requires that no possible alliances with other great powers be excluded, which provocative declarations easily tend to do.[42]

The spoken and written word is the main medium of parliamentary, electoral, and party politics.[43] Politicians weigh the strengths and weaknesses of alternatives in an open and public debate with the number of votes as the *ultima ratio*.[44] By contrast, diplomatic negotiations are oriented toward compromise between the great powers, similar to the old negotiations between estates.[45] In foreign policy Weber accordingly supports "holding your tongue" and "silent" action that would improve the chances for compromise. Diplomacy is also a politics of words, but its aim is to avoid, as Weber quotes Bismarck, "breaking the windows" toward other world powers.[46] Politics as a rhetorical activity should not be confused with the declarative style of the powerless *Reichstag*, in contrast to what he calls the "working parliament" or *Arbeitsparlament* of Westminster, which debates items in detail and where the members participate in committees that control the administration.[47]

Great powers and small states have different types of chances in their domestic politics. A *Machtstaat* has different callings or tasks (*Aufgaben*) in culture and history from the small states of "the Swiss, the Danes, the Dutch or the Norwegians."[48] Weber gives small states better chances to realize matters of civic virtues and democracy than great powers with their "duty and obligation to history," which they should not abandon.[49] Only in states such as Switzerland is a genuine democracy possible, as well as a genuine aristocracy based on personal trust and leadership.[50] In mass states the bureaucracy and the military are liable to extinguish both, Weber writes, referring to Jakob Burckhardt.[51] However, the freedom of small states is guaranteed only when several great powers are counterpoised to each other.

This disjunction is also visible inside Russia. Weber enumerates a number of non-Russian peoples in Russia whose *Kultur* is older and in some respects superior to that of the empire.[52] Russian hegemony in the world would mean a threat to the chances of *Kultur* within both Russia and western Europe. In his "universal historical" perspective, the future struggles in the West are marginal when compared to the decisive events of worldwide significance in eastern Europe.[53]

Weber analyzes the chances for political alliances and modus vivendi relationships in view of the prospects for a future peace. He is worried over the German wartime policy, which could preclude the very possibility of being able to pursue an advisable, appropriate, and practicable policy after the war, one that is *zweckmäßig* and will not squander the time still available for such a peace.[54]

For Weber the polity of the great powers in 1916 still offers the most viable vision for a more peaceful coexistence in the future. He takes for granted that the Great War will end in a negotiated peace similar to the kind made between the great powers in the wars of the Westphalian era. Instead of declaring normative principles or adapting his thought to the alleged exigencies of the current constellation, Weber analyzes political actions as comprising different types of temporally limited chances and the relationships of the chances to each other. The chances to maintain the European polity persisted for a time after the war, despite the threat of the annexationist policy of Germany to close them. His vision of the maintenance of the European order requires mutual recognition between the great powers, regular and active politicking between and within them, and consideration of the interests of the smaller states.[55]

The European polity of the great powers was for Weber both a product of a past momentum and an alternative to the hegemonic aspirations of any great power by itself. It was based on an order that included the strengths and weaknesses of the greater and smaller powers, and the relationships therein included intermediate degrees between enmity and alliance. The polity as a whole also created counterweights to the bureaucratization and militarization of the greater powers, and domestic measures that could be taken against them in parliamentary and democratic terms were discussed during the war in Weber's pamphlets "Suffrage and Democracy in Germany" and "Parliament and Government in Germany Under a New Political Order." In the latter Weber also strongly insists on the superiority of the Westminster-style parliamentary system over the rule of officialdom (*Beamtenherrschaft*) of the German Empire in the conduct of foreign policy.[56]

A Proposal for Regulating Warfare

Max Weber was pessimistic about the prospective outcome of the war, but, as Hinnerk Bruhns writes, the way the war ended in autumn 1918 was still worse than he expected.[57] Nonetheless, in the postwar months he wrote a number of articles on the future of German politics, participated (at the invitation of Hugo Preuss) in the committee to draft a republican constitution, and was a candidate of the liberal Deutsche Demokratische Partei for the Weimar National Assembly, although he did not have a chance of getting elected due to the maneuverings of local politicians.

Two months after the end of the war, Max Weber took up the topic of the postwar international order. The new German government of Social Democratic chancellor Friedrich Ebert brought an initiative on war guilt to the international commission on November 29, 1918. Seizing the momentum, Weber wrote the article "On the Question of 'War Guilt'" ("Zum Thema der 'Kriegsschuld'"), which was published in *Frankfurter Zeitung*, his "house newspaper," on January 17, 1919.[58]

Already in the weeks following the end of the war, Weber predicted that French generals and not US president Wilson would dominate the peace negotiations, and his Versailles experiences in spring 1919 confirmed this pessimism.[59] All this has left scholars uninterested in the constructive proposals Weber made for the planned League of Nations in January 1919.

Weber's initial point is to reject an a priori declaration of war guilt solely on the part of Germany that the "literati" had declared—elsewhere he mentions pedagogy professor Friedrich Wilhelm Foerster as a prominent exponent of such an attitude.[60] For Weber, losing the war should not be confused with the legal question of guilt. He declares that on both political and cultural grounds he had always supported an agreement with England that would have made the war impossible, and he had not changed this viewpoint.[61]

The point of the "War Guilt" article is Weber's insistence that US President Woodrow Wilson would be ready to negotiate with representatives of Germany and not impose a "forced peace," a *Gewaltfrieden*. Moreover, Weber sketched a "statute for an international law on war for consideration by the future League of Nations."[62]

In other words, Weber not only took seriously Wilson's proposal as a chance for a new momentum based on the League of Nations idea but also made his own proposals for its statutes regarding the regulation of war. In accordance with the Westphalian order, Weber still regarded war as a part of international politics, and he insisted on its regulation by international law within the framework of the new league. Equally obvious is that he thought of the great powers, including Germany, as forming the main pillars of the league.[63] Weber draws from the experiences of the war the lesson that stronger legal instruments against war crimes are needed, obviously also in order to reduce the threat of future wars.

His statute proposal contains four articles. The first declares, "A state that mobilizes for war while negotiations to prevent the war are continuing shall fall into international disrepute."[64] Weber's claim behind this article is that Russia's mobilization in 1914, and with it the entire tsarist system, bears the main responsibility for the outbreak of the Great War. Conceptually, the political and legal sanction lies in the "international disrepute" of the state in question. The claim is intelligible only within the polity of great powers, for the threat then exists that a rule-breaking state may be removed from full "membership" among the respected great powers and denied a voice in multipower diplomacy, the main form of political action within the international polity. In other words, the factual status of being a *Machtstaat* is not by itself sufficient to be a great power; a certain respect for international statutes is also necessary to be recognized as a full participant in the polity of great powers.

The second article reads, "A state that at the outbreak of a war does not clearly declare whether it will remain neutral shall fall into international disrepute."[65] Here the target of criticism is the French policy in 1914, as Bruhns remarks.[66] The threat is again merely disrepute. In this case, sanctioning might be more difficult to agree upon as a declaration of neutrality leaves more room for interpretation than does mobilization.

The third article is worded, "A permanently neutral state can appeal to its neutrality only if it is able to protect itself effectively and equally on all sides and in every direction."[67] Weber mentions Belgium as a small state that had "neglected" its defense in 1914, which appears to be a tacit acceptance of the German attack in 1914. The more general point, common to this and the previous article, is that the international war statutes also concern the small states. The target of criticism here is the non-justified use of not shouldering responsibility for one's own defense, though what degree of defense is sufficient again leaves much room for conflicting interpretations and how far the great powers would agree on this point remained uncertain.

The fourth article is one that Weber admitted to be a contested principle between the German and the US wartime interpretations, namely, concerning the duties of neutral states. Weber presented the interpretation that was supported by Germany during the war: "A neutral state that tolerates one state's war crimes without recourse to its own armed defence cannot then use violence against the other side by appealing to the other side's illegal counter-measures, even if the neutral state's violence is later judged to be the only means to meet the consequences of the enemy's breach of law."[68] Wilson's interpretation was that such a link of responsibility does not exist but must be decided separately. Weber admits that Wilson's legal interpretation prevailed after the outcome of the war but that the matter remains controversial. Germany's policy toward the United States was unwise but not a war crime.

Max Weber's proposals for an international law on war can, of course, be seen as directed against those who assigned Germany the sole culpability for starting the war. In more general terms, however, they were an attempt to seize the momentum at a time when the chances of international law to limit arbitrary acts by great and even small powers were recognized by the international polity. He admits, however, that due to the absence of any supranational enforcement apparatus, "international law" was not directly comparable to state-internal law.[69] The sanctions provided in his suggested articles do not, therefore, pose any absolute threats for a great power, but they do increase the political pressure on it.

In Weber's writings and comments from winter and spring 1919, there are a few remarks on the planned league (*Völkerbund*). In the brochure "Germany's Future Form of State" ("Deutschlands künftige Staatsform") Weber renounces any imperialistic dreams and commits himself to the cultivation of German ideals "within the framework of the League of Nations." He mentions, however, that annexation of German areas in the east would deal a deathly blow to the league.[70] Similar interpretations referring to *Völkerbund* can be found in Weber, for example, in one of his contributions to the Versailles conference and in his appeal to protect German interests in the Saar against the "French militarists."[71]

The partisan character of Weber's appeals and his seeing the League of Nations as a protector of the weak in world politics are less important than his recognition of the legitimacy of such a league. Insofar as the League of Nations transcends intergovernmentalism and approaches a supranational order, we can speak of a change in Max Weber's conceptualization of the European polity and a global polity.

Supranational Aspects of World Politics

As we have seen, Weber's discussion is consistently presented in a way in which the chances of the different participants in the actual situation are discussed and compared. Weber reinterprets the concept of *Weltpolitik* to include chances for a politics of different states within the Westphalian framework of the European polity, in times of both war and peace. He makes the west European type of *Kultur* a normative requirement for becoming a full-fledged world power, which also illustrates that he believed the polity should also contain a second historical reference to the west European politics of the preceding decades, that is, one that as a requirement for domestic politics includes an "individualistic" view of human rights and a democratized form of parliamentary government. The politicocultural order of the west European polity is a fragile one, and its fate depends for Weber largely on whether the foreign and domestic politics of Germany can be made to correspond to it.

The Westphalian order as the basis of the international polity implies an intergovernmental order. It is based on mutual recognition by members, exclusion of non-members, co-optation of new applicants, and exclusion of those who are no longer recognized as great powers. The criteria are by no means clear, and disputes among great powers over which parties are recognized as "members of the club" may persist.

In Wilson's proposal for the League of Nations, Weber identifies a chance to transcend the Westphalian momentum in some respects. The international polity is not necessarily a polity of the states. Weber's distinctions between great powers and lesser powers as well as between nation-states and other states already indicate a certain relativity in talking about "states." In his last lectures, Weber also analyzed how the chances of being legitimately recognized as a "state" contain degrees of difference, which he illustrates with the case of Bavaria in spring 1919, in which the *Räterepublik*, the Hoffmann government exiled to Bamberg, and the German *Reich* competed with each other for a time over which could legitimately use the title of "state," each of which had its own claims on power or "power shares" in the question.

To this picture we may add the rise of a number of international organizations, from the Red Cross and the World Postal Union to the Inter-Parliamentary Union and international academic organizations since the latter nineteenth century.[72] The Hague peace conferences of 1899 and 1907 had attempted to regularize not only multilateral diplomacy but also a parliamentary element on an international level.[73] Even if World War I interrupted much of their activities, a model of trans- or supranational political or protopolitical institutions had been created. Considering these new agencies in the international polity, Wilson's proposal of the league and Weber's application of it manifest the insight that the end of war provides specific occasions to create, activate, and strengthen such institutions.

Without doubt, Weber would have recognized that such institutions can further limit the chances of single states to establish a monopoly of violence in their areas. The Westphalian-style international polity already does this indirectly, as we have seen, by making all states dependent on receiving recognition by the great powers. Even if the League of Nations was based on the voluntary membership of states and on the acceptance of other member states, it was more than an intergovernmental organization. Nevertheless, it was still not a normative order of the kind that some pacifists and international law scholars had hoped it would be as it did not replace single states or the order of the great powers but rather contained certain *Chancen* to transcend them. The use of these chances depends on the political practices not only of governments but also of parliaments and international organizations. Some of the latter, such as the International Labour Organization, were soon included within the umbrella of the League of Nations.

To sum up, Weber is in his views on world politics neither a *Realpolitik* thinker, operating within the framework of the balance of the great powers, nor a normativist calling for an international legal order to replace world political struggles. This is closely related to Weber's political style of thinking in terms of *Chancen* as these allow him to discuss the possibilities and conditions of legitimizing certain practices or institutions, while leaving their acceptance to the acting politicians in the situation.

USING A WEBERIAN-STYLE IMAGINATION IN WORLD POLITICS

Applying Weber's counterfactual principle of historical interpretation to the present-day world, I now want to speculate how he would have assessed the political significance of two of the most important supranational political institutions today, the United Nations and the European Union.

Traditionally, foreign policy belongs in all countries to the *arcana imperii*, to the secrets of the realm, conducted originally by monarchs and their courts, around which a corps of professional diplomats was formed over time. Even in modern states, foreign policy has been the part of government that has most effectively resisted all attempts at becoming subject to parliamentary control. Or, to put it in "neo-Roman" terms, in foreign policy the arbitrary rule of government and administration has held citizens and parliamentarians in a state of dependence.[74]

Max Weber set forth ambitious formal criteria for his definition of parliamentary government, namely, the selection of ministers among members of parliament the government depends on for parliament's confidence, ministers having a duty to respond to members' questions in plenum and in committee, and the parliament exercising an efficient control of administration.[75] Regarding the last point, Weber's favorite measures to counter the allegedly superior knowledge of officials over parliamentarians included the power by parliamentary committees to cross-examine ministry officials, the possibility for these committees to carry out on-the-spot examinations of the sources of officials' knowledge, and setting up parliamentary examination commissions.[76]

The extension and intensification of parliamentary control of foreign policy implies one type of chance to politicize it from "below." From the Weberian point of view, foreign policy should be acknowledged as being as contingent and controversial as all politics, and therefore submittable to parliamentary oversight. To which degree and in which respects these chances of politicization are then used, while at the same time allowing the government to maintain particularly the possibility to take urgent action when necessary, is a matter of expediency and of the level of political competencies of the members of parliament.

Subjecting a country's foreign policy to oversight by supranational institutions contains a different chance for politicization, imposing limitations from "above" on the arbitrary foreign policy powers of national governments and diplomacies. The Westphalian system contains an indirect chance to recognize such limits, when not even the greatest powers can disregard the other powers. Weber's culture criterion gives an additional nuance to this chance. Multilateral intergovernmental organizations, such as the League of Nations, mark the next step, whereas supra- or transnational institutions provide still more radical chances to politicize the international polity through denationalization.

The two ways of politicization in foreign policy, parliamentarization and denationalization, are independent of each other. Both parliamentarization without denationalization and denationalization without parliamentarization are possible and have actually been practiced. Still, they do not exclude each other, and a double-check of the governmental-cum-administrative powers by supranational parliamentary institutions is also a realistic possibility, including, of course, a double risk that governments could be paralyzed when they need to take urgent action.

The United Nations is not merely an intergovernmental organization but one that deals also with the politics of non-member states and can exclude members that violate its charter. The General Assembly conducts its debates in a largely parliamentary style, but the votes are determined by the government representatives of members. The Security Council is an intergovernmental institution with a weak parliamentary element in the election of non-permanent members, while the veto power for permanent members' governments marks a limit to denationalization. The secretary-general is the main supranational office of the United Nations but depends on the election and range of possible actions of the Security Council, especially of its permanent members. From the Weberian perspective, the veto of the permanent members is an obstructive measure that can prevent the initiatives of Security Council majorities and restrict the independence of the secretary-general.

In the European Union the power struggle between the four main representative institutions is much more open. The European Council and to a large extent the Council of the European Union (which consists of ministers of the member states) combine intergovernmental, parliamentary, and presidential elements, whereas the European Commission is a supranational institution, combining the activities of a parliamentary cabinet, a superbureaucracy and a think tank. The European Parliament has gained power both through treaties since Maastricht (1993) and through the outcomes of its disputes on the election and the dismissal of the president and members of the commission. It is still lacking the parliamentary initiative for individual members and has little say in some policy fields. In matters of legislation the parliament is obliged to make compromises with the European Council which, along with the Council of the European Union, acts as the second chamber, while member-state parliaments act as the third chamber. Alongside the commission, the European Court of Justice and the European Central Bank also act as supranational institutions based on non-elected advocatory representation.

Despite this complex and open-ended "separation of powers" system, the European Union is probably the first polity in which both supranational and parliamentary aspects are present to some extent in all main institutions. Historically, supranational institutions have been those with the weakest parliamentary control (the European Commission, Court of Justice, and Central Bank) and the councils the stronghold of intergovernmental power. Denationalization initially took place largely at the expense of the member-state parliaments. Direct elections of the European Parliament since 1979, treaty revisions, and the de facto change of the commission in the direction of parliamentary government have contributed to a relative parliamentarization of the European Union. Leading in this direction as well has been the reduction in the requirements for unanimity in the councils, causing their status to resemble more that of a second chamber where other members must be persuaded in order to achieve a majority.

Looked at from this perspective, denationalization and parliamentarization no longer appear as mutually exclusive alternatives in the European Union. A politicization in terms of supranational parliamentary politics (including the cooperation between member-state parliaments) now appears to have real chances in the European Union. There exists no other analogous institution that has similar chances for politicization, for even the Inter-Parliamentary Union is still strongly based on the parliaments of its individual member states.

Andreas Anter claims that Weber would have regarded the European Union as a "superbureaucracy."[77] In contrast, I would rather think that Max Weber would today be among those of us who would support the politicization of the European Union via the two channels of parliamentarization and denationalization. The two channels also provide a chance to make the European Union a model for other supranational institutions.

NOTES

1. Max Weber, "Die 'Objektivität' sozialwissenschaftlicher und sozialpolitischer Erkenntnis" [The "objectivity" of knowledge in social science and social policy], in *Collected Methodological Writings*, trans. H. H. Bruun, ed. H. H. Bruun and S. Whimster (London and New York: Routledge, 2012), 102; *Zur Logik und Methodik der Sozialwissenschaften. Schriften 1900–1907, Max Weber-Gesamtausgabe* (hereafter *MWG*) I/7, ed. G. Wagner, with C. Härpfer et al. (Tübingen, Germany: Mohr [Siebeck], 2018), 147; discussed in Kari Palonen, *Das "Webersche Moment." Zur Kontingenz des Politischen* (Wiesbaden, Germany: Westdeutscher Verlag, 1998), 132–143; and *"Objektivität" als faires Spiel. Wissenschaft als Politik bei Max Weber* (Baden-Baden, Germany: Nomos, 2010), 77–85.

2. See the student notes of Weber's 1920 lectures, in which *Staat* refers to a *Gehorsamschance* [nicht: *Durchsetzungssetzungschance!*]: Weber, *Allgemeine Staatslehre und Politik (Staatssoziologie). Unvollendet. Mit- und Nachschriften 1920, MWG* III/7, ed. G. Hübinger, with A. Terwey (Tübingen, Germany: Mohr [Siebeck], 2009), 69. See also Kari Palonen, "The State as a *Chance* Concept: Max Weber's Desubstantialization and Neutralization of a Concept," *Max Weber Studies* 11 (2011): 99–117.

3. Martti Koskenniemi, *The Politics of International Law* (Oxford: Hart, 2011), 243.

4. Weber, "Zum Thema der 'Kriegsschuld,'" in *Zur Neuordnung Deutschlands. Schriften und Reden 1918–1920, MWG* I/16, ed. W. J. Mommsen, with W. Schwentker (Tübingen, Germany: Mohr [Siebeck], 1988), 179–190.

5. See Wolfgang J. Mommsen, *Max Weber and German Politics, 1890–1920*, trans. M. Steinberg, 2nd ed. (Chicago: University of Chicago Press, 1984); Wilhelm Hennis, *Max Weber's Central Question*, trans. K. Tribe, 2nd ed. (Newbury, UK: Threshold, 2000); also Catherine Colliot-Thélène, "Max Weber, la léçon inaugurale de 1895, ou: Du nationalisme à la sociologie comparative," *Les cahier de Fontanay* 58/59 (1990): 103–121; Hinnerk Bruhns, *Max Weber und der Erste Weltkrieg* (Tübingen, Germany: Mohr Siebeck 2017).

6. I refer especially to Weber's thinking in "Bourgeois Democracy in Russia," in *The Russian Revolutions* (hereafter *RR*), trans. and ed. G. C. Wells and P. Baehr (Cambridge: Polity Press, 1995), 41–147; also translated with the title "On the Situation of Constitutional Democracy in Russia," in *Political Writings* (hereafter *PolW*), trans. and ed. P. Lassman and R. Speirs (Cambridge: Cambridge University Press, 1994), 29–74; "Zur Lage der bürgerlichen Demokratie in Rußland," in *Zur Russischen Revolution von 1905. Schriften und Reden 1905–1912, MWG* I/10, ed. W. J. Mommsen, with D. Dahlmann (Tübingen, Germany: Mohr [Siebeck], 1989), 86–279.

7. Weber, "The Nation State and Economic Policy," in *PolW*, 1–28, cf. 20; "Der Nationalstaat und die Volkswirtschaftspolitik," in *Landarbeiterfrage, Nationalstaat und Volkswirtschaftspolitik. Schriften und Reden 1892–1899, MWG* I/4, ed. W. J. Mommsen, with R. Aldenhoff (Tübingen, Germany: Mohr [Siebeck], 1993), 545–574 cf. 565 ("uns ökonomische Nationalisten").

8. Weber, "Die ländliche Arbeitsverfassung," *MWG* I/4, 165–198, cf. 180 ("unter dem Gesichtspunkt der *Staatsraison*"); also Weber, "The Nation State," in *PolW*, 17; *MWG* I/4, 561.

9. Weber, "The Nation State," *PolW*, 26; *MWG* I/4, 571.

10. Weber, "Die ländliche Arbeitsverfassung," *MWG* I/4, 183; "The Nation State," *PolW*, 10–11; *MWG* I/4, 554–555.

11. Dirk Kaesler, *Max Weber. Eine Biographie* (Munich: Beck, 2014), 408; on Weber and Poland in this period, see also Hajime Konno, *Max Weber und die polnische Frage (1892–1920)* (Baden-Baden, Germany: Nomos, 2004, esp. 48–115.

12. Weber, "Die ländliche Arbeitsverfassung," *MWG* I/4, 182; "The Nation State," *PolW*, 15, 20; *MWG* I/4, 559 ("Qualität der Menschen"), 564 ("Typus des Menschentums").

13. Weber, "The Nation State," *PolW*, 13; *MWG* I/4, 558.

14. Weber, "The Nation State," *PolW*, 23; *MWG* I/4, 568.

15. Weber, "Stellungnahme zu der von der Allgemeinen Zeitung im Dezember 1897 veranstalteten Flottenumfrage," *MWG* I/4, 671–673.

16. S. J. Giwago, "Rezension von: Loi fondamentale de l'Empire Russe," republished in *MWG* I/10, 81–85.

17. Weber, "Bourgeois Democracy in Russia," in *RR*, 113n2; *MWG* I/10, 86–279, quotation 86n1; and "Russia's Transition to Pseudo-constitutionalism," in *RR*, 148–260; *MWG* I/10, 293–684.

18. Weber, "Bourgeois Democracy in Russia," in *RR*, 56–62; *MWG* I/10, 135–151; see Konno, *Max Weber und die polnische Frage*, 142–150.

19. Weber, "Bourgeois Democracy in Russia," in *RR*, 45–54, 65–66; *MWG* I/10, 108–129, 164–165.

20. Weber, "Bourgeois Democracy in Russia," in *RR*, 108 ("the empty shell for the new serfdom"); *PolW*, 68 ("The housing for the new serfdom"); *MWG* I/10, 269.

21. Weber, "Bourgeois Democracy in Russia," in *RR*, 109; *PolW*, 69; *MWG* I/10, 270.

22. Weber, "Russia's Transition to Pseudo-constitutionalism," in *RR*, 158–184 (incomplete translation); *MWG* I/10, 320–444.

23. Weber, "Russia's Transition to Pseudo-constitutionalism," in *RR*, 213–233 (incomplete translation); *MWG* I/10, 617–679.

24. See Weber, "Kaiser und Reichsverfassung," *Wirtschaft, Staat und Sozialpolitik. Schriften und Reden 1900–1912*, *MWG* I/8, ed. W. Schluchter, with P. Kurth and B. Morgenbrod (Tübingen, Germany: Mohr [Siebeck], 1998), 392–397.

25. See Bruhns, *Max Weber und der Erste Weltkrieg*, 28–50.

26. Weber, "Zur Frage des Friedensschließens," *Zur Politik im Weltkrieg. Schriften und Reden 1918–1920*, *MWG* I/15, ed. W. J. Mommsen, with G. Hübinger (Tübingen, Germany: Mohr [Siebeck], 1984), 54–67, cf. 54 (my translation).

27. Weber, "Soziologische Grundbegriffe," in *Wirtschaft und Gesellschaft. Soziologie*, *MWG* I/23, ed. K. Borchardt, E. Hanke, and W. Schluchter (Tübingen, Germany: Mohr [Siebeck], 2013), 147–215, cf. 161; "Basic Sociological Concepts," in *The Essential Weber*, ed. Sam Whimster (London and New York: Routledge, 2004), 312–358, cf. 321; see also the lectures from spring 1920 in Weber, *Allgemeine Staatslehre und Politik*, *MWG* III/7; and Palonen, "The State as a *Chance* Concept."

28. See Reinhart Koselleck, *Vergangene Zukunft. Zur Semantik geschichtlicher Zeiten* (Frankfurt am Main, Germany: Suhrkamp, 1979), 128–129.

29. Weber, "Zur Frage des Friedensschließens," *MWG* I/15, 63.

30. Ibid., 54–63.

31. Weber, "Bismarcks Außenpolitik und die Gegenwart," *MWG* I/15, 71–92: "Keine Großmacht darf sich ungestraft immer wieder vor vollzogene Tatsachen stellen und über sich zur Tagesordnung übergehen lassen" (78).

32. Ibid., 90 ("das Augenmaß für das Mögliche und politisch dauernd Wünschbare").

33. Ibid., 91.

34. Weber, "Der verschärfte U-Boot-Krieg," *MWG* I/15, 115–125: "Wir hätten unsere weltpolitische Zukunft für absehbare Zeit verspielt" (117).

35. Weber, "Between Two Laws," in *PolW*, 75–79, cf. 77; *MWG* I/15, 95–98, cf. 96.

36. Weber, "The Profession and Vocation of Politics," *PolW*, 309–369, cf. 316; *Politik als Beruf 1919*, *MWG* I/17, ed. W. J. Mommsen and W. Schluchter, with B. Morgenbrod (Tübingen, Germany: Mohr [Siebeck], 1992), 157–252, cf. 167; *PolW*, 77-78; *MWG* I/15, 97–98.

37. Weber, "Deutschland unter den europäischen Weltmächten," *MWG* I/15, 157–194; "Between Two Laws," *PolW*, 75–79; *MWG* I/15, 95–98, as well; for background and publication information, see the editorial reports that pretend the texts in *MWG* I/15; Bruhns, *Max Weber und der Erste Weltkrieg*, 18–20.

38. Weber, "Deutschland unter den europäischen Weltmächten," *MWG* I/15, 163–167.

39. See esp. Weber, "Parliament and Government in Germany Under a New Political Order," in *PolW*, 130–271; also translated as "Parliament and Government in a Reconstructed Germany," in Weber, *Economy and Society*, ed. and trans. G. Roth and C. Wittich (Berkeley: University of California Press, 1978), app. II, 1381–1469; *MWG* I/15, 432–596.

40. Weber, "Deutschland unter den europäischen Weltmächten," *MWG* I/15, 169.

41. Ibid., 170.

42. Ibid., 169–171.

43. See, e.g., Weber, "Politik als Beruf," *PolW*, 330; *MWG* I/17, 189.

44. Weber, "Suffrage and Democracy in Germany," in *PolW*, 80–129, cf. 102; *MWG* I/15, 347–396, cf. 368–369.

45. Weber, "Suffrage and Democracy in Germany," in *PolW*, 102–103; *MWG* I/15, 366–367.

46. Weber, "Deutschland unter den europäischen Weltmächten," *MWG* I/15, 164–165.

47. Weber, "Parliament and Government in Germany," in *PolW*, 176–177, 181, 191; *MWG* I/15, 486, 491, 502.

48. Weber, "Between Two Laws," *PolW*, 75; *MWG* I/15, 95.

49. Weber, "Between Two Laws," *PolW*, 75–76; *MWG* I/15: in Weber's words, "die verdammte Pflicht und Schuldigkeit vor der Geschichte" (96).

50. Weber, "Deutschland unter den europäischen Weltmächten," *MWG* I/15, 190–193.

51. Ibid., 191.

52. Ibid., 189.

53. Ibid., 180–181.

54. Ibid., 169.

55. See Bruhns, *Max Weber und der Erste Weltkrieg*, 183–197.

56. Weber, "Parliament and Government in Germany," *PolW*, 196–209, see also 235-236; *MWG* I/15, 507–524, see also 556.

57. Bruhns, *Max Weber und der Erste Weltkrieg*, 70.

58. Weber, "Zum Thema der 'Kriegsschuld,'" *MWG* I/16, 179–190.

59. See Weber, "Deutschlands politische Neuordnung," *MWG* I/16, 363–368, cf. 363–364; Wolfgang J. Mommsen, "Nachwort" in *MWG* I/16, 161–172; Bruhns, *Max Weber und der Erste Weltkrieg*, 70.

60. Weber, "Politik als Beruf," *PolW*, 362–363; *MWG* I/17, 240–241, 243.

61. Weber, "Zum Thema der 'Kriegsschuld,'" *MWG* I/16, 179–180.

62. Ibid., 180, 182, 184 (quotation).

63. See also Bruhns, *Max Weber und der Erste Weltkrieg*, 82–84.

64. Weber's exact words should be quoted: "Ein Staat, der mobil macht, während noch verhandelt wird, verfällt dem internationalen Verruf:" "Zum Thema der 'Kriegsschuld,'" *MWG* I/16, 184 (my translation of these passages).

65. In Weber's words, "Ein Staat, der bei Kriegsausbruch auf die Anfrage, ob er neutral bleiben werde, keine deutliche Erklärung abgibt, verfällt dem internationalen Verruf." Ibid., 185.

66. Bruhns, *Max Weber und der Erste Weltkrieg*, 83.

67. Quoting Weber, "Ein dauernd neutralisierter Staat kann sich auf seine Neutralität nur berufen, wenn er sich in den Stand gesetzt hat, sie nach allen Seiten hin gleichmäßig und möglichst wirksam zu schützen," "Zum Thema der 'Kriegsschuld,'" *MWG* I/16, 186.

68. In Weber's phrasing, "Ein Neutraler, der von einer kriegführenden Seite einen Rechtsbruch ohne gewaltsame Abwehr duldet, darf zur Gewaltsamkeit auch gegen die andere Seite nicht greifen wegen solcher rechtswidriger Gegenmaßregeln, welche das einzige Mittel sind, die Folgen des gegnerischen Rechtsbruchs wettzumachen." Ibid., 187.

69. Weber, "Soziologische Grundbegriffe," *MWG* I/23, 187; *Essential*, 338.

70. Weber, "Deutschlands künftige Staatsform," *MWG* I/16, 98–146, cf. 109.

71. Weber, "Gegen die Abtretung deutscher Gebiete im Osten," *MWG* I/16, 289–292, cf. 290; "Die wirtschaftliche Zugehörigkeit des Saargebiets zu Deutschland," *MWG* I/16, 236–242, cf. 241 ("Französische Militaristen"), also 237–238.

72. See Jo Leinen and Andreas Brummer, *Das demokratische Weltparlament. Eine kosmopolitische Vision* (Bonn, Germany: Dietz, 2016); Claudia Kissling, *Die interparlamentarische Union im Wandel. Rechtspolitische Ansätze zur repräsentative-parlamentarischen Gestaltung der Weltpolitik* (Frankfurt am Main, Germany: Peter Lang, 2006).

73. Evgeny Roshchin, "The Hague Conferences and 'International Community': A Politics of Conceptual Innovation," *Review of International Studies* 43 (2017): 177–198.

74. See Quentin Skinner, *Liberty Before Liberalism* (Cambridge: Cambridge University Press, 1998).

75. See Weber, "Parliament and Government in Germany," *PolW*, 166; *MWG* I/15, 473.

76. Weber, "Parliament and Government in Germany," *PolW*, 176–180; *MWG* I/15, 486–490; see the discussion in Palonen, *"Objektivität" als faires Spiel*, 146–167, and *A Political Style of Thinking. Essays on Max Weber* (Colchester, UK: ECPR Press, 2017).

77. Andreas Anter, *Max Weber und die Staatsrechtslehre* (Tübingen, Germany: Mohr Siebeck, 2016), 185–187.

CHAPTER 15

PLEBISCITARY POLITICS AND THE THREATS TO LEGALITY

*Some Classical Insights on a
Current Phenomenon*

CLAUDIUS HÄRPFER

IN contemporary diagnostics, the current situation is often understood as a crisis. The reasons for this are, of course, manifold.[1] One of these is the current insecurity in world politics, not least due to a referendum in which 51.9 percent of the electorate of the United Kingdom voted in favor of leaving the European Union on June 23, 2016 (with 72.2 percent voter turnout).[2] On the basis of the result of the vote, this is probably the most important referendum of recent years, and Brexit will figure significantly in the history of referendums. For the first time in the history of the European Union, a state has declared its withdrawal from the ever-expanding community. Immediately after this decision, citizens went out on the streets to demonstrate against the legitimacy of this decision, while in Scotland there were calls for another referendum to break away from the United Kingdom and stay in the European Union.

Despite all the political, economic, and cultural uncertainty that accompanies it, it is clear that this step involves an immense amount of legal effort because everything that was previously regulated by EU legislation is now open to re-legislation sooner or later. Nevertheless, this very spectacular British vote is, in terms of the formal process, just one of many plebiscitary acts that seek to democratically legitimize political processes in any direction. On the one hand, there are regular elections at all levels in democratic systems. On the other hand, we find large or at least highly emotionalized unscheduled decisions, whether this is a commitment to the political autonomy of a particular region (e.g., Scotland and Catalonia) or statements on planned or ongoing major public-sector construction projects (e.g., Stuttgart 21 in Germany). Certainly, public opinion polls also belong to this category to a certain extent because they also legitimize government action.

With these events, which are of course usually covered by the respective constitution and thus take place within the legal framework, the normal routine of representative democracies is more or less broken through and an extra-daily state of affairs is created, which entails not only direct but also indirect consequences.

In the age of big data, computational social sciences, and digital humanities the question arises why turn to Max Weber's work in respect of the broad and multimedia-based debate about the Brexit vote, instead of immediately plunging into the freely available data. Max Weber is considered a *fascinosum* and is a classic of enduring relevance around the world.[3] As such, he has the function of providing an orientation. He himself formulated the benefit of permanently important scientific achievements "as a didactic tool."[4] Anyone who takes Weber seriously and approaches a current symptom with his conceptual toolbox is, of course, faced with the problem that the scientific disciplines have continued to specialize.[5] In this case, Weber's perspective serves as the systematizing and linking achievement of a dilettante who directs the expert's attention to "useful *questions*."[6] The possible erosion of the legitimacy of legality as an indirect consequence of plebiscitary politics, which is discussed in this chapter on the basis of some of Weber's writings, is the attempt to generate such a question. For this purpose, I will, in accordance with the ideal-typical conceptualization, exaggerate individual aspects, which obviously are not to be found in this pure form but only tend to be found in the specifically treated example.

"Demands of the Day"

It is hard to say how Max Weber would have commented today on a process like Brexit, Certainly initially he was part of the spirit of the time of the decline of the liberal bourgeoisie[7] and had no illusions regarding the idea of popular sovereignty. On August 4, 1908, he wrote a letter to Robert Michels that is frequently cited after Wolfgang J. Mommsen's groundbreaking work *Max Weber and the German Politics.*[8] "Such concepts like 'will of the people', '*true* will of the people' and so on have not meant anything to me for a long time. They are *fictions*. It is just as if one wanted to speak of a 'will of the boot-consumer', which must be decisive for the manner *in which* the cobbler was to set up his technique.... The shoes consumers know where the shoe *pinches* them, but *never*: how to make it *better*."[9]

In Weber's work "Parliament and Government in Germany under a New Political Order," which was a compilation and revision of various articles that were published in the *Frankfurter Zeitung* in 1917, he speaks in the face of the immediate political background of his time.[10] There he states that the "democratisation of suffrage here, and particularly in the hegemonial state of Prussia" is a "compelling and urgent political necessity which cannot be postponed."[11] Nevertheless, according to him, the pure popular referendum—as an electoral and as a legislative instrument—has its "inner limits" in mass states that "follow from its technical peculiarity." Usually, the decision falls as a simple "yes" or "no." This makes more complex decisions, for example, the "determination of the budget," impossible, because any kind of "compromise," which is essential for any kind of legislative process, rests on a process of negotiation between "conflicting interests."[12] Weber denies the voter competence over professional decisions and decisions about professional qualifications. At the same time these processes "weaken the role of the party leaders and the responsibility of officials."[13] In the case of a negative decision by the masses, the individual is not in charge so as to make better proposals and to take responsibility. Instead, Weber describes the business of politics as "carried out by *interested parties*," which means that it is not the "politically passive 'mass'" that "gives birth to the leader." In fact, the political leader "recruits his following and wins over the mass by 'demagogy.'"[14]

In this process, Weber sees "the danger which mass democracy presents to national politics" in the "possibility" of "*emotional* elements" that might become "predominant in politics." That means, that the "'mass' as such…'thinks only as far as the day after tomorrow'. As we know from experience, the mass is always exposed to momentary, purely emotional and irrational influences."[15] His remarks on this remain cursory, but they reappear elsewhere. In "The Profession and Vocation of Politics"—while outlining something like a short history of the decline of democratic culture—he warns of those leaders who presently use the "purely emotive means like those of the salvation army" in order to "stir the masses."[16]

From this perspective, it may be only logical that he thought the will of the people as being incompatible with a transparent Parliament and especially a strong plebiscitary president of the Reich.[17] Since then few leading personalities have possessed the ideal qualities demanded by Weber—"passion, a sense of responsibility, judgement."[18] But that is another story, of course. This will probably remain so in the future, making Weber's concrete political recommendation only of limited use.

A Systematic View

Weber's position in this regard has been widely reconstructed in the context of his time.[19] To apply it to current phenomena, we certainly must understand it in its systematics. This becomes understandable when we take a look at his concept of the state, which he develops in *Economy and Society* beyond the political constraints of the day but according to the Prussian prototype. Weber conceptualizes the modern state as a "compulsory political organization with continuous operations" whose "administrative staff successfully upholds the claim to the *monopoly* of the *legitimate* use of physical force in the enforcement of its order."[20] Such a compulsory organization is characterized by the fact that it is an association in the form of an organization whose "order" is imposed with relative success "on all action conforming with certain criteria…within a specifiable sphere of operations." This imposition is carried out in the form of "continuous rational action."[21] According to Weber, an organization is characterized by the presence of a "chief" and an "administrative staff," which guarantee the maintenance of the organization's order by their "organized action". Thatmeans their behavior is specially committed to the order's execution.[22]

Weber thus conceptualizes the modern state as a compulsory bureaucratic organization with a territorial basis, which is formally characterized by "an administrative and legal order" that can be changed by legislation, "to which the organized activities of the administrative staff, which are also controlled by regulations, are oriented. This system of order claims binding authority, not only over the members of the state, the citizens ... but also to a very large extent over all action taking place in the area of its jurisdiction."[23]

The bureaucratic apparatus secures the legality of the leading actors and is—at least in its ideal typically developed form—highly efficient. However, like every bureaucratic administrative staff, there is "necessarily an element which is at least not purely bureaucratic."[24] This can be a traditional-monarchical remnant or, as is usually the case in the modern state, a leader of whatever charismatic qualities.

Plebiscitary acts, however, are not part of this "organized action," that means they are not part of the "action of the administrative staff itself or that which takes place under its direction." In this context, Weber also envisages a further category of action, a specific "action of the participants," that is "intended to uphold the authority of the order," which he calls "action oriented to organizational affairs."[25] If the mass of the people now votes on a fact or a personnel matter, then the members of the organization are not—as in the case of war—"deliberately directed" by the administrative staff which is equipped with professional competence. The organized action in this case is rather restricted to the "administration" and the "administrative procedure."[26] The actual, substantive decision is made by the masses. The transitions are, of course, fluent here, depending on the degree of direction of operations by the administrative staff. The higher the degree of decision-making of the other participants, the more the decision takes on the character of action oriented to organizational affairs and the less professional competence lies at the basis of the decision. Weber counts the pure " 'motion', which is passed by the members at the behest of its executive committee," still to be organized action.[27] In the case of a referendum, which Weber envisages as a means of resolving conflicts and disputes within an association,[28] the people voting on a restricted issue have a higher degree of autonomy, although their actions are also intended to uphold the authority of the order. This means that they do not necessarily break with the lawful order, which other (e.g., revolutionary) plebiscitary acts may do.

Since the decision of the people is not made on the basis of professional knowledge, Weber notes a clear connection between democracy and demagogy. As soon as "the masses" are "in some way active in throwing the weight of their own opinion into the balance" and can no longer be "treated purely as passive objects of administration," demagogic elements are involved in mass mobilization. The popularly elected leader does not gain the confidence of the masses by professional proof "but rather because he uses the means of *mass* demagogy," and this always implies that "the selection of the leader has shifted in the direction of *Caesarism*."[29]

More information about this construction can be found in "The Types of Legitimate Domination." Here, Weber describes the plebiscitary domination as a special form of charismatic domination, as its antiauthoritarian transformation. Charisma is a concept which Weber took over from contemporary literature on the history of ecclesiastical law.[30] In the time of the early Christian congregations, charisma was used to describe the pure prophecy. Weber applies the term in a broader meaning "to a certain quality of an individual…of which he is considered extraordinary and treated as endowed with supernatural, superhuman, or at least specifically exceptional powers or qualities. These as such are not accessible to the ordinary person, but are regarded as of divine origin or as exemplary, and on the basis of them the individual concerned is treated as 'leader'."[31] Thus, the concept of charisma forms a counterpoint to tradition and bureaucracy in Weber's typology. As a counterpoint to the tradition, whose legitimacy is "resting on an established belief in the sanctity of immemorial traditions and the legitimacy of those exercising authority under them,"[32] the concept of charisma stands for all that is new and cannot be sustained in pure form. Accordingly, charisma must either always prove itself again or somehow become routinized. In the modern state, where election campaigns are usually personalized to a certain extent and thus a charismatic component comes into play, the bureaucratic apparatus and the associated lawful order operates between campaigns. If this does not happen, Weber envisages the possibility of an antiauthoritarian transformation of charisma.

The antiauthoritarian reinterpretation of charisma is based on the idea that the charismatic authority, in its purest form, rests "on recognition by the ruled," which is caused by "'proof' before their eyes." On the other hand, this "recognition of a charismatically qualified, and hence legitimate, person is treated as a duty."[33] While Weber considers the implementation of forms of "'direct' or 'immediate democracy'" in smaller organizations as possible, he holds to the "principle of the small number" for mass states.[34] That is, a small, superior group dominates the political association, makes the decisions, and the others obey that decision. Given a certain rationalization of associational relationships, it is therefore natural that recognition, instead of being treated as "a consequence of legitimacy," is "treated as the basis of legitimacy: *democratic legitimacy*." Now the "designation of a successor by an administrative staff becomes 'preselection,' a 'recommendation' by the predecessor, whereas recognition by the group becomes an 'election.'"[35] As a result, the "personally legitimated charismatic leader becomes a leader by the grace of those who follow him." He is chosen or deposed by those who are "formally free to elect" or to depose him as he gains or loses his charisma. "Now he is the freely elected leader."[36] Of course, not everyone is chosen freely but only the one who is predestined by the catalyst effect of any kind of preselection. And the idea that modern politics are carried out by interested parties reinforces this effect even more.

Weber calls "plebiscitary democracy" the most important type of this Führer-Demokratie. Here, he includes the dictators of the ancient world and the modern revolutions, who, if they strove for legitimacy at all, searched for it in "recognition by the sovereign people through a plebiscite."[37] The loyalty and trust of the political followers in these cases directly apply to the person of the leader as such. Accordingly, the "highly emotional type of devotion to and trust in the leader" in general is a characteristic attribute of the Führerdemokratie. This leads to a "tendency to favor the type of individual" as a leader "who is most spectacular, who promises the most, or who employs the most effective propaganda measures in the competition of leadership."[38]

In the case of Brexit, the prime minister, David Cameron, who was suffering from domestic political problems, wanted his EU policy to be legitimized by the people and let the parliamentary routine be interrupted. Although this process may remind us of the above-mentioned motion, it goes beyond the organized action since the organization is not a voluntary association under whose executive committee unity prevails as in Weber's example. Apart from that, the decision concerns more than just a foreign policy issue but also has a domestic political component since the application of EU directives has a direct influence on life within the nation-state. It is immediately evident that, in view of the complexity of a multilateral, multilevel structure such as the European Union, the formation of opinion, at least for a large part of the voting citizens, with all its interdependencies, could not be achieved on the basis of professional competence. Rather, a number of leaders from the respective party elites have emerged, who were predestined by previous positions and who, due to their sometimes dazzling personalities, were in the focus of media attention. Some of them then fought for the legitimacy of their personal positions across party lines. Of course, this struggle was still within the framework of the constitution, but it had charismatic traits due to the incalculability of the consequences of the vote and the emotionalized discussion. Cameron, who campaigned to remain in the European Union, was no longer sufficiently legitimized by the outcome of the vote and resigned from his post as prime minister.[39]

DOMINATION AND LEGALITY

Weber observes a close connection between domination and law[40] because if the legitimate rules of action executed by the participants of the institutions apply to all actions in the controlled area, then they apply also to the sphere of law. The law is, if one follows Weber's basic concepts, a specific form of order, which is recognized as bindingly legitimate by regularities of action and the associated expectations of this regularity. In particular, law distinguishes itself by the fact that it is "externally guaranteed by the probability that physical or psychological coercion will be applied by a *staff* of people in order to bring about compliance or avenge violation."[41]

In our case of a charismatic political culture, however, this gives rise to a number of problems because charismatic domination as an antipole to tradition and bureaucracy breaks with the regular and expected. "There is no such thing as appointment or dismissal, no career, no promotion. There is only a call at the instance of the charismatic qualification of those he summons." The sentence "It is written...but I say unto you" applies to all genuinely charismatic leaders. "The genuine prophet, like the genuine military leader and every true leader in this sense, preaches, creates, or demands *new* obligations—most typically, by virtue of revelation, oracle, inspiration, or of his own will, which are recognized by the members of the religious, military, or party group because they come from such a source."[42]

Of course, Weber now also considers the possibility of an order's legitimation by "*affectual*, especially emotional, *faith*" that is the validity of the "newly revealed or exemplary."[43] Especially since not every "valid order" has to be of a "general and abstract character." A legal norm and a judicial decision in a concrete case were not always and everywhere distinct as clearly as we expect it today. "An 'order' may thus occur simply as the order governing a single concrete situation"[44]

If the charismatically gifted leader strives for legitimacy with his program of whatever kind, then he orients himself to the lawful order at best in the same way as the thief named by Weber, who orients himself to the valid criminal law by acting "surreptitiously."[45] If the leader thereby attains a basic level of legitimacy, contradictory drafts of regulations are competing. This inevitably violates regulations, be it in the form of radical rejection or partial violations. If the "evasion or contravention of the generally understood meaning of an order has become the rule," then the order is only " 'valid' " to a limited extent or not at all anymore. From a sociological perspective, the validity or non-application of an order is not a "rigid alternative" as it is for the law; instead, Weber sees a "gradual transmission between the two extremes,"[46] and every unsuccessful application weakens its legitimacy as every successful application strengthens it.[47]

Decisive for the concept of the law is the "presence of a staff engaged in enforcement," which can also be of different kinds. Weber talks about the fact that there does not necessarily have to be a " 'judicial' authority" but that, in the case of a blood vengeance, for example, the clan can also take over this task.[48] In the case of a charismatic relation of power, the administrative staff has a genuine character. Instead of the professionally trained civil servants, a selection according to charismatic qualities can be found here. There is "no such thing as appointment or dismissal, no career, no promotion. There is only a call at the instance of the leader on the basis of the charismatic qualification of those he summons."[49]

Now, in the case of plebiscitary leadership, of course, we are dealing not with pure charisma but with a "transitional type" in which "the chief feels himself to be acting on behalf of the masses and is indeed recognized by them." As such, it derives its legitimacy from the "confidence of the ruled."[50] In Weber's historical examples, the administrative staff often has the character of a mere "machine" with which the dictator puts the masses behind him.[51] In the case of the plebiscitary-charismatic order, the "recognition of charismatic decrees and judicial decisions" on the part of the congregation develops in a manner comparable to the legitimacy of the relations of power. Just as the revolutionary dictator ignores traditional legitimacy and formal legality to a certain extent, the community has the idea that it "has the right to enact, recognize, or appeal laws, according to its own free will, both in general and for an individual case."[52] In this context, the enforcement staff can also be recruited from the ranks of elected officials, which, however, always remain inferior to the specialist civil servants in terms of efficiency.

THE STRUGGLE OF THE GODS

If we recall the principle of the small number at this point, it becomes clear that of course the masses themselves do not create a new law or right. Rather, this requires a prese-lection by charismatically gifted individuals with leadership ambitions, who set out the possibilities of legislation, and the masses then make an indirect decision by legitimiz-ing the most convincing person. While Weber, in his system of domination, assumes that the charismatic person will break with rational, lawful legality, in the present case of Brexit, it is now the problem that not a single charismatically gifted potential leader questions the given order to a certain extent but rather that several charismatically gifted politicians enter the ring and compete for the chance that the action "will in fact be ori-ented" to their concepts of order.[53] Thus, the regulated competition, which is oriented (negatively) toward the lawful "order," becomes a "social selection" that leaves this orderly context.[54]

Of course, this has consequences for rationality. As already stated, Weber mentions on various occasions the emotional character of the leader's selection as a danger to mass democracy. According to the idea of charisma, it is completely indifferent how the charismatic quality of the leader can be "ultimately judged" from any point of view.[55] In Weber's view, "objectivity" is the subjective opinion of the individual on the world; there can therefore only be a relative consensus.[56] When different charismatic candi-dates for leadership, with whatever concrete followers behind them, find themselves struggling with each other, this consensus of common values and understanding for each other is only given to a certain extent, and the statements will sometimes be diffi-cult to accept for the other party.

In the process of the Brexit election campaign, the British constitution was of course not repealed, but the value orientations of the individual positions were so far from one another that observers found it difficult to understand the various statements. It is not for nothing that in the context of Brexit and the election of Donald Trump as president of the United States of America, the word "post-truth" was chosen by the *Oxford Dictionary* as the word of the year 2016, as "an adjective defined as 'relating to or denot-ing circumstances in which objective facts are less influential in shaping public opinion than appeals to emotion and personal belief.'" Decisive for the choice of this word was the strongly increasing frequency of the word in the media discourse from mid-2016, especially in the phrase "post-truth politics."[57]

THE EROSION OF LEGALITY

But to accuse politicians of being untruthful during an election campaign is, of course, only part of the problem. At the same time, the persons with leadership claims who have plebiscitary charismatic talents must already have a minimum degree of legitimacy and thus a minimum degree of allegiance—and therefore a minimum number of persons who recognize the respective concept of order associated with their person as legitimate.

Admittedly, this does not constitute a new law but merely a community of consent. In an attempt to describe the emergence of new orders, Weber introduces the category of consensus in his essay "On Some Categories of Interpretive Sociology."[58] By this he understands the fact "that an action oriented according to expectations concerning the behaviour of other persons has an empirically 'valid' chance of seeing those expectations realized, because there is an objective probability that these other persons will in practice treat those expectations as being, in terms of meaning, 'valid' for their behaviour, even though no agreement to this effect exists."[59] Accordingly, the individual within the consensus community legitimizes the one charismatic leader in the belief that there is an objective chance that others will also legitimize this leader. This goes beyond a subjective rational purpose calculation; in our case, it is rather an affective orientation toward a norm.

As far as the mass of the people is concerned, this means that there must be several competing consensus communities, each of which recognizes the legitimacy of its charismatic leader and the program associated with it. And the more these programs have broken with rationality and focus on the affective and emotional impulses, the less understanding among the different consensus communities is achieved. And the stronger the division of the masses will become.

This, of course, leads to longer-term problems as soon as the process of leader selection is completed and the charismatic episode is over. When it is now a matter of routinizing the concept of order and legalizing it through the consolidation of a bureaucratic apparatus, and at the same time imposing it on the inferior consensus communities, it becomes correspondingly more difficult to maintain the belief in legality that is "the compliance with enactments which are *formally* correct and which have been made in the accustomed manner."[60] This belief in legality, legitimized by externally guaranteed physical coercion, now conflicts with the legitimacy of the conventions of the consensus communities, which have developed from those orders—those resulting from purely internally guaranteed, current devotion.

Thus, there are inevitably several, partly contradictory ideas of legitimate order in play, which have reached the stage of a rule and thus mutually relativize each other. It is "authority" set "against authority, legitimacy against legitimacy," as Weber formulated in the context of his description of the tensions between occidental hierocracy and political power.[61] For the time being, the members of the British Parliament have prevented an escalation of this relativization of conflicting orders and the associated danger to their constitution by both the Conservatives and the Labour Party after Brexit, declaring that the result of the vote was binding on them, demonstratively acknowledging the current order. In order to be democratically legitimized at a time of supposedly good poll scores, Cameron's successor in the office of prime minister, Theresa May, ordered early elections for June 8, 2017. In these elections, May, who stood for a tough Brexit course— that means she refused to make any concessions to the large group of Brexit opponents—lost thirteen seats in the British House of Commons. Instead of the desired legitimization of her person and concept of order, she was thus only able to prove her worth to a limited extent and had to enter into coalitions in the course of the subsequent formation of a government in order to gain an absolute majority again and to be able to continue governing. It is not yet clear how the UK–EU Brexit negotiations will develop and what the resulting order will be.

Weber's concept of the state and his understanding of bureaucracy were often the subject of criticism, not least because of his ideal-typical constructs of terms which are rich in presuppositions, but they are still considered to be current.[62] His assessment of the masses, as thinking only as far as the day after tomorrow, was polemical and exaggerated at the time of the declining Kaiserreich, and today it is just as limited as his idealization of the leaders at that time. Nevertheless, it cannot be denied that the complex interrelationships of the "transnational fusion bureaucracy"[63] of the European Union at the national level cannot be judged by the citizens on the basis of professional competence. The emotionalization criticized by Weber has meanwhile grown into a major discourse around the buzzword "populism," in which, depending on the specification of the term used, there is disagreement about the impact of Weber's thinking and the concept of charisma on current research.[64]

Notwithstanding, a systematic look at Weber's thinking helps to understand the problems discussed here. The mechanism of democratic legitimacy described by Weber through the preselection of whatsoever instances has certainly become more complex in the meantime—in times of an increasingly interactive and confusing media landscape and a changing public sphere. For some time now, there has also been talk of an economy of attention,[65] which charismatically gifted persons make use of. The associated problem of poorly integrated consensus communities, which is nowadays more succinctly called "filter bubbles"[66] or "echo chambers"[67] depending on the perspective—although without theoretically penetrating the consequences—is without question more relevant than ever.

The question of how to deal with such a crisis-prone, charismatically re-enchanted world as an individual in the masses can be answered less with Weber's late political writings than with what he has developed quasi-simultaneously in "Science as a Profession and Vocation." Here, he writes that every single modern human being in the rationalized world is constantly confronted with elements of ignorance and incalculability and can nevertheless obtain a certain degree of clarity about the phenomena occurring by means of rudimentary logic and methodology in order to finally make its decisions and to meet the "demands of the day."[68]

Acknowledgment

I would like to thank Edith Hanke for her helpful suggestions. I dedicate this text to Gerhard Wagner on the occasion of his sixtieth birthday.

Notes

1. Cf. Heinrich Geiselberger, ed., *The Great Regression* (Cambridge: Polity Press, 2017).
2. BBC News, "EU Referendum: Results," http://www.bbc.com/news/politics/eu_referendum /results (accessed July 25, 2018).
3. Cf. Karl-Ludwig Ay and Knut Borchardt, eds., *Das Faszinosum Max Weber. Die Geschichte seiner Geltung* (Konstanz, Germany: UVK, 2006); Michael Kaiser, ed., *Max Weber in der Welt. Rezeption und Wirkung* (Tübingen, Germany: Mohr Siebeck, 2014).
4. Max Weber, "Science as a Profession and Vocation," trans. Hans Henrik Bruun, in *Collected Methodological Writings* (hereafter *CMW*), ed. Hans Henrik Bruun and Sam Whimster (London and New York: Routledge, 2012), 335–353, cf. 341; Max Weber, "Wissenschaft als Beruf," in *Wissenschaft als Beruf 1917/1919—Politik als Beruf 1919, Max Weber-Gesamtausgabe* (hereafter *MWG*), I/17, ed. W. J. Mommsen and W. Schluchter with B. Morgenbrod (Tübingen, Germany: Mohr [Siebeck], 1992), 71–111, cf. 85.
5. Weber, "Science as a Profession and Vocation," 338–339; *MWG* I/17, 80–81.
6. Weber, "Science as a Profession and Vocation," 339; *MWG* I/17, 82, 80.
7. Cf. Panajotis Kondylis, *Der Niedergang der bürgerlichen Denk- und Lebensform. Die liberale Moderne und die massendemokratische Postmoderne* (Weinheim, Germany: VCH, 1991).
8. Wolfgang J. Mommsen, *Max Weber und die deutsche Politik. 1890-1920*. 2nd rev. ed. (Tübingen, Germany: Mohr [Siebeck], 1974), 421.
9. Max Weber, "Letter to Robert Michels, 4. August 1908," in *Briefe 1906-1908, MWG* II/5, ed. M. R. Lepsius and W. Schluchter with B. Rudhard and M. Schön (Tübingen, Germany: Mohr [Siebeck], 1989), 615–620, cf. 615. Emphasis in the original.
10. Max Weber, "Parliament and Government in Germany under a New Political Order. Towards a Political Critique of Officialdom and the Party System," trans. Ronald Speirs, in *Political Writings* (hereafter *PolW*), ed. P. Lassman and R. Speirs (Cambridge: Cambridge University Press, 1994), 130–271, cf. 130; *Zur Politik im Weltkrieg. Schriften und Reden 1914-1918, MWG* I/15, ed. W. J. Mommsen with G. Hübinger (Tübingen, Germany: Mohr [Siebeck], 1984), 432–596, cf. 432. Emphasis in the original.
11. Weber, "Parliament," 233; *MWG*, I/15, 552.
12. Weber, "Parliament," 225; *MWG*, I/15, 544.
13. Weber, "Parliament," 226; *MWG*, I/15, 544.
14. Weber, "Parliament," 228; *MWG*, I/15, 547.
15. Weber, "Parliament," 230; *MWG*, I/15, 549.
16. Max Weber, "The Profession and Vocation of Politics," trans. Ronald Speirs, in *PolW*, 309–369, cf. 343; *MWG* I/17 157–252, cf. 211.
17. Cf. Mommsen, *Weber und die deutsche Politik*, 416–441.
18. Weber, "Profession of Politics," 352; *MWG* I/17, 227.
19. Cf. Wolfgang J. Mommsen, *The Age of Bureaucracy. Perspectives on the Political Sociology of Max Weber* (Oxford: Basil Blackwell, 1974); David Beetham, *Max Weber and the Theory of Modern Politics*. 2nd ed. (Cambridge: Polity Press 1985), 215–249; Sven Eliaeson, "Max Weber and Plebiscitary Democracy," in *Max Weber, Democracy and Modernization*, ed. Ralph Schroeder (Basingstoke, UK: MacMillan; New York: St. Martin's, 1998), 47–60; Joshua Derman, *Max Weber in Politics and Social Thought. From Charisma to Canonization* (Cambridge: Cambridge University Press, 2012), 176–215.

20. Max Weber, *Economy and Society. An Outline of Interpretive Sociology* (hereafter *E&S*), ed. G. Roth and C. Wittich (New York: Bedminster Press, 1968), 54; Max Weber, *Wirtschaft und Gesellschaft. Soziologie. Unvollendet 1919-1920, MWG* I/23, ed. K. Borchardt, E. Hanke, and W. Schluchter (Tübingen, Germany: Mohr [Siebeck], 2013), 212.

21. *E&S*, 52; *MWG* I/23, 209-210.

22. *E&S*, 48; *MWG* I/23, 204.

23. *E&S*, 56; *MWG* I/23, 214.

24. *E&S*, 222; *MWG* I/23, 462.

25. *E&S*, 48-49; *MWG* I/23, 204-205.

26. *E&S*, 49; *MWG* I/23, 205.

27. *E&S*, 49; *MWG* I/23, 205.

28. Cf. Max Weber, "Deutschlands künftige Staatsform," in *Zur Neuordnung Deutschlands. Schriften und Reden 1918-1920, MWG* I/16, ed. W. J. Mommsen with W. Schwentker (Tübingen, Germany: Mohr [Siebeck], 1988), 97-146, cf. 134-136.

29. Weber, "Parliament," 220-221; *MWG* I/15, 537-539. Emphasis in the original.

30. Thomas Kroll, "Max Webers Idealtypus der charismatischen Herrschaft und die zeitgenössische Charisma-Debatte," in *Max Webers Herrschaftssoziologie. Studien zur Entstehung und Wirkung*, ed. Edith Hanke and Wolfgang J. Mommsen (Tübingen, Germany: Mohr [Siebeck], 2001), 47-72.

31. *E&S*, 241; *MWG* I/23, 490.

32. *E&S*, 215; *MWG* I/23, 453.

33. *E&S*, 266; *MWG* I/23, 533.

34. *E&S*, 289; *MWG* I/23, 574; Weber, "Parliament," 174; *MWG* I/15, 483.

35. *E&S*, 266-267; *MWG* I/23, 533.

36. *E&S*, 267; *MWG* I/23, 533.

37. *E&S*, 268; *MWG* I/23, 535.

38. *E&S*, 269; *MWG* I/23, 538.

39. BBC News, "Brexit: David Camerons' Resignation Statement in Full," http://www.bbc.com/news/uk-politics-eu-referendum-36619446 (accessed July 25, 2018).

40. Werner Gephart, "Juridische Grundlagen der Herrschaftslehre Max Webers," in *Max Webers Herrschaftssoziologie*, 73-98.

41. *E&S*, 34; *MWG* I/23, 186.

42. *E&S*, 243-244; *MWG* I/23, 494.

43. *E&S*, 36; *MWG* I/23, 189.

44. *E&S*, 35; *MWG* I/23, 188-189.

45. *E&S*, 32; *MWG* I/23, 184.

46. *E&S*, 32; *MWG* I/23, 184.

47. Cf. Claudius Härpfer and Tom Kaden, "Weber and Simmel on the formation of norms, rules and laws," *Journal of Classical Sociology* 17 (2017): 116-126.

48. *E&S*, 35; *MWG* I/23, 187.

49. *E&S*, 243; *MWG* I/23, 493.

50. *E&S*, 267; *MWG* I/23, 533-534.

51. Weber, "Profession of Politics," 343; *MWG* I/17, 211.

52. *E&S*, 267; *MWG* I/23, 533.

53. *E&S*, 32; *MWG* I/23, 184.

54. *E&S*, 38; *MWG* I/23, 192.

55. *E&S*, 241-242; *MWG* I/23, 490-491.

56. Max Weber, "The 'Objectivity' of Knowledge in Social Science and Social Policy," trans. Hans Henrik Bruun, in *CMW*, 100–138, cf. 137; Max Weber, *Zur Logik und Methodik der Sozialwissenschaften. Schriften 1900–1907, MWG* I/7, ed. G. Wagner with C. Härpfer et al. (Tübingen, Germany: Mohr [Siebeck], 2018), 142–234, cf. 231–233.

57. Oxford Dictionaries, "Word of the Year 2016," https://en.oxforddictionaries.com/word -of-the-year/word-of-the-year-2016 (accessed July 25, 2018).

58. Cf. Klaus Lichtblau, "Die Bedeutung der Kategorie des 'Einverständnisses' in Max Webers Wissenschaftslehre. Ein (fast) vergessenes Kapitel innerhalb seiner Rezeption des Werkes von Ferdinand Tönnies," in *Max Webers vergessene Zeitgenossen. Studien zur genese der Wissenschaftslehre*, ed. Gerhard Wagner and Claudius Härpfer (Wiesbaden, Germany: Harrassowitz, 2016), 213–232.

59. Max Weber, "On Some Categories of Interpretive Sociology," trans. Hans Henrik Bruun, in *CMW*, 273–301, cf. 291; *Verstehende Soziologie und Werturteilsfreiheit, Schriften und Reden 1908–1917, MWG* I/12, ed. J. Weiß with S. Frommer (Tübingen, Germany: Mohr [Siebeck], 2018), 389–440, cf. 422.

60. *E&S*, 37; *MWG* I/23, 191. Emphasis in the original.

61. *E&S*, 1193; Max Weber, *Wirtschaft und Gesellschaft. Nachlaß. Herrschaft, MWG* I/22-4, ed. E. Hanke with Th. Kroll (Tübingen, Germany: Mohr [Siebeck], 2005), 650.

62. Cf. Peter Breiner, *Max Weber & Democratic Politics* (Ithaca, NY, and London: Cornell University Press, 1996); Ralph Schroeder, "From Weber's Political Sociology to Contemporary Liberal Democracy," in *Max Weber, Democracy and Modernization*, 79–92; Stefan Breuer, *Max Webers tragische Soziologie. Aspekte und Perspektiven* (Tübingen, Germany: Mohr Siebeck, 2006), 112–142; Hubert Treiber, "Moderner Staat und moderne Bürokratie bei Max Weber," in *Max Webers Staatssoziologie. Positionen und Perspektiven*, ed. Andreas Anter and Stefan Breuer (Wiesbaden, Germany: Nomos, 2007), 118–155; Andreas Anter, *Max Weber's Theory of the Modern State. Origins, Structure and Significance* (Basingstoke, UK: Palgrave Macmillan, 2014); Andreas Anter, "Max Webers Herrschaftskonzept, die EU-Superbürokratie und die Staatenwelt der Gegenwart," in *Alte Begriffe—Neue Probleme. Max Webers Soziologie im Lichte aktueller Problemstellungen*, ed. Thomas Schwinn and Gert Albert (Tübingen, Germany: Mohr Siebeck, 2016), 117–131.

63. Maurizio Bach, *Die Bürokratisierung Europas. Verwaltungseliten, Experten und politische Legitimation in Europa* (Frankfurt am Main, Germany; New York: Campus, 1999), 33.

64. Cf. Cas Mudde and Cristóbal Rovira Kaltwasser, *Populism. A Very Short Introduction* (Oxford: Oxford University Press, 2017), 66–67; Jan-Werner Müller, *What Is Populism?* (Philadelphia: University of Pennsylvania Press, 2016), 23; Breuer, *Max Webers tragische Soziologie*, 142–145.

65. Cf. Manfred Franck, *Ökonomie der Aufmerksamkeit. Ein Entwurf* (Munich: DTV, 1998).

66. Cf. Eli Pariser, *The Filter Bubble: What the Internet Is Hiding from You* (New York: Penguin Press, 2011).

67. Cf. Michela Del Vicario, Alessandro Bessi, Fabiana Zollo, Fabio Petroni, Antonio Scala, Guido Caldarelli, H. Eugene Stanley, and Walter Quattrociocchi, "Echo Chambers in the Age of Misinformation" (2015), https://arxiv.org/abs/1509.00189.

68. Weber, "Science as a Profession and Vocation," 345, 349, 353; *MWG* I/17, 94, 103, 111.

CHAPTER 16

....

POLITICS AND ETHICS, AND THE ETHIC OF POLITICS

....

HANS HENRIK BRUUN

POLITICS AND ETHICS

....

"POLITICS is a not a business which builds, or will ever be able to build, on moral foundations." This claim is made in a letter from Max Weber to some of his academic colleagues in 1911, and we find similarly uncompromising statements in his later writings.[1] He never wavers as far as this fundamental position is concerned.

The absolute character of these formulations should not, however, be taken to imply that Weber regarded the issue as a simple one. On the contrary: the question of how the concepts of ethics and politics relate to each other occupies Max Weber from the beginning of his academic career until the very end, shortly before his death in 1920. He deals extensively with it as early as 1895, in his "Inaugural Lecture" at Freiburg University. His thinking on this matter is influenced by his observation of the Russian Revolution in 1905. And he further develops his ideas on this topic, and more particularly on the question of the ethic of politics, in his 1917 article "Value Freedom" and his 1919 lecture/pamphlet "Politics as a Vocation."[2]

The Conflict of Ultimate Values

The central plank in the platform on which Weber's views of this matter rest is his claim that there is a fundamental *conflict* between the spheres of ultimate values.[3] We already find elements of this view expressed in a letter from Weber written years before the "Inaugural Lecture,"[4] but it is only given its full expression in a theoretical context after the turn of the century. In Weber's early methodological essays (1903–1906), these ultimate values are mostly identified with the traditional ones: truth, beauty, and morality (ethics). In his later, more profound treatment of the question,[5] other value spheres are added. The number and precise character of these value spheres do not seem to be fixed, and the criteria for defining them remain unclear. What is quite clear, though, is that there is no hierarchy between them and that their validity cannot be subjected to scientific proof: they must be *chosen* and *defended*. In this connection, Weber employs the dramatically strong metaphor of a conflict between "God" and the "Devil"; and he views the value conflict as a "fundamental fact"—one that not only is empirical, but must be acknowledged by any genuine philosophy of values.[6]

In Weber's view, each value sphere has its particular ethic and its specific "inherent laws" (*Eigengesetzlichkeiten*)[7] which are binding on everyone who chooses the value sphere in question. He never systematically discusses the grounds on which these "inherent laws" are defined; and considering the central importance of value spheres in his thinking, one may well agree with Guy Oakes[8] that his analysis on this point is "surprisingly casual."[9]

The Inaugural Lecture

Weber's inaugural lecture in many ways reads more like a political statement than an academic address. He does, however, make one central point of methodological importance: the ideals which the science of economic policy—in itself an amalgam between economic theory and value-oriented policy—should pursue cannot in his view be found within economic science itself. In Weber's pithy formulation, "The science of political economy is a *political* science."[10] Now, in itself this does not necessarily imply that political economy cannot be ethically oriented; and indeed, such an ethical orientation was precisely what many of Weber's older colleagues took for granted. But this approach, too, is rejected out of hand by Weber, who brands as "unspeakably philistine" the idea that it is possible to replace political with "ethical" ideals.[11] Economic and social policy, he insists,[12] cannot be conducted on the basis of a eudaemonistic approach (i.e., seeking the greatest happiness for the greatest number of people): this is an illusion since it ignores the fact that economic life is marked by a fundamental *struggle*. The supreme political value is, he insists, the interests of the *nation*.[13]

In the inaugural lecture, Weber's argument had been stated in crudely political terms; and he wrote to his brother Alfred that the "brutality" of his views had aroused "general consternation."[14] In the 1911 letter quoted at the outset, he admitted that the lecture had in many respects been "immature", but went on to say that, nevertheless, it already deliberately made a methodological point in affirming that ethics and politics were incompatible.[15]

THE ETHIC OF POLITICS

In some of his later writings, Weber enters into a philosophical analysis of the concept of ethics, and the result of this analysis turns out to be the mainstay of his view of the ethic of politics.

The Limits of Ethics

The conflict of principle between the value spheres of ethics and politics does not mean that politicians cannot in practice attempt to orient their action according to ethical norms. (As we have seen, Weber, in his inaugural lecture, castigated such attempts.) But what particularly interests him in relation to the sphere of politics are the cases where ethical norms *cannot* offer any substantive guidance for action. The central discussion of this kind is contained in Weber's essay "Value Freedom" from 1917.[16] He first points out that "the possibility of a normative ethic"—that is to say, of an independent ethical value sphere with its own specific dignity and laws—"is by no means called into question merely because there are problems of a *practical* kind for [the solution of] which such a normative ethic cannot by itself provide any unambiguous directives." As an example of such problems, Weber refers to the concept of (social–political) "justice": should one reward great talents or, on the contrary, balance out the consequences of the unequal distribution of mental capacities? This is "the type of *ethical* problem relevant to most of the questions concerning social policy;" and such questions "cannot be bindingly decided on the basis of 'ethical' premises."[17]

The Ethic of Conviction and the Ethic of Responsibility

The "social justice" problem concerns the difficulty of defining *what* should be the end of social–political action. But Weber goes on to discuss another, even more fundamental and far-reaching question, namely whether action should *at all* be guided by the wish to attain certain practical ends:

> [Is] the intrinsic value of ethical conduct (usually referred to as the "pure will" or the "conviction")...in itself sufficient to justify this conduct, in accordance with the maxim "The Christian acts rightly and leaves the outcome to God"...or [should] the responsibility for those *consequences* of the action that can be foreseen as possible or probable, because this action is enmeshed in the ethically irrational world...also be taken into account[?][18]

Weber claims that, like the well-known Kantian ethical maxims, the two orientations described have a "strictly formal character"; moreover, they are "in eternal conflict," which "no ethic can, in and of itself, provide the means for resolving." These alternatives—which we shall call the "ethic of conviction" and the "ethic of responsibility," respectively[19]—are at the core of Weber's reflections on the *ethic of politics*.[20]

As one can see from the definition of the two ethics, their essential point of difference lies in their attitude to the consequences of actions: a person acting according to the ethic of conviction judges his or her action solely by its intrinsic value, regardless of consequences, and thus takes no responsibility for those consequences; while a person acting in accordance with the ethic of responsibility will not only take those consequences—if they are foreseeable or probable—into account but also feel that he or she must accept responsibility for them.

This element, the *responsibility for the consequences* of one's actions, is at the heart of the ethic of responsibility, just as the refusal to be responsible for the consequences of one's action is crucial to the ethic of conviction.

Ethical Irrationality

In order fully to understand and compare the implications of these two political ethics, we need to look more closely at the concept of "ethical irrationality," which Weber introduces into the discussion. Why is the world "ethically irrational"? Because causality is, in principle, ethically neutral: an ethically positive action may have ethically negative direct or indirect effects, and vice versa. (In this connection, Weber sometimes refers to Schopenhauer's statement that "the law of causality is not so obliging as to let us use it like a hansom cab, which we can send home when we have arrived at our destination.")[21]

The Nature of Politics: Violence as the Essential Means

In this connection, the focus of Weber's discussion shifts from the nature of *ethics* to the nature of *politics*: in his view, the ethical irrationality of the world acquires a particular poignancy when it affects political action. Politics cannot, he claims, be defined by the *goals* that it pursues.[22] It has to be defined by its specific *means*. "The specific means of *legitimate violence per se* in the hands of human associations"—and, we may add, of their representatives—"is what gives all the ethical problems of politics their specific character. Anyone who makes a pact with the means of violence, for whatever purpose—and every politician does this—is at the mercy of its specific consequences" (italics in original).[23] In Weber's view, these "specific" consequences are not just theoretical possibilities but amount to an "inescapable pragma": "force and the threat of force unavoidably breed more violence."[24] In fact, this power pragma must be seen as nothing less than the inherent law of the political value sphere—something that Weber, with rhetorical pathos, repeatedly refers to as the "diabolical" quality of politics.[25] He particularly emphasizes the need for the political actor to be clear about the consequences which his or her action may have, not only externally—in the "world"—but also for his or her own inner being, and about his or her *responsibility* for these external and internal consequences. In fact, he specifically points out that the values governing the sphere of political action "can perhaps only be realized by assuming ethical 'guilt.'"[26]

Thus, in Weber's view, the exercise of political power will always be backed up by the *threat* of force and violence; but it may not always be characterized by the *use* of force. While physical violence is the backbone of politics, it is not necessarily its visage. This is especially true of domestic politics, where Weber's analysis concentrates on the *legitimacy* of rulership, which reduces the need for the overt exercise of physical force.

"Power States" in Foreign Policy

On the other hand, the "inescapable" importance of power and violence within the political sphere becomes especially salient when Weber discusses *foreign* policy.[27] This is a recurrent theme in his thought. As early as the inaugural lecture, he speaks of the *"reverberations of a position of world power"* (italics in original) which constantly confronts the state with great power-political tasks."[28] In an article more than twenty years later,[29] he further develops the same idea. There are, he says, nations which have very considerable amounts of physical force at their disposal: they are, in his terminology, "power states." And since a "power state," by its very existence, represents an obstacle and a threat to other "power states," it may, whether it wants to or not, be drawn into the maneuvers and conflicts of international politics. There is no binding way of settling international differences peacefully; consequently, the means of violence concentrated in the hands of the "power states" may come to be employed in armed conflicts against other states.

But the most striking element of Weber's thinking about the role of "power states" in international relations is his constant reminder that the "power state" has an "obligation" to use its power and, consequently, a *responsibility* for the way it is used (or left unused—in which case power states are particularly exposed to the power ambitions of their neighbors). Here, again, the element of responsibility is central to Weber's analysis.[30]

The Different Varieties of the Ethic of Conviction

Against this background, it is easy to see why Weber attaches special importance to that version of the ethic of conviction which he finds exemplified in the Sermon on the Mount and which is guided by the commandment "Resist not evil with force."[31] By always "turning the other cheek," a person may indeed escape the otherwise "inescapable" pragma of power: the violence necessitated by politics is countered by a passivity legitimated by ethics.

If carried to its ultimate conclusion, such an attitude may culminate in a complete rejection of *all* worldly things—what Weber calls "acosmism." The kingdom of the acosmistic ethic of conviction is simply "not of this world," and the adherents of acosmism will try to escape from the "world" altogether. They therefore cannot, strictly speaking, act as politicians in the ordinary sense of the word.

But Weber often discusses a less extreme variant of this ethic—what we may call the "pacifist-political" attitude.[32] Here, the "world," the general context of politics, is accepted in principle; but the practical policies adopted are based on the rejection of what Weber sees as the essential component of political action—the use, or the threat of use, of power; they are consistently pacifist. The adherents to this variant of the ethic of conviction act on the assumption that evil actions, like the use of power, can only have evil results, while good can only flow from good actions. The political pacifists close their eyes to the ethical irrationality of the world and take responsibility only for the ethical, non-violent political action as such. In Weber's view, they cannot, of course deny the ineluctability of the "power pragma"; but they will deny their responsibility for its "diabolical" consequences.

It is obvious why Weber concentrates on the convictional rejection of violence since violence is, in his view, the inescapable means of politics. There are other orientations than pacifism, however, which can be followed with the same single-mindedness and the same total disregard for consequences. (One example, quoted by Weber himself,[33] is that of the officer who, out of an absolute sense of duty and honor, prefers to be blown up together with his redoubt instead of surrendering.) A politician may, out of conviction, reject certain means of political action out of hand or, conversely, prescribe them as mandatory, irrespective of the consequences of this rejection or prescription.

There is yet another variant of the ethic of conviction, which Weber refers to as the "radical-revolutionary"[34] ethic. Unlike the pacifist, the radical revolutionary explicitly accepts, and may even have a special preference for, the use of violence. But like the pacifists, the radical revolutionaries will close their eyes to the ethical irrationality of the world: they will either—like the anarchists or syndicalists of Weber's times—assume that violent action is good *in itself* as a proof of commitment or faith, irrespective of its consequences, or use violent means to achieve the chosen goal—and to that extent consider the consequences of their actions—but dismiss any doubts, in themselves or others, as to their ethical justification, by claiming that the end always and totally justifies the means ("You cannot make an omelette without breaking eggs"). The radical revolutionaries only feel responsible for their overriding goal but not for the negative consequences of using violence to achieve it.[35]

Value Conflict and the Hierarchy of Values

It may be useful to keep in mind that the difference between the ethic of responsibility and the ethic of conviction can also be stated in terms of their respective implications with regard to the question of a possible hierarchy of values. As we have seen, Weber was convinced—and regarded it as an established element of scientific philosophy[36]—that the ultimate values of human existence are in fundamental conflict; thus, outside of the religious sphere, there can be no settled and binding hierarchy of values. The ethic of responsibility implicitly recognizes this fact: consequences, goals, and side effects have to be weighed against each other; the outcome of the deliberations is never given in advance but takes the form of a decision on the part of the politician—a decision for which he or she must then take and feel responsibility. The ethic of conviction, on the other hand, implicitly presupposes a hierarchy of values in the form of the general pre-eminence of a particular value. For the acosmist, this value is the negation of all worldly things; for the political pacifist, it is ethical conduct as such; and for the radical revolutionary, it is the overriding goal which must be pursued by all available means.

The Relationship between the Two Ethics of Politics

The ethics of conviction and responsibility have here been described in their purest form, as absolute opposites. But Weber himself points out that the ethic of conviction includes an element of responsibility (i.e., for maintaining the ethical quality of the action in itself). Similarly, the ethic of responsibility normally includes an element of principled conviction since the "responsible" politician will regard his or her goals as values to be realized.[37] It is, of course, possible that certain politicians have no principled convictions at all and practice their politics as "the art of the possible." Weber has little sympathy with this attitude, which, as he notes, is in Germany sometimes glorified with the name of *Realpolitik*.[38] And he is even less enamored of self-proclaimed "power politicians": "there is no more pernicious distortion of political energy than when [the politician] boasts of his power in the manner of a parvenu and vainly mirrors himself in the feeling of power—or indeed every worship of power for its own sake."[39]

One further point should be noted is this respect: there will in many cases be an analytical asymmetry between the ethic of conviction and the ethic of responsibility. The ethic of conviction, since it disregards the consequences, is essentially concerned with the purity of the *individual* act. The responsibility pertaining to that ethic will be a responsibility "before the forum of one's own soul." On the other hand, the ethic of responsibility, in accepting responsibility for the consequences, will regularly have to answer to a *wider* forum: the community, the state, or even "history."[40] In this context, however, we should remember Weber's remark that politicians also need an awareness of how they are affected by their own political actions. The burden of responsibility will grow ever heavier for any politician who is *aware* of the outward and inward costs of his or her actions and compromises.

The "Combined" Ethic of Politics

In accordance with his general value-free approach, Weber stresses that it is not possible to claim with any logically binding force that one or the other of the two ethics—the ethic of conviction or the ethic of responsibility—is the right one for a politician to adopt. But it does not seem difficult to discern which one he himself prefers. Politics, he says, should be made with both passion and a sense of judgment[41]; and this corresponds neatly to the combination of conviction-based goal-setting and thorough calculation of consequences which characterizes the politician committed to an ethic of responsibility. One might also think that Weber's emphasis on the necessity of being *aware* of the "diabolical" consequences of political action would in itself be a strong indication of his preference for the ethic of responsibility.

Against this background, the final (but often overlooked) step in Weber's analysis acquires especial importance. He describes it in a passage worth quoting in full:

> On the other hand it is immensely moving when a *mature* person (whether old or young) who actually feels with his whole soul the responsibility he bears for the consequences of his actions, and who acts on the basis of an ethic of responsibility, at some point says: "Here I stand, I can do no other".[42] That is something genuinely human and deeply moving. For it must be *possible* for *each* of us to find ourselves in such a situation at some point, if we are not inwardly dead. In this respect, the ethic of conviction and the ethic of responsibility are not absolute opposites, but complementary to one another; and only in combination do they produce the genuine human being, who is *capable* of having a "vocation for politics".[43]

So, in the final analysis, the ethic of responsibility is not sufficient for a true politician. Over and above it, when the calculations and weighing of consequences become too much, he or she must be capable of performing the "quantum leap" into the ethic of conviction. As Weber sees it, the ethic of politics at its fullest and most genuine is therefore neither the ethic of conviction nor ethic of responsibility, taken by themselves, but a "combined" ethic based on the *awareness* that one's political commitment and its realistic implementation may at some point "cost" too much, not only in relation to other political goals but also, and in the last resort more importantly, in relation to one's own "inner being." Political responsibility, under this construction, includes not only the political rationality of one's actions but also the decision whether to remain within the framework of political rationality *at all*: it is the responsibility to one's own conscience.[44]

The Relevance Today of the Weberian Analysis

Can the concepts "ethic of conviction" and "ethic of responsibility" still be seen as relevant for the analysis of politics and the action of politicians? The answer to this question will fall in two parts. First, I shall summarize the results of searches in a number of databases of public media and books written in English, German, and Danish. Some of these databases are selective, covering only certain newspapers, periodicals, and books; but they still cover a fairly large sample of the relevant material.[45] Second, I shall analyze a number of topical examples, chosen to illustrate particularly interesting features in connection with the two ethics of politics. In this connection, it should be borne mind that these ethics are described by Weber in their purest form, as borderline cases, and that they will in practice usually be intermingled.[46] Few participants in ordinary political life will behave *only* according to an ethic of conviction (if they did, they would encounter great difficulties); and equally, most "responsible" politicians will to *some* extent—over and above the fact that they have committed themselves to the realization of a goal—orient their action according to their convictions and conscience and not just choose the course which seems to them most expedient and trouble-free.

CONTEMPORARY USAGE:
DATABASE RESULTS

The database results make it clear that in English, the term "ethic(s) of responsibility" is found far more often than "ethic(s) of conviction." The Google Ngram graphs show that the "responsibility" terms occur from four to eight times more frequently than the "conviction" ones in the years from 1960 to 2000; in the most recent years recorded (2000–2008), the "responsibility" terms occur five to seven times more frequently. ProQuest Central K-12 records a number of hits almost ten times greater for "ethic(s) of responsibility" than for "ethic(s) of conviction." The reasons for this discrepancy are not hard to find: the term "ethic of responsibility" has a distinctly less academic air than "ethic of conviction" and is employed in contexts (e.g., business management) less directly related to the Weberian disjunction. However, in the German database DWDS, *Gesinnungsethik* ("ethic of conviction") still occurs two and a half times less often than *Verantwortungsethik* ("ethic of responsibility") in the most recent years, 2000–2017, although the contrast between the "academic" and the "non-academic" aspect is lacking in German.

Moreover, these results no doubt reflect the general impression—which one may indeed also, as we have seen, gain from Weber's own text—that the "ethic of responsibility" is simply seen as the more positive and desirable alternative. Looking through the corpus of examples, one frequently encounters the view that there should be more "ethic of responsibility" and less "ethic of conviction" in public life. The opposite wish, for more "conviction," is much less frequent, albeit not entirely absent.[47] It must be said, however, that the use to which Weber's concepts are being put tends to be of a much more everyday kind—narrowminded stubbornness versus broadminded realism—than in his own texts.

On the whole, the two Weberian ethical concepts are correctly understood in the large majority of articles examined.[48] (This may be connected with the fact that most of the texts in the databases which embody the terms "ethic of conviction/responsibility" are written by academics or public intellectuals. The ordinary contributor only rarely appears.) One notices, however, that the notion of the politician's personal responsibility, which is so central to Weber's own analysis, is usually trivialized or left completely out of the argument. This is surprising, given the broad general interest in Weber's discussion of the political leader, which definitely focuses on the notion of responsibility.

Similarly, it may be noted that Weber's idea of the conjunction of the two ethics—the willingness to accept that conviction and conscience may at some point come to be decisive for otherwise "responsible" politicians—is hardly ever reflected in the material.

The Danish-language database Infomedia yields interesting results. Here, unlike the English and German databases, "ethic(s) of conviction" (*sindelagsetik*) scores almost twice as many hits as "ethic(s) of responsibility" (*ansvarsetik*). At the same time, however, one finds a large number of examples where the ethic of conviction is contrasted not with the ethic of responsibility but with the "ethic of consequences" (*konsekvensetik*). To a certain extent, this seems to reflect the narrowness of the Danish public debate on these matters: there are a number of implicit references to the thinking of a popular philosopher, Peter Thielst, who in his work lists four kinds of ethics as relevant for the analysis of political action: ethic of conviction, ethic of consequences, ethic of rules (or duty), and ethic of dialogue.[49] Moreover, Thielst's concept of "ethic of consequences" includes both utilitarianism (seeking the happiness of the greatest number), adaptation (an aspect of the ethic of responsibility with which Weber shows little sympathy),[50] and action oriented toward "ends justifying the means"—which Weber, as we have seen, explicitly saw as the "radical-revolutionary" variant of the ethic of *conviction*. (The "ethic of duty" would also be grouped under the Weberian category of "ethic of conviction.") Generally speaking, there is a tendency in the Danish debate to focus on the choice between abstract good intentions and utilitarian action, while the "responsibility" element is almost wholly neglected. The ethic of consequences takes over from the ethic of responsibility.

THE WEBERIAN CONCEPTS APPLIED TO THE ANALYSIS OF CONCRETE CASES

The analysis of German political behaviour. It is not surprising that the two Weberian ethics have a larger place in German political discourse than in English-speaking countries.[51] This is explicitly noted in an article which appeared in the *Economist* in the autumn of 2016.[52] After giving a perfect and rounded account of the two concepts and their background, the anonymous author quotes a number of German commentators who specifically use these concepts in their analysis of German politics. (One of the commentators goes so far as to say that these ethics capture a moral tension specific to Germany, and another one states that "Germany has a surfeit of *Gesinnungsethik* [ethic of conviction].") The commentators' analysis of concrete policies yields somewhat paradoxical results, however. One, Thilo Sarrazin, argues that Germany, out of an ethic of conviction, refused to bail out Greece during its financial crisis, while another, Manfred Nowak, implies that this ethic of conviction (reflecting guilt feelings about the Second World War) could be a factor behind the eventual (slight) *softening* of the German stance toward Greece in that crisis. In the same way, Chancellor Merkel is said to have "galloped away with an ethic of conviction" in the 2015 refugee crisis, only to be confronted not just by realities on the ground but also by accusations—by other, less "convictional" countries—of "moral imperialism", so that she felt forced to return to her usual "ethic of responsibility."

In other concrete cases, the application of the Weberian scheme of ethical analysis can also yield interesting results.

The Fate of the Danish Jews during the German Occupation in World War II: The Paradox of Consequences

The Danish government had continued in office after the German Occupation in April 1940 but, under the pressure of unacceptable German demands, resigned on August 29, 1943. Executive power was then in practice transferred to the permanent secretaries of the various ministries. Toward the end of September, rumors of an impending German action against the Danish Jews grew ever more alarming, and on September 28 a high official from the German Legation, G. F. Duckwitz, confidentially revealed to central Danish politicians that the raid would take place in the night between October 1 and 2. The permanent secretaries were quickly informed, and in a series of meetings, over three whole days, they discussed among themselves how to react in the face of this impending tragedy. The choices were agonizing. One idea, which was quickly floated, was that the Danish authorities should offer to round up the Jews without German help and intern them on Danish soil, against a German guarantee that no further action would then be taken against the interned Jews. This idea was eventually accepted by a majority of the officials, led by the de facto prime minister, Permanent Secretary Svenningsen from the Foreign Ministry (who believed that he had the support of the representatives of the Jewish community). However, a few of the permanent secretaries staunchly opposed the proposal on grounds of principle; and when they finally, on October 1, reluctantly accepted the need for concerted action, one of them stressed that, if a decision of the majority went against his conscience, it could never bind him to act against his beliefs on such a grave and important issue. When the raid was actually launched on the night of October 1, Svenningsen, in a last desperate attempt to stop the action, presented the Danish internment proposal to the German plenipotentiary, Werner Best, but to no avail. The raid went ahead, but—as is well known—the vast majority of Jews, with the aid of their Danish countrymen, were able to reach Sweden in safety.[53]

This is an example of the operation of the ethic of responsibility at its finest. All of the Danish officials tried to evaluate, to the best of their ability, the uncertain consequences of proposed courses of action; and the consciousness of their responsibility before the Jewish community and Danish public opinion no doubt weighed heavily on all of them. But while the majority felt obliged, by their ethic of responsibility, to accept even such a controversial measure as the offer of Danish internment, a few others persisted in their refusal, out of principle—that is to say, out of an ethic of conviction. A quick agreement on the "responsible" internment offer *might* have forestalled the German raid, but the "convictional" opposition of the minority meant that the offer was delayed and came too late. The long-term result was that Denmark gained the respect of the whole world for the successful rescue of the Jews; on the other hand, if a Danish internment had actually taken place, Denmark would probably in international public opinion have been relegated to an ignominious position analogous to that of Vichy France. Thus, paradoxically, the unhampered application of the ethic of responsibility would have had dire consequences, which were in fact avoided by the countervailing operation of the ethic of conviction.

Sacrificing the Few for the Sake of the Many: The Ethic of Utilitarianism and the Ethic of Responsibility

In analytical philosophy, theoretical cases[54] have been constructed to demonstrate the ethical dilemma inherent in situations where accepting the death of a few may save the lives of many more. This kind of thinking was put into dramatic practice by the author Ferdinand von Schirach in his play *Terror* (2015). The plot is as follows: an aeroplane with 164 passengers is hijacked by a terrorist who wants to crash it in a football stadium with 70,000 spectators. The main character of the play is an air force pilot who decides to shoot down the plane before it reaches the stadium, thus sacrificing a relatively low number of lives for the sake of several thousands (but violating Article 1 of the German Constitution, which states that "the dignity of man is inviolable," as well as a decision of the Constitutional Court expressly denying the right to shoot down a plane under such circumstances). The twist was that the members of the audience were asked to vote on whether they approved of the pilot's action or not: was he a murderer or a hero? In the theater, 60 percent approved of his action; and when the play was filmed and shown on television, no less than 87 percent of those voting, on the Internet or by text messages, declared themselves in favor of the pilot's action. In itself, it is interesting—but perhaps not surprising[55]—that the majority approved of the pilot's decision (even though it was taken in express disobedience of the orders of the minister of defense and could therefore not be covered by an "ethic of duty"). It was, strictly speaking, the result of a utilitarian weighing of numbers of human lives, although the pilot's defending counsel also tries to argue in convictional terms ("the pilot did not act according to some principle, of whatever kind—he simply did what was right"). But the author's own view is particularly significant: the pilot might be a hero, Schirach said, but "heroes are always tragic and guilty, never happy. In this case, that means: shoot down the plane, and then—a life sentence."[56] This was the truly Weberian view of the pilot's action and of the concomitant guilt and responsibility. The vast majority of the public apparently took the responsibility aspect more lightly.

Freedom of Expression and the "Muhammad Cartoons": The Refusal to Consider Unacceptable Consequences

"Freedom of expression" is a principle which can be found enshrined in nearly all con-stitutions of Western societies. While it may legally be subject to certain limitations and restrictions, it has in political practice approached the status of a value which cannot be relativized. One particularly striking expression of this fact was found in the debate sur-rounding the so-called Muhammad cartoons, which appeared in a Danish newspaper in the autumn of 2005. The publication led to strong reactions in the Muslim world, includ-ing a boycott of Danish goods in the Arab world and the burning down of the Danish embassy in Damascus. In the ensuing debate, there was general support in the Western world for the view that freedom of expression was an inalienable right. But the question was raised whether this right should in practice be exercised with caution because of the foreseeable *consequences*. As the head of the Confederation of Danish Industries put it in an open statement (January 27, 2006) after the widening of the boycott of Danish goods: "the obvious consequences [of the publication] are that others feel aggrieved; and this now puts a strain on third parties." The parallel to the opposition between the ethic of conviction and the ethic of responsibility is clear.

Interestingly, the appeal to the "convictional" principle of free expression was in this case most prominent on the right side of the political spectrum, while the left side tended to argue that the consequences should be taken into account: Thus, the political right—normally deemed to be more "realist"—was here reluctant to take into account the foreseeable consequences of an action, simply because it strongly *disapproved* of these consequences. In essence, this attitude, by disregarding the ethical irrationality of the world, becomes an ethic of conviction.

House of Cards and the Weberian Ethics of Politics

The question of the ethic of politics has also been taken up, more or less directly, in certain television series. In particular, one episode[57] of the Netflix series *House of Cards* in fact, without acknowledging any actual inspiration from Max Weber,[58] presents a complete, didactically pure picture of all three Weberian variants of the political ethic: the ethic of conviction, the ethic of responsibility, and the "combined" variant (the ethic of responsibility "overwhelmed" by the ethic of conviction).

The setting is a journey to Moscow by the US president, Frank Underwood, who has a number of important matters to negotiate with Russian president Petrov; he is accom-panied by his wife, Claire, who has the separate mission of getting a jailed gay American, Michael Corrigan, out of prison so that he can return to the United States. The major part of the episode takes place in the prison. Claire tries to impress on Corrigan the need for him to sign a fulsome statement of thanks to President Petrov for treating him well and letting him go. Corrigan, in the spirit of the ethic of conviction, refuses to sign any text of this sort, however carefully worded ("You can't parse this. It's all or nothing"); and when Claire argues "That's not how politics works!" he replies "But that's how revolution works!" (18.25–40). In accordance with the ethic of responsibility, Claire carefully sets out all the arguments in favor of signing and all the negative consequences of *not* signing ("you'll help no-one; other people will suffer"). When Corrigan retorts "I can't betray myself. What would I be then?" Claire gives the devastatingly clear reply "You'd be a *politician*" (34.40–35.40). During the night, which Claire spends in the cell in the hope of finally convincing Corrigan, he manages to hang himself. This makes a deep impression on Claire. It is obvious that the matter must be papered over if the presidential mission to Moscow is not to fail entirely; and at a subsequent joint press conference with President Petrov, Claire starts out in the best "responsible" manner by reading out a bland prepared statement. But suddenly, she can stand this pretence no longer: she has reached the point (which occurs, with dramatic clarity, at 44.12) at which the "combined" ethic takes over, and she no longer bows to the logic of consequences. She tells the whole story, saying that Corrigan killed himself "because he didn't want to lie. . . . He was willing to die for what he believed in" and finishes off with an emotional outburst: "Shame on you, President Petrov!" (43.25–45.20). Obviously, against this background, the Moscow mission is an utter fiasco. President Petrov breaks off negotiations with Frank Underwood, who has to return empty-handed, and without Michael Corrigan, to the United States.

The didactic character of the episode is still further enhanced by an argument between Frank and Claire Underwood on the way home. Claire states her case: she needed to pay her respects to the action of Corrigan—the "action of a brave man." She admits that her frank speech at the press conference was a "political mistake," but when Frank contemptuously interjects "Was it some sort of moral epiphany, then?" she says that, yes, it was exactly that. Now it is Frank's turn: he rejects the idea that Corrigan's act showed courage ("Anyone can kill himself") and goes on, "What takes real courage is to keep your mouth shut when the stakes are that high." And to Claire's final outburst "We are murderers," he retorts "We are survivors." To end the episode, he turns to the camera and asks the viewers, "What are you looking at?" We are, of course, looking at a politician who does not, unlike his wife, have the moral fiber to realize that a politician's hands can get too dirty. In "keeping his mouth shut," he may be shouldering the responsibility toward the country that he serves; but he is unwilling—perhaps unable—to see that he also has a responsibility to his own conscience.

CONCLUSION

The types of political ethic that Weber described in 1919 are still perfectly recognizable in the political landscape of today: the radical-revolutionary ethic of conviction still animates terrorists of all persuasions; consistent pacifism may be less commonly met with, but many people reject the whole world of politics as a self-seeking struggle for power; on the other hand, some "power politicians" still emit vain and boastful claims of personal or national grandeur; and the utilitarian version of the ethic of responsibility, shading over into policies of adaptation or technocratic "necessity," is widely applied. Less commonly met with are politicians who accept the fundamental responsibility— and possible guilt—with which all exercise of political power is burdened. And still less common are those politicians who in practice conjugate their responsibility to the community with their responsibility to their own ethical standards and thus live up to the complete, "combined" ethic of politics. Weber's analysis of the relationship between ethics and politics, and of the ethic of politics, remains as relevant as ever, both empirically and as a benchmark for judgment.

Notes

1. For example, "Certainly, politics is not an ethical business," in Max Weber, "Suffrage and Democracy in Germany," (1917) in *Political Writings* (hereafter *PolW*), ed. Peter Lassman and Ronald Speirs, 6th ed. (Cambridge: Cambridge University Press, 2008), 80–129, quotation at 83; *Zur Politik im Weltkrieg. Schriften und Reden 1914–1918, Max Weber-Gesamtausgabe* (hereafter *MWG*) I/15, ed. W. J. Mommsen with G. Hübinger (Tübingen, Germany: Mohr [Siebeck], 1984), 347–396, 350.
2. Max Weber, "Inaugural Lecture," in *PolW*, 1–28; *Landarbeiterfrage, Nationalstaat und Vokswirtschaftspolitik. Schriften und Reden 1892–1899, MWG* I/4, ed. Wolfgang J. Mommsen with Rita Aldenhoff (Tübingen, Germany: Mohr [Siebeck], 1993), 535–574; writings on Russian Revolution of 1905: Max Weber, *The Russian Revolutions* (hereafter *RR*), trans. and ed. Gordon C. Wells and Peter Baehr (Cambridge: Polity Press, 1995), 41–240; *Zur Russischen Revolution 1905. Schriften und Reden 1905–1912, MWG* I/10, ed. W. J. Mommsen with D. Dahlmann (Tübingen, Germany: Mohr [Siebeck], 1989); "The Meaning of 'Value Freedom' in the Sociological and Economic Sciences," in *Collected Methodological Writings* (hereafter *CMW*), trans. Hans Henrik Bruun, ed. H. H. Bruun and S. Whimster (London and New York: Routledge, 2012), 304–334; *Verstehende Soziologie und Werturteilsfreiheit, MWG* I/12, ed. J. Weiß with S. Frommer (Tübingen, Germany: Mohr [Siebeck], 2018), 445–512; "The Profession and Vocation of Politics," in *PolW*, 309–369; *Wissenschaft als Beruf 1917/1919—Politik als Beruf 1919, MWG* I/17, ed. W. J. Mommsen and W. Schluchter with B. Morgenbrod (Tübingen, Germany: Mohr [Siebeck], 1992), 157–252.
3. Max Weber, "Science as a Profession and Vocation," in *CMW*, 335–353, 350; *MWG* I/17, 71–111, 104–105.
4. Max Weber's letter to Emmy Baumgarten, July 5 and 12, 1887, in *Briefe 1887–1894, MWG* II/2, ed. R. Aldenhoff-Hübinger with Th. Gerhards and S. Oßwald-Bargende (Tübingen, Germany: Mohr [Siebeck], 2017), 96–106, 101–103.
5. In particular, Weber's "Intermediate Reflections" (1915, revised 1920), in *From Max Weber: Essays in Sociology* (hereafter *FMW*), ed. H. H. Gerth and C. W. Mills (New York: Oxford University Press, 1946), 323–357; *Die Wirtschaftsethik der Weltreligionen. Konfuzianismus und Taoismus. Schriften 1915–1920, MWG* I/19, ed. H. Schmidt-Glintzer with P. Kolonko (Tübingen, Germany: Mohr [Siebeck], 1989), 479–522.
6. Max Weber, "Value Freedom," *CMW*, 314; *MWG* I/12, 469; "Science as a Profession and Vocation," *CMW*, 350; *MWG* I/17, 104. In "Intermediate Reflections," Weber goes thoroughly

into the question of the *empirical* relationship between the value sphere of monotheist salvation religions, with its demand for brotherly love, and the spheres of other values, including that of politics. In this context, he again emphasizes the "mutual strangeness" between politics and the ethical implications of the Sermon on the Mount (*FMW*, 335; *MWG* I/19, 492).

7. Weber, "Intermediate Reflections," *FMW*, 339 (translation changed from "laws of their own"); *MWG* I/19, 497.

8. Guy Oakes, "Weber on Value Rationality and Value Spheres," *Journal of Classical Sociology* 3 (2003): 27–46, 29.

9. Weber was thoroughly familiar with the philosophy of Kant, but his views on ethics and politics differ from, and are in some respects diametrically opposed to Kant's; see H. H. Bruun, "The Incompatibility of Values and the Importance of Consequences: Max Weber and the Kantian Legacy," *Philosophical Forum* 41 (2010): 51–67. Nor did Weber's acknowledged debt to the thinking of neo-Kantian philosophers, in particular Heinrich Rickert, extend to the question of ethics and politics. Wolfgang Schluchter, in *Paradoxes of Modernity* (Stanford, CA: Stanford University Press, 1996), 48–101, adopts a "systematizing" approach to Weber's views on values. For a critical appraisal of Schluchter's interpretation, see H. H. Bruun, *Science, Values and Politics in Max Weber's Methodology* (exp. ed.) (Aldershot, UK: Ashgate, 2007), 33–34, 49–54.

10. Weber, "Inaugural Lecture," *PolW*, 16; *MWG* I/4, 561.

11. Weber, "Inaugural Lecture," *PolW*, 27; *MWG* I/4, 573.

12. Weber, "Inaugural Lecture," *PolW*, 14, 27; *MWG* I/4, 558, 572.

13. Weber, "Inaugural Lecture," *PolW*, 17; *MWG* I/4, 561.

14. Weber's letter to Alfred Weber, May 17, 1895, quoted in Wolfgang J. Mommsen, *Max Weber and German Politics 1890–1920*, trans. Michael S. Sternberg (Chicago and London: University of Chicago Press, 1984), 37; *Briefe 1895–1902*, *MWG* II/3, ed. R. Aldenhoff-Hübinger with U. Hinz (Tübingen, Germany: Mohr [Siebeck], 2015), 80–83, 82.

15. Weber's letter to the colleagues in Freiburg, November 15, 1911, quoted in Mommsen, *Max Weber and German Politics*, 38; *Briefe 1911–1912*, *MWG* II/7, ed. M. R. Lepsius and W. J. Mommsen with B. Rudhard and M. Schön (Tübingen, Germany: Mohr [Siebeck], 1998), 352–357, 356.

16. Weber, "Value Freedom," *CMW*, 313–315; *MWG* I/12, 466–470. The article is based on an earlier memorandum from 1913, in which the passages referred to here can already be found (edited as "Beitrag zur Werturteildiskussion im Ausschuß des Vereins für Sozialpolitik," in *MWG* I/12, 336–382, 354–356.

17. Weber, "Value Freedom," *CMW*, 313; *MWG* I/12, 467. Weber's general point seems to be that, because of the conflict of ultimate values, the choice between the various ideologies of social justice, natural law, etc. cannot be bindingly resolved, even in terms of Kantian formal ethics.

18. Weber, "Value Freedom," *CMW*, 313; *MWG* I/12, 467–468.

19. The terms "ethic of ultimate ends" and "ethic of intentions" are also sometimes used in English translations, but "ethic of conviction" is the one usually adopted.

20. In substance, the description of the opposition between these two ethics of politics makes its appearance already at an early stage in Weber's empirical work, in one of his studies (1905–1906) on the Russian Revolution of 1905 (Weber, "Bourgeois Democracy in Russia," *RR*, 51–52; *MWG* I/10, 123–124). But while the ethic of conviction, with its rejection of responsibility for the consequences of one's action, is easily recognizable in that study, the

ethic of responsibility is theoretically underdeveloped: it appears as a "success ethic," which lacks the crucially important element of responsibility. For a fuller discussion of this aspect of Weber's "Russian writings," see Schluchter, *Paradoxes of Modernity*, 53–56.

21. Arthur Schopenhauer, *Über die vierfache Wurzel des Satzes vom zureichenden Grunde. Eine philosophische Abhandlung* in Arthur Schopenhauer (ed. Julius Frauenstädt), *Sämmtliche Werke*, Bd. 1, 2. Aufl. (Leipzig, Germany: F.A. Brockhaus), § 20. (My translation). It has even been argued that, because of this essential unpredictability of the consequences of political action—and, in particular, of their acceptability—the politician must in fact take responsibility for (all) the *actual* consequences of his action, not just for the foreseeable or probable ones. See Nick O'Donovan, "Causes and Consequences: Responsibility in the Political Thought of Max Weber," *Polity* 43 (2011): 84–105.

22. Weber, "The Profession and Vocation of Politics," *PolW*, 309–310; *MWG* I/17, 157.

23. Weber, "The Profession and Vocation of Politics," *PolW*, 364; *MWG* I/17, 245.

24. Weber, "Intermediate Reflections," *FMW*, 334; *MWG* I/19, 492.

25. Weber, "The Profession and Vocation of Politics," *PolW*, 362, 365, 366; *MWG* I/17, 241, 247, 248–249.

26. Weber, "Value Freedom," *CMW*, 313; *MWG* I/12, 466. This fundamental view is not contradicted by Weber's claim, in his address to students after the German defeat in 1918, that the "ethical" question of Germany's war guilt is "politically sterile" (*PolW*, 356; *MWG* I/17, 232): what he is arguing against in that connection is the tendency to see Germany's defeat as the result of the *ethical* deficiency of her actions—in other words, to *substitute* ethical values for political ones.

27. Weber, "Intermediate Reflections," *FMW*, 334; *MWG* I/19, 491.

28. Weber, "Inaugural Lecture," *PolW*, 26; *MWG* I/4, 571.

29. Weber, "Between Two Laws," *PolW*, 75–79, 75–77; *MWG* I/15, 95–98, 95–97.

30. See the contribution of Kari Palonen in this volume.

31. Weber, "Intermediate Reflections," *FMW* 334; *MWG* I/19, 491 (see also *FMW*, 148, 336; *MWG* I/19, 494; Weber, "The Profession and Vocation of Politics," *PolW*, 358; *MWG* I/17, 235).

32. Weber himself does not use this term.

33. Weber, "Value Freedom," *CMW*, 319; *MWG* I/12, 480.

34. The term is used by Weber himself ("Value Freedom," *CMW*, 313; *MWG* I/12, 468).

35. If Weber dwells particularly on this violent variant of the ethic of conviction, this obviously reflects political events in Germany at the time of writing. For references to the political situation in this context, see, for instance, Weber's letters to Robert Michels, August 4, 1908, and May 12, 1909, *CMW*, 394, 399; *Briefe 1906–1908*, *MWG* II/5, ed. M. R. Lepsius and W. J. Mommsen with B. Rudhard and M. Schön (Tübingen, Germany: Mohr [Siebeck], 1990), 615–620, 616–616; *Briefe 1909–1910*, *MWG* II/6 (1994), 124–126, 125; Weber, "The Profession and Vocation of Politics," *PolW*, 357, 360–361; *MWG* I/17, 233, 238–239.

36. Weber, "Science as a Profession and Vocation," *CMW*, 347, 350; *MWG* I/17, 99, 104.

37. It is significant that Weber often uses the terms "value" and "goal" interchangeably. This seems to imply that the goals set by the actor will normally have some identifiable relation to ultimate values. See Weber, "Basic Sociological Terms," in *Economy and Society. An Outline of Interpretive Sociology*, ed. G. Roth and C. Wittich (New York: Bedminster Press, 1968), 3–62, 26; *Wirtschaft und Gesellschaft. Soziologie*, *MWG* I/23, ed. K. Borchardt, E. Hanke, and W. Schluchter (Tübingen, Germany: Mohr [Siebeck], 2013), 147–215, 176.

38. Weber, "Value Freedom," *CMW*, 318–319; *MWG* I/12, 468–469. See also Weber's reference ("Bourgeois Democracy in Russia," *RR*, 101–102; *MWG* I/10, 252–253) to "the type of "complacent" German who cannot bear not to be "on the side of the victors," [and who is] puffed up by the elevating consciousness of his quality as a *realpolitiker*."

39. Weber, "The Profession and Vocation of Politics," *PolW*, 354 (translation changed); *MWG* I/17, 229.

40. In practice, Weber took a drastic view of the consequences of this responsibility. In a conversation in 1919 with General Ludendorff, he is reported (Marianne Weber, *Max Weber. A Biography*, trans. Harry Zohn [New York: Wiley and Sons, 1975], 653) to have said, "In a democracy the people choose a leader whom they trust.... Later the people can sit in judgement. If the leader has made mistakes—to the gallows with him!"

41. Weber, "The Profession and Vocation of Politics," *PolW* 353, 369; *MWG* I/17, 227–228, 251–252.

42. This reported statement by Luther at the Diet of Worms, which continues "God help me. Amen," could hardly be more precise as a link to the "convictional attitude" described: "The Christian does what is right, and leaves the results to God."

43. Weber, "The Profession and Vocation of Politics," *PolW*, 367–368 (translation changed); *MWG* I/17, 250.

44. The "combined" ethic obviously cannot be applied as a general principle, but serves as a guideline in the extreme case when the strain imposed by the ethic of responsibility becomes overwhelming. Even so, the fact that it combines two political ethics which are "irreconcilably opposed" (*PolW*, 359; *MWG* I/17, 237) has puzzled some commentators (see Shalini Satkunanandan, "Max Weber and the Ethos of Politics beyond Calculation," *American Political Science Review* 108, no. 1 [2014]: 169–181, 174).

45. These databases are ProQuest (English-language newspapers, worldwide, reaching back to the mid-1980s); New York State Newspapers (reaching back to at least 1992); Historical *New York Times* (covering 1990–2007, with a few older hits); DWDS (a German-language "corpus" dictionary, which includes coverage of a couple of daily newspapers and the weekly *Die Zeit*); and the Danish database Infomedia, which covers all Danish-language newspapers and periodicals from 1980 onward. Google Ngrams, giving relative frequencies of occurrence of a particular term in English-language books, has been used for the period 1900–2008. Scholarly articles and books have, for the purposes of the present study, been excluded from the analysis (apart from the Ngrams, where they form a major part of the underlying corpus of books). I am indebted to Sybille Bruun Moss for facilitating access to some of these databases.

46. Weber himself explicitly acknowledges this fact when he says ("The Profession and Vocation of Politics," *PolW*, 367; *MWG* I/17, 249) that one cannot give instructions to anybody about *when* they should act on the basis of an ethic of conviction and *when* they should act according to the ethic of responsibility.

47. See, for instance, the review ("In Politics Begin Responsibilities," *New York Times Book Review* (June 7, 1992) by the German sociologist Ralf Dahrendorf of a book by Vaclav Havel.

48. One interesting exception is President George W. Bush, who exhorts his audience at an Ohio business college to "[embrace] some cause larger than his or her profit"—an attitude which he then labels an "ethic of responsibility" (*New York Times*, June 15, 2002).

49. Peter Thielst, as reported by Morten Mikkelsen," Moral i alle retninger," *Kristeligt Dagblad*, February 24, 2004.

50. Weber, "Value Freedom," *CMW*, 318; *MWG* I/12, 477.

51. An analysis of the relevant NGrams seems to indicate a difference between the two of at least a factor of 10.

52. "Charlemagne" (pseudonym), "A Tale of Two Ethics," *The Economist*, October 1, 2016.

53. For a compelling narrative of the whole sequence of events, see chaps. 3–6 of Bo Lidegaard, *Countrymen: The Untold Story of How Denmark's Jews Escaped the Nazis* (London: Atlantic Books, 2014).

54. For a useful discussion of such cases, see Judith Jarvis Thomson, "The Trolley Problem," *Yale Law Journal* 94 (1985): 1395–1415.

55. For one thing, if he had not done so, it would seem inevitable that the lives of the 164 passengers would still have been lost when the plane crashed into the arena.

56. "Sind Soldaten Mörderer, Herr von Schirach?" (Are soldiers murderers, Herr von Schirach?). (Interview with Ferdinand von Schirach), *Bild-Zeitung*, October 17, 2016.

57. Season 3, episode 6. The numbers in brackets refer to points in that episode, in minutes and seconds.

58. Unfortunately, it has not been possible to elicit from the manuscript writer of the episode, Melissa James Gibson, any information as to whether she might, directly or indirectly, have been influenced by knowledge of Weber's thinking on the political ethic.

PART IV

RELIGION

CHAPTER 17

MAX WEBER'S ETHICS FOR THE MODERN WORLD

PETER GHOSH

WHAT WEBER SAID

AMONG many instances of incomprehension in the reception of Max Weber's thought, the reception of his ethical ideas is one of the bleakest. One might think it obvious that a man whose most famous work was entitled *The Protestant Ethic and the Spirit of Capitalism* (1904–1905) had something important to say about ethics, especially when we find that "ethic" and "spirit" were essentially equivalents. For example, Weber described his argument as designed to show how "A constitutive component of the capitalist spirit . . . was born out of the spirit of *Christian asceticism*."[1] Elsewhere, he referred to the capitalist "ethic" that had descended from a Protestant "ethic," before adding in the extra label of Puritan and capitalist "ethos" in 1919.[2] Now, whatever the significance of these terminological variations might be, this fussing makes it plain that ethics were indeed at the forefront of his mind, and the *Protestant Ethic* is by far his most important statement in this area. As he stated in 1919–1920, his subject was "the universal history of the ethics of Occidental Christianity;" more specifically, "the interconnections between the modern economic ethos and the rational ethic of ascetic Protestantism."[3] Yet Weber's twentieth-century readers found his thinking on ethics alien and incomprehensible. It was unflinchingly realistic and radically original, so they marginalized it. Today, however, we can see that he identified patterns of behavior of fundamental importance within the social phenomena of his day which are to a large extent ours as well.

The best-informed contemporary in regard to Weber, modern ideas about religion, and the ethical theory of the philosophers was Ernst Troeltsch. For him Weber was ultimately a mystery: he embodied "a union of scepticism, heroism and moral severity at root alien to me."[4] It was a commendably honest response by a Christian and idealist thinker to Weber's seemingly incomprehensible combination of passionate ethical conviction in his personal life, belief in irreconcilable value-pluralism and conflict in society, and a call for "value-freedom" in intellectual inquiry (*Wissenschaft*)—but it left the field wide open to misrepresentation. This set in with a vengeance after 1945 when, understandably, it became axiomatic that the only good German was one who espoused conventional ethical values: that is, values which were eternal, universally applicable, and harmonious. So Weber's ethical thought was located within mainstream Kantian and post-Kantian tradition, as if he were a philosophical idealist, who "holds firmly...to the possibility of specifying universal, comprehensive ethical commands."[5] Indeed, his entire sociology has been characterized as "Kantianizing," and this remains an observable theme in commentary to this day.[6] Now, this was no doubt an understandable response to the ethical problems raised by Nazism, the Berlin Wall, or Baader-Meinhof; and it was certainly no worse than Leo Strauss' alternative: that Weberian "value-freedom" "necessarily leads to nihilism."[7] But still the Kantian label was a drastic denial of the ideas of a man who announced himself as one of "the spokesmen for value-collision,"[8] and its textual foundation was equally eccentric. Insofar as it discussed Weber's ethics at all, a strongly secular generation studiously ignored the *Protestant Ethic* and focused instead on two outlying and largely unconnected areas: his methodological writings— that is, the academic ethics implied by his radical demand for analytical "value-freedom," a subject distinct from social ethics—and the discussion of ethics in the famous lecture "Politics as a Vocation" (1919).[9] Here, Weber's appraisal of politicians motivated by ethics of conviction and responsibility seemed to present something substantial and accessible, on the assumption that responsible behavior was a self-evident good. Yet such an assumption overlooked his dictum in the same lecture that politics was the most morally empty or "diabolical"[10] of all ethical contexts, so it could hardly supply a model for society as a whole. It also overlooked the fact that the origin of Weber's argument lay with the "ethic of conviction," which was a religious category, because the root of all his ethical thought lies in ideas about religion.

What then were these ideas? For Weber it was an evident historical fact that religion (and not idealist philosophy) had been the great generator of ethics in all eras and societies previous to his own. The precursor to modern ethics lay in "salvation" or "ethical" religions. These were "ethically rationalized religions," based on an "ethical postulate: that the world was a divinely ordered cosmos, hence that it had some form of ethically meaningful direction."[11] Religious salvation (whether in an afterlife, reincarnation, or annihilation) and the creation of ethical meaning in a rational earthly cosmos were seamlessly fused, and these benefits were available to all believers. Under the auspices of religion such ethics could present themselves, and were received, as universal and eternal. However, in seventeenth-century Europe and New England ("the Occident") there was a unique departure from this model. Within the Christian tradition of this area there arose a radically new, deviant religious form: ascetic Protestantism with its own "Protestant ethic." Ascetic Protestantism was still a religion; but unlike Catholicism and Lutheranism it was "no longer...an actual 'salvation religion,'" so it gave rise to an entirely new ethic which created the "modern *Kultur*" or value-scheme on which twentieth-century Western society and its social relations were based.[12] This radical modernizing departure was of course Weber's principal concern, so this was the aspect of his thinking that he outlined first, in the *Protestant Ethic*. The historical and comparative context to occidental modernity would then follow later in his writings on the sociology of religion and the "world religions" after 1910.

The crucial novelty of modern Western ethics was that the principal social determinants of ethical conduct had ceased to be personal; they had become impersonal and, in that sense, amoral. The rise of modern capitalism was the outstanding example of this[13]:

> The characteristic feature of modern historical development is the lapse of *personal relationships of rule* as the basis for the organization of labor…Modern development increasingly replaces these with the *impersonal* rule of the propertied *class*, purely business connections instead of personal ones, and tributary obligations to an unknown power which cannot be seen or grasped [shareholders] instead of personal subordination. It thereby eliminates the possibility of comprehending the relationship of ruler and ruled in ethical and religious terms.

Conversely, the Lutheran Church "always adopted a position of extreme mistrust in relation to what we customarily call the money economy.… Why has it done so? For this reason: because it recognised instinctively that the money economy necessarily eliminated direct relationships of rule from one individual to another, and set in their place relations of a purely 'business,' that is, impersonal kind."[14] At the end of the nineteenth century the Lutheran and Catholic Churches continued to suppose that traditional personal ethics, understood in terms of the relationship between one individual and another and founded on the biblical principles of "love thy neighbor" (*Nächstenliebe*)[15] and Christian "brotherhood" (*Brüderlichkeit*), were sufficient for the needs of a modern, mass society—as if being good or loving was sufficient to explain and cope with such phenomena as the conflict of class interests, the pitiless discipline of market forces, or the disintegrative effects of specialization based on the division of labor. To Weber this was nonsense, and this lies at the heart of his (and our) diminished conception of the position occupied by religion in Western society.

By contrast, in Calvinists and Protestant sectarians he found doctrines and practices that inaugurated a new ethical world based on a radical denial of "personal" and previously "unconstrained" (*unbefangene*) humanity.[16] The Calvinist postulate of a transcendental, impersonal, inscrutable, and ethically meaningless *deus absconditus*, or hidden god, had generated an ethic that promoted the rise of a "transcendental" and "meaningless" capitalism and had begun the process of training which enabled men and women to cope with its demands. Calvinists turned the doctrine of "love thy neighbor" on its head. "'Love of one's neighbour' is expressed…in the *first* instance by fulfilment of the…tasks prescribed by one's *job* or *calling*; at the same time it takes on a characteristically objective and *impersonal* character, that of service to the *rational* formation of the social *cosmos* that surrounds us." One "loved" one's fellow men not by reaching out to them but by ignoring them, by accepting a "happy limitation" of one's perspectives and devoting oneself to one's job, which was also a religious calling.[17] This rather than personal relationships was the real religious calling, and those who observed this ethic were the "steel-hard" individuals whose institutionalized residue or "*congealed spirit*" created the twentieth-century "steel-hard housing" that placed enforcement of the new ethic on the "mechanical foundation" supplied by the demands of servicing capitalism—it was no longer a matter of personal initiative.[18] Sectarianism performed a similar function in an associational context. A sect was not (as one might think) a "community" (*Gemeinschaft*) based on emotional warmth between its members but an impersonal "society" (*Gesellschaft*). The crucial rite of admission to the sects was based on a detached, meritocratic assessment of a person's individual ethical "*qualities*," and the sectarian life was one of continual self-assertion of those qualities before one's peers. So its ethical legacy was not communitarianism; rather, it was "one of the most important historical foundations of modern 'individualism.'" In these ways ascetic Protestantism dismissed the traditional Christian ethic based on love, personal warmth, and "cosiness" (*Gemütlichkeit*) and created instead the impersonal and exclusively self-reliant "ethic" which modern capitalism and other organizations required in a public context.[19]

It will be clear that Weber's use of the term "Protestant ethic" was doubtful since the ascetic Protestant ethic was no longer an ethic in the traditional, personal sense, even if in the first instance it retained a "religious root" like the "actual" salvation religions—the psychological stimulus contained in the threat of damnation. The departure from ethical tradition was more obvious in the case of the capitalist economy and its market, which on any conventional understanding was "neither ethical, nor anti-ethical, but simply non-ethical."[20] Yet capitalism, like Protestantism, *was* "ethical" in the elementary sense that it regulated conduct; and this was why Weber resorted to a miscellany of substitute terms in this context, "spirit," "ethic," and "ethos," as well as the ethically detached terminology of "norms."[21] Capitalism worked in two principal ways. First, the capitalist "housing" exercised an external disciplinary function on conduct that could not be ignored:

> It forcibly imposes its norms of economic conduct on the individual, insofar as he is caught up in the relationships of the "market." The manufacturer who persistently contravenes these norms will just as infallibly meet with economic elimination, as the worker who cannot or will not adapt to them, will be thrown unemployed onto the street.[22]

Second, and more comprehensively, the individual was governed by an internalized "ethical" commitment to the *Beruf* (calling, job, profession) as an "absolute *end in itself*": that is, the conduct of one's social life was limited toward performing a narrowly specialized function within the division of labor, where a person was "ultimately concerned only with himself, thinking only of his own salvation."[23]

The modern ethic was not simply a capitalist ethic but (as Weber had noted) a "rational ethic," just as his conception of modernity was a continual oscillation between distinct yet overlapping ideas of capitalism and rationality.[24] In the transition to modernity,

"The ethical practice of everyday man was stripped of its lack of plan and system and shaped into a consistent *method* for the entire conduct of life." A rational life was a remorselessly systematized life, where all one's life—"the entire conduct of life" or *Lebensführung*—was organized to one end, the "absolute *end in itself*." Hence, Weber emphasizes in a capitalist context Benjamin Franklin's maxim *"time is money*," where not a moment was to be wasted or to go unconsidered.[25] For the same reason Weber also considers "lifestyle," "that powerful tendency towards making lifestyle uniform which today stands side by side with the capitalist interest in 'standardization' of production," and traces behavior down to quite minor symptoms such as dress and short haircuts. Another great engine of Western rationalization was the law. Here again seventeenth-century Puritans anticipated modernity in that they did not necessarily observe the law because it was right—"the agent can never have a conscience"—but practiced "formal legality": they observed the letter of the law because it was a necessary requirement in a rationalized society. In the same way capitalists practiced the traditional virtue of "honesty" not only or even because it was a virtue but because it was "the best policy." For example, when you "*appear* as both a careful and an *honest man*... it increases your *credit*."[26]

In this way Weber made an extremely important and original statement about modern ethics or codes of conduct. In a social or public sphere, such as the workplace, the factors governing conduct do not compel because of their moral force. Instead, one is presented with a rationalized, homogenized, and "impersonal" environment, where one yields to the command of what is understood to be functionally, legally, and technically correct, hence rational. Ethically "correct" conduct is not defined substantively as right or wrong or in terms of outcomes (such as the biblical Ten Commandments) but primarily in terms of procedure: what is formally legal or rational—hence what Weber calls "the *formalism* of the Puritan ethic."[27] The attributes of correct behavior are not enthusiasm, human warmth, or sympathy but being "cool," "reserved," "hard," and "sober," with conduct as a whole governed by personal "control" or "self-control."[28] This is the human face of "ascetic" and "rational" conduct which in a capitalist context serves the "categorical imperative" of systemic, humanly meaningless acquisition.[29] (Such an impersonal and unintended "imperative" is surely a sufficient comment on Weber's alleged Kantianism.) Any display of a personal, emotional, or moralizing kind is out of place; and this modern "ethical" code is very much the one by which we live today in most public spaces.

However, the impersonal "ethic" only applies in public or social contexts. Weber did not suppose that men and women ceased to have values—this is the one point where he coincides with Kantianism—and there is a second tier of ethical behavior manifested primarily in the private and personal spheres. One component comes from the vestiges of religious behavior, where what was once public has retreated into the private sphere: the "prophetic pneuma" which had swept through "great communities" now "beats only within the smallest community circles, passing from one person to another in pianissimo."[30] Flight into mysticism (in principle, a wholly isolated state) and even erotically charged passion were further alternatives of this kind, and Weber also saw an analogy to the collapse of a public religion in the change from public and monumental art to one that was more intimate and domestic.[31] All were part of a more general development of personal behavior which, far from being a product of historical decline, was very much in the ascendant; and it too is mentioned, however fleetingly, in the *Protestant Ethic*. When Weber asks who might live in the "steel housing" of rationalism and capitalism in the future, his final answer is that the future state might be one of "'Chinese' (or 'mechanised') petrifaction, garnished by a . . . frantic self-importance."[32] Reference to "self-importance" here is not just vague rant but quite precise. What Weber means is that the complement to an impoverished rationalism ("petrifaction") is an ostentatious, "self-important" display of personal identity *outside* the workplace or other rationalized public spaces. Elsewhere he went so far as to describe his age as one of "subjectivist *Kultur*" or values, where the younger generation in particular had "an inevitable and strongly developed predisposition in favour of its own self-importance."[33] We must presume that Weber himself did not take himself so seriously, but when he was asked by a student, "Max Weber, what is your supreme and leading value?" he answered, "I have no supreme and leading value" and itemized a miscellany instead.[34]

So alongside impersonal uniformity in public and professional life, there was a marked assertion and proliferation of personal values. Weber's most sustained treatment of this development appears in his better-known, yet insufficiently appreciated, remarks from 1917–1919, when he describes the modern condition as one of "polytheism": "The old plurality of gods, devoid of magic and so in the form of impersonal powers, climb out of their graves, strive for power over our lives, and begin again their eternal struggle with one another."[35] At first sight this might suggest that modern religious and ethical life had somehow reverted to that of ancient Greece and Rome. But this is not Weber's meaning, as the characteristic reference to modern "impersonal powers" makes plain. The essence of his thinking is that once the control exercised by the socially agreed scheme of traditional Christian ethics has lapsed (this lapse is our one and only point of common ground with the ancient world), diversity of values and conflict between them proliferate. In the modern situation there is not only irreducible political conflict between nations, for example, French and Germans, or between different religious views; there is also conflict between the value priorities one allocates to different "life orders" (or spheres) since all of these are now driven by their own inner laws. Given the different values of art, religion, sexual pleasure, the economy, and politics, which does one prefer? Is beauty "better" than moral goodness? There can be no authoritative answer to such questions, only an individual one. Religion itself is just a single component of the modern "polytheism"—a stark contrast to the "ethic of brotherhood" of the salvation religions, which brought all of these differing areas of life under a single, controlling standard.[36]

Perception of the breakdown of traditional values was already widespread in the Germany of Weber's day, far more so than in any other European country. In a famous phrase Ernst Troeltsch referred to "the anarchy of values,"[37] and discussion of the subject was carried on with great energy throughout Weber's adult life. A seminal figure here was Friedrich Nietzsche, whose concern with this subject is announced very clearly in such books as *Beyond Good and Evil* (1886) and *The Genealogy of Morality* (1887).

Weber's references to "self-importance" are a jaundiced reference to Nietzsche's elitism of "higher beings" and still more to the "Nietzsche cult" that set in after c. 1890 with its emphasis on personal identity and what was in fact an assertion of social elitism.[38] But while Weber was surely a beneficiary of Nietzsche's destructive criticism of established values (though there were many other forces pointing to the same conclusion), he was no "Nietzschean" in any positive sense. He had an abhorrence of any elitism in regard to values or "the goods of *Kultur*"—universal access to such goods is the foundation of all his ideas about "bourgeois democracy"[39]—as of the personal exhibitionism that accompanied it. Though he received the collapse of unified religio-ethical codes of value as a fundamental fact, he was dismissive of what followed in its wake: a situation where the choice of fundamental values, a choice that was once that between God and the devil and which should still define "the meaning of one's being and doing," had become a banal "everyday" continuum, where meaningful choice was now evaded and replaced by a flight into visceral and anti-intellectual "experience" (*Erlebnis*).[40] However, unlike Nietzsche, Troeltsch, and indeed all other ethical thinkers of his day, Weber was the only significant thinker who took it for granted that the breakdown of traditional, universally prescribed personal ethics was radical and irreversible. The purpose of reflection on ethics and *Kultur* was not to restore or reform authoritative values (as with Troeltsch, Nietzsche, and Heinrich Rickert) but to understand the new situation and its implications.[41] Outside Germany, Emile Durkheim anticipated Weber at one important point when he insisted that the social fact of the division of labor was also a moral fact; but still his understanding of "the general formula of morality" was wholly conventional so that the social ethic of the "collective conscience" was simply an extension of the Kantian ethics of the individual and in no way a challenge to them.[42]

After 1905 the original ethical conception of the *Protestant Ethic* was unchanged. Weber's theoretical focus shifted away from conjoint promotion of capitalism and rationalism toward a clear-cut emphasis on rationalism in 1907–1908[43]—hence the increased prominence of bureaucracy in his thinking, such that bureaucracy rather than capitalism appears as the principal modern form of *Herrschaft* (rule) in *Economy and Society*. However, whereas he viewed Western capitalism as a distinctly modern phenomenon whose ethical significance required explanation, bureaucracy was age-old (albeit subject to a process of rationalizing purification over time); and since it was based on a principle of command, it carried no ethical significance. It is true that its latest, most purely rational character and its reliance on obedience to the impersonal agency of law meant that it now abutted modern capitalism very nearly and created a similar "ethical" environment de facto; yet there was little novelty in the idea that bureaucratic command was "not in the name of a personal authority, but in the name of an impersonal norm."[44] Accordingly, it never occurred to him to speak of, or write about, the ethics of bureaucracy as distinct from those of formal legality.

Furthermore, the theoretical shift toward bureaucracy did not mean that capitalism ceased to be important. Because of its specifically modern character and ethical significance, it remained "the most fateful power of our modern life."[45] The principal "late" presence of capitalism in Weber's work comes in his analysis of contemporary German politics in 1917–1918, where he supposed that a healthy polity should rest on three distinct foundations: rational bureaucracy; political parties and a parliament which would foster charismatic political leadership; and an independent capitalist economy and *Kultur*, which was largely rational but not purely so (unlike bureaucracy). Confronted by the threat of bureaucracy, capitalism was one of the few chances "to rescue *any* remnant in *any* sense of 'individualistic' freedom of movement," and so it was precious.[46] Hence, much of what was said about capitalism in the *Protestant Ethic* was recycled in *Suffrage and Democracy in Germany* (1917), where Weber praises the appeal to "the ethic of professional duty and honour" and the capitalist embodiment of the principle that "honesty is the best policy." And, in contrast to a ubiquitous, politically supported capitalism which was both unstable and unethical, "it is precisely the *rational-capitalist business ethic* of this second [modern, Western] type of 'capitalism' which stands the highest—on the whole far higher than the average economic ethic of any period that really existed in history."[47]

This positive view of the "ethical" qualities of capitalism casts fresh light on the *Protestant Ethic* and shows the error of reading too much tragedy into its famous conclusion. There was much about modern ethics that Weber did not *like*, not least because from his youth he had hated the narrowing of horizons implied by specialization: "I have never had any respect for the concept of a 'profession' [*Beruf*], since I believed that in fact I was broadly suited to a fairly large number of positions."[48] But while there is a lament in the *Protestant Ethic* and Weber undoubtedly yearned for "mankind's Faustian universality," he then dismisses his emotional outburst for what it is: a collapse into private "value judgements." Yet today's readers prefer tragedy.[49] Hence, a tenacious insistence that when Weber wrote about the "steel housing" (*stahlhartes Gehäuse*) of capitalism and rational specialization, his underlying idea was not that of a "housing" (an image which implies constraint rather than coercion as well as the supply of the means of life) but that of the "iron cage" bestowed upon him in translation by Talcott Parsons.[50] However, Weber knew exactly what he was writing, and he would have had no time for Gothic romanticism of this kind. By his "hard" realism and distaste for personal advertisement he *identified* with much of the impersonal *Kultur* he outlined, where questions of personal preference or "happiness" were irrelevant.[51] For him impersonal capitalism and rationalism were the outcomes of a historically irreversible process, and whatever limitations they might place on a maximal conception of human freedom, it was now simply not possible to function in a technical, specialized, rationalized, mass society on any other basis than that of impersonal constraint and regulation. Weber's views, like those he attributed to Puritans in the seventeenth century, were "*without illusion* and *pessimistically* tinged"; but they were not simply pessimistic.[52]

The one tangible supplement to the *Protestant Ethic* is the discussion of ethics in "Politics as a Vocation." However, we should not be misled by the canonical status of this lecture today. It may look like a valuable synoptic statement, being the one and only theoretical text where Weber put "politics" in the title; but such reticence can be read in more than one way.[53] The discussion of the need for a political "ethic of responsibility" is indeed new, but paradoxically in the case of a thinker whose thinking is so remorselessly continuous in its evolution, this novelty is questionable. There is an obvious contrast here with "Science as a Vocation," which appeared in the same lecture series and which has clear roots going back to the "Objectivity" essay in 1904. Why then had he never discussed political ethics or even "politics" before?

In fact, the idea for "Politics as a Vocation" was not Weber's. The lecture was given in response to an outside request (from the Freistudentischer Bund),[54] and its argument was by no means well worked out. The root of the lecture lies not in the "ethic of respon-sibility" but its alternative, the religious "ethic of conviction"; and this is its point of contact with his established ideas. For Weber any authentic ethic, for example, the Protestant and Catholic ethics, was an "ethic of 'conviction'"[55]; so the ethical question that underlies the lecture (which is about much else besides) is whether there could be an authentic political ethic at all. His lifelong belief was that there could not because of the stark contrast between politics as a realm of debased, contingent, and local ethics where physical force was the final court of appeal and any universal ethical claims, whether they be those of the ethical and salvation religions or the impersonal and inter-national ethic of Western capitalism.[56] Furthermore, the time for any extraordinary incursion of religious ethics into politics, such as the seventeenth-century introduction of ethical natural law and human rights by Puritan agency, was long since past.[57] Weber's principal concern in 1917–1919—as is well known—was not to promote ethical politi-cians but charismatic ones, capable of exercising decisive leadership in a sphere where rule-bound, ethical, and legal prescriptions were a positive hindrance. Possession of personal charisma was "the highest form" of the political vocation.[58] Given such prem-ises he takes an extremely skeptical view of "conviction" politicians. Action on the basis of ethical conviction is seen as an illegitimate importation of non-political ideas, and nine out of ten of such persons are "windbags."[59] But then, giving way to his own moralism and the possible needs of the new Weimar Republic,[60] he accepts that there may be room for the tenth case: he imagines the politician who tempers inflexible and unworkable "conviction" by a "responsible" awareness of the worldly consequences of his actions. But logically such a person remains a contradiction in terms, and he is really "a prophet," whose gifts are purely personal and who can strike no permanent root. In other words, he is a "genuine," charismatic "leader."[61]

Given the evanescent nature of any ethical component in this argument, we can hardly be surprised to find Weber reverting subsequently to his normal or default position: that politics was a diabolical arena, that alliance with the devil in power politics was entirely permissible, and that the only sin in politics was not a matter of ethics but "stupidity."[62] Not only is "Politics as a Vocation" an extremely fragile construction, but it offers only a fragment of Weber's ethical thought, just as the arena of political conflict is only a small and unusual subset of social behavior as a whole. It says nothing about the rational and impersonal context which is the principal basis of modern ethics in the "everyday" public, social, and non-political sphere: that is, the realms of capitalism, bureaucracy, law, and the professions, in comparison to which the sphere of "politics," strictly defined, is actually very limited: that is, the realm of irrational power struggle and international relations above all.[63] The family resemblance between Weber's understanding of "politics" as adversarial and unethical and Carl Schmitt's famous statement of "The Concept of the Political" is frequently noted, but this overlooks the stark contrast between the space and prominence the two men allot to "politics." Where Schmitt wanted to establish "the *total* state" that would render all of society political, Weber wished to squeeze "state" and "politics" into a corner, so far as possible under the overall aegis of "society"—as Schmitt recognized.[64] Weber's true originality lay in the admission that there was an ethical divide between politics and the rest of the public sphere, and in this he anticipated the perceptions of the affluent, stable, and disillusioned democracies that emerged in the West after 1945.

WHAT WEBER MIGHT SAY TO US TODAY

Weber's rationally homogenized yet ethically fragmented modernity is generically the same as ours. That there has been a collapse of traditional, universal, and religiously founded ethics has long been obvious; and we do not need him to remind us. What is radically new about his thought is his identification of two distinct ethical tiers. On the one hand, there is the "impersonal," sober, self-controlled code of conduct which dominates so much of public life in the economy, law, bureaucracy, and the professions generally. Here there is little moral sense or discourse, and the primary "values" are the observance of what is procedurally correct, formally legal, and logically and technically rational. On the other hand, there is the "subjectivist *Kultur*" of the private individual which, in the sharpest contrast, is about the assertion of individual values in all their variety. But though it is a contrast, it can only exist as a complement or balancing antithesis to the first. It too can only be understood as a socially determined phenomenon, operating in relation and reaction to the constraints imposed by the public sphere. But if Weber's social construction of ethics has something substantial to say, it raises a question whether much of today's moral philosophy is not rendered otiose by its relentlessly traditional and individual premises. Here society exists only as an offstage presence, a source of external "consequences" which serve as a possible measure of the rightness of the actions of the sovereign individual (though this is not to deny its testimony to the entrenchment of asocial individualism in Anglophone culture).[65] Even those who take the modern economy as their starting point make a category error when they seek to set "*moral* limits" to markets.[66] In a word, the premises of much of today's ethical theory have remained unaltered since the days of Troeltsch and the neo-Kantians (or even Aristotle and Aquinas).[67] Can this be right?

The contemporary relevance of what Weber says about the public sphere will be clear. When we talk of "professional conduct" or "behaving in a professional manner," it is an unconscious imitation of Weber's focus on the *Beruf*; and our meaning is essentially the same as his: an implicit appeal to an incontrovertible norm of great power, yet one that is colorless and limited to a specific context. Less colorless is the apotheosis of what is "cool" in popular culture, another unconscious conjunction with Weber. Not to be "cool" is "to lose it," to lose the emotional "self-control" in public spaces that Weber prized so highly; and it is notable that it should be a code of great importance in youth culture. This thereby serves as an "ethical" training for a more middle-aged public sphere, with which at first sight it has nothing to do. The most obvious test of the border between private and public ethics lies for us, as for Weber, in the sharp boundary drawn between kinship and family groups and the "impersonal" sphere. This boundary remains far less developed in many societies outside the West,[68] and its weakness renders the whole fabric of public life precarious and corrupt in our eyes. Still the boundary is also transgressed in the West. Organized crime and "gangs" ultimately founded on personal connection are an extreme example[69]; the suggestion by corporate law firms that female employees might like to display "loyalty" by marrying male partners within the firm is a smaller one yet equally flagrant. The boundary is not absolute: consider the family business. But though this may have inscrutable private consequences (how does business life affect family life?), in public it is only an extension of individual agency, whose position in an impersonal marketplace is conventional.

The operation of "formal legality," where the only incontestable action is that which follows the letter of the law, is widely acknowledged, not merely in "professional life" and tax avoidance but also, for example, in sport. What is the definition of foul play? Does sports equipment conform to the weight limit or chemical compound prescribed? Is the blood composition of an athlete within prescribed limits? The minute regulation of such questions, based jointly on law and impersonal technology, determines the decision; and ideas about right and wrong are ever more closely tied to the letter of the law. Meanwhile the infinity of laws and rules constantly changes in all spheres, which further enhances the priority of technically informed behavior and the relegation of any "moral" sense. On the other hand, the ethical status of law is contested, and one salient objection to Weber's position would be that there is an ethical component to human rights law.[70] Now, Weber's regard for "the rights of man" was extremely high, so high that in practice his formalism is hardly different from others' ethical commitment[71]; but still the force of a Weberian and formalist analysis of twentieth-century human rights is considerable. It only applies to "the Occident" where the rule of law is established, but still most of the articles of the European Convention on Human Rights (1948) can be analyzed in Weberian terms: that is, as the establishment either of formal rights—for example, "formal freedom" rather than physical servitude,[72] which does not exclude a myriad of social, economic, and cultural oppressions—or of private rights—such as freedom of conscience—or procedural rights—like the right to a fair trial.

As regards "capitalism," it may be said that with the concept of the *Beruf* Weber had identified the distinctive ethics of the professional and corporation man whose world-view was primarily determined by the requirements of the professional career long before this idea was taken up by sociology and journalism after 1945.[73] It also marked out a more socially comprehensive phenomenon: the idea that possession of a job was an essential source of "ethical" legitimacy or self-esteem. Weber was one of the first to understand from personal experience that absence of a job specification— "unemployment" (a new term from the 1880s) or a gap on the CV—could be internalized as an ethical failing in modern Western society.[74] More broadly still, while Weber was no apologist for the "steel housing" of capitalism, the explanation he offers of why it is "ethically" acceptable—it is founded on formal, technical, and rational strengths which are "unarguable," separate from politics, yet make no moral claim—is of the utmost relevance to the hold capitalism exercises both on western European societies which long nurtured a deeply critical attitude toward it as well as on the more sympathetic cultural terrain of Britain and America.

On the debit side Weber failed to theorize the relationship between diabolical and ephemeral politics and a quite differently formed public sphere. In particular, he was so keen to keep apart state bureaucracy and industry in his own day that he refused to create a sociology of the "two types" of capitalism that he himself identified: an unethical and unregulated "political," "robber," and "adventure" capitalism and an industrial capitalism which was largely rational and possessed of a specifically "economic ethic."[75] Yet today the interface between capitalism and its political supports is a central issue, though it has been set aside a priori by neoliberalism.[76] An ever more bureaucratized economy has rendered even the illusion of the "free" market (which had, of course, to be based on law) illusory, and its regulation cannot be regarded simply as formally rational and politically neutral. So neo-Weberian analysis of the extent to which capitalism is rational, "ethical," and apolitical and of the extent to which it has departed from a Weberian model rooted in an idealized conception of laissez-faire Britain c. 1846— "the affinity of innerworldly asceticism with the minimization of state intervention ('Manchesterism')"—is now a pressing need.[77]

Another kind of exception to a conception of public behavior as rational and ethical lies in organized sport and mass entertainment, where it is legitimate and expected that audiences give vent to emotion in a social context. Weber, like most continental intellectuals of his generation, had no interest in sport; and he identified the sports of early seventeenth-century England as pre-rational symptoms of "the *spontaneous enjoyment of existence*" doomed to be obliterated by the Puritans. The one place he witnessed modern, mass spectator sport was in America where, in accordance with this conception, he took it to be an expression of the youthfulness (i.e., primitiveness) of American *Kultur* as it belatedly followed the path of "Europeanization": the passions it evoked were those of the classical Greek *agon* or "amphitheater." Of course, such views are quite unsustainable today, especially when we consider that the other pioneer of organized sport was England—very much one of "the old capitalist countries" of Europe and the epicenter of Puritan "reserve" and "self-mastery."[78] Nonetheless, neo-Weberian analysis of mass spectator sport is eminently feasible. It would rest on the facts, first, that sport is a site of entertainment and consumption, distinct from the world of employment (the *Beruf*), which dominates the *Protestant Ethic*; but, even so, any such public entertainment (as distinct from the domestic, television audience) is organized, rationalized, and commercialized. The release (*Abreaktion*) of emotion by the audience must be confined within a regulated time period and physical location, it must conform to law (violence is strictly proscribed), and it must be paid for.[79] Something similar could be said of music—by far the most developed entertainment industry known to Weber. Here again he had no interest in its passive consumption, but still his interest in demonstrating the rational components at work in the mass performance of classical music is a pointer, at a time when live performance was also a principal form of its consumption.[80]

In general, we live in a Weberian world, where the incursion of unregulated private emotion into the public sphere is profoundly unsettling. The outstanding current example is the radical breach in the boundaries between private and public communication created by social media. Through technology, the public and social forms of durable record and impersonal interchange have become attached to an enormous range of utterance, of which the large majority is conceived and expressed as private conversation with its attendant emotion, exposed sensitivity, and want of restraint. The format of private–public citizens' gossip then permeates, or is taken into, the mainstream of public discourse, whether by existing media, politicians, or cybercriminals; and combustion, outrage, and abuse are the result—hence the widely noted degradation of public debate in twenty-first-century America above all, the original home of social media. (This is not to overlook the political forces in play here, where there is no novelty.)[81] It is an unusual instance of mass technology with an "anti-Weberian" tendency—it releases and does not "standardize" personality—and the level of threat is accordingly high. Unless we consent to the degradation of an impersonally "ethical" public sphere, then Weberian analysis would suggest that some regulation must take place and a sufficient boundary between the public and private spheres be restored. However, as Weber observed, we cannot make predictions here; we can only estimate "chances" and make probabilistic estimates of "objective possibility."[82]

The other face of Weberian ethics is that of the proliferation of subjective values in areas that were once seen as fundamental, and hence of public concern and regulation, but which are now allowed to be private and plural. (Note, however, their status as values, as well as the defense or establishment of their privacy, still entails a large volume of public discussion today.) This relates above all to questions of religion, marriage, sexuality, and gender or "identity politics," questions which, though broached in Weber's lifetime and familiar to him through a wide range of personal acquaintance ranging from Else Jaffé to Georg Lukács, only became a central feature of western European and American society from the 1960s on. In some areas, such as race and gender, Weber was much more interested in public uniformity and legal equality than private diversity, though even here some recognition of diversity is present.[83] The one point at which his agenda has clearly dated is the prominence he gives to aesthetic values as an area where prescriptive norms were breaking down.[84] This was an area of obvious interest given art's importance to the culture of the educated bourgeoisie and because of the incursion of aesthetic modernism which was bringing about the final destruction of any belief in classical artistic norms, but neither consideration applies today.

Weber's principal achievement was to situate this development as a whole, but he also produced an exceptionally powerful analysis of religion in particular. He never tried to offer "a definition of what religion 'is,'"[85] being all too aware of its historical transformations and variations. His core unit was not religion but values, just as his one and only "transcendental presupposition" was that "we *are persons of Kultur*": humans are holders of values who render selected parts of empirical reality meaningful by attaching value to them, and this is *Kultur*.[86] He did not claim (as is sometimes supposed) that religion would be eliminated by modernizing rationalization, and he was not a theorist of "secularization" in this sense. What he claimed was that due to the modern reconfiguration of values, religion had lost its claim to provide a single, universal code of ethics, accepted by all members of society. This is surely correct and is essential to understanding the diminished social and institutional position occupied by religion today, regardless of the retained position occupied by many churches "in public" for portions of the public,[87] or the personal significance of religious thinking to individuals across a wide plurality of viewpoints. Churches and individuals adopting a "religious" perspective (a perspective outwardly continuous with past forms yet subject to the reconfiguration of values) are simply one set of contributors to the debate about personal values alongside a larger number who ignore the religious label. In this debate all are equal in principle and all except terrorists must accept that there is a plurality of views outside their own.

One possible objection to Weber's presentation of "subjectivist *Kultur*" is that he was too much of a strenuous moralist to be wholly modern. The fact that religious codes of value had broken down or that values themselves were historically mutable and could be a matter of personal choice did not mean (in his eyes) that they had ceased to serve the elementary function they had always served: of working out "the meaning of [one's] doing and being." Accusations of "relativism" were utterly misplaced for someone who, though a moral pluralist, was also a passionate moral absolutist.[88] As we saw, he could be dismissive of the banality and hedonism of the lifestyle radicals of his own days, and experiments in living regarding sexuality were unlikely to appeal to someone whose modernism here consisted in upholding (and practicing) birth control, as a means of protecting women's health and making a breach in "patriarchalism."[89] (As noted, public equality rather than private diversity was his principal concern here.) But though our culture (and perhaps any mass culture) is more relaxed than Weber might have liked, it would be a mistake to underestimate either his tolerance of diversity or the seriousness of today's views on religion, sexuality, and gender. The ethically strenuous wrestlings of existentialism that Weber foreshadowed[90] have long since passed away, and we acknowledge our moral relativism almost unthinkingly; but this does not mean that values have gone away—postmodernism has proven quite as ephemeral as moral strenuousness—and if Weber were alive today, it must be supposed that in principle he would have been a staunch supporter of "identity politics."

There was, however, a more significant difficulty which Weber understood very well: that the ethical bequest of the Protestant past was split. He insisted with all possible force that the modern capitalist "ethic"

> is so completely stripped of any eudaemonist, let alone hedonist thoughts, it is conceived so *purely* as an end *in itself*, that in relation to the "happiness" or "utility"

of the single *individual* (at any rate), it appears as something wholly transcendental and simply irrational.[91]

But there were obvious problems with such an assertion. Concentration on the ethic of "the single *individual*" obscured the fact that the aggregate reward of modern capitalism was an unsurpassed provision of industrial goods for "the *mass*" of ordinary people.[92] Technically rational capitalism was comparable to bureaucracy in its superior provision of services, and here is a fundamental respect in which capitalism is a housing, not a cage or prison. Because it was a distraction from his ethical argument, Weber did not mention this in the *Protestant Ethic*, preferring instead to make the alternative point that systemic pursuit of profit was not the same as "satisfaction of [people's] material needs"—but he was not so mean-spirited as to deny the value of mass material comforts. Elsewhere he was happy to second a mixed "democratic" ideal: seeking "to make possible the increasing participation of [the working masses] in the material *and* intellectual goods of our *Kultur*," always provided it was participation and did not derive from paternalist welfare provision.[93]

Materialism posed an obvious problem at the individual level. The central feature of the capitalist "ethic" may have been impersonal, ascetic-rational discipline; but its "highest good" was "the *acquisition of money* and ever more money." However much Weber insisted that "innerworldly Protestant asceticism...brings its whole weight to bear against the unconstrained *enjoyment* of possessions," that "it is a straitjacket on *consumption*, and especially luxury consumption," its capitalist offspring was continually multiplying possessions, consumption, and exposure to hedonism. Conscious recognition of a mass "affluent society" may have been unknown in Weber's Germany, but he knew full well that "asceticism" as the creator of unprecedented material wealth was a force "which always wills the good and always produces evil" in the form of "property and its temptations." So once the ascetic ethic ceased be the product of personal assertion and came to rest on a "mechanical foundation," it was subject to a "dissolution into pure utilitarianism," "the striving for worldly goods, conceived as an *end in itself*" which was practically a denial of the original.[94] This commonsense recognition of the prevalence of modern materialism by no means subverts Weber's principal argument (though it tells us once more that a "Kantian" Weber is nonsense). Neither the disciplined and impersonal ethic of professional life nor the subjective assertion of private values is canceled thereby. On the contrary, hedonism or materialism is just one more private value or "end in itself," and Weber deserves credit for recognizing a central modern reality that he found personally distasteful. But his message is more mixed than might appear at first sight, and the *Protestant Ethic* is about more than just the Protestant and capitalist ethics.

The conclusion is simple: Weber worked out a brilliantly original analysis of modern ethics which has been shamefully ignored. His world is not perfectly congruent with ours, but it is close to it; and he supplies an extremely powerful model with which to analyze this world. Accordingly, his work opens a wide field for reflection and inquiry.

NOTES

1. *The Protestant Ethic and the Spirit of Capitalism* (hereafter *PESC*), trans. Talcott Parsons (New York: Scribner's, 1930), 180; "Die protestantische Ethik und der 'Geist' des Kapitalismus," in *Asketischer Protestantismus und Kapitalismus. Schriften und Reden 1904–1911, Max Weber- Gesamtausgabe* (hereafter *MWG*) I/9, ed. W. Schluchter with U. Bube (Tübingen, Germany: Mohr [Siebeck], 2014), 420; this is the text originally published in 1904–1905 in the *Archiv für Sozialwissenschaft und Sozialpolitik*. The correlation between published and linguistically accurate English translations of Weber's work is, with honorable exceptions, often only moderate. Thus, translations are my own as I have prioritized linguistic accuracy in translation.

2. *PESC*, 51–52, 53–54, 165–166, 180; *Die Protestantische Ethik und der Geist des Kapitalismus/ Die protestantischen Sekten und der Geist des Kapitalismus. Schriften 1904–1920, MWG* I/18, ed. W. Schluchter with U. Bube (Tübingen, Germany: Mohr [Siebeck], 2016), 155–157, 159–161, 444–449, 485–486 (the revised 1920 text).

3. *PESC*, 27, 186–187n1; *MWG* I/18, 117, 123–125n1.

4. Ernst Troeltsch, "Max Weber," *Frankfurter Zeitung*, June 20, 1920, in *MWG*, ed. J. Winckelmann and R. König (Opladen, Germany: Westdeutscher Verlag, 1985), 46.

5. Dieter Henrich, *Die Einheit der Wissenschaftslehre Max Webers* (Tübingen, Germany: Mohr [Siebeck], 1952), 117. See also Wolfgang Schluchter, *Die Entwicklung des okzidentalen Rationalismus* (Tübingen, Germany: Mohr [Siebeck], 1979), VIII–IX; Jürgen Habermas, *The Theory of Communicative Action*, trans. T. McCarthy (Boston: Beacon Press, 1984), 1:154–156.

6. Wolfgang Schluchter, *Grundlegungen der Soziologie* (Tübingen, Germany: Mohr Siebeck, 2006), pt. 1, c.3, cf. idem, *Religion und Lebensführung* (Frankfurt am Main: Suhrkamp, 1988), 1:80–88.

7. Leo Strauss, *Natural Right and History* (Chicago: University of Chicago Press, 1953), 42.

8. Max Weber, "The Meaning of 'Value-Freedom' in the Sociological and Economic Sciences" (hereafter "Value-Freedom"), in *Collected Methodological Writings* (hereafter *CMW*), trans. H. H. Bruun and ed. H. H. Bruun and S. Whimster (1917; New York: Routledge, 2012), 315; *Verstehende Soziologie und Werturteilsfreiheit. Schriften und Reden 1908–1917, MWG* I/12, ed. J. Weiß with S. Frommer (Tübingen, Germany: Mohr [Siebeck], 2018), 470.

9. See my "Beyond Methodology: Max Weber's Conception of *Wissenschaft*," *Sociologia Internationalis* 52 (2014): 157–218; also Wolfgang Schluchter, *Wertfreiheit und Verantwortungsethik* (Tübingen, Germany: Mohr [Siebeck], 1971); Hans Henrik Bruun, *Science, Values and Politics* (Copenhagen, Denmark: Munksgaard, 1972); Weber, *Wissenschaft als Beruf 1917/1919—Politik als Beruf 1919, MWG* I/17, ed. W. Schluchter and W. J. Mommsen with B. Morgenbrod (Tübingen, Germany: Mohr [Siebeck], 1992), which pairs "Politics" and "Science as a Vocation"; Martin Endreß, "Ethik (Gesinnungs- und Verantwortungsethik)," in *Max Weber Handbuch*, ed. Hans-Peter Müller and Steffen Sigmund (Stuttgart, Germany: Metzler, 2014), 52–54. For a rare discussion of the "Protestant Ethic" in ethical terms, see Klaus Lichtblau, "The Protestant Ethic versus the 'New Ethic,'" in *Weber's Protestant Ethic*, ed. Hartmut Lehmann and Guenther Roth (Cambridge: Cambridge University Press, 1993), 179–193; cf. Lichtblau, "Die Kulturwerte des asketischen Protestantismus und die 'Neue Ethik,'" in *Kulturkrise und Soziologie um die Jahrhundertwende* (Frankfurt am Main, Germany: Suhrkamp, 1996), 315–345. However, the Protestant ethic remains "Christian" and "conventional," standing in contradiction to any concessions Weber made to ethical

modernism elsewhere (in the erotic sphere). So "tragedy" is the keynote of a broken-backed ethical scheme (185, 191–192).

10. Weber, "Politics as a Vocation," in *Political Writings* (hereafter *PolW*), ed. P. Lassman and R. Speirs (1919; Cambridge: Cambridge University Press, 1994), 362, 365, 366; *MWG* I/17, 241, 247, 249.

11. Weber, "Zwischenbetrachtung," in *The Essential Weber: A Reader* (hereafter *Essential*), ed. S. Whimster (1915/1920; London: Routledge, 2004), 221, 238 (under the title "Intermediate Reflection on the Economic Ethics of the World Religions"); *Die Wirtschaftsethik der Weltreligionen. Konfuzianismus und Taoismus. Schriften 1915–1920*, *MWG* I/19, ed. H. Schmidt-Glintzer with P. Kolonko (Tübingen, Germany: Mohr [Siebeck], 1989), 486, 512 resp.

12. Weber, "Zwischenbetrachtung," *Essential*, 223; *MWG* I/19, 490; *PESC*, 180; *MWG* I/18, 484–485.

13. Weber, "Review of Friedrich Naumann, *Was heißt Christlich-Sozial?*," in *Landarbeiterfrage, Nationalstaat und Volkswirtschaftspolitik. Schriften und Reden 1892–1899*, *MWG* I/4, ed. W. J. Mommsen with R. Aldenhoff (1894; Tübingen, Germany: Mohr [Siebeck], 1993), 356–357. Compare the sociology of *Herrschaft* in *Economy and Society* (hereafter *E&S*), ed. G. Roth and C. Wittich (c.1911–1914; Berkeley: University of California Press, 1978), 1186; *Wirtschaft und Gesellschaft. Nachlaß. Herrschaft*, *MWG* I/22-4, ed. E. Hanke with Th. Kroll (Tübingen, Germany: Mohr [Siebeck], 2005), 635.

14. Weber, "Die deutsche Landarbeiter" (1894), in *MWG* I/4, 328; cf. 356–357.

15. Leviticus 19:18, Matthew 22:39, etc.

16. A frequent usage not indexed in *MWG* I/9 and *MWG* I/18. It is supplemented by "natural" (in inverted commas), but almost never by 'natural' since Weber has no belief in an original natural state, only the vacant state of absence of *Kultur*.

17. Weber, "Sociology of Religion" (c.1913), in *E&S*, 548; *Wirtschaft und Gesellschaft. Nachlaß. Religiöse Gemeinschaften*, *MWG* I/22-2, ed. H. G. Kippenberg with P. Schilm (Tübingen, Germany: Mohr [Siebeck], 2001), 328.

18. References to *PESC*, 53, 108–109, 181, 221n12; *MWG* I/18, 159, 275n98, 291–293, 487. *Parliament and Government in a Restructured Germany* (1917–1918), in *PolW*, 158; *Zur Politik im Weltkrieg. Schriften und Reden 1914–1918*, *MWG* I/15, ed. W. J. Mommsen with G. Hübinger (Tübingen, Germany: Mohr [Siebeck], 1984), 464.

19. Weber, "'Churches' and 'Sects' in North America" (1906), *MWG* I/9, 455, 454n1; "The Protestant Sects and the Spirit of Capitalism," in *From Max Weber: Essays in Sociology* (hereafter *FMW*), ed. H. H. Gerth and C. W. Mills (1907/1919–1920; Oxford: Oxford University Press, 1946), 320–322; *PESC*, 127; *MWG* I/18, 344.

20. *PESC*, 176–177; *MWG* I/18, 479–481; *E&S*, 1186; *MWG* I/22-4, 635.

21. *MWG* I/9, Index q.v.

22. *PESC*, 54–55; *MWG* I/18, 161–162.

23. *PESC*, 62, 107; *MWG* I/18, 180, 287.

24. See my *Max Weber and the Protestant Ethic: Twin Histories* (Oxford: Oxford University Press, 2014) (hereafter Ghosh, *Twin Histories*), esp. 133–142.

25. *PESC*, 48, 117; *MWG* I/18, 151, 322.

26. References in *PESC*, 50, 151, 165, 169; *MWG* I/18, 153, 407, 443, 458–459.

27. Exodus 20:3–17; Deuteronomy 4:13, 5:7–21; *PESC*, 258n189; *MWG* I/18, 407n275.

28. All are frequent usages, but only "*Kontrolle*" and "*Selbstkontrolle*" are indexed in *MWG* I/9.

29. *PESC*, 276n79; *MWG* I/18, 462n358.

30. Weber, "Science as a Vocation" (1917/1919), *CMW*, 352; *MWG* I/17, 110.

31. Weber, "Sociology of Religion" (c.1913), *E&S*, 601; *MWG* I/22, 402; "Suffrage and Democracy in Germany" (1917), *PolW*, 108–109; *MWG* I/15, 375–376; "Sociology of Music" (1912) or *Zur Musiksoziologie, Nachlaß*, *MWG* I/14, ed. C. Braun and L. Finscher (Tübingen, Germany: Mohr [Siebeck], 2004), 275–280.

32. *PESC*, 182; *MWG* I/9, 422; *MWG* I/18, 488.

33. Respectively, Weber, "Der Begriff der Produktivität. Diskussionsbeiträge auf der Generalversammlung des Vereins für Sozialpolitik am 28. September 1909 in Wien]," in *MWG* I/12, 212; "Value-Freedom," *CMW*, 307; *MWG* I/12, 453.

34. Ghosh, *Twin Histories*, 279.

35. Weber, "Science as a Vocation," *MWG* I/17, 101; cf. "Value-Freedom," *CMW*, 348 cf. 314; *MWG* I/12, 469–470.

36. This clash is mapped out in Weber's "Zwischenbetrachtung," *Essential*, 215–244; *MWG* I/19, 479–522. However, this famous essay is limited by the fact that it takes the ethic of the salvation religions as its starting point and not that of the modern West. This is regrettable, but it is also a testimony to Weber's belief that views stated in the "Protestant Ethic" need not be repeated.

37. Ghosh, *Twin Histories*, 105.

38. Cf. Ferdinand Tönnies, *Der Nietzsche-Kultus* (Leipzig, Germany: Reisland, 1897).

39. This ideal is repeatedly stated in 1892–1894 when real social reform appeared to be a possibility and only rarely thereafter, but it had not gone away: see Marianne Weber, diary entry December 4, 1911, in *Max Weber: A Biography*, trans. H. Zohn (New Brunswick, NJ: Transaction, 1988), 462; *Max Weber. Ein Lebensbild* (Tübingen, Germany: Mohr [Siebeck], 1926), 470.

40. Weber, "Value-Freedom," *CMW*, 314–315, 348; *MWG* I/12, 469–470; "Science as a Vocation," *MWG* I/17, 101, respectively. On Weber and personal exhibitionism, Weber and "meaning," Ghosh, *Twin Histories*, 4–5, 277–293.

41. See my "Beyond Methodology," § I; "Max Weber and the *Literati*," Ghosh, *Max Weber in Context* (Wiesbaden, Germany: Harrassowitz, 2016), chap. 5.

42. Emil Durkheim, *De la division du travail social* (1893; Paris: PUF, 1930), 9; *The Division of Labour in Society* (Basingstoke, UK: Macmillan, 1984), 10.

43. Ghosh, *Twin Histories*, 162–174.

44. Weber, "Introduction" (1915/1919), *Economic Ethics of the World Religions*, in *FMW*, 294–295; *MWG* I/19, 119.

45. Weber, "Vorbemerkung" ("Prefatory Remarks to the Collected Essays in the Sociology of Religion"), *PESC*, 17; *Essential*, 103; *MWG* I/18, 105.

46. Weber, "Parliament and Government," *PolW*, 159; *MWG* I/15, 465–466; cf. Ghosh, *Twin Histories*, 331–332.

47. Weber, "Parliament and Government," *PolW*, 90; *MWG* I/15, 356–357; cf. Ghosh, *Twin Histories*, 329–335.

48. Weber's letter to Marianne Schnitger, Spring 1893: Marianne Weber, *Biography*, 185; *Lebensbild*, 197; *Briefe 1887–1894*, *MWG* II/2, ed. R. Aldenhoff-Hübinger with Th. Gerhards and S. Oßwald-Bargende (Tübingen, Germany: Mohr [Siebeck], 2017), 360.

49. *PESC*, 180, 182; *MWG* I/18, 485, 488; for Weber as tragic thinker, see Gerhard Wagner, *Geltung und normativer Zwang* (Freiburg and Munich: Karl Alber, 1987), 163, 168; Hinnerk Bruhns, "Science et politique au quotidien chez Max Weber," *Max Webers historische Sozialökonomie* (Wiesbaden, Germany: Harrassowitz, 2014), 210; Lichtblau, *Kulturkrise und Soziologie*.

50. *PESC*, 181; *MWG* I/18, 487; cf. Lawrence A. Scaff on "Parsons' fortunate imaginative mistake": *Weber and the Weberians* (New York: Palgrave Macmillan, 2014), 151. What Weber really feared was the invasion of industry by state bureaucracy, thereby choking off capitalist dynamism: "the housing of that future serfdom in which perhaps men will one day be compelled to an impotent submission," in "Parliament and Government," *PolW*, 158; *MWG* I/15, 464.

51. Weber, "Erhebungen über Auslese und Anpassung…der Arbeiterschaft der geschlossenen Großindustrie," *Zur Psychophysik der industriellen Arbeit. Schriften und Reden 1908–1912, MWG* I/11, ed. W. Schluchter with S. Frommer (1908; Tübingen, Germany: Mohr [Siebeck], 1995), 81; "Science as a Vocation," in *Essential*, 277; *MWG* I/17, 92; cf. Ghosh, *Twin Histories*, 4.

52. *PESC*, 105; *MWG* I/18, 281.

53. Weber, "The National State and Economic Policy/Politics" (1895) is explicitly not "explanatory and analytical *Wissenschaft*": *PolW*, 15; *MWG* I/4, 559.

54. Hence its opening, "The lecture which I have to give at your request…": *PolW*, 309; *MWG* I/17, 157. Cf. Wolfgang J. Mommsen, "Editorischer Bericht," *MWG* I/17, 120, 129.

55. *PESC*, 116; the Protestant ethic is frequently referred to as a *Gesinnung* or ethical conviction: *MWG* I/9, 915.

56. Ghosh, *Twin Histories*, 218–221.

57. See Weber to Adolf Harnack, February 5, 1906, in *Briefe 1906–1908, MWG* II/5, ed. M. R. Lepsius and W. J. Mommsen with B. Rudhard and M. Schön (Tübingen, Germany: Mohr [Siebeck], 1990), 32–33.

58. Weber, "Politics as a Vocation," *PolW*, 312; *MWG* I/17, 161.

59. Weber, "Politics as a Vocation," *PolW*, 367; *MWG* I/17, 250.

60. Compare *Suffrage and Democracy in Germany*: "Of course, politics is no ethical concern. But all the same there is a certain minimum sense of shame and obligation of decency which if transgressed cannot go unpunished, even in politics": *PolW*, 83; *MWG* I/15, 350.

61. Weber, "Politics as a Vocation," *PolW*, 365, 367; *MWG* I/17, 246, 250.

62. Weber, "*Sachliche*…Bemerkungen am 19.1.[1920]," *Zur Neuordnung Deutschlands. Schriften und Reden 1918–1920, MWG* I/16, ed. W. J. Mommsen with W. Schwentker (Tübingen, Germany: Mohr [Siebeck], 1988), 273.

63. Weber, "Politics as a Vocation," *PolW*, 311; *MWG* I/17, 159.

64. Carl Schmitt, *Der Begriff des Politischen* (Berlin: Duncker, 2009), 23; cf. 20n2 on Weber.

65. Compare Derek Parfit, *Reasons and Persons* (Oxford: Oxford University Press, 1984), and *On What Matters*, 3 vols. (Oxford: Oxford University Press, 2011–2017).

66. Cf. Michael Sandel, *What Money Can't Buy: The Moral Limits of Markets* (New York: Farrar, 2012).

67. Consider the loyalties of Alasdair Macintyre, author of *After Virtue* (London: Duckworth, 1981).

68. Compare Weber, "The City," *E&S*, 1222–1231; *Wirtschaft und Gesellschaft. Nachlaß. Die Stadt, MWG* I/22-5, ed. W. Nippel (Tübingen, Germany: Mohr [Siebeck], 1999), 107–112; Fei Xiaotong, *From the Soil. The Foundations of Chinese Society* (1948; Berkeley: University of California Press, 1992).

69. The compendious literature on the Mafia is the best-known case.

70. See Winfried Brugger, *Menschenrechtsethos und Verantwortungspolitik: Max Webers Beitrag zur Analyse und Begründung der Menschenrechte* (Freiburg, Germany: Karl Alber, 1980); Jürgen Habermas, *Faktizität und Geltung: Beiträge zur Diskurstheorie des Rechts und des demokratischen Rechtsstaates* (Frankfurt am Main, Germany: Suhrkamp, 1992); Samuel

Moyn, *The Last Utopia. Human Rights in History* (Cambridge, MA: Harvard University Press, 2010).

71. *PESC*, 245n118; *MWG* I/18, 358–359n204.

72. Compare *PESC*, 21–24; *MWG* I/18, 110–114 on "(formally) *free labour.*"

73. For example, see William Whyte, *The Organization Man* (New York: Simon & Schuster, 1956).

74. Cf. Marianne to Helene Weber, December 10, 1902, *Biography*, 261; *Lebensbild*, 274.

75. Weber, "Suffrage and Democracy," *PolW*, 89–90; *MWG* I/15, 356–357; *E&S*, 164–166; *Wirtschaft und Gesellschaft. Soziologie*, *MWG* I/23, ed. K. Borchardt, E. Hanke, and W. Schluchter (Tübingen, Germany: Mohr [Siebeck], 2013), 379–382; *PESC*, 17–22; *MWG* I/18, 105–111. Cf. Ghosh, *Twin Histories*, 337–338.

76. More reflective thinkers of this persuasion accept that long-established, *laissez-faire* political institutions provide the foundation for "free" economic activity, but still this tells us nothing about the workings of political economy today: Daron Acemoglu and James Robinson, *Why Nations Fail* (New York: Crown, 2012).

77. Weber, "Sociology of Religion," *E&S*, 593; *MWG* I/22-2, 390; cf. "Antikritisches" (1910), *MWG* I/9, 589n14, and "Antikritisches Schlußwort" (1910), *MWG* I/9, 672n2, on Cobden and the Anti-Corn Law League; *The Protestant Ethic Debate: Max Weber's Replies to His Critics, 1907–1910*, ed. D. J. Chalcraft and A. Harrington (Liverpool, UK: Liverpool University Press, 2001), 78n14, 121n2.

78. For references see *PESC*, 119, 166–167, 235n81, 268n47; *MWG* I/18, 325–327n167, 438n326, 449; also Max to Helene Weber, October 27/November 2, 1904, *Briefe 1903–1905*, *MWG* II/4, ed. G. Hübinger and M. R. Lepsius with T. Gerhards and S. Oßwald-Bargende (Tübingen, Germany: Mohr [Siebeck], 2015), 366–367.

79. Compare Allen Guttmann, *From Ritual to Record: The Nature of Modern Sports* (1978; New York: Columbia University Press, 2004), and *Sports Spectators* (New York: Columbia University Press, 1986), for a somewhat different employment of Weberian analysis in this area. Guttmann's belief in the importance of statistics and rational calculation to modern sport was well founded, but his emphasis on "records" distracted attention from a central point: that victory in sport now comes to a large degree through an accumulation of statistically measured achievement (leagues, championship series, world rankings, judges' panels) and not necessarily from the superior prowess of one individual over others.

80. Weber, *Zur Musiksoziologie*, *MWG* I/14, 253–280.

81. Cf. Sandel, *What Money Can't Buy*, 11–15.

82. Weber, "Critical Studies in the Logic of Sciences of *Kultur*" (1906), in *CMW*, 139–150, 169–184; *Zur Logik und Methodik der Sozialwissenschaften. Schriften 1900–1907*, *MWG* I/7, ed. G. Wagner with C. Härpfer et al. (Tübingen, Germany: Mohr [Siebeck], 2018), 288–412, 451–484.

83. See my *Max Weber in Context*, 119–31, on Weber, Georg Jellinek, and Judaism.

84. For example, Weber, "Zwischenbetrachtung," *Essential*, 230–232; *MWG* I/19, 499–502.

85. Weber, "Sociology of Religion," *E&S*, 399; *MWG* I/22-2, 121.

86. Weber, "The 'Objectivity' of Knowledge in Social Science and Social Policy," *CMW*, 119, cf. 116; *MWG* I/7, 188–189, cf. 181–182.

87. José Casanova, *Public Religions in the Modern World* (Chicago: University of Chicago Press, 1994), presents what is in practice a largely Weberian analysis. He may have a somewhat exaggerated thesis of the "*deprivatization* of religion" today, as if it had once been

excluded from the public sphere altogether and then returned to it; but still he accepts that "the liberal principle of the privatization of religion is ... unimpeachable" (57).

88. Weber, "Value-Freedom," *CMW*, 315; *MWG* I/12, 470.
89. *PESC*, 263n22; *MWG* I/18, 423–425n301.
90. See my *Max Weber in Context*, chap. 8.
91. *PESC*, 53; *MWG* I/18, 159.
92. See *E&S*, 165; *MWG* I/23, 381.
93. *PESC*, 53; *MWG* I/18, 159; "Objectivity," *CMW*, 107; *MWG* I/7, 159 (my emphasis).
94. References are to *PESC*, 53, 89, 170–172, 183; *MWG* I/18, 159, 253–254, 460–467, 489; Cf. J. K. Galbraith, *The Affluent Society* (Boston: Houghton Mifflin, 1958).

CHAPTER 18

....

MAX WEBER AND THE LATE MODERNIZATION OF CATHOLICISM

....

ROSARIO FORLENZA AND BRYAN S. TURNER

IN this chapter we present Max Weber's critical but scattered account of Roman Catholicism and describe how he viewed Catholic ritual such as the sacraments as a set of practices with magical characteristics. Weber never wrote extensively about Catholicism, but we can assemble his views from various sources in his sociology of religion.[1] Despite the importance in Weber's sociology of religion of the Reformation and hence the contrast between Protestantism and Roman Catholicism, the literature on Weber's view of Catholicism is, in English-language publications, slight. We refer in this chapter, for example, to publications by Anthony J. Carroll and Werner Stark.[2] The extant literature points to the fact that Weber appears to express a critical understanding of Catholicism that is drawn primarily from liberal Protestantism. In other words, his accusations about magical assumptions behind the sacraments and the polytheistic tendencies within Mariology and veneration of the saints were conventional in the late nineteenth century. Rodney Stark is critical of Weber and more generally of mainstream sociology of religion for what he sees as its anti-Catholic bias.[3]

In this chapter we first examine developments in nineteenth-century Catholicism that lay behind Weber's critical commentary. The second half of our chapter asks how changes in Catholicism after the Second Vatican Council (informally known as Vatican II, 1962–1965) have brought about a modernization of Catholicism. How might Weber have responded to these developments? We examine the relevance of Weber's views today by considering the impact of Vatican II on Catholic teaching and practice, arguing that it represents the political modernization of Catholicism. Vatican II represented a radical departure from the political conservatism of the nineteenth century. In principle, the church was no longer critical of secular democracy, pluralism, the party system, and state sovereignty. This modernization, however, began to undermine the universalism of the church and pushed Catholicism toward denominationalism. A denomination does not claim universal relevance, being satisfied to service its local community. Its ministers are also more inclined to accept the secular values and beliefs of the surrounding society. In the absence of an established church, America was basically a society of denominations. By accepting the secular values and institutions of modern politics, the Catholic Church exposed itself to denominationalization. However, the church did not modernize its teaching on contraception, abortion, marriage, divorce, and family life. This tension between political modernization and what we might simply call "familial conservatism" still haunts the church today.

WEBER AND THE GERMAN *KULTURKAMPF*

We locate Weber's critical views on Catholicism in the context of Otto von Bismarck's anti-Catholic politics, namely the *Kulturkampf*. This "cultural struggle" was a response to developments in church doctrine. In 1832 the encyclical *Mirari Vos* by Pope Gregory XVI had condemned liberalism and questioned free speech and free thought. In 1864 the Vatican published the *Syllabus of Errors*, which attacked the separation of church and state, civil marriage, the sovereignty of the people, and democracy. In 1870 the Vatican Council declared the dogma of papal infallibility. The loyalty of the Catholic laity was not to the secular state but to the gospel and the church over which the pope now exercised authoritative control. For Bismarck, these developments in Catholicism represented a challenge to the unitary sovereignty of the German state. In this respect, Germany followed similar struggles between state and church in Switzerland in the 1840s and in Austria–Hungary. In Great Britain Prime Minister William E. Gladstone wrote in 1874 that the doctrine of papal infallibility undermined the allegiance of English Catholics to the secular state. The *Kulturkampf* came to a climax in Germany around 1871–1878. With the unification of Germany in 1871 the German Empire was made up of a Protestant majority (62% of the population) and a Catholic minority (36.5%). There was little interconnection between the two communities, for example, by intermarriage.

Unsurprisingly the struggle against Catholic conservatism gained traction among liberal, secular, and anticlerical elites. As with many liberals of his age, Weber respected the secular democratic cultures of Protestant America and Britain against conservatism in France and southern Europe. The *Kulturkampf* was in this respect the logical conclusion of the Reformation. Not only had Martin Luther challenged the church as an institution, but his contribution to German culture was through his translation of the Bible. Thus, the critical date in the unfolding of the *Kulturkampf* was the four hundredth commemoration in 1883 of Luther's birth. The Catholic Church responded through ultramontanism as a strategy for overcoming the negative impact of Protestantism. However, historians abandoned the idea that the Counter-Reformation was a direct response to the Reformation and now argued that Catholicism was going through its own internal renewal that was not tied to the Protestant Reformation. The history of Catholicism has been distorted through the lens of Protestant reformism, which has implied that Catholicism prior to Luther was unchanging and that subsequently the history of Catholicism was bound up exclusively with the Protestant challenge. The "Counter-Reformation" is too general and imprecise a term, and instead it is more accurate to speak of "early modern Catholicism."[4]

WEBER, KANT, NIETZSCHE

Weber's sociology of religion in this respect was influenced by Immanuel Kant's pietism and his attempt to root religion in morality. In *Religion Within the Limits of Reason Alone* of 1793 Kant distinguished between rational religion (Protestantism) and cultic religion (Catholicism). In cultic religions, the individual seeks to influence God (or other divine powers) through prayer, offerings, sacrifice, and submission. Rational religion is faith alone, or *sola fides*, as Max Weber repeated time and again in the *Protestant Ethic*. However, as with Weber's sociology as a whole, any simplistic view of the *Protestant Ethic* thesis is misleading. Weber's views about rationalization and capitalism were also influenced by Friedrich Nietzsche, who of course was profoundly critical of Christianity in his God-is-dead philosophy. Nietzsche and Weber shared a common view of modern society as an iron cage. Nietzsche was profoundly critical of modern society, especially of the growing influence of Prussian militarism, and he feared the negative consequences of capitalist industrialization. There could never be any comfortable relationship between modernity and individual happiness. Indeed, he anticipated much of the criticism of capitalism that characterized the work of Weber, whose analysis of resentment and disenchantment in modernity had a distinct dependence on Nietzsche. Thus, Nietzsche's criticism of the shallow optimism of economic measures of human endeavor could be taken from Weber's *Politics as a Vocation* and *Science as a Vocation*, in which the modern world is characterized as meaningless or more exactly that human beings struggle to give reality meaning in a world that is subject to rationalization processes.[5] Weber's characterization of Western rationalization is not so much a celebration of rationality as an awareness that social reality harbors irrationality and that, thus, human actions can have negative unintended consequences. In short, Weber's views about Catholicism were influenced by the political struggle against the church within German society, by his reception of Kantian ethics, and by Nietzsche's critique of the religions of subordinated groups as manifestations of resentment.[6]

WEBER AND THE RISE OF MODERNITY

Weber was in general terms concerned to understand the social conditions that made possible the rise of modernity as a specific form of rationalization of the world. Famously, in *The Protestant Ethic and the Spirit of Capitalism* Weber had examined how

Protestant beliefs about salvation and ascetic practices had ultimately promoted capitalist accumulation, individualism, and personal discipline. On the basis of his notions about inner-worldly and other-worldly religious traditions, Weber undertook comparative sociological investigations of the "world religions" to see how far their economic ethics promoted or prohibited pathways to rationalized modernity. Weber established four ideal types of religious orientation along mysticism and asceticism and inner-worldly and other-worldly. Catholicism was more inclined to mysticism and hence exercised less leverage over social change than was the case with ascetic Protestantism.[7]

For him, Catholicism was traditionalistic in spirit, as exemplified by its relationship to traditional capitalism as described in the *Protestant Ethic*. In contrast to Protestantism, it was split into a religious elite and a laity. Again, in principle, the Reformation had promoted the idea of "the priesthood of all believers," thereby reducing the space separating a calling to the ministry and the everyday world of laypeople. Protestantism promoted the idea that the ordinary laity had a calling and that a religious vocation was not exclusively a priestly calling. In contrast, the emphasis in Catholicism was on institutional grace. The church hierarchy had a monopoly over the "means of grace" such as confession, baptism, marriage, and so forth. The hierarchical bureaucracy and structure of the Catholic Church are certainly pertinent to Weber's definition of church as opposed to its theoretical counterpart, the sect. Specific religious qualifications are needed to become a member of the sects. One typically becomes a member of a church through birth. In *The Religion of India*, Weber writes, "a 'sect' in the sociological sense of the word is an exclusive association of religious virtuosos or of especially qualified persons recruited through individual admission after establishment of qualification."[8] In the church–sect typology, the church had less capacity to achieve a methodical impact on its lay members.[9] Weber was critical of the confessional tradition in Catholicism because the confession of sins considerably lessened the potential for effectively shaping the lives of the believers.[10] He wrote, "The psychological effect of the confessional was everywhere to relieve the individual of responsibility for his own conduct, that is why it was sought, and that weakened the rigorous consistency of the demands of asceticism."[11]

In *The Sociology of Religion* Weber noted that "the viewpoint of the Catholic church has oscillated between a relatively magical and a relatively ethical and soteriological orientation."[12] His theory of secular modernity rejected cultic or magical practices in favor of religions of personal discipline and piety. Indeed, for Weber we might conclude that religion starts where magic ends. He also claimed that Catholic theology promotes a version of polytheism by elevating the status of the saints as charismatic figures who mediate between the laity and God and by treating the Virgin Mary as co-redemptrix. Thus, while Weber's personal attitude to ascetic Protestantism was positive, his view of Catholicism was negative. According to Paul Honigsheim, Weber was "an unconditional opponent of Catholicism," but nonetheless "he was [also] in the habit of using every opportunity to learn more about Catholicism."[13] Werner Stark is equally critical of Weber's argument that the sacraments in Catholicism are exclusively magical.[14] In fact, Weber's critical perspective on the sacraments in the Catholic Church is consistent with John Calvin's views on "the corruption" of the sacraments. In 1544 Calvin had written his short treatise *The Necessity of Reforming the Church*, in which he complains "in regard to the sacraments, ceremonies devised by men were placed in the same rank with the mysteries instituted by Christ. For seven sacraments were received without any distinction, though Christ appointed two only, the others resting merely on human authority."[15] The communal Lord's Supper involved the biblical injunction "take eat" and encouraged the laity to share the bread and wine among themselves. However, this communal rite had been taken over by the priesthood, and there was no longer an invitation. The priest "prepares it for himself alone."[16] This, Weber's critique of Catholicism, reflected many of the assumptions of Protestants and secular liberals for whom the Catholic Church had not emerged from the medieval world. The juxtaposition of Calvinism and Catholicism was thus a commonplace.

CATHOLICISM AND MODERNITY

Max Weber's views on Catholicism largely follow the standard picture drawn by nineteenth-century Protestant historians who typically overlooked the actual practices and spirituality of early modern Catholicism, some of which (the increasing bureaucratization, the development of rationalization procedure for the regulation of church business, the social disciplining of the faithful, and the spirituality and practices of the Jesuits) contributed, often unintentionally, to modernization.[17] There was also a long process by which magic was rationalized. While the sociology of Roman Catholicism was one of "missing" components of Weber's comparative sociology of rationalization, the debate concerning the relative impact of Protestantism and Catholicism on the modern world was an ongoing issue in Weber's sociology.

Weber wrote in a context where Protestantism was regarded as superior to Catholicism and the statistics on the contrasted employment characteristics of Protestants and Catholics in Baden that occupied the opening section of Weber's *The Protestant Ethic and the Spirit of Capitalism* demonstrated, among other things, the over-representation of Protestants in positions of economic leadership. Weber adopted the statistical data in the work of Martin Offenbacher on employment by religion in Germany and disarmingly claimed that the findings were well known. Thus, Weber's account of modernity tends to see modernization as resulting from Protestant sources but eventually moving away from Protestantism to a more secularized modernity. However, the reasons for Weber's vision of Catholicism, as we have suggested, arise from the dominant antimodern attitude of the church in the nineteenth century and at the beginning of the twentieth century.

It would indeed be tempting and not entirely incorrect to place Catholicism as an adversary to modernity, democracy, and nation-state politics, siding with tradition and being an outspoken critique of the modern project as a work of the devil. With the advent and impact of the Enlightenment, the church had officially condemned modernity for its godlessness. The French Revolution pitted the church against modern politics in ways that at the time seemed irreconcilable. While repeated attempts were made to reconcile Catholicism with the modern world and national politics (the French priest and philosopher Félicité Lamennais had even spoken of "baptizing the Revolution," and the Italian journalist and priest Davide Albertario had proposed to "sanctify" democracy), the Vatican remained locked in a battle with modernity, national politics, and liberal democracy. Throughout the eighteenth century, clericalism and anticlericalism divided many countries in Europe and Latin America, sometimes even turning into confrontational ways of life. The result was a continuous cultural and political war between the Vatican and the liberal states, between Catholics and their opponents. The anticlerical French would aggressively defend the ideals of lay education and ostentatiously eat meat on Friday and *tête de veau* on January 21 (the day of the beheading of the king). In the context of the process of nation formation in Italy, the Vatican issued the *non expedit*, a decree which, with the formula "no representative, no voters," forced Catholics to stay out of the political realm, at least at the national level.[18]

THE DOCTRINAL GROWTH
OF PAPAL AUTHORITY

In 1832, Gregory XVI's encyclical letter *Mirari Vos: On Liberalism and Religious Indifferentism* condemned Lamennais' proposal to welcome the new society and its civil liberties as an opportunity for Catholicism, or to "baptize" in Lamennais' term, the Revolution. The text reads, "At the present moment a brutal malevolence and imprudent science, an unrestrained arbitrariness prevail" ("Alacris exultat improbitas, scientia impudens, dissolute licentia").[19] In 1864 Pius IX concluded his *Syllabus Errorum*, attached to the encyclical *Quanta Cura*, by condemning the idea that "the pope would have to learn to accept progress, liberalism and modern civilization" ("Romanus Pontifex potest ac debet cum progressu, cum liberalismo et cum recenti civilitate sese reconciliari et componere"). As the pope stated in the opening lines of the encyclical, modernity must be seen as the result of "criminal plans by malevolent people" ("nefariis iniquorum hominum molitionibus"). This general outlook did not change until the Second Vatican Council in the 1960s and certainly explains the Vatican's weak position toward rightwing dictatorships emerging in the twentieth century and its general distrust of political modernity and national-democratic politics.

True, Pius XII, during the war, had expressed a favorable predisposition and an opening toward the values of political modernity and had begun to draw direct links between freedom, democracy, and the Christian message. Yet even when he praises democracy, the pope warned of possible abuses. In his famous 1944 Christmas radio message "True and False Democracy" he distinguished between "the people" and "the mass," describing the latter as "the main enemy of true democracy and of its ideal of liberty and equality." He continued, "A democratic state left to the arbitrary will of the mass…becomes a pure and simple system of absolutism. State absolutism consists as a matter of fact, in the wrong principle that the authority of the state is unlimited…and there is not left any appeal whatever to a superior and morally binding law." Pius seemed to have been thinking of communist invocation of the name of the people to justify its oppression, but there was also an effort to maintain continuity with the criticism of democracy made by his predecessor. In 1950 the pope, aware of the theological stirring in France, responded with the encyclical letter *Humani Generis*, in which he remarked sternly that "some [Catholic teachers]…desirous of novelty, and fearing to be considered ignorant of recent scientific finding, tend to withdraw from the sacred Teaching Authority," with the risk of "departing from revealed truth" and "drawing others along with them into error."

FROM POLITICAL CATHOLICISM
TO CHRISTIAN DEMOCRACY

However, from the middle of the nineteenth century, an alternative model for Catholicism started to be seen. While always serving as a critique of political modernity and democracy, Catholic thought on the modern also started to undergo profound transformations. This happened very much in the context of the process of nation-state formation which took place in Italy (a traumatic event for the church as the pontiffs lost their territorial domains and Rome became the capital of a new secular state in 1870), in Europe, and in Latin America. Everywhere liberal political elites attempted to reduce the influence of the church in society and abolish its ancient rights, at the time increasing the authority and power of the state. As a reaction, Catholics entered into the secular political scene, increasingly engaging with public matters and the defense of their own interests, and those of the church, through a vast array of organizations such as political clubs, peasant leagues, youth and recreational associations, and, eventually, proper political parties.

The direct consequence of this phenomenon was the emergence of a proper Catholic political civilization milieu, which turned Catholicism into a political identity. This process was reinforced and further promoted by Pope Leo XII and his "social encyclical" *Rerum Novarum* (1891). Catholics were now urged to actively unite, to engage themselves in all kinds of social domains, and to respond to the threat of liberal and anti-clerical governments as well as to the challenge of socialism. By then it had become clear that modern society was more than a revolutionary chaos soon to collapse. A full-fledged and well-organized Catholic subculture, a Catholic "pillar" or compartment within society, was established in anticipation of a Catholic modernity proper. The movement in many ways resembled what the socialist labor movement was achieving around the same time in Europe and beyond.

Nevertheless, the Vatican continued to condemn modernity and democratic politics. Between the end of the nineteenth century and the beginning of the twentieth century the Vatican was forced to face a new challenge from *within* its own ranks, incidentally called "modernism." Modernism was an intellectual, amorphous movement which developed among Catholics in the late nineteenth century and early twentieth century, first in France and England, with the proclaimed aim of bringing the church into harmony with modernity and with the post-Enlightenment world. Interestingly, the term "modernist" was first employed condemningly by the church authorities. The official condemnation of modernism in 1907, with Pius X's encyclical *Pascendi Dominici Gregis*, signaled a victory for Catholic anti-modernists, and an anti-modern position that would last in most of Europe throughout the first half of the century.

After World War I, political Catholicism and Catholic-inspired parties flourished everywhere in Europe and Latin America and soon were to compete with socialists, communists, and fascists and with new emerging authoritarian regimes. The Vatican itself maintained a highly ambiguous relationship with Catholic political organizations, as in the past, remaining skeptical of Catholic political activity. After all, pluralism as such was bound to remain a problem for an institution with universalistic aspirations. The Vatican continued to deal with secular governments, even when they were authoritarian or fascist regimes. Rather than put its affairs in the hand of groups and parties which could become independent, the Vatican realized that the more prudent approach was to sign concordats to solve issues concerning the place and roles of the church in the state and to above all else guarantee the fundamental prerogatives and rights of the church, especially in the realm of religious education. Thus, the Vatican entered into agreement with fascist regimes to protect ecclesiastic influence. Crucially, on February 11, 1929, a historic treaty was signed between the Fascist Italian government and the Vatican, re-establishing the political power and diplomatic standing of the Catholic Church, which had been lost when Italy seized Rome. The Lateran Pacts established Vatican City as an independent state, restored the civil sovereignty of the pope as a monarch, and regulated the position of the church and the Catholic religion in the Italian state. Furthermore, a financial convention compensated the Holy See for the loss of the Papal States.[20]

But the interwar years were crucial for the development of a Catholic modernity. Catholic intellectuals and politicians—at first not necessarily opposed to fascist and authoritarian regimes but then more and more disappointed and distraught by fascist racial politics, by the acceleration of the totalitarian dynamics, and by the war and the political–existential uncertainty that it entailed—began to search for a Catholic response to the problem of mass politics. The French intellectual Jacques Maritain became the compass of this political and intellectual search.[21]

Maritain had been close to the quasi-fascist Action Française in the 1920s but had abandoned the movement when it was condemned by the Vatican in 1926. Working within a neo-Thomist philosophical framework, in the 1930s he started to embrace human rights and modern democracy. In particular, his 1936 study *Humanisme Intégrale* and his 1942 pamphlet *Christianisme et démocratie* (which was dropped by Allied planes over Europe in 1943) had constituted a cautious but nevertheless decisive endorsement of the ultimately Christian nature of democracy. Central to Maritain's theory and definition of democracy was the concept of the "person" and its opposition to the "individual." However, critics have argued that the Catholic notion of the dignity of the person retained an element of hierarchy that was not entirely compatible with the idea of equal citizenship.[22] The "person" has a spiritual and transcendent quality, not reducible to material and biological nature; it flourishes only within a community, when open to God. It is via the transcendent principle that the good of all can be articulated in the first place. Many Catholics, who had been sympathetic to Fascism, found in Maritain an antidote to fascism, authoritarian politics, and totalitarianism. Maritain made the conceptual incompatibility between Catholicism and totalitarianism clear to Catholic intellectuals, serving as a powerful antidote to clerico-fascism. It freed Catholics (or a large sector of Catholicism) from the medievalist, anti-modern utopia that drove many of them to adhere to fascist or authoritarian regimes, seen as a sort of ally in the fight against modernity and for the Catholic regeneration of the world.

Maritain had a direct influence on Christian democracy, the new "political animal"[23] that in the post–World War II era dominated the political scene in western Europe and in Latin America. Via Christian democracy central principles of political Catholicism and Catholic social teaching, as well as the personalist and communitarian language of Maritain, were introduced into the constitutions of Italy, West Germany, France, and other European countries: the centrality of the person, a social view on economy, the defense of non-statal entities from the family to the church, and the validation of forms of organization which were both political (parties) and corporatist (trade unions). Via Christian democracy, the Catholic philosophical-political luggage and some of its important federalist principles (such as subsidiarity)[24] were also translated into the nascent process of European supranational integration.[25]

Christian democracy was also at the forefront of the struggle against authoritarian regimes in Latin America for the entire post–World War II period. In short, resting on the tradition of Catholic social teaching, as re-elaborated by Maritain, Christian democracy became a central actor in the process of building a modern mass and post-totalitarian democracy and a welfare state. With Christian democracy in the post–World War II era the purpose of Catholic action changed dramatically. Christian democrats were in the political realm not to protect the church from anticlerical assault but to articulate and develop (in competition or in cooperation with non-Catholic forces) political and socioeconomic platforms and plans implementing a Christian democratic and Catholic response to the challenge of modernity and democracy. Thus, Christian democracy achieved what traditional political Catholicism had until then only dreamt about: to gain a leading role within the modern world.

THE SECOND VATICAN COUNCIL

With the Second Vatican Council, as José Casanova has written, Catholicism became a "public religion."[26] This event is certainly the most significant change in the history of the relation of the Catholic Church with secular culture. The council served to shape a new self-image of the church as interpreter of the sign of the times, as a companion traveler, partner, or guide of modernity. The church recognized freedom of religion, pluralism, and human rights as central to its doctrine and encouraged its members to engage with the political realm. The final pastoral document, *Gaudium et Spes*, expressed hopes that the church and the good forces of the modern world united would be able to build a common house for all people. Science and faith were defined by Paul VI in the closing address of the council as "mutual servants of one another in the one truth."

To what extent did the development of Christian democracy influence the church and its attitude toward modernity? And to what extent were Christian democrats controlled by the Vatican? Catholic writers in particular but also scholars such as Casanova have seen the council, implicitly or explicitly, as the moment when the Catholic Church finally accepted a changing world, shook off its reactionary past, and adapted to reality. But matters were more complex than that. The changes in attitude were not simply caused by external pressures. Catholic philosophers and political thinkers and activists were actively seeking out, and had sought out since the 1930s, a position on the crucial social issues of the day from within a Christian-inspired worldview.[27] Their argument was that the church should take moral leadership with respect to questions of social justice, the welfare of citizens, the dignity of the person, peace, and democracy. Put briefly, Christian democracy became agenda-setting. And this happened in a continuous dialogue between the Vatican and Catholic politicians, a dialogue that took place across an institutional divide which crystallized within the same historical process. Christian democracy developed outside the control of the Vatican, but the mutual influence that took place in formulating a stance toward the modern is at the same time clear.

The redefinition of Catholicism as a modern intellectual–cultural project advanced by Christian democracy as a basis for new politics and practices, reinforced by the wider social, economic, and cultural transformation of the 1950s, certainly impinged upon the church's attitude on democracy and modernity. The council, in particular with the final pastoral document, *Gaudium et Spes*, encouraged Catholics to enter the stage of pluralism and democracy; but in fact, European and Latin American Christian democrats had engaged the political realm and embraced the cause of democracy at least from World War II. Here it is also worthy to note that Maritain, who was a central figure in drafting the United Nations' Declaration of Human Rights, played a crucial role in the Vatican Council. It was Maritain who presented Paul VI (Montini) with the "Message to the Philosophers" at the closing of the council, and there is no doubt that Paul VI was profoundly influenced by his reading of Maritain. This influence shines through, for example, in Pope Paul's encyclical "Development of Peoples" (*Populorum Progressio*, 1967). Here Pope Paul refers explicitly to Maritain's writings, for example, in notes 17 and 44. Several central passages are literally transcribed versions of Maritain's "integral humanism" and draw on his image of "modern man":

> If further development calls for the work of more and more technicians, even more necessary is the deep thought and reflection of wise men in search of a new humanism which will enable modern man to find himself anew by embracing the higher values of love and friendship, of prayer and contemplation.

Weber and Catholic Modernity in the Late Twentieth Century and Beyond

What would Max Weber have made of Catholicism in the late twentieth century and at the beginning of the twenty-first century? What would he have made of the church's realignment with political modernity? As we have seen, from the French Revolution to the Vatican Council, the Catholic Church and Catholicism (writ large) went through a process of transformation which developed from radical *rejection* of modernity to *hesitant embracement* and, finally, *critical co-articulation* of the modern project. Or, employing kindred terms in the wider multiple modernities literature: the church moved from a position of anti- and counter-modernity to one of alternative or parallel modernity.[28] What would Max Weber have made of this historical trajectory and of Vatican II seen as an internal renewal of the church, which inaugurated not only a rapprochement of Catholicism with modernity but also the culmination of a complex historical trajectory?

The council's understanding of the church in the modern world has undermined the spirit of anti-modernism that Max Weber, and other scholars in his footsteps, saw in the church and in Catholicism in the nineteenth and early twentieth centuries. It is noteworthy that the mature project of one of the most important political philosophers, Charles Taylor, has been to seek a convergence between post-liberal thought, communitarianism, and Catholicism. Taylor has insisted that a religious dimension gives shape to how human beings experience and make an image of the world. Here Taylor is not just aligning Catholicism with modernity and democracy: he is situating Catholicism as a foundational platform for recognizing and accepting pluralism and difference, within the context of the modern multicultural society.[29] Likewise, in a famous debate with a Catholic pope, one theoretician and staunch defender of modernity has recognized the role of religion within the modern world and in the public sphere.[30]

Catholicism and Sexual Modernization

Vatican II refashioned the church in terms of political modernization. It is now around the family, procreation, gender, sex, and homosexuality that the church has not modernized its view. It is important to realize that the Catholic Church is not a proselytizing church. Rather, it has relied on a high birth rate, marriage for life, and baptism. In the secular West, people are getting married late (if they get married at all) and having relatively few children. On this basis one can understand that, for practical reasons as well as theological arguments, the church is committed to defending a traditional view of marriage.[31]

In his contributions to the study of human rights, Samuel Moyn is skeptical of many of the conventional explanations of their rise and growing influence. He suggests that the Catholic idea of "dignity" was in the 1930s set within the church's understanding of hierarchy and rank. The human subject, while bathed in dignity, was still subordinated to authority and hierarchy. Rank was especially important in the hierarchy of men and women. The Irish Constitution of 1937, while celebrating "the freedom and dignity of the individual," proposed that women should find their place in the home.[32]

Now that the ground of modernity is understood as sexual modernization, the conflicts between the church and the secular or post-secular society remain largely and acutely controversial. This is why the Vatican decided to devote the Synod of the Bishops of October 2015 to the topics of family and sexual morality. The assembly had been anticipated in October 2014 by an extraordinary session of the synod, which then prepared and paved the way for the subsequent gathering. The path to the synod, in fact, had begun in 2013, when Pope Francis first announced the event. The announcement was accompanied with the elaboration of a preparatory working document. Ever since, other documents and reports have been drafted and questionnaires sent to Catholics of all ages in dozens of countries and several continents to collect views at the grassroots level. Later, speeches by cardinals and bishops, interviews, and inevitable controversies have followed one another. In short, the intense debate has put the church under considerable strain and distress. The end of the synod did not terminate the debate. Quite the opposite, polemics and controversy still loom large on the quite often very tense relationship between the church and the modern world society.[33]

The continuity of Catholic Church teaching on family, marriage, and divorce can be illustrated by encyclicals—from *Casti Connubii* by Pius XI (1931), later taken up by fascist propaganda on the prolific family, to the pronouncements of Wojtyla and Ratzinger and through *Humanae Vitae* by Paul VI (1968)—and by recent statements of the bishops following, for example, the Irish referendum on same-sex marriage (May 2015). To brutally simplify a topic which has involved generations of theologians and required conceptual subtlety and sophistication, the church treats marriage as a sacrament ("to make" or to "render sacred") in which the principal aim is procreation and family life. It may be tempting to see how Christ and the canonical and apocryphal gospels *really* treat and engage with family, marriage, and sex.

In any event, in the secular world marriage is a contract between consenting adults that can be terminated in most Western societies by no-fault divorce (consensual divorce). The struggle between the Catholic model and the secular model takes place at different levels. Firstly, this is the model of marriage as a sacrament that is embedded in Genesis, where God created man and woman, and which cannot be broken. The secular model of contract allows for multiple divorces and marriages and is seen as a companionate arrangement for the emotional and sexual satisfaction of the partners but not necessarily for life. The longevity of modern partners is a significant challenge to lifelong fidelity. The secular model is not necessarily a modern invention because the Protestant view of marriage as a companionate relationship based on a contract can be traced back to John Milton, the seventeenth-century English poet and author not only of the famous

Paradise Lost but also of four tracts on divorce interpreted in a contractual fashion.[34] In any case, the procreation of children is not essential to the secular model; children are simply an expression of that companionship. The contract can be broken once there is little affection supporting the relationship. With no-fault divorce, divorce is no longer a social stigma and the couple is free to remarry. In this secular model the core of marriage is the couple. The modern recognition of same-sex marriage can be seen as the logical extension of the idea of the companionate couple based on gender equality and thus available to gay men and lesbian women This secular model of marriage and family does not assume that the family is the basic unit of social life and political institutions such as the state.

A further level of struggle is the difference between a language of rights and the language of morality. Many cases can illustrate this fundamental point. Recent court decisions in the United States have decriminalized sodomy, defended the right to homosexual identity, and recognized same-sex marriage in the name of equal treatment of citizens regardless of sexual orientation. The logic behind such decisions is in terms of racial equality. Race is not accepted as a basis for discrimination; therefore, there are no consistent legal grounds for discrimination in terms of gender. Whether or not individual judges approve or disapprove of homosexuality becomes irrelevant. If people of color have achieved the protection of the law against discrimination, then the same protection, in order to avoid arbitrary legal judgments, should be accorded to people whose sexual orientation is gay. In the debate about same-sex marriage in the United States, the judges dismissed the argument that the Bible offers no defense of marriage between people of the same sex, they dismissed arguments about tradition or human history, and finally they rejected arguments that children would suffer in same-sex marriages. The overriding principle was one of equality of treatment. In short, while the church has historically defended family and marriage by reference to theology and morality, the courts and gay social movements have fought their case on the basis of secular notions of rights.

However, if the church modifies its position to recognize same-sex marriage (and other sexual rights such as the decriminalization of sodomy), it may defend its relevance to society and to the politics of (at least) some states but at the cost of its orthodox theological content. It can modernize its teaching but will undermine the credibility and strength of its theology. Theological orthodoxy provides acclaim to universality against the prevailing global diversity. Catholicism will then eventually become a denomination and slowly turn into a *low-intensity religion*,[35] that is, a religion lacking normative demands, freed from the concerns of orthodoxy, flexible and open, and thus able to effectively compete on the "market" with other religious entrepreneurs. In fact, Catholicism as a low-intensity religion could dominate and control the market in several countries in southern Europe, Latin America, or the Philippines, thanks to its profound understanding of the context and its reservoir of symbols and rites, which still hold a certain weight on a variety of social sectors. In short, Catholicism as a low-intensity religion would mean the commodification of religious practices and beliefs, and thus their transformation in a product, a merchandise, a good to consume at the individual's convenience. This is a form of religiosity which does not require significant time, effort, and existential commitment: a subjective and post-institutional religion, which eventually will have not a lasting and significant impact on the social structure and popular culture of a country. Thus, an uncontrollable and unpredictable process could unfold, putting under strain some doctrinal certainties and thus culminating in the weakening of the church's claim to universality. Likewise, the church's prestige and influence on the public and political spheres will weaken.

Conclusion: The Last Frontier of Orthodoxy

We have argued that Vatican II amounted to a profound modernization of the Catholic Church in terms of its relationship to other religions, its liturgy, and its political orientation to authoritarian regimes and to human rights concerns. It modified the relationship between laity and priesthood. However, the church has not been able to modernize its attitudes toward a range of sexual issues, most notably same-sex marriage and abortion. Pope Francis has attempted to manage these challenges by regarding them as pastoral problems and not as a challenge to theological orthodoxy. However, the decision of the Supreme Court in the United States to recognize same-sex marriage and the Irish referendum in 2015 have challenged this pastoral solution to the problems presented by the transformation of marriage, procreation, and divorce within secular society.

The external challenge of secular modernity (understood as sexual modernization and creation of new personal rights) and the internal challenge in the conflict between conservatives and liberals is a double crisis that will determine whether the Catholic Church can preserve or even relaunch its claims to universality or whether it will be transformed into a Catholic denomination alongside mainstream (American) Protestant denominations. Denominationalism in essence means that religious organizations adapt to secular society without significantly challenging that society and that denominations compete with each other for members in a religious market. Denominations draw their members from social groups that are basically comfortable with secularity and do not demand that their denomination has other than national relevance. The denomination is neither a sect nor a universal church.[36] With denominationalization, the Catholic Church would remain relevant to secular society and to its congregations but at the cost of its orthodox core. It is for this reason that the "war" over same-sex marriage and abortion represents the "last frontier" between universalism and denominationalism.[37]

While Weber held strong views about Catholic traditionalism and bureaucracy and was critical of what he saw as the magical assumptions of the sacraments, he had little to say about gender, family, and procreation in his general sociology. We assume Weber would not have predicted Vatican II, but he may have seen it as one step toward "the disenchanted garden" that had eventually overtaken liberal Protestantism.

NOTES

1. For an overview, see Bryan S. Turner, "Max Weber and the Sociology of Religion," *Revue international de philosophie* 276, no. 2 (2016): 141–150; Christopher Adair-Toteff, *Fundamental Concepts in Max Weber's Sociology of Religion* (New York: Palgrave MacMillan, 2015); Adair-Toteff, *Max Weber's Sociology of Religion* (Tübingen, Germany: Mohr Siebeck, 2016).

2. Anthony J, Carroll, "The Importance of Protestantism in Max Weber's Theory of Secularization," *European Journal of Sociology* 50, no. 1 (2009): 61–95; Werner Stark, "The Place of Catholicism in Max Weber's 'Sociology of Religion,'" *Sociological Analysis* 2, no. 4 (1968): 202–210.

3. Rodney Stark, *The Victory of Reason: How Christianity Led to Freedom, Capitalism and Western Success* (New York: Random House, 2005); *Bearing False Witness. Debunking Centuries of Anti-Catholic History* (West Conshohocken, PA: Templeton Press, 2016).

4. John O'Malley, *Trent and All That: Renaming Catholicism in the Early Modern Era* (Cambridge, MA: Harvard University Press, 2000).

5. Max Weber, "Politics as a Vocation" and "Science as a Vocation," in *From Max Weber: Essays in Sociology*, trans. and ed. H. H. Gerth and C. Wright Mills (New York: Oxford University Press, 1946), 77–128, 129–156; *Wissenschaft als Beruf 1917/1919—Politik als Beruf 1919, Max Weber-Gesamtausgabe* (hereafter *MWG*) I/17, ed. W. J. Mommsen and W. Schluchter, with B. Morgenbrod (Tübingen, Germany: Mohr [Siebeck], 1992).

6. Georg Stauth and Bryan S. Turner, *Nietzsche's Dance: Resentment, Reciprocity and Resistance in Social Life* (Oxford: Basil Blackwell, 1988); Bryan S. Turner, "Max Weber and the Spirit of Resentment: The Nietzsche Legacy," *Journal of Classical Sociology* 11, no. 1 (2011): 75–92.

7. Max Weber, *Economy and Society: An Outline of Interpretive Sociology*, ed. G. Roth and C. Wittich (New York: Bedminster Press, 1968), 542–544; *Wirtschaft und Gesellschaft. Nachlaß. Religiöse Gemeinschaften, MWG* I/22-2, ed. H. G. Kippenberg with P. Schilm (Tübingen, Germany: Mohr [Siebeck], 2001), 320–324.

8. Max Weber, *The Religion of India: The Sociology of Hinduism and Buddhism*, ed. and trans. H. H. Gerth and D. Martindale (Glencoe, IL: Free Press, 1958), 6; *Die Wirtschaftsethik der Weltreligionen. Hinduimsus und Buddhismus. 1916–1920, MWG* I/20, ed. H. Schmidt-Glintzer, with K.-H. Golzio (Tübingen, Germany: Mohr [Siebeck], 1996), 56.

9. Max Weber, "'Churches' and 'Sects' in North America," in *The Protestant Ethic and the Spirit of Capitalism and Other Writings*, trans. and ed. P. Baehr and G. C. Wells (London: Penguin, 2002), 216; *Asketischer Protestantismus und Kapitalismus. Schriften und Reden 1904–1911, MWG* I/9, ed. W. Schluchter, with U. Bube (Tübingen, Germany: Mohr [Siebeck], 2014), 460.

10. Weber, *The Protestant Ethic and the Spirit of Capitalism* (hereafter *PESC*), trans. Talcott Parsons (New York: Scribner's, 1930), 180; *MWG* I/9, 262–264; see also *Max Weber's Replies to His Critics, 1907–1910*, ed. D. J. Chalcraft and A. Harrington, trans. A. Harrington and M. Shields (Liverpool, UK: Liverpool University Press, 2001), 108–109; "Antikritisches Schlußwort," *MWG* I/9, 712–713.

11. Weber, *PESC*, 250, n. 149; *MWG* I/9, 336, n. 111.

12. Max Weber, *The Sociology of Religion*, intro. T. Parsons, foreword A. Swidler (New York: Beacon Press, 1993), 188; *MWG* I/22-2, 345; on this see also Bryan S. Turner, "Ritual, Belief and Habituation: Religion and Religions from the Axial Age to the Anthropocene," *European Journal of Social Theory* 20, no. 1 (2017): 132–145, 138.

13. Paul Honigsheim, *The Unknown Max Weber*, ed. A. Sica (New York: Transaction Publishers, 2000), 216–217.

14. W. Stark, "Place of Catholicism," 204–205.

15. John Calvin, *The Necessity of Reforming the Church*, trans. H. Beveridge (Dallas, TX: Protestant Heritage Press, 1995), 29.

16. Calvin, *Necessity*, 68.

17. Carroll, "Importance of Protestantism," 81; Wolfgang Reinhard, "Gegenreformation als Modernisierung? Prologomena zu einer Theorie des konfessionellen Zeitalters," *Archive for Reformation History* 68 (1977): 226–252, 231, 240.

18. Rosario Forlenza and Bjørn Thomassen, *Italian Modernities: Competing Narratives of Nationhood* (New York: Palgrave, 2016), 64.

19. The texts of all encyclicals and papal documents and speeches quoted in this chapter are available at the official websites http://papalencyclicals.net and http://www.vatican.va.

20. Forlenza and Thomassen, *Italian Modernities*, 74.

21. Rosario Forlenza and Bjørn Thomassen, "Catholic Modernity and the Italian Constitution," *History Workshop Journal* 81 (2016): 231–251, 238–241; Forlenza and Thomassen, "Global Connections: Catholicism and the Alternatively Modern" (2018, forthcoming).

22. For further reflections on this point, see Samuel Moyn, *Human Rights and the Uses of History* (London; Verso, 2017).

23. Tony Judt, *Postwar: A History of Europe Since 1945* (London: Heinemann, 2005), 80; Rosario Forlenza, "A Party for the Mezzogiorno: The Christian Democratic Party, Agrarian Reform and the Government of Italy," *Contemporary European History* 19, no. 4 (2010): 331–349.

24. In Catholic social teaching, the principle of subsidiarity designated the idea that powers which individuals can exercise adequately themselves should not be arrogated to a central authority. In the context of Europeanism, it refers to the principle that the supranational community should only make law in situations where individual nations were incapable of acting.

25. Forlenza and Thomassen, "Catholic Modernity"; Rosario Forlenza, "The Politics of the *Abendland*: Christian Democracy and the Idea of Europe After the Second World War," *Contemporary European History* 2, no. 2 (2017): 261–286.

26. José Casanova, *Public Religions in the Modern World* (Chicago: University of Chicago Press, 1994).

27. Rosario Forlenza and Bjørn Thomassen, "Rethinking Christian Democracy: Transcendence as Transformation, 1930–1950" (paper presented at the American Historical Association annual meeting, Washington DC, 2018); Forlenza and Thomassen, "Global Connections."

28. Forlenza and Thomassen, "Global Connections"; see also Bill McSweeney, *Roman Catholicsim; The Search for Relevance* (Oxford: Oxford University Press, 1980), xiii–xv, 236–239.

29. Charles Taylor, "A Catholic Modernity?," in *A Catholic Modernity: Charles Taylor's Marianist Award Lecture*, ed. J. H. Heft (Oxford: Oxford University Press, 1999), 13–39; *A Secular Age* (Cambridge, MA: Harvard University Press, 2007); see also Wolfgang Schluchter, "Dialectics of Disenchantment: A Weberian Look to Western Modernity," *Max Weber Studies* 17, no. 1 (2017): 24–47.

30. Jürgen Habermas and Joseph Ratzinger, *The Dialectics of Secularization: On Reason and Religion* (San Francisco: Ignatius Press, 2006).

31. This section is based on Bryan S. Turner and Rosario Forlenza, "The Last Frontier: The Struggle over Sex and Marriage Under Pope Francis," *Rassegna Italiana di Sociologia* 57, no. 4 (2016): 689–710.

32. Samuel Moyn, *Christian Human Rights* (Philadelphia: University of Pennsylvania Press, 2015), 26.

33. The Anglican Church has had the same issue in its synods. One of the major reasons for internal conflicts has been the contrast between the African bishops who have followed a customary and conservative moral code and the liberal mores of English society and parishes.

34. The four tracts (titled *The Doctrine and Discipline of Divorce*, *The Judgment of Martin Bucer*, *Tetrachordon*, and *Colasterion*) are in *Complete Prose Works of John Milton*, vol. 2, *1643–1648*, ed. E. Sirluck (New Haven, CT: Yale University Press, 1959).

35. Bryan S. Turner, *Religion and Modern Society: Citizenship, Secularization and the State* (Cambridge: Cambridge University Press, 2011).

36. Ernst Troeltsch, *Die Soziallehren der christlichen Kirchen und Gruppen* (Tübingen, Germany: Mohr [Siebeck], 1912).

37. Turner and Forlenza, "The Last Frontier."

CHAPTER 19

THE "DISENCHANTMENT OF THE WORLD" OR WHY WE CAN NO LONGER USE THE FORMULA AS MAX WEBER MIGHT HAVE INTENDED

KENICHI MISHIMA

"Nothing is ever lost."

Robert Bellah[1]

"…strongly exposed to the imperative of consistency."

Max Weber[2]

WALTER BENJAMIN'S RESERVATIONS ABOUT "DISENCHANTMENT"

IN his essay in literary criticism "Goethe's Elective Affinities," Walter Benjamin sees the decline of the novel's main characters preprogrammed, so to speak, by their construction of a false relationship to nature. This is true above all for Charlotte and Eduard, both landed gentry, on account of their "cultivation," or *Bildung*. Immediately at the beginning of the novel, with the reorganization of the estate in mind, "Without scruple, indeed without consideration, they line up the gravestones along the church wall, wound through by a footpath, for the minister to sow clover in."[3] For these characters, who later on will suffer under the complex relationship of an elective affinity, the world is already *entzaubert*, disenchanted and devoid of magic. "The principals, as cultivated human beings, are almost free of superstition."[4] For those with *Bildung* the gravestones are merely stones. Although Benjamin does not use the term *Entzauberung*, it is crystal clear that is what he means in the phrase "without consideration." He continues, "One cannot imagine a more conclusive liberation from tradition than that liberation from the graves of the ancestors, which, in the sense not only of myth but of religion, provides a foundation for the ground under the feet of the living."[5] For Benjamin the departed ancestors prepare a foundation for the living, the ground on which life is possible. And that is a matter of myth and religion. In the novel only the philistine Herr Mittler, who as his name suggests, tries to mediate between the protagonists, is described as "held back not by a pious reluctance but by a superstitious one—while to the friends it does not appear either scandalous to stroll there or forbidden to do as they please."[6]

Benjamin sees problematic aspects of disenchantment both in the inconsistency that Mittler shows by presenting himself as a man of reason, while still unable to free himself from the superstitious fear of the violation of the graves, as well as in the consistency that Charlotte and Eduard demonstrate with the destruction of the ground prepared by ancestors, thus with the destruction of "religion," seeing *Bildung* as the only means for disciplining the passions. "At the height of their cultivation, however, they are subject to the forces that cultivation claims to have mastered, even if it may forever prove impotent to cure them."[7] In these sentences we can read a conclusion: the world can become disenchanted, or it has already been disenchanted. However disenchanted it may be, humans cannot be liberated from their inner nature. Goethe knew as much: the entire cultural-Protestant practice of using *Bildung* against one's own nature proves to be deceitful. The immanent objectification of a disciplined, enlightened, and cultivated form of life is subjected to the power of fate, an expression that Weber applied not only to capitalism but also to the erotic life and "sexual love."

Thus we have the problematization of disenchantment by Walter Benjamin, who presumably knew Max Weber's important work. But for now we can set Benjamin aside, although I shall return to his ideas in addressing an issue arguably ignored by Weber's disenchantment thesis.

PROTESTANT RELIGIOSITY AND THE RADICAL CONSEQUENCES OF DISENCHANTMENT

In the context of numerous lines of argument Weber characterizes the "disenchantment of the world" initially as a twofold process: religious-historical and scientific. Concerning the religious-historical process, a long quotation is appropriate:

This, the complete elimination of salvation through the Church and the *sacraments* (which was in Lutheranism by no means developed to its final conclusions), was what formed the absolutely decisive difference from Catholicism. That great historic process in the development of religions, the *disenchantment* of the world which had begun with the old Hebrew prophets and, in conjunction with Hellenistic scientific thought, had repudiated all *magical* means of salvation as superstition and sin, came here [in the ascetic sects of Protestantism] to its logical conclusion. The genuine Puritan even rejected all signs of religious ceremony at the grave and buried his nearest and dearest without song or ritual in order that no "superstition," no trust in the effects of magical and sacramental forces on salvation, should creep in.[8]

In the course of history humanity gradually came to realize that there was no direct line between God or the gods and life on earth, not even for the clergy. For a long time magic ruled as one of the "primordial methods of influencing supernatural powers."[9] Previously gods were "strong beings, whose passions resemble those of man; they may be brave or treacherous, friendly or hostile to one another and to man; at any rate, like man they are completely amoral, amenable to bribery through sacrifices and subject to magic influences, which may make the human manipulator even stronger than they are."[10] Humanity, or when appropriate the clergy, can win over the gods for its own advantage through magic or sacrificial acts. "Throughout the world the magician is in the first instance a rainmaker, for the harvest depends on timely and sufficient rain, though not in excessive quantity."[11] Because of disenchantment this is no longer the case, though the learning process took considerable time.

With the triumphal march of monotheism the "magical means" characteristic of polytheism were progressively constrained. But there was no internal connection between the disappearance of magic and the dissemination of monotheism. As Weber's remarks show, he emphasized the "peculiar position of the old Hebrew ethic, as compared with the closely related ethics of Egypt and Babylon, and its development after the time of the prophets."[12] Weber understood the difference established by the peculiar position of Jewish prophecy primarily through the repudiation of magic, not simply in monotheism. In this respect it is helpful to consider his reference to the "universalistic transition" of Amenhotep IV (Ikhnaton) in ancient Egypt. Ikhnaton prevailed with his idea of a single god, at least for a while. Weber pointed to a relationship between world empire and a fondness for monotheism that could be observed everywhere, but added that this transition revealed in essence "a purely naturalistic character."[13] In contrast to Sigmund Freud in his essay *Moses and Monotheism*, Weber did not think highly of Ikhnaton's reforms because they remained "naturalistic" and still enmeshed in magic rituals. He did not see monotheism as the only factor at the beginning of a long process of disenchantment. Perhaps monotheism is less prone to magic, but it alone cannot exclude magical practices, which subsequently could still be practiced up to the present in the Catholic sacraments.

Weber continually emphasized that disenchantment of the world was not consistently implemented in the Catholic tradition: "The 'disenchantment' of the world, the elimination of *magic* as a means to salvation, was not extended in its consequences nearly as far in

Catholic piety as it was in Puritan (and before that only in Jewish) religiosity."[14] From Weber's point of view what was important was not only the repudiation of magic as such but that such repudiation was carried through consistently in its "radical consequences." The rejection of magic can be half-hearted. The Catholic Church had tried to control the process of disenchantment with a mixture of magic and ritual. According to another passage in the *Protestant Ethic*, "The Baptist denominations along with the predestinationists, especially the strict Calvinists, carried out the most radical devaluation of all sacraments as means to salvation, and thus accomplished the religious 'disenchantment' of the world in its most extreme consequences."[15]

Three comments are necessary at this point. First, there is the erratic character of the radical disenchantment. In general, Weber's interpretation starts from the view that the history of religion must be understood in developmental or evolutionary terms, although the concept of "evolution" should never be identified with that of Charles Darwin. Always skeptical of his own time, Weber almost always placed the word "progress" in quotation marks. He wrote about the "process of disenchantment, which has continued to exist in Occidental culture for millennia, and, in general, this 'progress.'"[16] He also referred to this continuing process that "set in" and then reached its "conclusion." On the whole, the presence of a developmental perspective cannot be denied, as in his assertion, "The magician has been the developmental-historical precursor of the prophet."[17] On closer inspection two mental leaps can be established in the process of the disenchantment of the world. We may even speak of a discontinuity. What is decisive is the emergence of Jewish prophecy and the Calvinist or old Protestant sects. Weber does not envisage an underlying linear trend connecting the two that never ceased to exist beneath the flourishing Catholic sacraments and then re-emerged following the Reformation.

Thus, second, something becomes clear in Weber's discussion of disenchantment: namely, the emphasis on radical consequences and consistency. In every cited passage the word *Konsequenz* ("consequence," "consistency") appears. When Weber speaks of the old Protestant sects, this figure of speech appears again and again, often combined with "radical," "ultimate," and "absolute." The affiliated verb is always *durchführen*, "to carry through" or "implement." This means it is not the case that disenchantment takes place (*geschieht*), as Heidegger would say, but rather that it is "carried through" or "implemented" and to be sure "in all its consequences" or "in its ultimate consequences." Because of its still "naturalistic character," Ikhnaton could not "carry through" his revolutionary new religion "in its ultimate consequences." Thus, disenchantment appears to be a reflexive and thereby precipitous or volatile act of will, even though it emphasizes immanent evolutionary processes. It is a reflexive act of will in so far as the heretofore familiar, the entire set of time-tested conventions, becomes problematized. This view remains consistent with the emergent properties of disenchantment. As supporting evidence, consider Weber's comment about ascetic Protestantism in the conclusion of *The Religion of China*: "In principle, magic was eradicated even in the sublimated form of sacraments and symbols, so much so that the strict Puritan had the corpses of his loved ones dug under without any formality in order to assure the complete elimination of 'superstition.' That meant, in this context, cutting off all trust in magical manipulations. *Only* here has the complete *disenchantment of the world* been carried through with absolute consistency [*in alle Konsequenzen durchgeführt*]."[18]

Third, the disenchantment of the world in its radical consequences does not simply mean the waning of religiosity. The opposite is more likely the case. The intensification of religiosity accompanied the rise of the old Protestant sects. "The radical disenchantment of the world inwardly allowed no other path than inner worldly asceticism."[19] The result was a religious acosmism of love and the puritanical ethic of conviction. The religion of brotherliness originated beyond the community of the "natural *sib*" or other similar groups. "Prophecy has created a new social community, particularly where it became a soteriological religion of congregations. Thereby the relationships of the sib and of matrimony have been, at least relatively, devalued. The magical ties and exclusiveness of the sibs have been shattered, and within the new community the prophetic religion has developed a religious ethic of brotherliness."[20]

Thus arose the tension between the ethic of brotherliness and the world. Disenchantment is not eo ipso the death of God, to borrow Nietzsche's phrase. However, the tension between life in this world and salvation religion led to the differentiation of the different value-spheres in modern society, as Weber's splendid analysis showed in the *Zwischenbetrachtung*, the "Intermediate Reflection." The hallmark of the modern that commences with the disenchantment of the world is connected to the conscious awareness of "the *internal and lawful autonomy* [*Eigengesetzlichkeit*] of the individual spheres" and their "tensions which remain hidden to the originally naive relation with the external world."[21]

Disenchantment of the World Through Science: Calculability and Intellectualization

For Weber the process of the disenchantment of the world is still a scientific-historical process, as against the religious-historical process that can be described, generally speaking, as one of erratic reflection, a demand for consistency, and growth in religiosity. According to Weber, after Hellenism science sought to recognize law-like regularities beneath the manifold of appearances and the normal play of forces in nature beneath the violence of nature. He always emphasized the essential contribution modern science had made to the disenchantment of the world. In this respect, we can cite the famous sentences from "Science as a Vocation": "The increasing intellectualization and rationalization do *not*, therefore, indicate an increased and general knowledge of the conditions under which one lives. It means something else, namely, the knowledge or belief that if one but wished one *could* learn it at any time. Hence, it means that principally there are no mysterious incalculable forces that come into play, but rather that one can, in principle, master all things by calculation."[22]

As the sociologist of *Verstehen*, Weber sees the result of the disenchantment of the world through science less in technical calculability as such than in the knowledge about it—that is, in the widely shared insight that there are no higher powers to guide human fortunes. Furthermore, the most important result appears in the independence and autonomy of the individual value-spheres. Outside our own specialty everyone is only a layperson. But as a layperson we know that technical achievements are based on the application of the laws of nature that have been discovered in the process of collective learning. "Unless he is a physicist, one who rides on the streetcar has no idea how the car happened to get into motion. And he does not need to know. He is satisfied that he may 'count' on the behavior of the streetcar, and he orients his conduct according to this expectation; but he knows nothing about what it takes to produce such a car so that it can move."[23] Differentiation of the value-spheres and adaptation to them in everyday life are important concomitant phenomena accompanying the disenchantment of the world.

However, Weber does not explore in detail these complex historical relationships that led to the emergence of modern science. As Jürgen Habermas has noted in considering the sociological viewpoint in Weber's work, "The history of science and technology is certainly an important aspect of Western culture; but in his *sociological* attempt to *explain* the origins of modern society, Weber treats it rather as a boundary condition."[24] In Weber's own words in "Science as a Vocation," "Scientific progress is a fraction, the most important fraction, of the process of intellectualization which we have been undergoing for thousands of years."[25]

WHAT IS THE VALUE OF THE DISENCHANTMENT FORMULA TODAY?

The question becomes, to what extent today, a century later, does the formula "disenchantment of the world" have epistemological value or a knowledge-enhancing function? To be sure, the formula has served as the basis of discussion for many theoreticians, such as Horkheimer and Adorno in the *Dialectic of Enlightenment*, where in the introductory chapter they declare, "The program of the Enlightenment was the disenchantment of the world."[26] In their view the cunning of "reason" brings together the process of disenchantment with the mastery of nature. The sirens of temptation are *disenchanted* and doomed by the cunning of Odysseus. For the founders of critical theory, the dominating power of myth was most important, whereas for Weber myth was absorbed into the concept of magic. Moreover, for the exiles, Horkheimer and Adorno, religion as an element of priestly domination, executed by nonworking priests, was more important than for Weber.

Today, however, we must renew our questioning of the epistemological value of the Weberian concept. To do so requires two steps. First, we must place the thesis of the disenchantment of the world in historical context—a context in which Weber, seemingly removed from his times, represented the disenchantment process as having universal-historical significance, at least in the historical experience of the Occident. In this regard the historically conditioned thematic and limited outlook becomes evident, which even a mind like Weber's could not escape. Second, based on this context we can attempt to emerge from such a constraining perspective, though without being able consciously to know our own limiting tendencies, which can only become visible later on. Weber himself writes with a measure of sadness and resignation:

> In an age of specialization, everyone who works in the field of the cultural sciences, having decided to deal with a certain material in order to throw light on a particular set of problems, and having worked out the methodical principles [that he wants to apply], will regard his work with this material as an end in itself: he will not constantly and deliberately check whether each fact, measured against the ultimate value ideas, is worth knowing, and may even lose his awareness that it is anchored in those value ideas. That is as it should be. But, at some point, the coloring changes: the significance of those points of view that have been applied unreflectingly grows uncertain, the way forward fades away in the twilight. The light shed by the great cultural problems has moved on. Then science, too, prepares to find a new standpoint and a new conceptual apparatus, and to contemplate the stream of events from the summits of thought.[27]

The spirit of the times moves on, and thus the problematics change, altering even the vocabulary with which problems are formulated. Our questions have a limited horizon. And the limits of our questioning, irksome enough for the participant in scientific discussions, only become clearly visible for later generations.

The Misleading Connection Between Disenchantment and Loss of Meaning

Above all, one can see the most striking evidence of a bounded and limiting perspective in the close connection that Weber established between disenchantment and the loss of meaning. In relation to the problem of disenchantment, he speaks of "salvation" from "inner need" but also of the conception of "the 'world' as a problem of 'meaning,'" even "pervasive 'meaning'":

> The salvation sought by the intellectual is always based on "inner need," and hence it is at once more remote from life, more theoretical and more systematic than salvation from external distress, the quest for which is characteristic of nonprivileged strata.

The intellectual seeks in various ways, the casuistry of which extends into infinity, to endow his life [*Lebensführung*] with a pervasive "meaning," and thus to find "unity" with himself, with his fellow men, and with the cosmos. It is the intellectual who conceives of the "world" as a problem of "meaning." As intellectualism suppresses belief in magic, the world's processes become "disenchanted," lose their magical significance, and henceforth simply "are" and "happen" but no longer "signify" anything. As a consequence, there is a growing demand that the world and the total "pattern of life" [*Lebensführung*] be subject to an order that is significant and "meaningful."[28]

Correspondingly, in the words of "Science as a Vocation": "The fate of our times is characterized by rationalization and intellectualization and, above all, by the 'disenchantment of the world.' Precisely the ultimate and most sublime values have retreated from public life." Weber then comments ironically that those who cannot bear this fate "like a man" should return to "the arms of the old churches [which] are opened widely and compassionately for him."[29] What is also immediately suggestive is the self-intoxicating and suspect heroizing of the intellectual life.

Symptomatic for this way of thinking are not only expressions like the "fate" of bearing up "like a man" but also "totality." Invoking totality comes easily. It is the language of a generation that was deeply affected by Nietzsche,[30] perhaps also by Dostoevsky—a generation that after the collapse of metaphysical systems nevertheless continued to cling to residual needs for metaphysics and remained disoriented in the face of accelerating industrialization. With the "death of God" following the dissolution of the formative power of Christianity, Nietzsche had also dramatized the loss of meaning with an inflated, radicalized, and indeed consequential language: "All is the same, nothing is worth it, the world is without meaning, knowledge chokes," proclaims his own shadow in the fourth part of *Zarathustra*. The title of this chapter is "The Cry of Distress."[31] In Weber's reformulation such "meaninglessness" appears as follows: "The fate of a cultural epoch that has eaten from the tree of knowledge is that it must realize that we cannot read off the *meaning* of events in this world from the results—however complete they may be—of our scrutiny of those events, but that we ourselves must be able to create that meaning."[32] In the close connection between the loss of transcendence and loss of meaning, Charles Taylor sees a sign of the "spiritual vision" embedded in "modern humanistic consciousness." In this respect both Max Weber and Marcel Gauchet appear as successors to Nietzsche.[33]

For Weber the fact that there is no hidden world, no "secret powers" who intervene in this world, no functioning magical forces, is a result of a learning process at work for millennia, progressing from animism (rainmakers), polytheism, and monotheistically oriented prophecy to the Reformation and Calvinism. It is difficult to understand why this process, strengthened further by modern science, should lead to the meaninglessness of life, to a metaphysical longing for meaning. This is especially true because monotheism's rejection of magic actually sharpened the sense of totality, either with a sense of mission or in the Protestant conception of calling. Why should we speak of "meaning" in the singular after the decline of Christianity induced in part by science? The zeitgeist-conditioned connection became possible only through the gradual dissolution of the confessional integration of society that was accomplished after the revolutions of 1848.[34] One contributing factor was the specific residual need for metaphysics, for religion in European and above all in late nineteenth-century German circles. The other consideration was the world-historical learning process, starting with animism, that endowed life with meaning. And both are mixed together and confused in Weber's brilliant formulation.

In this regard Nietzsche and Weber have something in common: different dimensions are combined in the love for *Konsequenz*, for consequences and logical consistency. Both obscure the possibility of seeing the interactive negotiation of meaning in modernity. In saying this, I mean to suggest that, even after the death of God, people can still discuss moral principles, norms, and cultural values—that is, questions of meaning—without being burdened metaphysically by the word "meaning." Indeed, only after the removal of this transcendental cover can they engage in unconstrained discussion of important topics, assuming symmetrical conditions of communication, and without supposing naively that the "totality" is ordered "meaningfully" and endowed with "significance." To be sure, with his dispassionate sociological outlook Weber often places the concept of "meaning" in quotation marks. But that does not prevent the confusion just cited.

Furthermore, in the contemporary setting a deep entanglement in the relationship between disenchantment and loss of meaning is more than evident when Weber speaks of the "experience [of] a consecrated meaning of death which is characteristic only of death in war." He means death in "the community of the army standing in the field."[35] This characteristic style reminds one of the relevant comments in *Being and Time* on the "resoluteness" of death and the communal experience of a generation marching off to war in August 1914, though not mentioned explicitly by Heidegger.[36] That Weber is ensnared in his own times is also evident in "Science as a Vocation" when he mounts a defense against the aesthetic cult of experience promoted in the Stefan George circle, where rational science "is usually judged in such an extremely negative way."[37] A similar observation applies when he considers erotic love "in terms of intellectualist cultures." For the modern individual the "tension between the erotic sphere and rational everyday life, specifically extramarital sexual life" makes eroticism appear "as the only tie which still linked man with the natural fountain of all life."[38]

> This boundless giving of oneself is as radical as possible in its opposition to all functionality, rationality, and generality. It is displayed here as the unique meaning [!] which one creature in his irrationality has for another, and only for this specific other. However, from the point of view of eroticism, this meaning [!], and with it the value-content of the relation itself, rests upon the possibility of a communion which is felt as a complete unification, as a fading of the "thou." It is so overpowering that it is interpreted "symbolically:" as a *sacrament*.[39]

This pietistically inclined apotheosis of extramarital relations, a secularized glorification of the *unio mystica*, belongs to the many contemporary intellectual attempts at life-reform of the era. Only in the context of the times before the Great War can we understand this description of a sensibility chained to the altar of an eros with religious connotations. Death in war, the aesthetics of lived experience, erotic excitation as consequences of the disenchantment of the world (as Weber would have judged such phenomena) no longer belong to the vocabulary of our time, nor does his naive opposition between the everyday and the extraordinary. Such expressions belong to the context of the intellectual circles, dominated by masculinity, and their efforts at orientation prior to, during, and after the First World War. The British Weber scholar Richard Jenkins writes not by accident of the "definitively masculine character of Weber's thought."[40]

These notions are related to the special position of purposive rationality or *Zweckrationalität* in Weber's conception of rationality, an aspect of his thinking revealed in the urge for logical consistency, for *Konsequenz*. The relationship likely emerged from practical experience with industrial capitalism, which spread quickly and was specific to the times. The omnipresence of this development in society, labeled "instrumental reason" later by Max Horkheimer, encouraged a consequential objectification and led to the thesis that the result of disenchantment would be loss of meaning. Thus, the dimension of human interaction became underappreciated and ignored. As many activities in civil society demonstrate, it is through human interactions that actual "meaning" is negotiated, rather than some larger half-metaphysical "meaning." For example, many civic activists see the actual and current but not the ultimate "meaning" of life in their ecological engagement or in their voluntary participation in the acceptance and social integration of immigrants. The disenchantment of the world need not lead to a nihilistic backward glance while teetering on the edge of the abyss.

A WRONG TURN: RE-ENCHANTMENT OF THE WORLD THROUGH CONSUMERISM

In no way can we reduce such a grand conception as the disenchantment of the world to the context of its origins, just as we cannot make sense of Aristotle's concept of politics wholly within the context of the ancient polis. So we can take a *second* step to attempt a critical revision of the conception and one relevant to the present.

In search of a critical revision, many sociologists and cultural theorists believe they can identify a re-enchantment of the disenchanted world in the realm of capitalist consumerism, as well as in the nationalistic hyped-up symbols and rituals of the state. A Weberian like Richard Jenkins is concerned with the rituals that every organization requires: for example, on the one hand, the governmental practices of self-representation and, on the other hand, the glittering world of consumption and the media. "Formal organizations are not insulated containers of rationality. What is more, as institutions with boundaries, authority structures which require legitimation, and memberships which have to be required and retained, bureaucracies are themselves constitutive of a broad panoply of collective enchantments, in the form of rituals, symbols, legends, traditions and so on." Moreover, he speaks of "the mundane daydreams of advertising and consumption: cinematic escapism; science fiction and fantasy; and, not least, the virtual attractions available on the internet." In his concise formulation, "we are back to disenchanted enchantment again."[41]

In my view, however, the concepts of disenchantment and re-enchantment are overextended by such generalizations, for it is hardly a matter of an event or occurrence in which some sort of "secret powers" intervene in our mortal world when marketing strategies produce attractive products, such as automobiles or personal computers, or when political consultants stage acts of state. Other conceptual strategies are better suited to analyzing these phenomena. For example, in his analysis of the world of commodities in the Parisian arcades, Walter Benjamin spoke not of a new enchantment but of a *phantasmagoria* inherent in commodities. Out of it he tried dialectically to read a symbol of prehistory or, as he formulated it, a classless society. It is no counterevidence for Weber's disenchantment thesis that today a president of a state can review an honor guard and that this public display of pomp can have a certain aura, and thus an enchanting effect. In no sense do such ceremonies aspire magically to banish evil spirits. Thus, in the conjuring hocus-pocus of the present, the evidence for the re-enchantment strategy in the world of consumption and public state ceremonies hardly reaches the level of detached criticism. For this criticism one does not need to apply Weber's concept of disenchantment.

Against the Disenchantment Formula: "Nothing Is Ever Lost"

The effort of the sociologist of religion Robert N. Bellah to relativize the Weberian understanding of disenchantment is a completely different matter that should be seriously considered. Bellah bases his view on a precise microsociological observation in the sociology of religion: "Just as the face-to-face rituals of tribal society continue in disguised form among us, so also the unity of political and religious power, the archaic 'mortgage.'" Today the king of "God's grace" arrives in a modified form as a president "who claim[s] to act in accordance with a 'higher power.'" Bellah's thesis is that "Nothing is ever lost."[42] According to Bellah, precise observation of our everyday rituals leads us to the conclusion that everyday life consists of "endless 'interaction ritual chains.'"[43] And many rituals presuppose the physical presence of persons. For example, from shaking hands to marriage ceremonies to burial services, Bellah shows how many archaic factors still shape our everyday life. At the altar one cannot say "yes" using Skype. The presence of a congregation is also indispensable for important ceremonies that mark a passage in life, such as a marriage or a death. That has been the case throughout human history: a reflexive breakthrough at the beginning of the Axial Age, ushering in the process of disenchantment, "does not mean the abandonment of what went before. Theoretic culture is added to mythic and mimetic culture."[44]

In Weber's view all magical means in the search for salvation were rejected as "superstition and sacrilege" in the great religious-historical process of the disenchantment of the world. Bellah instead emphasizes the always present chains of everyday rituals and their archaic character, which are never-ending and indeed always returning, typically in altered forms. In the long sweep of history the intellectual breakthrough does not signify a turning away from the archaic dimension. In his phrasing, the theory cannot replace the "story." Bellah notes in his sardonic way, "There are even anti-ritual rituals."[45] However, in no way does Bellah's standpoint signify a negation of Weber's thesis. It represents much more a supplement, as he proposes that in the disenchanted world as well, nothing of the archaic dimension to life has disappeared. Once again, nothing is ever lost.

As a sober sociologist, Weber of course knew that human beings do not live exclusively with thoughts of their salvation and that everyday life requires rituals which are not unconditionally bound up with questions of salvation. He refers not just to societies before the Axial Age when he writes, "religious or magical behavior or thinking must not be set apart from the range of everyday purposive conduct, particularly since even the ends of the religious and magical actions are predominantly economic."[46] Only contemporaries of the time can judge, either partly or fully enlightened, whether magic is involved in one or another ritual action or whether a kernel of rationality resides within it. A "naturalistic outlook" always accompanies all theorizing. In Weber's words, "To this day, no decision of church councils…has succeeded in deterring a south European peasant from spitting in front of the statue of a saint when he holds it responsible for withholding a favor even though the customary procedures were performed."[47] Nevertheless, from Weber's perspective, in terms of rationality this southern European leaves something to be desired; he is still backward in comparison with the Protestant northern European.

Weber's hierarchies and oppositions are no longer valid for Bellah: to bear the fate of the disenchanted world "like a man" *or* to return to the "arms of the old churches," to lead a methodical life guided by principle *or* to relapse into the "magic garden," to live free from superstition *or* to be trapped in the occult. These polar opposites are the result of thinking driven by objectifying consistency. But today, two centuries after the Enlightenment in the age of biotechnology and innovative science, we actually still find many actions and explanations in the everyday world that inhabit the gray zone between "superstition" and rituals validated communally.

Consider some examples. After forgetting someone's birthday, the "rule" is always better late than never with a salutation. For friends departing on a skiing holiday, we extend the ironic missive to "break a leg!" so that nothing bad will happen. In many Western countries the number 13 is omitted in hotels for well-known reasons, though no rational guest would be convinced by them, but which most nevertheless gladly accept. In both Japan and Korea the room number 4 is often missing, because the homonym of the number (*shi* in Japanese or *sa* in Korean) can mean "death." At the Russian space center in Baikonur a Russian Orthodox priest always gives a ritual blessing before the launch of a manned spaceship. The main airport of Haneda in Japan has a Shinto shrine devoted to the safety of a flight and its passengers. The shrine honors three gods from Japanese mythology, who are said to have helped the first emperor achieve a victory with an aircraft they cobbled together themselves. In his speech to flight personnel and the pilots' association at Fiumicino airport in Rome, Pope Benedict XVI, a level-headed rational theology professor, reminded his audience of the protective patron of flight safety, the Mother of God of Loretto. In both cases it is a matter of a so-called functional deity, to speak with Weber. Another example would be the insignia C+M+B, *Christus mansionem benedicat* (Christ blesses this house), which one can see on many house doors in rural southern Germany as a vestige of epiphany. Many still believe in the legend of the Black Madonna of Altötting, or shall we say that they behave as if they believe in the legendary miracle. That is also true of the legend passed down at Klosterneuburg, a suburb of Vienna. On New Year's Day in Japan many citizens go to a famous Shinto shrine or a Buddhist temple and pray for happiness and health for themselves and their families in the New Year. Most do not believe in the effect of their prayers, but they do it anyway because it creates a positive feeling and uplifting mood for the year ahead. This practice became a mass phenomenon only in the 1920s. In Korea on the day of the national achievement test for entrance to the university, many parents gather at a temple in Seoul and pray together for their children's success. Based on the price of admission, the best and second-best seats are allocated just as in the opera. In no sense do parents believe in a miraculous outcome, but for children it is reason enough to concentrate on the task at hand when they know their parents have sacrificed an entire day for them. Finally, in Russia too there are many female faith healers, who reputedly can heal severe illnesses by a laying on of hands.

"MULTIPLE MODERNITIES" AND THE NEED TO REVISE CLASSICAL CONCEPTS

We can see how extensive the gray zone is. Of course, these impromptu examples display quite different characteristics. Only a few belong to the line of thought expressed by Bellah's sentence, "Nothing is ever lost." Many tall stories and deceptions are involved too. There are also episodes that only invite a smile, along with historical habits that seem a bit homely and commonplace. If a person is involved in one of these rituals, she or he must be prepared to discuss what can be accepted, or even welcomed, and what can be politely avoided or strongly repudiated. Most readers of this essay will not believe in faith healers, for example: "Most of us ... no longer seek the curing powers of a wise-woman or a cunning man if we are ill. We go to our doctor."[48] Most readers will also smile if in the newspaper they see a picture of a priest in front of a spacecraft, even though they find nothing objectionable about the doorway inscription on a half-timbered home in southern Germany. Observing the consecration of the most modern spacecraft, some may offer critical remarks about the church's adaptation to the state, though without distancing themselves from their own pieties at Christmas. Naturally it is hypocrisy when in Arthur Schnitzler's drama *Professor Bernhardi* a colleague named Professor Filitz, an ambitious and honor-seeking philistine, proclaims, "But I can assure you that belief and science go together nicely. I would even like to say that science without belief will always remain a somewhat uncertain affair, for then the moral foundation, the ethos, is missing." On the other hand, however, among natural scientists a considerable number are practicing Christians.

Weber ignored this gray zone, or he spoke of compromises. In his view it can only be a matter of a compromise if a natural scientist declares his faith in a religion. There is considerable discussion of compromises in the *Zwischenbetrachtung* as well as *Economy and Society*. In Weber's vocabulary, and not his alone, compromise has a negative connotation, whereas the "imperative of consistency" sounds elevated and sometimes even heroic. Weber's thinking begins with idealistic constructions like disenchantment versus "magic garden" or life conduct guided by principles versus compromise. For this reason, important thematic content for sociology, from which I have drawn examples, remains a broad uncultivated field occupied by the "underprivileged strata" of ordinary humanity. And this field of inquiry is decisive for the comparative sociology of culture and religion!

In this regard, with his thesis "Nothing is ever lost" Robert Bellah can provide us with further assistance, above all with respect to the problem of secularization.

The classical model of secularization, recognized as dominant in northwestern Europe, can no longer be applied to other parts of Europe, such as Poland, not to mention other parts of the world. In terms of the exceptional character of northwestern Europe, this appears as the consensus even in the discussion of "multiple modernities" (S. N. Eisenstadt). The sinologist Rudolf G. Wagner notes that for Buddhism the world was never anything other than secular. For this reason, it had "fewer problems with secularization in modernity than with the accompanying world-wide obsession with wealth and power."[49] Moreover, José Casanova contends that even in the classical West the narrative of secularization can be called into question. For the Spanish sociologist, precisely the debate over Turkey's entry into the European Union demonstrates how entrenched a secularized western Europe remains with regard to its Christian religious tradition.[50] If caution is advisable in using the concept of secularization in the West and a more complex understanding is attempted, then for other parts of the world the concept is scarcely usable. In sum, there are very different types of "secularization," for which the conception of the disenchantment of the world hardly retains any scientific meaning or utility.

THE NARRATIVE OF COMMEMORATION IN A DISENCHANTED WORLD

The concept of multiple modernities can be easily misapplied, above all politically by those in power and their cultural apologists in defense of normatively unacceptable abuses, as in the case of Singapore. The concept can also be made to serve the cultural self-assertion of an emerging nation.[51] But it also presents the possibility of another thesis, namely, that multiple modernities means multiplicity in the *semantics of resistance* to the distortions of the modern.[52] For the discussion of disenchantment in the context of multiple modernities, it is important to have a narrative of commemoration that remembers those who have been unjustly sacrificed by brutal modernization.

Numerous literary texts provide evidence for such a claim. One example would be the texts in Japanese literature that have been written about the surviving victims of the atomic bomb, Minamata disease (mercury poisoning), or the atomic reactor catastrophe in Fukushima. Joined to this literature are also texts written by those who take care of the victims, those who have died, and those who suffer from unspeakable pain and handicaps. Notwithstanding differences in the causes and the character among these authors, a common thread is found in discussion of the departed souls of those who had to endure unjustified suffering and death. Their souls still wander aimlessly, without the prospect of admission to the beyond. The description of the encounter with these restless souls often occurs in a language that borders on the animistic and pre-animistic dimensions of life. This is true even for the *Hiroshima Notes* of Ōe Kenzaburō, winner of the Nobel Prize for literature, as well as for Michiko Ishimure and her book *Paradise in the Sea of Sorrow*, in which she describes the fate of those afflicted with mercury poisoning, the victims of ecological catastrophe in a fishing village.[53] She is the author who speaks knowingly of the "animistic" and "pre-animistic" in her own commentaries. Her prose mixes together resignation determined by fate and cries of desperation but also social criticism and critical analysis of capitalism. In this prosaic form the light of a paradise understood in Buddhist terms shines through, seen with this many-sided combination of desperation and anger, resignation and retreat, clear analysis and rational juridical speech. On the existence of such a paradise—and this is the most important point in our discussion—scarcely anyone *actually* believes, though almost everyone believes a little in its partial existence. The world is indeed disenchanted but still not thoroughly disenchanted, above all when it comes to contact with its victims. "In order to understand the quiet resignation, the composure, and even serenity of many patients in face of their unbearable suffering, their pride in refusing financial support, compensation, or medical help, we have to kind of reenact their attitude towards life, their religiosity, and their strong bonds with nature and their community." These are the words of Irmela Hijiya-Kirschnereit, the Japanese specialist, in her introduction to the German translation of Ishimure.[54]

The narrative of commemoration that has spread throughout East Asia, with its pre-animistic phase of life, is of course not limited to a single region of the world. Something similar is found in the commemorative myths related to those who perished in the slave ships crossing the Atlantic. In the 2017–2018 program for Berlin's Deutsches Theater, we find this account: "The underwater world between Africa and America, Drexciya by name, forms a powerful myth, a place populated with sea creatures produced by African women who threw themselves overboard during the dreadful passage, before they could be sold as slaves in America. According to the myth, the dying women brought children of the sea into the world who created a new population beneath the surface of the sea."[55] The language of resistance is produced by this non-disenchanted relationship of the departed to an already disenchanted world. In a ceremony in May 2015, Vienna's Museum of Ethnology returned the recently discovered human remains of Maoris to a Maori delegation so that they could be buried at home in the circle of their descendants. In 1822 these remains were taken from a Maori burial ground by the naturalist Andreas Beischek "without a lot of moral reservations," according to the museum's information guide. For Austrian ethnologists the world then was already disenchanted.

A DIALECTIC PATH TO MODERNITY: REASSESSING RELIGIOUS POTENTIAL WITHIN THE BOUNDS OF RATIONALITY

We return to the beginning passages of this chapter, where through Walter Benjamin's questioning we addressed the Protestant, enlightened, objectifying way of dealing with deceased ancestors. Benjamin knew, just as did Robert Bellah, that the old religious potentiality will never be lost. In relation to Weber's "Protestantism" essay, and in opposition to it, Benjamin writes that

> One can behold in capitalism a religion, that is to say, capitalism essentially serves to satisfy the same worries, anguish, and disquiet formerly answered by so-called religion. The proof of capitalism's religious structure as *not only* a religiously conditioned construction, as Weber maintained, but as an *essentially religious* phenomenon, would still mislead one today into a boundless, universal polemic.[56]

In addition, he contends that capitalism is a pure religious cult, "perhaps the most extreme that has ever existed." The religion called "capitalism" distinguishes itself in opposition to other religions through "the permanent duration of the cult."[57] In classical religion, for example, in Christianity, the "cult" makes its presence known on Sundays, whereas in capitalism it occurs every day and at every moment with the creation of new commodities and with every advertisement. Against this permanent cult, Benjamin attempts in another way than capitalism to mediate the archaic-mythical with the language of modern rationalism—and perhaps in vain. In this attempt he saw the only possibility of avoiding the catastrophe preprogrammed into capitalism. For this reason, Benjamin would gladly connect with the discursive culture of remembrance, as found in the briefly cited literature of mourning. It is a culture in which the old semantics of departed, though not completely dead, souls can become reinstated after a lengthy dose of disenchantment, as a means of opposition to the brutality of the modern. "The only writer of history with the gift of setting alight sparks of hope in the past," writes Benjamin, is the person who sees that "The past carries a secret index within it, by which it is referred to its resurrection. Are we not touched by the same breath of air which was among that which came before? Is there not an echo of those who have been silenced in the voices to which we lend our ears today?"[58]

To render Weber's strong disenchantment thesis serviceable today, or to reactivate it, we must be able to reflect simultaneously on his view of the irreversibility of the learning process, together with Bellah's conception of the continuity of magical rituals. For this purpose, we need to take up aspects of religion in everyday life, animated by the discussion of multiple modernities. Thus, it is a matter of mediating the historical and intellectual repudiation of magic and ritual with the continuity of magical-mythic thinking and to do so, to be sure, in order to rescue the past in the spirit of Walter Benjamin. Otherwise we will remain trapped in Weber's agonistic thought and unable to escape the suspect attraction of heroic words and deeds.

We find the metaphor of heroic engagement in the famous sentences about the struggle of the gods in "Science as a Vocation":

> We live as did the ancients when their world was not yet disenchanted of its gods and demons, only we live in a different sense. As Hellenic man at times sacrificed to Aphrodite and at other times to Apollo, and, above all, as everybody sacrificed to the gods of his city, so do we still nowadays, only the bearing of man has been disenchanted and denuded of its mystical but inwardly genuine plasticity. *Fate*, and certainly not "science," holds sway over these gods and their struggles....
>
> Many old gods ascend from their graves; they are disenchanted and hence take the form of impersonal forces. They strive to gain power over our lives and again they resume their eternal struggle with one another.[59]

Since David Hume there has been thought inclined toward anti-monotheism or, better stated, the tradition of a thought experiment that gives preference to polytheism over monotheism. Weber knew the measured reflections of John Stuart Mill about whether polytheism would be perhaps a more natural expression of the human spirit.[60] In one of his aphorisms (which Weber certainly knew), Nietzsche also spoke of "the greatest advantage of polytheism" for the benefit of individualism and the "free-spiriting and many-spiriting" of humankind and "the strength to create for ourselves our own new eyes—and ever again new eyes that are even more our own."[61] People knew that coexistence of the gods is possible, that they are not just locked in an eternal struggle. Nevertheless, Weber spoke of a struggle of the gods because of his "remarkably Christian-monotheistic profile," as Hartmann Tyrell has said[62] and, I would add, a remarkable pattern of Christian-monotheistic views specific to the fin de siècle. Weber surely knew not only that gods can coexist but that monotheism can survive alongside polytheism, even partly of an animistic type. This possibility exists because of the imperative of consistency, although it is a completely different kind of consistency. This different kind of consistency, as Aby Warburg could plausibly make visible in his work on the Renaissance, was something Weber could not comprehend very well, despite the fact that he would have had to take it seriously in Italy, at least at the theoretical level, where the coexistence of a Catholic God and many saints, above all the Virgin Mary, was a feature of everyday life. But for Weber, all of this was ultimately "compromises."

Today, nevertheless, in the elevation of the heroic which has become foreign to us, there is something hidden in the previously cited sentences about the struggle of the gods ascending from their graves. It is the insight, perhaps not fully evident to Weber, that surely binds him to Benjamin and Bellah: namely, that nothing is lost, that disenchantment does not unconditionally compel a loss of meaning, but that precisely in the disenchanted world religious potential in a transfigured form can still become visible, and even in a rational way. This means taking a critical stance against the brutality of modern systems, but without romanticizing the past.

Translated from the German by Lawrence A. Scaff

NOTES

1. Robert N. Bellah, "What Is Axial About the Axial Age?" *European Journal of Sociology* 46, no. 1 (2005): 69–89, 72.
2. Weber, "Religious Rejections of the World and Their Directions," in *From Max Weber: Essays in Sociology* (hereafter *FMW*), ed. H. H. Gerth and C. W. Mills (New York: Oxford, 1946), 324; "Zwischenbetrachtung," in *Die Wirtschaftsethik der Weltreligionen. Konfuzianismus und Taoismus. Schriften 1915–1920, Max Weber-Gesamtausgabe* (hereafter *MWG*) I/19, ed. H. Schmidt-Glintzer, with P. Kolonko (Tübingen, Germany: Mohr [Siebeck], 1989), 480.
3. Walter Benjamin, "Goethe's Elective Affinities [Wahlverwandtschaften]," *Selected Writings*, vol. 1, *1913–1926*, ed. M. Bullock and M. W. Jennings (Cambridge, MA: Belknap Press, 2002), 302.
4. Ibid.
5. Ibid, 302–303.
6. Ibid, 302.
7. Ibid, 304.
8. Weber, *The Protestant Ethic and the Spirit of Capitalism* (hereafter *PESC*), trans. Talcott Parsons (New York: Scribner's, 1958), 104–105 (translation modified according to the original); *Die protestantische Ethik und der Geist des Kapitalismus/Die protestantische Sekten und der Geist des Kapitalismus. Schriften 1904–1920, MWG* I/18, ed. W. Schluchter, with U. Bube (Tübingen, Germany: Mohr [Siebeck], 2016), 280–281.
9. Weber, *Economy and Society* (hereafter *E&S*), ed. G. Roth and C. Wittich (Berkeley: University of California Press, 1978), 432; *Wirtschaft und Gesellschaft. Nachlaß. Religiöse Gemeinschaften, MWG* I/22-2, ed. H. G. Kippenberg, with P. Schilm (Tübingen, Germany: Mohr [Siebeck], 2001), 167.
10. *E&S*, 1179; *Wirtschaft und Gesellschaft. Nachlaß. Herrschaft, MWG* I/22-4, ed. E. Hanke, with Th. Kroll (Tübingen, Germany: Mohr [Siebeck], 2005), 622.
11. *E&S*, 448; *MWG* I/22-2, 190.
12. *PESC*, 221–222n19; *MWG* I/18, 280.
13. *E&S*, 419; *MWG* I/22-2, 152–153.
14. *PESC*, 117; *MWG* I/18, 320 (translation modified according to the original).
15. *PESC*, 147; *MWG* I/18, 398 (translation altered).

16. Weber, "Science as a Vocation," in *FMW*, 139; *Wissenschaft als Beruf 1917/1919—Politik als Beruf 1919, MWG* I/17, ed. W. J. Mommsen and W. Schluchter, with B. Morgenbrod (Tübingen, Germany: Mohr [Siebeck], 1992), 87.

17. Weber, "Zwischenbetrachtung," *FMW*, 327; *MWG* I/19, 484 (translation modified).

18. Weber, *The Religion of China: Confucianism and Taoism*, trans. H. H. Gerth (New York: Free Press, 1951), 226; *MWG* I/19, 451 (translation modified; italics in the original).

19. *PESC*, 149; *MWG* I/18, 403 (sentence retranslated).

20. *FMW*, 329; *MWG* I/19, 485–486.

21. *FMW*, 328; *MWG* I/19, 485. See Robert N. Bellah, "Max Weber and World-Denying Love: A Look at the Historical Sociology of Religion" (lecture, University of California at San Diego, San Diego, CA, October 30, 1997), http://www.robertbellah.com/articles_2.htm (accessed December 10, 2017).

22. *FMW*, 139; *MWG* I/17, 86–87. There is a certain conceptual similarity, scarcely noticed previously, to Martin Heidegger in his Zürich lecture of 1938, "The Age of the World Picture," in which he speaks of calculation and mastery but also of enterprise, an important figure of speech in "Science as a Vocation." It is well known that Heidegger ignored Max Weber, so it cannot be a matter of "swiping" his ideas. Instead, it is a matter of a shared conceptual strategy, common to the German *Geisteswissenschaften*, whose transformation engaged Nietzsche with his fondness for the word "mastery."

23. *FMW*, 139; *MWG* I/17, 86.

24. Jürgen Habermas, *The Theory of Communicative Action*, vol. 1, *Reason and the Rationalization of Society*, trans. T. McCarthy (Boston: Beacon Press, 1984), 159.

25. *FMW*, 138; *MWG* I/17, 86.

26. Max Horkheimer and Theodor W. Adorno, *Dialectic of Enlightenment*, trans. J. Cumming (1944; New York: Continuum, 1987), 3.

27. Weber, "The 'Objectivity' of Knowledge in Social Science and Social Policy," in *Collected Methodological Writings* (hereafter *CMW*), ed. H. H. Bruun and S. Whimster, trans. H. H. Bruun (London: Routledge, 2012), 138; *Zur Logik und Methodik der Sozialwissenschaften. Schriften 1900–1907, MWG* I/7, ed. G. Wagner, with C. Härpfer et al. (Tübingen, Germany: Mohr [Siebeck], 2018), 233–234.

28. *E&S*, 506; *MWG* I/22-2, 273 (translation modified according to the original).

29. *FMW*, 155; *MWG* I/17, 109–110.

30. On Nietzsche's inspiration for Weber, see Wilhelm Hennis, *Max Weber: Essays in Reconstruction*, trans. Keith Tribe (London: Allen & Unwin, 1988), 146–162.

31. Nietzsche, *Thus Spoke Zarathustra*, trans. Adrian del Caro (Cambridge: Cambridge University Press, 2006), 194.

32. *CMW*, 104; *MWG* I/7, 153.

33. Charles Taylor, *A Secular Age* (Cambridge, MA: Belknap Press, 2007), 572, 678.

34. On re-confessionalization in the nineteenth century, see Olaf Blaschke, "Das 19. Jahrhundert: Ein zweites konfessionelles Zeitalter," *Geschichte und Gesellschaft* 26 (2000): 38–75.

35. *FMW*, 335; *MWG* I/19, 492.

36. To the reader's amazement, in this passage Heidegger addresses the significance of the nation and the *generation* as a community willed by fate, so to speak: *Being and Time*, trans. J. Macquarrie and E. Robinson (Oxford: Blackwell, 1962), 436.

37. *FMW*, 138–139; *MWG* I/17, 86.

38. *FMW*, 346; *MWG* I/19, 506.

39. *FMW*, 347; *MWG* I/19, 507 (author's emphasis).

40. Richard Jenkins, "Disenchantment, Enchantment and Re-Enchantment: Max Weber at the Millennium," *Max Weber Studies* 1, no. 1 (2000): 11–32, 22.
41. Jenkins, "Disenchantment," 14, 18. Johannes Weiß traces the thirst for re-enchantment to romanticism in "Wiederentzauberung der Welt? Bemerkungen zur Wiederkehr der Romantik in der gegenwärtigen Kulturkritik," in *Kultur-Soziologie. Klassische Texte der neueren deutschen Kultursoziologie*, ed. Stephan Moebius and Clemens Albrecht (Wiesbaden, Germany: Springer, 2004), 347–366.
42. Bellah, "What Is Axial About the Axial Age?," 72.
43. Ibid., 84; in this regard Bellah appeals to Durkheim and Goffman.
44. Ibid., 83.
45. Ibid., 85.
46. *E&S*, 400; *MWG* I/22-2, 122.
47. E&S, 401; *MWG* I/22-2, 123.
48. Jenkins, "Disenchantment," 18.
49. Rudolf G. Wagner, "Säkularisierung: Konfuzianismus und Buddhismus," in *Säkularisierung und die Weltreligionen*, ed. H. Joas and K. Wiegand (Frankfurt am Main, Germany: S. Fischer, 2007), 242–243; Wagner criticizes Weber for failing to see the "prejudices and biases" about China entrenched in the scientific literature of the time (245).
50. José Casanova, "Die religiöse Lage in Europe," in *Säkularisierung und die Weltreligionen*, 345–346.
51. On the concept of cultural self-assertion and affirmation, see Iwo Amelung et al., *Selbstbehauptungsdiskurse in Asien: China, Japan, Korea* (Munich: Iudicium, 2003), and above all my essay therein: Kenichi Mishima, "Ästhetisierung zwischen Hegemoniekritik und Selbstbehauptung," 25–47. See also Michael Lackner, ed., *Zwischen Selbstbestimmung und Selbstbehauptung: Ostasiatische Diskurse des 20. und 21. Jahrhunderts* (Baden-Baden, Germany: Nomos, 2008).
52. For the "semantics of resistance," see my essay, "Eine Moderne-viele Modernen. Zwischen normativem Leitbild, Verbrechen und Widerstand," *Zeitschrift WestEnd, Neue Zeitschrift für Sozialforschung* 1 (2014): 147–162; in what follows I have reworked a couple of passages from this essay.
53. Ōe Kenzaburō, *Hiroshima Notes*, trans. D. L. Swain and T. Yonezawa (New York: Grove Press, 1981), and Michiko Ishimure, *Paradise in the Sea of Sorrow: Our Minamata Disease*, trans. L. Monnet (Ann Arbor: University of Michigan Press, 2003).
54. Michiko Ishimure, *Paradies im Meer der Qualen. Unserer Minamata-Krankheit*, trans. U. Gräfe (Frankfurt am Main, Germany: Insel, 1995), 10.
55. Deutsches Theater Berlin, *Welche Zukunft* (2017): 87.
56. Walter Benjamin, *Gesammelte Schriften* (Frankfurt am Main, Germany: Suhrkamp, 1986), 6:100 (fragment 74 on "Capitalism as Religion") (author's emphasis).
57. Ibid.
58. Walter Benjamin, "On the Concept of History," trans. D. Redmond, http://www.marxists .org/reference/archive/benjamin/1940/history.htm; *Gesammelte Schriften* (Frankfurt am Main, Germany: Suhrkamp, 1991), 1-2:695, 693 (theses VI and II).
59. *FMW*, 148, 149; *MWG* I/17, 100, 101 (author's emphasis). On Weber's metaphor, see Hartmann Tyrell's excellent discussion, in which he sees it as a cure for disillusionment, emphasizing that ultimately Weber moves within a Christian-monotheistic framework: "'Kampf der Götter'–'Polytheismus der Werte'. Variationen zu einem Thema von Max

Weber," in *"Religion" in der Soziologie Max Webers*, ed. H. Tyrell (Wiesbaden, Germany: Harrassowitz, 2014), 251–272.

60. See esp. J. S. Mill's essay "Theism" in *Three Essays on Religion* (Peterborough, Canada: Broadview Press, 2009 [1874]).

61. Nietzsche, *The Gay Science*, trans. W. Kaufmann (New York: Vintage, 1974), 191–192 (III.143).

62. Tyrell, "'Kampf der Götter,'" 275.

CHAPTER 20

THE LITERATI AND THE DAO

Vernacular and Nation in China

SCOTT LASH

INTRODUCTION

THE central figure of the first part of Max Weber's *General Economic History* is the clan. The clan is a lineage group that has or claims a common ancestor. In southern China, a village of say 1,500 people may only have three clans or lineage groups. There are a number of Western mechanisms of individualization and universalization that bypass the clans in China. These mechanisms are clan destroyers in the West. Weber ties the clan not to Daoism or Confucianism, which are more or less world religions, but instead more or less to magic. Magic, in this context for Weber, stands as the polar opposite of Protestantism.[1]

The first destroyer of the clan in Western rationalization is feudalism itself. The one-to-one quasi-contractuality of Hegel's *Herrschaft und Knechtschaft*—of lord and vassal—already presumes the dissolution of the clan. Clan and *mir*, unlike in western Europe, persist in China and Russia. In China, when rule is fragmented in the Shang dynasty and in the Spring and Autumn and Warring States, there existed a more feudal, manorial division of land. The Qin dynasty restoration of Zhou "absolutism" overcame feudal fragmentation; hence, clan and village ownership of property persisted and have lasted until this very day. Weber observed that the strength of the clan in contrast to the weakness of the state meant that the state did not bureaucratize as in the West, where this was driven not by Confucian humanists but by jurisprudential knowledge. The main source of this jurisprudence is Roman private and civil law. The origins of rational, which Weber called "formal," law were not in Greece but in Rome, in what Hannah Arendt termed the ultimate political space of Rome. Formalism of law was a precondition for the later calculability crucial for the modern capitalist.[2] This stands in contrast to the not formal but instead "material" formations of Chinese law. Weber gives the example of someone who purchases a house. Were the previous owner to fall into poverty, there was a strong convention that the purchaser was obligated to take him back as a free renter.

The second clan destroyer in the West is the city. In Confucian China the Mandarin, who had his seat much like the western bishops in every city, knew nothing of statecraft. There was no rationalization of a centralized state bureaucracy, as achieved in France under Louis XIV. A legal-rational bureaucracy needs the application of rational jurisprudence, whereas the provincialized Mandarin was oriented to the *Analects* or the writings of Mencius. State rationalization in the West penetrates the population at large and leads to an instrumental and individualizing attitude. In China, Weber notes, the state stays largely separate from the people, and the clan structure, closely tied to magic and not religion, persists. One basis of Western capitalism for Weber is the independence of the city. In China, in contrast, the army of the prince is older than the city. The empire and not the city principle dominates, at least as far back as the Zhou dynasty (1050–750 BCE) and through to modernity. With no city and the hegemony of the clan there can be no Western oikos/polis dichotomy that thinkers from Arendt to Foucault but also Weber have thematized. Indeed, there is no (political) polis and its military "phratry" but only the lineage-based clan of multigenerational family and the dominance of the "prince."[3]

There is a second, anti-clan movement in the West, namely the medieval guild city, a development the Chinese clan did not experience. Craftsman-based urban Christianity was another anti-clan formation, whereas Confucianism partly reinforced clan structure and in particular its lineage base. Paul the Apostle and the other apostles were wandering tradesmen and carriers of prophetic religion. Weber's prophet intones, "it (tradition) is written, but I (prophecy) say unto you." Indeed, as the Evangelist John says, you follow me and you have to "say goodbye to your family," your hearth, your magic and wider kinship and clan. Paul promotes universalism, ordering that the uncircumcised may sit down and eat with the Jew, which stands against the particularism of clan and magic. Weber brings this out more strongly in the *General Economic History* than in the *Religion of China*, where he places the emphasis on Confucian elites. Magic stands in the path of a rational capitalism. So there seems to be a chasm between the "magic" of the clans and indeed the guilds with their preference for geomancy.[4] The famous Confucian five relationships do bear a marked resemblance to the everyday family life of the clan.

In contrast, the *I Ching* was a divining manual yet had what Leibniz saw as its own rationality in the yin and yang combinations in trigrams and hexagrams. China's unification via the script of a written language represented iconically and penetrating to a few in each village is a step in the direction of rationalization, though not so much as the more abstract phonetic alphabets in Indo-European languages. In Durkheim and Mauss's *Primitive Classifications* Chinese classifications are seen as less rational than Western modernity, yet more rational than hunting and gathering social formations. Major decisions in regard to selling land and land redivisions needed clan approval.[5]

How then did China enjoy such great economic success until c. 1750? It was the Qing dynasty (1636–1912 CE) that rationalized the Chinese economy and society. Without the Qing, there would not have arisen a Cantonese overseas monopoly guild of merchants. In the Tang and Song dynasties markets were already developing in foreign trade. But Weber had no interest in writing a history of China and the exact place of the Qing dynasty in rationalizing the immanent forces within Chinese civilization, just as he had no interest in writing a history of the West. He was interested instead in the peculiar rationalism of the West and its instrumentalization of rationality. Weber never extended this interest to Marcel Mauss's anthropological argument that all social relations embody some, and different forms of rationality. Clan shrines are still everywhere in rural China, yet all work takes place in cities. Clans and lineages remain important. While Weberian exact calculability may be absent in Chinese history, we have to accept the operation of a quasi-calculability that allowed lineage and business to coexist, a relationship capable of a rationalization process in its own right.

This chapter, while drawing on all of the above, will argue that Weber's Confucianism is neither this worldly nor otherworldly but, with François Jullien, an "in between" or "between worldly:" between the *wu wei* and instrumental rationality, between sacred and profane, between ideal and material. In making this point I will bring in the linguistic dimension which Weber largely ignores, supplementing his understanding of China and its relationship to the West. I will introduce a number of linguistic concepts— *langue-pensée*, analogical culture—in order to contrast Indo-European languages with Chinese language. This produces a civilizational difference and a new site to locate civilizational rationalization. The contrast, on the one side, is the more analytic and propositional Western *langue-pensée*, especially the clarity and precision of phonological Sanskrit, and, on the other side, the comparatively alexical and antigrammar of ancient Chinese. In such a context, I will draw substantially on Sheldon Pollock's *The Language of the Gods in the World of Men: Sanskrit, Culture and Power in Premodern India*.[6]

If we think in terms of Kant's three critiques, we can identify Weber with instrumental and practical rationality of the first two critiques and Pollock with the third critique of the rationality of aesthetic judgment. Pollock is concerned with the poetics of culture— in Sanskrit culture and south Asian culture more generally, extending also to the whole of southeast Asia. The larger point is that if we were to speak in terms of "world cultures" rather than "world religions," we could generalize or ideal-typify Western cultures as organized by the epistemology, and hence instrumentality of Sanskrit cultures, and Chinese culture by the poetic lack of finality and the moral cosmology of an embedded ethics of Confucianism, importantly driven by the way of the Dao.[7]

Pollock also gives us as a theory of rationalization, not the rationalization of knowing and changing the world (Weber's theory of knowledge) but a rationalization of the poetic. What is meant by this? The answer lies in Jullien's concept of the *langue-pensée*. For Jullien the language of a culture or civilization is inextricably linked to its way of thinking. Thus, the pictographic Chinese script in part signifies through resemblance of its referent (i.e., analogically), in comparison to European alphabetic script, which signifies much more abstractly and indeed rationally. The unit of meaning in Chinese, especially up until the 1920s, is in many respects the single character, whereas in European languages it is the sentence. The absence of morphology and inflection in Chinese entails that meaning must be grasped more through context.[8] In comparison to the subject–verb–object or subject–predicate structure of the West, Chinese foregrounds the adverbial of time and place. Chinese language situates the Western abstract pronoun, the "I" or "she," in quasi-familial context so that students call fellow students *xuemei* or *xuejie* ("student little sister," "student big sister"). In the West, such linguistic assumptions structure our thought in its derivation from Aristotelian logic of substance and its predications (qualities); in the East, such assumptions promote a mode of thought derived from the Daoist–Confucian moral cosmology.

CONFUCIANISM AND DAOISM: THE MAGIC GARDEN

Let us look at Weber's Confucianism. The Confucian bureaucrat-gentleman was responsible for maintaining the unity of Chinese culture. He was schooled in the rites and protocols and was responsible for the maintenance of tradition. The Confucian literati-office holder was the model for Weber's traditional authority (*Herrschaft*), which was not mostly Western feudalism, but patrimonial authority. Patrimonial authority presumes a central state apparatus, a written language and settled agriculture, and thus is less enchanted than hunting and gathering or nomadic societies. Hunting–gathering is fully "enchanted" and with continual movement has not developed institutions of property and is more totemic than ancestor-worshipping. It is ancestor-worshipping patriarchy that is the legitimizing glue for patrimonial *Herrschaft*.

Ideal-type Confucianism has two "peaks," first in the Han dynasty (206 BCE to 220 CE) and second with Zhu Xi's reforms in the Southern Song dynasty in the late twelfth century. Confucian influence was evident in both the full systematization of the office-holding framework, and the spread of Confucian teaching to overlay the more fully magical and already patriarchal (but not yet patrimonial) rural village life. The development entailed a partial *Entzauberung* (a de-magicalization) with the disappearance of the *I Ching* among the new classics. This partial *Entzauberung* is Duan Lin's argument using Weber in his *Konfuzianische Ethik und Legitimation der Herrschaft im alten China*.[9] The point is that this happened at about the same time as Pollock's "vernacularization" and the beginnings of nation-state formation in the West. In China Zhu Xi's partially rationalized neo-Confucianism instead reinforced imperial central power and inhibited both vernacularization and nation-state formation, despite the rise of science and technology and markets in the Song.

In legal-rationalism respect is given to the law and the duties of the office, while Chinese patrimonial power entailed the personalization of authority, with respect owed to the temporary inhabitant of the office. Legal-rationalism enables entrepreneurs to make reliable calculations, and contracts are enforceable. In China the personal *guanxi* of the people making the contract is more important. Weber notes that China does not have the pervasive spread of civil law, but instead often a temple court in which dispute resolution is by personally respected notables instead of based on abstract legal rules. There was codification of law, but decisions were based on the interpretations of the Confucian bureaucrat. The bureaucrat's obligation was not to professional competence, but personally to his superior.[10]

Weber's second central dimension of traditional Chinese culture-power lies in religion. Unlike Durkheim and Mauss,[11] Weber sees a strong dimension of magic in Chinese beliefs. He points to the role of magician as rainmaker, in particular in drought-prone northern China. The gods, and especially the god of heaven, were the arbiters of rain. The magician was closer to the gods than everyday people: a mediator between them and the gods. If the Confucian literati was the maintainer of normative order, the magician had the power to restore cosmic order.

For Weber otherworldly religiosity could entail asceticism. Thus, the early Christians "escaped this world to the desert" and medieval Christians to the monastery. In China otherworldly Buddhist and Daoist ascetics stood in contrast to the this-worldly Confucian. Weber's Calvinist ascetic, for his part, escaped neither to the desert of the early Christian nor to the medieval Catholic monastery, but into his own interiority— hence the radical anxiety of Protestant guilt in comparison with "confessionable" Catholic guilt. In Confucian culture, however, there was not guilt but only shame, and not for sin but only because of the bad taste of breaking social norms. Inner loneliness was unknown.

Adair-Toteff observes that Weber's Confucian China resembles Leibniz's theodicy, in which this world is the best of all possible worlds, mocked by Voltaire in *Candide*. Theodicies have much to do with doctrines of free will, and as Hans Blumenberg has shown, Enlightenment notions of free will have their roots in Augustinian Christianity. For the Greeks everything was caused by some combination of formal, final, material, and efficient causation. In Christianity, God as prime mover or "uncaused cause" granted powers of free will to humans. Thus, Augustinian Catholics could see the evils of this world as human-made. Weber's predestined Calvinist Protestant does not have free will at all. He does not need to justify God in regard to the evils of this world but is fully focused on the next world. The magical world is seen as chaos and needs to be mastered. The Protestant inner-worldly ascetic is an instrument of an all-powerful God. He in turn treats the world instrumentally. Hence, there is Weber's instrumental rationality. The Protestant ascetic imposes on this world the order and calculability of the rational business enterprise. He does this in the interest of the Eden-like order and reason of the next world. God's justice is then understood wholly in terms of the next world.[12]

The Confucian, in contrast, without a transcendental God or original sin, sees this world as neither evil nor disordered but instead as ordered. In place of the Greek four causes there are the five Confucian relations: emperor–subject, husband–wife, older sibling–younger sibling, friend–friend, teacher–student. The relations are governed by the *li* (礼), which are called rites but are just as much conventions or protocols. Our

Western idea of free will comes from Plato's prime mover in the context of Greek epistemic causation. China is not primarily an epistemic culture, but for Weber, a moral culture.[13]

Confucianism is driven by this-worldly rites that are largely court protocols, extending to the everyday in the five relations (*wu lun* 五伦) of emperor–subject, father–son, etc. But such this-worldliness should not be misunderstood along the lines of Western materialism. Unlike Copernicus' and Galileo's West, Chinese thought has no categories for the radically material. Materialism is *wuzhizhyui* (物质主义), matter is *wuzhi* (物质), physics is *wulixue* (物理学); but all of these are loan words in modern Chinese. The key root is *wu* (物), or "thing," as in the *wan wu*, the "ten thousand things." And the ten thousand things which share in the Dao are not primarily material but part of Daoism's moral universe.[14]

In the West, Voltaire understood Calvinism as abolishing priestly chastity to put the entire society into a convent, fully chiming with Weber's inner-worldly asceticism. Yet the Calvinist subject, alongside the Cartesian cogito, is otherworldly in the sense that he no longer possesses free will but is now only an extension of God's will. The Buddhist or Daoist monk is also not in possession of free will: he is instead more or less will-less. The ascetic Protestant for whom the world is one of suffering and sin listens to God, whereas the Daoist ascetic is in tune with a happy and harmonic nature of the Dao, the way.[15] In contrast to Western epistemic cosmology, in China at stake are otherworldly and this-worldly moral spaces, the former in Daoism and the other in Confucianism. Daoism is characterized by a near Buddhist will-lessness of the *wu wei*, which is a refusal of social stratification and asceticism. The difference with the West, as Parsons underscored, is that Daoism's otherworldliness is immanent in its adaptation to the flow of nature, whereas Protestantism is otherworldly and transcendental.[16]

Weber spoke of China as a "magic garden" in the chapter "Orthodoxy and Heterodoxy" in *The Religion of China*.[17] He rightly sees a measure of *Entzauberung* in Confucianism. Unpacking this insight further and drawing on Duan Lin's work on Confucian ethics, the religion of the Shang dynasty was very much a combination of a transcendental god, *shangdi* (上帝), feudal rule, and magic in the sense of the power of divination and of rites that were closely coupled with sacrifice. There was in Weber's sense no ethics and not yet the emergence of the characteristic Chinese moral cosmology. The massive change came in the Zhou dynasty with the shift from *shangdi* to *tian* (天), from a personal god to a god in heaven. The Shang dynasty (*shangdai*, 商代) personal god was the governing instance of a pantheon of gods, *di*, using his magical powers to control the other gods. *Di* (帝) also means emperor. And on the oracle bones and turtle shells of the Shang dynasty, it was invariably this one character, *di* (帝), that is encountered most often. The *shang* (上) means that he is above the emperor. The emperor shared in the divinity of a personal god but in the sense of a son. The personal god was not a creator god. He and the emperor together constituted magical power and political power. There was not a sense of duty or even a contract or covenant with the people which Weber selects as a central feature in ancient Judaism. In that work Weber identifies the beginnings of *Entzauberung* with the move from Baal-worshipping Israel's tribes to an ethics-based covenant with a god, Jahwe. There are similarities between the covenant and the Zhou dynasty's Mandate of Heaven, *tianming* (天命). But in Judaism it was a move from immanence to a transcendental personal god, while in China the move was away from Shang's personal god to the space of heaven.

The key to these developments lies in the Zhou dynasty, in the centuries before Confucius' Spring and Autumn middle sixth century BCE and a further two centuries before Zhuangzi's Warring States ironic attacks on Confucian society. The Five Classics of the Han dynasty were preceded by a book of songs and a book of documents of the Zhou. In these, as Lin notes, scholars perceive that the heavenly mandate is made explicit. Even under Shang, Zhou kings are benevolent rulers.

Chinese scholarship changed definitively after Weber's *Religion of China* appeared, with Wang Guowei's scholarship in the 1920s on Shang dynasty oracle bones and on bronze culture in the Shang and Zhou dynasties. Even in the preceding Xia dynasty, there was settled agriculture and hence ancestor shrines and property relations, paralleling similar developments in Mesopotamia. But Wang's work and subsequent work confirm the importance of the Weberian ideal types of magic, on the one hand, and ethics, on the other.

The Zhou dynasty, heavily influenced by the customs of the "Ji" tribe, operated with the rule of primogeniture. But this was not the case with the Shang dynasty, where the most virtuous or ablest male and not the eldest succeeded as king. This led to contestable succession and instability. Zhou primogeniture rules set up one single family as the ruling bloodline, and it is at this point that the rule of rites and "role ethics" appeared. The stability of social order then depended on the stability of the moral order, on honoring ancestral lineages and respecting ministers. Confucius witnessed the partial breakdown of this order during the Spring and Autumn period that opened into outright rebellion of non-Ji states in the period of Warring States. After the brutal legalist unification of the Qin state came the 400 years of stability of the Han dynasty and with that the centrality of the Confucian classics. Confucius redacted and systematized the Zhou dynasty books of documents and songs, which only became dominant 300 years later in the Han dynasty.

Consider the nature of "ethics" in the context of what Weber termed the "magic garden." Whereas a number of Confucian philologists in China tend to privilege the *li* (礼) or rites, the Weber scholar Duan Lin focuses on *ren* (仁). In the Shang dynasty there was no clear hierarchy of virtues. In Zhou, later emphasized by Confucius, *ren* is the cardinal virtue. For Lin, *ren* presumes a personal and moral inner-worldliness, achieved through cultivation. According to Lin, this is not individualistic but a humanist ethic of the relation between people, creating a relation between *ren* and *li*. The latter is legitimated by the former, while at the same time, *ren* generates *li*. This can be seen as a post-magical ethic that still bears traces of divination. The *I Ching* does not disappear but is central to cosmology and cosmogony, as the Dao works through *qi* and *yin/yang* to constitute the cosmos.

What is the Daoist moral universe, and what is its cosmology and cosmogony? The *Dao de Jing* is first found as written in about 350 BCE—during the Warring States some

300 years after Confucius' Spring and Autumn period. The *Dao de Jing* makes common cause with the School of Yin/Yang and the School of Nature. This is not a "philosophy of nature" as found in Newton or Hegel. It is "nature" as the ground of a moral universe. There are large doses of magic-like shamanism: the *I Ching* is about divination and arises in the late Shang dynasty or early Zhou, about 1150 BCE. It uses the eight trigrams, each with its yin/yang composition, and then the sixty-four hexagrams for divination of the future.[18] The shaman is a bit different, with Manchu—that is Paleolithic and not (Chinese) Neolithic—origins. And the shift from Paleolithic to Neolithic—settled agriculture, the state, written language—brings with it a sea change in the direction of disenchantment. Shamanism mediates between individuals and the spirits for fortune telling and exorcism. There are very important shamanic origins in the *I Ching* and Daoism, though both undergo substantial Neolithic rationalization, the *I Ching* in its binary rationalization. Since Moses' termination of Baalism for the commandments of the transcendental God, soothsaying is rooted out of Jewish and Christian traditions. Of all the Five Classics in the Confucian orthodoxy of the Han dynasty, only the *I Ching* engaged with divination. The others were already more disenchanted. After the Confucian Han dynasty, Daoism arose to a hegemonic role in the Three Kingdoms and the Jin dynasty. The subsequent Tang dynasty saw the reception and predominance of Buddhism, yielding to the neo-Confucian hegemony—and disappearance of the *I Ching* from the classics—in the Song dynasty.

But what kind of *cosmology* are we talking about? For example, eight unbroken *yang* lines are "force," while eight broken *yin* lines are "field." This along with *feng shui* (geomancy) and other methods, such as palm reading and astrology, will more or less accurately predict futures. In other combinations, this will ultimately yield the ten thousand things. *I Ching* divination with its "combinatorics" as Leibniz put it, are ways of putting order on an otherwise preexistent chaos. Combined with the Five Phases or Five Elements (*wu xing* 五行)—air, water, earth, wood, fire—they give rise to what Needham saw as a basis for all Chinese sciences.[19] Without a creator god, cosmogony comes from the Dao itself. The Dao, which is not a being, much less a personal god, and is universal harmony, is the one that generates the two that then generate the three which finally generates the ten thousand things. For their part, the ten thousand things are not a chaotic but instead an ordered multiplicity: ordered less by classification than by generation from the Dao through the poles of yang and yin, positive and negative.

Cognitive psychologist Eleanor Rosch developed a culture-specific schema of experience, giving a paradigm of identification of all beings for a given culture, a schema of perception and the imagination.[20] Chinese "analogical culture" foregrounds the imagination: still a mode of representation but analogic in its representation. The Dao itself is immanent and does not represent at all. Before Zhou unification there was a more or less transcendental god, the old *shangdi* of the "feudal" Shang dynasty. Even before Daoism there was a sort of dualism of *shen* (神) and *gui* (鬼), in which *gui* is at the same time ghost and disorder, while *shen* gives order. The Dao, as Matthews notes,[21] for its part is monist. The *I Ching* and the Dao work through *qi* (气) as matter energy, a sort of monist "materialism" which the Hangzhou diviners see as big bang–like matter energy. The

Daoist moral cosmos then keeps self-generating in a seemingly "self-organizing" process, in which the Dao itself is present in each of the ten thousand things. This Dao is also present in the highest levels of consciousness, in the *wu wei* of the person who withdraws from politics and joins nature in a monasticism classically portrayed by the poets of the Three Kings era in the "Seven Worthies in the Bamboo Forest."

Weber saw the Dao and Confucianism as in many ways consistent. How then is the otherworldly yet immanent Dao brought into conjunction with the this-worldly—and, indeed, in some sense Promethean Confucianism? First, as Yuk Hui notes, this is achieved by technology as *qi* (器), which we encounter in the *Book of Rites* as literally containers for the rites themselves. The implication, as Hui notes using Plato's discussions of at least partial fusion of technics and praxis, is that the rites themselves become technics, that is, a technology which bring the Dao into court society and forms of life more generally in the relationships of filial piety.[22]

There is an additional development, for in China the reception of Buddhism took place within a Daoist set of presuppositions and modes of identification. The massive difference between Buddhism and Daoism is that Buddhists see the world as suffering, while Daoist nature is happy and harmonic. Hence, Buddhist thought, like Hindu and Vedic, features reincarnation, while Daoism does not. Mahayana rather than Theravada Buddhism came into China along the Silk Road. In Tibet this took the form of Zen and emphasized meditation. In China it took a somewhat less ascetic form, featuring the bodhisattvas and especially Guanyin. The bodhisattva works through *tathata* or "suchness," the "and thus and thus and thus," very much akin to the Daoist "way." This suchness also informs the Confucian cultivation of the self. The modes of identification in the Chinese moral universe are schema through which we see the world as a suchness and not as Western quiddity. In the West things are seen in their "whatness," but in the East in their "thusness." Western ontology, as Jullien insists, is a mode of thought foregrounding the *qu'est-ce que c'est*—indeed, the "whatness" or true nature of things that Aristotle and Aquinas understood as "quiddity." In the Chinese moral universe, however, it is not epistemic quiddity that is at stake, but instead suchness. China's variety of Mahayana Buddhism has been *wei shi* or consciousness-only Buddhism. It works from eight levels of consciousness, the seventh being willful and instrumental and the eighth storehouse consciousness that approaches will-lessness or *wu wei*. There is still cultivation of the self, but things are seen in terms of their thusness, their suchness.[23]

LANGUAGE AND THOUGHT: THE MISSING VERNACULAR

In contrast to Daoism, Confucianism favors rules. Confucianism gives us a quasi-determination, not in Daoism's *wu ming* but instead in the *mingfen* (analytic name) that brings harmony. It is not a matter of law, but of more or less formalized custom. If

Weber's West universalizes through the teachings of Jesus versus the clans, then Confucian China universalizes through written language. The universalizing trend was very state-centric; even large factories in China, Weber noted, produced porcelain for the king in state enterprises. We could consider the trend Chinese *langue-pensée*, or what Walter Benjamin saw as a "mimetic" language and Philippe Descola as "analogical."[24]

Keeping in mind Weber's tripartite division of China, the religion of India, and the Abrahamic ethos of *Ancient Judaism* and the *Protestant Ethic*, we should note that Indian *langue-pensée* also stands in contrast with the analytic and propositional West. What is at stake are Indo-European and Dravidian languages more generally, especially within Weber's *The Religion of India*[25] where phonological Sanskrit, whose clarity and precision, lexicon, and grammar stood in contrast to the alexical and antigrammar of ancient Chinese. With regard to Sanskrit, Sheldon Pollock's reflections see its vernacularization as a poetic or aesthetic rationalization. Vernacularization presages the rise of nation-states, though not with capitalism. Vernacular language spreads from 900 to 1300 along with the "pre-capitalist world system," with trade but also with the vast extension of agriculture, especially single-crop grains. The spread of written language and "civilization" itself took place with large-scale grain cultivation. But it seems as if a single-crop agrarian economy spread not just the numeracy of calculation, as described by Giovanni Arrighi as "Adam Smith's" China, but also literacy.[26] Pollock describes two stages, a "cosmopolitan" epoch that corresponds to Weber's world religions and an epoch of vernacularization that leads to a shift from empire to nation. In the West the cosmopolitan stage corresponds with Rome and empire, while vernacularization aligns with nation and the modern.

We can find parallels to the West in Wang Hui's work on China and modernity in *The Rise of Modern Chinese Thought*. Wang's argument concerns a partial transition from empire to nation. The backward-looking Zhou dynasty's Heavenly Principle inspires "empire," while the forward-looking universal principle (*gongli*), a paradigm of Western progressive thought, becomes the basis of nation. The Heavenly Principle entails Zhou unification of the much more splintered previous Shang dynasty, and it is also enunciated at the time of the fragmented Spring and Autumn periods. China is reunified in the Qin dynasty, but Qin's legalist culture was not enough to create harmony and sustained unity. This required Confucianism, which married an ideology, a way of life, with bureaucratic structure.[27]

For Pollock, in the cosmopolitan stage there are lexicons and grammars, works on meter and phonology. The epic becomes pivotal to Sanskrit and Greco–Roman culture, giving rise to cosmologies and mythic lineages whose descendants are the people of a nation. Epics presume something like the equivalent of bards, feature complex rhetorical and metrical schemes, and comprise not only a narrative but also a journey. The dactylic hexameter of classical epic also provides an aide-memoire. In this respect the great Sanskrit epics, the *Ramayana* and the *Mahabharata*, were more influential even than the Western epics of (in the cosmopolitan age) the *Iliad* and the *Odyssey* and (in the vernacular age) the German *Nibelungenlied* and the French *Chanson de Roland*.[28]

In China, however, there was no epic poetry. The closest approximation is *The Epic of Darkness* (*hei an zhuan*, 黑暗转), which addresses myths of world creation rather than the journey of the epic hero. It dates not from the mid-first millennium BCE like the Sanskrit and Western epics, but only from the mid-seventh-century Tang dynasty. Is there no space for heroes or the heroic in China? Using Aristotle's tripartite epic/dramatic/lyric distinction, there surely was lyric poetry in China in the Shijing (诗经) or *Classic of Poetry* or *Book of Odes*, derived about 1000 BCE from folk songs mediated through literati in the Zhou dynasty. Such lyric poetry was a specialty of the courts, with court aristocracy collecting the poems. There were two types of poems: the affairs of state, and short lyrics using simple language. These were not devotional songs as in classical Sanskrit poetry, the *kavya*, which were never entirely oral but always recorded by literati. The Chinese *Classic of Poetry* also consisted of poems and not commentaries on poems, whereas in Sanskrit and Latin, the poets followed quickly with analytics, grammars and lexicons, and the discipline of meter and genre. In China, despite books of rhymes and the addition of pronunciation radicals to meaning radicals, such analytics were far less common. We may attribute this fact to Confucian rejection of formal definition, not to mention the Daoist devaluation of the designation of the name: *ming ke ming fei chang ming v* (名可名非常名). Another reason may be the absence of inflection and morphology in the language, with meaning made possible only through word order and context.

In contrast to Greek, Roman and oracle-bone written language, Sanskrit started with the religious community which "universalized" from near Iraq to much of south and southeast Asia, a sacerdotal transmission through priests to the "world of man." Moreover, Sanskrit poetry has only two genres: *kavya*, written poetry, and *prasati*, or royal panegyrics. It was not a language of documents, as was common in Latin and the middle Chinese realm. However, the Chinese *Book of Documents* did not literally comprise *documents*, consistent with Weber's category of legal-rational *Herrschaft*, but instead speeches by Zhou dynasty figures. In India *kavya*'s overlords were patrons of grammarians, lexicographers, metricians and schools for grammatical studies. In the West, by contrast, there was a Platonic focus not on correct grammar or the shape of the phrase, but instead on the ontological or epistemic truth of the thing, an emphasis not on syntax but on definitional semantics. But Chinese thought-language focused on neither: neither clear and distinct lexical meaning, nor clear and distinct syntax. Expression in Chinese instead is at home in Wittgenstein's *Philosophical Investigations*: as neither philological content nor grammatical form, but as the unclear and indistinct, the characteristic Jullien has understood as "fadeur" or blandness.[29]

What drives the universalization of cosmopolitan thought-language? In the Indian world, with Sanskrit it was the homogeneous language of political poetry, which became transregional not through military conquest but through the spread of Vedic thought from 1500 to 500 BCE. There were the Vedas as liturgical texts of customary public worship, similar to Christian liturgy and unlike Judaism or Islam, in which there is not so much liturgy as rites. Vedic rites were exclusive and practised by an elite, providing a monopoly on the religious until about 500 BCE with the rise of

Buddhism and Jainism, the world religions proper of the "Axial Age." In the West, by contrast, it was Roman armies—and later the Roman Catholic Church—following in the tracks of Alexander the Great's organized military, that underwrote cosmopolitan universalism. Chinese development was distinctive: it relied on the propagation of a analogical written language, supported by Confucian literati in the service of a rationalizing dynastic state.

VERNACULAR

Vernacularization for Pollock takes place from 1,700 to 2000 years later than the "cosmopolitan" epoch, the period that aligns with the precapitalist world system of about 800 to 1350 (CE) and the Black Death. This is the precapitalist world system of settled agriculture that follows the Arab and Muslim conquests and is circumscribed in China by the Mongols' eclipse of the Southern Song. In the post-Sanskrit world, it is often in documents rather than literature, the sphere of Weber's legal-rational authority, that the vernacular first emerges. In the post-Latin world, by contrast, an analogous "vernacular revolution" proceeded essentially through literary texts.[30]

With vernacularization there is a break with the classical and preclassical world of the epic. For Mikhail Bakhtin the epic world is constructed in the zone of an absolute distanced imaginary. Latin itself becomes distant as it becomes literary. The no-longer place of Latin is matched by the "non-place" of the "unintimate and unforgiving" Sanskrit, which may never have had a place. These changes represent the move from empire to not-yet emergent nation, indeed from *Zivilisation* to *Kultur*, from the civilizations of cosmopolitan Greece and Rome and Sanskrit to the culture of the national vernaculars: English, French, German, Italian, Spanish, Hindi, Bengali, Marathi, Urdu, Tamil, Kannada. *Zivilisation* was universal, *Kultur* particular and even singular. *Zivilisation* was *Gesellschaft*, *Kultur Gemeinschaft*; *Zivilisation* maps onto social anthropology, *Kultur* onto cultural anthropology.[31]

But China was the exception. Chinese never vernacularized, never produced a written language or documents in the variety of idioms in Cantonese, Shanghainese and Wu dialects that originated mainly in the Southern Song. Why? This outcome is associated with what Wang Hui notes as an only partial transition from empire to nation-state, from the Heavenly Principle that always points back to Zhou to the universal principle (*gongli*) that points forward and is associated with modernity. The Zhou had already brought harmony and unity after the feudal Shang, and from the chaos of the Spring and Autumn, Confucius could look back to the Zhou. Vernacularization would have meant a large number of states with different written languages and their own lexicons and grammars. The Heavenly Principle itself was one of unity and anti-vernacular. Vernacular would have destroyed the hegemony of Confucian culture, of the tax-collecting literati bureaucracy. These literati were not fully a court literati. They were more a *noblesse d'épée* without the *épée*, shuffled about every three or four years, as the communist officers are now, yet not located in the capital or the court cities. Empire was just too strong for nation to settle in.[32]

What is going on in vernacularization? In Europe in the era of Frankish kings from 600 to 1000, Latin is still the language of political expression. Revived under Charlemagne, it is the language of literary and document production, the imperial language of the Holy Roman Empire. This stands in contrast to Sanskrit, whose origins were religious and not military-religious or military-political. Literature itself written in Latin begins only about 240 BCE, some 200 years before *The Aeneid*. Roman laws, but not literature were written in Latin from 540 BCE. The political context of cosmopolitan language was empire, and both India and Rome, though not China, were influenced by the imperial model taken from Achaemenid Persia, where centralized administration approached Weber's understanding of rational bureaucracy.[33]

Later in the Tang dynasty, Indian religion in Buddhism and even literature and grammar would flow to China along the Silk Road. The age where China could have vernacularized in the late Song with Zhu Xi's Confucianism was preceded by Buddhism, a great leveler in India and China, as was Daoism against which Confucianism was always able to rally. Zhu Xi's neo-Confucianism was thus a reassertion of stratification and class power that would tend to preserve empire and inhibit the transition to nation-state. Hinduism and Confucianism recognize social stratification and inequalities in their this-worldliness that monastic Buddhism and Daoism did not.

Global integration of trade from the eighth to the eleventh centuries saw vast routes extended from Bruges to Hangzhou. International trade peaked in 1350 with the Black Death and the isolation of Ming China. The Arab conquest of Sindh from the eighth century was part of this global trade integration, to which India was tied through export of spices and finished cloth. This development was a triumph of settled agriculture, yet China had single-crop growing some 800 years earlier. It did not need to vernacularize in order to "modernize." China was already prepared for the "Neolithic" precapitalist world system. In Pollock's Weberian formulation, "the breakthrough to vernacularization was absent throughout the Chinese world, including in China itself" not because of economic factors, but because of "the specific character of the imperial polity, its language politics, and its neo-Confucian ideology."[34] Political and socio-cultural factors, especially the powerful enduring position of the literati, account for the unique path forged by China.

The patrons of the literati all over Europe and India were no longer satisfied with Latin and Sanskrit. In Europe, experimentation began with romance languages as a writing medium, aided by the paper revolution of the twelfth and thirteenth centuries, and accompanied by "the production of philological appurtenances appropriate to literary culture."[35] In the Latin West, its missionizing priests, literacy, and Romanization accompanied Christianity everywhere, and with literacy came literarization in the secular French *chansons de geste*. In India, vernacular arrived in political transactions, durable deeds, records of endowment. The law of distance held as Dravidian Sanskrit first vernacularized in south India, both Tamil and Kannada in the ninth century, and in Karnataka by court elites in the tenth century, though in north India only from the fifteenth century. In Europe distance privileged England, starting about 990 with Aelfric's glosses on his Latin "Grammatica," while King Alfred in 878 sponsored state-directed translation into English of Augustine's soliloquies. The first romantic productions, however, were political documents in the Oath of Strasbourg of 842 following the dispute of the sons of Charlemagne. Only 250 years later is there literary vernacular. But the point is that vernacular literarization in Europe produced entire literary traditions that were "intentional, reflexive, memorialized, circulating, continually reproduced, and philologized."[36]

What about China? Do changes occur with Zhu Xi's reimposition of the imperial? The *Book of Songs* moved in the direction of Sanskrit poetic grammaticality. It featured odes in syntactically related couplets, in stanzas with rhymes between the second and fourth lines, written in four-syllable meter. Its hymns and eulogies were accompanied by bells, drums, and stone chimes. The songs were collected from the regions and passed through the courts. With Zhu Xi's reimposition, the *I Ching* disappeared, as did the *Book of Documents*. The *Mencius* with its focus on the goodness of human nature is added, as well as the *Analects*, mostly sayings and ideas of Confucius previously seen as commentaries on the Five Classics. The parts of the *Book of Rites* dealing with protocols are less present. Instead, two chapters of the *Book of Rites* become two of the four books: the *Doctrine of the Mean* and the *Great Learning*. Zhu Xi emphasized a kind of rationalism, in which all things are made from *qi* and *li*: *li* was the structure of all things, present in all human beings and the basis for cultivating the person, whereas *qi* was mostly an obstacle.

Zhu Xi also encouraged the investigation of things (*gewu, gewuzhizhi*). He stood against both Daoism and Buddhism, even though the *Great Learning* featured the Dao. Yet his *li* (理, or reason) itself stemmed from the *taiji*, the "supreme ultimate" that was considered not a god, but a dynamic and constantly creative principle, unlike the stillness and silence of the Dao or Buddhism. This was surely a partial rationalization of thought. But was it also a move toward modernity, to vernacular and the nation-state? Because it reinforced the power of the Confucian literati and bureaucracy for the following 700 years, it surely was not.

Why the extraordinary grammatization in India and its relative absence in China? Sanskrit Veda and later Hinduist *langue-pensée* are more grammatized, systematized, and hence rationalized than even Greek and Latin. Pānini's commentaries and Pantanjali's grammar of about the third or fourth century BCE are often thought to be the founding documents of linguistics, whose discoveries were only surpassed in the twentieth century. Pānini developed transformation rules, compound nouns, and rules of syntax and semantics. His syntax, morphology and lexicon had a metalanguage. Patanjali's great commentary on Pānini's *Astadhyayi* added etymology and semantic explanation. In India grammatization was not about knowing the truth of the thing, as with European *langue-pensée*, but about achieving ritual purity. It was Patanjali, after all, who insisted on the removal of "impurities" in the mind through yoga, in speech through his grammar, and in the body through medicine.

Chinese thought does not have its origins in either ritual purity or morphological purity, indeed not in the clear and distinct, but in the vague and indistinct of everyday life. Chinese language lacks a morphology or clitics. Only with modern Chinese after about 1910 do we find something like compound nouns bound by morphemes, such as with a word like *dongxi* (东西; thing, object) where there is at long last some phonological dependency. Or consider the *Doctrine of the Mean*, one of the four books of Confucianism. The doctrine proper is not so much the "golden rule" as taught in the West, not "do unto others as you would have others do unto you," but rather a "principle of reciprocity" that we are meant to cultivate in our natures. It is the *zhongyong* (中庸), where *yong* refers to both ordinary and use or function. What you do not like when done to yourself, do not do to others, which Confucius immediately embeds in the precept that I should serve my father as I would require my son to serve me, or I should serve my prince as I would require my minister to serve me. The doctrine of the mean is not an arithmetic relation or logical proposition. There is nothing clear and distinct about it. It comes from the *Book of Rites*, but does not seem a sacred rite at all. It works not through definition or clarification, not through saying but through showing and examples. Moderns like Lu Xun and Mao Zedong could thus oppose the *Doctrine of the Mean* because it was profoundly undialectical, a threat to impede progress for China.

In India, Weber's conceptualization of religion plays out between a more this-worldly Hinduism and otherworldly Buddhism. But in China, Confucianism was victorious. This meant, for example, that the five relations of filial piety, of the *ciaojing* or *xiaodao* (孝经, 孝道) through the five virtues following from the five elements—benevolence, righteousness, reverence, wisdom, and sincerity—replaced the non-self of the Buddhists and the monks. Confucianism coopts the Dao but not the *wu wei* of Daoism, and is neither religious nor secular, but somehow in between. In India reason was not propositional, but poetic and most of all religious. Indian *langue-pensée* was about the city of the gods, expressed in the sacerdotal. By contrast, in the West Aristotle's famous modes of reason—episteme, technics, and praxis—were all phenomena of the city of man. In China, we find instead neither a city of man nor a city of the gods, but no city whatsoever. As Weber noted, generational ancestor worship and familial sovereignty prevented the Chinese polity from taking on city form in either its ancient or modern incarnation.[37] Instead, we have empire—neither city nor nation, but empire; neither city-state nor nation-state, but empire-state. Based on the Confucian looking backward to the Heavenly Principle and heavenly mandate of Zhou, the Confucian ideology-bureaucracy of the literati was its glue with its anti-grammatology in either the Indian or Aristotelian sense. In sum, the Confucian beliefs and rites were not logical propositions or rituals. They represented a way of life.

India tried to unify, notably in the short-lived Maurya and longer Gupta empires (300–600 CE). But these efforts could not integrate the Huns into the sacerdotal Hindu and at times Buddhist culture and polity. China on the other hand unified via its far-from-rational language: through its non-grammatological language, non-religious religion, and unique language-politics of dynastic rule. Yet China today, still suffering from more than 100 years of humiliation from the Opium Wars to the Japanese invasions, is intensely nationalist. Chinese intellectuals espouse a sense of "national" identity that would make people blanch in the United Kingdom, France, the United States, or Germany. But it is nationalism in large part without a nation. Nationalist sentiment is still rooted in empire. It is as if the West had kept to the Latin of the Holy Roman Empire, never vernacularized, and continued to identify with the glory of imperial Rome.

Does this outcome matter in an age in which English has become the cosmopolitan *Weltsprache*, with Mandarin waiting in the wings? For capitalist modernity as understood by the original comparativist and analyst of the Chinese literati, Max Weber, it was a matter of immense significance. On the level of economy, thought, and geopolitics today it still matters a great deal.

Notes

1. See Nicholas Gane, *Max Weber and Contemporary Capitalism* (Basingstoke, UK: Palgrave Macmillan, 2012). Max Weber, *General Economic History* (hereafter *GEH*), trans. Frank H. Knight (London: George Allen & Unwin, 1927), 161; Max Weber, *Wirtschaftsgeschichte. Abriß der universalen Sozial- und Wirtschaftsgeschichte. Mit- und Nachschriften 1919/20, Max Weber-Gesamtausgabe* III/6, ed. W. Schluchter with J. Schröder (Tübingen, Germany: Mohr [Siebeck], 2011), 227.

2. *GEH*, 342; *MWG III/6*, 372. The Chinese language literature refers to these periods literally in terms of feudalism (*fengjian*). They are feudal in terms of Weber's "decentralization of the means of destruction." But they do not exhibit the emergent contractual nature that Weber notes in his ideal type of feudalism in *Economy and Society*.

3. *GEH*, 339–340; *MWG III/6*, 370–371.

4. *GEH*, 161, 322; *MWG III/6*, 226–227, 356.

5. *GEH*, 44–45; *MWG III/6*, 135.

6. François Jullien, *De l'Être au Vivre: Lexique euro–chinois de la pensée* (Paris: Gallimard, 2014); Sheldon Pollock, *The Language of the Gods in the World of Men: Sanskrit, Culture and Power in Premodern India* (Berkeley: University of California Press, 2006).

7. Pollock, *Language of the Gods*, 10ff.

8. Jullien, *De l'Être au Vivre*, 19.

9. Duan Lin, *Konfuzianische Ethik und Legitimation der Herrschaft im alten China: Eine Auseinandersetzung mit der vergleichende Soziologie Max Webers* (Berlin: Duncker & Humblot, 1997), 83; also Christopher Adair-Toteff, "Max Weber on Confucianism versus Protestantism," *Max Weber Studies*, 14, no. 1 (2014): 79–96, 83.

10. Adair-Toteff, "Max Weber on Confucianism versus Protestantism," 87–88; Hans Kelsen, *Pure Theory of Law* (Berkeley: University of California Press, 1967).

11. Emile Durkheim and Marcel Mauss, *Primitive Classification* (London: Routledge, 2009).

12. Adair-Toteff, "Max Weber on Confucianism versus Protestantism"; G. W. Leibniz, *Theodicy* (New York: Cosimo Classics, 2010).

13. Max Weber, *The Religion of China: Confucianism and Taoism* (hereafter *RC*) (New York: Free Press 1968); *Die Wirtschaftsethik der Weltreligionen. Konfuzianismus und Taoismus. Schriften 1915–1920, MWG* I/19, ed. H. Schmidt-Glintzer with P. Kolenko (Tübingen, Germany: Mohr [Siebeck], 1989); Reinhard Bendix, *Max Weber: An Intellectual Portrait* (Berkeley: University of California Press, 1977), 114.

14. A. C. Graham, *Disputers of the Tao: Philosophical Argument in Ancient China* (Chicago: Open Court, 1989).

15. See G. W. F. Hegel, "Introduction," in *The Phenomenology of Spirit* (Cambridge: Cambridge University Press, 2019), 49–59; Max Weber, *The Protestant Ethic and the Spirit of Capitalism* (Oxford: Oxford University Press, 2010), esp. ch. 4; *Die Protestantische Ethik und der Geist des Kapitalismus. Schriften 1904-1920*, *MWG* I/18, ed. W. Schluchter with U. Bube (Tübingen, Germany: Mohr [Siebeck], 2016), esp. 257–411, "die religiösen Grundlagen der innerweltlichen Askese."

16. Talcott Parsons, *The Structure of Social Action* (New York: Free Press, 1968), 551.

17. *RC*, 227; *MWG* I/19, 450.

18. On ambiguities in the concept of "nature" (*hsing*), see Graham, *Disputers of the Tao*, parts II and III.

19. Joseph Needham, *Science and Civilization in China*, vol. 4 (Cambridge: Cambridge University Press, 1965).

20. Eleanor Rosch, "Cognitive Representations of Semantic Categories," *Journal of Experimental Psychology* 104, no. 3 (1975): 192–233.

21. William Matthews, "Ontology with Chinese Characteristics: Homology as a Mode of Identification," *HAU: Journal of Ethnographicl Theory* 7, no. 1 (2017): 265–285.

22. Yuk Hui, *The Question Concerning Technology in China: An Essay in Cosmotechnics* (Cambridge, MA: MIT Press, 2016).

23. See Dan Lusthaus, *Buddhist Phenomenology: A Philosophical Investigation of Yogācāra Buddhism and the Ch'eng Wei-shih lun* (London: Routledge, 2002).

24. Walter Benjamin, "On the Mimetic Faculty," *Reflections: Essays, Aphorisms, Autobiographical Writings*, transl. E. Jephcott (New York: Schocken, 1978): 333–36; Philippe Descola, *Beyond Nature and Culture*, trans. J. Lloyd (Chicago: University of Chicago Press, 2013); also David Gellner and D. N. Gellner, "Max Weber, Capitalism and the Religion of India," *Sociology* 16, no. 4 (1982): 526–543.

25. Max Weber, *The Religion of India. The Sociology of Hinduism and Buddhism*, trans. Hans H. Gerth and Don Martindale (New York: Free Press, 1958); *Die Wirtschaftsethik der Weltreligionen. Hinduismus und Buddhismus. 1916-1920*, *MWG* I/20, ed. H. Schmidt-Glintzer, with K.-H. Golzio (Tübingen, Germany: Mohr [Siebeck], 1996).

26. Giovanni Arrighi, *Adam Smith in Beijing:Lineages of the 21st Century* (London: Verso, 2009).

27. Wang Hui, *From Empire to Nation-State*, trans. M. Hill (Cambridge, MA: Harvard University Press, 2014), the introduction to his magnum opus, *The Rise of Modern Chinese Thought* [*xiandai zhongguo aixiang de xingqi* (现代中国思想的兴起] (Beijing, 2004-2009).

28. See the discussion in Pollock, *Language of the Gods*, ch. 6; 449, 469, 544–545.

29. Pollock, *Language of the Gods*, 68 f.; François Jullien, *In Praise of Blandness: Proceeding from Chinese Thought and Aesthetics*, trans. P. Versano (Cambridge, MA: MIT Press, 2004).

30. Pollock, *Language of the Gods*, 451.

31. Scott Lash, *Experience: New Foundations for the Human Sciences* (Cambridge: Polity Press, 2018).

32. The main point of Wang Hui, *From Empire to Nation-State*.

33. On the Achaemenid influence, see Pollock, *Language of the Gods*, 59, 482, 537.

34. Ibid., 487.

35. Ibid., 438–439.

36. Ibid., 451. Perhaps not to the extent of Sanskrit and ancient Greek, China had dictionaries and compendia of syllables that look back to the Zhou dynasty, in particular the 说文解学 (*shuowenjiexue*) and the *erya*, 尔雅, *The Literary Expositor*.

37. *GEH*, 161; *MWG* III/6, 226f.

CHAPTER 21

CLASS, CASTE, AND SOCIAL STRATIFICATION IN INDIA

Weberian Legacy

HIRA SINGH

IT has been claimed that Max Weber was the first to undertake a strictly empirical comparison of social structure and normative order in world-historical depth. He disagreed with the systems and "isms" of the time, such as social Darwinism and Marxism that remained essentially speculative notwithstanding their claim to a science of society. Similarly, he was opposed to the evolutionary and monocausal theories—idealist or materialist. While he did recognize the significance of economic factors and their role in group conflicts, he rejected the thesis of class contradictions and class struggle in society and history. Finally, "Unlike Engels, he saw no grounds for assuming an 'ultimately determining element in history.'" To the contrary, he approached sociological theory and historical generalization on the concrete level.[1]

This statement about Weber's general approach is useful in examining the particular strands of his theory. My particular interest in this chapter is to underline the salience of Weber's conceptual and theoretical contributions to the study of the caste in India as a system of social stratification.

Caste is unarguably a most studied and at the same time a most contentious subject in sociological enquiry of India, by Indians and non-Indians alike. Max Weber's distinction between class and status is the single most important influence on the mainstream sociology of caste. Caste appears in this work as a particular case to illustrate his general theory of the distribution of power. Caste is not determined by economic and political power. Rather, it is a source of economic and political power. Another work by Weber that deals directly with caste is his study of Hinduism and Buddhism, which formed

Volume II of the "Economic Ethics of the World Religions" (and was translated by Hans H. Gerth and Don Martindale as *The Religion of India. The Sociology of Hinduism and Buddhism*).[2] This was part of his larger study, that is, the development of capitalism in the West. We may be reminded that the larger question Weber was interested in was why it was in the West and only in the West that "modern capitalist conditions" emerged. Why did they not emerge in India or China? We may note that this question is central to Weber's wider theoretical goal, rooted in his rejection of the role of class contradictions and class struggle in history. Some sixty years before Weber, Marx had emphasized the role of class struggle under feudalism leading to the expropriation of the direct producers from land, the means of their subsistence, as a decisive factor in the transition from feudalism to capitalism, replacing serfdom with wage labor, the distinguishing feature of the capitalist mode of production. He had also emphasized the role of violence in the process: the rosy dawn of capitalism was anything but idyllic, he noted. Weber rejects that and offers an alternative explanation of the genesis of capitalism in his *Protestant Ethic and the Spirit of Capitalism* as peaceful pursuit of acquisition determined by the economic ethic of Calvinism and the Puritan sects. How did caste as embodiment of the work ethic of Hinduism determine "the pursuit of life conduct" of Indians, and how did that impact on the development of capitalism in India, was Weber's question.

Caste in India was not peripheral but central to Weber's theoretical scheme. Two important, arguably the most important, components of Weber's theoretical contributions include the distribution of power and the emergence of capitalism in the West; and caste figures prominently in both. I propose to critically examine Weber's contribution to the study of caste, particularly the distinction between class and status, identifying caste as the latter, and the relationship between caste and religion (Hinduism).

CLASS AND STATUS

Max Weber's seminal essay "Class, Status, and Party" is hailed as "perhaps the most influential single essay in the sociological literature...the embryo of...a multidimensional approach to social analysis...primary alternative and antidote to Marx's strong emphasis on material factors in social economic formations." His main concern in this essay, we are told, was "to avoid confusing different forms of power that served as the bases for different types of social formation."[3] Weber's main concern in the aforementioned essay is the distribution of power in society. He identifies class (economic), status (cultural), and party (political) as three different phenomena of the distribution of power. He argues that economically conditioned power is not identical with "power" as such. Nor is it the primary source of power in all cases. In some cases, economic power may be the consequence of other sources of power. It is further argued that power is not merely a source of enrichment but frequently also a source of social honor. The source of social honor is cultural as opposed to economic and may frequently be a source of the latter.[4]

There are two component parts of class recognized by Weber: one, property and lack of property as the basic categories of all class situations and, two, class situation is ultimately the market situation. Those who cannot have a chance of using goods or services for themselves on the market (e.g., slaves or serfs) are not classes but status groups. Caste is characterized as status group, based on cultural power, in contrast to class, based on economic power.

Following on the distinction between economic power and cultural power, Weber distinguishes economic order from social order. One, concerned with the distribution of goods and services, is the realm of class. The other, concerned with the distribution of social honor, is the realm of status. Caste belongs to the realm of status as opposed to class.

Property as such is not always recognized as a status qualification, but in the long run it is, and with extraordinary regularity. However, status honor need not necessarily be linked with a "class situation." It is so since both the propertied and the propertyless can belong to the same status group. This equality of social esteem (without equality of property) may, however, in the long run become quite precarious.[5] If property becomes a status qualification in the long run, does that mean that status, albeit social honor, without property is a phenomenon only in the short run? The same holds for status equality between the propertied and the non-propertied: what happens in the long run when equality between the propertied and the non-propertied, the very essence of status in contrast to class, becomes precarious? There is no satisfactory answer to these and other—more serious—questions arising from Weber's distinction between class and status.

STATUS AS STYLE OF LIFE

It is argued that the status group is not to be confused with the "occupational status group." Status group is distinguished by style of life, not the occupation per se. Thus, for example, military service as a knight is status, but military service as a mercenary is not. The difference between the two lies in their different styles of life.[6] What is missing here is that a knight lived off his estate where he had monopoly of economic–political power and social esteem, a privilege which was not available to a mercenary. That was the basis of his lifestyle as distinct from that of the mercenary's.

Weber provides two other examples of status group distinguished by their respective styles of life—blacks during slavery in the United States and the nobility in medieval Europe. Very much like the example of the knight and the soldier, the lifestyle of blacks during slavery in America and that of the nobility in medieval Europe was determined by their respective access to avenues of economic and political power. Focusing on style of life as exclusively cultural independent of economic and political power is problematic. Style of life and social esteem, the quintessence of status as cultural power, are intrinsically connected to economic and political power, underlining the connectedness of economic–political power and social honor.

Status Usurpation

Weber argues that status groups set themselves apart by adopting certain characteristics or badges indicative of social honor. Usurpation may begin in conflict, but it must be converted into legal privilege, which, we are told, happens only after it has become a "lived-in" reality by virtue of a stable distribution of economic power.[7] It is not clarified whether usurpation of status occurs only after the economic power has already been usurped or prior to that. If stabilization of economic (and political) power normally leads to usurpation of badges of status, does that not make the distinction between class and status rather problematic in the sense that cultural power in that case is a result of economic power? If stabilization of economic power is a condition for the transition from usurpation by convention to usurpation by law (as argued by Weber), what does that say about status without property, the basis of distinction between status and class, to begin with?

Status, the Opposite of Stratification by Market

Status stratification is opposed to stratification by market. Every rational economic pursuit, especially entrepreneurial activity, is looked upon as a disqualification of status. If mere economic acquisition and naked economic power bearing the stigma of extra-status origin could bestow upon anyone the same honor as enjoyed by those who have earned it by virtue of style of life, the status order is threatened to its very core. Precisely because of the rigorous reaction against the claim of property per se, the "parvenu" is never accepted, without reservations, by the privileged status group. However, the succeeding generation of the "parvenu" faces little resistance to acceptance by the status group. Having been educated in the conventions of their status group, they are easily assimilated provided that they have never compromised status honor by engaging in manual labor for subsistence.[8] What this means is that admission to the status group is dependent on stabilization of a family's position in the existing economic–political order. Education in the conventions of the status group as a condition of admission is well taken if it is noted that stabilization of the economic eminence and corresponding political and cultural position was a necessary condition for training in the convention of status. Slaves and serfs could not be educated in the convention of the master and the lord. The low-caste landless laborer could not be educated in the convention of the Brahman whose status qualification was to abstain from physical labor.

The hindrance of the free development of the market, the argument goes on, occurs first for those goods which are monopolized and withheld from free exchange by status groups, for example, the inherited estate in Hellenic cities and in Rome and the estates of knights or the clientele of the merchant guilds in medieval Europe. To that we may add the landed estates in India until the end of colonial rule. The principle at work is that the market is restricted, and the power of naked property per se, which gives its stamp to "class formation," is pushed into the background. Where stratification by status permeates (antiquity and the Middle Ages), one can never speak of a genuinely free-market competition, as we understand it today.[9] If status is a feature of non-market, albeit pre-capitalist, societies, it is well taken. If, however, it is argued that status is independent of property and political power per se, that is problematic. Status in pre-market society (antiquity, feudalism) was based on ancient and feudal forms of property as opposed to bourgeois forms of property characteristic of market (capitalist) society. The basic principle of the intrinsic connection between property and social honor at work is, however, the same in pre-market and market societies: the group having monopoly of economic and political power enjoys the highest social honor. It applies to antiquity, medieval society, and capitalism in the West, as well as to the caste system in India.

Relations of Production and Consumption

The distinction between class and status comes out sharply in Weber's concluding remarks: "classes are stratified according to their relations to the production and acquisition of goods; whereas status groups are stratified according to the principles of their *consumption* of goods as represented by special 'styles of life.'"[10] The problem is that consumption, marker of style of life of the status group, is not isolated from relations of production and acquisition of goods. Production, acquisition, and consumption are determined by the social relations of production, which bind the producers and consumers in unequal economic–political relations justified by dominant ideology with religious and secular components. It is as true of class society as of status societies.

To his credit, Weber admits that separation of status from economic power is not a general condition. He writes that they are separate at one point, connected at another, and separate at yet another. The differences between classes and status groups frequently overlap. It is precisely those status communities most strictly segregated in terms of status honor (e.g., the Indian castes) that there is a high degree of indifference to pecuniary income. However, the Brahmans seek such income in many different ways, he admits.[11] It may be added that the Brahman, barring an ascetic or renouncer (a rank which was in fact not closed to other castes including the lowest castes), indifferent to pecuniary income, is a mythical creature. Going back to Vedic times, Brahmans claimed their share of gold, garments, cows, and maidens acquired by warrior chiefs in return for praying for the latter, a relationship that continued after pastoralism gave way to settled agriculture with warrior chiefs turning into territorial landlords and princes. Brahmans were the first recipients of land grants once land became the private property of the prince and landlords, not only for praying but also for expanding agricultural production on newly colonized lands.[12] In addition, Brahmans monopolized education, a perennial source of pecuniary income, in addition to social honor. In accounting for the eminence of the Brahman in Indian society and history, his spiritual eminence is analytically disconnected from his privileged access to material resources. Social honor of the Brahman in the caste system was not in contrast to economic power. One may argue, following Weber, that the economic power enjoyed by the Brahman was a result of the social honor he enjoyed. That does not, however, negate the fact that social honor and economic power in the caste system were intrinsically connected and mutually reinforcing rather than being contradictory.

The other examples of status group cited by Weber—estate holders in antiquity and medieval times—were distinguished by their style of life premised on consumption. The question is why it is that those who produced (slaves and serfs in the West and lower castes in India) did not consume, while those who did not participate in production (masters in antiquity and modernity, lords in medieval times, and upper castes in India) consumed. The answer lies in the social relations of production. Stylization of life by status group with positive honor: there is no dispute with that, if we remember that status groups with positive honor become bearers of convention and stylization of life only after they have already become bearers of exclusive rights to economic, political, and cultural power. That makes the contrast between class and status problematic.

STATUS AND PERFORMANCE
OF PHYSICAL LABOR

Among privileged status groups there is status disqualification that operates against the performance of common physical labor. Any activity, including artistic and literary, is considered degrading if it is exploited for income or connected with hard physical exertion.[13] When did physical labor become associated with negative social honor in human history? Only when the means of production became the private property of a particular class was the class without property rights compelled to engage in manual labor, freeing the other class to devote itself to mental labor and the symbolic boundaries between the two types of labor with their roots in the material conditions of existence drawn and sanctioned by convention, law, and religion. Manual labor became the condition of status disqualification and mental labor, of status qualification. As Richard Lee writes, "For most of the long history of human society, however, there were no leisure class, few machines and no distinction between the mental and manual laborer. Everyone worked and everyone used both hands and mind."[14]

A digression: status disqualification is now setting in America against the old tradition of esteem for labor, writes Weber.[15] The tradition of esteem for labor in America noted by Weber is interesting. How well does that sit with the real history of the degradation of labor in America, a degradation that included slaves, indentured servants, indentured whites, and immigrants including Irish, Russians, and Jews at the turn of the twentieth century?[16] What masters in antiquity, landlords in medieval Europe, dominant castes in India, and bourgeoisie in America have in common is their disdain of (manual) labor in the process of production—a disdain that is extended to the laborer, as rightly noted by Sharma[17] in the specific context of the caste system in India.

Finally, as to the general economic conditions making for the predominance of stratification by status, Weber only says the following: "When the bases of the acquisition and distribution of goods are relatively stable, stratification by status is favored."[18] We may be reminded that the separation of cultural power from economic power is the very starting point of the distinction between status and class. It follows that separating cultural power from economic power and disconnecting consumption from relations of production and acquisition, the core of status–class distinction, is untenable.

STATUS AND MISCEGENATION

Tambiah writes that the classical theory enshrines timeless truths about certain basic features of the Indian caste system. One such timeless truth he mentions is the differential privilege and dominance coded in the traditional theory in terms of sexual access to women of different varna status. Hypergamy (*anuloma*) and concubinage, prevalent in different parts of India at different times, were among the institutionalized forms of this privilege, he writes. Going back to ancient days, Manu prescribed that a Brahman may take three more wives, in addition to one from his own varna and three from the other three varnas; Kshatriya two more, Vaisya one more, and the Sudra only one (from his own).[19]

Milner argues that while many status groups are concerned about the regulation of sexual relations in general, they are especially concerned with the regulation of marriage.[20] They may, however, be excused for sowing "wild oats." In the specific context of caste, it refers to upper-caste men having sexual relations with lower-caste women, with no obligation to marry. As Rajshekhar puts it, "while our men are untouchables, our women can be enjoyed by the high caste men."[21] In characterizing this as "sowing wild oats," Milner is dismissive of it as individual deviance. It was not individual deviance but a systemic issue. It happened in medieval Europe, the antebellum South, and the caste system on a daily basis. Status groups with positive honor—upper castes in India, masters in the antebellum South, and the aristocracy in medieval Europe, given their control over the means of subsistence of the lower caste, race, and class—"usurped the privilege" (to borrow Weber's words) of access to the female bodies of the latter, while zealously guarding the sexuality of their own women, particularly against access by men of the latter. As a systemic issue, it was an embodiment of asymmetrical power relations between the higher and the lower in the caste system. It was the same between the master and the slave in slavery and the lord and the serf in feudalism. Sexual access by men of privileged groups to women of unprivileged groups in different social economic formations across cultural boundaries is a phenomenon of power as defined by Weber, that is, to impose one's will against the resistance of the other.

Social Honor in Caste: Consequence or Cause of Economic–Political Power

In distinguishing status from class, Weber argued that, indeed, social honor, or prestige, may even be the basis of political or economic power and very frequently has been. This argument is commonly used in mainstream sociology, that it is not economic power (or a lack of it) that makes a particular caste higher or lower in status. To the contrary, it is their status (with a positive or negative association with honor) which determines their access to economic (and political) power or a lack of it. It is thus argued that Marx on occasion overstated the effect of people's relationship to the means of production. In doing that, we are told, he did not give adequate attention to the reverse causal relationship, that is, the way social–cultural factors determine the available resources.[22] In order to determine whether social honor in the caste system results from, or results in, economic power, one has to study caste hierarchy not only as it exists at a particular point of time but also over time including times of social change. Take, for instance, the case of the Rajputs and Jats in Rajasthan until the 1940s and afterward. Until end of the 1940s, the Jats as peasants were dependent tenure holders in subordination to the Rajput landlords and consequently lower in caste hierarchy. Following the abolition of the age-old land tenure system following the abolition of landlordism in the 1950s, the Jats became independent proprietors of lands according to their occupation, which also enhanced their political power and social honor. It is the same with Ahirs and Kunabis in Uttar Pradesh and Bihar.

Historically, the most obvious case of economic power resulting in social honor is that of the Kshatriyization or Rajputization of the various groups of amorphous origin who after establishing dominion over a territory staked claim to the Kshatriya (Rajput) status and found pliable Brahmans or bards to legitimize their claim in return for material gain. As Romila Thapar notes, the rise of families of relatively obscure origin to high social status, usually through the channel of landownership and administrative office, is amply shown by historical records. Those who became economically and politically powerful had genealogies fabricated for themselves, bestowing on the family Kshatriya status, linked with royal lineages.[23]

As argued by R. S. Sharma,[24] the members of the higher castes could claim a number of exploitative privileges only when manual work was separated from non-manual (religious, intellectual, and administrative) work. The main condition for that to occur was to separate the laboring groups from the land, the most important means of production of the time, which allowed the higher castes to perpetuate their power and position by socially–culturally distancing themselves from the former—artisans and agricultural laborers. Rituals of purity and pollution were devised to mask the division of property and political power, turning a social–historical process into a divine creation. Thus, only after particular castes were dispossessed of the means of their subsistence were they associated with negative social honor and a lower rank in caste hierarchy, which became self-perpetuating with the passage of time. Conversely, caste or castes gaining access to productive resources and political power moved up, becoming more power-ful not only economically and politically but also culturally in terms of social honor. Mainstream sociology of caste confined, by and large, to studying caste as it exists at a particular period rather than over a course of different periods turns the relationship between economic power and social honor in the caste system upside down, making the latter cause the former.

DISTINCTION OF CASTE AS STATUS: RELIGIOUS USURPATION

As a status group, caste has a specific feature that makes it rather distinct from other types of status group. As noted, status distinctions in caste are guaranteed not only by conventions and laws but also by rituals. This occurs in such a way that every physical contact between members of higher and lower castes results in ritualistic impurity—a stigma that must be expiated by a religious act.[25] Usurpation by religion, in addition to convention and law, in the caste system noted by Weber is beyond doubt an important, arguably the most important, of Weber's observations about caste. It may be mentioned that apart from usurpation, the relationship between religion and caste in general is unarguably the most controversial and debated issue in the sociology of caste.[26] Mainstream sociology of caste, following Weber, turned his valuable insight about the role of religion in usurpation into religion as the very essence of caste and the caste sys-tem, stamping the latter with cultural uniqueness—Indian exceptionalism, with Louis Dumont's *Homo Hierarchicus* being the most famous example of this. In what follows, I discuss some of the issues arising from the centrality of religion in isolation from economic–political power in conceptualizing caste as status.

SUBORDINATION OF POLITICAL POWER TO RELIGIOUS POWER IN CASTE: INDIAN EXCEPTIONALISM

The distinction between status (priest/Brahman) and power (prince/Kshatriya) is at the core of Louis Dumont's *Homo Hierarchicus*, unarguably one of most important and talked about books on caste. It may be noted here that Dumont borrows the idea of status from Weber and gives it his own interpretation to make it purely religious—a distortion of Weber's conceptualization of status and of the reality of caste, past and present. Dumont writes that some eight centuries perhaps before Christ, Hindu tradition established an absolute distinction between power and hierarchical status. Indian culture, he argues, is characterized by the probably unique phenomenon of a thoroughgoing distinction between hierarchy and power. As a result, hierarchy appears there in its pure form.[27] Milner echoes Dumont in saying that, strange as it may seem, the culture of premodern India has been relatively successful over a long period of time at insulating status from economic–political power.[28] Status and moral worth have been less directly dependent upon economic and political power than in most other complex societies. Hence, Milner asks, is status more important in India than in most societies? This is a case of Indian exceptionalism.

PRIEST AHEAD OF PRINCE: BRAHMANOCENTRIC VIEW OF CASTE

It has been argued that Brahman (spiritual power) in the caste system does not fall under the jurisdiction of the Kshatriya (economic–political power). The relationship between the spiritual principle and the principle of imperium is fully seen in the institution of the *purohit* (priest) with whom the king must have a "permanent personal relationship." *Purohit* literally means "the one placed in front." The king depends on him for all the actions of his life, for these would not succeed without him. *Purohit* is to the king as thought is to will.[29] If one goes by historical and ethnographic evidence, there is scant support for the precedence of priest over prince. The prince was not dependent on the priest for "all actions." In economic, political, juridical, and military matters—the main spheres of kingly duty (*rajdharma*)—there was little involvement of the priest. Priests' activities were confined to rituals in temples. Kingdoms were not founded on rituals or for rituals but on the monopoly of land, the main form of property and principal source of subsistence; the main function of kings was the administration of land and people within their territory. In administering the land and people, the prince was dependent on peers—the fraternity of landlords—who were members of his class and caste. In the administration of land and people, the priest was not to the fore. The priest and the prince were united and separated. The prince provided for the priest in return for the spiritual and ideological service the latter rendered. But the prince and the priest belonged to two separate spheres when it came to the main affairs—economic, political, juridical, military, and social–cultural—of the state. They belonged to the realm of the profane, separate from the realm of the sacred belonging to the temple. The prince was the eminent owner of all land in the state, on which depended the survival of all including that of the priest. To collapse the court into the temple and privilege the temple over the court and the priest over the prince is distortion of historical reality.

WAS THE PRIEST–PRINCE
RELATIONSHIP IN INDIA UNIQUE?

It is argued that, driven by religion, the alliance between priest and prince in India was unique, separating it from other historical cases. To the contrary, the alliance between prince and priest in the caste system was not basically different from the alliance between king and priest in feudal societies in Africa, Asia, and Europe. The driving force behind the alliance was not religious but secular. The prince and the priest together constituted the dominant class (and caste), an alliance against the rest of society. As Huberman writes about the Middle Ages in Europe, the church and nobility were the ruling classes, which seized the land and the power that went with it. The church provided spiritual aid and the nobility, military protection. In return for this they squeezed the laboring classes.[30] As in the case of the church and the nobility in Europe, the function of the priest was to provide spiritual service in return for military protection and material rewards guaranteed by the prince. Together, they seized the land and the political power to squeeze the peasants and artisans in the caste system.

THE PROBLEM OF LEGITIMATION

Hermann Kulke writes that Weber focuses his analysis of the Hindu social system on the order of the castes, but his definition of the caste system had little influence on actual anthropological research on caste, Dumont's *Homo Hierarchicus* being a prime example.[31] I disagree. Weber is the single most important influence on mainstream sociology and social anthropology of caste, with Dumont's *Homo Hierarchicus* being the most important. Weber's distinction between status and class is at the very core of *Homo Hierarchicus*. Weber's influence is even stronger on the relationship between caste and Hinduism in mainstream sociology of caste in general, Dumont in particular. It is the same with the Brahmanocentric view of caste and the centrality of commensality and connubium in defining the caste system. Affinity between Weber, Dumont, and mainstream sociology of caste is not incidental. Rather, it is based on their common objective to find an alternative to Marxism as an explanatory model of society and history, as Sara Farris argues.[32]

Weber's concept of legitimation is considered "an intrinsic and seminal aspect of his study on the Hindu social system and processes of state formation and Hinduization." It has been argued that the centrality of religion and the preeminence of Brahman in the caste system was due to the role of the priest in the legitimation of princely rule.[33] Weber wrote,

> Legitimation by a recognized religion has always been decisive for an alliance between politically socially dominant classes and priesthood. It provided the "barbarians"

with recognized rank in the cultural world of Hinduism. By transforming them into castes it secured their superiority over the subject classes with an efficacy unsurpassed by any religion.[34]

Apart from the sacred texts of Hinduism, if one looks at historical and ethnographic evidence, it is clear that the legitimation of kingship was not exclusively or even primarily a religious phenomenon. It was rather predominantly political–economic outside the spiritual domain of the Brahman priest. The role of the priest (Brahman) and the religious nature of coronation of the king and legitimation of the kingship are exaggerated, suppressing the secular and contingent character of kingly power, most importantly, the role of peers—the fraternity of landlords. A king could not rule without the consent of his peers on whom he was dependent for the military support to conquer and defend the kingdom in the first instance and subsequently for their political support to administer it.

In the Rajput princely states of Rajasthan, the coronation ceremony was not complete until and unless the peerage (the fraternity of land grantees in return for military, political, and judicial services) took the oath of allegiance. The coronation of the ruler of Marawar (a premier princely state of Rajasthan) was not complete unless the landlord of Bagari (a prominent land grantee of the state) put the *tilak* (the red mark of sovereignty) with the blood of his thumb on the forehead of the would-be king. In the state of Mewar (another premier state of Rajasthan), the privilege of putting the *tilak* with his blood on the forehead of the king at coronation belonged to the Bhil chief, member of a tribal group outside the fold of Hinduism and the caste system. Kulke mentions similar cases of the special role played by tribal chiefs, outside the fold of Hinduism and caste, in the coronation in the princely states of Orissa.[35] The participation of tribal chiefs in the coronation of Hindu kings, he points out, can be interpreted as a demonstration of the power of the dominant tribes as the real or original owners of the land and the mutual dependence between the king and the tribe.

In the princely states of Rajasthan the Jain monks of the monastic lineage, in addition to the Charans and the Bhats, had a prominent role in royal affairs including coronation and legitimation. The Brahmans, Jain monks, Charans, and Bhats competed in providing alternative narratives of major historical events relating to the kings and kingdoms. What is interesting is that the Jain monks, Charans, and Bhats did not identify with the Brahmans. Rather, they identified with and emulated, by and large, the lifestyle of the Rajputs, the dominant caste.[36] Legitimation and coronation were not sacred, rooted in religion, but dictated by political, economic, and administrative contingencies: they were profane.

It may be pointed out that the most important change in the transition from tribe to caste was the dissolution of tribal property rights in land and its replacement by feudal land rights. Conversion to Hinduism and caste was the secondary step. Sociologists following Weber focused on the latter, ignoring the former altogether. Integration of tribes took place at the top (Kshatriya) and at the bottom (Shudra) of the caste hierarchy. The difference between the two did not lie in Hinduization but in their differential land rights, political power, and social esteem—one having monopoly of all powers, the other dispossessed and powerless. The sociology of legitimation in caste is confined to the top, ignoring the bottom. It is the story of the upper caste. Its main failure is evading the question of land, the very basis of stratification by caste and class. Inability to deal with the land question is more serious in Weber's theory of stratification by caste. To deal with that, we turn to the question of feudalism.

CASTE AND THE LAND QUESTION: THE PROBLEM OF FEUDALISM

Weber relates the peculiarity of the caste system, in which spiritual authority of the Brahman reigns supreme, to the absence of feudalism in India. How does he establish that relationship? The Hindu social order, he argues, more than anywhere else in the world (another instance of Indian exceptionalism!) is organized in terms of the principle of clan charisma. This form of charisma was not absent in the West. The hereditary divine right of kings and the legend of blue blood are examples of charisma in the West, he admits. However, in the West the charisma was routinized and institutionalized in the offices of the prince, the elector, and the cardinal. To the contrary, in India it was confined to the sib. Sib charisma prevented the development of feudalism in India, which in turn kept the "rural idiocy" of the priest intact.[37]

In order to show how sib charisma prevented the development of feudalism in India, Weber argues that feudal ties in Europe developed in response to the military need of the time: feudal relationships were made by a "free contract" among sib strangers. Increasingly, feudal lords developed the in-group feeling of a unitary status group and eventually into the "closed hereditary estates of chivalrous knights." This relationship grew on the basis of sib estrangement among men who viewed themselves not as sib, phratry, or tribe but simply as "status peers." Indian development, to the contrary, took quite a different turn. There the feudal status formation did not rest on land grants. Rather, it was derived from the sib, clan, phratry, and tribe, as correctly emphasized by Baden-Powell. The conquering classes in India were comprised of a circle of phratries and sibs of lords dispersing over the conquered territory under the rule of the tribe, writes Weber. Feudal prerogatives were enforced by the head of the phratry (*raja*) or a tribal king (*maharajah*) only, as a rule, to his agnates. It was not a freely contracted trusteeship. Fellow sib members claimed their land grant as a birthright.[38]

Romila Thapar points out that Weber ignored the evidence showing that land grants in India were feudal rather than prebendal. The *Dharmasastras* and *Arthashastra*, she points out, discuss the laws and regulations for the sale, bequest, and inheritance of land and other forms of property. Inscriptions on stone and copper plates after 500 CE, recording the grant of land to religious beneficiaries by the king or wealthy persons, are even more precise. So are the secular grants made by the king in return for service. These inscriptions were deciphered in the nineteenth century but read primarily for chronology and dynastic purposes. Land grants in India broke the clan charisma going back to the first millennium CE, she writes.[39]

Early centuries (Christian era) in India were a period of transition, when land and other agrarian resources came to be privately controlled by a considerable class of beneficiaries, religious and secular, which resulted in a division of society into two basic classes: (1) landlords having titles to land grants and (2) peasants, the basic producers. The landlords restricted the free access of the peasants to lands. This led to the emergence of the two principal classes—(1) landlords with a monopoly of economic–political powers and (2) dependent peasantry having the right to possess lands in return for rent and tributes. This constituted feudalism.[40]

It may be added that a serious problem with Weber's position on feudalism in India, or the West for that matter, is that he confines himself to considering the political relations between landlords, ignoring the relations between landlords and serfs, the two principal classes of feudalism and its very foundation. Instead, consistent with his approach, he isolates a particular cultural feature, fealty, from its structural roots and turns it into the defining feature of feudalism. Whether feudalism ever developed in India depends on an answer to the most important question: were the relations between lords and peasants in India feudal, as defined in a generic sense?

Whether relations between a prince and his sib and clan members were feudal came up in the famous controversy between James Tod and Alfred Lyall in the nineteenth century. Tod maintained that the relations between rulers and landlords in the princely states of Rajputana (now Rajasthan) were analogous to the relations between lords and vassals in medieval Europe.[41] Lyall, to the contrary, argued that Tod failed to make a distinction between two forms of society, tribal and feudal, and mistakenly introduced into his writings on Rajputana such medieval terms as "feuds" and "subinfeudation." Rather than comparing "the Rajput tribal system" to that of medieval Europe, it should appropriately be compared to the system of kindred tribes like the Pathans and Afghans or a widely spread tribe of professional thieves, the Meenas of Rajputana. Lands held by the subchiefs of Rajputana must not be confused with the service grants—the fiefs—of medieval Europe. They were instead part of the clan occupation. The clannish origin of their tenures makes them tribal, rather than feudal. The subchiefs, rather than being the dependent tenure holders of the ruler of the state, were indeed their co-parceners. As clan members, they were equal partners in landownership,[42] which is the same as Weber's argument.

Contrary to Lyall, historical evidence from the 1870s shows that landlords in the princely states of Rajputana held their grants as service tenures. The two most important conditions attached to these grants were *rekh* (tribute) and *chakari* (service), the latter being more important.[43] There are innumerable instances where a land grantee was forgiven for defaulting the payment of *rekh*, but in no single instance was he forgiven the default of *chakari* since it included military service, among a whole host of other services symbolic of inequality between the prince and the landlords holding their grants at the sufferance of the former. The subordinate status of the subchiefs (land grantees) was clearly demarcated not only by the lower economic, political, and juridical rights they held of the king but also by the symbolic boundaries that set the chiefs and sub-chiefs apart, notwithstanding their common kinship and caste ties. The obligations of the land grantees (subchiefs) in Rajasthan involved the duties of kindred in addition to those of obedience ranging from attending the court and guarding the fort to giving themselves as hostages for their lord.[44] It contradicts Weber's claim that the position of subchiefs in India was dependent upon sib or clan, denoting equality rather than a feudal hierarchy.[45]

There were other features of land grants in India that made them feudal, most important being the primogeniture, which in feudalism was a device to prevent par-celization of the estate to enable it to meet the public obligations attached to the land grants.[46] More importantly, it was indicative of the precedence of class interests over those of kinship.[47] The justification of primogeniture in Hindu law rested on a distinc-tion between private property and a chiefship. In the case of the former, all of the sons had an equal share in family estates, but this did not apply to chiefships. Chiefship was a public estate, and the owner had to discharge the responsibilities of kingly office. It was for this reason that a land grant in return for military service was not allowed to die: "[sub]chief, like his sovereign never dies.... The great fiefs of Rajasthan never become extinct."[48] The distinction between private and public is absent in social for-mations based on the sib.

The basic principle of landholding in the feudal system is defined as follows:

> The feudal system in the last resort rested upon an organization, which, in return for a protection...placed the working classes at the mercy of the idle classes, and gave the land not to those who cultivated it, but to those who had been able to seize it.[49]

Seizure of land in India by those who did not labor was not negated by the caste system. To the contrary, it was the very basis of caste hierarchy, very much as it was the basis of class hierarchy in feudal regimes elsewhere.

Our disagreement with Weber is on the wider implications of his argument in this context; that is, Indian society organized by the caste system rooted in Hinduism did not move beyond the tribal stage, while society in the West moved from tribalism to slavery to serfdom (feudalism), finally culminating in capitalism. To the contrary, the introduction of plough agriculture in various regions marked the transition from a clan-based to a class- and caste-based society going back to the first millennium BCE. The Mauryan Empire controlling the Indian subcontinent, contemporary to the Hellenic regime, was not a tribal polity and economy. The evolution of the state proper (premised on the disintegration of the sib and clan as the basis of socioeconomic organization) took place in the Ganga Valley in the mid-first millennium BCE.[50] The most important change in the transition from the clan to the state society was the dissolution of the communal property and its replacement by hierarchical rights in land, with the ruler of the state having the highest rights. Weber does recognize the difference between tribe and caste in terms of different modes of subsistence (based on different property rights), but in distinguishing the tribe from the caste he shifts the focus to rituals in isolation from the mode of subsistence and property rights.[51]

Conclusion

In conceptualizing class and status, Weber's main objective was to provide an alternative to the Marxist notion of class and class struggle in history. By defining class as a market situation, Weber provides an alternative view of history and the role of class and class struggle in the making of it. If class is a market situation, it could not have existed in pre-market, albeit pre-capitalist, societies; and the origin of capitalism could no more be attributed to class contradictions and class struggle under feudalism.

Weber's challenge in conceptualizing status as cultural power in contrast to class as economic power was to find empirical–historical examples of status groups. The examples of slave and master, serf and lord in Western history were open to interrogation in the sense that these divisions were also divisions between the propertied and the propertyless. The Brahman in the Indian caste system, assumed to have social honor without economic (and political) power, ideally meets the criterion of status. The Brahman in the caste system also meets the other criterion of status, that is, entitlement to economic power on account of social honor.

The Brahman serves yet another function in Weber's other project, "The Economic Ethics of the World Religions," which can be seen as a follow-up to his Protestant ethic thesis. If capitalism did not develop in India, the reason must be found in the absence of a rational economic ethic in Hinduism. In *The Religion of India*, caste is presented as predominantly religious and a creation of Hinduism. Inseparability of Hinduism and caste—no Hinduism without caste and no caste without Hinduism—emphasized in the *Religion of India* has to be seen in that light. Subsequent studies of caste in mainstream sociology rather than critically examining Weber's conceptualization of caste as status and separating the rational elements in his thesis from the irrational elements according to modern scholarship, turned it into a formula. This is not what Weber aimed at, as outlined by Roth (quoted at the start of this chapter).

Hinduism has played and continues to play an important role in shaping caste consciousness, and Weber's contribution in that regard remains valuable. It is equally important to emphasize that religion (read Hinduism) is *not* the basis of caste stratification. Indian exceptionalism due to the uniqueness of caste rooted in Hinduism is based on myth. True, caste is not class. But caste is not negation of class in Indian society and history. Historically, class developed in India before caste, and class relations are the very foundation of caste hierarchy. Neither the structure of caste at a particular time in a particular region nor the struggles and changes in the caste system over millennia can be understood in isolation from class relations.

In Weber, caste is part of a universal-historical system of stratification. In mainstream sociology, apparently following Weber, caste is peripheralized to uniquely Indian cultural phenomena, a case of Indian exceptionalism. Bringing caste from the periphery to the center of the comparative historical study of social stratification will enrich the Weberian legacy. It will also liberate mainstream sociology of caste from narrow ethnocentrism.

NOTES

1. Guenther Roth, "Introduction" to Max Weber, *Economy and Society: An Outline of Interpretive Sociology* (hereafter *E&S*), ed. G. Roth and C. Wittich (New York: Bedminster Press, 1968), xxvii, xxix.

2. Max Weber, *The Religion of India. The Sociology of Hinduism and Buddhism* (hereafter *RI*), trans. Hans H. Gerth and Don Martindale (New York: Free Press, 1958); *Die Wirtschaftsethik der Weltreligionen. Hinduismus und Buddhismus. 1916–1920, Max Weber-Gesamtausgabe* (hereafter *MWG*) I/20, ed. H. Schmidt-Glintzer, with K.-H. Golzio (Tübingen, Germany: Mohr [Siebeck], 1996).

3. Murray Milner, *Status and Sacredness: A General Theory of Status Relations and an Analysis of Indian Culture* (New York: Oxford University Press, 1994), 7.

4. Max Weber, "The Distribution of Power Within the Political Community: Class, Status, Party," *E&S*, 926–940; "'Klassen,' 'Stände' und 'Parteien,'" *Wirtschaft und Gesellschaft. Nachlaß. Teilband 1: Gemeinschaften, MWG* I/22-1, ed. W. J. Mommsen, with M. Meyer (Tübingen, Germany: Mohr [Siebeck], 2001), 252–272.

5. *E&S*, 932; *MWG* I/22-1, 259–260.

6. *From Max Weber: Essays in sociology*, ed. and trans. Hans H. Gerth and C. Wright Mills (New York: Oxford University Press, 1958), 39.

7. *E&S*, 933; *MWG* I/22-1, 262.

8. *E&S*, 935-936; *MWG* I/22-1, 266–267.

9. *E&S*, 936–937; *MWG* I/22-1, 267–268.

10. *E&S*, 937; *MWG* I/22-1, 268.

11. *E&S*, 937; *MWG* I/22-1, 268.

12. R. S. Sharma, *Rethinking India's Past* (Delhi, India: Oxford University Press, 2009), 176–177.

13. *E&S*, 936; *MWG* I/22-1, 266.

14. Richard B. Lee, *The !Kung San: Men, Women, and Work in a Foraging Society* (Cambridge: Cambridge University Press, 1990), 250.

15. *E&S*, 936; *MWG* I/22-1, 266.

16. Karen Brodkin, *How Jews Became White Folks and What That Says About Race in America* (New Brunswick, NJ: Rutgers University Press, 1998).

17. Sharma, *Rethinking India's Past*, 7.

18. *E&S*, 938; *MWG* I/22-1, 269.

19. S. J. Tambiah, "From Varna to Caste Through Mixed Unions," in *The Character of Kinship*, ed. Jack Goody (Cambridge: Cambridge University Press, 1973), 191–230.

20. Milner, *Status and Sacredness*, 39–40.

21. V. T. Rajshekar, *Hinduism vs Movement of Untouchables in India* (Bangalore, India: Dalit Sahitya Academy, 1983), 4.

22. Milner, *Status and Sacredness*, 7.

23. Romila Thapar, *Cultural Pasts* (Delhi, India: Oxford University Press, 2000), 13; Sekhar Bandyopadhyay, *Caste, Culture, and Hegemony: Social Domination in Colonial Bengal*

(Delhi, India: Sage, 2004) 51; Weber, *RI*, 65; *MWG* I/20, 131; Hermann Kulke, "Max Weber's Concept of Legitimation in Hinduism Revisited," *Max Weber Studies* 18, no. 1 (2018): 55–57.

24. Sharma, *Rethinking India's Past*, 7.
25. *E&S*, 933; *MWG* I/22-1, 262.
26. For more on this, see R. S. Khare, ed., *Caste Hierarchy, and Individualism: Indian Critiques of Louis Dumont's Contributions* (Delhi, India: Oxford University Press, 2006).
27. Louis Dumont, *Homo Hierarchicus: The Caste System and Its Implications*, trans. Mark Sainsbury et al. (Chicago: University of Chicago Press, 1980).
28. Milner, *Status and Sacredness*, 16, 28.
29. Dumont, *Homo Hierarchicus*, 289–290.
30. Leo Huberman, *Man's Worldly Goods: The Story of the Wealth of Nations* (New York and London: Monthly Review Press, 1963), 15.
31. Kulke, "Max Weber's Concept of Legitimation," 41.
32. Sara R. Farris, "New and Old Spirits of Capitalism," *International Review of Social History* 55 (2010): 297–306.
33. Kulke, "Max Weber's Concept of Legitimation," 40–46.
34. *RI*, 16; *MWG* I/20, 68–69 (translation altered).
35. Kulke, "Max Weber's Concept of Legitimation," 57–64.
36. Ramya Sreenivasan, *The Many Lives of a Rajput Queen: Heroic Pasts in India c. 1500–1900* (Seattle: Washington University Press, 2007), 77–79.
37. *RI*, 50–51; *MWG* I/20, 110–111.
38. *RI*, 53–54; *MWG* I/20, 114–115.
39. Thapar, *Cultural Pasts*, 12, 41.
40. Sharma, *Rethinking India's Past*, 18–19.
41. James Tod, *Annals and Antiquities of Rajasthan* (1832; London: Routledge, 1920), 153.
42. Alfred Lyall, *Asiatic Studies, Religious and Social: First Series* (London: John Murray, 1882).
43. G. D. Sharma, *Rajput Polity: A Study of Politics and Administration of the State of Marwar, 1638–1749* (Delhi, India: Manohar Publishers, 1977).
44. Tod, *Annals and Antiquities*, 146.
45. *RI*, 63; *MWG* I/20, 128.
46. F. L. Ganshof, *Feudalism*, trans. P. Grierson (New York: Harper & Row, 1964), 45.
47. Marc Bloch, *Feudal Society* (London: Routledge, 1961), 204.
48. Tod, *Annals and Antiquities*, 153.
49. Huberman, *Man's Worldly Goods*, 16.
50. Sharma, *Rethinking India's Past*, 34–37; Thapar, *Cultural Pasts*, 377–379.
51. *RI*, 30–31; *MWG* I/20, 88–89.

CHAPTER 22

INCLUDING ISLAM

STEFAN LEDER

THE legacy of Max Weber's observations on Islam resides in his transcultural approach, and the evaluation of his assessments concerning Islamic culture, society, and political order, scattered in his work, has to consider this orientation.[1] Weber's theoretical inquiry combines the epistemic value of comparison with the ambition of conceiving an abstract typology that defines characteristics of specific cultures. His comparative sociology thus intends to develop a comprehensive understanding of transcultural relationships. Instrumental to the understanding of how modernity emerged in the West from a background of traditions formed by antiquity, Christianity, and the premodern European polity, his inquiry into concepts, attitudes, and configurations of power in Chinese, Indian, Jewish, and Islamic civilizations offered a new conceptual framework. The historical context of his work was the unrivaled world hegemony that Europe, or more generally the West, enjoyed at the beginning of the twentieth century. It made anthropologists, historians, philosophers, and social theorists embark on explaining this triumph in self-congratulatory terms. Yet the analytical properties of his work and its methodical innovation and comprehensive outlook surpassed the established discourse of "othering" in nineteenth-century *Weltgeschichte* in Germany.[2] Weber's concepts have to be repositioned today in a way that reflects postmodern discourse and globalized outlooks skeptical of Europe's uniqueness.[3] This requires transcending Weber's typology and reconsidering the analytical perspectives that inform it. Aspects of his approach then constitute a suggestive, challenging, and inspiring research agenda until this day.

WEBER AND ISLAM

The importance of Islamic religion and Muslim society in Weber's thought is hard to establish. According to what we know from his work as it has come down to us,[4] Islam was not a central interest of his, nor was his attempt to incorporate Islamic civilization into his intellectual venture marginal to his work. Weber assigned to Islam a cultural specificity informed by its difference. That particular lens magnified details, distorted proportions, and thus impaired his perception. His approach, however, beyond the contingency of historical and intellectual conditions that helped to give shape to his vision, is inductive and offers impulse and guidance for a comparative and transcultural work that includes Islam.

Weber's pivotal idea, that the transformation of specific traditions in Europe induced the dynamics of rationalization foundational to modernity and that this dynamic was effective in particular through the elective affinity between Calvinist ascetic Protestantism and the routines and mentality of rational capitalism, owes much to the stimuli he received from contemporary (German) studies of economy and theology.[5] Although he perceived Calvinism and Islam as similar with respect to how the belief in the unconditionally transcendent almighty God is sustained,[6] he ascribes to Islam a plain predeterministic belief in contrast to the more complex Calvinist doctrine that emphasizes salvation and rational work ascetics.[7] As a cultural factor, inner-worldly asceticism contributes to a disciplined and order-based lifestyle and way of life.[8] His selective view of Islam emerges as a substantial addendum to this agenda and is instrumental for his purpose of elaborating the European particularity through comparison. This approach tends to construe the Islamic "other" as being defined by the lack of preconditions for a development comparable to the European. Despite this obvious tendency, it may offer a theoretical framework that invites further exploration also on the Islamic side.

Inspired by Weber's *Protestant Ethic*, one study of Islamic theology explored a sideline of the Islamic acquisition ethic, namely the concept of acquisition of merit, which shows striking similarity to Weber's Protestant asceticism.[9] The significance of such a parallel phenomenon remains limited, however, because Weber suggests a complex inner relationship between belief, comportment, mentality, and institutional order that results from a particular constellation of convergent historical sociocultural factors.[10] The impact of religious belief in this model relies on the role of a (bourgeois) milieu of carriers whose lifestyle and practices produce a lasting sociocultural impact. We may therefore conclude that attempting to identify analogous constellations in the Islamic environment is problematic, if not fruitless, but that paying attention to striking similarities regarding aspects of it challenges the underlying concept of distinction and separation.

The potential of Weber's peculiar and suggestive notion of "elective affinity" (*Wahlverwandtschaft*) is not limited to the historical model. He also refers to the notion in terms of adequacy,[11] in a way that is vague enough to avoid a narrow definition of this relationship. Accordingly, Weber interpreters suggest that he was not trying to demonstrate causal primacy of values but affinity, congruency, and mutual reinforcement.[12] The interest in the impact of religion and cultural traditions and, more generally, the relationship between culture, institutional patterns, and political order stand in the center of Weber's work.[13] This approach invites us to reassess the impact of religion and its relationship with political order in terms adequate to the Islamic context. As reading Weber demands going beyond the boundaries of his thought, this also implies the necessary reorientation of his discourse in terms of a plurality of pathways to modernity.

The Eurocentric outlook which informs Weber's account of—or rather scattered remarks on—religion, political order, and social and economic matters of Islamic civilization is an inherited imprint and pervasive flaw that inspired anti-orientalist and anti-essentialist criticism, as well as criticism of historians of the Near East emphasizing the complexities, subtle differentiations, and interpretations that Weber missed or ignored.[14] As Weber's characterization of Islamic society might be summarized as a series of lacks and absences in Islamic civilization, regarding inter alia the autonomous city, private property, democratic rights, rational law, natural sciences, and social revolutions, it is an inborn reaction of the specialist to verify the underlying data and to correct accordingly the lopsidedness of this overall picture. The task also appeals to the theorist who does not subscribe to the supposed inevitability of defining modernity singularly as a European endeavor.[15] However, in this perspective, the essentialist argument that gives priority to certain perceived characteristics meant to represent the nature or spirit of Islam or Islamic society may appear as a heuristic instrument appropriate for the delineation of distinction and unavoidable in comparative work.[16] It is moreover a means of exploring the self in a perceived context of plurality, which in fact constitutes an arena of contact with the other and thus goes beyond the notion of cultural singularity.[17] In this vein, essentialism per se, despite its ambivalence, does not necessarily delegitimize the intellectual endeavor. Weber's use of the ideal type as a conceptual idealization and an instrument to bridge the gap between theory and history is not an issue that would justify contempt.[18]

The ideal type remains problematic, however, as long as the context of its deployment is not transparent, when it serves tacitly established perspectives and a preconditioned "logic of making a difference" aiming at establishing distinction and separation.[19] Qualifying Islam as a warrior religion may thus seem faulty by the normative and ideological nature of the term. It may also appear to presuppose a unitary character not only of Islam, which evidently is a contestable notion in the light of the changing diversity of "Islam," but of modern civilization in general.[20] Yet the ideal type may be functional to the questions asked and derived from it so that various ideal types are conceivable depending on the particular orientation of the inquiry.[21] Historically, in terms of a representative cultural orientation that molded the relationship between the spheres of religion, law, and political order, the role of Islamic religious authority (*'ulamā'*) stands out, much more than that of warriors. The problem here then is not primarily the essentializing character of the ideal type but rather that it may fail to grasp a central dynamic that gave shape to Islamic history.

The framework of Weber's approach was indeed tentatively applied to Islamic society, that is, society historically influenced by Islamic religion. Ernest Gellner's renowned distinction of the "great tradition" of urban, scriptural Islam from the "little tradition" of rural, tribal, heterodox Islam presents Islam as a coherent, unitary, and dynamic entity, distinct from European civilization but in part comparably structured. He thus recognizes a reverberation of Weber's concept of the "Protestant ethic" in the disciplined urban Islam ("monistic, puritan, scripturalistic") promoted by religious scholars ('*ulamā*'). He also regarded the rise of urban high Islam with its puritanical tendencies in modernity as a phenomenon convergent with Weber's idea of the compatibility between the "Protestant ethic" and a rational economy, an idea that he also applied in his study of the emergence of the nation and the nation-state more generally.[22] The apparent incoherence in this distinction of two traditions, which omits large parts of Islam, as well as the questionable comparison of Islamic scholarly puritanism with Weber's idea of Protestant inner-worldly asceticism, gave reason to contest this conception.[23] While addressing the conflict between simplifying tendencies of theory and detail-oriented history, this critique implicitly relates to the difficulty of how to approach characteristic traits of Islamic civilization in its own terms *and* in a manner that relates to a universal framework.

REFRAMING THE WEBERIAN PERSPECTIVE

In this vein, the ubiquitous conceptualization of legitimation and accountability, for instance, is recognizable in the Islamic context by use of notions such as law (*sharʿ, fiqh*) and justice (*ʿadāla*), and thus relates to the relationship between religious and political order. The assessment of difference in comparative analysis must avoid statements of static deficiency. The assertion that democratic constituencies in many societies of the Middle East are scarce and preconditions for the application of the Western model of democracy precarious, however true, must translate into a contextualized vision of how forms of political participation occur or may occur and to what degree we have to be attentive to impediments from outside.[24] This implies expanding the horizons of our perception beyond the institutional structures and model idiosyncrasy of Western political order. Such an approach may be functional to making sense of the Weberian concept of relating values and lifestyles to power in the context of non-European societies, if we recognize the democratic politics of everyday life where "moral virtue as the specific accumulation of habits and becomings" may play a significant role.[25]

While observations of difference may have a matter-of-fact value, they may at the same time enhance the construed dichotomy between the Western tradition of democracy and the Eastern/Islamic tradition of autocracy, which reappears in contemporary sets of contrarian beliefs, such as secularity as a universal faith and the authenticity or "alterity" of Islam. Statements such as "fully institutionalized effective checks on the decision making of the rulers did not develop in these [i.e., non-Western] societies" and "there was no machinery other than rebellion through which to enforce any far-reaching 'radical' political demands" cannot be disqualified as arbitrary attributions to premodern societies of the Near East.[26] At the same time, they may not reveal the whole story. Conceptually, such assertions relate to a presumed historical tendency of separating the moral and the political spheres, culture and power, the limited radius for the authority of religious scholars and the inaccessible arena of rulers. This perception recognizes the traditional Islamic concepts of autonomous religious authority and the accountability of holders of worldly power to a supreme transcendental lordship. Yet it implies the deficient character of Islamic tradition in as far as that tradition failed to turn the tension between the two spheres into a productive, dynamic societal and political differentiation similar to the dynamics of rationalization postulated by Weber as fueled by religious and cultural tradition.[27] In a practical sense, statements of this kind may impede the realization of the potential resulting from the overlapping of the two spheres, which indeed established a tradition manifest in institutionalized discourse. Premodern polyphonic political thought produced by literati, scholars, and rulers and continued and revised by reformist authors of the nineteenth and twentieth centuries presumes the moral, religious, and governmental accountability of rulers. The concern for human and material resources and the manner in which political administration would protect and develop them was indeed a continuous preoccupation of Islamic scholars and part of their conceptualization of legitimacy.[28]

Acknowledging the principle that cultural traditions constituted by the ensemble of practices and arguments "influence contexts in which power is conceptualized"[29] should entail looking beyond the historical contingency resulting from the interaction of the two spheres and searching instead for the dynamics that relate past and present in the perspective of an ongoing process. Conceptualizing the open horizons of modernity from this point of view and accepting the plurality of cultural traditions then permit thinking along the lines of different properties without getting involved in statements of alterity. For instance, the assertion that revolution in the modern sense of popular uprisings leading to political movement developed in the Near East in the context of resistance against foreign domination, rather than being based on a conception of rights and the notion of liberty,[30] although justified, would need completion. This qualification applies not only to historical events but also to the broad campaigns of civil resistance in the recent past (2009–2011), such as the Iranian election protests, the Jasmine revolution, and the Arab spring, the legacy of which is not yet apparent.

In a Weberian sense, set into a universal perspective disregarding the uniqueness of the Western pathway to modernity as he perceived it, the tension between moral value as part of cultural and religious tradition and politics reveals a powerful dynamic. The elaboration of a Weberian approach derived from his interest in a comparative characterization of European particularities is justified by Weber's intended universalism. In this vein, scholars have suggested that in terms of a democratic politics of everyday life we have to recognize the preconditions of political participation as they rely "on moral virtue as the specific accumulation of habits and becomings in everydayness (habitus)."[31] More generally, religion constitutes a rational approach to the unsatisfiable desire for meaning and salvation, which according to Weber may be regarded as a key to understanding social dynamics. Salvation religion is foundational for communal interaction, or *Vergemeinschaftung*, which by nature is exposed to rationalization and social forces, thus constituting a medium through which the process of disenchantment of the world extends itself.[32]

Weber's comparative perspective invites an effort to verify his assessments of Islamic religion or revise the judgments derived from it. His approach implies the idea that

Western modernity emerges from the individual's total institutional involvement based on the rational interdependence between immanence and transcendence leading to ever greater maximization of self-control.[33] Part of this concept is the doctrine of election by grace, which belongs to the foundations of Calvinism. Its significance resides according to Weber in the relationship between religious ethics and conduct molded not only by the substance of ideas but also by the need for consistency and (personal) religious legitimation. Compared to Calvinism, Islam has a deterministic belief in providence and never attains the same rational coherence.[34] Weber's Islam is devoid of a consistent salvation concept in its ethical dimension, which implies the relationship between ethic and *Lebensführung*, or the conduct of life.[35] There is, of course, a concept of salvation or definitive success (*falāḥ*) in Islamic doctrine, presented as the ultimate purpose in life of the believer attained through practicing the faith.[36] Yet even if the classical Islamic debate on salvation should not be seen as isolated from life conduct, as some have maintained,[37] it is difficult, if not impossible (or simply has not been done yet), to re-create a context that matches Weber's sociology linking personality and life orders in their relationship to economy and politics.[38] It might be a vain effort in any case as thinking along the lines of plurality seems much more promising.

Multiple Modernities

The paradigm of multiple modernities helped to overcome the impasse of classical modernization discourse and gave further impulse to the idea of dropping the habitual postulation of Western properties functioning as exclusive historical conditions for the rise of rational capitalism and modernity: free labor market, autocephalous urban corporations, money economy, rational legal system, science-based technology, world mastery–Protestantism. Thinking along these lines and according to the established wisdom of contrasting juxtaposition produces a stereotyped image of Islam, namely the view that in Islamic societies the separation between private and public spheres did not occur, Islam was a religion of obligation calling for the conquest of the world, and Islamic law did not create the tensions and oppositions between law and practice necessary for further rationalization.[39] In contrast, voting for the nonidentity of westernization and modernity postulated a multiplicity of cultural programs in a wider context of modernity, and it abolished the idea that newcomers to modernization would have to emulate the cultural program of modernity and the basic institutional constellations as they came together in Europe. Shmuel Eisenstadt recognized general trends to structural differentiation of various social arenas in many of the modernizing societies, and he observed that the variety of ways in which these arenas were defined and organized gave rise to multiple institutional and ideological patterns. Notwithstanding anti-Western or anti-modern attitudes, social movements in these non-Western societies were distinctively modern. He also considered that such modernities are changing and that the upsurge and reconstruction of the religious dimension are best understood within the framework of such transformations.[40] The distinct visions of fundamentalist movements thus evolved not only *in* a modern context but rather by use of notions common to the discourse of modernity. They have attempted to appropriate modernity in their own terms.[41]

This approach is consistent with Weber's idea of a productive tension between value-spheres (politics, religion, science, economy) as the dynamics resulting from the conflictual character of modernity give shape to a plurality of realizations corresponding to the diversity of the factors involved and their interrelation in a transcultural context. Whether cultural traditions have the impact assumed in accordance with Weber's theory[42] or whether, alternatively, structural conditions, possibly emerging from long-standing historical legacies, may play a more decisive role is indeed a matter of debate.[43] Two aspects encourage reservations against emphasizing the genuine religious factor. One is the ongoing politicization of religion. Radicalized Islamist political confessionalism today operates in the historical context of colonial and postcolonial power relations[44] and in the framework of a globalized Islamist crusade furthered by the antagonistic interests of funding organizations and states. The other concerns the doctrinal and attitudinal characteristics of Calvinist Protestantism as they are pivotal for Weber's theory of the emergence of capitalism in Europe. All of these characteristics can be detected in fundamentalist Islam too, differing somewhat in form and degree.[45] These perspectives do not exclude each other. Weber's point of departure is to consider the social relevance of religion as a certain kind of communal (inter)action and the dynamics of rationalization to which it is exposed.[46] This concept does not divide West and East, Europe and the Islamic world.

The discursive context of analyzing different societies through the lenses of the multiple modernities thesis is primarily aimed at rejecting the idea of a universal type of modernity. Recognizing "the dynamics specific to particular civilizations" is its epistemic ambition, and confronting "the problem of the fruitfulness—and limits—of applying concepts developed in the Western social science discourse to the analysis of non-Western societies" is its pragmatic and moral aspiration.[47] The pluralistic concept of modernities tends to consider difference instead of observing deviance. It tries to identify the common grounds of quite different and even antagonist appearances, including Islamic fundamentalism as a signature of modernity.

Under the premise that values, beliefs, attitudes, and associated lifestyles are formative elements that give shape to the project of modernity, Islamic fundamentalism relates to the wider context of how tradition is processed in modern contexts. Generally speaking, concepts of social order referring to a premodern tradition formulate standardized systems consisting of conduct (norms and practices) and basic patterns of civilization that influence attitudes and orientations of people. As modernity does not eliminate basic inherited orientations, these are transposed into the modern context and thus alter and lose their original meaning. In this manner, non-Western fundamentals—fragmented schemes of a generalized meaning—aspire to replace the pluralism of modern styles and produce the notions of difference and identity.[48] Historically considered, Islamic reform movements of the nineteenth and twentieth centuries were "fundamentalist" in so far as they advocated the return to the fundamental sources against accustomed practices. Differences between law schools and strict adherence to their methodologies contributed to introducing a rationalization of access to the tenets of belief and precepts of religious law.[49] Reform movements integrated Islam into the general pattern of modernization, crystallized as the imposition of rationality and reason which function as the instrumental regulation of human conduct.[50]

FUNDAMENTALISM AND SECULARIZATION

Identifying the role of Islamic fundamentalism within the framework of modernity is the guiding idea in Bryan S. Turner's interpretation of Weber's sociology, where he qualifies Islamic fundamentalism as representing the communal type of relationship based upon traditional and affectual bonds in contrast to the rationality of the associational relationship organized by contracts. Unlike the Calvinist moment in European history that created an "external world of discipline, vocations and rational mastery" through "the inner quest of meaning," Islamic fundamentalism had an unremitting political stance in its opposition to colonialism and later to postmodernist relativizing of religion, thus establishing a "global Islamdom," a "new version of the traditional household."[51] The term "fundamentalism" here serves as a broad label meant to connect Islamic beliefs and attitudes, including contemporary Near Eastern Islamist factions and their predecessors, to fundamentalist movements more generally. This perspective illustrates what the distinct visions of fundamentalism share: a relationship with the cultural and political program of modernity enabling them to appropriate modernity on their own terms.[52]

The complex and foundational relationship between religious fundamentalism and modernity, which relates the European and Islamic variants,[53] is articulated also in the rapport of secularism and Puritan reformist fundamentalism. Whereas the separation between the private and the public spheres, and in particular Luther's notion of the separation between the spiritual and the temporal, are constitutive of Weber's concept of rationalizing disenchantment that occurred in Europe exclusively, comparable notions indeed are notable in the Islamic context, partly in the framework of colonial rule and the hegemony of Western nation-states. Within the religious realm, not directly coupled to structural aspects of secularization, a trend toward a puritanical form of Islam took hold, furthering a process of rationalization.[54] The revision of Islamic law by reformist *salafī* Islam in the early twentieth century seems to have been driven by the idea of creating an all-embracing jurisdiction in adaptation to European institutions of the nation-state.[55] The tacit acceptance of a secular framework is recognizable where religious authority excludes modernist Muslim scholars advocating secularism. Defending authority in the public space and constructing "deviance" in fact give consent to competition in a public arena and imply that religious truth is contingent.[56]

Islamic law itself adapted to the model of a secular comprehensive legal code covering all aspects of life by way of new interpretations of the tradition of Islamic law in the early twentieth century.[57] So long as the authority of the sacred law had not been challenged in classical tradition, there was no need to justify the rules with general moral or rational concepts. In the latter half of the nineteenth century, however, a discursive shift occurred furthering a less legalistic approach that emphasized moral justifications and the underlying ethical values.[58] Various translations of the cultural construction of "secularity" (i.e., culturally, symbolically, and institutionally anchored forms of distinction between religious and non-religious spheres and material spaces) that did not need to be expressed in a neat separation of secular and religious spheres thus emerged under the conditions of globalization and intercivilizational encounter.[59] Related issues, such as individual freedom, religious heterogeneity, integration, and development of the institutional domain constitute a demanding agenda and indeed entail normativity. When Talal Asad insists that "secularity" is not a neutral category but deploys a normative dimension in defying deviant Muslim practices, he refers to the background of Western/ non-Western power relations and to the systemic character of secularity which appears as a marker and ingredient of "conquering" Western hegemonic modernity.[60] More pertinent than this assumed political antagonism probably is the experience structured by secularization in contemporary multicultural society. The encounter between subjects and communities in this framework entails a—possibly frustrating—relativizing of familiar norms and assumptions.[61]

ISLAMIC CIVILIZATION:
WARRIORS, RELIGIOUS AUTHORITY,
AND POLITICAL RULE

The plurality of appearances of the secular in a transcultural framework illuminates the specificities of cultural–historical pathways, which fuel religious–secular dynamics in their own terms. In Weber's vision, the important cultural role of jihad in Islam is a clue for understanding the difference between European and Near Eastern societies.[62] This approach seems to confirm the cliché of a warrior religion bound by the simplicity of its religious and ethical requirements and its belief in a predetermined fate in this world. Weber's notion of asceticism and its sociocultural impact applies to the Islamic worldview in a primitive form, reduced to a military discipline following largely external and ritual demands; and it is thus alien to the dynamics of modernity. Accordingly, the relation between the individual and the transcendent sphere is mainly political in character and stands in contrast to the Calvinist striving for personal salvation. The alternative mystical quest for salvation in Islam does not offer an ethic that inspires an active relationship to the world.[63]

Weber's interest in the relationship between belief and economy identifies the warrior seeking to conquer the world as a representative type in Islamic culture, which emerged historically with the sociological shift from the faith of an entrepreneurial class in Mecca to a world-conquering religion beginning with the subsequent Medinian period.[64] In contemporary Weber reception, this narrowing down of Islamic civilization to the notion of warrior religion was met with embarrassment for its supposed essentialist character, even if some historical evidence for Weber's conception was conceded with reference to the historicity of the era of conquests.[65] Yet there was also careful confirmation that the status ethics of warriors and the supposed meaningfulness of death in battle may attain the level of a worldview in the Weberian sense, and warrior Islam is a cornerstone of the uncritical reproduction of Weber's narrative.[66] Attempts to explain Weber's notion with reference to history do not provide ample detail and instead misinterpret its intention. The cultural pattern of warrior Islam cannot represent the historical dynamics of Islamic civilization and is not meant to do so.[67] But it is instrumental to Weber's purpose of laying out a historical macrosociology of the economic ethics of world religions.[68] One may further relativize his notion by pointing out that it was not Weber's only argument for explaining why Western rationalism did not emerge under Islam. In his view, capitalism and the ensuing industrialization were impeded by the religiously determined structure of the Islamic state, its officialdom and jurisprudence. This aspect seems instead to be the key to his interpretation of the relation between Islamic society and social change.[69]

This twofold perspective in Weber's work inspired the distinction of "internal" (ethical) and "external" (structural) factors inherent in his conception of the essential impact factors that gave shape to the particularities of Islamic history.[70] Yet even if this may seem to increase the plausibility of his conclusions, both of its main aspects miss their point in a characteristic manner. His concept of warrior Islam conceals the dynamics resulting from the tension between religious and ethical attitudes and worldviews and the political realm of the organization of power and statehood. Many aspects of this process were unknown to Weber and thus remained unconsidered. The epistemic value of Weber's jihad–warrior–Islam typology, coined as a distinct ideal type in contrast to European history, can be seen as a representation of an essential and productive trait of Islamic history. But it cannot establish an analytical perspective allowing engagement in critical comparison. Weber's notion omits the rise of religious scholars as a moral and juridical authority connected with jihad as concept and practice. Widening the perspective implied by his notion enables us to perceive the larger framework of religious–secular dynamics in which jihad is situated, if it is understood beyond the Weberian focus on war and warriors and if it includes the discourse on moral order and its carriers in the arena of jihad. Historical evidence supports this perspective and demonstrates its dynamics in a way that underscores the potential of Weber's initial concept.

Islamic conquest resulting from jihad, it seems, changed the cultural configurations producing legitimacy since the conversion of elites did not necessarily respond to political constraint.[71] The scholarly discourse on jihad went well beyond the issue of war-making and contributed to establishing moral order.[72] With the privatization of jihad as it occurred during the eighth century, the authority of religious scholars ('ulamā') in moral and religious issues was established on the basis of their discourse on jihad and asceticism, or religious, world-renouncing discipline. This process led toward the end of any notion of a caliphal role in the definition of Islam, thus accentuating the distinction between religious authority and political rule.[73] The Islamic scholars' authentication of the authorized religious memory centered upon their control of the foundational texts, their moral conduct, and their access to "the immediacy of the meaning of things."[74]

While the authority of military rulers leading a military movement can be seen as characteristic of the early Islamic period, during the subsequent three centuries, scholarly authority gradually came to challenge this initial order. Tensions between judicial authority (*qadis*) and rulers' interventions in judicial practices—in contrast to the continuous tension in administrative matters—seem to have ceased from the middle of the ninth century onward.[75] Religious authority thus came to play a distinct role in public spheres. But its autonomy and the normative supremacy of *shari'a*, which gradually gained the systematic character displayed in the fourteenth century, did not establish any sort of autonomous access to the rulers' domain. Whereas guardianship over the moral order was conferred to religious authority, participation in policymaking remained rather limited.[76] The decoupling of public moral order and the domain of political power was articulated in the separation of truth and order.[77] The relationship with jihad, both in practice and in discourse, for the emergence and occasional reformist revival of religious authority, justifies the role of religious scholars in the public sphere in general and their legitimating function in the realm of political order in particular. Since this stance reduces the importance of the institutional form of Islamic governance and at the same time emphasizes the importance of religious authority in upholding moral norms, it acknowledges the ambivalent character of political rule that cannot achieve an unambiguous good. The painful insight into the inescapability of injustice in political practice and the necessity of submitting to inchoate rule that maintains order is counterbalanced by the normative frame of "enjoining the good," which is ultimately based upon the consensus of the believers.[78]

In light of this tension, Weber's conception of the Islamic warrior ideal type, grounded in the status ethic of warriors and the meaningfulness of death in battle, requires elaboration. The ideal type may constitute an ingredient and background of a more civilized and developed version of the Islamic worldview as interpreted by Weber. Yet such a worldview would mainly consist of immersion in the discipline of scholarly religious authority, especially scriptural discipline and moral practices, including those expressed in personal conduct and the manner of conducting one's life (*Lebensführung*).[79]

CONCLUSION: PATRIMONIALISM AND LEGITIMACY

The role of religious authority, which of course is a heterogeneous entity with different schools, orientations, social practices, and many transitions between its idiosyncrasies, has implications for Weber's concept of patrimonialism, in so far as the Islamic concept of legal limitation of government depends on the functioning of religious authority.[80] While rulers were obliged, in theory, to observe the principle of commanding what the law required and what it prohibited, it was the role of religious authority to provide legitimacy by asserting the lawfulness of the rulers' regime.[81] The discourse on rulers' responsibilities and key values, such as justice and probity ('adl),[82] contributed to creating and maintaining moral standards that could not be ignored. In practice, there was a contested field open to intervention from both sides, particularly with respect to the interpretation and administration of pious endowments (awqāf), where personal, public, and juridical interests often collided. For instance, the Maliki school of Islamic law was especially inclined to defend private property.[83] In brief, various fields of activity, including the investiture of rulers, contributed to producing the legitimacy provided by religious authority.[84]

Religious authority and political rule were intersecting domains connected by mutual dependencies. The potentially conflictual relationship between the two domains did not produce institutionalized arenas of juridical conflict resolution, and direct access to policymaking remained weak. Mainly on this basis Weber's notion of patrimonialism gained wide acceptance and application to the history of the Islamic world.[85] Yet here, too, the typology used to create distinction and separation must be repositioned in the analytical perspective of society–state relations. This would help to prevent misunderstandings, such as using his notion of "sultanism" to characterize Islamic rule in general, whereas the concept was meant to denote purely arbitrary patrimonial rule not bound by substantive rationality and was thus an extreme version of autocracy.[86] In the context of Weber's purpose of exploring the plurality of developmental histories,[87] from a historical perspective the abstract concept of patrimonialism signifies and construes a type of deficient institutionalization. According to Weber, it is responsible for precluding "the emergence of capitalist pre-conditions, namely rational law, a free labor market, autonomous cities, a money economy, and a bourgeois class."[88] Patrimonial rule as such, following Weber, is not incompatible with the emergence of a rational system of administration under specific conditions as they developed in the European legal framework of feudalism,[89] conditions that were, as one may suppose, absent in the Islamic context.

For Weberian theory or a sociology of Islam inspired by Weber's impulse, the general traits of the Islamic type of patrimonial rule are characterized by prebendalism and, as a consequence, by the lack of the legal framework of feudalism. In addition, the bureaucracy, dependent on the lavish imperial household, is said to have absorbed a huge part of the tax yield. Yet this vision construes history in a way that seems to be at odds with the evidence. In what respect such conditions really limited the productivity of merchant capital, as some scholars have asserted,[90] is doubtful in light of more recent research. The verdict against the rationality of institutions that the notion of patrimonialism conveys is not substantiated, when empirical data from economic, legal, and institutional history are considered. To give just a few examples, the wide range of monetization, beginning with the early Islamic period, early capitalistic features in Egypt under Abbasid rule, and resettlement policies in response to the observation of population decline, speaks against a general malfunctioning of institutions.[91] The enforceability of contracts in Islamic law, the protection of property rights, the dynamics of enhancement of the law, as well as the legal status of *waqf* endowments point in the same direction.[92] Religious authority was involved and augmented in the administration of this institution that served private, public, and sometimes hybrid purposes.[93] The features that define Islamic patrimonial domination seem hard to specify in the premodern context, at least to a degree that justifies a generalizing classification concerning the malfunctioning of institutions. Even if Weber concedes that all types of domination—legal, traditional or patrimonial, charismatic—depend on consistent and persistent administrative practice for the execution and enforcement of order,[94] methodical and systematic traits of premodern governance do not confirm the negative image of "Islamic" institutionalization related to a normative understanding of the notion of patrimonialism. Given that types of domination rarely ever existed in a pure and ideal form, reality rather provides examples for a synthesis of various features.

Weber's concept of patrimonialism, more particularly neo-patrimonialism, is also applied in the context of developing countries, certainly in the Islamic world. In this context the term refers to the large extent of informal networks and communication channels coexisting with a low level of institutionalization. The variety and efficiency of mechanisms establishing bonds of loyalty counterbalance the deficient legitimacy of the state and its agencies.[95] Such occurrences, of course, are not engendered by a certain type of domination but are part of complex society–state relations showing patrimonial features. These may be favorable for a pluralistic structure in a Weberian sense, such as segregated regional, ethnic, and religious sectors; the weak permeation of the center into the periphery; as well as multiple patterns of legitimation.[96]

Weber's inspiring approach of linking culture, society, and institutional order may not only encourage studying the impact of belief systems in terms of Western uniqueness.[97] The challenge that results from his work lies in understanding cultural traditions beyond the West as being vital and connected to modernity in their own terms.

Notes

1. Max Weber, *Economy and Society* (hereafter *E&S*), ed. G. Roth and C. Wittich (Berkeley: University of California Press, 1978), 231–232, 237–241, 259, 280; 574–575, 581, 623–627, 909–910; Weber, *Wirtschaft und Gesellschaft. Soziologie. Unvollendet 1919–1920, Max Weber-Gesamtausgabe* (hereafter *MWG*), pt. 1, vol. 23, ed. K. Borchardt, E. Hanke, and W. Schluchter (Tübingen, Germany: Mohr [Siebeck], 2013), 476–477, 485–490, 520, 559; Weber, *Wirtschaft und Gesellschaft. Die Wirtschaft und die gesellschaftlichen Ordnungen und Mächte. Nachlaß. Teilband 2: Religiöse Gemeinschaften, MWG* I/22-2, ed. H. G. Kippenberg, with Petra Schilm (Tübingen, Germany: Mohr [Siebeck], 2001), 365–366, 373–374, 432–437; Weber, *Wirtschaft und Gesellschaft. Die Wirtschaft und die gesellschaftlichen Ordnungen und Mächte. Nachlaß. Teilband 1: Gemeinschaften, MWG* I/22-1, ed. W. J. Mommsen, with M. Meyer (Tübingen, Germany: Mohr [Siebeck], 2001), 216–217.

2. Richard Heigl, *Wüstensöhne und Despoten: das Bild der Vorderen Orients in deutschsprachigen Weltgeschichten* (Regensburg, Germany: Lehrstuhl für Neuere deutsche Literaturwissenschaft, 2000).

3. Jack Goody, *The Theft of History* (Cambridge: Cambridge University Press, 2006), 181, 293, 300.

4. Wolfgang Schluchter, "Hindrances to Modernity: Max Weber on Islam," in *Max Weber & Islam*, ed. T. E. Huff and W. Schluchter (New Brunswick, NJ: Transaction Publishers, 1999), 53–138, 27.

5. Wolfgang Schluchter, "Einleitung," in Max Weber, *Asketischer Protestantismus und Kapitalismus. Schriften und Reden 1904–1911, MWG I/9*, ed. W. Schluchter, with U. Bube (Tübingen, Germany: Mohr [Siebeck] 2014), 1–89. Friedrich Lenger, *Werner Sombart 1863–1941, Eine Biographie* (Munich, Germany: C. H. Beck, 1995), 129–135 on the proximity of Weber's approach to Werner Sombart's *Der moderne Kapitalismus*.

6. Schluchter, "Hindrances to Modernity," 74.

7. Armando Salvatore, "Beyond Orientalism? Max Weber and the Displacements of 'Essentialism' in the Study of Islam," *Arabica* 43, no. 3 (1996), 457–485, 465.

8. Georg Stauth and Bryan S. Turner, "Nietzsche in Weber oder die Geburt des modernen Genius' im professionellen Menschen," *Zeitschrift für Soziologie* 15, no. 2 (1986), 81–94, 90.

9. Stefan Leder, "Max Weber in der arabischen Welt," in *Max Weber in der Welt. Rezeption und Wirkung*, ed. M. Kaiser and H. Rosenbach (Tübingen, Germany: Mohr Siebeck, 2014), 23–31, 29, with reference to the work of Ridwan as-Sayyid (in Arabic).

10. Michael Löwy, "Le concept d'affinité élective chez Max Weber," *Archives de Sciences sociales des Religions* 27, no. 3 (2004), 93–103, 94, 99–101.

11. In his "Second Reply to Rachfahl" of 1910, Weber explains that certain attitudes "seem to us somehow to be specifically 'adequate' to just those forms of organisation. For *inner* reasons, they seem to possess an 'elective affinity' to them": Weber, *The Protestant Ethic Debate: Max Weber's Replies to His Critics, 1907–1910*, ed. D. J. Chalcraft and A. Harrington, trans. A. Harrington and M. Shields (Liverpool, UK: Liverpool University Press, 2001), 94; *MWG I/9*, 668.

12. Bryan S. Turner, "Islam, Capitalism and the Weber Theses," in *The Sociology of Islam. Collected Essays of Bryan S. Turner*, ed. B. S. Turner and K. M. Nasir (Farnham, UK: Ashgate, 2013), 23–36, 26. First published in *British Journal of Sociology* 25, no. 2 (1974): 230–243.

13. Shmuel N. Eisenstadt, "Concluding Remarks: Public Sphere, Civil Society, and Political Dynamics in Islamic Societies," in *The Public Sphere in Muslim Societies*, ed. M. Hoexter, S. N. Eisenstadt, and N. Levtzion (Albany: State University of New York Press, 2002), 139–161, 146; Armando Salvatore, "Tradition and Modernity Within Islamic Civilization and the West," in *Islam and Modernity: Key Issues and Debates*, ed. M. K. Masud, A. Salvatore, and M. van Bruinessen (Edinburgh, UK: Edinburgh University Press, 2009), 3–35, 6.

14. For instance, concerning the oriental city, Jürgen Paul, "Max Weber und die 'Islamische Stadt,'" in *Max Weber's Religionssoziologie in interkultureller Perspektive*, ed. H. Lehmann and J. M. Ouédrago (Göttingen, Germany: Vandenhoeck & Ruprecht, 2003), 109–138; and Islamic law, Patricia Crone, "Weber, Islamic Law and the Rise of Capitalism," in *Max Weber & Islam*, 247–272.

15. Bryan S. Turner, "State, Science and Economy in Traditional Societies: Some Problems in Weberian Sociology of Science," in Turner, *Sociology of Islam*, 53–73, 55–61. First published in *British Journal of Sociology* 38 (1987): 1–23.

16. Salvatore, "Beyond Orientalism?," 458.

17. Salvatore, "Tradition and Modernity," 14.

18. Toby E. Huff, "Introduction," in *Max Weber & Islam*, 1–52, 21; Schluchter, "Einleitung," in *MWG* I/9, 19–21; Michael Curtis, *Orientalism and Islam: European Thinkers on Oriental Despotism in the Middle East and India* (Cambridge: Cambridge University Press, 2009), 263–264.

19. Salvatore, "Beyond Orientalism?," 482.

20. Mohammad R. Nafissi, "Reframing Orientalism: Weber and Islam," in *Islam: Critical Concepts in Sociology*, vol. 2, *Islam, State and Politics*, ed. B. S. Turner (London: Routledge, 2003), 1–22, 3, 15. First published in *Economy and Society* 27, no. 1 (1998): 97–118.

21. Ibid., 18.

22. Ernest Gellner, *Muslim Society* (Cambridge: Cambridge University Press, 1995; reprint from the paperback edition 1981), 15–16, 89, 170. Similarly, he applied this concept to his study of the nation and the nation-state in general: Athena S. Leoussi, "Max Weber in the Thought of Edward Shils (1910–1975) and Ernest Gellner (1925–1995): The Paradox of Two Weberian Approaches to the Understanding of Nations and Nationalism?" *Ethnic and Racial Studies* 36, no. 12 (2013): 1957–1976, 1969.

23. Sami Zubaida, "Is There a Muslim Society? Ernest Gellner's Sociology of Islam," in *Islam: Critical Concepts in Sociology*, vol. 2, 21–69, 38–44, 53. First published in *Economy and Society* 24, no. 2 (1995): 151–188.

24. Walid Kazziha, "The Fantasy of Arab Democracy Without a Constituency," in *The Struggle over Democracy in the Middle East. Regional Politics and External Policies*, ed. N. J. Brown and Emad Eldin Shahin (London: Routledge, 2010), 42–61.

25. Ali Mirsepassi and Tadd Graham Fernée, *Islam, Democracy, and Cosmopolitanism: At Home and in the World* (New York: Cambridge University Press, 2014), 34–35.

26. Eisenstadt, "Concluding Remarks," 154.

27. Salvatore, "Tradition and Modernity," 13–14; cf. Bryan S. Turner, "Classical Approaches: Understanding Islam," in *Sociology of Islam*, 11–22, 13.

28. Stefan Leder, "Sultanic Rule in the Mirror of Medieval Political Literature," in *Global Medieval: Mirrors for Princes Reconsidered*, ed. R. Forster and N. Yavari (Cambridge, MA: Harvard University Press and Ilex Foundation, 2015), 94–111, 95–96.

29. Salvatore, "Tradition and Modernity," 6–8.

30. Ami Ayalon, "From Fitna to Thawra," *Studia Islamica* 66 (1987): 145–177, 168.

31. Mirsepassi and Fernée, *Islam, Democracy, and Cosmopolitanism*, 35.

32. Hans G. Kippenberg, "Religiöse Gemeinschaften. Wo die Arbeit am Sinnproblem der Welt und der Bedarf sozialen Handelns an Gemeinschaftlichkeit zusammenkommen," in *Das Weber-Paradigma*, ed. Gert Albert et al. (Tübingen, Germany: Mohr Siebeck, 2005), 211–233, 222–224.

33. Georg Stauth, "Islam and Modernity: The Long Shadow of Max Weber," in *Islam—Motor or Challenge of Modernity*, ed. G. Stauth (Hamburg, Germany: LIT Verlag, 1998), 163–186, 166.

34. Schluchter, "Hindrances to Modernity," 71–77.

35. Salvatore, "Beyond Orientalism?," 465.

36. Maurice Borrmans, "Salvation," in *Encyclopaedia of the Qur'ān*, vol. 4, ed. J. D. McAuliffe (Leiden, The Netherlands: Brill, 2002), doi:10.1163/1875-3922_q3_EQSIM_00368 (accessed February 20, 2018).

37. Muhammad Hassan Khalil, *Islam in the Faith of Others: The Salvation Question* (Oxford: Oxford University Press, 2012), 14.

38. Turner, "State, Science and Economy in Traditional Societies," 16–17.

39. Stauth, "Islam and Modernity," 174.

40. S. N. Eisenstadt, "The Reconstruction of Religious Arenas in the Framework of 'Multiple Modernities,'" in *Islam: Critical Concepts in Sociology*, vol. 4, *Islam and Social Movements*, ed. B. S. Turner (London: Routledge, 2003), 1–22, 2–5. First published in *Journal of International Studies* 29, no. 3 (2000): 591–611.

41. Shmuel N. Eisenstadt, "Multiple Modernities," *Daedalus* 129, no. 1 (2000): 1–29, 19, 22.

42. Schluchter, "Hindrances to Modernity," 122.

43. Thomas Schwinn, "Gibt es eine multiple Moderne?," in *Globale, multiple und postkoloniale Modernen*, ed. M. Boatca and W. Spohn (Mering, Germany: Rainer Hampp Verlag, 2010), 105–131, 108, 114, 122; Rudolph Peters, "Paradise or Hell? The Religious Doctrine of Election in Eighteenth and Nineteenth Century Islamic Fundamentalism and Protestant Calvinism," in *Max Weber & Islam*, 205–216, 206.

44. Pierre-Jean Luizard, *Die Falle des Kalifats. Der Islamische Staat oder die Rückkehr der Geschichte* (Hamburg, Germany: Hamburger Edition, 2017).

45. Peters, "Paradise or Hell?," 215.

46. Kippenberg, "Religiöse Gemeinschaften."

47. Eisenstadt, "Concluding Remarks," 146.

48. Georg Stauth, "Islam als Selbstbegriff nicht-westlicher Modernität," in G. Stauth, *Islamische Kultur und moderne Gesellschaft. Gesammelte Aufsätze zur Soziologie des Islams* (Bielefeld, Germany: transcript, 2000), 103–130. Reprint from *Modernität zwischen Differenzierung und Globalisierung*, ed. H. Buchholt et al. (Münster, Germany: Lit, 1996), 125–126.

49. Peters, "Paradise or Hell?," 213; Johanna Pink, "Where Does Modernity Begin? Muḥammad al-Shawkānī and the Tradition of Tafsīr," in *Tafsīr and Islamic Intellectual History: Exploring the Boundaries of a Genre*, ed. A. Görke and J. Pink (Oxford: Oxford University Press, 2014), 323–360.

50. Stauth, "Islam and Modernity," 175; Bryan S. Turner, "Politics and Culture in Islamic Globalism," in *Religion and Global Order. Religion and the Political Order*, ed. R. Robertson and W. R. Garrett (New York: Paragon House, 1991), 4:161–181, 163.

51. Turner, "Politics and Culture in Islamic Globalism," 167, 172, 175.

52. Eisenstadt, "The Reconstruction," 11; "Multiple Modernities," 19.

53. "Max Weber discovered a fascinating paradox in Occidental reasoning, namely that secularization of society was brought upon by religious fundamentalism": Stauth, "Islam and Modernity," 167.

54. Francis Robinson, "Secularization, Weber, and Islam," in *Max Weber & Islam*, 231–246, 236.

55. Ahmad Dallal, "Appropriating the Past: Twentieth Century Reconstruction of the Premodern Islamic Thought," *Islamic Law and Society* 7, no. 3 (2000): 325–358.

56. Daniel Kinitz, "Deviance as a Phenomenon of Secularity: Islam and Deviants in Twentieth-Century Egypt—A Search for Sociological Explanations," in *Multiple Secularities Beyond the West: Religion and Modernity in the Global Age*, ed. M. Burchardt, M. Wohlrab-Sahr, and M. Middell (Boston: De Gruyter, 2015), 97–118.

57. Dallal, "Appropriating the Past."

58. Rudolph Peters, *Jihad in Classical and Modern Islam* (Princeton, NJ: Markus Wiener Publishers, 1996), 111.

59. Marian Burchardt, Monika Wohlrab-Sahr, and Matthias Midell, "Introduction," in *Multiple Secularities Beyond the West*, 1–15, 15.

60. Talal Asad, *Formations of the Secular. Christianity, Islam, Modernity* (Stanford, CA: Stanford University Press, 2003).

61. Christopher Craig Brittain, "The 'Secular' as a Tragic Category: on Talal Asad, Religion and Representation," *Method & Theory in the Study of Religion* 17 (2005): 149–165, 164.

62. *E&S*, 623–627; *MWG* I/22-2, 432–437.

63. Ralph Schroeder, *Max Weber and the Sociology of Culture* (London: Sage, 1992), 65–70.

64. Bryan S. Turner, "Origins and Tradition in Islam and Christianity," in Turner, *Sociology of Islam*, 37–52, 37–40. First published in *Religion* 6, no. 1 (1976): 13–30.

65. Huff, "Introduction," in *Max Weber & Islam*, 7–8.

66. Stephen Kalberg, *Max Weber's Comparative-Historical Sociology Today: Major Themes, Mode of Causal Analysis, and Applications* (Farnham, UK: Ashgate, 2012); Curtis, *Orientalism and Islam*.

67. Turner, "Origins and Tradition in Islam and Christianity," 40.

68. Turner, "Classical Approaches: Understanding Islam," 12; Bryan S. Turner, *Weber and Islam: A Critical Study* (London: Routledge, 1974), 2.

69. Schroeder, *Max Weber and the Sociology of Culture*, 68; Turner, *Weber and Islam*, 75.

70. Schluchter, "Hindrances to Modernity," 68, 84ff.; Huff, "Introduction," in *Max Weber & Islam*, 9.

71. Alan Strathern, "Global Patterns of Ruler Conversion to Islam and the Logic of Empirical Religiosity," in *Comparative Perspectives from History*, ed. A. C. S. Peacock (Edinburgh: Edinburgh University Press, 2017), 21–55, 39.

72. Paul L. Heck, "Jihad Revisited," *Journal of Religious Ethics* 32, no. 1 (2004): 95–128, 123.

73. Deborah Tor, "Privatized Jihad and Public Order in the Pre-Seljuq Period: The Role of the Mutatawwi'a," in *Jihad and Martyrdom*, ed. D. Cook (London: Routledge, 2010), 1:123–142, 123–126, 131.

74. Christian Découbert, "L'Autorité religieuse aux premiers siècles de l'islam, " in *Archives de sciences sociales des religions* 125 (2004): 2–12, 20, https://www.cairn-int.info/article -E_ASSR_125_0002-religious-authorities-in-theearly.htm.

75. Mathieu Tillier, "Judicial Authority and Qāḍīs' Autonomy Under the Abbasids," *Al-Masaq* 26, no. 2 (2014): 119–131, 120, 126.

76. Shmuel N. Eisenstadt, "Sectarianism and the Dynamics of Islamic Civilization," in *Islam— Motor or Challenge of Modernity*, 31; Eisenstadt, "Concluding Remarks," 152–153.

77. Bernard Haykel, *Revival and Reform in Islam. The Legacy of Muhammad al-Shawkānī* (Cambridge: Cambridge University Press, 2003), 84–85.

78. Navid Hassanzadeh, "The Canon and Comparative Political Thought," *Journal of International Political Theory* 11, no. 2 (2015): 184–202, 192–193.

79. Gudrun Krämer and Sabine Schmidtke, "Introduction," in *Speaking for Islam: Religious Authorities in Muslim Societies. International Symposium "Religious Authorities in Middle Eastern Islam"* (Leiden, The Netherlands: Brill, 2000), 1–15, 12.

80. Bettina Dennerlein, "Asserting Religious Authority in the Late 19th/Early 20th Century Morocco. Muḥammad b. Ja'far l-Katānī (d. 1927) and His Kitāb Salwat al-Anfās," in *Speaking for Islam. Religious Authorities in Muslim Societies*, ed. G. Krämer and S. Schmidtke (Leiden, The Netherlands: Brill, 2006), 128–152.

81. Jeremy Kleidosty, *The Concert of Civilisations. The Common Roots of Western and Islamic Constitutionalism* (Burlington, VT: Ashgate, 2005), 39.

82. Linda T. Darling, "The Circle and the Tree. Visions of Justice in the Middle East," in *Historical Dimensions of Islam, Pre-Modern and Modern Periods, in Honor of R. Stephen Humphreys*, ed. J. E. Lindsay and J. Armajani (Princeton, NJ: Darwin Press, 2009), 155–156.

83. Maya Shatzmiller, "Economic Performance and Economic Growth in the Early Islamic World," *Journal of the Economic and Social History of the Orient* 54 (2011): 132–184, 138.

84. Bettina Dennerlein, "Legitimate Bounds and Bound Legitimacy. The Act of Allegiance to the Ruler (bai'a) in 19th Century Morocco," *Die Welt des Islams* 41, no. 3 (2001): 287–310.

85. *E&S*, 231–241; *MWG* I/23, 475–490; cf. Ahmad Ashraf, "Historical Obstacles to the Development of a Bourgeoisie in Iran," in *Studies in the Economic History of the Middle East: From the Rise of Islam to the Present Day*, ed. M. A. Cook (London: Oxford University Press, 1970), 308–332, 311–312.

86. Turner, "Islam, Capitalism and the Weber Theses," 31; *E&S*, 231–232; *MWG* I/23, 475; for the concept of "material" or "substantive rationality" see *E&S*, 85–86; *MWG* I/23, 251; Curtis, *Orientalism and Islam*, 270.

87. Schluchter, "Hindrances to Modernity," 57.

88. Turner, *Weber and Islam*, 2; Huff, "Introduction," in *Max Weber & Islam*, 43; Schluchter, "Hindrances to Modernity," 122; cf. Georg Stauth, "Anmerkungen zur Soziologie des Islams," in *Islamische Kultur und moderne Gesellschaft*, 239–251, 239. First published in *Der Orient* 28, no. 2 (1997).

89. Schluchter, "Hindrances to Modernity," 101.

90. Ibid., 92; Turner, "State, Science and Economy in Traditional Societies," 66–68.

91. Shatzmiller, "Economic Performance and Economic Growth," 146–155, 174.

92. Ibid., 136–139; Doris Behrens-Abouseif, "The Waqf: A Legal Personality?," in *Islamische Stiftungen zwischen juristischer Norm und sozialer Praxis*, ed. A. Meier, J. Pahlitzsch, and L. Reinfandt (Berlin: Akademie-Verlag, 2009), 55–60; cf. Ana Maria Carballeira-Debasa, "The Role of Endowments in the Framework of Andalusian Society," in *Stiftungen in Christentum, Judentum und Islam vor der Moderne. Auf der Suche nach ihren Gemeinsamkeiten und Unterschieden in religiösen Grundlagen, praktischen Zwecken und historischen Transformationen*, ed. M. Borgolte (Berlin: Akademie Verlag, 2005), 109–121.

93. Jonathan P. Berkey, "There are 'ulamā' and Then There Are 'ulamā': Minor Religious Institutions and Minor Religious Functionaries in Medieval Cairo," in *Histories of the Middle East. Studies in Middle Eastern Society, Economy and Law in Honor of A. L. Udovitch*, ed. R. E. Margariti, A. Sabra, and P. M. Sijpesteijn (Leiden, The Netherlands: Brill, 2011), 9–22, 14–15.

94. *E&S*, 262–265; *MWG* I/23, 527–530.

95. Peter Pawelka, "Einleitung: Konstitution, Geschichte und Funktionsweise des Staates im Vorderen Orient," in *Der Staat im Vorderen Orient. Konstruktion und Legitimation politischer Herrschaft*, ed. P. Pawelka (Baden-Baden, Germany: Nomos, 2008), 27–36.

96. Eisenstadt, "Sectarianism and the Dynamics of Islamic Civilization," 32.

97. Avner Greif, "Cultural Beliefs and the Organization of Society: A Historical and Theoretical Reflection on Collectivist and Individualist Societies," *Journal of Political Economy* 102, no. 5 (1994): 912–950.

CHAPTER 23

THE STUDY ON ANCIENT ISRAEL AND ITS RELEVANCE FOR CONTEMPORARY POLITICS

EDUARDO WEISZ

WHEN Max Weber began his work on the historical importance of the relationship between the Protestant ethic and modern capitalism, subsequently published in 1904 and 1905, he committed himself to the most enduring of his theoretical interests, the economic ethic of the most important religions. This uninterrupted commitment lasted until his death in June 1920.

Weber focused on a specific rationality in Western modernity throughout his sociology of religion, as well as on the different rationalities developed in other cultures. That is why he can state that, rather than a sociology of religion, his should be considered a sociology of rationalism.[1] As I will develop, Weber found in his study of ancient Judaism key elements for the understanding of the Western rationalization process.

Ancient Judaism cannot be considered just a study on the historic precedent of Western modern culture, but there is, of course, a historical process connecting ancient Judaism and Western modernity. As Wolfgang Schluchter wrote, in Weber "the general developmental direction for religious *ethic* was attained through the religion of ancient Israel. Here lies its outstanding cultural significance."[2] I think that looking at Weber's sociology of religion from the standpoint of this *general developmental direction* allows for a better understanding of it, without leaving aside the immediate link between that and our civilization: it is Weber himself who reminds us of this link. In *General Economic History*, for example, he asserted that Judaism played an important role in transmitting to modern capitalism its enmity toward magic.[3]

I do not intend to discuss *Ancient Judaism* as a whole or its historical accuracy, which has been widely addressed since its publication. I refer though to some of these discussions, given their implications for my topic. What I try to do instead is show this text's importance in two specific fields: first, as a crucial part of Weber's analysis of modernity. It is not necessary to expand here on the importance of Weber's concern with crucial features of the modern world. His early interest in its relation with Protestantism draws on trying to grasp a world that was so drastically changing German society around the turn of the century. Neither is it necessary to expand here on the decisive significance he assigned to this society's specific rationality, a key feature of it. His discussions on bureaucracy as an unavoidable tendency of modern societies and his somber view on modern capitalism as a *stahlhartes Gehäuse* ("shell as hard as steel") are wholly dependent on his perspective on the consequences of Western rationality. In this sense, *Ancient Judaism* sheds light on Weber's understanding of this characteristic and decisive component of modern culture.

For Max Weber, the prophet was the ancestor of the charismatic leader. This opens up the second problem I want to address. Weber referred explicitly to Rudolf Sohm's *Kirchenrecht* (1892) as the source of his concept of "charisma." As Adair-Toteff has shown, the subsequent debate between Sohm and the church historian Adolf Harnack was undoubtedly an important influence for Weber.[4] It has also been stressed how his concept of charisma was influenced by the importance of the personality in German culture. As Stefan Breuer explained, Goethe, Schiller, and Hölderlin and later Nietzsche, Wagner, and Stefan George were revered as outstanding personalities—*genii*. This cannot be left aside when trying to grasp Weber's conceptualization of charisma.[5] However, his studies on Judaism were at least as important for this conceptualization. Weber's grasp of the importance of a charismatic leader was strongly influenced by his understanding of the Old Testament prophets. He defined the prophet as a bearer of charisma and was specifically attracted by the political role each played. Meanwhile, Sohm's treatment of charisma stressed its sole religious character. So, while the phenomenon was introduced to Weber by Sohm's work, his research on ancient Judaism was where he found the features that allowed for the use of charisma in social and political issues.

Peter Berger claimed that Weber considered charisma and rationalization as "the two great innovating forces in history."[6] Agreeing with this statement, these are precisely the two aspects I look for in his essay on pre-exilic Israel.

The last part of this chapter will further advance these aspects by dealing with some suggestions on how Weber's understanding of these great forces can aid in assessing an outstanding issue in today's politics: populism. As I show, some of the inaccuracies in Weber's assessment of Judaism—pointed out by later Old Testament scholars—allow, however, for an increased potentiality of his concepts in contributing to this contemporary political discussion. Populism can be related to Weber's study on ancient Judaism along two lines.

On the one hand, it has often been stressed that populism is an expression of the irrationality of the masses and for this reason opposed to modern legal-rational domination. I discuss this assertion from the perspective we can obtain from Weber's assessment of the rationality of the prophets.

On the other hand, the religious background of the affinity between the prophet and the political leader sheds light on another issue raised by the discussions on populism, namely, the role of charisma. I focus on those elements from the role of the prophets in *Ancient Judaism* that can provide us with theoretical tools to think about and assess contemporary populism.

As my subject is Weber's study of ancient Israel, I mainly resort to populism as a way essentially to develop relevant aspects of his essay. But this back and forth will also allow me to stress the potentiality of thinking the political through the isomorphism between it and religion: secular politics frequently uses discursive mechanisms of religious origin to gain support and loyalty.

ANCIENT JUDAISM AS THE CRADLE OF WESTERN RATIONALITY

Like many of his contemporaries, Weber found important common features in the civilizations that developed in the first millennia BCE, an epoch he called a "prophetic era."[7] However, the emergence in Israel of an ethic and magic-free monotheism was the consequence of aspects in that process that differed from those that took place at the same time in China and India. While Weber saw the rise of salvation religions as a stage in a universal rationalization process, with consequences in the making up of life-conducts, the specific form of its occurrence in each civilization depended on the concrete historical conditions in which it developed.[8]

For Weber, the external conditions—for example, attacks by the surrounding powers—were decisive in the appearance in Israel of a rational reply to the problems they posed. This rationality can be assessed by Weber's own criteria. In his essay on China, he explained that the rationality of a religion can be appraised by the degree to which, first, it eliminated magic and, second, it systematized the relationship between its god and the world.[9] In relation to the first criterion, Weber stressed the differences between this Levite-centered religion and the cult of death in Egypt or the orgiastic practices in the cult to Baal among the Canaanites. With respect to the second criterion, in ancient Israel the rituals as a way to accomplish religious mandates were replaced by a set of ethical commandments that had to be fulfilled by each believer in his or her behavior toward the world. These led to a religion whose rational systematization was certainly unique in comparison with the surrounding cultures.

This difference was based, for Weber, in the belief in a covenant between the people of Israel and Yahweh. Socially, this alliance was the sole associative force in a complex social and economic stratification that resulted in an "entire maze," in a "permanent relationship of landed warrior sibs with guest tribes as legally protected metics."[10] And it is to this alliance that Weber conferred the fact that fulfilling religious obligations was more important than following rites or sacrifices, as in other cultures. Together with the rejection of magic, this meant an important drive toward the rationalization of conduct.[11] When Yahweh did not help the nation or a person, what followed was the question of which obligations were not fulfilled. And the answer would come not through irrational means of prediction but through the knowledge of the obligations. Thus, the alliance allowed that any inquiry on God's will was channeled "toward an at least relatively rational mode of raising and answering the question."[12]

Old Israel's Levitical priests were similar to other religions' priests in several aspects, but they did not practice magical therapies, nor did they use irrational therapeutic methods; rather than magicians, they were bearers of knowledge. Their prestige was based on the purely rational knowledge of Yahweh's commandments.[13] And there was nothing in them that was beyond comprehension: world events were seen as having a rational nature.[14]

As summarized by Ladrière, "the ethical rationalism of Moses, who coherently opposed agrarian cults and orgiastic rites, was continued in an increasing rationalization that mitigated ephemeral moments of emotion and religious euphoria to become a permanent *habitus* of ethical and rational nature,"[15] therefore leading to a certain kind of rational life-conduct. For my purpose, what is important is that, as it was underlined by the biblical scholar Irving Zeitlin, "Hebrews initiated the process of breaking magic's hold upon the world"; their prophets never made peace with the magicians.[16] By doing so, in Weber terms, they "have created the basis for our modern science and technology, and for capitalism."[17]

This is the reason Weber stressed repeatedly the affinity between ancient Judaism and Protestantism. He saw that both the period between the ninth and tenth centuries BCE and that between the fifteenth and seventeenth centuries CE were times of historically decisive innovations. In this context, Protestantism inherited the "perfectly unemotional wisdom of the Hebrews... its rational suppression of the mystical, in fact the whole *emotional* side of religion, has rightly been attributed... to the influence of the Old Testament."[18]

For this reason, after having done his research on ancient Judaism, Weber could add in the 1920 version of *Die protestantische Ethik und der Geist des Kapitalismus*: "That great historic process in the development of religions, the elimination of magic from the world which had begun with the old Hebrew prophets and, in conjunction with Hellenistic scientific thought, had repudiated all magical means to salvation as superstition and sin, came here to its logical conclusion."[19] With this assertion we can see the full scope of Judaism's importance for Weber. When he aimed at depicting the specificity of the modern West, as in the *Vorbemerkung*, or "Preface," for his *Gesammelte Aufsätze zur Religionssoziologie*, he showed how every single value sphere is characterized by a particular type of rationality, one that, as he stated and as I have shown here, had its origins in ancient Judaic culture.

THE HEBREW PROPHETS AS MODELS FOR THE CHARISMATIC POLITICAL LEADER

In *Economy and Society* Weber defined the prophet as a "purely individual bearer of charisma, who by virtue of his mission proclaims a religious doctrine or divine commandment."[20] This is why he stands close to "the popular leader (*demagogos*) or political publicist."[21] Weber's insight on the prophets was deeply influenced by the school led by Julius Wellhausen, a German biblical scholar. For this group of intellectuals, the classical prophets of the eighth century BCE initiated the struggle against magic, differentiating themselves from the established priests. Weber assumed this, underlining emphatically the contrast between those bearers of charisma and the ritualism of the priests: "as a rule, the prophet or the savior personally has stood in opposition to the traditional hierocratic powers of magicians or of priests."[22] The former brought the words of Yahweh and had no respect for the latter—despite their office charisma (*Amts-Charisma*)—or for their rituals.[23] The prophet represented nobody except Yahweh, confronting the traditional religious order. One can see in Weber's stressing of Wellhausen's distinction, as well as in other aspects of *Ancient Judaism*, a clear political bias, and that is specifically what I want to emphasize—because it is the personal charisma of the political leader, depicted in *Economy and Society* as an institutional outsider, that Weber will oppose to the *Amts-Charisma* of the bureaucracy in his political interventions.

No less politically biased is Weber's emphasis on the social politics of the prophets. He considered Moses, the first prophet of Israel, as someone whose function was to "resolve the conflicts between status groups," and the later prophets were also "concerned with social reform."[24] Prophets emerged in a context of profound social changes, with increasing differences between rich and poor, between patrician groups in the towns and rural-based tribes of peasants and shepherds, having a consistent social-ethical attitude in defense of the humble people, being coherent with the charity he considered as a characteristic feature of the Torah.[25] As Zeitlin posed it, the prophets arose to oppose the unjust policies of the kings.[26] He showed this through his analysis of the role played by prophets such as Amos, Isaiah, Micah, and Zephaniah, who fought the battle of the poor and the oppressed against the injustices of the ruling classes.[27]

From a political point of view, another relevant feature of the prophets Weber pointed out is that they typically addressed the nation as a community. Prophecy "promotes systematic unification, by relating the people's life as a whole [*Gesamtleben des Volks*] and the life of each individual to the fulfillment of Yahweh's positive commandments."[28] Weber explained that although the prophet dealt with the destiny of individuals— though, regularly with those politically important—he did take on "the destiny of the state and the people."[29] Weber added that "this concern always assumed the form of emotional invectives against the overlords." Thus, prophets engaged in political opposition but by appealing strongly to the believers' feelings.

Indeed, relying on their charismatic inspiration, prophets inspired deep feelings in their followers; the relationship between them and the prophet was fully shaped by its emotional nature. A distinct characteristic of the prophets, Weber made clear, was their "vital emotional *preaching*."[30] The prophet, we read in *Ancient Judaism*, "discharges his glowing passion and experiences all the abysses of the human heart."[31] So, despite their crucial role in confronting magic and, by this, constituting a decisive step in the world-historical process of rationalization, the prophets' importance had nevertheless a significant non-rational component in the affective drive that grounded their relationship with the believers.

We can see in Weber's analysis of the Hebrew prophets an emphasis on three aspects, which are highly relevant for the understanding of contemporary political issues. These are the place of charismatic leaders as relative outsiders of the political institutional scene; the social bias of their politics, claiming the overcoming of an unequal and corrupted social order; and their appeal to the affective involvement of broad sectors of the population, giving birth to communal bonds.

THE IMPORTANCE OF WEBER'S ANALYSIS OF ANCIENT JUDAISM FOR TODAY'S POLITICS

In line with Berger, I have stressed two issues in Weber's *Ancient Judaism* that are of the greatest importance as historical forces. Therefore, these can be used as guidelines for the understanding of relevant political matters. There is no doubt that populism has become a political issue of the utmost importance in this century. Since 1989, and in a much more acute form since the world economic crisis in 2008, various political movements have been seen as different forms of populism. Post-neoliberal movements in Latin America, nationalistic right-wing parties in many European countries, strong alternatives to the long-established two-party system as in Spain, and even the rise of Donald Trump have all been labeled as "populist."

Given the vastness of this concept, and its use in so many settings, it could not but give rise to an extended bibliography, becoming a relevant issue and subject of an important amount of theoretical publications in the past years. Much has been written to tackle this extremely complex issue. There is a common agreement on the difficulty of defining it, as was already acknowledged at the famous conference on populism in 1967 at the London School of Economics, with Isaiah Berlin as the main referent, among many other important scholars.[32]

Max Weber, and in particular his comprehension of the historical role of the prophets, can aid in grasping this widespread political issue. In a recent article Carlos de la Torre tackled populism from a standpoint that paves the way for its study with Weberian categories.[33] However, he focuses only on Latin American populist experiences. And what is more important here, he does not make much use of Weber's analysis of the prophets, and none at all of his essay on ancient Judaism. What I try to show here is precisely how important features from the German thinker's analysis of that civilization can help in the comprehension of this theoretically and politically relevant movement.

There is, however, one previous aspect that has to be tackled, and it derives from the rooting of Weber's conception in Wellhausen's understanding of the Old Testament. Weber refers to this Lutheran scholar many times in *Ancient Judaism*, and it is usually accepted that his grasp of old Israel was highly influenced by this Protestant theologian.[34] This has a specific importance for the issues I focus on. The prophet–priest antinomy underlined by Weber had a clear origin in Wellhausen's writings, but it was strongly relativized in later studies. As others stressed, including Zeitlin, the revolutionary role of the prophets, radically opposing the established priesthood, was contradicted by new generations of Old Testament scholars: "the view that ethical monotheism appeared in Israel for the first time with the eighth-century prophets can no longer be taken seriously. This was the position of Wellhausen and his followers and it dominated biblical criticism well into the present century."[35] As Peter Berger has shown, from the 1920s onward—after Weber's death—the classic Protestant interpretation of the canonical prophets has been seriously challenged.[36] New evidence made clear that they cannot be thought of as isolated from the priests' established religion; therefore, Weber's emphasis on the non-institutional character of the prophets should be, in Berger's opinion, relativized. For this reason, the very character of charisma, as understood by Weber, enters the discussion, for "the contra-position of prophet and priest, which Weber knew from the Wellhausen school, vibrates through the entire theory of charisma."[37] As this eminent sociologist of religion concluded, this "does *not* weaken the Weberian notion of the innovating power of charisma. On the contrary, it strengthens it."[38] It does so, in his opinion, because it shows that charisma may also be a trait of individuals located within the institutions.

Rudolf Sohm's analysis also provided much for this distinction, as Martin Riesebrodt has shown. Within a Protestant framework as well, Sohm attempted to show that Catholicism represented a fundamental break with early, charismatic Christianity. For him, in Riesebrodt's words, "*Charisma* is contrasted to organization and administration. It knows neither legal regulation nor economic rationality."[39] Also in Sohm, therefore, Weber found a basis for his sharp distinction between prophets and established institutions.

Notwithstanding the historical inaccuracy inherited from Wellhausen and Sohm, Weber's approach must be considered in the context of his interest in building an ideal type of prophet and, along the same line, of a political charismatic leader. His construction allowed for a clear-cut distinction of the prophet from a priesthood, whose *charisma-of-office* placed it close to his own well-known understanding of bureaucracy. Due to this distinction, the edges of the political leader, heir of the prophet, became more clearly defined for his typology of domination, as different from the legal-rational type.

Stephen P. Turner has pointed out that the purest form of charisma is so unstable that it is probably negligible in historical terms because of the weakness of an authority solely based on it. Therefore, he concludes, "one could only use charisma as a way of understanding something that naturally occurs solely in combination, as a tincture, or as a hybrid."[40]

What matters here is that this combination is also to be found in modern populism. Any ideal-type construction for an understanding of domination needs to be built leaving aside some features of actual regimes and emphasizing others. That is therefore the case when assessing the charismatic leadership of a populist movement. In fact, none of the examples given earlier, nor any other expression of Western populism of the twentieth or twenty-first century, has or has had a leadership that was independent of legal-rational (i.e., constitutional) domination. Perón, Haider, or Trump; Chavez, Pablo Iglesias, or Le Pen, all moved and move within constitutional rules. Karin Priester, analyzing different kinds of populist regimes, spoke of a dualism of a charismatic and a bureaucratic domination structure when populism emerges in modern, complex societies.[41] This is why Weber's analysis of charisma, based on his research on ancient Israel, provides us with important insights for the understanding of contemporary populist leaders. Even when his study was shown to be partially wrong, the misunderstandings he inherited from the Protestant scholars allow for a clearer distinction of these actual movements.

Together with the sharp differentiation Weber made between prophets and priests, other traits of the prophet have to be considered: the novelty of his message and, along with this, his independence of all established powers. Depicting the ideal type of prophet in *Economy and Society*, Weber wrote that "[t]he genuine prophet, like the genuine military leader and every true leader in this sense, preaches, creates, or demands *new* obligations."[42] In *Ancient Judaism*, he asserted that "none of them raised the claim to annunciate new commandments," opposing this to Jesus' "It is written but I say unto you."[43] In his study on Israel he also found evidence that prophets were many times part of old structures of power and that their legitimation was based in the Torah. The charisma of the prophet comes out of his relation with Yahweh, therefore out of a traditional creed. Despite resorting to the just mentioned quote by Jesus when defining the charismatic ideal type of leadership, thereby stressing its novelty, when studying actual prophets Weber showed this combination with features associated to the traditional ideal type of legitimacy. Actual prophets, as well as actual charismatic populist leaders, combine tradition, charisma, and legal-rational domination.

The newness of the prophetic message can also be relativized by an important conclusion Weber arrived at in his research. The message often referred to a glorified past, to "the hallowing of the brotherliness and plain manner of the confederates during the desert period, appropriately called the 'nomadic ideal.'"[44] This ambiguity, being a novelty but resorting to a traditional, glorified past, also shifts the prophet closer to the populist charismatic leader, who very often recalls an early stage of happiness and fraternity, as was highlighted, among others, by Berlin in the conference at the London School of Economics.

What is of the utmost importance for this approach to populism is that both prophets and populist leaders raise their voices against the established powers. Weber stressed the political character of the pre-exilic prophecy and its standing against those in power.[45] Even when subsequent studies relativized their independence of kings and established powers, the role of the prophets in Israel's history, as Weber understood it, made of them an important pattern to define charismatic leadership. Contemporaneous populist leaders might come out of an institution as traditional as the army, as did Hugo Chavez; but they nevertheless represent something new that stands against the existing structure of political parties that held power, usually continuously until the rise of the populist movement. That is characteristic of this kind of movement, which emerges to close down a crisis-ridden regime that has lost its legitimacy. The similarity to the role of prophets, as depicted by Weber, is useful to understand ambitious contemporary regimes that confer on themselves the role of turning the page of history in their countries. In this sense, as was underlined by Berger, the fact that prophets and leaders cannot be considered complete outsiders strengthens the Weberian notion of the innovating power of charisma because they are "a power of 'radicalization' from within rather than of challenge from without."[46]

The possibility of presenting themselves as a hinge in the historical process, common to prophets and populist leaders, lies in the fact that they arise in historical times ridden by crises. As Abraham Malamat maintained, for Weber the charismatic leader appears in a time of necessity—psychic, physical, economic, ethical, religious, or political—and the same can be seen, following this Jewish history professor, in the charismatic characters depicted in the book of Judges: they rescued Israel from a national crisis.[47]

This allows for a further resemblance: as Weber stressed, the prophetic message, as a response to crisis, had a strong political bias. Among the people of old Israel, "salvation as well as promise concerned actual political, not intimate personal affairs"[48] because "[t]he whole attitude toward life of ancient Jewry was determined by this conception of a future God-guided political and social revolution."[49] That is what lies behind the prophets' political view—for Weber, a utopian view; they aimed to achieve a dreamed kingdom of peace in the future.[50] This did not make them politicians; they "were concerned with social and other types of injustice as a violation with the Mosaic code primarily in order to explain god's wrath, and not in order to institute a program of social reform."[51] Populism, as Loris Zanatta summarized it, aims at a social harmony by confronting "those who are seen as guilty because of having acquired too much power and wealth."[52]

Another analogy between prophets and populist leaders concerns the place occupied by the leader himself. One of the features that have been pointed to in populist movements is their lack of democratic functioning. This has often been a crucial target for their critics. It is noteworthy that Weber underlined this not only in the prophets of Israel—"no prophet was a champion of 'democratic' ideals. In their eyes, the people need guidance; hence, everything depends on the qualities of the leader"[53]—but also in his political positions. He was fully skeptical about the role of the people in democracy: after the November revolution in Germany in 1918, he stood for a democratic leader, heading the masses and even having the right to dissolve the Parliament, which lost increasing importance in his proposals after the war.

As we have seen, Weber gave great importance to the rationalizing role the prophets played in history. However, for him rationality was to be understood in relative terms. If prophecies broke with magic and therefore with the incapability of consistently systematizing life-conduct, they were nevertheless expressions of aspects that, from a modern standpoint, are fully irrational. However, notwithstanding the rationalistic tendencies he highlighted in modern societies, they cannot be considered as exclusive. And this brings forth an interesting relationship between ancient Judaism and populism—the affection involved in them.

For Weber, the demagogue appeared, for the first time in history, in the "emotional invectives against the overlords" used by the prophets, discharging their glowing passion.[54] Affection and feelings are crucial components of a prophecy, especially in times of disarray, such as when the Yahwistic community had to keep together after the destruction of Jerusalem, when the "pressing emotional timeliness of the eschatological expectation" was the main binding force.[55] And this view can be found when Weber analyzes the group that is organized around a charismatic leader, one he depicts as emotional communalization (*emotionale Vergemeinschaftung*).[56]

The idea of a community as a welding force in populist movements has been emphasized in many studies, and it has been highlighted by Berlin as well. Ernesto Laclau, drawing on Le Bon and Freud, has shown that affection is the social cement that allows for the joining together of heterogeneous sectors of society. Populism, in his view, has always been associated with a dangerous crossing of the lines of a rational bond.[57] Affection for the leader, longing for an often imagined glorious brotherly past, and confidence in an ideal future for the people constitute the irrational foundations of these movements; and they can be traced back to Weber's study on ancient Israel.

CONCLUSION

I have tried to show the structural homologies between populism and the features Weber found in ancient Israel. This analogy allows for a better understanding of populism, one of the fundamental issues in today's world politics.

The comparison between the irrational aspect of any religious movement—and of the prophetic one shown here—and the affective irrationality characteristic of contemporary populism may help in the comprehension of the strength and extension of these movements in past years. It is worth recalling here Weber's comparison between Israel's prophecies and the political system in ancient Greece. In Athens, "the firm military structure of the city was averse to free emotional prophecy," whereas in Jerusalem, "on the other hand, the purely religious demagogue was spokesman and his oracles highlighted obscure fates of the future like lightning out of somber clouds."[58] Weber's powerful metaphor is an indication of the strength he assigned to emotion in political issues, a feature he reserved, in his typology of domination, to the charismatic type.

In Weber's view, the masses are emotional and irrational; as Cavalli stressed, this makes the charismatic process possible. When there is a political or social crisis, this irrationality becomes decisive, and the feeling that only somebody coming from outside can overcome it spreads among the people.[59] This is recurring in populist movements, which are usually defined as being a consequence of the irrationality of the masses, as in the case of the populist movements that arose in Latin America after the economic crisis in 1930.

However, irrationality is for Weber a necessary component of politics, and its religious origins are clearly depicted in *Ancient Judaism*. The ethic of conviction, necessary in every politician, involves ultimate "values" and "meanings" of life that cannot be defined by scientific rationality. Weber's own positions toward issues related to German nationality were frequently driven by his values, more than by a rational, scientific approach.[60] On the one hand, irrationality is inescapable in politics, even in a society as rationalized as ours; and any approach to populism has to depart from this fact, avoiding the contempt that, due to it, can frequently be found in many analyses of contemporary political situations. On the other hand, *Ancient Judaism* can aid in the understanding of the rise of charismatic leaders present in almost any populist movement. The situation in which they appear, their relationship with the established elites, the masses' involvement with them, their appeal to their emotions to build an "us" against "others" were present in the historic cases Weber used to build his notion of charisma.

The structural and functional isomorphism between religion and politics has attracted considerable attention. It is even present in sociology's origins, in the work of Saint-Simon and Comte. Furthermore, the social sciences have thought of religion as a source of analytical tools that transcend the religious sphere. From this source spring categories that aid in the comprehension of modern issues that are religiously embedded, issues that cannot fit into a purely secular framework. Weber's sociology of religion, and his study of ancient Israel in particular, demonstrate religion's utmost importance as a source for understanding these categories, which the contemporary study of populism should not overlook.

NOTES

1. Max Weber, "'Zwischenbetrachtung' or 'Intermediate Reflection,'" in *From Max Weber: Essays in Sociology* (hereafter *FMW*), trans. and ed. H. H. Gerth and C. W. Mills (New York: Oxford University Press, 1946), 324; *Die Wirtschaftsethik der Weltreligionen. Konfuzianismus und Taoismus. Schriften 1915–1920*, ed. Helwig Schmidt-Glintzer with P. Kolonko. *Max Weber Gesamtausgabe* (hereafter *MWG*) I/19 (Tübingen, Germany: Mohr [Siebeck], 1989), 481.

2. Wolfgang Schluchter, "Altisraelitische religiöse Ethik und okzidentaler Rationalismus," in *Max Webers Studie über das antike Judentum*, ed. W. Schluchter (Frankfurt am Main, Germany: Suhrkamp, 1981), 56.

3. Max Weber, *General Economic History* (hereafter *GEH*), trans. F. Knight (Glencoe, IL: Free Press, 1950), 360; *Abriß der universalen Sozial- und Wirtschaftsgeschichte, MWG* III/6, ed. W. Schluchter with J. Schröder (Tübingen, Germany: Mohr [Siebeck], 2011), 388.

4. Christopher Adair-Toteff, "Max Weber's Charismatic Prophets," *History of the Human Sciences* 27, no. 1 (2014): 4–5.

5. Stefan Breuer, *Burocracia y carisma. La sociología política de Max Weber*, trans. J. N. Pérez (Valencia, Spain: Alfons el Magnànim, 1996), 142 ff.

6. Peter L. Berger, "Charisma and Religious Innovation: The Social Location of Israelite Prophecy," *American Sociological Review* 28, no. 6 (1963): 949.

7. Max Weber, *Economy and Society* (hereafter *E&S*), ed. G. Roth and C. Wittich (Berkeley: University of California Press, 1978), 447; *Wirtschaft und Gesellschaft. Die Wirtschaft und die gesellschaftlichen Ordnungen und Mächte. Religiöse Gemeinschaften, MWG* I/22-2, ed. Hans G. Kippenberg with P. Schilm and J. Niemeier (Tübingen, Germany: Mohr [Siebeck], 2001), 189.

8. I have analyzed some of these differences in Eduardo Weisz, "Le judaïsme Antique aux origines de la modernité: les desseins de l'étude wébérienne," in *Max Weber et les paradoxes de la modernité*, ed. M. Löwy (Paris: Presses Universitaires de France, 2012), 13–36.

9. Max Weber, *The Religion of China. Confucianism and Taoism*, trans. H. H. Gerth (Glencoe, IL: Free Press, 1951), 226–227; *MWG* I/19, 450–451.

10. Weber, *Ancient Judaism* (hereafter *AJ*), trans. and ed. H. H. Gerth and D. Martindale (New York: Free Press, 1952), 79; *Die Wirtschaftsethik der Weltreligionen. Das antike Judentum. Schriften und Reden 1911-1920, MWG* I/21 ed. Eckart Otto with J. Offermann (Tübingen, Germany: Mohr [Siebeck], 2005), 354.

11. *AJ*, 135–136; *MWG* I/21, 432–433.

12. *AJ*, 167; *MWG* I/21, 476.

13. *AJ*, 175, 178, and 219; *MWG* I/21, 486, 490, and 547.

14. *AJ*, 314; *MWG* I/21, 666.

15. Paul Ladrière, "La fonction rationalisatrice de l'éthique religieuse dans la théorie wébérienne de la modernité," *Archive de Sciences Sociales des Religions* 61, no. 1 (1986): 106–107.

16. Irving Zeitlin, *Ancient Judaism. Biblical Criticism from Max Weber to the Present* (Cambridge: Polity Press, 1984), xi–xii.

17. *GEH*, 362; *MWG* III/6, 389.

18. Weber, *The Protestant Ethic and the Spirit of Capitalism* (hereafter *PESC*), trans. T. Parsons (London: Allen & Unwin, 1930), 123; *Die protestantische Ethik und der Geist des Kapitalismus/ Die protestantischen Sekten und der Geist des Kapitalismus. Schriften 1904-1920, MWG* I/18, ed. W. Schluchter with U. Bube (Tübingen, Germany: Mohr [Siebeck], 2016), 336.

19. *PESC*, 105; *MWG* I/18, 280.

20. *E&S*, 439; *MWG*, I/22-2, 27.

21. *E&S*, 445; *MWG*, I/22-2, 32.

22. *FMW*, 328; *MWG* I/19, 484.

23. *AJ*, 284; *MWG* I/21, 629.

24. *E&S*, 443; *MWG*, I/22-2, 30.

25. *AJ*, 255; *MWG* I/21, 595–596. See also John Love, "Max Weber's *Ancient Judaism*," in *The Cambridge Companion to Weber*, ed. S. Turner (Cambridge: Cambridge University Press, 2000), 203.

26. Zeitlin, *Ancient Judaism*, 157.

27. Ibid., 212, 226, 233, 236.

28. *AJ*, 255; *MWG* I/21, 594.

29. *AJ*, 269; *MWG* I/21, 611.

30. *E&S*, 445; *MWG*, I/22-2, 32.

31. *AJ*, 273; *MWG* I/21, 614.

32. Berlin's interventions at this conference can be read at http://berlin.wolf.ox.ac.uk/lists /bibliography/bib111bLSE.pdf

33. Carlos de la Torre, "Los avatares del carisma en el estudio del populismo latinoamericano," in *Max Weber en Iberoamérica*, ed. Álvaro Morcillo and Eduardo Weisz (Ciudad de México: Fondo de Cultura Económica, 2016), 469–493.

34. In the first footnote in *Ancient Judaism*, Weber writes, "all *Old Testament* study today is based on the splendid work of J. Wellhausen" (426); *MWG* I/21, 236.

35. Zeitlin, *Ancient Judaism*, 96–97.

36. Berger, "Charisma," passim.

37. Ibid., 949.

38. Ibid., 950.

39. Martin Riesebrodt, "Charisma in Max Weber's Sociology of Religion," *Religion* 29 (1999): 7.

40. Stephen P. Turner "Charisma Reconsidered," *Journal of Classical Sociology* 3, no. 1 (2003): 9.

41. Karin Priester, *Rechter und linker Populismus* (Frankfurt, Germany: Campus Verlag, 2012), 73.

42. *E&S*, 243; *MWG* I/23, 494.

43. *AJ*, 304; *MWG* I/21, 653.

44. *AJ*, 114; *MWG* I/21, 400.

45. *AJ*, 267–278; *MWG* I/21, 607–611.

46. Berger, "Charisma," 950.

47. Abraham Malamat, "Charismatische Führung im Buch der Richter," in *Max Webers Studie über das antike Judentum*, 119.

48. *AJ*, 126; *MWG* I/21, 418.

49. *AJ*, 4; *MWG* I/21, 242.

50. *AJ*, 321; *MWG* I/21, 676.

51. *E&S*, 443: *MWG*, I/22-2, 30.

52. Loris Zanatta, *El populismo* (Buenos Aires: Katz, 2014), 61.

53. *AJ*, 278; *MWG* I/21, 621.

54. *AJ*, 269, 273; *MWG* I/21, 611, 614.

55. *AJ*, 334; *MWG* I/21, 692.

56. *E&S*, 243; *Wirtschaft und Gesellschaft. Die Wirtschaft und die gesellschaftlichen Ordnungen und Mächte. Recht, MWG* I/22-3, ed. Werner Gephart and Siegfried Hermes (Tübingen, Germany: Mohr [Siebeck], 2010), 174.

57. Ernesto Laclau, *La razón populista* (Buenos Aires: Fondo de Cultura Económica, 2005), 10.

58. *AJ*, 271; *MWG* I/21, 612.

59. Luciano Cavalli, "Charisma and Twentieth-Century Politics," in *Max Weber, Rationality and Modernity*, ed. S. Whimster and S. Lash (London: Routledge, 2006), 324.

60. Eduardo Weisz, "Nación y racionalización: dos focos en tensión en los escritos políticos de Max Weber," *Estudios Sociológicos* 32, no. 96 (2014): 681–708.

PART V

CULTURE

CHAPTER 24

....

THE RATIONALIZATIONS
OF CULTURE AND THEIR
DIRECTIONS

....

THOMAS KEMPLE

AMONG Counter-Enlightenment thinkers from the late eighteenth century to the present, the advance of rationality is often characterized as a serious threat to freedom, and the dominant form of modern Western rationality is said to have had unintentionally irrational consequences. Although Max Weber was influenced by these intellectual countercurrents, his stance on the relation between the cultures of reason and freedom is for the most part ambivalent or even ironic. Noting that reason may offer a powerful justification for either emancipation or domination, for example, he argues that rational industrial capitalism creates the conditions for formally free labor but also for the exploitation of labor by capital, and that modern bureaucracy requires space for personal discretion while placing individuals under the rule of legal-rational domination. At the same time, he points out, prevalent rational attitudes in occidental culture may have their sources in non-rational habits or deeply felt passions, and the cultural effects of rational actions may be decidedly irrational and incalculable. In the best-known version of this double perspective, he discusses how the secular values of early modern capitalism were partly motivated by strict adherence to ascetic religious principles and that the modern nation-state formally monopolizes the rational means of force and the administration of violence, sometimes with unpredictable or even explosive consequences. Generally speaking, rationality in its many forms provides the basic framework for Weber's theory of culture in its many ancient and modern as well as Western and global manifestations.

Less known are his ideas on how these tendencies affect the rational development of a variety of other value spheres as well, in particular the aesthetic sphere. The present chapter elaborates on Weber's general concept of culture, illustrated by his scattered remarks on aesthetic culture, from the perspective of his relatively overdeveloped yet more precise theory of rationalization.[1] At issue for him is how the spheres of human civilization and culture, including painting, architecture, music, and literature, become relatively autonomous over time while exhibiting their own logics of rationalization. The starting point for Weber's approach, and for any consideration of its significance for us today, is expressed in one of his last statements on this theme, from the "Prefatory Remarks" to his collected essays on the sociology of religion:

> For one can "rationalize" each of these areas under quite different points of view and directions, and what is "rational" from one point of view may well be "irrational" from another. There have thus been rationalizations in the most varied areas of life and in all cultural circles. The distinction between them in terms of cultural history, however, depends upon precisely *which* spheres and in which direction they were rationalized. The first problem is therefore once again to recognize the distinctive *characteristic* of Occidental rationalism, and, within this, of modern Occidental rationalism, and to explain its emergence.[2]

This passage is remarkable for how it presents the argument that rationalization is not a unitary or unilinear historical process. Rather, it develops *in multiple spheres, in many directions, to varying degrees*, and *at different rates*. Since the rationalization of culture is a plural process, how we assess the directions it takes in any instance will depend upon the value spheres we focus on and from which standpoint we view it. This process is also uneven and relative with respect to where one locates particular life orders within the stages of cultural history. In any case, throughout the "Prefatory Remarks" Weber explicitly states that he is mainly interested in the cultural spheres shaped by *modern Western* rationalism.

In what follows I consider the emergence and implications of Weber's focus on the rational cultures of modernity first by tracing how he took up this theme from the cultural sciences of his day. Weber's approach challenges a monolithic concept of rationality and at the same time undermines a rigidly normative Eurocentric view of cultural history. Ultimately he adopts a kind of "heuristic Eurocentrism" for methodological purposes. These broader arguments form the backdrop to his focus on the rationalization of particular life orders and value spheres, such as those that motivate and give direction to the aesthetic sphere, including architecture, the plastic and fine arts, painting, music, literature, and theater. Although his comments on particular artworks and cultural movements are not systematically developed, they illustrate, complicate, and deepen his broader concern with the differentiation and rationalization of occidental culture. As he notes in the "Prefatory Remarks," for example, the mathematical foundation of astronomy or the biochemical basis of medicine in modern science, as well as the training of a cadre of specialized officials in the political sphere, all have their counterpart in the development of the principles of spatial perspective in painting, the theory of harmony and counterpoint in music, and the solution to the technical problems of domes and arches in architecture.[3] Drawing on Weber's larger argument and the ideas of cultural historians and philosophers who influenced him, I extend his cultural sociology of literature and painting with reference to particular works and artists, from Rembrandt and Milton in the early modern era to Stefan George and Leo Tolstoy in his own day. I conclude by noting how Weber's cultural sociology anticipates some of the ideas of his contemporaries and successors, such as Alfred Weber and Norbert Elias, and is challenged in recent critical studies of cultural fields and disciplinary cultures of power.

THE RATIONALIZATIONS OF MODERN OCCIDENTAL CULTURE

Just as there is no unidirectional or homogenous process of rationalization, so too there is no single or uniform culture. Weber's writings follow the German usage of his day in conceiving *Kultur* as "civilization," and thus as a shorthand term for the characteristic institutional patterns and organizational arrangements of (typically modern) techno-logical, economic, and political developments. At the same time, he understands *Kultur* to refer more narrowly to bourgeois artistic and literary expressions of "culture" in their objective, subjective, material, or ideal dimensions. Generally speaking, culture is there-fore a cover concept for diverse and shifting constellations of action, beliefs, values, and meanings in terms of which reality is considered significant from particular standpoints. Weber developed these ideas about the plurality of cultural realities and culture as a "value concept" (*Wertbegriff*) in the 1890s and early 1900s, when he was formulating his early methodological ideas on the problems of irrationality in historical economics and the objectivity of knowledge in the social and cultural sciences.[4] In his 1904 essay "Objectivity" he offers a very broad definition of the *Kulturwissenschaften* that encompasses a wide variety of specialized sciences for studying reality (*Wirklichkeitswissenschaft*): "We have designated as 'cultural sciences' those disciplines which strive to know the cultural *significance* of the manifestations of life."[5] From a disciplinary perspective, he argues, "significance (*Bedeutung*)" always suggests a way of understanding (*Verstehen*) that is based on both a principle of emphasis or selection (*Auslese*) and a criterion of relevance or value relationship (*Wertbeziehung*). In the cultural sciences the kinds of causal explanations, historical laws, and general concepts that are central to the natural sciences can only meaningfully be employed as "heuristic devices," that is, as lenses that refract, focus, or magnify some aspects of reality over others for the purposes of careful analysis and closer study.[6]

Weber is particularly interested in studying cultural phenomena from the viewpoint of "the historical epoch distinguished by the advancement of capitalism," especially how such phenomena are socially and economically conditioned.[7] His own scientific approach can therefore itself be considered a cultural artifact or conceptual construction. Like any competent social being, an investigator selects from an infinity of experiences and empirical realities in order to understand and assess actual relationships. As he formulates this general point, " 'culture' is a finite segment of the meaningless infinity of events in the world that is regarded with meaning and significance from the standpoint of *human beings*."[8] The cultural sciences are likewise governed by particular logics, distinctive rules of operation, and frameworks of perception that have their own history and conditions of emergence. Toward the end of the "Objectivity" essay he acknowledges, for example, that "the belief in the value of scientific truth is the product of certain cultures, and is not given by nature."[9] The particular branch of the cultural sciences that ultimately concerns Weber—sociology—therefore finds its focus "under the light of the great cultural problems" of the time, and these problems in turn are illuminated by values and meanings that are subject to change or reinterpretation.[10] Although Weber did not comment extensively or systematically on the literary and visual arts, several intriguing statements in both his published and unpublished writings allow us to extend these ideas on the rationalization of culture in general to a consideration of the aesthetic sphere in particular.

The ethical beliefs and cultural values of an epoch are inevitably reflected (like a mirror) or refracted (like a prism) in the methodological choices and evaluative ideas of the sociologist or historian who analyzes them. As Weber argues, "knowledge of culture is determined by *value* ideas," and "all knowledge of cultural reality is always knowledge from specific and *particular points of view*."[11] Without the investigator's cultural interests and even personal values there is no way of selecting certain topics for study over others or of determining which knowledge is meaningful and relevant: "Just as any attempt to gain knowledge of individual reality is simply meaningless if the investigator does not believe that some elements of culture are significant, so the direction of his or her personal belief, the refraction of values in the prism of his or her soul [*die Farbenbrechung der Werte im Spiegel seiner Seele*], will give direction to his or her work."[12] Although individual intentions and cultural standards always underpin scholarly inquiry, subjectively intended (*gemeinte*) meanings must be distinguished from objectively valid (*gültig*) meanings, at least for the purposes of analysis. In short, Weber's selection of some cultural problems over others necessarily reflects (and refracts) his own value choices and conceptual commitments. In "Remarks on 'Technology and Culture,'" his reply to Werner Sombart's lecture at the first meeting of the German Sociological Society in 1910, for example, he asserts that "a belief in the value of science" is a necessary precondition for science, whether or not this assumption is explicitly acknowledged as a topic of intellectual debate and discussion.[13]

From around 1910 onward, Weber narrowed his focus on the directions and dimensions of rationalization by turning from the broadly cultural science of modern capitalism to a more specialized sociological investigation of world civilizations and specifically Western culture, along with the particular value spheres that give shape to this culture.[14] Each of his two multivolume studies, *Economy and Society* and *The Economic Ethics of the World Religions*, draws from earlier methodological essays and *The Protestant Ethic and the Spirit of Capitalism*, where he acknowledges that "'rationalism' is an historical concept which includes a whole world of contradictions" and must therefore be examined in terms of its ambiguity (*Vieldeutigkeit*) and many-sidedness (*Vielseitigkeit*).[15] By formulating a clear analytical distinction between subjective and objective aspects of knowledge and understanding, he shows how even irrational intentions may give rise to rational social orders. As he illustrates with reference to the early modern economic system, the subjective orientations, motives, and desires of the Protestant reformers unintentionally gave rise to and in turn were shaped by the objective orders of capitalist institutions, norms, and systems. His general point about the cultural consequences of modern capitalism is then developed from another perspective in *Economy and Society* with reference to the illogical, unjust, or incalculable effects of expropriating workers from the means of production: "That the highest degree of *formal* rationality in capital accounting is only possible with the subjection of workers under the domination of entrepreneurs is a further *substantive* irrationality of the economic order."[16] Generally speaking, modern industrial capitalism is a material force driving the rationalization of Western culture-as-civilization (*Kultur*). At the same time, this process is propelled by irrational motives that inadvertently give rise to class conflict, bureaucratic domination, and industrial exploitation. Invoking Marx's topographical imagery of base and superstructure in his reply to Sombart's lecture, he concludes that the materialist thesis that economic conditions somehow lie at the end of the line of causes has been definitively discredited: "If we lay the causal chain before us, it will...go quickly from technological to economic and political, and then from political to religious and then to economic etc. factors. At no point do we have any resting place."[17]

To gain some conceptual orientation to these issues and their particular ramifications, it is useful recall Weber's canonical outline of the four pure ideal types of social action in the opening chapter of *Economy and Society*, "Basic Sociological Concepts."[18] Instrumentally rational (*zweckrational*) and value-rational (*wertrational*) actions are each based on the conscious deliberation of ends and means, and thus form an idealized conceptual pair in contrast to action based on emotions and feelings (*affektuell*) or on habit and custom (*traditional*). Besides suggesting a two-dimensional understanding of rational motives, this scheme also implies that rationalization may lead either away from non-rational or toward irrational modes of behavior. For example, habitual routines and emotional reactions in religious practices can potentially be replaced by carefully formulated rituals and plans, just as rationalization "can ultimately also work in favor of nihilistic [*wertungläubigen*], instrumentally rational action at the expense of action linked rationally to absolute values."[19] Likewise, time-honored religious customs and rituals of belief may eventually be supplanted by consciously enacted rules, just as familial bonds of love and affection can be transformed into sublimated communal relationships and aesthetic ideals may be driven by careful calculations and technical operations.

In empirical reality, of course, instrumental rationality and value-rationality do not exhaust the possible directions of rationalized culture. In the "Introduction to the Economic Ethics of the World Religions" Weber sketches a further typology of rationalism that appears to supplement and expand on the fourfold schema of social action presented in *Economy and Society*:

> "Rationalism" can mean very different things:
> [1] an increasing theoretical mastery of reality by means of increasingly precise abstract concepts;

[2] the methodical attainment of a particular given practical end by means of an increasingly precise calculation of adequate means;

[3] rejecting traditionalist conditions [in favour of more formal ones...]

[4] ordered according to plan [*Planmäßigkeit*] [rather than amorphous feelings].[20]

Although these conceptual distinctions are not fully or consistently worked out, they suggest a framework for refining and elaborating on the simple contrast between rational and irrational views of cultural reality. By way of example, Weber contrasts the *theoretically rational* mastery of reality in Western metaphysics and modern science with the *practically rational* standards of utilitarian ethics. He also considers how *formally rational* ideals that inspired early modern art and natural philosophy rejected earlier traditional beliefs and how *substantively rational* methods of systematic and ascetic contemplation displaced ecstatic or emotionally charged religious expressions. These examples suggest that social actions and cultural values become more intense and precise as they follow a potential path of rationalization, at least in the Western context: instrumentally rational action tends to move toward an ideal of theoretical mastery; value-rational action toward a principle of practical ethics and methodical calculation; affective action toward the passionate application of substantive standards of value and principles of judgment; and traditional action toward formulaic routines and refined cultural rituals (see Figure 24.1).[21]

Although this expanded and differentiated scheme of types of rationality and their directions does not exhaust all conceivable possibilities, it at least allows Weber to see beyond the Eurocentric assumption that the development of rationalism is a unitary process or an exclusively modern and occidental phenomenon. His principal objective is to identify the adequate causes or possible motives of human action in historical and cross-cultural perspective, as he notes in the celebrated metaphor of the railway tracks (*Bahnen*) of history in the "Introduction to the Economic Ethics of the World Religions": "Interests (material and ideal), and not ideas, have immediately governed the actions of human beings. But the 'world images' that have been created by 'ideas' have very often,

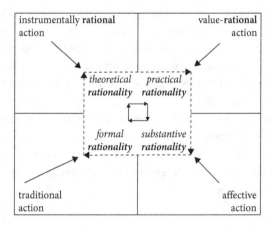

FIGURE 24.1. Directions of Rationalization.

Originally published in Kemple (2012).

like switchmen, determined the tracks on which the dynamic of interests has propelled action."[22] The figure of the cultural switchmen (*Weichensteller*) suggests that *human interests* and not just ideal values or material conditions in the abstract often drive social actions and cultural developments and that these particular interests in turn are propelled by images of the world constructed by human actors. This historical axis is combined with the cultural axis of comparison between culture-bearers (*Kulturträger*) that serve as vehicles for certain value ideals, ethics, and sensibilities. In short, Weber deliberately presents a methodologically "occidentocentric" view of global culture in an effort to trace historical genealogies, cross-cultural comparisons, and causal analyses of the dynamic autonomy of the ruling ideas of leading social groups and dominant cultural strata.[23]

THE RATIONALIZATIONS OF AESTHETIC CULTURE

The art world is arguably the birthplace of Weber's theoretical insight into the rationalizations of the cultural value spheres as they are differentiated from and enter into conflict with one another over time. A first indication of this idea can be found in his reply to Sombart's lecture "Technology and Culture" at the German Sociological Society meeting. Weber and his contemporaries picture the emergence of the aesthetic sphere as a problem for sociological discussion with respect to the social organization of the production and reception of artworks among members of particular social strata, especially the educated middle classes (*Bildungsbürgertum*). Weber is especially concerned with the conditions that give rise to new aesthetic *forms* and how the realm of art exhibits its own inner logic and relative autonomy (*Eigengesetzlichkeit*). Not only are modern artists finding new subject matter, such as the representation of industrial workers in drama and sculpture, but an emerging aesthetic culture is also giving rise to *new forms of expression and techniques of performance*, especially in lyric poetry and orchestral music. Echoing some of Georg Simmel's ideas, who also attended the conference in Frankfurt, Weber singles out the modern metropolis as the impetus and condition for an unprecedented cultural movement of technical rationalization and artistic innovation:

> the modern metropolis with its railways, subways, electric and other lights, shop windows, concert and catering halls, cafés, smokestacks, and piles of stone, the whole wild dance of sound and colour impressions that affect sexual fantasy, and the experiences of variations in the soul's constitution that lead to a hungry brooding over all kinds of seemingly inexhaustible possibilities for the conduct of life and happiness. Partly as a protest, a specific means of fleeing from this reality: the highest aesthetic abstractions, the deepest forms of dream, or the most intense forms of frenzy; and partly as an adaptation to this reality: apologies for its own fantastic and intoxicating rhythms.[24]

As this lyrical passage asserts (and even seems to enact with its fragmentary effusions), the social and technological organization of modern life seems to induce refinements in aesthetic form, as well as the rational transformation of cultural values more broadly. At the same time, the social, cultural, and material conditions of city life inspire irrational expressions of outrage, delirium, and frustrated desire among artists who react against this tendency toward rationalization, often by challenging the principle of artistic form itself. Such aesthetic responses to the conditions of modern life are among the many possible paths that rationalism and anti-rationalism may take.

As Weber wrote to his publisher upon realizing the enormity of his work on *Economy and Society*, "*Later* I hope to give you a sociology of cultural *contents* (art, literature, worldview) apart from *this* work or as an independent supplementary volume."[25] Although the posthumously published study of the rationalization of music was his most fully developed contribution to such a project, his remarks on the aesthetic sphere in "Intermediate Reflection on the Economic Ethics of the World Religions" outline a more expansive cultural sociology of the arts.[26] He begins by describing how religion, and specifically magical religiosity, has been a source of aesthetic stylization in rituals and artifacts and in liturgical dance and song. These practices have often existed in tension with rigorous rules or refined ethical principles that place moral content over artistic form. Viewed against the background of the intellectualization and rationalization of life in Western culture, however, "art ... constitutes itself as a cosmos of ever consciously grasped, free-standing autonomous values (*Eigenwerte*)."[27] In other words, artworks may compete with or function as surrogates for religious salvation, especially when they promise inner-worldly redemption or when ethical judgments are reformulated as matters of aesthetic taste. To illustrate this tension, he goes on to mention how the Council of Trent in the late sixteenth century deliberated over whether free expression and artistic creativity may be unbrotherly, immoral, or irresponsible, and thus whether certain kinds of organ and choir music in particular should be considered deceptive, blasphemous, or idolatrous.

At the same time, conflicts within modern culture may also inspire renewed alliances between art and religion, such as when artworks serve as emotion-laden propaganda for the transformation of religious beliefs or as a source of legitimation for dominant ethical ideas. In *The Protestant Ethic and the Spirit of Capitalism*, Weber notes how the shift from the value-rational axioms of the early Protestants to the practical rationalism of secular utilitarian ethics is manifested in specific works of art (the pattern depicted in the upper right quadrant of Figure 24.1). Despite the hostility of some religious reformers toward the fine arts and the frosty ascetic attitudes that descended on the warmth and spontaneity of previous periods, certain artworks may convey how discipline and specialization supplement or compensate for the disenchantment of the world. As evidence of this positive relationship, Weber cites Luther's and Gerhard's chorales, Shakespeare's plays, Bunyan's *Pilgrim's Progress*, and Goethe's *Faust Part II* and *Wilhelm Meister's Journeyman Years*.[28] Drawing on the work of his colleague, the art historian Carl Neumann, he highlights how the genius of Rembrandt was profoundly marked by the religious culture of seventeenth-century Holland, even though his personal conduct and aesthetic sensibilities would not have been acceptable to God in the eyes of the Puritans: "Standing before Rembrandt's *Saul and David* (in the Mauritshuis), one seems directly to feel the powerful influence of Puritan emotions," he notes.[29] Although Weber does not provide any detailed examination of Rembrandt's painting of David playing the harp to Saul (inspired by a passage in 1 Samuel 16:23), this work is remarkable for how it displays sensual exuberance (through luxurious clothing and soothing music, for instance) while asserting an austere spirituality (in Rembrandt's characteristic depiction of light radiating out of darkness). In Weber's letters to his wife from his travels to the Netherlands, he writes of the profound impression that this and other works had on him, praising Rembrandt as a "virtuoso portraitist and technician" and a "soulful artist."[30] In general terms, he is interested in describing the contradiction between the productive influence of ascetic Protestantism on painting, on the one hand, and its repudiation of fleshly idolatry and hostility to beauty, on the other.

In his remarks on the aesthetic sphere Weber's primary concern is to ask "why just here in the West?" and thus to inquire into how particular artworks and cultural movements developed historically as they did and not otherwise.[31] Against the backdrop of the panorama of Western and world history, he traces the trajectory from traditional action ruled by religious customs and rituals to their formal rationalization in the institutionalization of legal statues, bureaucratic procedures, formally "free" labor, and capital accounting (the path represented in the lower left quadrant of Figure 24.1). This general tendency is evident on a smaller scale from changes in literary form, language use, and aesthetic ideals that either replace or reinforce moral principles of salvation. Here Weber is following the lead of another colleague, Karl Vossler, a scholar of romance literatures and languages who published studies of the social conditions that gave rise to troubadour poetry and the late medieval cultural milieu of Dante's poetry.[32] In particular, Weber's intriguing quotations in *The Protestant Ethic* from Milton's *Paradise Lost*, which he refers to as "The Divine Comedy of Puritanism," illustrate Vossler's concern with how both the cultural spirit of a people and the artistic will of a poet may draw upon a common reservoir of thoughts, emotions, and linguistic conventions. In contrast to the ending of Dante's great poem, where the poet stands speechless in Paradise while contemplating the secrets of God, Milton portrays Adam and Eve being expelled from Eden while accepting their fate as a worldly task, assured by the angel Michael that they possess "a Paradise within ... happier far":

> The world was all before them, where to choose
> Their place of rest, and Providence their guide.
> They hand in hand with wandering steps and slow
> Through Eden took their solitary way.[33]

Milton's use of blank verse and iambic pentameter appears here as a formal innovation insofar as he rejects the rhyming practices employed by Dante in post-classical Europe while at the same time reviving the technique of unrhymed verse characteristic of classical poetry. Although Milton vehemently rejected Calvin's doctrine of predestination in favor of a more free expression of Christian faith, he also reaffirms a commitment to traditional values in classical and Christian art while embracing modern expressions of selfhood.[34] As in Weber's discussion of Rembrandt, here too his general concern is with how these tensions not only inhibit but are also conducive to aesthetic production.

Weber intended his comparative study of the world religions to serve as a contribution to the cultural sociology of rationalism more broadly and of specific value spheres, as he states in the "Intermediate Reflection": "The rationalization and the conscious sublimation of the relation of human beings to the various spheres, in which external and inner, religious and worldly goods were possessed, then forced into the open a *consciousness* of the consistency of the *inwardly autonomous workings* [*innere Eigengesetzlichkeiten*] of the individual spheres."[35] His objective in these essays on world culture is to trace elective affinities (*Wahlverwandtschaften*) and multi-causal relationships between relatively autonomous value spheres (*Wertsphären*) and life orders (*Lebensordnungen*), rather than to determine one-to-one correlations or a single line of causal development. He argues that social action directed against secular interests or away from worldly concerns may itself be a factor in the advance or retreat of rationalization.

With this idea in mind, Weber refers to the charismatic appeal of the expressionist poet Stefan George, whose influence among his contemporaries extended beyond conventional religious and political patterns of leadership into a modernist aesthetics and a new substantive ethics (the direction depicted in the lower right quadrant of Figure 24.1). By offering his readers and followers a kind of formal prophecy as well as emotional inspiration, George's poetry rejects the modern world by preaching an aesthetic flight from rationalism. His circle of admirers thus forms a kind of "ascetic and aesthetic cloister" with all the characteristics of a sect, insofar as he "demands, announces, promises, preaches and propagates '*salvation*'" and calls his disciples to "regenerate and master the world."[36] In one of George's most popular poetry collections, *The Year of the Soul*, published in 1897, he combines techniques of rhyme and rhythm with an idiosyncratic use of punctuation and lowercase letters in a way that evokes feelings of both solitude and solidarity:

Noch zwingt mich treue über dir zu wachen	Your beauty while you mourn, my loyalty
Und deines duldens schönheit dass ich weile	Compel me to remain and cherish you.
Mein heilig streben ist mich traurig machen	That I may share your grief more perfectly
Damit ich wahrer deine trauer teile.	I try devoutly to be mournful too.[37]

In asserting the primacy of refined artistic form over raw emotional content, George's poetry expresses a protest against the present and a prophecy about the future while promising a line of escape from the past through the medium of art. George and his followers appear to want to transform the fleeting and intimate life of the artist into an enduring monument. Against this view, Weber scornfully declares in the conclusion of "Science as a Vocation" that "our greatest art is intimate rather than monumental."[38]

Similar points about the expressionist movement of aesthetic formalism are also made by the young Hungarian philosopher and literary critic Georg Lukács, who describes how George's lyric poetry "makes its own music, it is text and sound, melody and accompaniment all at the same time: something closed within itself and needing no further addition."[39] Early on in his correspondence with Weber, when he had hoped to complete a second doctoral dissertation (*Habilitation*) in Heidelberg, Lukács sent Weber the German version of his essay collection *Soul and Form* along with drafts of his evolving aesthetic theory. In these works, he develops his own ideas on the formative power of aesthetic culture to elevate life into art by unifying the diverse and divergent forces of reality. For Lukács, the critic's task is not just intellectual but also ethical and artistic, insofar as it seeks out "the mystical union between the outer and the inner, between soul and form."[40] Advising the young student to leave these essayistic experiments behind to pursue more disciplined and systematic work, Weber nevertheless acknowledges the correctness of Lukács' guiding research question: "how are artworks possible?"[41] In order to explain the conditions under which particular works arise, aesthetic theorists and art historians take the existence of works of art as given and then ask "how is that (meaningfully) possible?" A scholarly approach to these questions offers valuable conceptual and empirical insights but cannot judge whether such works *should* exist or whether art is a realm of diabolical magnificence and inimical to God. Nor can aesthetic theory alone decide if aristocratic aspirations are hostile to human fellowship or how to reconcile the tension between rational technique and emotional expression.[42] In "Science as a Vocation" and "Politics as a Vocation," Weber invokes these themes with reference to the scientific aspirations of Leonardo in his notebooks, the musical experiments with keyboards by innovators like Bach, the poetic paradoxes expressed by Baudelaire in *Les Fleurs du Mal*, and the ethical aporias in Dostoevsky's story "The Grand Inquisitor."[43] In each instance, he seems to suggest that these works are somehow symptoms of the theoretical rationalism that has come to dominate the aesthetic sphere in Western modernity, ironically as a result of their exquisitely refined application of technical and aesthetic innovations (as represented in the upper left quadrant of Figure 24.1).

In some ways the culmination of this tendency toward theoretical mastery in art is embodied in the later novels and philosophical writings of Leo Tolstoy, to whom Weber had planned to devote a book and who profoundly influenced many of his contemporaries and personal acquaintances.[44] What Weber calls "the keynote of the Tolstoyan art" is marked by the resolute path (*Konsequenz*) of an ethic centered on inner convictions rather than on a commitment to political revolution and by adherence to a strict morality based on the Sermon on the Mount rather than the achievements of modern science.[45] As Lukács notes in *The Theory of the Novel*, a draft of which Weber read before it was published as a book, Tolstoy's art is distinguished by the close relationship of literary form to its historical-philosophical substratum: "Tolstoy's truly great and epic mentality, which has little to do with the novel form, aspires to a life based on a community of feeling among simple human beings closely bound to nature, a life which is intimately adapted to the great rhythm of nature, which moves according to nature's cycle of birth and death and excludes all structures which are not natural, which are petty and disruptive, causing disintegration and stagnation."[46] Tolstoy's literary and broadly ethical sentiments are canonically expressed in the epilogue to *War and Peace* and even more forcefully in his last major work published in 1899, *Resurrection*, which Weber recommended to his mother as a work that is "magnificent of its kind, despite its heavy and utopian tendencies."[47] In what is perhaps Tolstoy's most didactic work of fiction, and a dramatic expression of his own ideals of universal brotherhood and communal sharing, he presents a scene in which the protagonist Nekhlyudov explains to a bewildered and suspicious gathering of peasants on his estate why he is handing his property over to them: "Because I consider...that land shouldn't belong to someone who does not work on it, and that everybody has a right to enjoy the benefits of the land."[48] Inspired by the New Testament and economic philosophies of agrarian reform, Tolstoy adopts the novel form to preach an ethic of love over violence and the desire for a more pure and natural state of humanity over the requirements of civilization. In departing from the expectations of his own aristocratic roots (Tolstoy himself gave his lands over to the peasants and donated the proceeds of his book to religious causes), he also breaks with the literary conventions of both narrative fiction and moral philosophy.

In a sense, the modern aesthetic sphere epitomizes the tendency toward the inward intensification of experience in response to the economic conditions of capitalism and the social advance of the metropolis. Apart from observing the relative autonomy of aesthetic practices and the artistic will (*Kunstwollen*) of particular artists and eras, Weber refrains from offering a causal explanation of the cultural changes or a detailed discussion of the social forces that shape this sphere. Rather, in "Science as a Vocation" he draws an intriguing comparison between the historical evolution of the arts and aesthetics and how progress is measured in science and technology:

> Science has a fate that profoundly distinguishes it from artistic work. Scientific work is harnessed [*eingespannt*] to the course of progress. In the realm of art there is no progress in that sense. It is not true that the work of art of a period that has worked out new technical means, such as the laws of perspective, stands therefore artistically higher to a work of art that is devoid of all knowledge of such means and laws—*if* its form does justice to the material, that is, if its object has been chosen and formed so that it could be artistically mastered without applying those conditions and means. A work of art that genuinely achieves "fulfillment" is never surpassed; it will never grow old. The individual can assess its significance for himself personally in different ways, but no one will ever be able to say of such a work that it has been "superseded" by any other work which achieves genuine "fulfillment."[49]

A work of art may be deemed successful in view of the pleasure it gives to an audience or the satisfaction experienced by its creator, for instance, but can hardly be evaluated as superior only on the basis of how effectively it applies technical innovations or theoretical principles to its subject matter. Rembrandt's *Saul and David*, Milton's *Paradise Lost*, George's *Year of the Soul*, and Tolstoy's *Resurrection* are each appreciated for how skillfully they express the spirit of the age or how intensely they evoke certain feelings, but they do not for that reason "surpass" other works of art. Apart from how we judge their aesthetic value, these works can be examined for how effectively they give form to content and place rational-technical means into the service of the will to expression, often in new, surprising, or virtuosic ways. Although each work may advance the theory, practice, form, and substance of artistic representation to a level that other works had previously been unable to attain, other works are not for that reason necessarily inferior to them.

Perhaps these are the cultural-scientific and historical issues that Weber might have addressed more fully if he had the opportunity to write a "sociology of cultural contents" as he had planned or if he had been given the occasion to present a lecture on "art as a vocation."[50]

The Afterlives of
Rationalized Culture

The "inwardly autonomous workings (*Eigengesetzlichkeiten*)" of the various cultural value spheres, including art and literature, can be understood from the perspective of either the subjective intentions that motivate individuals who act within them or the objective order of the institutions, forces, and structures that define their boundaries. In his 1917 essay "Value-Freedom" Weber stresses the methodological requirement to distinguish subjectively rational from objectively rational aspects of cultural development:

> *Subjectively* "rational" conduct is not identical with rationally "correct" action—that is to say: [action] utilizing those means that are, according to scientific knowledge, the objectively correct ones. It only means that the *subjective* intention is to orient oneself systematically [*planvoll*] towards the [utilization of] means that one *believes* to be the correct ones, in order to attain a given goal. A progressive subjective rationalization of action therefore does not necessarily also constitute objective "progress" in the direction of rationally "correct" action.[51]

Only by specifying whether actions are intended on a personal level or accomplished on a social level is it possible to assess the relative pace or possible directions of rationalization. In other words, understanding the "progressive" or "advanced" character of the rational consistency of any given cultural value sphere depends upon whether one's framework of reference is within or outside that sphere and on whether "progress" is understood in a strictly empirical-analytical or a broadly evaluative-critical sense. The criteria for considering a work successful, excellent, or innovative in the realm of the arts, whether from the perspective of an insider or the institution as a whole, for example, will hardly apply to the field of science or politics. Even within the aesthetic sphere technical improvements and creative advancements in painting, poetry, and music are often understood very differently from the viewpoints of variously located practitioners in these fields and at distinct historical stages of their development.

As a particularly outstanding example of this approach, Weber cites the book *Classical Art* by his contemporary Heinrich Wölfflin, who examines innovations in artistic ideals, images of beauty, and pictorial forms introduced in the Italian Renaissance.[52] In particular, Wölfflin discusses the shift from the fifteenth century (Quattrocento) to the sixteenth century (Cinquecento), where new techniques in architecture and pictorial representation were developed for cultivating and educating the eye in the perception of depth, open space, physical surroundings, and corporeal movement. Where Wölfflin offers detailed and in-depth analyses of these technical and perceptual shifts, Weber touches only briefly on the social construction and aesthetic composition of particular artworks and aesthetic styles.

In some ways, Weber's approach to cultural sociology both anticipates and offers an alternative to what in his day were called the *Geisteswissenschaften*, literally, the sciences of the spirit or mind, especially the rational intellect and higher faculties and cultural achievements. His method of cultural and historical understanding also lays a foundation for what today is called *cultural studies*, with their focus on mass media, popular and consumer culture, and culture industries. Despite their differences in emphasis and attention, these approaches share Weber's commitment to navigating a third way between the sciences of explanation and the arts of interpretation.[53] The revised map of disciplinary knowledge that he helped to draw in the nineteenth and early twentieth centuries placed the social and cultural sciences (especially political economy, sociology, and history) *between* the empirical methods of the natural sciences (such as physics, biology, and chemistry), on the one hand, and the evaluative criteria employed in the humanities (including philosophy, aesthetics, and jurisprudence), on the other. In order to justify their existence as legitimate scholarly disciplines, these "empirical sciences of social action" must undergo the trial of *rhetorical appeal* with respect to values and meanings while also passing the test of *empirical validity* with respect to evidence and causes. In addressing this double demand of science and literature, Weber avoids the temptation to take an objectivist view of collective behavior (as in the functionalist studies of Karl Escherich) or to embrace a merely subjectivist expression of human uniqueness (as in the lyricism of Stefan George).[54]

Since the end of the "classical" period of the late eighteenth and mid-twentieth centuries, the cultural sciences have attempted to investigate and produce knowledge about the plurality of cultures emerging from within and beyond modernity: among the educated and working classes, entrepreneurial and business strata, sexualized and gendered groups, ascetic and artistic movements, not to mention a myriad of non-Western worlds and experiences. These novel topics were taken up by others in Weber's lifetime and afterward: in the work of his wife Marianne on the tension between the domestic duties and professional aspirations of women and in the writings of his brother Alfred on the conflict between the civilizing ambitions of the practically oriented middle and lower classes and the culturally refined sensibilities of upper-class and educated elites.[55] Many of these issues are also taken up by Alfred Weber's young assistant Karl Mannheim on the sociology of knowledge and culture and of Mannheim's student Norbert Elias, who traces the genesis of the antithesis between the German emphasis on intellectual, artistic, and religious *Kultur* and English, French, and American attitudes toward political, economic, and technical *Zivilisation*.[56] Weber's approach to the rationalization of culture is likewise evident in Pierre Bourdieu's concept of the bureaucratic field in terms of the habitus or disposition of specialized agents of symbolic power and in Michel Foucault's method of examining the formulation and inscription of regimes of rationality in practices of governmental and disciplinary power.[57]

Like Weber, these thinkers and those following in their footsteps are concerned with how a realm of freedom is both enabled and constrained in political and economic life as well as in the arts and sciences. Against the grain of Weber's often pessimistic assessments yet still inspired by his framework of analysis, they have continued to raise critical questions of perennial significance for our twenty-first century about the prevailing rule of reason and the future prospects of its cultures of freedom and expression.

NOTES

1. Wolfgang Schluchter, *Rationalism, Religion, and Domination: A Weberian Perspective*, trans. N. Solomon (Stanford, CA: Stanford University Press, 1989), 100, calls Weber's use of the concept of rationalization "inflationary." Rogers Brubaker, *The Limits of Rationality: An Essay on the Social and Moral Thought of Max Weber* (London: George Allen & Unwin, 1984), identifies sixteen different kinds of rationality in Weber's work. A full discussion of rationality and culture is developed in S. Lash and S. Whimster, eds., *Max Weber, Rationality, and Modernity* (London: Allen and Unwin, 1987).

2. Max Weber, "Prefatory Remarks to the Collected Essays in the Sociology of Religion," in *The Essential Weber: A Reader*, trans. S. Whimster (London: Routledge, 2004), 101–112, 109; "Author's Introduction," in *The Protestant Ethic and the Spirit of Capitalism*, trans. T. Parsons (New York: Scribner's, 1930), 26; "Vorbemerkung," in *Die protestantische Ethik und der Geist des Kapitalismus*, Max Weber-Gesamtausgabe I/18, ed. W. Schluchter with U. Bube (Tübingen, Germany: Mohr [Siebeck], 2016), 101–121, 116. Hereafter *Essential*, *PESC*, and *MWG*, respectively. Note that I have modified the translation when both English and German editions are cited.

3. Weber, "Prefatory Remarks," in *Essential*, 101–103; *PESC*, 13–16; *MWG* I/18, 101–104.

4. See especially Max Weber, "Roscher and Knies on the Logical Problems of Historical Economics," "The 'Objectivity' of Knowledge in Social Science and Social Policy," and "Critical Studies in the Logic of the Cultural Sciences," in *Collected Methodological Writings* (hereafter *CMW*), trans. H. H. Bruun, ed. H. H. Bruun and S. Whimster (London: Routledge, 2012), 3–94, 100–128, 139–184; *Zur Logik und Methodik der Sozialwissenschaften. Schriften 1900–1907*, *MWG* I/7, ed. G. Wagner with C. Härpfer et al. (Tübingen, Germany: Mohr [Siebeck], 2018), 41–101, 243–379, 142–234, 384–480.

5. Weber, "'Objectivity'" in *CMW*, 116; *MWG* I/7, 181; Lawrence A. Scaff, "Culture and Significance: Toward a Weberian Cultural Science," *Current Perspectives in Social Theory* 11 (1991): 97–116.

6. Thomas Kemple, *Intellectual Work and the Spirit of Capitalism: Weber's Calling* (Basingstoke, UK: Palgrave Macmillan, 2012), 76–80.

7. Weber, "Accompanying Remarks [Geleitwort]," in *CMW*, 95–99, 96; *MWG* I/7, 125–134, 127.

8. Weber, "Objectivity" in *CMW*, 119 (translation altered); *MWG* I/7, 188.

9. Weber, "Objectivity" in *CMW*, 137; *MWG* I/7, 231.

10. Weber, "Objectivity" in *CMW*, 138; *MWG* I/7, 234.

11. Weber, "Objectivity" in *CMW*, 119; *MWG* I/7, 189.

12. Weber, "Objectivity" in *CMW*, 120; *MWG* I/7, 190–191.

13. Max Weber, "Remarks on 'Technology and Culture'," trans. Beatrix Zumsteg and Thomas Kemple, *Theory, Culture & Society* 22, no. 4 (2005), 23–38, 26; *Verstehende Soziologie und Werturteilsfreiheit. Schriften und Reden 1908–1917*, *MWG* I/12, ed. J. Weiß with S. Frommer (Tübingen, Germany: Mohr [Siebeck], 2018), 226–236, 226.

14. Schluchter, *Rationalism, Religion, and Domination*, 430.

15. *PESC*, 78, 194n9; *MWG* I/18, 159n32, 208.

16. Max Weber, *Economy and Society* (hereafter *E&S*), ed. G. Roth and C. Wittich (Berkeley: University of California Press, 1978), 138; *Wirtschaft und Gesellschaft. Soziologie*, *MWG* I/23, ed. K. Borchardt, E. Hanke and W. Schluchter (Tübingen, Germany: Mohr [Paul Siebeck], 2013), 336. On the contradiction between formal and substantive rationality, see also Hans-Peter Müller, "Rationalität, Rationalisierung, Rationalismus," in *Max Weber-Handbuch: Leben, Werk, Wirkung* (Stuttgart, Germany: Metzler, 2014), 109–111; Richard Swedberg, *Max Weber and the Idea of Economic Sociology* (Princeton, NJ: Princeton University Press, 1998), 36–39; and Herbert Marcuse, "Industrialism and Capitalism in the Work of Max Weber," in *Negations: Essays in Critical Theory*, ed. J. Shapiro (Boston: Beacon Press, 1968), 210–212.

17. Weber, "Technology and Culture," 31; *MWG* I/12, 236. Earlier in these remarks he attributes the idea that economic forces cause social and cultural life in the last instance to a line from Marx's *Misère de la philosophie* (*The Poverty of Philosophy*).

18. *E&S*, 24–25; *Essential*, 329; *MWG* I/23, 175.

19. *E&S*, 30; *Essential*, 334; *MWG* I/23, 182.

20. This passage from the "Introduction" is translated in *From Max Weber: Essays in Sociology* (hereafter *FMW*), ed. and trans. H. H. Gerth and C. W. Mills (New York: Oxford University Press, 1946), 267–301, 293–294; *Die Wirtschaftsethik der Weltreligionen. Konfuzianismus und Taoismus. Schriften 1915–1920*, *MWG* I/19, ed. H. Schmidt-Glintzer with P. Kolonko (Tübingen, Germany: Mohr [Siebeck], 1989), 83–127, 117–118. See also the translation in Donald N. Levine, *The Flight from Ambiguity: Essays in Social and Cultural Theory* (Chicago: University of Chicago Press, 1985), 221–222.

21. Figure 24.1 is based on the diagram I call "Weber's Window" in Kemple, *Intellectual Work and the Spirit of Capitalism*, 20, which expands the scheme presented here outward in mapping the mid-twentieth-century post-Weberian theoretical traditions of American sociology and German critical social theory. In the present context I elaborate on the distinctions identified by Levine, *Flight from Ambiguity*, 203–205, while employing the simplified terminology proposed by Stephen Kalberg, *The Social Thought of Max Weber* (London: SAGE, 2017), 216, 221, 226, and 227.

22. Weber, "Introduction," *Essential*, 69; *FMW*, 280; *MWG* I/19, 101.

23. On Weber's "methodological occidentalism" or "heuristic Eurocentrism," see Jürgen Habermas, *The Theory of Communicative Action*, vol. 1, *Reason and the Rationalization of Society*, trans. T. McCarthy (Boston: Beacon Press, 1984), 186–215; Stephen Kalberg, *Max Weber's Comparative-Historical Sociology Today: Major Themes, Mode of Causal Analysis, and Applications* (Farnham, UK: Ashgate, 2012), 43–72; Schluchter, *Rationalism, Religion, and Domination*, 139–174, and *The Rise of Western Rationalism: Max Weber's Developmental History*, trans. G. Roth (Berkeley: University of California Press, 1981). Acknowledging this aspect of his method does not absolve Weber from charges of "Orientalism" in the use

he makes of scholarly sources, whether intended or unintended, as I argue in *Intellectual Work and the Spirit of Capitalism*, 13–15, 233–234.

24. Weber, "Technology and Culture," 29; *MWG* I/12, 232.

25. Weber to Paul Siebeck, December 30, 1913, *Briefe 1913–1914*, *MWG* II/8, ed. M. R. Lepsius and W. J. Mommsen with B. Rudhard and M. Schön (Tübingen, Germany: Mohr [Siebeck], 2003), 450.

26. Weber, "Intermediate Reflection [Zwischenbetrachtung]," in *Essential*, 215–244, 230–232; *FMW*, 323–359, 340–343; *MWG* I/19, 479–522, 499–502.

27. Weber, "Intermediate Reflection," *Essential*, 231; *FMW*, 342; *MWG* I/19, 500.

28. *PESC*, 88, 107, 168–170, 180–181, and 272–275n64–74; *MWG* I/18, 251, 286–287, 452–462, 484–487.

29. *PESC*, 169 and 273n66; *MWG* I/18, 454n345. See Carl Neumann, *Rembrandt* (Berlin: Spemann, 1902), especially the discussion of religious life in Holland, 523–581.

30. See, for example, Weber's letter to Marianne, June 7, 1903, *Briefe 1903–1905*, *MWG* II/4, ed. G. Hübinger and M. R. Lepsius with T. Gerhards and S. Oßwald-Bargende (Tübingen, Germany: Mohr [Siebeck], 2015), 96–100, 97.

31. *PESC*, 13; *Essential*, 101; *MWG* I/18, 101; "Objectivity," *CMW*, 114; *MWG* I/7, 174.

32. See Weber's letters to Vossler in *Briefe 1906–1908*, *MWG* II/5, ed. M. R. Lepsius and W. J. Mommsen with B. Rudhard and M. Schön (Tübingen, Germany: Mohr [Siebeck], 1990), 556–563; *Briefe 1909–1910*, *MWG* II/6, ed. M. R. Lepsius and W. J. Mommsen with B. Rudhard and M. Schön (Tübingen, Germany: Mohr [Siebeck], 1994), 727–740; and *Briefe 1910–1911*, *MWG* II/7, ed. M. R. Lepsius and W. J. Mommsen with B. Rudhard and M. Schön (Tübingen, Germany: Mohr [Siebeck], 1998), 358–360; and Christoph Braun, "The 'Science of Reality' of Music History: On the Historical Background of Max Weber's Study of Music," in *Max Weber and the Culture of Anarchy*, ed. S. Whimster (New York: St Martin's Press, 1999), 186–,189.

33. John Milton, *Paradise Lost*, ed. S. Orgel and J. Goldberg (Oxford: Oxford University Press, 2004), 315, 317. Weber emphasizes the lines in italics when quoting from the German translation of Milton in *PESC*, 87–88; *MWG* I/18, 250–251. Also see the comment on Milton and the rise of metropolitan London in Weber, "Technology and Culture" 29; *MWG* I/12, 233.

34. *PESC*, 101, 220n10; *MWG* I/18, 272–273.

35. Weber, "Intermediate Reflection," *Essential*, 219; *FMW*, 328; *MWG* I/19, 485.

36. Weber's letter to Dora Jellinek, June 9, 1910, in *MWG* II/6, 559–563, 561; and Marianne Weber's remarks on George in *Max Weber: A Biography*, trans. H. Zohn (New Brunswick, NJ: Transaction, 1988), 457–459. Weber raises these points explicitly in "Technology and Culture," 29; *MWG* I/12, 232; *E&S*, 245; *MWG* I/23, 497; and implicitly in his use of George's translation of Shakespeare's Sonnet 102 in "Politics as a Vocation," *FMW*, 128; *Wissenschaft als Beruf 1917/1919 - Politik als Beruf 1919*, ed. W. J. Mommsen and W. Schluchter, with B. Morgenbrod (Tübingen, Germany: Mohr [Siebeck], 1992), *MWG* I/17, 251. For discussions of Weber and George, see Edith Weiller, *Max Weber und die literarische Moderne: Ambivalente Begegnungen zweier Kulturen* (Stuttgart, Germany: Metzler, 1994), 61–81; Lawrence A. Scaff, *Fleeing the Iron Cage: Culture, Politics, and Modernity in the Thought of Max Weber* (Berkeley: University of California Press, 1989), 104–107; and Kemple, *Intellectual Work and the Spirit of Capitalism*, 178–180.

37. Stefan George, *The Works of Stefan George*, trans. O. Marx and E. Morwitz (Chapel Hill: University of North Carolina Press, 1949), 87; and Stefan George, "Das Jahr der Seele," in *Sämtliche Werke* (Stuttgart, Germany: Klett-Cotta, 1981), 2:942.

38. Weber, "Science as a Vocation," in *The Vocation Lectures*, trans. R. Livingstone (Indianapolis, IN: Hackett, 2004), 1–31, 30; *MWG* I/17, 71–111, 110.

39. Georg Lukács, "The New Solitude and Its Poetry," in *Soul and Form*, trans. A. Bostock, ed. J. T. Sanders and K. Terezakis (New York: Columbia University Press, 2010), 85–86.

40. Lukács, *Soul and Form*, 23–24. Also see Lukács' 1910 essay "Aesthetic Culture," in *The Lukács Reader*, ed. A. Kadarkay (Oxford: Blackwell, 1995), 146–159.

41. See Lukács, *Heidelberger Ästhetik*, ed. G. Markus and F. Benseler (Darmstadt, Germany: Luchterhand, 1974), 9, quoted in Weber's letter to Lukács, in *MWG* II/8, 116, and paraphrased in "Science as a Vocation," 29; *MWG* I/17, 107.

42. On Weber's versus Simmel's views on this point, see Klaus Lichtblau, " 'Innerweltliche Erlösung' oder 'Reich diabolischer Herrlichkeit'? Zum Verhältnis von Kunst und Religion bei Georg Simmel und Max Weber," in *Die Eigenart der kultur- und sozialwissenschaftlichen Begriffsbildung* (Wiesbaden, Germany: VS Verlag), 153–172.

43. Weber, "Science as a Vocation," 15, 22; *MWG* I/17, 90, 100; and "Politics as a Vocation," in *The Vocation Lectures*, trans. R. Livingstone (Indianapolis, IN: Hackett, 2004), 32–94, 85; *MWG* I/17, 157–252, 247.

44. Marianne Weber, *Max Weber: A Biography*, 466; Edith Hanke, *Prophet des Unmodernen: Leo N. Tolstoi als Kulturkritiker in der deutschen Diskussion der Jahrhundertwende* (Tübingen, Germany: Max Niemeyer Verlag, 1993), and Hanke, "Max Weber, Leo Tolstoy and the Mountain of Truth," in *Max Weber and the Culture of Anarchy*, 144–161.

45. Weber, "Science as a Vocation," 13, 17, 27; *MWG* I/17, 87–88, 93, 105; and "Politics as a Vocation," 90; *MWG* I/17, 247.

46. Georg Lukács, *The Theory of the Novel*, trans. A. Bostock (Cambridge: Cambridge University Press, 1971), 145–416.

47. Weber to Helene Weber, April 13–14, 1906: *MWG* II/5, 74–76, 75.

48. Leo Tolstoy, *Resurrection*, trans. R. Edmonds (London: Penguin Books, 1966), 290. For further commentary, see Kemple, *Intellectual Work and the Spirit of Capitalism*, 151–159, 181–188.

49. Weber, "Science as a Vocation," 11; *MWG* I/17, 85.

50. On how Weber's remarks on "Technology and Culture" might be read as the outline of a possible lecture on "art as a vocation," see Kemple, *Intellectual Work and the Spirit of Capitalism*, 47–48, 210–211.

51. Weber, "The Meaning of 'Value-Freedom' in Sociological and Economic Sciences," in *CMW*, 304–334, 325; *MWG* I/12, 445–512, 492. In *The Flight from Ambiguity* Levine develops this distinction: 160–161, 203–205.

52. Weber, "Value-Freedom," *CMW*, 324; *MWG* I/12, 489. See, for example, Part II of Heinrich Wölfflin, *Classical Art: An Introduction to the Italian Renaissance*, trans. Peter and Linda Murray (London: Phaidon, 1984), 207–289; and Lawrence A. Scaff, "Weber, Art, and Social Theory," *Etica & Politca/Ethics & Politics*, 1–12, http://www2.units.it/etica/2005_2/SCAFF.pdf.

53. Wolf Lepenies, *Between Science and Literature: The Rise of Sociology*, trans. R. J. Hollingdale (Cambridge: Cambridge University Press, 1988).

54. *E&S*, 16, 245; *MWG* I/23, 164, 497; and "Technology and Culture," 29; *MWG* I/12, 232. On Weber's rejection of these extremes, see Niels Werber, "Sense per Simplicity: Ant Societies as a Self-description Formula of Society," *Modern Language Notes* 130, no. 3 (2015), 430–467, 437; and Weiller, *Max Weber und die literarische Moderne*, 138–162, respectively.

55. Colin Loader, "The Cultural Sociology of Alfred Weber and Karl Mannheim," in *The SAGE Handbook of Cultural Sociology*, ed. D. Inglis and A.-M. Almila (London: SAGE, 2016), 48–59; and Ralph Schroeder, *Max Weber and the Sociology of Culture* (London: SAGE Publications, 1992).

56. Norbert Elias, *The Civilizing Process*, trans. E. Jephcott (Oxford: Blackwell, 2000), 5–30. On Mannheim, see Austin Harrington, *German Cosmopolitan Thought and the Idea of the West: Voices from Weimar* (Cambridge: Cambridge University Press, 2016), 271–299.

57. Pierre Bourdieu, "Rethinking the State: Genesis and Structure of the Bureaucratic Field," in *Practical Reason* (Stanford, CA: Stanford University Press, 1998), 55–58; Michel Foucault, "Questions of Method," in *Essential Foucault*, ed. P. Rabinow and N. Rose (New York: New Press, 2003), 251–254.

....

CHAPTER 25

MAX WEBER AND THE SOCIOLOGY OF MUSIC

....

BRANDON KONOVAL

WHAT could the "sociology of music" be taken to mean? And what could a sociology of music possibly be? These questions would have been anything but academic for the select guests invited to the Heidelberg villa of Max Weber early in the summer of 1912, questions that evidently lingered long after hearing an extended private lecture for which Weber had provided the enticing, if mysterious, title "Sociology of the Muses."[1] Marianne Weber was among several witnesses who described the event in terms of astonishment and sheer intellectual inundation: writing to her mother-in-law, Marianne recalled how her husband spoke "for two and a half hours like a waterfall on the most challenging music-theoretical topics and their connections to economic and sociological matters," prompting a decisive intervention to rescue her husband's audience—not to mention, the waiting asparagus—before they drowned.[2]

Over a century later, and as preserved in a manuscript left unfinished at his death,[3] Weber's sociology of music has not lost its capacity to astonish and to bewilder, to inundate and even to infuriate, provoking critical response of such polarity at times that it can prove challenging to discern a common text under consideration. In the commentary literature, one encounters both a "minor work" that is testament to the very apex of Wilhelmine amateurism[4] as well as "a discovery . . . of such importance" that it helped to inaugurate a new phase of Weber's thought and research[5]; an account that is straightforwardly "Eurocentric"[6] yet offers a "resolutely universalist perspective" wholly exceptional for its time and place[7]; a "music study, the scope of which has hardly been attempted before or since,"[8] which nonetheless prompted the indignant inquiry as to how Weber, "on such an important topic," could "author so apparently myopic a text."[9] Myopia may well be in the eye of the beholder, but there is no overlooking a central question for all who grapple with the idiosyncrasies of the *Musiksoziologie*: what could a sociology of music have possibly meant to Max Weber?

If there is no succinct answer to such a question, the most comprehensive engagement with it remains Christoph Braun's *Max Weber's Musiksoziologie* (1992), a singular critical and scholarly endeavor that prepared several further articles,[10] as well as informing the editorial apparatus for the *MWG* publication of *Zur Musiksoziologie: Nachlaß 1921*. Nevertheless, "sociology of music" has not proven a popular term of reference for readers exposed to the work through the only English version currently available, *The Rational and Social Foundations of Music*,[11] and not solely due to the absence of "sociology" from that title. Indeed, a popular refrain rising from the chorus of secondary literature maintains that there is scarcely any "sociology" per se to be found in the *Musiksoziologie*, regardless of Weber's own use of the term (as reflected in the work's title for the *MWG*).[12] What modern readers of any version encounter in the music study is a curious amalgam that integrates aspects of music theory, music history, tuning practices and associated mathematics, music technologies (including forms of instrumentation and notation, as well as phonogram recordings), music ethnography, and reference to acoustic and psychoacoustic or cognitive studies of musical phenomena, reflecting the central role of music in these fields during the later nineteenth and early twentieth centuries.[13] The aspects of Weber's account that are more recognizable in conventional social or socio-logical terms—and as principally focused upon European music traditions and practices—emerge only gradually, acquiring prominence later in the text: these include Weber's attention to varieties of musical performing forces or ensembles, social classes and status groups, social institutions or milieux like the church and the court, modes of music edu-cation and musical acculturation more generally, professional training and professional associations for musicians, as well as market forces and venues for music production and music consumption that significantly contributed to music as a cultural practice in general, and as a vocation in particular—all this in just under one hundred pages of the original text that was posthumously edited and published by Marianne Weber.

Thus, while comparatively short, the music study plunges into a myriad of topics and details that would strain the core competencies of many practicing musicians and musi-cologists, whether in Weber's day or in our own. Furthermore, such a bare listing of subject matter fails to convey the structure of the text, a polyphonic interweaving of diverse threads of discussion that intensively explore, rapidly exchange, and frequently recall multiple themes, with source materials that range widely both in cultures and in chronology. With Weber's narrative flow not readily channeled on the page or in the mind, the editors of the English translation chose to incorporate a series of seven chapter headings, further subdivided with section headings (occasionally somewhat misleading) and scores of paragraph breaks added beyond those of the original manu-script, to highlight and conveniently parse the most linear trajectory that could be drawn through its contents.[14]

The discussion begins with Weber's attention to more technical aspects of music theory and mathematics—an "inside knowledge"[15] that Weber establishes at the center of the domain of music, identifying core challenges to musical practice that persist through the contingencies of history and culture—before gradually surfacing into the more recognizably "sociological" features that enclose this cultural sphere. Tracing mul-tiple pathways through this domain, the music study recalls what Thomas Kemple has referred to as Weber's "commitment to *perspectival seeing* as both a mode of knowing and a method of understanding,"[16] associated with Weber's reading of Nietzsche in general, and of "that brilliant essay" as Weber himself described it,[17] the *Genealogy of Morality* (1887), in particular.[18] David Inglis suggests that this perspectival, "multidimensional mode of analysis" ought to be "particularly appealing to scholars today who want to try to develop understandings of phenomena which go beyond older disciplinary and sub-disciplinary specialisms, and the forms of blindness to multi-causality which they entail."[19]

To approach Weber's music study in terms of the *Genealogy of Morality* is to reorient the associations that have been conventionally drawn between Weber and Nietzsche in this context, which have focused upon Nietzsche's *The Birth of Tragedy out of the Spirit of Music* (1872).[20] Nevertheless, Nietzsche's genealogical approach characterizes both the idiosyncrasies of the *Musiksoziologie* itself—in the multiple interacting developmental factors with which it engages and the internal tensions and discontinuities highlighted by these factors, contributing to a distinctive result (*Sonderentwicklung*) that is not immanent in prior phases of development—as well as the music study's relationship to Weber's critical projects more generally.[21] Lawrence A. Scaff has argued that "it is most improbable...that Weber could have pursued the twists and turns in the momentous career of asceticism in the 'sociology of religion' without Nietzsche's achievements in the *Genealogy*,"[22] and we might ask whether the often surprising twists and turns of the *Musiksoziologie* itself were similarly inspired: readers anticipating a royal road of occidental rationalization that will guide them straight to a final destination in modern Western musical practices will be startled by countless curves thrown in their path as Weber navigates multiple musical cultures through diverse eras of practice.

With a view to corralling such complexities, Nietzsche and Weber could be said to have framed their respective undertakings as an engagement with a central question. For Nietzsche, the challenge was to account for the distinctive and surprising ascendance of an ascetic, specifically Christian morality, despite the historical evidence of alternative pathways for moral development; for Weber—recalling the emergence of Western *Kapitalismus*—the challenge was to account for the distinctive and surprising emergence of occidental harmony, a strikingly ascetic phenomenon itself in several respects (above all in the restrictions it placed upon melodic freedom), despite the extant historical and growing ethnological evidence of alternative pathways for musical development. As Weber formulated it in the "Value Freedom" essay (1917), "why was it only in Europe, and during a certain epoch, that the polyphony which had almost everywhere emerged in the area of folk music developed into harmonic music, whereas everywhere else the rationalization of music took another, and mostly quite the opposite direction."[23] Though both Weber and Nietzsche could thereby orient their studies with respect to a central objective for interpretation, neither assumed the historical destiny or absolute value of the outcome they addressed, whether found in an ascetic morality or a harmonic tonality.

In this sense, genealogy served as antidote to teleology, consistent with Weber's critical response to the historiography and musicology of Karl Lamprecht's *Deutsche Geschichte*.[24] The fortuitous developments of Weber's account are encountered in some of its most telling details: a central component of harmonic practice, for example, is the use of a distinctive combination of intervals called a "chord" or, more narrowly, a "triad," the mathematical proportions of which Weber details right near the start of the *Musiksoziologie*[25]; nevertheless, though rationalized with such precision, Weber maintains that triads "arose to a certain extent accidentally, out of the progressions of several independent voices requiring harmonic regulation" (that is, to serve their contrapuntal integration).[26] The triad thus originated as a creative possibility latent within polyphonic practice, more the child of chance than of necessity.

The inherent complexities of his project notwithstanding, Weber identified an overarching concern of the music study in the "Value Freedom" essay that has often been highlighted as a principal source of unity for the text and has likewise been used to cast it in a teleological light: namely, music as a peculiarly fertile domain for rationalization. As Theodor Adorno framed it in 1959, "it was Max Weber...who first identified 'rationalization' as the crucial concept for the sociology of music....There can be no doubt that the history of music exhibits a progressive process of rationalization."[27] The *Musiksoziologie* is a particularly inviting text for such characterization, not least in view of its frequent mathematical references, but above all given its appreciably dense employment of the terms "rationalized" and "rationalization": of the 455 uses of these terms that Joachim Radkau was able to uncover in Weber's oeuvre on CD-ROM, just over 10 percent—forty-six uses—occur in the music study alone.[28] At the same time, however, the multiple analytic strands of the *Musiksoziologie* highlight the complex texture of rationalization, tracing its distinctive forms or processes not only through different stages of musical development or in diverse cultures but also where distinctive modes of rationalization were in productive counterpoint or even in direct conflict with one another. For example, observing that melody, even when "harmonically conditioned and bound...is not reducible to harmonic terms"[29] and that the chords of harmony "grow out of melodic needs,"[30] Weber concludes that "chordal rationalization lives...in constant tension with melodic realities that it can never completely digest."[31]

Thus, on Weber's account, modern harmonic tonality remains caught between axes of rationalization that are governed, on the one hand, by a "melodic distance" principle and by a "harmonic division" principle, on the other: these principles were used to pursue fundamentally different aesthetic ends via distinctive pathways, melodic rationalization being principally associated with subdivision of the interval of the perfect fourth, as in the ancient Greek tetrachords (the four-pitch segments providing the basic building blocks for ancient Greek melody and tuning systems), and harmonic rationalization emerging from the perfect fifth.[32] Correspondingly, Weber's study highlights the role of these intervals in framing a further interval that is central to his account: namely, a dissonant Pythagorean third (64:81) in the subdivision of the perfect fourth, serving melodic aims while obstructing harmonic development,[33] and a consonant major third (4:5) in the subdivision of the perfect fifth, a core component of modern triadic harmony.[34] In seeking out the conditions that made possible the emergence of modern harmony—a heuristic rather than historically determinist teleology in this sense (cf. note 24)—Weber traces distinctive pathways of rationalization that, with "a division of labor partly in cooperation, partly in competition,"[35] arrived at a serendipitous outcome from the standpoint of occidental harmony.

With the music study, therefore, Weber evidently heeded his own advice from the original text of *The Protestant Ethic and the Spirit of Capitalism*:

> One may—this simple proposition, which is often forgotten, should be placed at the head of every study that deals with "rationalism"—rationalize life from fundamentally different points of view and in very different directions. "Rationalism" is an historical concept which includes a whole world of contradictions.[36]

Rather than the vehicle for a fundamentally uniform, cumulative process of rationalization that gradually overcame irrational factors—a characterization that has sometimes been conflated with a singular *Entzauberung*, or "disenchantment"[37]—music evidently presented Weber instead with a peculiarly dynamic matrix of rationalizing processes that shared both affinities and antinomies, fueling creative enterprises that found expression through multiple, interacting outlets. If rationalization marks a key concern of Weber's sociology more generally, the domain of music therefore offered an exceptionally enticing venue for probing its varieties and extent and, at the same time, one that introduced relatively precise coordinates with which to map corresponding features and developments of rationalization in distinctive societies or cultures around the globe or distinctive phases of development within a single culture itself. Such an undertaking presented a bracing challenge to anyone convinced that a properly founded sociology of music was obliged to engage idiosyncratic, highly technical features that could not be straightforwardly reduced to social relations or material conditions as conventionally understood. This presented a challenge that Weber plainly found himself unable to resist.

ON THE GENEALOGY OF *MUSIKSOZIOLOGIE*

That Weber felt equal to such a challenge reflects more than just the confidence of an experienced and voraciously trained mind. In tracing Weber's pathway to the *Musiksoziologie* and the impact of that journey on the text itself, we might adopt the schematic of the "vocation lectures" and consider those conditions both internal and external that informed the genesis of the work. A lifelong devotee of Viennese classicism and an aficionado of *Tristan und Isolde* (whatever his reservations about the Bayreuth mystique cultivated by Wagnerians), Weber was passionately involved with European art music long before he came to engage it in more stringently analytic terms, along with music from much further afield. His close associate, Paul Honigsheim, recalled that when starting to recover from a lengthy setback in his mental health, one of Weber's first excursions was to hear *Die Meistersinger von Nürnburg*—indeed that, "for Weber, music was almost a necessity of life."[38] In her biography (1926), Marianne Weber likewise recorded frequent conversations concerning both music and musicians who included the pianist Mina Tobler, who Honigsheim recalled as having fed (or possibly whet) Weber's appetite for Liszt, among other shared interests.[39] Although Marianne observed a notably increased interest in music in 1911, a couple of years after Tobler had entered his circle[40]—with Braun even suggesting that, "without Mina Tobler, the music study would not have come into being"[41]—that intensification built upon a notably deep foundation in Weber's emotional, aesthetic, and intellectual life.

Nonetheless, the specific timing of Weber's study is telling, not least for its association with a seminal period in musical modernism: the *MWG* identifies 1912—the year in which Weber was deluging guests with his lecture on the Muses—as the year in which the manuscript itself began to take shape[42]—correspondingly, a year in which Schoenberg produced *Pierrot Lunaire* and Debussy and Stravinsky composed emblematically modernist scores for Diaghilev's Ballets Russes, *Jeux* and *The Rite of Spring*, respectively. With its ambitious breadth of historical and geographical references, Weber's music study was therefore acutely attuned to the seismically shifting cultural sensibilities of a time and place in which the apparent "inner logic" of harmonic tonality was increasingly placed under pressure by searching reconsiderations of the very foundations of music, out of which brave new worlds of creative possibility burst forth on all sides.

Likewise, when reading the *Musiksoziologie*, one is struck over and over again by the sheer press of possibilities Weber reveals to have been available to musicians of the present or of the past and whether of Europe or, indeed, of any place in the world from which indigenous music—whether "folk" or "art" or ritualistic—had reached European awareness in some form, often in a colonial context.[43] These forms included written reports of musical encounters; attempts to notate the music itself; phonogram recordings made either in the field or of performers brought to European centers and subsequently analyzed in periodical publications and books; live performances introduced to European settings, whether through world fairs (such as had introduced Debussy to gamelan music) or other forms of cultural exchange like the Meiji reforms that brought Japanese music and musicians to Europe and within close orbit of researchers like Hermann von Helmholtz (1821–1894) and his inheritors[44]; or even as incorporated in musical settings by Europeans themselves, a widespread practice that had initially grown out of a Romantic, Herder-inspired interest in *völkisch* identity[45] and which became a topic of close interest for leading music theorists whose publications were consulted by Weber.[46]

Therefore, far from focusing with myopic single-mindedness upon occidental harmony—and the technologies of tuning, notation, and instrumentation that ultimately supported its emergence—Weber took pains to begin to survey the untold wealth of alternative foundations and forms of music being revealed all around him, an approach already modeled for him to a great extent by Helmholtz in the pathbreaking study *Die Lehre von den Tonempfindungen als physiologische Grundlage für die Theorie der Musik* (first edition, 1863; first translated into English by Alexander J. Ellis in 1875 as *On the Sensations of Tone as a Physiological Basis for the Theory of Music*). Indeed, as Honigsheim recorded, Weber could be deeply annoyed when a fellow devotee of music like Ernst Bloch (the philosopher and cultural critic, not the composer) had, in making "all sorts of assertions which 'transcended into the metaphysical,'" simply "ignored facts which Weber considered empirically verifiable...concerning the music of Asiatic peoples."[47] In this sense, Weber appears to have stepped back from the more tightly circumscribed Nietzschean genealogy of morality of 1887 to embrace the vision of its prequel, *Beyond Good and Evil* (1886), in which Nietzsche raised the importance of comparative study to found a proper "science of morals":

> Precisely because moral philosophers had only a crude knowledge of moral *facta*, selected arbitrarily and abbreviated at random—for instance, as the morality of their surroundings, their class, their church, their *Zeitgeist*, their climate and region—precisely because they were poorly informed (and not particularly eager to learn more) about peoples, ages, and histories, they completely missed out on the genuine problems involved in morality.[48]

Were we to substitute "music" or "musical" for "moral" or "morality," the passage would no less cogently characterize the critical framework in which the ethnographic features of Weber's *Musiksoziologie* are set and the overarching empirical orientation (emphasized by Braun, 1992) to which they were tributary.

Although there are crucial distinctions between the views and claims of Weber and Helmholtz (to which Weber himself repeatedly attests), we might nevertheless recognize in Weber's music study a genealogy that is as much Helmholtzian as it is Nietzschean. When turning from the first half of the *Sensations of Tone*—principally concerned with acoustics, psychoacoustics, and the anatomy of the hearing mechanism—to musical traditions and practices, Helmholtz promptly cautions those readers who might think that music could be comprehended by a singular, rational grounding in scientific principles:

> *the system of Scales, Modes, and Harmonic Tissues does not rest solely upon inalterable natural laws, but is also, at least partly, the result of esthetical principles, which have already changed, and will still further change, with the progressive development of humanity.*[49]

Helmholtz was thereby preparing his readers to encounter Arabic and Abyssinian, Chinese and New Caledonian, Japanese and Javanese musics. By Weber's time, Ellis had already critiqued Helmholtz' portrayal of these musical traditions,[50] and phonogram archiving and corresponding analyses published by leading researchers associated with the Berlin Phonogram Archive—Carl Stumpf (1848–1936), Erich Moritz von Hornbostel (1877–1935), and Otto Abraham (1872–1926), among several other researchers cited by Weber—had vastly expanded the repertoire of musical *facta* that Weber was keen to take account of.[51] Michael Fend has noted that, in fact, "the majority of [Weber's] contemporary sources were ethno-musicological studies on musical cultures outside northwestern Europe."[52]

Such cross-cultural features of the *Musiksoziologie* contributed no less to Weber's historical ambitions. With frequent use of the term "primitive" throughout the text, the music study simultaneously emphasized the empirical and genealogical import of currently observable indigenous cultures, taking their musical practices for a window in time: "only now, on the basis of phonograms, has the strictly empirical knowledge of primitive music found an exact basis."[53] His critique of Wilhelm Wundt (1832–1920) notwithstanding,[54] Weber's *Musiksoziologie* found alignment with the general empirical sensibilities of German ethnological or cultural psychology such as were evident in Wundt's *Probleme der Völkerpsychologie* (1911), which suggested that psychological faculties beyond the reach of experimental procedures might yet be accessed through the behaviors and cultural productions of "natural" peoples, whose minds were held to be comparatively uncontaminated by modernity. At the same time, indigenous cultures could present suggestive evidence not just of a fixed, aboriginal state of music but furthermore of significant points of transformation: seeking evidence of the impact on traditional melodic cadential formulae by "virtuoso" artistic development (*Virtuosenkunst*), Weber referred to phonogram recordings of the Nyamwezi people under colonial rule in German East Africa, songs analyzed by von Hornbostel in 1909.[55] With its tremendous expansion of both cultural and temporal horizons, therefore, Weber's music study can be seen to have followed the path he came to envisage in the aftermath of critical reception to *The Protestant Ethic and the Spirit of Capitalism*: namely, "to correct the isolation of this study [PESC] and to place it in relation to the whole of cultural development."[56] The comparative studies undertaken for *Economy and Society* and *The Economic Ethics of the World Religions* thus found their correlative and precedent in the *Musiksoziologie*: while venturing beyond the pale of Protestant asceticism, the appeal of the music study for Weber evidently lay as much in the opportunity to look outside the domain of occidental music and assess alternative musical cultures and formations, as in the ways such alternatives could enrich Weber's understanding of the varieties and scope of rationalization.

If the music study reflects the omnivorous intellectual appetites of its author, therefore, it bears witness no less to the veritable explosion of interrelated scholarly and scientific endeavors that fed those appetites, newly emerging beneath the aegis of *Musikwissenschaft* in the later nineteenth and early twentieth centuries. Such endeavors included both music theory and historical musicology—intimately related pursuits with respect to accounts of tonality, epitomized by the foundational work of François-Joseph Fétis (1784–1871) and Weber's profoundly influential contemporary Hugo Riemann (1849–1919)—as well as comparative musicology (*Vergleichende Musikwissenschaft*) and its inheritor, ethnomusicology, but furthermore, anthropology and ethnology, acoustics and psychophysics,[57] physiology and evolutionary biology, as well as cognitive and cultural psychology—a polyphony of disciplines, the contrapuntal agents of which could be highlighted in a title like Georg Simmel's "Psychologische und ethnologische Studien über Musik" (1882). As nexus for such an astonishing disciplinary array, the scholarly and scientific study of music at the dawn of the twentieth century already presented in itself a paradigm of rationalization worthy of Weber's attention.

Furthermore, between 1907 and 1910, Weber's engagement on behalf of the *Verein für Sozialpolitik* (Association for Social Policy) with psychophysics and factory productivity—industrial work as a vocation—likewise brought him in simultaneous contact with practical economic and ethnomusicological concerns. The economist appointed to head the subcommittee charged with developing a workers' survey was no less than Karl Bücher, the author of a surprisingly popular 1896 study comparing clock-timed factory labor with the *rhythmische Gestaltung* (rhythmical patterning) of *Naturvölker* (natural peoples). *Arbeit und Rhythmus*—"one of the most diverting reads ever produced by the dismal science"[58]—opened up questions concerning the productive use of time, entertaining the prospect that research into pre-industrial societies could guide productive reform in worker satisfaction and efficiency within a fully industrial context.[59] Bücher's "Rhythmus" included actual musical practices such as the use of singing, chanting, and dance in the social context of pre-industrial work; at the same time, *Arbeit und Rhythmus* engaged in current debates concerning music and *Ursprungsphilosophie* (philosophy of origins), for Bücher's account was founded upon a claim relating the social function of music with the origins of music, which he had connected with the repetitive actions of work among *Naturvölker*, promoting common cause between the sociology and the genealogy of music.

Bücher's approach was nonetheless problematic in ways that would prove to be of particular concern for Weber. In public lectures and their subsequent publication as *Die Anfänge der Musik* (1911)—a key resource for the *Musiksoziologie*, among several other cited publications by the same author—Carl Stumpf argued that Bücher had fundamentally mischaracterized indigenous music: providing examples from the Tehuelche people in Patagonia, Stumpf remonstrated, "anyone who takes the trouble to analyse in more detail just one single song of this type" would "certainly no longer be able... to accept Karl Bücher's view that they only valued rhythm."[60] Thus, by narrowly attributing the origins of music to practical social origins, Bücher was held to be unable to account for the development of characteristic pitch features or structures of music, a fatal weakness from the standpoint of many would-be genealogists of music.[61] The rationalization of pitch materials played a crucial role in the development of *Mehrstimmigkeit*, a key term for Weber that is conventionally translated as "polyvocality" to reflect the genealogical perspective it seeks to capture. On Weber's account, polyvocality would differentiate in the West in two principal, interrelated dimensions: initially, toward a polyphony that had begun to evolve with considerable sophistication during the twelfth century and would continue to flourish through the *Ars Nova* and Renaissance and, later, through the Baroque period beneath the growing hegemony of harmony.

In this regard, Weber joined a wider community of scholars, often highly nationalistic, who were "at pains to show how the origin of music [was] tantamount to the origin of *Mehrstimmigkeit* (polyphony and harmony) and indeed tonality[62]—often in the face of plentiful evidence to the contrary, such as Greek and medieval monophonic music and various non-Western musical systems."[63] Unlike such teleologies of *Mehrstimmigkeit*, however, Weber made substantial efforts to acknowledge and conceptualize the distinctive processes of rationalization that did *not* necessarily arrive at such an end: in this respect, as Alexander Rehding observes, Weber attended no less to ancient Greek tetrachords or Christian chant formulae than he did to Arabic or Asiatic scales and tuning systems, as if occidental music could in some sense provide its own domain of cross-cultural data between the monophonic and the varieties of *Mehrstimmigkeit* or polyvocality. In contrast to Bücher's account, therefore, Weber's music study—aspects of which were first publicly shared in that Heidelberg soirée, the year immediately following Stumpf's lectures and publication critiquing *Arbeit und Rhythmus*—focused on the development of rationalized pitch structures that ostensibly emerged when musical horizons expanded beyond mere practical applications, developing an aesthetic orientation.[64]

The essential role of that aesthetic orientation, along with the *künstlerische Wollen* or artistic will directing its development, had recently been emphasized by Weber at the inaugural conference for the *Deutsche Gesellschaft für Soziologie* (German Society for Sociology) in October 1910. When responding to Werner Sombart's lecture "Technology and Culture," Weber found the interrelationship of the technological and the aesthetic introduced in a way that was promising in certain respects but vulnerable to a somewhat vulgar materialism. Referring to the professional context of Joseph Haydn (1732–1809) as a court composer at the Esterhazy estate—which Haydn had famously credited for the extraordinary opportunity it presented for experimentation with a professional orchestra—Weber observed:

> Development of the Haydn orchestra was made possible by conditions of a sociological, and partly an economic character. But its underlying idea is his most personal possession and is not technologically motivated. As a rule, the artistic will (*das künstlerische Wollen*) itself gives birth to the technological means for problem-solving.[65]

These comments proved prophetic and in relatively short order. Material conditions—social, economic, technological—as conventionally understood offer key contributions but are largely left for last in the *Musiksoziologie*. What Weber will ask as he commences his music study will not be, "what are the social or material conditions for the production of music?" but, rather, "what conditions are material to music making?"—a platform upon which a credible and suitably flexible sociology of music might be founded. And, thus, Weber would first seek out those features of an aesthetic domain that provided the working conditions proper to music as vocation, the *materia musica* which made possible the diversity of musical *facta* encountered not only in cross-cultural comparison but within the genealogy of occidental music itself.

RATIONALIZATION AND THE "INNER LOGIC" OF MUSIC

The deep personal experience that defined Weber's relationship with music—music as "a necessity of life"—provides context for Weber's observation in the "Intermediate Reflection" (1920) that, "[c]ertainly music, which is the most 'inward' of the arts, has the capacity in its purest form of instrumental music with its own internal development

(*Eigengesetzlichkeit*) to feign a realm that does not reside within the soul (*eines nicht im Innern lebenden Reiches*) and to appear as an irresponsible surrogate form of the primary religious experience."[66] The "purest form of instrumental music" highlights the development of structural principles that could stand independently of extra-musical frameworks, such as those conveniently supplied by texts—whether as the framework for songs or for opera, for ritual chant or for prominent liturgical genres like the mass, the sacred cantata, and the oratorio—as well as the social functions or occasions with which they were often associated. Furthermore, the music study repeatedly stresses how the use of instruments typically compels the rational organization of pitch materials, a fixing of pitch relationships that the unaccompanied voice was not immediately constrained by:

> Historically, the rationalization of tones is regularly based upon instruments: the length of the bamboo flute in China, the tension of the kithara strings in Hellas, the lengths of lute strings in Arabia, of the monochord in Occidental cloisters—all have served for the physical measurement of consonances.[67]

However, Weber likewise raises a deeper, strikingly affective concern in the "Intermediate Reflection," the sensibility of which is succinctly captured by Benjamin Steege (albeit not directly addressing the passage): namely, that an "appropriate response to the contemporary 'disenchantment of the world' was a retreat into new forms of private experience and intimacy," a haven of meaning that could be sought through the inner life of music[68] (cf. Weber, "Art takes over the function of a this-worldly salvation").[69] But what structural principles sustained the vault of this alternate heaven?

The Janus-faced character of music as both a socially embedded activity and an autonomous art form—one that could powerfully impact individual, subjective experience—presented a challenging profile for any scholarly portrait seeking to integrate such features. The transition from serving particular social functions to the *eigengesetzlich* nature of art more generally was a theme addressed by Georg Simmel in a 1910 lecture, "Sociability," at a conference attended by Weber (later incorporated in Simmel's *Grundfragen der Soziologie*, 1917), highlighting their shared concern with the aesthetic realm and its boundaries. Simmel observed that "in both art and play, forms that were originally developed by the realities of life have created spheres that preserve their autonomy in the face of these realities."[70] In the music study, Weber observes such a transition taking place under the auspices of a kind of de-enchantment: it is in opposition to magical practices—apotropaic and exorcistic, securing physical and spiritual health—as mediated by particular melodic formulae, that music's "rationalization proper commences . . . reaching beyond the purely practical use of traditional tone formulae, thus awakening purely aesthetic needs."[71] This departure from a purely pragmatic (if ostensibly magical) function correspondingly gave birth to music as a vocation, a distinctive role among other social functions, in which rationalization begat professionalization. Thus, to reincorporate the practice and vocation of music following its successful detachment from a culturally subservient anonymity, Weber's music study set out to engage music as an autonomous cultural sphere such as Simmel had emphasized in his remarks on art and play:

> their significance and their very nature derive from that fundamental change through which the forms engendered by the purposes and materials of life, are separated from them, and themselves become the purpose and the material of their own exist-ence. From the realities of life they take only what they can adapt to their own nature, only what they can absorb in their autonomous existence.[72]

For Weber, the codes by which that autonomous existence was conducted in music would sometimes reflect eminently practical concerns familiar "from the realities of life," but these realities would have to be assessed in context—that is, in terms of the "internal conditions" engaged by an inner logic of music.

In fact, Weber directly refers to an "inner logic" (supplying quotation marks, "*innere Logik*"), which he associates with the expansion of the Guidonian hexachord system toward modern (octachord) scales during the Medieval era, for which the *MWG* notes an apparent reference to Hugo Riemann's *Geschichte der Musiktheorie im IX.–XIX. Jahrhundert* (1898).[73] However, the concept associated by Riemann himself with such logic is encountered earlier in the music study, where Weber writes that "strict chordal harmony comprises only a regular conclusion of a tonal construction or one of its segments through a chord succession [*Akkordfolge*] that clearly characterizes a key (cadence [*Kadenz*])"[74]: the passage recalls Riemann's "*immanent logic of harmonic succession* [*immanenten Logik der Harmoniefolgen*]" as the expansion of a "theory of cadential construction [Die Lehre von der Kadenzbildung]."[75] "Cadence" is to be under-stood here not in its more narrow, modern sense as the structural conclusion to a phrase or passage but rather as a much deeper structural principle, a "succession of chords that establishes a tonic"[76]—tonality itself as an inner harmonic logic. (For a simplified illus-tration, one might imagine the opening harmonic sequence of the Pachelbel Canon, which departs from and returns to a central or "tonic" chord, repeating this sequence and reinforcing its tonal impetus throughout the work—with the harmony changing on the lowest pitches, heard once every four notes—while the actual canonic melody is sub-sequently introduced and overlaid with itself.)[77] Thus, whether the product of an *innere* or *immanenten Logik*, the concept of harmonic tonality as an *eigengesetzliches* phenomenon had become central to German theoretical discourse; but "strict chordal harmony" was a comparatively recent and culturally localized phenomenon, an expression of "inner logic" distinct from earlier traditions of occidental music or from the rationalized practices of music found outside the West. For Weber's account, on the other hand, identifying core, enduring challenges to the rationalization of music would provide a stable framework not only for drawing comparisons between different musical cultures but for revealing the dynamic tensions highlighted by rationalization within occidental music itself—the kinds of tensions that had in fact produced modern harmony and tonality. What kinds of issues could be exposed and brought into contention by musical rationalization, pro-viding the internal conditions with which a musical inner logic had to contend?

In his introductory comments to *The Economic Ethics of the World Religions*, Weber observed that, among the "very different things" that it could be taken to mean, "rationalism" could refer to "the methodical attainment of a definitively given and practical end by means of an increasingly precise calculation of adequate means."[78] Not surprisingly, Weber highlights the calculation of pitch relationships—a feature of all the musical cultures recognized as "non-primitive" by Weber—as a primary characteristic of musical rationalization, serving attunement as its end; however, it is a calculation that frequently reveals competing or conflicting demands and, correspondingly, the potential to arrive at different solutions or attunements that meet differing cultural or aesthetic preferences—choices that can facilitate or motivate momentous change in musical style and production, as it did in the transition from Renaissance to Baroque music. Weber's concern with such matters is not readily appreciated even by modern-day musicians or musicologists, who can spend an entire career sheltered from any conscious engagement with such issues, the beneficiaries of a kind of vocational amnesia made possible by received technologies of attunement. This is perhaps where a Weberian "amateurism" reveals itself as among the greatest assets of the music study, in which Weber's determination to penetrate beyond the familiar boundaries of his own musical milieu reveal hidden chasms of incommensurability that have sometimes played a decisive role in the genealogy of music.

The torrent of musical and mathematical arcana with which the music study begins finds its source in such contentious terrain, the original province not of modern harmony but of ancient harmonics or canonics, named after divisions of the *kanon* or monochord, conventionally a single-string instrument with inscribed calibrations and a movable bridge, which was used to assess the musical intervals formed by relative lengths of vibrating string.[79] In brief, harmonics can be understood as the attempt to create feasible, acceptable, or preferable attunements—that is, a means of selecting and determining a fundamental framework of pitch relationships for musical use, whether by singers or instrumentalists—and to articulate the principles that govern them. This has remained a long-standing challenge because our aesthetic response to tuning—in particular, our preference for intervals in a best possible, "pure" (Weber's conventional term), or just form—often uncovers conflicting preferences that an attunement must seek to reconcile. The issues at stake in attunement are highlighted by Weber as standing among the "foundational facts for all musical rationalizations"[80] and play a critical role in his account of modern harmony: one possible solution to the challenges presented by attunement is the use of temperament (of which there are many varieties), without which Weber asserts that "the whole of modern chordal harmonic music is unthinkable."[81] The core challenge addressed by any form of attunement, including temperament, is what Weber characterizes as "the fatal 'comma,'"[82] the gap that emerges between distinct sequences of intervals which depart from a shared starting pitch and which "can never again coincide on one and the same tone no matter how long the procedure be continued"[83]: that is, they will never arrive at a unison with one another, and thus divide up musical "space" in fundamentally incommensurable ways.

Weber's account reflects long-standing tradition in music theory—the incommensurability he highlights is prominently featured in Plato's *Timaeus*—but is not readily grasped by those unfamiliar with that tradition. The disharmony of the spheres can perhaps provide a helpful analogy at this point, for the creation of a calendar addresses a challenge similar to that of attunement. Both the calendar and attunement are concerned with reconciling different intervals that appear to provide self-evident tools or components on their own and which might be plausibly combined in a mutually supportive way: in the case of a calendar, these intervals are the lunar month and the solar year; in the case of attunement, they are different types of consonant interval, such as the perfect fifth and the perfect octave in "pure" or just tuning. The use of twelve pure lunar phases to subdivide the pure solar year presents a familiar challenge as the pure lunar year that would result falls approximately eleven days short of the solar period (in the approximate ratio 354:365 rather than 1:1); likewise, to use one series of consonant intervals (such as perfect fifths in just tuning) to subdivide the compass established by another interval series (such as perfect octaves in just tuning) produces one of those "fatal" commas highlighted by Weber. There are various types of comma, but a central one—moreover, one that invites closest analogy with calendar attunement—is the "Pythagorean" comma, where twelve perfect fifths fail to reconcile with seven perfect octaves, producing an approximate frequency ratio of 77:80 between the ultimate pitch arrived at by each interval series, rather than the desired unison, 1:1, as though the start of the tuning "year" would never again align after the first cycle.[84]

The Pythagorean comma is of particular consequence because it emerges between two interval sequences—of the perfect octave and of the perfect fifth—that are of foundational significance. The octaves' sequence is what provides the stability of the "tone," a conventional term used by Weber that is more precisely termed the "pitch-class relationship" in modern music theory: a designation like "the note C" refers to pitch class since it may be expressed at a number of distinct frequencies—a class of pitches so closely related that they sound like higher or lower versions of each other, as if in virtual unison. The fifths' sequence, on the other hand, is what generates *different* pitch classes, the twelve "tones" or pitch classes that have become conventional in Western music. These two sequences are characterized in the *Timaeus* as representative of the foundational principles of the "the same" (the pitch-class relationship) and "the different" (producing new pitch classes), which succinctly captures their vital role in music and their concern for Weber. Thus, the central challenge of attunement could be described as the attempt to find a satisfactory reconciliation of intervals that are desirable in themselves—thereby providing a calculable aesthetic basis for attunement—but which are ultimately incommensurable in their most desirable or "pure" form, an empirical antinomy represented by the comma lurking at the heart of any form of attunement. In a note to "On Some Categories of Interpretive Sociology" (1913), Weber observed that the study of music history could reveal "the seams at which tensions between empirical [facts] and the correctness type may burst open," demanding a "compromise or a choice between several such bases of rationalization"[85]: such tensions, and the choices or compromises they demand, are epitomized by the Pythagorean comma and the ways in which both attunement and the creation of music itself respond to it.

A significant part of the discipline of harmonics or attunement therefore involves the judicious, rational distribution of the effects of a comma, just as a calendar that seeks to reconcile lunar and solar intervals must find ways to suitably distribute the approximately eleven-day comma that falls between the solar and the lunar year. To make such accommodations in music, either more pitch locations need to be added within the span of an octave or intervals themselves may be slightly adjusted in size or "tempered," just as months can be given different lengths to synchronize with a solar year: the standard Western calendar could thus be characterized as a "tempered" calendar (albeit not "equal-tempered" since the months are not each comprised of the same number of days). Weber recognized that the complexities of harmony could be navigated in attunements that sought to avoid temperament by greatly expanding the number of available pitch classes, an approach that had precedent in the Renaissance and had indeed found more recent proponents[86]; however, Weber argued that both instrumental design and the physical demands of performance it entailed promoted a concentration rather than expansion of pitch materials. Referring to radically modified keyboard designs for the piano or organ, Weber noted that "in principle, no upper limit can be set to the number of keys [of a keyboard] in the octave if one wants to construct pure intervals for each interval cycle" but that "the difficulty of using pianos with some thirty to fifty keys per octave" provided a powerful motivating force that favored temperament in their stead,[87] amplified by the industrial production and wide commercial distribution of the piano in the nineteenth century (and particularly in a cooler northern European climate with a pronounced indoor social life). Although Weber himself does not make the point, the arbitrarily uniform distribution of the Pythagorean comma through twelve equal semitones of the octave suggests a measure of industrial standardization in itself, establishing an equal-tempered foundry that would reliably serve the chromatic harmony of Wagner through to the serialism of Schoenberg.

Thus, what could be understood in terms of "internal conditions"—of attunement itself, of the types of tonal materials derived from attunement, and of a growing aesthetic drive toward the composition of harmonic music—had met with "external conditions"— such as idiosyncratic developments in bourgeois musical culture (Weber highlights the piano as a domestic musical technology par excellence) and technologies of industrial production—setting the stage for a serendipitous, genealogical convergence: namely, at occidental harmony, which could not be adduced to any single cause or component or to any singular process of rationalization. Indeed, when temperament emerged in the later sixteenth century as a strong contender among forms of attunement—in particular, for fixed-pitch instruments that lacked the spontaneous tuning flexibility of the voice— one of its leading proponents, Vincenzo Galilei (c.1520–1592), characterized it as but one alternative provided by a "generous Nature" that could at the same time sustain other rationalizations of attunement.[88] Galilei correspondingly portrayed a venerable predecessor like Pythagoras as a theorist guided by certain aesthetic preferences—specifically, for perfect consonances (the octave, fifth, and fourth) in just tuning—who consciously chose one such rationalization of pitch materials even while recognizing alternative aesthetic objectives, which an alternative rationalization could realize in musical practice.[89]

Thus, for Galilei no less than for Weber, the rationalization of music could not be understood or plausibly represented in terms of a singular, monolithic process. Galilei himself acknowledged justifications on behalf of both just tuning and temperament, as he was obliged to do, for temperament ultimately draws its very purpose from serving and securing the just tuning of the pitch-class relationship. It was just such a combination that Weber portrayed as making possible the emergence of occidental harmony, even though Galilei's own proposal was not ventured with that objective in mind. In this sense, one of the most striking features of rationalization in music is the way in which the offspring of calculation—engendered by interacting conditions, both internal and external—may transform or transcend the more immediate goals envisaged by their parents, the often surprising products of a genealogy of causes and contingencies that could only be traced through multiple perspectives.

Weber's critics notwithstanding, Christoph Braun contended that the music study "reveals a breadth and depth of thinking and a synthetic achievement which is as yet unequalled, and which now more than ever can serve as the model for a sociology of culture."[90] What, then, could the "sociology of music" be taken to mean, and what could a sociology of music possibly be? If Weber himself left these questions open, his *Musiksoziologie* nonetheless recorded a provocative attempt to frame them and leaves a compelling template for their further pursuit.

NOTES

1. Max Weber, *Zur Musiksoziologie. Nachlaß 1921, Max Weber-Gesamtausgabe* (hereafter *MWG*) I/14, ed. C. Braun and L. Finscher (Tübingen, Germany: Mohr [Siebeck], 2004), 128.

2. Letter, Marianne Weber to Helene Weber, May 12, 1912, quoted in *MWG* I/14, 128.

3. *Die rationalen und soziologischen Grundlagen der Musik* was first published in 1921 (Munich: Drei Masken Verlag) and next appeared in 1925 as an appendix in the second edition of *Wirtschaft und Gesellschaft* (Tübingen, Germany: Mohr [Siebeck]).

4. Leon Botstein, "Max Weber and Music History," *Musical Quarterly* 93 (2010): 183–191, 183.

5. Wolfgang Schluchter, *Rationalism, Religion, and Domination: A Weberian Perspective* (Berkeley: University of California Press, 1989), 45.

6. Alan C. Turley, "Max Weber and the Sociology of Music," *Sociological Forum* 16, no. 4 (2001): 633–653, 634.

7. Simha Arom, "'À Plusieurs Voix': La conception wébérienne de la plurivocalité vue par un ethnomusicologue," *Revue de synthèse* 129, no. 6.2 (2008): 285–296, 289.

8. Michael Fend, "Witnessing a 'Process of Rationalisation'? A Review-Essay of Max Weber's Study on Music," *Max Weber Studies* 10, no. 1 (2010): 101–120, 105.

9. James Wierzbicki, "Max Weber and Musicology: Dancing on Shaky Foundations," *Musical Quarterly* 93 (2010): 1–35, 271.

10. Christoph Braun, "Grenzen der Ratio, Grenzen der Soziologie. Anmerkungen zum 'Musiksoziologen' Max Weber," *Archiv für Musikwissenschaft* 51, no. 1 (1994): 1–25; "Vom Clavichord zum Clavinova. Kulturanthropologische Anmerkungen zu Max Webers Musik-Studie," *Historische Anthropologie* 3 (1995): 242–266; "Max Weber und die Suche nach dem musiksoziologischen Gründervater," in *Wege zu einer Wiener Schule der Musiksoziologie: Konvergenz der Disziplinen und empiristische Tradition. Musik und Gesellschaft* B.23, ed. Irmgard Bontinck (Vienna: Verlag Guthmann & Peterson, 1996), 119–147; "The 'Science of Reality' of Music History: On the Historical Background to Max

Weber's Study of Music," in *Max Weber and the Culture of Anarchy*, ed. Sam Whimster (London: Macmillan, 1999), 176–195.

11. Max Weber, *The Rational and Social Foundations of Music*, trans. and ed. Don Martindale, Johannes Riedel, and Gertrude Neuwirth (New York: Southern Illinois University Press, 1958). The English edition lacks the depth of support offered to readers by the *MWG* edition—with its extensive scholarly introduction and copious footnotes, technical glossary (*MWG* I/14, 299–353), and biographical and citation appendices (283–298, 354–368)—or, for that matter, by the French translation prepared under the direction of Jean Molino. Furthermore, Weber, *The Rational and Social Foundations of Music*, shies away from resolving confusions in terminology otherwise readily clarified, rendering Weber's account more obscure than the material already merits. All future references to the *Musiksoziologie* will provide corresponding pagination for Weber, *The Rational and Social Foundations of Music* and *MWG* I/14, with the translation usually modified in light of the original text. For the reception of Weber's music study in the United States (and in association with the publication of Weber, *The Rational and Social Foundations of Music*), see K. Peter Etzkorn, "Aspekte der Rezeption von Max Webers Musiksoziologie in den Vereinigten Staaten," in *Wege zu einer Wiener Schule der Musiksoziologie: Konvergenz der Disziplinen und empiristische Tradition. Musik und Gesellschaft* B.23, ed. Irmgard Bontinck (Vienna: Verlag Guthmann & Peterson, 1996), 149–158.

12. Braun recorded that the original title planned for the *MWG* publication had been *Rationale und soziale Grundlagen der Music*: see Braun, "The 'Science of Reality' of Music History," 192n24.

13. Cf. Albrecht Schneider, "Psychological Theory and Comparative Musicology," in *Comparative Musicology and Anthropology of Music: Essays on the History of Ethnomusicology*, ed. Bruno Nettl and Philip V. Bolman (Chicago: University of Chicago Press, 1990), 293–317.

14. Fend, "Witnessing a 'Process of Rationalisation'?" provides a helpful concordance with the pagination of the *MWG* for readers familiar with the English translation.

15. Thomas Kemple, *Intellectual Work and the Spirit of Capitalism: Weber's Calling* (Basingstoke, UK: Palgrave Macmillan, 2014), 7.

16. Ibid., 77.

17. Max Weber, "The Social Psychology of the World Religions," in *From Max Weber: Essays in Sociology* (hereafter *FMW*), ed. and trans. H. H. Gerth and C. W. Mills (London and New York: Routledge, 2009), 267–301, 270; "Einleitung," in *Die Wirtschaftsethik der Weltreligionen. Konfuzianismus und Taoismus. Schriften 1915–1920*, *MWG* I/19, ed. Helwig Schmidt-Glintzer with P. Kolonko. Max Weber Gesamtausgabe (Tübingen, Germany: Mohr [Siebeck], 1989), 83–127, 88.

18. Cf. Friedrich Nietzsche, *On the Genealogy of Morality*, trans. Maudemarie Clark and A. J. Swensen (1887; Indianapolis, IN: Hackett, 1998), III, §12, 85: "there is only perspectival seeing, *only* a perspectival 'knowing'."

19. David Inglis, "Max Weber's Presences: On the Cultural Sociology of the Long-Term," in *The SAGE Handbook of Cultural Sociology*, ed. David Inglis and Anna-Mari Almila (London: SAGE, 2016), 26–47, 44.

20. In "Weber and the Rationalization of Music," *International Journal of Politics, Culture and Society* 1, no. 2 (1987): 337–352, Ferenc Feher briefly addresses the more obvious connection with Nietzsche's juxtaposition of the Apollonian/Dionysian with the rational/irrational. In "Weber, Nietzsche and Music," in *Nietzsche: A Critical Reader*, ed. Peter R. Sedgwick (Oxford: Blackwell, 1995), 84–103, Andrew Edgar offers a rich discussion fully devoted to

the Nietzsche comparison. On Weber's relationship to Nietzsche more generally, see Eugène Fleischmann, "De Weber à Nietzsche," in *Archives européenes de sociologie: 40ème anniversaire* (1964; Cambridge: Cambridge University Press, 2001), 243–291; Roger Häußling, *Nietzsche und die Soziologie: Zum Konstrukt des Übermenschen, zu dessen anti-soziologischen Implikationen und zur soziologischen Reaktion auf Nietzsches Denken* (Würzburg, Germany: Königshausen & Neumann, 2000), 165–203; Wilhelm Hennis, *Max Weber: Essays in Reconstruction* (London: Unwin Hyman, 1988), 146–162; Klaus Lichtblau, *Kulturkrise und die Soziologie um die Jahrhundertwende: Zur Genealogie der Kultursoziologie in Deutschland* (Frankfurt am Main, Germany: Suhrkamp, 1996), 158–177; and Franz Graf zu Solms-Laubach, *Nietzsche and Early German and Austrian Sociology* (Berlin: Walter de Gruyter, 2007), 75–92.

21. In the "Objectivity Essay," Weber observes that the synthesis or selective "accentuation of *one* or *a number* of viewpoints and…a great many diffuse and discrete *individual* phenomena" may be used to "attempt to comprehend historical individuals, or their component parts, in *genetic* concepts" (emphasis in original): see Max Weber, "The 'Objectivity' of Knowledge in Social Science and Social Policy," in *Collected Methodological Writings* (hereafter *CMW*), ed. H. H. Bruun and S. Whimster, trans. H. H. Bruun (London: Routledge, 2012), 100–138, 125, 127; *Zur Logik und Methodik der Sozialwissenschaften. Schriften 1900–1907, MWG I/7*, ed. G. Wagner with C. Härpfer et al. (Tübingen, Germany: Mohr [Siebeck], 2018), 142–234, 203–204, 208.

22. Lawrence A. Scaff, *Fleeing the Iron Cage: Culture, Politics, and Modernity in the Thought of Max Weber* (Berkeley: University of California Press, 1989), 131.

23. Weber, "The Meaning of 'Value Freedom' in the Sociological and Economic Sciences," *CMW*, 304–334, 323; *Verstehende Soziologie und Werturteilsfreiheit. Schriften und Reden 1908–1917, MWG I/12*, ed. J. Weiß with S. Frommer (Tübingen, Germany: Mohr [Siebeck], 2018), 445–512, 487. The formulation in the music study—buried in the midst of the text— is somewhat less pointed: "why did polyphonic as well as harmonic-homophonic music and the modern tone system develop out of the rather widespread distribution of polyvocality in only one place on earth" (Weber, *The Rational and Social Foundations of Music*, 83, and *MWG I/14*, 232).

24. By "teleology," I refer here to a "theory of objectively necessary and progressive stages," rather than a heuristic or "conditional" teleology that identifies stages of development for the purposes of analysis, in terms of a final condition (Schluchter, *Rationalism, Religion, and Domination*, 40–41; cf. Max Weber, "Roscher and Knies and the Logical Problems of Historical Economics," in *CMW*, 3–94, 54–59; *MWG I/7*, 41–101, 243–379, 298–308), although the latter may impinge on the former through "causal imputation" (*CMW*, 56; *MWG I/7*, 306). On Weber and Lamprecht, see *MWG I/14*, 77–79, and Sam Whimster, "Die begrenzten Entwicklungsmöglichkeiten der Historischen Soziologie im 'Methodenstreit': Karl Lamprecht und Max Weber," in *Max Weber und seine Zeitgenossen*, ed. W. J. Mommsen and W. Schwentker (Göttingen, Germany: Vandenhoeck & Ruprecht, 1988), 380–402 (in English, *Max Weber and His Contemporaries*, ed. W. J. Mommsen and J. Osterhammel (London: Allen & Unwin, 1987, 268–283).

25. Weber, *The Rational and Social Foundations of Music*, 4; *MWG I/14*, 146.

26. Weber, *The Rational and Social Foundations of Music*, 68; *MWG I/14*, 214.

27. Theodor W. Adorno, "Some Ideas on the Sociology of Music," in *Sound Figures* (Stanford, CA: Stanford University Press, 1999), 1–14, 5.

28. Joachim Radkau, *Max Weber: Die Leidenschaft des Denkens* (Munich and Vienna: Carl Hanser, 2005), 577.

29. Weber, *The Rational and Social Foundations of Music*, 8; *MWG* I/14, 150.

30. Weber, *The Rational and Social Foundations of Music*, 9; *MWG* I/14, 152.

31. Weber, *The Rational and Social Foundations of Music*, 10; *MWG* I/14, 153.

32. Weber, *The Rational and Social Foundations of Music*, 30; *MWG* I/14, 176. For further discussion of this fundamental divide in avenues of rationalization—"the structuring of music systems through a dynamic of tensions between opposed poles...two equally possible logics of rationalization"—see Isabelle Darmon, "Weber on Music: Approaching Music as a Dynamic Domain of Action and Experience," *Cultural Sociology* 9, no. 1 (2015): 20–37, esp. 24–26.

33. Weber, *The Rational and Social Foundations of Music*, 63; *MWG* I/14, 209.

34. Weber employs frequency ratios, an updated application of classical string length ratios that were historically associated with the monochord, now represented in inverse relation: for example, where an interval like the major third in just tuning can be represented by the ratio of lengths of string that produce it, 5:4—that is, with the longer string producing the lower pitch—the same interval in the same tuning can be represented by the frequency ratio 4:5—namely, with the shorter string moving faster than the longer string, to produce a correspondingly higher pitch. Frequency measurements themselves were established as Hertz numbers or cycles per second, by the former Helmholtz student Heinrich Hertz (1857–1894). Weber's use of frequency ratios was nonetheless somewhat out of step with contemporary practice in acoustics and comparative musicology, for which ratios had proven increasingly cumbersome: Alexander J. Ellis had developed a logarithmic scale, the "cent" system—of 1,200 cents per octave, or 100 cents per equal-tempered semitone—to create a common metric that could clearly differentiate scales and their attunements in cross-cultural comparison, the value of which had been highlighted by Helmholtz's study.

35. Weber, *The Rational and Social Foundations of Music*, 52; *MWG* I/14, 198.

36. Max Weber, *The Protestant Ethic and the Spirit of Capitalism* (hereafter *PESC*), trans. T. Parsons (London: George Allen & Unwin, 1930), 78 (translation modified); *Die Protestantische Ethik und der Geist des Kapitalismus/Die protestantischen Sekten und der Geist des Kapitalismus. Schriften 1904-1920, MWG* I/18, ed. W. Schluchter with U. Bube (Tübingen, Germany: Mohr [Siebeck], 2016), 208.

37. Cf. Daniel K. L. Chua, *Absolute Music and the Construction of Meaning* (Cambridge: Cambridge University Press, 1999); for critique of this position, see Brandon Konoval, "Pythagorean Pipe Dreams? Vincenzo Galilei, Marin Mersenne, and the Pneumatic Mysteries of the Pipe Organ," *Perspectives on Science* 26, no. 1 (2018): 1–51, esp. 3–5, 46.

38. Paul Honigsheim, *Memories of Max Weber*, ed. J. Allan Beegle and William H. Form, trans. Joan Rytina (Toronto: Collier-Macmillan, 1968), 87, 83.

39. Honigsheim, *Memories of Max Weber*, 84.

40. Marianne Weber, *Max Weber: A Biography*, ed. H. Zohn (New York: John Wiley & Sons, 1975), 496.

41. Braun, "The 'Science of Reality' of Music History," 192n14.

42. *MWG* I/14, 128–129.

43. For the German context in particular, see Vanessa Agnew, "The Colonialist Beginnings of Comparative Musicology," in *Germany's Colonial Pasts*, ed. Eric Ames, et al. (Lincoln: University of Nebraska Press, 2005), 41–60.

44. Cf. Jonathan Service, "Harmony Outside the Iron Cage: Tanaka Shóhei's Strategic Deconstruction of the Music-Theoretical Edifice," *History of Humanities* 2, no. 2 (2017): 375–387.

45. Cf. Philip V. Bohlman, "Johann Gottfried Herder and the Global Moment of World-Music History," in *The Cambridge History of World Music*, ed. Philip V. Bohlman (Cambridge: Cambridge University Press, 2013), 255–276.

46. See Alexander Rehding, *Hugo Riemann and the Birth of Modern Musical Thought* (Cambridge: Cambridge University Press 2003), 172–176, on Riemann's "Six Original Chinese and Japanese Songs" (1902).

47. Honigsheim, *Memories of Max Weber*, 28.

48. Friedrich Nietzsche, *Beyond Good and Evil*, ed. Rolf-Peter Horstmann and Judith Norman, trans. Judith Norman (Cambridge: Cambridge University Press, 2002), §186, 75–76.

49. Hermann von Helmholtz, *On the Sensations of Tone as a Physiological Basis for the Theory of Music*, ed. and trans. Alexander J. Ellis (New York: Dover Publications, 1954), 235 (emphasis in original).

50. See Alexander J. Ellis, "On the Musical Scales of Various Nations," *Journal of the Society of Arts* 33 (1885): 485–532, as well as the appendices he provided for his translations of Helmholtz.

51. Cf. *MWG* I/14, "Introduction," 42–51; see also Dieter Christensen, "Erich M. von Hornbostel, Carl Stumpf, and the Institutionalization of Comparative Musicology," in *Comparative Musicology and Anthropology of Music: Essays on the History of Ethnomusicology*, ed. Bruno Nettl and Philip V. Bolman (Chicago: University of Chicago Press, 1990), 201–209; Alexander Rehding, "Wax Cylinder Revolutions," *Musical Quarterly* 88 (2005): 123–160; Kay Kaufman Shelemay, "Recording Technology, the Record Industry, and Ethnomusicological Scholarship," in *Comparative Musicology and Anthropology of Music*, 277–292. Stumpf founded the Berliner Phonogramm-Archiv in 1902 at Friedrich Wilhelm Universität, as part of the Institute for Psychology. One of the principal motivations behind the phonogram archive was to provide cross-cultural data through which evidence of musical cognition might provide insights into human cognition more generally.

52. Fend, "Witnessing a 'Process of Rationalisation'?," 112.

53. Weber, *The Rational and Social Foundations of Music*, 33; *MWG* I/14, 179.

54. Weber, "Roscher and Knies," *CMW*, 33–41; *MWG* I/7, 253–273.

55. Weber, *The Rational and Social Foundations of Music*, 48; *MWG* I/14, 194.

56. *PESC*, 284 n119; *MWG* I/18, 491 n394.

57. Cf. Alexandra Hui, *The Psychophysical Ear* (Cambridge, MA: MIT Press, 2013).

58. Robert Michael Brain, "The Ontology of the Questionnaire: Max Weber on Measurement and Mass Investigation," *Studies in History and Philosophy of Science* 32, no. 4 (2001): 647–684, 655.

59. Cf. Brain, "The Ontology of the Questionnaire," 655–656.

60. Carl Stumpf, *The Origins of Music*, ed. and trans. David Trippett (Oxford: Oxford University Press, 2012), 131. Weber's own interest in phonograms of Patagonian melody notably drew attention to the sometimes problematic empirical basis provided by such data, where "there are latitudes for intonational deviations from a naturalistic scale of up to a halftone" (Weber, *The Rational and Social Foundations of Music*, 33; *MWG* I/14, 179).

61. "Pitch" is a psychoacoustic term referring to our perception of a particular sound frequency, albeit allowing for some flexibility in tuning. (For example, modern musicians would recognize a narrow range of frequencies around 440 Hz as a particular pitch, "A.") Pitch features can include relationships formed between pitches that are relatively immediate to

perception—such as the formation of an interval or a combination or sequence of intervals like a chord or melody or the contrapuntal relationship between melodic lines—or they may cumulatively establish a deeper level of structure and interrelationship that orients our listening experience, as in the case of tonality (see following note).

62. "Tonality" is a complex concept that may be either more narrowly or more broadly defined, depending upon how strictly one wishes to constrain its meaning (with corresponding impact on its historical application). In general, the term may be applied to various components of musical hierarchy, whether assigning a focal role to a particular note (like "the note C"), chord (like "a C major chord"), or collection of notes (a "diatonic" collection, itself ordered in terms of a preeminent note, thereby defining a mode) that is perceived as a reference component or "tonic" for all other pitch activity in a particular work or in a defined section of a musical work. Like many music historians and theorists, Weber was keenly interested in the genealogy of tonality, a developmental relationship that could be traced between forms of tonal hierarchy in pre-harmonic and in harmonic music, for which a tonic note, tonic chord, and diatonic collection are constituent elements that may be used to define a "key." Weber's use of "Tonart" or "Tonarten"—which might be translated as either "key(s)" or "mode(s)," depending on context—is routinely translated as "key(s)" in the English edition (*The Rational and Social Foundations of Music*) of the *Musiksoziologie*, reflecting conventions in German terminology (cf. Beethoven String Quartert Op. 132, third movement, "in der lydischen Tonart"/"in the Lydian key"), while avoiding the problematic key/mode distinction that many musicologists observe (namely, that only certain types of mode, "major" and "minor," may be appropriately applied to the concept of key, thus translating Beethoven's quartet movement as being "in the Lydian mode").

63. Alexander Rehding, "The Quest for the Origins of Music in Germany Circa 1900," *Journal of the American Musicological Society* 53, no. 2 (2000): 345–385, 349.

64. As *MWG* I/14 notes, Weber here follows the account of A. W. Ambros' *Geschichte der Musik* (Leipzig, Germany: Leuckart, 1880), 1:218. Ambros emphasizes that music as an art form is no longer purely the servant of social activities like dance, festivals, or ritual sacrifice.

65. Max Weber, "Remarks on Technology and Culture," trans. Beatrix Zumsteg and Thomas Kemple, *Theory, Culture and Society* 22, no. 4 (2005): 23–38, 31; *MWG* I/12, 226–236, 234.

66. Max Weber, "Intermediate Reflection on the Economic Ethics of the World Religions," in *The Essential Weber: A Reader*, ed. Sam Whimster (London: Routledge, 2004), 215–244, 231–232; *MWG* I/19, 479–522, 501.

67. Weber, *The Rational and Social Foundations of Music*, 94; *MWG* I/14, 243.

68. Benjamin Steege, *Helmholtz and the Modern Listener* (Cambridge: Cambridge University Press, 2012), 250.

69. Max Weber, "Religious Rejections of the World and Their Directions," in *FMW*, 323–359, 342; "Zwischenbetrachtung," *MWG* I/19, 479–522, 500.

70. Georg Simmel, *The Sociology of Georg Simmel*, ed. and trans. Kurt H. Wolff (Glencoe, IL: Free Press, 1950), 43.

71. Weber, *The Rational and Social Foundations of Music*, 41–42; *MWG* I/14, 188.

72. Simmel, *The Sociology*, 43.

73. Weber, *The Rational and Social Foundations of Music*, 61; *MWG* I/14, 207. The hexachord (six-note) system was one of the great theoretical innovations developed to serve the performance of liturgical chant repertoire—complex, lengthy melodies that could challenge the accuracy both of singing and of memory—as demanded by the standardization

of the Christian liturgy. Conceptualized by Guido d'Arezzo early in the eleventh century, hexachords mapped the larger gamut of twenty-two pitches used by the chant repertoire into overlapping regions of six-pitch segments sharing an identical interval sequence (that is, the distances between successive pitches), symmetrical around a central semitone: singing this shorter interval sequence could be perfected using solmization (ut/do-re-mi-fa-sol-la), enabling singers to translate vocal facility developed within a comparatively narrow range of pitches into a command of the entire gamut itself—the epitome of transferable skill, and a triumph of rationalization in practical music theory at a time of intense bureaucratic organization of sacred music.

74. Weber, *The Rational and Social Foundations of Music*, 5–6; *MWG* I/14, 148.

75. Riemann, Hugo Riemann, *Geschichte der Musiktheorie im IX.—XIX. Jahrhundert*, 2nd ed. (Berlin: Max Hesse, 1921), 473 (emphasis in original).

76. Rehding, *Hugo Riemann and the Birth of Modern Musical Thought*, 67.

77. It should be noted that the most familiar version of the Pachelbel Canon is an arrangement: as is typical for accompaniments provided by Baroque *basso continuo*, Pachelbel simply indicated chord types built upon a bass line (as one would for a jazz rhythm section that provides the harmonic underpinning for improvisation). The result of the popular arrangement is that the stretched-out, slow plucking of the chord components encourages many listeners to mistake the initial statement of the accompaniment for the "theme" of the work; the statement of the actual melody notes which subsequently enter is so distended that it becomes nearly impossible to perceive the canonic imitation of the three melodic parts that provides the title of the piece.

78. Weber, "The Social Psychology of the World Religions," 293; *MWG* I/19, 117.

79. Cf. David Creese, *The Monochord in Ancient Greek Harmonic Science* (Cambridge: Cambridge University Press, 2010).

80. Weber, *The Rational and Social Foundations of Music*, 3; *MWG* I/14, 145.

81. Weber, *The Rational and Social Foundations of Music*, 101; *MWG* I/14, 251. Weber refers to "chordal-harmonic music" (*akkordharmonische Musik*) to distinguish the use of actual chords from intervals derived by harmonic or arithmetic mean, which can either contribute to or be used independently of chord structures.

82. Weber, *The Rational and Social Foundations of Music*, 99; *MWG* I/14, 248.

83. Weber, *The Rational and Social Foundations of Music*, 3; *MWG* I/14, 145.

84. Another important comma to which Weber refers is the "syntonic" comma (80:81), not quite as appreciably dissonant as the Pythagorean comma that offers a greater discrepancy from the unison but emerging after far fewer interval cycles: a syntonic comma is produced after a sequence of only three major thirds (tuned in their most pure, consonant form).

85. Weber, "On Some Categories of Interpretive Sociology," *CMW* 273–301, 280n1; *MWG* I/12, 389–440, 403n2.

86. Daniel K. S. Walden, "Emancipate the Quartertone: The Call to Revolution in Nineteenth-Century Music Theory," *History of Humanities* 2, no. 2 (2017): 327–344; cf. Service, "Harmony Outside the Iron Cage," 380.

87. Weber, *The Rational and Social Foundations of Music*, 100; *MWG* I/14, 249.

88. Vincenzo Galilei, "A Discourse Concerning the Various Opinions that the Three Most Famous Sects of Ancient Musicians had Concerning the Matter of Sounds and Tunings," in *The Florentine Camerata: Documentary Studies and Translations*, ed. Claude V. Palisca (c.1589; New York: Hamilton Printing, 1989), 164–179, 169.

89. Galilei, "A Discourse," 167, 171.

90. Braun, "The 'Science of Reality' of Music History," 190.

CHAPTER 26

....

CONTEMPORARY LIFE CONDUCT AND EXISTENTIAL CULTURES

....

BARBARA THÉRIAULT

THE concept of lifestyle appears in Max Weber's writings under the guise of *Lebensführung*, or life conduct. It is closely linked to the spirit of capitalism and to a religious work ethic Weber tracks in life maxims influencing daily practices. Not unlike Simmel's style of life in the *Philosophy of Money*, Weber's concept is concerned with individual meaning in a world characterized by objective forces.[1] Both authors offer a social diagnosis typical of the beginning of the twentieth century, one centered on the fate of the individual in an increasingly objectified, rationalized, and disenchanted world. Although still pervasive in social theories, this diagnosis framed in terms of loss is at odds with the contemporary world; indeed, most of today's readers do not share the angst so characteristic of the atmosphere surrounding the first and second generations of sociologically informed intellectuals.

While challenging this diagnosis of loss and void, this chapter argues that Max Weber's approach is still inspiring today. His notion of life conduct, and the specific attention he pays to life maxims underlying action and to their carriers, is fruitful for a sociology of religion concerned with the influence of religious or "existential" ideas on daily life conducts. Indeed, the program bodes well with recent attempts to map out what Lois Lee calls "existential cultures,"[2] a concept that will be introduced further in this chapter after a brief return to Weber's notion of life conduct. Offering a reflection on methodological imagination and the manner in which to grasp it empirically, this chapter then presents an example drawn from an east German town, one involving imaginary tattoos.

MAX WEBER'S APPROACH

In the *Protestant Ethic and the Spirit of Capitalism*, Weber sets himself to sound out ideas that "stand in some sort of adequate relationship" with modern capitalism and, more generally, modern culture.[3] More specifically, Weber was concerned with methodical life conduct (*Lebensführung*) and organizations resonating with these ideas.

The thesis of the *Protestant Ethic* is well known and does not need to be explained in any more detail. What has been less reflected upon is *the way* Weber goes about studying the "spirit" (the "subjective culture," in Simmel's words). In his famous essay, he is attentive to maxims—life maxims that guide action and influence practice (maxims such as "time is money" or "honesty is the best policy"). Such maxims represent, for the observers, external traces that enable them to delineate the motives underlying actions. Incidentally, delineating motives, and the ideas behind them, is what Weber's interpretative sociology—as put forth in the *Protestant Ethic*—is all about; as such, Weber's endeavor is reminiscent of the work of a detective uncovering motives based on evidence, clues.[4]

Two points should be stressed with regard to such clues. First, Weber observes them not in theological treatises but in widely read books, tracts of advice, such as Benjamin Franklin's *Advice to a Young Tradesman*.[5] The use of such documents constitutes a methodological innovation, something comparable to the study of etiquette books by Norbert Elias or blockbuster movies by Siegfried Kracauer.[6] Second, Weber is also attentive to the bearers or *carriers* of a particular ethos and their social characteristics—in the case of the *Protestant Ethic*, members of the middle classes.

It has often been noted that Weber's concepts and methods—the ideal type—have greatly influenced sociology as a discipline; indeed, they have generated a great deal of commentaries and stimulated the imagination, as the myriad of intertextual nods bears witness to.[7] Yet, his *general* approach, attentive to individual meaning and its lived dimensions, has rarely informed empirical studies—and when it has, those studies were neither claimed nor readily considered as bearing a Weberian heritage. The sociology of religion, which has long been indebted to a "Weberian" secularization thesis—derived more from the *reception* of Weber's work than from the actual approach informing it—is no exception.

This apparent oversight is what makes the publication of a recent book, *Recognizing the Non-religious: Reimagining the Secular*, especially noteworthy. Although Lois Lee, its author, does not explicitly refer to Weber,[8] she seems to pick up his line of inquiry. In outlining "existential cultures," she is thinking along Weber's fundamental concern: meaning-giving ideas and their *practical* dimensions or, in today's wording, their "lived" dimensions. She thus links her endeavor to trends that have been prevailing in the discipline for the past twenty years and that stress the study of the everyday dimensions and materiality of religion. This perspective puts the question of meaning in what could be called a post-Weberian context, one largely dominated by an often challenged secularization paradigm.

CONTEMPORARY EXISTENTIAL CULTURES

Although they leave open the question of a resurgence of meaning—through prophets or great individuals, for instance—Weber and his contemporaries offer a diagnosis of modernity framed in terms of loss, one which has durably influenced the way in which we think about contemporary culture. Commentators have noted this pessimistic imprint or birthmark of European sociology that portrays the secular world as a place largely devoid of meaning.[9]

This take has long been commonplace in German sociology; the second generation of social theorists was largely imbued with the idea. Perusing through the literary, social sciences, and journalistic writings, Georg Lukács' metaphor of the world's "spiritual homelessness" (*transzendentale Obdachlosigkeit*)[10] appears as a sign of those times. It finds expressions in a "metaphysical suffering," an "alienation from the absolute," a "fear of emptiness," reminiscent of an ambience, a *Stimmung*, characteristic of the literary landscape of the time: Musil's *The Man without Qualities*, Broch's *Sleepwalkers*, Mann's *Buddenbrooks*. This diagnosis is accompanied by a longing for meaning, for a homeland of the soul (*Seelenheimat*). Siegfried Kracauer, to take but one example, extensively uses the term "shelter" (*Asyl*) to refer to a substitute for a system of absolutes, be it religious, philosophical, or aesthetical. An intellectual class lived in angst while the salaried masses—or so these same intellectuals assumed—were fleeing reality through consumption and popular distractions (cinema, dance, travel).[11] The reception of Weber's work has contributed to these two components—the anguish and the class that is said to have borne it. Engrossed in these somber considerations, sociologists have, for a long time, been blind to the religious vibrancy of the world[12] but also to the possible vibrancy of the secular. This is what the notion of "existential culture" attempts to remedy.

In her book, Lois Lee challenges this still prevalent pessimistic view of reality. Instead of seeing secularity strictly in the negative light that most researches have so far cast on it (presenting secularity itself as something residual to religion, the secular as a space bereft of meaning, secularization as loss, or the seculars as "nones"), she grasps it as something that is—at least in part—substantial, full of meanings and tensions. She calls the substantial modes of secularity the "non-religious."[13] While the term itself is not devoid of ambiguity, it still aims to reject the binary opposition usually stressed between religion and the secular (and atheism) as well as between intellectuals and the "masses." Lee's approach is open to elements that actually link the two and to individuals' will to purposely distance themselves from organized religions without completely rejecting them (for individuals who identify, say, as "non-practicing Catholics," "non-Muslim Muslims," "non-religious, but not atheists," or "spiritual, but not religious").[14]

This shift toward the substantial dimension of the secular represents a major turn in the sociology of religion and the study of the "secular moderns." After all, the non-religious represent the largest segment of the population in contemporary Western societies.[15] Lee is not alone in her endeavor, but—unlike most—she has developed an approach that aims to go beyond organized groups, such as atheists or humanists, and an intellectual stratum. In studying the "non-religious," Lee enjoins us to dive into the heart of society to investigate those who are so numerous that they often remain unseen.

In addition to her significant conceptual contribution to the field, Lee attempts to make an empirical one, tracing the contours of what she called "existential cultures."

> Existential cultures incarnate ideas about the origins of life and human consciousness and about how both are transformed or expire after death—what has been called "ultimate questions" in the literature before now. These existential beliefs are bound up with the distinctive notion of meaning and purpose of life, as well as with epistemological theories about how it is that humans are able to take a stance on existential matters. Finally, these existential positions are manifest in particular ethical practices—not the unspecified ethics imagined when people speak of "religion and ethics," but ethics that can be identified concretely as anchored in existential principles and cultures and distinct from other ethical forms.[16]

Although they need not be based on religion, the existential cultures do borrow from the religious, the spiritual, and the non-religious. Like Weber's "spirit," the existential cultures manifest themselves in ethical principles and commitments as well as in practices—such as secular rituals, forms of sociality and communities—pertaining to the "existential."[17] They are not always acknowledged as such specific cultures by their carriers; it is the sociologist who frames what often remains not-institutionalized and unnamed. In other words, existential cultures require sociologists to think across conceptual categories and recast them.[18]

To achieve this, Lee compellingly advocates for a qualitative approach. Non-religious or existential cultures should, she argues, be approached ethnographically—that is, in their lived dimensions and materiality, as embodied practices and as new forms of belief, ethical conviction, and aesthetic expression. As convincing as her conceptual exposition is, her empirical analysis—a study among young educated men and women in Cambridge and the greater London area, often loosely attending atheist activities—tends to associate non-religion with atheism or humanism and, most importantly, is reduced to a few illustrations and gets buried under her formidable conceptual apparatus. Lee seems to anticipate criticism when she enjoins readers to methodological creativity,[19] stresses that non-religion is not restricted to atheism—although atheists are at the center of most of the literature[20]—and encourages us to think together existential cultures and class identities or, in Weber's words, to pay attention to the carriers of ideas and their characteristics.

Weber's question, but also his methodological insights, can prove useful in studying non-religion and individual meaning in conjunction with life conducts of the middle class. Without being exhaustive, the following section undertakes a Weberian-inspired attempt to study empirically non-religion.

AN EAST GERMAN TOWN
AND IMAGINARY TATTOOS

Since 2014, a study has been being conducted among a small group of parents living in a mid-size town of what used to be the German Democratic Republic (GDR).[21] Most of them are employees, civil servants, and pedagogues, aged between forty and fifty-five, representatives of a stratum that defines itself as middle class and is busy with family and work as well as with sport or artistic activities. Since east Germany is known as one of the most secular regions in the world, it will not come as a surprise that most of the participants do not identify as religious. Still, it would be misleading to describe them as atheists. When asked to describe themselves, they often hesitate. As he talks about his family, one participant typically mentions that they are Catholics, though "his wife is an athe… eh not affiliated with a church I mean." Later, his wife describes herself as a spiritual and religiously interested person.

All parents were interviewed. Also, and in addition to ethnographic observations in town, the researcher accompanied them in their daily life and attended special occasions such as rituals and family celebrations. In an attempt to grasp forms of belief, ethical conviction, and aesthetic expression, a small experiment was undertaken: the participants were asked what they would write if they had a tattoo made.

Because they are indelible and because they are worn directly on one's skin, tattoos usually involve much reflection. Tattoos are—beyond their signification as individual ornaments—meaningful objects.[22] When observing townspeople bearing real tattoos, one can glance at inscriptions like "All that you have is your soul," "All you need is love," or simply "Love"; these mostly attempt to reduce life—or the individual's take on it—to one basic principle. At the heart of the researcher's experiment was an intuition: today's tattoos could well be a contemporary's equivalent of Weber's material, life maxims encompassing a kind of guiding principle or ethos. Likewise, then, imaginary tattoos could be read as signposts, expressions of what the participants say they are, of what they aspire to, and what they value.[23]

Although tattoos are very widespread in the east German town at the center of the study, most of the people interviewed did not have any. While insisting that they would never get one, they nevertheless engaged in what turned out to be a thought experiment about "imaginary tattoos".

Gelassenheit: "to be able to let go," "to be able to relax," "to be spontaneous."[24] This is what Marlene immediately said, when asked what inscription she would like to have as a tattoo. Claudia said something similar. She would have tattooed a quotation from a bestseller: "It is as it is and it comes as it comes."[25] Given the hectic pace of their everyday life, the two women—as well as many others interviewed who mentioned expressions such as "carpe diem" as possible inscriptions—wished they could be more relaxed. At once admonition and encouragement, their tattoos would be reminders, a counterweight to the numerous social obligations and expectations characteristic of their active life conduct. As such, life conduct and maxims seem to mirror each other, if only negatively: the latter enable us to delineate, by contrast, the former.[26]

Sources

If you walk through the town and raise your head, you can see many inscriptions. A building in the main street also has a tattoo. Like people, not all buildings are tattooed, but this one (anno 1898) has one, even two—on each side. These are also life maxims, admonitions, encouragements, or diagnoses: *Ohn' Gottes Gunst all Bauen umsunst* ("Without God's favor no building is worthwhile") and *Durch Müh' und Fleiß kommt Nutz und Preis* ("Through effort and hard work come benefits and price").

While the rhyming inscriptions on houses echo Bible quotations and bourgeois maxims of a medieval merchant town, today's inspiration for such inscriptions—tattoos, real or imaginary—derive from a mix of self-help literature (not unlike Franklin's tracts of advice) and Eastern philosophy mediated through pop culture: songs, bestsellers, and TV series. Part of Claudia's chosen quotation, "It is as it is," is also John Watson's favorite saying in the newest *Sherlock Holmes* TV adaptation. Those inscriptions, in turn, also resonate in pop culture, to which they stand in a dialectical relation: they mirror individuals, and individuals copy them while revealing their desire, the way they want to see themselves.

Tattoos echo prescriptive maxims, principles, "worldly wisdom"[27]; but they do not hold the same level of psychological or ethical sanctions and are not as socially effective as Weber's Protestant work ethic—nor are they as reliable to understand and explain the action's motives. Yet, they might well represent a first step toward an empirical inquiry into today's non-religion and link them, in this particular case, with the life conduct of busy, middle-class people.

Non-religious Conceptual Repertoire

Tattoos can also represent a methodological asset to the sociologist in that they are significantly easier to broach than direct considerations about meaning or (non-)religious identification. When it comes to meaning, we often notice a lack of concepts, both on the side of research participants and on the side of those who study them.[28] As Lee notes, there is "an appetite for some codification and circulation of non-religious cultural resources."[29] If people like to chitchat about tattoos, the subject also opens a door toward deeper conversations and reflections.

The study participants answered strikingly quickly to the tattoo question. They had a linguistic arsenal for attitudes (*Haltungen*) that conferred sense and meaning to their lives. Yet, they sometimes felt uneasy: it was as though their repertoire lacked the depth of meaning or the kind of luster that an institutional and sanctioned religious language may more easily confer. This is probably the reason tattoos in a foreign language, ornamental writings, abstract symbols and arabesques seem somewhat more meaningful and appropriate: their very ambiguity leaves place for multiple interpretations and helps avoid the awkwardness that can derive from more straightforward maxims or phrases.

Marlene, the woman who would consider having the word *Gelassenheit* as a tattoo, liked the idea but not the word itself—not in German in any case. It sounds, she said, outdated, old-fashioned. She thought it might sound more mysterious, enigmatic, in a foreign language. Often, tattoos were or ought, it was said, to be in English. As the conversation moved on, attempts were thus made to find an English or French word for *Gelassenheit*—but an expression like "to be chill about things" somehow did not seem to suit a forty-two-year-old civil servant with three children. The endeavor was soon abandoned, and no attempts were even made to find a French translation.

A similar type of hesitation was palpable in formal speeches or addresses at coming-of-age ceremonies, the *Jugendweihe*, a civil consecration ceremony for fourteen-year-olds that Communists (re)introduced in 1954 in the GDR as a state atheist competing ceremony for the Protestant and Catholic confirmation. With a humanist touch, minus the militant state atheism, the *Jugendweihe* has survived the fall of the regime with great success.[30] As Lee mentions on several occasions in her book, life-cycle rituals are possible *loci* to observe non-religion; they present forms of sociality and communities one cannot observe through the tattoos experiment and could very well complement it.

A Glimpse at Some Rituals

Jugendweihe ceremonies splendidly highlight the overall difficulty with which questions of meaning are tackled: in one observed instance, the main speaker ventured into the meaning of life but quickly renounced and went on to talk about life in general. At a different ceremony, the speaker, facing a similar challenge, used for his part humor to talk about life and its meaning. Interestingly enough, humanism, as an organized set of beliefs, does not seem to hold an important role in the ceremonies or to provide a helpful conceptual repertoire.

If one listened to them with the tattoo question in mind, though, the speakers at ceremonies seemed to have lexical tools; indeed, they could give examples of good behaviors and stress: "This is strength, a good attitude!" (*Das ist Haltung!*), but it did not seem to be legitimate, to enjoy the necessary aura. Another ritual, the *Lebenswende*—a ceremony the Catholic Church designed for youth with no religious affiliation and that often takes place in the cathedral—did not have such a problem. The lay speakers presiding at the ceremony could draw on liturgy, light, the history of the building.

The question of vocabulary is not the only thing one can observe at such ceremonies; they also instruct us on the members of the group and their aesthetic preferences. Up in the balconies, at one of the *Jugendweihe* ceremonies, a father, a mother, or a friend had simply thrown a jacket over everyday clothes. One could see, worn as ornaments, a number of tattoos. The interviews unveiled some light criticism regarding the *Jugendweihe*, one reminiscent of the attitudes toward tattoos. In spite of its popularity, the slightly low-middle class aesthetics of the *Jugendweihe* seems to put off some study participants, more so than its Communist heritage. In contrast, the *Lebenswende*

Box 26.1 The "Tattoo-less:" A Specific Segment of the Middle Class

Do the study participants, the tattoo-less fragment of society, have no style, carry no life maxim? On the contrary. As we know from non-religion, "nothing" need not mean meaningless. Tattoos seem so widespread these days that those who do not have any sometimes see themselves as "dissidents." After openly condemning graffiti, one of the participants compared—in quite colorful language—some tattooed people to advertising pillars. Without wanting to offend them, most of the tattoo-less distance themselves from those who do have one—or many—and their aesthetic taste. In so doing—and without saying it or even thinking about it—they express a specific attitude: "I am both self-confident and reserved, and that is good."[31]

The untattooed segment of society can be related to a specific life conduct: one of activities, obligations and duties—participants talk to the researcher in part because they feel obligated to. The effects of this life conduct stand in a dynamic relation with an attitude (*Haltung*) calling for *Gelassenheit* (letting go). Helmuth Plessner's philosophical anthropology hinted at such a dynamic between a need of recognition (*Geltungsdrang*, *Ausdrucksdrang*) and reserve (*Verhaltenheit*, *Schamgefühl*). What the author describes as a human psyche is indeed more a characteristic of the middle class or bourgeois—a label the study participants reject—segment of society.[32]

---

seemed to enjoy a good reputation among the participants. For Jens, a father whose daughter took part in the ritual, such a ceremony is better suited to his identity—as a non-confessional individual from a Catholic background—than would be the *Jugendweihe* and the sacrament of confirmation. Andreas and Claudia are not affiliated to any confession—they call themselves, as would most sociological observers, *konfessionslos*, or "confession-less"—and while their oldest daughter had taken part in the *Jugendweihe*, their twin daughters for their part participated in the *Lebenswende*. When commenting on this choice, they talked about a parents' meeting in the cathedral, the church bells, and the city tradition. In their choice transpires a desire to belong to a good society, one associated with the religious and local past, and the children's future.

The *Lebenswende* and the *Jugendweihe* can be seen as manifestations of non-religion. More than forms of belief and ethical conviction, they point to identification, aesthetic attitudes, and forms of sociability. Talking about them with interviewees reveals what is dearest and most meaningful to the study participants, their children (Box 26.1).

CONCLUSION

In making a critical assessment of Weber's diagnosis and presenting Lee's notion of existential culture, this chapter draws the contours of what a Weberian-informed sociology of a (non-)religious world might look like. Investigating the interplay between life conducts and meaning—forms of belief, ethical conviction, and aesthetic expression—it enjoins to an investigation of a fragment of the middle class, with methodological creativity based on classical sociology, minus the pathos.

Not unlike Lee, Kracauer outlined in his 1930 text "Those Who Wait" ideal-typical intellectual positions, existential answers to the shared "spiritual homelessness," approaches leading to new "homelands of the soul." Next to the old doctrines and religions, he saw a kind of polytheism at play: anthroposophy, communism, and mysticism.[33] As serious alternatives, he considered the "hesitant openness" of those who waited and the "skepticism as a matter of principle" which he saw represented in Weber's position as an "intellectual desperado" rejecting new gods, but whose sociology, it might be added, nonetheless clung to subjective meaning and its interpretation.[34]

With her concept of non-religion, Lee has shown that a different diagnosis is possible. She has not set herself an easy task: the east German example shows it is difficult to find a new language and pin down ideas; the tattoo question is an attempt at sounding out meaning, non-religious maxims. Henrietta, the sixteen-year-old daughter of two study participants, got money for a tattoo on her birthday. Engraved under her breast, where it cannot be seen by all, it will bear the inscription "still waters run deep" (*Stille Wasser sind tief*), as if she was inviting us to find original ways to trace meaning-giving ideas and their impact on daily life.

NOTES

1. Wilhelm Hennis, *Max Weber's Central Question*, trans. K. Tribe (Newbury, UK: Threshold Press, 2000).

2. Lois Lee, *Recognizing the Non-religious: Reimagining the Secular* (Oxford: Oxford University Press, 2015).

3. Max Weber, *The Protestant Ethic and the Spirit of Capitalism* (hereafter *PESC*), trans. T. Parsons (1930; London: Routledge, 2007), 27; *Die protestantische Ethik und der Geist des Kapitalismus/Die protestantischen Sekten und der Geist des Kapitalismus. Schriften 1904–1920, Max Weber-Gesamtausgabe* (hereafter *MWG*) I/18, ed. W. Schluchter with U. Bube (Tübingen, Germany: Mohr [Siebeck], 2016), 185. Parsons also translates *Lebensführung* as "manner of life," "life," or "standard of life."

4. Weber's very definition of "sociology" involves a police or detective word, *ermitteln*: "it is the task of the sociologist to be aware of this motivational situation and to describe and analyse it" ("diesen [Motiv-]Zusammenhang zu ermitteln und deutend festzustellen"): Max Weber, *Economy and Society*, ed. G. Roth and C. Wittich (Berkeley: University of California Press, 1978), 9–10; *Wirtschaft und Gesellschaft.Soziologie. Unvollendet 1919–1920, MWG* I/23, ed. K. Borchardt, E. Hanke, and W. Schluchter (Tübingen, Germany: Mohr [Siebeck], 2013), 156.

5. *PESC*, 14–16; *MWG* I/18, 151–155.

6. Cf. Norbert Elias, *The Civilizing Process* (1939; Oxford: Blackwell, 1982); Siegfried Kracauer, "On the Task of the Film Critic," in *The Weimar Republic Sourcebook*, ed. Anton Kaes, Martin Jay, and Edward Dimendberg (Berkeley: University of California Press, 1994), 634–635; "Über die Aufgabe des Filmkritikers," in *Werke*, vol. 6.3, *Kleine Schriften zum Film 1932–1961*, ed. I. Mülder-Bach (1932; Frankfurt am Main, German: Suhrkamp, 2004), 61–63, and "The Little Shopgirls Go to the Movies," in *The Mass Ornament* (1925; Cambridge, MA: Harvard University Press, 1995), 291–304; "Die kleinen Ladenmädchen gehen ins Kino," in *Werke*, vol. 6.1, *Kleine Schriften zum Film 1921–1927*, ed. I. Mülder-Bach (1927; Frankfurt am Main, Germany: Suhrkamp, 2004), 308–322.

7. See Laurence McFalls, Augustin Simard, and Barbara Thériault, "Conclusion: The 'Objectivist' Ethic and the 'Spirit' of Science," in *Max Weber's "Objectivity" Reconsidered*, ed. L. McFalls (Toronto: University of Toronto Press, 2007), 351–373; cf. other articles in this volume.

8. Lee quotes Weber's sociology of religion in *Economy and Society*, where she refrains from defining religion at the outset and rather chooses to look at the "conditions and effects of a particular type of social behavior [BT: *Gemeinschaftshandeln*]": Lee, *Recognizing*, 23.

9. Johannes Weiß, "Negative Soziologie. Grundlagenprobleme einer Wissenschaft," *Ethik und Sozialwissenschaft* 6, no. 2 (1995), 241–246; see also Klaus Lichtblau, *Kulturkrise und Kultursoziologie um die Jahrhundertwende* (Frankfurt am Main, Germany: Suhrkamp, 1996).

10. Georg Lukács, *The Theory of the Novel*, trans. A. Bostock (1916/1920; Cambridge, MA: MIT Press, 1971).

11. One finds the expression "shelter for the homeless" (*Asyl für Obdachlose*) with regard to overarching systems of ideas (Siegfried Kracauer, *The Salaried Masses. Duty and Distraction in Weimar Germany* [1929/1930; London: Verso, 1998], 88); and the search for comfort in, for example, activities like gambling ("Glück und Schicksal," *Straßen in Berlin und anderswo* [1964; Frankfurt am Main, Germany: Suhrkamp, 2013], 89) or by retreating to luxurious lifestyles ("Riviera-Napoli-Express," *Berliner Nebeneinander. Ausgewählte Feuilletons 1930–33*, ed. Andreas Volk [1931; Zürich, Switzerland: Epoca, 1996], 283–285); or to places like steam baths and bars (Joseph Roth, "Im Dampfbad bei Nacht," *Trübsal einer Straßenbahn* [1921; Salzburg and Wien, Germany: Jung und Jung, 2013], 94–97, and "Asyle der Heimatlosen," 125).

12. See Peter L. Berger, ed., *The Desecularization of the World. Resurgent Religion and World Politics* (Grand Rapids, MI: W. B. Eerdmans, 1999).

13. Surveys on religion often reduce the "others" or "seculars" to one undifferentiated residual category contrasting the various religious categories. The census in England and Wales includes, next to the religious and none/no religion categories, the possibility to abstain from answering. This option turned out, both in the 2001 and the 2011 censuses, to be the third most favored one: see Lee, *Recognizing*, 153.

14. "Secular people are probably more likely to identify with a religious culture than a non-religious one in settings where the former is or has been predominant: to do so is to follow the path of least resistance": Ibid., 143.

15. Ibid., 142.

16. Ibid., 159–160.

17. Lee aims to go further than the study of great transcendence and middle-range transcendences as investigated by Monika Wohlrab-Sahr, Uta Karstein, and Thomas Schmidt-Lux in *Forcierte Säkularität: Religiöser Wandel und Generationendynamik im Osten Deutschlands* (Frankfurt am Main, Germany: Campus, 2009). Based on interviews and discourses, their analysis follows Thomas Luckmann's approach while challenging it; for them, middle-range transcendences are not considered "religious."

18. Lee identifies five types of existential culture: humanist, agnostic, theist, subjectivist, and anti-existential. In so doing, she goes beyond the idea of "religion à la carte," that is, to assemble oneself a religion—without consideration of more general patterns and the characteristic of their carriers.

19. Lee, *Recognizing*, 186.

20. See J. Eccles and Rebecca Catto, "The Significance of Secular Sacred Space in the Formation of British Atheist Identities," in *Materiality and the Study of Religion. The Stuff of the*

Sacred, ed. Timothy Hutchings and Joanne McKenzie (London: Routledge, 2017), 151–165; Roberto Cipriani and Franco Garelli, eds., *Sociology of Atheism* (Leiden, the Netherlands: Brill, 2016); Matthew Engelke, "Humanist Ceremonies: The Case of Non-Religious Funerals in England," in *The Wiley Blackwell Handbook on Humanism*, ed. Andrew Copson and A. C. Grayling (Oxford: Wiley, 2015).

21. The core sample includes twenty-two persons, both women and men.

22. Sometimes, tattoos are not thought to mean anything, if only that one's body is a means of expression.

23. If Frank had a tattoo, it would read: "confidence, passion, trust, self-confidence." Nicole, a high school ethics teacher, mentioned something she sometimes used while teaching: "It is not because things are difficult that we do not dare, it is because we do not dare that they are difficult" ("*Nicht, weil es schwer ist, wagen wir es nicht, sondern, weil wir es nicht wagen, ist es schwer*").

24. It was later pointed out to the researcher that, with regard to Amish studies, *Gelassenheit* can also mean a submission to God's will.

25. "*ist wie es ist, und es kommt, wie es kommt*," in Jonas Jonasson, *Der Hundertjährige, der aus das Fenster stieg und verschwand* (Munich: Carl's Books, 2011); English-language edition as *The Hundred-Year-Old Man Who Climbed Out the Window and Disappeared*, trans. R. Bradbury (New York: Hyperion, 2012).

26. For an account of the contemporary German middle class, without references to issues of meaning, see Cornelia Koppetsch, *Die Wiederkehr der Konformität. Streifzüge durch die gefährdete Mitte* (Frankfurt am Main, Germany: Campus, 2013).

27. *PESC*, 144n12; *MWG* I/18, 169n35.

28. Although in a minority position, church representatives are still continuously asked to publicly comment on ethical issues.

29. Lee, *Recognizing*, 125.

30. Most children of the East German town at the center of the study take part in the *Jugendweihe*, among them some Christian youths too.

31. For this reason, Plessner's writings, as well as those from Simmel whom he drew upon, remind us today of etiquette books: Helmuth Plessner, *Die Grenzen der Gemeinschaft. Eine Kritik des sozialen Radikalismus*, in *Gesammelte Schriften*, vol. 5: *Macht und Menschliche Natur*, ed. Günter Dux, Odo Marquard and Elisabeth Ströker (Frankfurt/M., Germany: Suhrkamp, 1981 [1924]), 7–133; see also Gregor Fitzi, *Grenzen des Konsenses: Rekonstruktion einer Theorie "transnormativer Vergesellschaftung"* (Weilerswist, Germany: Velbrück, 2015).

32. This attitude is not unlike the one of down-to-earth John Watson, the counterpart to the unconventional Sherlock Holmes.

33. According to Kracauer, Simmel made out of the process of life an absolute, "Those Who Wait," in *The Mass Ornament. Weimar Essays*, trans. and ed. Thomas Y. Levin (1930; Cambridge, MA: Harvard University Press, 1995), 131.

34. Siegfried Kracauer, "Those Who Wait," in *The Mass Ornament. Weimar Essays*, trans. and ed. Thomas Y. Levin (1930; Cambridge, MA: Harvard University Press, 1995), 138.

CHAPTER 27

....

FROM OCCIDENTAL RATIONALISM TO MULTIPLE MODERNITIES

....

JOHANN P. ARNASON

THE idea of multiple modernities was coined by S. N. Eisenstadt in the mid-1990s, and together with the civilizational turn that had been developing in his work since the late 1970s, it can be understood as a synthesis of themes on which he had been working for several decades. Although he drew on a wide range of sources, classical and contemporary, the Weberian background to these results seems more important than any other influence. Conversely, a closer look at Eisenstadt's arguments will help to clarify some understated aspects of Weber's problematic; and Eisenstadt's comparative study of civilizations, closely linked to the notion of multiple modernities, is the only twentieth-century project that bears comparison and reflects a fundamental affinity with the Weberian one.

THE WEBERIAN PROBLEMATIC AND ITS REVISION

....

A brief glance at Weber's unfinished genealogy of modern European culture will show affinities as well as contrasts with Eisenstadt's later lines of argument. The "concatenation of circumstances" stressed by Weber at the beginning of his last summarizing statement is best understood as a concatenation of processes.[1] The specific conceptual problems of processual analysis are not raised, but in substantive terms, Weber interpreted all the cases in question—from historiography and science to bureaucracy and capitalism—as rationalizing developments. They are disparate enough to prompt an unending discussion about types of rationality and their relative weight in the formation of modernity. In addition to the rationalizing processes, the more or less pronounced diversity of their intrinsic principles signals a pluralism that foreshadows Eisenstadt's emphasis on underlying cultural patterns that shape the horizons and directions of rationality. Finally, Weber's concrete analyses reconstruct complex historical processes, conducive but not reducible to rationalizing trends; they combine and converge in a macrohistorical dynamic that culminates in the modern condition. The late revised version of the *Protestant Ethic* contains a much-quoted mention of *Entzauberung* (inadequately translated as "disenchantment") as a very long-term development going back to Greek and Jewish origins and reaching its climax in radical Protestantism.[2] This great and protracted transformation is inseparable from successive rationalizing breakthroughs, but its overall human significance extends beyond that context.

These multiple paths and processes are discussed in Eisenstadt's writings, both in the historical overview of European civilization and in the texts outlining comparisons with other civilizations.[3] The conceptual tools used to theorize them go beyond Weber's frame of reference, and three points are particularly noteworthy. Eisenstadt analyzes religious as well as broader cultural impulses to change in relation to the differentiation and interaction of orthodoxy and heterodoxy; these categories occur in Weber's work but are not systematically applied. Eisenstadt also links transformations within and differences between civilizational patterns to the dynamics of centers and peripheries, with an emphasis on the plurality of centers and the possibility of peripheral forces claiming central status. Both categories are applicable to cultural, political, and social spheres. They can grasp the changing relationship between church, empire, and kingship in Western Christendom; the contested trajectory of city states and territorial states; and the emergence of revolutionary movements aiming at a radical rebuilding of society. Here, the Weberian connection is more complicated. Eisenstadt's concepts of center and periphery draw on the work of Edward Shils, and Shils' idea of center grew out of his efforts to translate the Weberian concept of charisma into more stable and circumscribed terms. A center in Shils' sense is a dominant and durable source of integrative and authoritative meaning; it can only play that role in relation to a periphery, and this conceptual pair thus becomes a distinctive alternative to the uncontrollable proliferation and unresolved religiopolitical ambiguity that troubled Weber's understanding of charisma. Finally, Eisenstadt places a strong emphasis on the autonomization of sociocultural spheres, from the economic and the political to the cognitive and the aesthetic. This is a problematic adumbrated in Weber's *Zwischenbetrachtung* but not given its due in later readings and sometimes interpreted in ways alien to Weber's basic assumptions.[4] In Eisenstadt's version, it becomes clearer that the divergence of spheres presupposes constitutive meanings inherent in each of them and is thus irreducible to a general trend of rationalizing differentiation. His study of Japan shows that he also allows for cases where specific cultural barriers to the autonomization of spheres remain in force.

UNITY AND DIVERSITY

The autonomization of spheres is relevant to the next step of the argument. The multiple paths and processes discussed in the previous section are a crucial part of the background to diverse modernities, but to move closer to the core of Eisenstadt's thesis, we must consider the patterns of modernity and their scope for pluralization. Eisenstadt's notion of multiple modernities rests on two presuppositions which may be described as "analytical" and "substantive." The first has to do with the very idea of modernity as both one and many. If it is to be tenable to speak of multiple modernities, we must allow for multiple components of an underlying common field and for the possibility of varying relations between them. It is not difficult to identify the outlines of such a view in Weber's work. Capitalism is for him "the most fateful force of modern life" and therefore the most emphatic focus of his comparative inquiry.[5] Another crucial component of modernity is bureaucratic statehood. A third emerging theme of this kind is modern science, seen as an institutionalized and continuously pursued growth of knowledge. In his "Science as a Vocation, " Weber describes it as the most important part of a broader process of intellectualization.[6] That term seems more or less synonymous with the more frequently mentioned rationalization, and there is no doubt that if Weber had lived longer, he would have dealt more extensively with the origins, institutions, dynamics, and effects of modern science. All three historical forces—capitalism, bureaucracy, and organized science—represent constellations of self-empowering and self-rationalizing human action resulting paradoxically in the expansion of structures less and less amenable to human control and understanding. But there is a further component: the individual freedom that enables actors to reflect on the human origins of meaning as well as on the human loss of sovereignty over a human-made environment. Both of these aspects of the human condition in modernity are indicated by Weber's remark on a culture that has eaten off the tree of knowledge.[7]

Weber's vision of modernity does not exclude significant shifts in the balance between these components. A strengthening of bureaucracy, fuelled both by an expanding state and by trends within the very core structures of capitalism, was in his view an obvious and threatening possibility. This is most clearly expressed in his comments on the Russian Revolution of 1905, where he notes that an impending transformation of the Russian Empire, involving a more rapid capitalist development, might disappoint those who expect that capitalism will—as in earlier Western cases—be favorable to political and personal freedom.[8] Another hint in this vein appears at the end of the revised version of the *Protestant Ethic*, where Weber allows for the possibility that future charismatic outbreaks might disrupt the established structures of modern society.[9] Such outbreaks did in fact leave their mark on twentieth-century history, but when Weber wrote his last statement, he did not see the Bolshevik revolution in that way. Finally, it is easy to read the analysis of "world orders" in Weber's *Zwischenbetrachtung* as keys to a pluralistic interpretation of modernity.[10] It is true that the idea of divergent and potentially conflicting orders is neither limited to modern societies nor developed into a theoretical paradigm of modernity, but the reference to the rival orders as disenchanted versions of old gods suggests that Weber had in mind a conceptual scheme that would in appropriately different ways be applicable to both modern and premodern constellations. And if the modern world is seen as a field of tensions between multiple orders, it is plausible to envisage variations to the overall pattern. Weber did not pursue that line of argument.

One important aspect of the later debate on multiple modernities is entirely absent from Weber's work. His analyses of non-European civilizations do not raise the question of their ability to modify the Western patterns which European expansion or the efforts to resist it led them to adopt. He did to some extent distinguish between responses to Western capitalism. Japan is singled out as a culture that has proved eminently capable of importing capitalism, although it had shown no signs of inventing it; the verdict on China is that it is likely to show a similar ability, although the massive sociocultural forces that ruled out an indigenous road to capitalism have so far also blocked its import; in the case of India, Weber emphasized the penetration of capitalism due to colonial rule but also the resistance of conservative social structures that limited its impact but remained capable of minimal adaptation. In no case is there a reference to a possible "reinvention of capitalism," to use a later term.

Eisenstadt's approach to the problematic of multiple modernities shows some basic affinities and contrasts with Weber. The first thing to note is that Eisenstadt reinforces Weber's emphasis on the rupture that marks the modern condition; quoting an author who attributes to Weber the notion of an "existential threshold," he takes the point even further and describes the advent of modernity as an "epiphany," or as we might say an inverted epiphany, consisting in the collapse of an imagined meaningful cosmos and a corresponding empowering of the human subject that emerges as the source of meaning.[11] Another difference is that for Eisenstadt the transition to modernity is not associated with anything as clear-cut and conclusive as Weber's *Entzauberung*. Rather, the hallmark is uncertainty and controversy, "antinomies and contradictions,"[12] different in kind and degree from the experience of earlier historical epochs. The tension described as "perhaps the most critical, both in ideological and political terms"[13] calls for a closer look. It is the conflict between the recognition of different values and rationalities, corresponding to distinct sociocultural spheres, and the vision of an all-encompassing synthesis or common denominator of such values and rationalities. Although Eisenstadt refers to the alternatives as totalistic and pluralistic, it seems that the unifying vision is not to be reduced to the political phenomenon known as totalitarianism. In historical terms, Eisenstadt traces the contrasting projects back to early modern thought and associates the totalizing conception of reason with Descartes. In regard to contemporary trends (which Eisenstadt does not discuss), it can be argued that those who envisage a generalized market rationality are following a totalistic line; the notions of markets for political parties and religions go together with a comprehensive utilitarianism. As for totalitarianism in the strict sense, it is highly debatable whether it necessarily involves a totalistic model of rationality. The Marxist–Leninist version certainly did, but the radical particularism of fascist movements and regimes does not fit into the same category.

The contrast between pluralistic and totalistic interpretations raises further questions about Eisenstadt's relationship to Weber. References to values and rationalities show that Weber's conception of different spheres with their own built-in evaluative and rationalizing orientations is taken for granted, but their unfolding is accompanied by the totalizing countercurrent. The latter is a response to the development of pluralistic patterns and an attempt to impose unity on diversity, but for Eisenstadt this response accompanies the pluralistic trend from the outset and can achieve historical successes but not a definitive victory. Both the totalistic and the pluralistic versions have ideological as well as institutional consequences. In this respect there is an interesting contrast with Weber, whose analyses of rationality and rationalization proceed on two levels without a clear definition of each or of the relationship between them. On the one hand, Weber works with a series of dichotomies: logical versus teleological (in other words, the rationality of thought and of action), formal versus material, and instrumental (or purposive) versus value-oriented. On the other hand, he suggests, as we have seen, that different forms of rationality are built into the "world orders," as he labels the multiple spheres of sociocultural life. Eisenstadt's account, however condensed, seems more structured. He posits a historical constellation of different contextual rationalities, divergent interpretive responses to that experience, and expressions of these alternative interpretations across the ideological and institutional spectrum of modern societies. The interpretive dimension of rationality, thus foregrounded, also implies embeddedness in broader cultural settings. That aspect must be examined in light of Eisenstadt's turn to civilizational analysis.

THE CIVILIZATIONAL CONTEXT

The idea of multiple modernities grew out of Eisenstadt's long and critical engagement with modernization theory. His interest in the comparative analysis of civilizations, strongly evident from the late 1970s onward, was also rooted in earlier work, most obviously in a comparative study of empires, the first work of that scope and kind.[14] It linked up with Weber's perspectives on bureaucracy in different historical formations but combined this approach with an emphasis on imperial visions, a theme left unexplored in Weber's work, due primarily to the overextended category of patrimonialism. Civilizations are the initially unacknowledged background of such visions. To clarify the meaning of Eisenstadt's move to explore that field, we must turn to retrospective formulations in later writings. The most revealing one is to be found in a text first published in 2000. Eisenstadt defines what he calls the civilizational dimension of human societies, latently inherent in them from the beginning of history but only articulated gradually and relatively late on the level of specific large-scale and long-term formations. The core constitutive feature is the intertwining of articulated world horizons, also characterized as ontological or cosmological visions, with the "definition, structuration and regulation of the major arenas of institutional life, of the political arena, of authority and its accountability, of the economy, of family life, social stratification, and of the construction of collective identity."[15]

In making this assertion, Eisenstadt is neither advocating a cultural determinism of the Parsonian type nor positing a single and direct line from a cultural program through values to norms. The link between articulations of the world and institutions of society is described in terms of interrelations, rather than a unilateral determination; and that suggests an institutional and practical input into the social projections of cultural visions. There is, in other words, an emphasis on interpretive patterns related to contexts of action, especially relevant to the cultural definition as more fundamental than normative regulation. Where interpretation is involved, the conflict of interpretations is not far away. And there are further indications of conflict in Eisenstadt's statement. He does not refer to subsystems, as did Parsons and his followers; instead, he uses the metaphor of "arena," clearly connoting a field of conflict and power, less reducible to rational or normative frameworks than are the traditionally conceived subsystems. Moreover, Eisenstadt's comments make it clear that a closed list of arenas is not to be envisaged. To sum up, it is reasonable to argue that Eisenstadt structures his paradigm of the civilizational dimension around the interplay of culture and power, with an emphasis on the interpretive links shaped by both sides.

There is no comparable conceptual summary in Weber's work. That has not prevented Eisenstadt and other recent civilizational analysts from recognizing Weber as a preeminent pioneer in the field. This view, based on the historical and theoretical content of his comparative studies, can gain further support from some significant but underdeveloped sketches and passing comments in his writings. There are three particularly suggestive openings of this kind that can be linked to the idea of the civilizational dimension.

The first such hint is the definition of culture in the exceptionally rich but often cryptic and inconclusive essay "Objectivity."[16] This is an early text, written at a time when Weber situated his project within the framework of the cultural rather than the social sciences, and he was very conscious of the philosophical background to the notion of *Kultur*. He defined "culture" as an always specific way of lending meaning to the world and adopting an attitude to it. Although this claim is neither cited nor otherwise reaffirmed in his later writings, it is implicit in Weber's use of the term "cultural world" to describe the historical formations of China, India, and the Occident. Cultural ways of relating to the world are central to his analyses of contrasts and divergences between them. The affinity with Eisenstadt's emphasis on cultural articulations of the world is obvious. But it is also noteworthy that—compared to the original formulation—Weber narrows the focus of his approach. He stresses the attitudes to the world more than the ways of making sense of it; within the former category, he works with a stark dichotomy of world-accepting and world-rejecting orientations; the more specific differentiations that interest him are varieties of world rejection, leading to flight from the world, efforts to master it, or, less explicitly, ideas of changing it.

The definition of culture does not refer to the interconnections with society that are crucial to Eisenstadt's line of argument. A certain shift in that direction can be found in Weber's introductory essay on economic ethics of world religions:

> It is interests (material and ideal), and not ideas, which have directly governed the actions of human beings. But the "worldviews" that have been created by ideas have very often, like switches, decided the lines on which the dynamic of interests has propelled behaviour.[17]

Interests are the direct primary determining factor, ideas a more broadly orienting one. This is one of his most quoted passages but frequently taken out of the context. If we consider it in connection with the following studies of religions and their civilizational settings, it becomes obvious that the societies embedded in cultural worlds are also constellations of interests. The social strata that figure in Weber's analyses—rulers, priests, warriors, merchants, artisans, peasants, intellectuals—are groups with distinctive sets of interests; their positions and interrelations also represent ways of distributing social power, operating within overall patterns of domination (*Herrschaftsverbände*). Such structural complexes are integrated through institutions, although Weber did not thematize that aspect to the same extent as did the French sociological tradition. Institutional frameworks are in turn grounded in configurations of meaning, notably religious ones; and Weber's reference to orienting ideas has mainly to do with this level. Such key institutions as the Chinese imperial rulership, the Indian caste order, or the occidental urban community cannot be understood without linking them to religious presuppositions. In conjunction with institutions, world-articulating ideas can not only define the paths along which interests are pursued but also influence the very under-standing of the interests. The quest for wealth and power has a different meaning in the Chinese context of utilitarian social ethics based on a cosmic order and in the Indian caste regime dominated by priests and legitimized by otherworldly visions of salvation. Last but not least, the distinction between material and ideal interests varies from case to case, in kind and degree. The Daoist notion of immortality blurs the contrast more than do Christian visions of the afterlife; Buddhist ideas of liberation have proved less assimilable to the Western paradigm of salvation than Weber thought.

All of these considerations suggest points of contact with Eisenstadt's problematic. The third and last affinity to be noted concerns the notion of arena. It is reminiscent of Weber's reflections on the "world orders," the sociocultural spheres that interact and diverge in different ways in different historical and civilizational contexts. Weber's orders are not subordinated to any systemic unity or evolutionary logic, and his enu-meration of them is neither a constant nor a closed model. Moreover, and in addition to the tensions between orders, conflicts within each order are easily conceivable and in part indicated by Weber. In the economic sphere, there is an obvious possibility of conflicts between the formal rationality of economic organization and the rival models of material rationality that can enter into disagreements about property, distribution, and regulation. As for politics, the conflictual relationship between charisma and bureaucracy and the problem of balancing their roles in the conditions of modern statehood are familiar to all readers of Weber. Although the intellectual sphere is not discussed as extensively, it is not difficult to identify the makings of a conflict in Weber's account of modern science: the progress of knowledge becomes a prime example of human ability and initiative, but the results of scientific inquiry also give rise to deterministic models that cast fundamental doubt on human agency.

MODERNITY AS A DISTINCT
TYPE OF CIVILIZATION

If Eisenstadt's general conception of civilizational patterns can be shown to be indebted to Weberian sources, it also constitutes a step beyond them in its implications for the theory and historical analysis of modernity. Eisenstadt never formulated his idea of modernity as a new civilization in the systematic way that would have clarified the relationship between unity and diversity. But the main lines of reasoning are quite clear. The key innovation is a major "shift in the conception of human agency, of its autonomy and of its place in the flow of time... a conception of the future in which various possibilities which can be realized by autonomous human agency—or by the march of history—are open."[18] The concept to be underlined is that of autonomy, understood in a very broad and non-normative or more precisely meta-normative sense: it denotes a horizon within which rival normative projects can emerge but does not constitute a normative principle or presupposition. It is true that Eisenstadt sometimes refers to a modern project or cultural program, but that seems to be a case of terminology lagging behind conceptual content. A more adequate description might focus on a mutation of horizons, with implications and consequences that mature through long-term processes and affect multiple aspects of the human condition.

For Eisenstadt, Weber's work is the most significant anticipation of this approach to modernity. The inclination to describe the modern turn as an abrupt shift and a kind of revelation may be seen as a sign of overreliance on Weber's most provocative formulations. A closer reading of his work as a whole will support a more processual perspective. But when it comes to the patterns that emerge from a concatenation of processes, Eisenstadt relates the vision of autonomy to a more explicitly multidimensional and polysemic context than Weber did. The modern orientation to autonomy entails a new degree and an expanding role of inquiry, intervention, and imagination in multiple fields. On the other hand, it also leads to unintended consequences with structuring power, disputes about the meaning and destiny of human empowerment, and encounters with the limits of autonomous insight and conduct. Human mastery over nature expands, but at the same time, conceptions of the order of nature are transformed and new dimensions of the natural world are discovered. Both of these trends are, in the longer run, conducive to awareness of unintended effects and destructive dynamics. The social world and its political order are increasingly seen as human constructs, questionable and transformable in more or less radical ways; developments along such lines also include the exploration of paths that come to be rejected as blind alleys or self-defeating options and may delegitimize broader perspectives with which they are associated. In the intellectual sphere, the accumulation of knowledge is accompanied by enhanced reflexivity but also by attempts to recompose a unified and up-to-date worldview, on the one hand, and varying versions of relativism, on the other.

It may not be obvious how this emphasis on autonomy fits with Eisenstadt's conception of civilizations grounded in ontological or cosmological visions. Whatever his allusions to a radical inaugural break may imply, both theoretical arguments and historical evidence speak against any notion of modernity as a domain of the sovereign subject. Interpretations of autonomy, implicit or explicit, theoretical or practical, intertwine with world articulations; the modern transformation therefore does not deactivate or randomize the latter aspect but results in a major, unprecedented, and continuously redefined shift in the balance, toward the subjective side and with pluralizing effects on the world-related one. This shift is the main reason why it seems more adequate to describe modernity as a distinct type of civilization, rather than just a distinct civilization. To sum up, the civilizational dimension of modernity is defined by an empowerment of the human subject but with a contested interpretive background and ambiguous practical consequences. The diversifying impact of this constellation is particularly visible in the ideological currents that draw on visions of autonomy. Individualist and collectivist projects share some basic cultural premises, but their divergent aspirations and direct conflicts play a noteworthy role in the formation of multiple modernities.

One aspect of Eisenstadt's argument on autonomy and modernity reveals a particularly interesting connection to Weber. The chapter on "sociological foundations" in Weber's study of China ends with comments on a major contrast between the historical trajectories of China and the Occident. Beginning with the observation that Chinese efforts to rationalize administrative and economic practice were more limited than Western efforts, Weber mentions two main reasons for this. The first is that the absence of interstate competition after the rise of a unified empire weakened the incentives to such measures. This point calls for some qualifications. Historians of East Asia have increasingly stressed the need to study Chinese developments in connection with inner Asian empires, their periodic conquest of Chinese territories, in some cases rivalries between states set up by such intruders, and temporary fragmentation of the inner core as a result of defeats suffered by the imperial center. There was, in other words, an outer circle of interstate competition, emerging at roughly the same time as the inner one was brought under central control (around 200 BCE). But this broader picture also shows that explanations in terms of interstate competition should take due note of specific factors and not reduce the matter to general virtues of rivalry. The struggle with inner Asian neighbors and conquerors often imposed geopolitical and military imperatives that were not necessarily in harmony with reformist visions. This was clearly the case with Wang An-shih's policies in the second half of the eleventh century, which Weber rightly saw as a landmark episode in Chinese history.

Weber's second point is more directly linked to the question of roads to modernity. In addition to interstate competition, he mentions internal processes that accelerated the overall rationalizing trend. The rise of independent social forces, primarily urban-based, opened up two possible paths of development. It could either enable ruling monarchs to build alliances that broke the hold of traditional authorities or turn against patrimonial power, as "was the case in the five great revolutions which decided the destiny of the Occident: the Italian revolution of the 12th and 13th centuries, the Netherland revolution of the 16th century, the English revolution of the 17th century, and the American and the French revolutions of the 18th century. We may ask: were there no comparable forces in China?"[19] The whole following analysis of Chinese civilization answers the final question in the negative. But the remark about revolutions deciding the destiny of the Occident signals a problematic that was not taken further: if revolutionary upheavals play a key role in the history of occidental rationalism, that is an obvious reason to enlarge the frame of reference used in Weber's final statement on the concatenation of rationalizing processes.

Eisenstadt's discussion of revolutions is much more extensive and more conceptually grounded. The comparative study of revolutions was already of major importance for his civilizational turn and went beyond the Weberian approach by examining the impact of different civilizational backgrounds on the possibilities and ideological articulations of revolutionary change. His last publication on this subject discussed "great revolutions" and included non-Western cases (Russia, China, occasionally Vietnam) in that category.[20] In his view, revolutions are not obligatory passages to modernity. There are non-revolutionary paths, and Eisenstadt can in principle accept the Weberian idea of a state-dominated alliance that transforms society from above, without the upheavals associated with revolution. His analysis can also link up with the influential school of thought that has interpreted modern revolutions as processes beginning with state breakdown, marked by acute social conflicts and culminating in the rebuilding of stronger state structures on new foundations.[21] That model seems eminently applicable to the Russian Revolution, where an imperial state was reconstructed after an exceptionally thoroughgoing collapse under the leadership of a counter-elite with uncompromising aspirations to unchecked power. But the outcome cannot be explained without taking the ideology behind these aspirations into account, and this factor is generally downplayed by state-centered theories of revolution. Here we can draw on Eisenstadt's approach as a corrective.

The specific historical role of the great revolutions, as analyzed by Eisenstadt, is that their ideological aspects express the civilizational problematic of modernity in the most radical and controversial way, thus articulating issues and projects that also affect the course of events in non-revolutionary settings. These revolutions are the most concentrated effects of the transformative dynamic that characterizes modernity. This applies most obviously to the two democratic revolutions par excellence, the North American and the French. In particular, the much-invoked ideas of 1789 liberty, equality, fraternity—can be understood as variations on the theme of autonomy. In the case of liberty, that goes without saying; equality is about the generalization or universalization of autonomy, and fraternity is about the mutual recognition of autonomous subjects. Both liberal and socialist patterns of political ideology grow out of attempts to define the relationship between these principles. At the same time, the French Revolution produced a model of transformative politics that turned out to be adaptable to opposing projects. The Jacobin notion of radical change guided by an ideologically inspired vanguard has, as Eisenstadt argues, left its mark on very different movements and regimes, including Bolshevism and its radical right-wing antagonists as well as builders of capitalism on the ruins of communist regimes and the current first known as Islamic fundamentalism but now more widely labeled as Islamism.[22] Finally, Eisenstadt spells out an unstated implication of Weber's remark on the sequence of revolutions: this history gives rise to a revolutionary tradition, a memory work that involves learning from experience as well as mythologizing of key episodes and the construction of archetypal models. The influence of interpretive schemes derived from the French Revolution on the Russian Revolution is a prime example of such connections.

EMERGENCE, EXPANSION, AND DIFFERENTIATION

Eisenstadt repeatedly referred to modernity as "rooted...in the transformation of the late medieval European civilization and polities" and crystallizing through early European expansion as well as the revolutions that marked the beginning of more advanced modernity.[23] This view is more or less in line with Weber's account of the occidental breakthrough. But a closer look at Eisenstadt's work and its various themes reveals two significant moves beyond the Weberian frame of reference. The first has to do with the emergence of modernity as a new civilization. Eisenstadt's participation in the debate on early modernities clearly suggests that he was willing to extend the genealogy of the new formation beyond Europe.[24] This is especially important for state formation in East Asia and the Muslim (Ottoman, Safavid, and Mughal) empires that emerged around the middle of the second millennium. It is in Eisenstadt's spirit to suggest, following the Weberian view, that if early modern patterns emerged in different parts of Eurasia, this was probably the outcome of interconnections, parallels, and collisions in the long history of the macro-region. But modern beginnings took a more markedly civilizational turn in Europe than elsewhere. Several historical innovations from the sixteenth century onward contributed to this epoch-making shift. A new phase of European expansion led to the formation of transoceanic empires for the first time in history and at the same time gave rise to global trade connections that opened up new perspectives for capitalist development. New steps of state formation, spearheaded by the new monarchies in western Europe, had an all-around impact on social life; and interstate competition appears to have been a particularly important factor. Two rival reformations, one of them somewhat misleadingly known as the Counter-Reformation, put an end to the unity of Western Christendom and transformed the religious culture of Europe in a fundamental fashion. Finally, the beginnings of the scientific revolution set in motion an ongoing change to ways of interpreting the world.

The other point that distinguishes Eisenstadt's approach from Weber's is much more systematically formulated and central to the problematic of multiple modernities. Weber did not raise the question of reinvented modern patterns in non-Western socio-cultural settings, whereas for Eisenstadt this becomes a central problem. He considers it, first of all, in the context of European expansion as a long-term process that enabled or forced societies and civilizations on the receiving end to adapt European patterns in a more or less creative way. The conditions of possibility for such encounters were present on both sides. The ambiguities of autonomy and its practical manifestations provide a space for further variations. First responses to European expansion are frequently marked by attempts to match the most visible strengths of the adversary while main-taining the identity and independence that keeps the threat at bay. The emphasis on self-preservation implies a more consciously agonistic relationship to other cultural worlds than was traditionally the case and can result in further steps toward reinterpre-tation of modern horizons. The record of Chinese responses to Western challenges, from late imperial strategies of self-strengthening through a Confucian reformist alter-native to the victory of a revolutionary paradigm grounded in Western countercultural sources, is perhaps the most spectacular case. It is currently continuing with an unfin-ished attempt to synthesize two models that previously proved irreconcilable: a capitalist strategy of development and a Leninist conception of statehood. But the Chinese trajec-tory also exemplifies the role of another factor. In a short essay on European expansion, Eisenstadt criticized the reductionism of world system theory and argued that the process of expansion gave rise to three different global systems: economic, political, and ideological, mutually irreducible and each with its own dynamic.[25] This claim does not involve a strong concept of system; we might more adequately speak of constellations. Such broader connections decisively affected the course of Chinese history during the transformative period commonly dated from 1840.

However, Eisenstadt's analysis of interactive roads to modernity is not limited to specific episodes and global conjunctures. He links the question to a much more general and long-term perspective. The presuppositions of multiple modernities are traced back to very early beginnings. Eisenstadt singles out the "Axial Age," roughly identifiable with the period from the eighth to the third centuries BCE, as a time of changes that set the scene for later civilizational developments and encounters. The idea that this was an epoch of exceptional dynamism and creativity is not new, and Weber took note of it, although there was no continuous discussion until Karl Jaspers coined the term "Axial Age" (*Achsenzeit*) in 1949. Weber referred to an age of prophecy, and he stressed the emergence of autonomous intellectuals; but he saw no need to move toward a more unified picture or theory of the age.[26] Drawing on Jaspers, Eisenstadt proposed such a theory, emphasizing a cultural rearticulation of the world based on a distinction between higher and lower reality, between the transcendental and the mundane. The two levels are not defined in the same way in all the Eurasian worlds, but the distinction always involves reforming mundane life and its social frameworks along lines defined by a higher order, which entails more or less explicit prefigurations of autonomy. To put it another way, the Axial turn generates a transformative potential, and Eisenstadt's thesis is that this cultural resource is essential to the formation of specific modernities.

The distinctive legacies of axial breakthroughs and later elaborations of their respective problematics set their mark on the practically operative visions of modernity. In the Chinese case, a traditional emphasis on political power as a link between cosmic and social order first obstructed and then facilitated a modern reception of revolutionary projects. Another example of Axial backgrounds affecting entries to modernity is the long-term impact of affinities and divergences between monotheistic religions, where different cleavages between orthodoxy and heterodoxy result in varying trajectories. But in general terms, Eisenstadt's theory posits an Axial type of civilization, invariably characterized by an enhanced self-questioning and self-transformative capacity. That approach makes his focus on the preconditions and obstacles to modern types of change very different from Weber's. The main emphasis is on civilizational frameworks of centers and peripheries.[27] He thus highlights the general modalities of change and the possibilities of radicalizing it, rather than concrete innovations in particular spheres. From this point of view, the European premises of modernity have to do with a plurality of centers and a strong tendency to ideologize them, hegemonic and even universal claims growing out of their rivalry, recurrent emergences of new centers from the periphery, and the association of separate centers with different sociocultural spheres. The modern transformation is, first and foremost, a matter of radical rupture, principled discontinuity, and realized or at least imagined alternative orders. All of these aspects are outlets for the vision of autonomy that defines modernity as a civilization. If a particular sphere can be credited with a privileged role, it seems to be the political one. The genesis of modern capitalism is, by contrast, a much less central theme for Eisenstadt than for Weber.

Similarly, the specific problematics of other civilizations and their relationship to modernity can be analyzed in terms of centers and their dynamics. Eisenstadt's view of the Chinese tradition as marked by an exceptional ideological and institutional emphasis on a dominant center is not incompatible with Thomas Metzger's critical comment that this center was organizationally inhibited; the distinction between institutional and organizational levels, which Eisenstadt uses in his more conceptual analyses, can help to clarify this.[28] The center that came to preside over the twentieth-century wave of Chinese modernization attempted to outmatch its predecessor, up to and including the deification of its leader. But as the monumentally self-defeating excesses of the Cultural Revolution showed, it also reproduced the dysfunctionalities, albeit in a very different shape. As for India, Eisenstadt agrees with Weber on the exceptionally other-worldly orientation of this civilization but links it more directly to institutions than to conduct. The other-worldly stance was anchored in a hierarchy that ensured the primacy of priests but also the prerogative of rulers; the comprehensive ritual framework that sustained this two-peaked power structure was embodied in the caste regime. Inherent in the whole configuration is a general weakening and fragmentation of centers, as well as structural limits to the cumulation and ideologization of conflict and change. As a result, obstacles to the development of statehood were more fundamental than in Europe and China. But these observations did not prevent Eisenstadt from noting links between aspects of the Indian tradition and key features of Indian modernity; for example, he adopted and elaborated the argument that the stability of Indian democracy is in part due to the caste regime and its potential for political mobilization in a new environment.

The First Western and Non-Western Multiple Modernities

In an essay on the Americas as the first multiple modernities, Eisenstadt analyzed the settler societies of the western hemisphere as variations on the European civilizational complex in transition to modernity.[29] This argument links up with a point Eisenstadt made in other writings, namely, that we need to distinguish between religion as one institution among others and as a "meta-institution," that is, a framework within which institutions take shape, and thus more or less identical with a civilizational pattern. The distinction applies to the two estranged branches of Western Christendom, the Reformation and the Counter-Reformation, whose innovations and conflicts shaped the early modern scene in Europe. Eisenstadt's main thesis is that in the space opened up by the conquest of new territories and the destruction of indigenous societies, each of the two confessions was able to unfold its civilizational implications in more comprehensive ways than had been possible in the European context of entrenched traditions. In both Americas, this shaped the premises of social and political order. Protestant hegemony in the north was marked by a shift toward more radical positions and an ongoing strengthening of sects. This resulted in a sociocultural emphasis on egalitarian and achievement-oriented individualism, notions of a chosen people in secularized versions, and a high relative weight of society vis-à-vis the state. In Latin America, a region made up of former colonies of the Spanish and Portuguese empire, the alliance of the Counter-Reformation with absolute monarchs created a situation that led to long-term strengthening of hierarchic and centralist models. In practice that translated into an entrenched patrimonial state, compromising with local oligarchies.

This point of view has an important Weberian connection. Weber's essay on the Protestant sects in the United States, written as a kind of afterword to the *Protestant Ethic*, deals with the broader sociocultural implications of a Protestantism more inclined to doctrinal radicalization and sectarian proliferation than the original European versions.[30] Weber argued that the influence of the sects contributed to the spread of a morality conducive to proper functioning of a capitalist economy. The sects became models for a variety of associations, and the latter in turn become the backbone for an articulated civil society. Weber described this indirect impact of the sects as a secularizing turn, but as in other contexts, the concept of secularization is inescapably ambiguous: overtly non-religious projects are still drawing on a residual but enduring religious legacy. This line of argument is obviously akin to Eisenstadt's approach; what the latter added was a more comprehensive civilizational perspective and a comparative reference to Latin America, whereas Weber had taken no significant interest in that continent.

Eisenstadt's critics have accused him of coming too close to conventional notions of two Americas, one dynamic and the other stagnant, and called for more differentiated models. Eisenstadt was not unaware of major differences within each of the two regions. He noted the "continental divide" between Canada and the United States, already discussed by Lipset, and the contrasts between the Andean countries and the more Europeanized Southern Cone. The most explicit and detailed alternative to Eisenstadt's interpretation is Wolfgang Knöbl's discussion of the Americas, which suggests at least seven historical regions: Canada, the northern states that shaped the destiny of the United States after the Civil War, the US South, the Andean and the southern parts of Hispanic Latin America, Brazil, and the Caribbean.[31] This emphasis on regional divisions does not invalidate Eisenstadt's point about the civilizational potential of the two reformations, but their role must be analyzed in different contexts and in connection with other factors that vary from region to region. Geographical pluralization thus also entails a stronger focus on the plurality of factors that is a defining theme of Weber's historical sociology and that is in principle integrated into Eisenstadt's comparative project.

Another important corrective to Eisenstadt's view of Latin America (and an extension of Weberian perspectives) is Laurence Whitehead's description of the continent as a "mausoleum of modernities."[32] The metaphor refers to a historical pattern that differs from Weber's observations about the import of modern capitalism. Whitehead's claim is that on the whole Latin America has been characterized by exceptionally strong dependence on European models and visions of modernity. But this orientation does not lead to any straightforward transfer; rather, the result is a sequence of inconclusive and inconsistent modernizing initiatives, whose cumulative effects mark a long-term trajectory. The implication is that for all the importance of the two reformations, it would be misleading to see them as civilizational matrices of subsequent history. They represent alternative versions of early modernity, in both cases centered on an ambiguous containment of modernity, neither outright affirmation nor wholesale denial. Their long-term imprint depends on interaction with later phases of modernity, including the externally inspired and internally disrupted sequence described by Whitehead.

There is another side to this constellation. A particularly troubled and discontinuous process of state formation affected both domestic developments and the responses to lessons from abroad. One aspect of the resultant path raises interesting questions in relation to Weber's comparative sociology of domination as well as to Eisenstadt's civilizational frame of reference. The phenomenon of "caudilloism," rule by strongmen, often but not always of military origin, is a persistent feature of Latin American history and can most plausibly be explained as a result of the incomplete and fragile efforts of state formation in the wake of the wars for independence.[33] It did not enter into Weber's field of research, and the very few attempts to deal with it on a Weberian basis seem to hesitate as to whether the main focus should be on charismatic, patrimonial, or even traditional characteristics.[34] As for Eisenstadt's analysis of Latin America, caudilloism is strangely absent, but twentieth-century developments have not only underlined its importance but also highlighted a fact that invites comparison with other themes in his work. Like Jacobinism, but on a more restricted regional scale, caudilloism has a record of variations across the political spectrum. Some of the regimes in question defended an established oligarchic order, others aimed at more personal or dynastic rule, and others moved toward the positions of Latin American populism, or even further to the left, with the Cuban adaptation of communism as the most extreme case.

The other exemplary case among multiple modernities is very different and looms much larger in Eisenstadt's work. He refers to Japan as the first non-Western modernity, and his book about Japanese civilization in comparative perspective is probably the most detailed civilizational study ever written.[35] Its main thesis is that Japan represents a non-Axial civilization that, interacting with Western challenges, has proved capable of shaping its own version of modernity. Given Eisenstadt's emphasis on connections between Axial and modern transformations, this seems paradoxical, as does his particular interest in the case. Although his study does not draw directly on Weber's work, Weber's approach to Japan nevertheless offers a useful starting point for a critical discussion.

Weber was interested in Japan and suggested an explanation for its exceptional record of modernization. His analysis is not on the same scale as the studies of India and China but is a short section in the survey of Buddhist expansion east of India in his study of Indian religions.[36] Two observations are important. On the one hand, Weber worked with an inadequate image of Japan. He took for granted a simple model of feudalism, applied to a longer period and more assimilated to European patterns than historians of Japan would now accept. On the other hand, he did not appreciate the significance of the early Japanese transformation of the Chinese imperial paradigm. The inclination to stress analogies to Europe became evident in the treatment of Japanese religion, where Weber found analogies to Lutheranism and the Counter-Reformation but not to radical Protestantism. When it came to explaining the modernizing turn after 1868, including the importation of capitalism as a ready-made "artefact," the emphasis was on feudal structures modified by bureaucratization. The transition was made easier by the absence of a clearly defined religious background. Weber even used the metaphor tabula rasa, which certainly does no justice to the originality of Japanese religious culture.

Elaborating Weber's interpretation, we can suggest that he saw Japan as a case of feudalism developing without urban and clerical counterweights, charting its own path toward bureaucratization and on that basis initiating an imitative strategy of modern capitalist development. To a certain extent, Japan thus seems to have inverted the European relationship between capitalism and bureaucracy. However, it is also possible to read Weber's text on Japan as a first sketch of a historical interpretation open to additions and corrections. He stresses the multiple foreign sources of Japanese culture.

In premodern times, China towered above all other models; but its influence was partly channelled through Korea and partly based on beliefs and institutions of Indian origin, which left room for direct contact with both Korean and Indian sources. Yet the process of cultural transfer between China and Japan was more complex, proceeding through different phases and with Japanese responses more inventive than Weber believed. The nineteenth-century shift to openness and transformation involved a learning process relating to experiences in the whole East Asian region and a selective reinvention of Western precedents. Weber noted the interaction of imported cultural patterns with indigenous power structures but went much too far in identifying the latter with the dynamics of feudalism. In fact, the feudal component was only one part of a more complex constellation, which also included processes of state formation of varying kind and strength. The similarities with Europe were more limited than Weber thought.

It is this kind of a more complex and nuanced Weberian perspective that works best as an alternative to Eisenstadt's view. The idea of Japan as a non-Axial civilization with its own version of modernity is not only based on an analysis of the nineteenth-century transition. The main claims concern developments preceding the encounter with the West by more than a millennium. Eisenstadt argues that the original Japanese adoption of Chinese models, from the sixth to the eighth centuries CE, went hand in hand with the consolidation and institutionalization of an older and indigenous mode of thought, marked by assumptions of continuity between nature and culture, society and state, familial and political relationships, myth and history. In more negative terms it did not encompass the distinctions between levels and domains of reality that had been the key Axial innovations, and the contrast that Eisenstadt defines in terms of transcendental and mundane was therefore alien to Japanese civilization. His thesis is that despite structural changes, power struggles, and institutional differentiation, this cultural framework remained in force and set limits to social transformations. Cultural borrowings were "de-axialized," that is, adapted to the preexisting ways of world-understanding.

Eisenstadt's stress on continuity across domains of reality and phases of history is directly reflected in his conception of Japanese modernity. He regards the notion of the "family state," *kazoku kokka*, as a core component of modern Japanese political culture. "Familistic" models derived from traditional kinship units are also central to the organization of Japanese capitalism, characterized by patterns of "interlocking" that include governmental guidance of the economy, extended networks of economic units, and a close relationship between firms and unions. Eisenstadt does not use the term "reinvention of capitalism," but it seems easily compatible with his argument.

However, the crucial question is whether this analysis of the sixth- to eighth-century transformation is tenable. There are good reasons to express reservations. Recent scholarship about Japan suggests a comprehensive appropriation of Chinese traditions. The reception of Daoism was less openly articulated than in the case of Confucianism, but it seems to have been decisive for the constitution of Shintō, the supposedly indigenous religion.[37] There was, in other words, no straightforward perpetuation of a more archaic mode of thought. The results of the overall transformation induced by closer contact with China were not preharmonized, and their development along divergent lines was an important aspect of later Japanese history. This critique is further supported by revised interpretations of the Axial Age. It now seems plausible to regard the transformations of that epoch as a set of changes within several major civilizational centers. Some of these changes were more or less akin to Eisenstadt's distinction between transcendental and mundane; but they intertwined or contrasted with others, and there is no uniform common denominator of axiality. The civilizations of the Axial Age were more a historical group than a category, and another group can be added to the picture: civilizations—or, more loosely speaking, civilizational formations—that emerged within the orbit of the original Axial civilizations but took distinctive forms and directions. The relationship between Greece and Rome is the most familiar case, but China and Japan may be seen in a similar light.

The upshot of this discussion can be summed up in a few words. Shmuel Eisenstadt was Max Weber's most legitimate and most autonomous heir, but Weber's work still seems the most rewarding source of complements and correctives to Eisenstadt's project. A confrontation of the two classics reveals strengths and merits on both sides.

Notes

1. Max Weber, "Vorbemerkung" [Author's introduction], in *The Protestant Ethic and the Spirit of Capitalism* (hereafter *PESC*), trans. T. Parsons (New York: Scribner's, 1958), 13; *Die protestantische Ethik und der Geist des Kapitalismus. Schriften 1904–1920*, ed. W. Schluchter with U. Bube. *Max Weber Gesamtausgabe* I/18 (hereafter *MWG*) (Tübingen, Germany: Mohr [Siebeck], 2016), 101.
2. *PESC*, 105, 117; *MWG* I/18, 280, 320.
3. S. N. Eisenstadt, *European Civilization in a Comparative Perspective* (Oslo, Norway: Aschehoug AS, 1987); "Japanese Historical Experience in a Comparative Framework," in *Japanese Civilization: A Comparative View* (Chicago: University of Chicago Press, 1995), 396–426.
4. Max Weber, "Zwischenbetrachtung: Theorie der Stufen und Richtungen religiöser Weltablehnung" [Religious rejections of the world and their directions], in *From Max Weber: Essays in Sociology* (hereafter *FMW*), trans. and ed. H. H. Gerth and C. W. Mills (Oxford: Oxford University Press, 1946), 323–359; *Die Wirtschaftsethik der Weltreligionen. Konfuzianismus und Taoismus. Schriften 1915–1920*, ed. H. Schmidt-Glintzer with P. Kolonko. *MWG* I/19 (Tübingen, Germany: Mohr [Siebeck], 1989), 209–233.
5. *PESC*, 17; *MWG* I/18, 105.
6. Max Weber, "Wissenschaft als Beruf" [Science as a vocation], in *FMW*, 138–139; *Wissenschaft als Beruf 1917/1919*, ed. W. J. Mommsen and W. Schluchter with B. Morgenbrod. *MWG* I/17 (Tübingen, Germany: Mohr [Siebeck], 1992), 86–87.
7. Max Weber, "Die 'Objektivität' sozialwissenschaftlicher und sozialpolitischer Erkenntnis" [The 'objectivity' of knowledge in social science and social policy], in *Collected Methodological Writings* (hereafter *CMW*), ed. H. H. Bruun and S. Whimster, trans. H. H. Bruun (London: Routledge, 2012), 104; *Zur Logik und Methodik der Sozialwissenschaften. Schriften 1900–1907*, ed. G. Wagner with C. Härpfer et al., *MWG* I/7 (Tübingen, Germany: Mohr [Siebeck], 2018), 156.

8. Max Weber, "Bourgeois Democracy in Russia," in *The Russian Revolutions*, trans. and ed. G. C. Wells and P. Baehr (1906; Ithaca, NY: Cornell University Press, 1995), 108–109; *Zur Russischen Revolution von 1905. Schriften und Reden 1905–1912*, ed. W. J. Mommsen with D. Dahlmann. *MWG* I/10 (Tübingen, Germany: Mohr [Siebeck], 1989), 269–272.

9. *PESC*, 182; *MWG* I/18, 488.

10. Max Weber, "Zwischenbetrachtung," in *FMW*, 327–357; *MWG* I/19, 483–520.

11. S. N. Eisenstadt, "The Civilizational Dimension of Modernity: Modernity as a Distinct Civilization," in *Comparative Civilizations and Multiple Modernities* (Leiden, the Netherlands: Brill, 2003), 2:495.

12. Ibid., 499.

13. Ibid., 499.

14. S. N. Eisenstadt, *The Political Systems of Empires* (1963; New Brunswick, NJ: Transaction Publishers, 1993).

15. Eisenstadt, "The Civilizational Dimension in Sociological Analysis," in *Comparative Civilizations*, 1:34.

16. See Max Weber, "Objectivity," in *CMW*, 100–138; *MWG* I/7, 142–234.

17. Max Weber, "Introduction to the Economic Ethics of the World Religions," in *The Essential Weber*, ed. S. Whimster (London: Routledge, 2004), 69; cf. *FMW*, 280; *MWG* I/19, 101.

18. Eisenstadt, "Civilizational Dimension of Modernity," 494.

19. Max Weber, *The Religion of China: Confucianism and Taoism*, trans. and ed. H. H. Gerth (New York: Free Press, 1951), 62; *MWG* I/19, 236.

20. S. N. Eisenstadt, *The Great Revolutions and the Civilizations of Modernity* (Leiden, the Netherlands: Brill, 2005).

21. The most seminal work in this vein is Theda Skocpol, *States and Social Revolutions. A Comparative Analysis of France, Russia and China* (1978; Cambridge: Cambridge University Press, 2015).

22. S. N. Eisenstadt, *Fundamentalism, Sectarianism and Revolution. The Jacobin Dimension of Modernity* (Cambridge: Cambridge University Press, 1999).

23. Eisenstadt, "Civilizational Dimension of Modernity," 502.

24. S. N. Eisenstadt and Wolfgang Schluchter, eds., "Early Modernities," *Daedalus* 127, no. 3 (Summer 1998).

25. S. N. Eisenstadt, "European Expansion and the Civilization of Modernity," in *Expansion and Reaction*, ed. H. L. Wesseling (Leiden, the Netherlands: Leiden University Press, 1978), 167–186.

26. Max Weber, *Wirtschaft und Gesellschaft. Die Wirtschaft und die gesellschaftlichen Ordnungen und Mächte. Nachlaß. Religiöse Gemeinschaften*, ed. H. G. Kippenberg with P. Schilm. *MWG* I/22 (Tübingen, Germany: Mohr [Siebeck], 2001), 189 ("prophetisches Zeitalter"), 266–290 (Intellektuelle); *The Religion of India*, trans. and ed. H. H. Gerth and D. Martindale (New York: Free Press, 1958), 137–143 on intellectuals (hereafter *RI*); *Die Wirtschaftsethik der Weltreligionen. Hinduismus und Buddhismus. Schriften 1916–1920*, ed. H. Schmidt-Glintzer with K.-H. Golzio. *MWG* I/20 (Tübingen, Germany: Mohr [Siebeck], 1998), 224ff.

27. Eisenstadt, *Japanese Civilization*, 396–426.

28. For Metzger's critique, see Thomas A. Metzger, "Eisenstadt's Analysis of the Relations between Modernization and Tradition in China," *American Asian Review* 2 (1984), 1–87.

29. S. N. Eisenstadt, "The First Multiple Modernities: The Civilization of the Americas," in *Comparative Civilizations*, 2:701–722.

30. See Max Weber, "The Protestant Sects and the Spirit of Capitalism," in *FMW*, 302–322; *MWG* I/18, 493–545.

31. Wolfgang Knöbl, *Die Kontingenz der Moderne: Wege in Europa, Asien und Amerika* (Frankfurt am Main, Germany: Campus, 2007).

32. Laurence Whitehead, *Latin America: A New Interpretation* (London: Palgrave, 2006).

33. On this point, see Alain de Vayssière, *Les révolutions d'Amérique latine* (Paris: Points, 2002).

34. See, e.g., Peter H. Smith, "The Search for Legitimacy," in *Caudillos: Dictators in Spanish America*, ed. H. M. Hamill (Norman: University of Oklahoma Press, 1992), 87–96.

35. Eisenstadt, *Japanese Civilization*.

36. Weber, *RI*, 270–282 (on Japan); *MWG* I/20, 432–449.

37. See especially Herman Ooms, *Imperial Politics and Symbolics in Ancient Japan: The Tenmu Dynasty, 650–800* (Honolulu: University of Hawaii Press, 2008).

CHAPTER 28

MAX WEBER AND THE IDEA OF THE OCCIDENT

JOSHUA DERMAN

MAX Weber believed that all scholarly inquiry in the human sciences presupposed a standpoint, a perspective that situated the scholar in a particular time and place. Without some subjective criterion of interest or relevance, he argued, it was impossible to frame a research agenda or even form analytical concepts in the face of the "absolutely infinite multiplicity of events." As he explained in his seminal essay "The 'Objectivity' of Knowledge in Social Science and Social Policy," the investigator's perspective was manifested at the most basic level in the choice of "ideal types," the conceptual tools that formed the basis of all social scientific research. Ideal types presented a simplified model of reality based on maxims or traits of exaggerated consistency, constructed from the vantage point of a limiting case that was subjectively relevant to the investigator. They served as yardsticks for discerning "*the distinctive character* of the reality of the life in which we are placed and which surrounds us" or as building blocks of broader theories. Ideal types and the theories they generated were necessarily "one-sided" since they accentuated features of the world that the investigator found significant as an object of inquiry. But, if properly constructed, they were also unbiased: they excluded any normative judgments about which elements of the phenomena under investigation were desirable or disagreeable. Only then could social science claim to offer the kind of "objective" knowledge that was capable of confirmation by other scholars, even by those who were motivated by very different ideas about what was worth investigating.[1]

There were only a few occasions in Weber's life when he openly expressed the subjective interests that motivated his scholarship. The last instance can be found in the "Prefatory Remarks" to the first volume of his *Collected Essays in the Sociology of Religion*, which he composed in the months before his death.[2] Weber began by articulating the approach that an individualizing science of universal history would invariably adopt in the hands of a modern European scholar:

The child of the modern European cultural world [*Kulturwelt*] will inevitably and justifiably approach problems of universal history from the standpoint of the following problematic: What chain of circumstances led to the appearance in the Occident, and only here, of cultural phenomena which—or so at least we like to think—came to have *universal* significance and validity?[3]

The tasks that Weber set himself—to identify a set of distinctive occidental cultural phenomena and then account for their historical emergence—were consistent with his general understanding of the aims of social science. It now remained for him to define a particular subjective interest, or point of view, that would facilitate the first part of this operation, the identification of uniqueness. Only toward the end of his "Prefatory Remarks" did he spell it out. "The first problem is therefore once again to recognize the *distinctive characteristics* of occidental rationalism," he declared, "and, within this, of modern occidental rationalism, and to explain how it came into being."[4] By investigating occidental cultural phenomena from the perspective of their rationalism, Weber aimed to identify what made them unique. In the last decade of his life, this was an enterprise that he increasingly came to identify with the discipline of sociology. Having established their distinctiveness through the analytical use of ideal types, he then planned to explain how they "came into being," the proper task of the historian.[5]

When Weber spoke about the "European cultural world," his preferred term of reference was the Latinate *Okzident,* or "Occident," a choice that reflected his classical education and his early career as a scholar of Roman and medieval history.[6] He sometimes used the term *Abendland* to refer specifically to the culture of medieval Christian Europe; only on rare occasions did he speak of "the West" (*der Westen*). Though he presented his scholarly perspective as seemingly self-evident, his idea of the Occident, as well as his approach to discerning and accounting for its alleged uniqueness, raise several questions that are central to our understanding of his work and its legacy for the social sciences. What did he think were the distinctive features of the Occident, a concept whose geographical scope, in his hands, encompassed the Mediterranean, western and central Europe, the British Isles, and the Anglo-Saxon settler colonies, from classical antiquity until the present? More specifically, where did he situate his own "modern European cultural world" within the trajectory of occidental development? Did he succeed in expunging normative judgments from his theorization of universal history, or did he import "Eurocentric" biases that distorted the objectivity of his conclusions? Even if one accepts that partial perspectives are intrinsic to the social sciences, must we regard his choice of perspective as inevitable and justifiable, as he assumed we would? At a time when many historians, economists, and sociologists are once again turning to the kinds of macro-historical questions that animated Weber's scholarship, it is worth reflecting on the nature of his comparative project and the kinds of pitfalls and potentials it contains.[7]

Weber's idea of the Occident comprised two main claims. He argued that the Occident had produced a set of unique cultural phenomena of "*universal* significance and validity," whose distinctiveness could be characterized using ideal types that accentuated their type and degree of rationalization. The rise of modern capitalism, one element within this set of unique cultural phenomena, was conditioned by the presence of other elements, he asserted, none of which had indigenously arisen anywhere else in the world. Such sweeping claims are difficult, perhaps impossible to prove or conclusively disprove in their totality, though many scholars have attempted to do so. It must fall to specialists in Near Eastern and Asian history to judge whether Weber's individual claims of cultural uniqueness and causal dependency can be supported on the basis of today's scholarship.[8] Like any scholar in the social sciences, Weber may have been empirically wrong about a great number of things. What I would like to consider here, however, are the ways in which his comparative enterprise might have been wrong-footed from the very beginning. It is worth examining three methodological critiques that have been directed at his attempt to discern the nature of occidental rationalism and to account for its origins, each of which contains valid objections to his approach. All of them take Weber to task for proceeding in a Eurocentric manner that yields a distorted picture of other cultures. The first holds that Weber violated his own principle of value freedom by importing a normative bias into his investigations. The second regards his preoccupation with discerning the uniqueness of the Occident as an impediment to perceiving more fundamental similarities among Eurasian cultures. Finally, the third argues that Weber's use of ideal types, derived largely from occidental experiences, tends to obfuscate the dynamics at work in non-European societies.

Let us begin by considering how Weber framed his problem. Did he mean to say that *only* the Occident had produced any cultural phenomena that were universally significant and valid? The ambiguity of his phrasing makes it possible that he was proposing such a radical claim, but it is not necessary to interpret him in this light, based on what he went on to say. Weber wanted to direct his readers' attention to a particular set of cultural phenomena with "*universal* significance or validity," at least as judged by their apparent ubiquity or attraction at the turn of the twentieth century, and then inquire why *they* emerged in the Occident and nowhere else. These he went on to enumerate in the subsequent pages of his "Prefatory Remarks." They included empirical natural science and the European research university; jurisprudence based on civil or common law models; classical music and its compositional forms of the sonata, symphony, and opera; the use of linear and aerial perspective in the visual arts; specialized, trained officialdom as the core of public and private administration; the state as an impersonal political institution; and modern capitalism as a "rational, capitalist organization of (formally) free labor."[9]

If Weber had wanted to discuss all the European practices with universal significance, he might have included many other phenomena typically associated with "westernization," such as sartorial conventions, cuisine, or pastimes. It was not his intention to be exhaustive. Weber chose the aforementioned set for a particular reason: the character of its elements, and their relationship to each other, could be heuristically analyzed with ideal types that accentuated different types and degrees of "rationalism." Weber acknowledged that rationalization processes—understood generally to mean systematization, abstraction, or quantification in the service of mastering reality—were common to all societies; they could take place in different cultural spheres and for different goals.[10] The particularity of the Occident's cultural phenomena, he argued, could be framed in terms of the types of rationalism or rationalization processes that were peculiar to them. This epiphany may have first occurred to him around 1910 as he conducted investigations into the history of European music.[11]

It is important to appreciate what Weber was *not* interested in explaining. Unlike many historians and social scientists who have offered accounts of the "great divergence," Weber was not trying to understand why European output and living standards had outpaced the rest of the world in recent centuries.[12] Had this question been at the forefront of his mind, one would have expected him to devote more attention to the Industrial Revolution, the obvious motor of many of these quantitative changes. Yet Weber had very little to say about the nature of the Industrial Revolution or why it first took place in Britain.[13] He was fascinated not so much by the measure of modern Europe's wealth and power but rather by what he regarded as its unique cultural formations: its highly bureaucratized and specialized social order, its "demagified" and impersonal way of life, and the premium it placed on calculability and predictability. Without minimizing the revolutionary significance of modern technology or the shift to inorganic sources of energy, Weber portrayed the Industrial Revolution as only one among many factors that had facilitated a social order based on specialization, bureaucracy, and rational bourgeois capitalism. Occidental rationalism as a cultural phenomenon was the explanandum of his sociological inquiries; he did not adduce it to explain something else, such as a divergence in gross national product.

Though Weber referred to occidental rationalism as a singular noun in his "Prefatory Remarks," he in fact discussed a variety of types of premodern rationalization, taking place at different times and in different geographical locations. European harmonic music, linear perspective, and double-entry bookkeeping were products of rationalization in the form of quantification and measurement. Ascetic Protestantism drove the *"rationalization* of the conduct of life in the world" by encouraging believers to suppress their impulses and systematize their moral choices in the service of a transcendent calling; it rationalized the content of Christian religion by rejecting magical practices; it impelled its adherents to submit "the creatural world" to God's will and thus achieve "rational mastery of the world."[14] Early modern occidental rationalism consisted in a variety of types of rule-governed action, none of which were identical but which nonetheless evinced a common emphasis on calculation, measurement, systematicity, and logical ordering.

When it came to the distinctive features of *modern* occidental rationalism, as distinct from occidental rationalism tout court, Weber seemed to portray a unitary process at work. "Our European-American social and economic life is 'rationalized' in a specific way and in a specific sense," he observed.[15] Though he never explicitly identified the form of rationalization specific to contemporary Europe and the United States, his characterization of modern bourgeois capitalism and bureaucracy suggests that "formal rationality" was what he had in mind: a kind of social action based on general rules and procedures that were highly calculable or quantifiable, predictable, and impersonal.[16] Within the European-American condominium of modernity, Weber thought that Europe's entrenched and highly developed public bureaucracies put it in the vanguard position, at least for the time being. As he understood it, the United States in the early twentieth century was still largely governed by amateur administrators as opposed to trained officials with technical expertise. He nonetheless expected that the United States would eventually develop a robust and ubiquitous public administration. As its abundant land and resources became scarcer with the closing of the frontier, its citizens would cease to tolerate the corruption and waste that accompanied a spoils-based distribution of offices. More immediately, the First World War would stimulate the formation of a large American army and civil service, along with a demand for university-educated specialists to serve as professional administrators.[17]

Contrary to the view of many of his contemporaries, who were preoccupied with the extent to which Europe was succumbing to American practices and norms, Weber believed that the tendency of capitalist development under conditions of limited resources, combined with geopolitical pressures, would make the rest of the industrial world increasingly resemble the older and denser societies of Europe.[18] "Inescapable universal bureaucratization" was driving a process whereby "America become[s] 'Europeanized' just as quickly as people say Europe has become Americanized."[19] In this context, Weber's concept of Europe functioned as little more than an empty placeholder. Neither in his political nor in his sociological writings did he develop a substantive notion of what the various nations of modern Europe possessed in common. Instead, the process of "Europeanization" (*Europäisierung*), in the sense of long-term social convergence, meant something much more along the lines of "Germanization." Weber regarded the Prussian army and civil service, along with the German Social Democratic Party, as paradigmatic institutions of modern specialized bureaucracy.[20] Imperial Germany represented for him the epitome of a society in which bureaucratization and specialization had come to predominance in all spheres of economic and political life. "It was…the *Germans* who developed to a virtuoso degree the rational, *bureaucratic* organization of all human associations of rule, on the basis of expertise and the division of labor, whether in factory, army, or state," he claimed. The First World War had only accelerated the bureaucratization of the national economy. Germany's fate would soon befall the entire modern Occident and eventually the rest of the world. "The present World War means above all the victory of this form of life throughout the whole world. It was under way in any case."[21]

Weber's comparative project aimed not only to discern the distinctive features of occidental rationalism in its premodern and contemporary forms but also to causally explain their historical emergence. Yet he never lived to write—or perhaps never wished to write—a comprehensive account of the rise of the Occident. Eight months before his death, he announced that his forthcoming *Collected Essays in the Sociology of Religion* would include "a sketch devoted to the rise of the social singularity of the Occident, i.e., an essay on the development of the European bourgeoisie in antiquity and the Middle Ages"; a volume on "primitive Christianity, Talmudic Judaism, Islam, and Oriental Christianity"; and "a concluding volume [that] will treat the Christianity of the Occident." The "sketch" may have referred to his posthumously published manuscript on the occidental city; in any case, the projected two volumes on occidental Christianity never appeared.[22] As a result, readers who wish to understand Weber's historical account of the "social singularity of the Occident" must engage in a work of reconstruction, drawing on the *Economic Ethics of the World Religions, Economy and Society*, as well as his *General Economic History*, arguably the closest of any of his texts to a conventional narrative account of the development of European institutions.

From these works it is possible to construct a causal explanation for the emergence of one distinctive feature of the modern Occident, bourgeois rational capitalism, in terms of rationalized practices or institutions that were *also* unique to the Occident.[23] Modern capitalism was unique by virtue of its "formal rationality of capital accounting," its ability to calculate profit and loss with a high degree of quantitative accuracy and reliability. The social and economic prerequisites for rational capital accounting included the private disposal of the means of production, managerial freedom, market freedom, industrial mechanization, free labor, freedom of contract, "rational" bookkeeping, separation of the business enterprise from the household budgetary unit, and the commercialization of assets.[24] Weber devoted particular attention to three institutions that he thought had functioned as preconditions for economic rationalism in the Occident: the development of highly predictable and rule-governed forms of law and public administration, and the emergence of a distinctive kind of urban community. Another equally important prerequisite for economic rationalism, he argued, was "the ability and disposition of people in favor of certain kinds of practical, rational *conduct of life*."[25] This vocational ethic, which Weber believed had first emerged among the ascetic Protestants of seventeenth-century Europe, provided the organizing theme of *The Protestant Ethic and the "Spirit" of Capitalism*, the *Economic Ethics of the World Religions*, and the sections on the sociology of religion in *Economy and Society*.

Having considered the framework of Weber's idea of the Occident, let us now turn to some of the most trenchant objections to his approach. Though Weber believed that his comparative sociological project yielded "objective" knowledge, one might question whether he violated his cherished principle of value freedom in the course of setting up his inquiry. The reader does not need to look far in his oeuvre to find statements that portray non-European societies as relatively static or undynamic compared to those of the Occident. His repeated references to the "Chinese ossification" of cultural life, a fate which he hoped the modern Occident would avoid, represent a case in point.[26] Weber's approach to forming ideal types of non-European cultural phenomena contributed greatly toward creating this impression of immutability. By leaping across centuries in search of data to construct his models, he frequently failed to treat Near Eastern or Asian societies with the same attention to periodization that he applied to the Occident. "The implication of not treating historical chronology seriously is that the social structure of Asia is frozen," Bryan S. Turner observes. "For example, in his outline of Islam Weber quotes evidence from the seventh century on the Prophet and the twelfth century on feudalization of land tenure and the nineteenth century on Tunisian law reform. It appears as if evidence from any century is equally germane to the sociology of Islamic stationariness."[27] When we consider this kind of discriminatory treatment, there is a strong case to be made that Weber's comparative project contains an underlying normative bias in favor of the dynamism of the occidental world.

It is another matter to suggest, as the geographer J. M. Blaut has done, that Weber was an unreflective booster of occidental culture, who "held to the typical conceit of his time and place, and class, in thinking that contemporary European capitalism is the culmination of social evolution—if not the end product of evolution, at least its highest achievement thus far."[28] This interpretation is difficult to sustain. The "modern European cultural world," as Weber portrayed it in his writings, rarely appears in an unambiguously favorable light. The famous final sentences of *The Protestant Ethic* depict a society in which "the outward goods of this world gained increasing and finally inescapable power over men, as never before in history," thereby forming a "shell as hard as steel." Within it live those "last men" of European civilization, "specialists without spirit, hedonists without a heart, these nonentities imagine they have attained a stage of humankind never before reached."[29] The ubiquity of modern bureaucracy, which Weber regarded as the hallmark of contemporary European life, threatened to snuff out the remaining sparks of human initiative. "How is it *at all possible* to salvage any remnants of 'individual' freedom of movement *in any sense*, given this all-powerful trend towards bureaucratization?" he wondered in the midst of the First World War.[30] These statements hardly amount to a triumphalist portrait of modern European culture.

Perhaps a more persuasive argument can be made that Weber personally identified with the early modern Atlantic world, where ascetic Protestants "with a calling" generated cultural energies that, in his telling, eventually transformed economy and society.[31] Yet one must keep in mind that Weber wrote *The Protestant Ethic* at a time when he had largely renounced the kind of relentless professional duties that had contributed to his early psychological breakdown. Did he admire the Puritans as vectors of the Promethean energy latent in occidental culture? Or was his interest in them conditioned by their role as unwitting engines of the processes of specialization and professional compulsion that ultimately burdened him? There are no unambiguous answers to these questions. Besides, there is room in his oeuvre to find still other objects of admiration and even emulation. "If we look not only at the content but also at the language, we notice unmistakable signs of sympathy, even identification, in his account of China's and India's intellectual elites," his biographer Joachim Radkau observes. "Evidently he saw the noble educated Confucian as a model for himself, one whose mentality and emotional economy he could comprehend especially well."[32] Weber's self-recognition as a "child of the modern European cultural world" did not preclude the capacity to appreciate the values cultivated by other cultural traditions.

A second major criticism of Weber's comparative project addresses his quest to discern the uniqueness of the Occident. Weber believed that social scientists misinterpreted their calling if they tried to develop laws of historical development or abstract generalities about the human condition. Instead of "aim[ing] at finding 'analogies' and 'parallels,' as is done by those engrossed in the currently fashionable enterprise of constructing general schemes of development," scholars engaged in comparison ought to accomplish "precisely the opposite: to identify and define the individuality of each development, the characteristics which made the one conclude in a manner so different from that of the other."[33] Weber considered it inevitable and justifiable that a modern European social scientist would proceed from this perspective. We might question, however, whether his dogged pursuit of cultural peculiarity invariably foreclosed the possibility of yielding other insights that were equally real and significant. Did Weber's conception of social science as an individualizing discipline generate a kind of empirical myopia, which permitted him to clearly discern the features of only those phenomena that were culturally closest to him but rendered him unable to recognize similarities in more distant societies?

Following in this line of criticism, the anthropologist Jack Goody has argued that an unspoken assumption of the Occident's "'miraculous' Uniqueness" forms the basis of Weber's comparative sociology. In his view, Weber and his followers erroneously drew distinctions that "overemphasized and deepened historically the differences... between the two parts of the Eurasian landmass" and in the process "often overlooked the common heritage of the major societies of that region in the great Near Eastern civilizations."[34] Goody has made it his mission to assemble empirical evidence that challenges these alleged differences. Without formulating the kinds of universal laws of development that Weber regarded as invariably associated with historical analogies, his research program seeks to underscore "the relative unity of the European and Asian continents rather than their differences, a relative unity that began with the Bronze Age Revolution."[35] To disprove the claim that Europeans developed a unique form of rationalism, Goody points to evidence of syllogistic reasoning in ancient Mesopotamian, Buddhist, and Mohist writings and argues that versions of double-entry bookkeeping existed in China. If Chinese society was suffused with magical beliefs that inhibited innovation, as Weber asserted, how did it manage to develop forms of science and technology that exceeded anything found in Europe for many centuries?[36] To undermine Weber's argument that early modern Europeans developed a unique attitude toward professional and economic life, Goody refers to the work of scholars who have claimed to find functional equivalents of the Protestant ethic among merchants in diverse communities in early modern Eurasia. The presence of vocational attitudes in other cultures would mean that either seventeenth-century Europe was not unique in this regard or that these ethics mattered less for social development than Weber thought.[37]

As scholars acquire new empirical knowledge and challenge old certainties, many of the ostensible peculiarities of the Occident may indeed dissolve in comparison; this is one way in which the alleged Eurocentrism of Weber's comparative project might be confirmed and corrected. At the same time, Weber's critics must reckon with the fact that long-term divergence was only one of his scholarly interests. Goody fails to mention a distinctive and crucially important feature of Weber's comparative method: his assumption that many basic cultural institutions, especially political and economic ones, were widely shared by societies whose developmental trajectories ultimately turned out to be very different. Weber believed that the literate societies of premodern Eurasia exhibited powerful similarities. "In the traits relevant for us, the further back one goes in history, the more similar the Chinese and Chinese culture appear to what is found in the Occident," he observed.[38] As a common default state for all economic societies, regardless of time or place, Weber posited the general propensity to act in accordance with the dictates of economic traditionalism:

> At the beginning of all ethics and the economic relations which result, is traditionalism, the sanctity of tradition, the exclusive reliance upon such trade and industry as have come down from the fathers. This traditionalism survives far down into the present; only a human lifetime in the past it was futile to double the wages of an agricultural laborer in Silesia who mowed a certain tract of land on a contract, in the hope of inducing him to increase his exertions. He would simply have reduced by half the work expended because with this half he would have been able to earn twice as much as before [sic]. This general incapacity and indisposition to depart from the beaten paths is the motive for the maintenance of tradition.[39]

According to Weber, traditionalism was able to persist for two main reasons: the recalcitrance of organized groups, who blocked any changes that challenged their power or interests, and the tenacity of magical beliefs, which produced "a deep repugnance to undertaking any change in the established conduct of life because supernatural evils are feared."[40] What was different about the modern Occident, he conjectured, was that it ultimately broke free from this basal state of culture and embarked on a historically unique path of rationalization.

According to a third line of criticism, the underlying error in Weber's comparative project arises not so much from his assumption of occidental uniqueness but rather from his conviction that occidental development constituted a departure from common starting points. An important illustration can be found in a case study of Weber's concept of patriarchalism by the sociologist Gary Hamilton. For Weber, patriarchalism was one of the most basic forms of traditional domination: it was a "primeval" form of rulership, carried out without any administrative staff, representing "the master's authority over his household." Its legitimacy derived from personal loyalty to the master and acquiescence to the force of tradition. Though patriarchalism had functioned as a core element of authority during classical antiquity, most notably in Roman law, its power in the Occident attenuated over time. The universalist claims of the Christian church and the growing power of the state weakened the ties of family and lineage group.[41] In China, however, Weber believed that patriarchalism maintained its strength from ancient times until the present. The "cardinal virtue of filial piety" structured the relations between sons and fathers and between officials and emperor; the "fetters of the sib [viz. clan or lineage group]" continued to exert a restraining force on individual initiative.[42] As Hamilton observes, Weber concluded "not only that China and the ancient societies in the West had similar patriarchies, but also that China, if anything, was more patriarchal and remained that way long after the West left patriarchalism behind."[43]

A major problem for Weber's comparison, Hamilton argues, is that Chinese patriarchalism fails to conform to the logic of his ideal type. The penalties for disobeying the head of the family indeed grew more extreme toward the end of late imperial China, but it is hard to say that patriarchal authority had been bolstered as result. As the duties of family members were increasingly concretized in custom and law, the family's "discretionary power" to determine what constituted a breach of obedience became progressively weaker; the state was now empowered to intervene to uphold norms in cases where the family or lineage group proved unable to do so. The codification of familial duties in late imperial China served the power interests of government administrators and hardly produced the kind of unlimited household authority that Weber associated with both Rome and China.[44] Moreover, the laws that punished violations of filial duties became stricter during an epoch—the Ming and Qing dynasties—when the economic institutions that Weber associated with patriarchalism, such as the manorial household (*oikos*) and the government regulation of the market, dramatically weakened.[45] The authority of the Chinese family was subject to neither the linear development nor the economic affinities that Weber's ideal type presumed.

According to Hamilton, Weber's analysis of Chinese patriarchalism went wrong by trying to assimilate Chinese experiences to an ideal type derived from European cases. Weber based his ideal type of patriarchalism on the kind of historical data that he, a trained historian of classical antiquity, knew best: the position of the master of the household in Roman law. The distinctive feature of Roman patriarchalism was the master's personal power to command obedience. The male family head possessed absolute jurisdiction over his children and successors, his wife and his sons' wives, and household property.[46] While Chinese fathers also possessed considerable authority over their households, Hamilton argues, there was nonetheless a fundamental distinction between the Roman legal concept of *patria potestas* and the Chinese concept of *xiao*, which Weber translated as "filial piety." The former expresses the power of an individual to command within a delimited jurisdiction (i.e., the sphere of the household), whereas the latter signifies the duties defined by a role or set of relationships. Hamilton explains the difference thus:

> With *patria potestas*, a person obeys his father; with *xiao* a person acts like a son. *Patria potestas* defines jurisdictions within which a person can exercise personal discretion, and accordingly defines *relations of authority between people. Xiao* defines roles, and actions and values that go with roles, and accordingly defines a *person's duty to a role.*[47]

Hamilton argues that Weber's insistence on interpreting Chinese patriarchalism in terms of European experiences was symptomatic of a larger blind spot in his comparative sociology: an inability to see how social order could be constructed, or how rationalization could take place, on the basis of "roles and duties" rather than "jurisdiction and wills." Weber failed to understand that China represented "an independent vision of how a society can be put together."[48] He did not recognize the significance of the norms that structured the dynamism of late imperial Chinese society, primarily because they had played a less prominent role in the institutional development of Europe. It was not the courts or the state that provided most of the regulatory framework for commerce in late imperial China but rather urban associations of non-local merchants (*huiguan*), who saw themselves as fulfilling moral roles. These associations established standards for inputs and outputs, settled disputes, disciplined their members, and provided networks of trust that helped regulate commerce.[49] Weber interpreted the ubiquity of merchant associations as symptomatic of "the absence of fixed, publicly recognized, formal and reliable legal foundations for a free and cooperatively regulated organization of industry and commerce, such as is known in the Occident."[50] Whether these associational forms could have promoted the indigenous development of modern capitalism, as he understood it, is an open question. Nonetheless, the rapid growth of private enterprise in China since the late 1970s , oftentimes in the absence of legal protections or robust public institutions to regulate them, suggests that informal networks of trust, such as lineage groups, can play a much more important role in modern economic life than Weber might have imagined.[51]

Weber would have been the last person to be surprised by the fact that later specialists deemed his scholarship in need of revision or reorientation. It was the fate of all empirical knowledge, he believed, to become obsolete with each passing generation. The process of scholarly innovation was driven by an expanding pool of empirical knowledge about the world but also by the advent of new priorities and perspectives, new understandings of the Occident's place in contemporary affairs. His famous "Objectivity" essay anticipated these developments in powerful and evocative language:

> Some sciences are fated to remain eternally youthful, namely all *historical* disciplines: all those that are constantly confronted with new questions by the ever-advancing flow of culture. The very nature of the task of those disciplines implies that *all* ideal-typical constructions are transitory, but that, at the same time, one inevitably needs ever-*new* ones.... In the sciences of human culture, the formation of concepts is dependent on how the problems are configured, and in its turn, this configuration changes with the substance of the culture itself.[52]

For all the immodesty of his grand historical conjectures, Weber's understanding of his own place in the advancement of scholarship was a humble one. He recognized that our idea of the Occident would change over time and that this changing concept had the potential to generate new empirical knowledge and, in turn, revisions to the standpoint that initiated the inquiry. Weber wanted to participate in the process of pushing the social sciences onward—not by uttering the final word, an impossible task, but rather by framing "ever-*new*" concepts and vantage points and encouraging others to do the same. In responding to his invitation, the modern social sciences grow with him and beyond him, just as he hoped they would.

Acknowledgment

I am grateful to Peter Baehr for his comments on an earlier version of this chapter.

Notes

1. Max Weber, "The 'Objectivity' of Knowledge in Social Science and Social Policy," in *Collected Methodological Writings* (hereafter *CMW*), ed. H. H. Bruun and S. Whimster, trans. H. H. Bruun (London: Routledge, 2012), 114, 125; *Zur Logik und Methodik der Sozialwissenschaften. Schriften 1900–1907, Max Weber-Gesamtausgabe* (hereafter *MWG*) I/7, ed. G. Wagner with C. Härpfer et al. (Tübingen, Germany: Mohr [Siebeck], 2018), 175, 224–225. On the use of ideal types as "yardsticks" and explanatory models, see the helpful discussion in Stephen Kalberg, *Max Weber's Comparative-Historical Sociology* (Chicago: University of Chicago Press, 1994), 81–142; and Thomas Burger, *Max Weber's Theory of Concept Formation: History, Laws, and Ideal Types* (Durham, NC: Duke University Press, 1976), 115–179.
2. For an earlier passage in which he enunciates "the standpoint of the *interest of the modern European*," see Max Weber, "The Meaning of 'Value Freedom' in the Sociological and Economic Sciences," in *CMW*, 323; *Verstehende Soziologie und Werturteilsfreiheit. Schriften und Reden 1908–1917, MWG* I/12, ed. J. Weiß with S. Frommer (Tübingen, Germany: Mohr [Siebeck], 2018), 487.
3. Max Weber, "Prefatory Remarks to *Collected Essays in the Sociology of Religion*," in *The Protestant Ethic and the "Spirit" of Capitalism and Other Writings* (hereafter *PEOW*), ed. and trans. Peter Baehr and Gordon C. Wells (New York: Penguin, 2002), 356; *Die protestantische Ethik und der Geist des Kapitalismus/Die protestantischen Sekten und der Geist des Kapitalismus. Schriften 1904–1920, MWG* I/18, ed. W. Schluchter with U. Bube (Tübingen, Germany: Mohr [Siebeck], 2016), 101. I have occasionally modified this translation to make it more literal. Baehr and Wells translate *der Okzident* as "the West" and *Kulturwelt* as "civilization."
4. *PEOW*, 366; *MWG* I/18, 116.
5. For Weber's views on the division of labor between history and sociology, see his letter to the historian Georg von Below, June 21, 1914, quoted in Max Weber, *Economy and Society: An Outline of Interpretive Sociology* (hereafter *E&S*), ed. G. Roth and C. Wittich (Berkeley: University of California Press, 1978), lxiv; *Briefe 1913–1914, MWG* II/8, ed. M. R. Lepsius and W. J. Mommsen with B. Rudhard and M. Schön (Tübingen, Germany: Mohr [Siebeck], 2003), 724.
6. Peter Ghosh, *Max Weber and The Protestant Ethic: Twin Histories* (Oxford: Oxford University Press, 2014), 242–243. "Occident" comes from the Latin *occidens* (the region where the sun sets, i.e., the west); see the verb *occidere*, meaning "to go down, set." In late antiquity the terms *oriens* and *occidens* were associated with the distinctions between (a) the eastern and western divisions of the Roman Empire and (b) the Greek and Latin churches. On the history of these concepts, see Jürgen Fischer, *Oriens—Occidens—Europa: Begriff und Gedanke "Europa" in der späten Antike und im frühen Mittelalter* (Wiesbaden, Germany: Steiner, 1957), 26–39; and H. Hühn, "Westen; Okzident," in *Historisches Wörterbuch der Philosophie*, ed. Joachim Ritter, Karlfried Gründer, and Gottfried Gabriel (Basel, Switzerland: Schwabe, 2005), 12:661–668.
7. For insightful interpretations and surveys of recent scholarship on the "rise of the West," see Jack Goldstone, *Why Europe? The Rise of the West in World History, 1500–1850* (New York: McGraw-Hill, 2009); and Ian Morris, *Why the West Rules—For Now: The Patterns of History, and What They Reveal About the Future* (New York: Farrar, Straus and Giroux, 2010). A critical appraisal of the literature can be found in Peer Vries, "The California

School and Beyond: How to Study the Great Divergence?" *History Compass* 8, no. 7 (2010): 730–751.

8. For a survey of the state of current scholarship, see Thomas C. Ertman, ed., *Max Weber's Economic Ethic of the World Religions: An Analysis* (Cambridge: Cambridge University Press, 2017).

9. Weber, "Prefatory Remarks," *PEOW*, 356–365, quotation on 362; *MWG* I/18, 101–116, 110.

10. *PEOW*, 365–366; *MWG* I/18, 116–117. On the different types of rationality in Weber's work, see Stephen Kalberg, "Max Weber's Types of Rationality: Cornerstones for the Analysis of Rationalization Processes in History," *American Journal of Sociology* 85, no. 5 (1980): 1145–1179.

11. See Marianne Weber, *Max Weber: A Biography*, trans. and ed. Harry Zohn (New Brunswick, NJ: Transaction, 1988), 333–334; and Wolfgang Schluchter, *Rationalism, Religion, and Domination: A Weberian Perspective*, trans. Neil Solomon (Berkeley: University of California Press, 1989), 44–48, 411–432.

12. The term has been popularized by Kenneth Pomeranz, *The Great Divergence: China, Europe, and the Making of the Modern World Economy* (Princeton, NJ: Princeton University Press, 2000).

13. Weber's comments were largely restricted to the hypothesis that ascetic Protestantism had made an important contribution to the Industrial Revolution. While the major discoveries of the scientific revolution largely took place in Catholic countries, he argued, Protestants particularly excelled at applying them for economic and technological purposes. See Max Weber, "The Protestant Ethic and the 'Spirit' of Capitalism," in *PEOW*, 194n285; *Asketischer Protestantismus und Kapitalismus. Schriften und Reden 1904–1911*, *MWG* I/9, ed. W. Schluchter with U. Bube (Tübingen, Germany: Mohr [Siebeck], 2014), 405–406n59; "A Final Rebuttal of Rachfahl's Critique of the 'Spirit of Capitalism,'" in *PEOW*, 317; *MWG* I/9, 738–739; and *General Economic History* (hereafter *GEH*), trans. Frank H. Knight (Mineola, NY: Dover, 2003), 368; *Abriß der universalen Sozial- und Wirtschaftsgeschichte. Mit- und Nachschriften 1919/20*, *MWG* III/6, ed. W. Schluchter with J. Schröder (Tübingen, Germany: Mohr [Siebeck], 2011), 395.

14. Weber, "The Protestant Ethic," 104; *MWG* I/9, 365; *The Religion of China: Confucianism and Taoism* (hereafter *RC*), trans. and ed. Hans H. Gerth (Glencoe, IL: Free Press, 1951), 226, 240, 248; *Die Wirtschaftsethik der Weltreligionen. Konfuzianismus und Taoismus. Schriften 1915–1920*, *MWG* I/19, ed. H. Schmidt-Glintzer with P. Kolonko (Tübingen, Germany: Mohr [Siebeck], 1989), 450, 467, 476.

15. Weber, "The Meaning of 'Value Freedom,'" 325; *MWG* I/12, 492.

16. Weber, *E&S*, 85–86, 107–111, 118, 161–165, 223–226; *Wirtschaft und Gesellschaft. Soziologie*, *MWG* I/23, ed. K. Borchardt, E. Hanke, and W. Schluchter (Tübingen, Germany: Mohr [Siebeck], 2013), 251–252, 285–290, 303, 375–380, 463–468; Weber, "Intermediate Reflection on the Economic Ethics of the World Religions," in *The Essential Weber: A Reader*, ed. Sam Whimster (London: Routledge, 2004), 222; *MWG* I/19, 488. See Wolfgang J. Mommsen, "The Two Dimensions of Change in Max Weber's Sociological Theory," in *The Political and Social Theory of Max Weber* (Chicago: University of Chicago Press, 1989), 161–164; and Rogers Brubaker, *The Limits of Rationality: An Essay on the Social and Moral Thought of Max Weber* (London: Allen & Unwin, 1984), 36–44.

17. Max Weber, "Parliament and Government in Germany under a New Political Order," in *Political Writings* (hereafter *PolW*), ed. Peter Lassman and Ronald Speirs (Cambridge: Cambridge, University Press, 1994), 152; *Zur Politik im Weltkrieg. Schriften und Reden*

1914–1918, MWG I/15, ed. W. J. Mommsen with G. Hübinger (Tübingen, Germany: Mohr [Siebeck], 1984), 457–458; "Socialism," in *PolW*, 276–279; *MWG* I/15, 603–607; "Politics as a Vocation," in *The Vocation Lectures*, ed. David Owen and Tracy B. Strong, trans. Rodney Livingstone (Indianapolis, IN: Hackett, 2004), 44, 69, 71–72; *Wissenschaft als Beruf 1917/1919—Politik als Beruf 1919, MWG* I/17, ed. W. Schluchter and W. J. Mommsen with B. Morgenbrod (Tübingen, Germany: Mohr [Siebeck], 1992), 176, 214–215, 217–218; *E&S*, 971; *Wirtschaft und Gesellschaft. Nachlaß. Herrschaft, MWG* I/22-4, ed. E. Hanke with Th. Kroll (Tübingen, Germany: Mohr [Siebeck], 2005), 181–182. See Claus Offe, *Reflections on America: Tocqueville, Weber and Adorno in the United States*, trans. Patrick Camiller (Cambridge: Polity, 2005), 43–68; and Lawrence A. Scaff, *Max Weber in America* (Princeton, NJ: Princeton University Press, 2011), esp. 188–189.

18. See P. Ghosh, "Max Weber on 'The Rural Community': A Critical Edition of the English Text," *History of European Ideas* 31 (2005): 327–366.

19. Weber, "Socialism," *PolW*, 279; *MWG* I/15, 606–607.

20. Wolfgang J. Mommsen, "'Toward the Iron Cage of Future Serfdom'? On the Methodological Status of Max Weber's Ideal-Typical Concept of Bureaucratization," *Transactions of the Royal Historical Society* 30 (1980): 170–171.

21. Weber, "Parliament and Government," *PolW*, 155; *MWG* I/15, 461. See also "Science as a Vocation," in *The Vocation Lectures*, 24; "Politics as a Vocation," 72; *MWG* I/17, 101–102, 219; *E&S*, 999; *MWG* I/22-4, 230. For a Weber-inspired interpretation of early twentieth-century Germany as the most modern of countries, with all its attendant pathologies, see Detlev J. K. Peukert, *The Weimar Republic: The Crisis of Classical Modernity* (New York: Hill and Wang, 1993).

22. Schluchter, *Rationalism*, 425.

23. See Randall Collins, "Weber's Last Theory of Capitalism: A Systematization," *American Sociological Review* 45, no. 6 (1980): 925–942.

24. *E&S*, 85, 91–92, 161–166; *MWG* I/23, 251, 259–260, 375–382; *GEH*, 276–278; *MWG* III/6, 318–320; "Prefatory Remarks," *PEOW*, 359–366; *MWG* I/18, 106–117.

25. Weber, "Prefatory Remarks," *PEOW*, 366; *MWG* I/18, 116–117.

26. Weber, "Objectivity," *CMW*, 121; *MWG* I/7, 194. See also Weber, "The Protestant Ethic," *PEOW*, 121; *MWG* I/9, 423.

27. Bryan S. Turner, *For Weber: Essays on the Sociology of Fate*, 2nd ed. (London: SAGE, 1996), 278.

28. J. M. Blaut, *Eight Eurocentric Historians* (New York: Guildford Press, 2000), 19.

29. Weber, "The Protestant Ethic," 121; *MWG* I/9, 422–423.

30. Weber, "Parliament and Government," *PolW*, 159; *MWG* I/15, 465–466.

31. See Harvey Goldman, *Max Weber and Thomas Mann: Calling and the Shaping of the Self* (Berkeley: University of California Press, 1988); and Sung Ho Kim, *Max Weber's Politics of Civil Society* (Cambridge: Cambridge University Press, 2004).

32. Joachim Radkau, *Max Weber: A Biography*, trans. Patrick Camiller (Cambridge: Polity, 2009), 198–200, 470.

33. Max Weber, *The Agrarian Sociology of Ancient Civilizations*, trans. R. I. Frank (London: Verso, 1988), 385; *Zur Sozial- und Wirtschaftsgeschichte des Altertums. Schriften und Reden 1893–1908, MWG* I/6, ed. J. Deininger (Tübingen, Germany: Mohr [Siebeck], 2006), 747.

34. Jack Goody, *The East in the West* (Cambridge: Cambridge University Press, 1996), 4, 5.

35. Jack Goody, *The Eurasian Miracle* (Cambridge: Polity, 2010), 1.

36. On Weber's ignorance of the achievements of Chinese science and technology, even as judged by the scholarly standards of his day, see N. Sivin, "Max Weber, Joseph Needham,

Benjamin Nelson: The Question of Chinese Science," in *Civilizations East and West: A Memorial Volume for Benjamin Nelson*, ed. E. V. Walter et al. (Atlantic Highlands, NJ: Humanities Press, 1985), 37–49.

37. Goody, *East in the West*, 22–39, 79–81, 241; *Capitalism and Modernity: The Great Debate* (Cambridge: Polity, 2004), 56, 91. An important study not cited by Goody is Ying-shih Yü, "Business Culture and Chinese Traditions—Toward a Study of the Evolution of Merchant Culture in Chinese History," in *Dynamic Hong Kong: Business & Culture*, ed. Wang Gungwu and Wong Siu-lun (Hong Kong: University of Hong Kong Centre of Asian Studies, 1997), 1–84. For a more skeptical view, see Timothy Brook, "Weber, Mencius, and the History of Chinese Capitalism," *Asian Perspective* 19, no. 1 (1995): 79–97.

38. Weber, *RC*, 231; *MWG* I/19, 455. At the same time, Weber was keen to point out what he believed were important prehistoric differences: the early "pattern of settlement" in Europe, unlike in eastern Asia, continued to involve milk-cattle breeding and thus developed unique forms of communal property based on the mark and the commons. "Nor does one find among East Asians the 'individualism' connected with ownership of herds, with all its consequences." Weber, *Agrarian Sociology*, 37; *MWG* I/6, 321.

39. Weber, *GEH*, 354–355; *MWG* III/6, 384. Weber presumably meant that by working half as much, the laborer could still earn the same amount as before.

40. Weber, *GEH* 355; *MWG* III/6, 384.

41. Weber, *Agrarian Sociology*, 274–275; *MWG* I/6, 615–616; *RC*, 86; *MWG* I/19, 258; *E&S*, 231; *MWG* I/23, 475; *E&S*, 645; *Wirtschaft und Gesellschaft. Nachlaß. Recht, MWG* I/22-3, ed. W. Gephart and S. Hermes (Tübingen, Germany: Mohr [Siebeck], 2010), 282–283; *E&S*, 1006, 1008; *MWG* I/22-4, 247, 252; *E&S*, 1243–1244; *Wirtschaft und Gesellschaft. Nachlaß. Die Stadt, MWG* I/22-5, ed. W. Nippel (Tübingen, Germany: Mohr [Siebeck], 1999), 112–114; *GEH*, 43–50; *MWG* III/6, 134–139.

42. Weber, *E&S*, 1050; *MWG* I/22-4, 333; *RC*, 14, 157, 237; *MWG* I/19, 151–152, 352, 463.

43. Gary G. Hamilton, "Patriarchy, Patrimonialism, and Filial Piety: A Comparison of China and Western Europe," *British Journal of Sociology* 41, no. 1 (1990): 77–104, cf. 83.

44. Gary G. Hamilton, "Patriarchalism in Imperial China and Western Europe: A Revision of Weber's Sociology of Domination," *Theory and Society* 13, no. 3 (1984): 393–425, cf. 418.

45. Hamilton, "Patriarchy," 88–92.

46. Hamilton, "Patriarchalism," 405–409.

47. Ibid., 411.

48. Gary G. Hamilton, "Why No Capitalism in China? Negative Questions in Historical, Comparative Research," in *Max Weber in Asian Studies*, ed. Andreas E. Buss (Leiden, the Netherlands: Brill, 1985), 65–89, cf. 84, 85.

49. Ibid., 72–74, 78–83.

50. Weber, *RC*, 20; *MWG* I/19, 158.

51. Yusheng Peng, "Lineage Networks, Rural Entrepreneurs, and Max Weber," *Research in the Sociology of Work* 15 (2005): 327–355. See Jack Barbalet, *Confucianism and the Chinese Self: Re-Examining Max Weber's China* (Singapore: Palgrave Macmillan, 2017), 41.

52. Weber, "Objectivity," *CMW*, 133, 134; *MWG* I/7, 224, 225.

PART VI

SCIENCE AND
KNOWLEDGE

....

CHAPTER 29

INTELLECTUALS, SCHOLARS, AND THE VALUE OF SCIENCE

....

GANGOLF HÜBINGER

WHEN Max Weber died in June 1920, he left behind an impressive but incomplete body of work. Marianne Weber played the most important role for the first generation that appropriated the vitality in his writings and determined their potential for the future. In 1926 she published the first biography of her husband and informed us of events and conversations about which we otherwise would never have known. She also supplied an account of Weber's great "discovery" that around 1910 gave a new direction to his investigations and until his death formed the core problematic of his work.

Weber identified the "process of rationalization" and a "methodical way of thinking" as the most decisive forces in the Occident from antiquity to modernity. They revealed a historical process of universal significance that had determined all the human orders of life. The rationalization process "moves on several tracks, and its autonomous development encompasses all creations of civilization—the economy, the state, law, science, and art." With this shrewd observation Marianne Weber set the course for studying Weber's thought in the future: "Weber regarded this recognition of the special character of Western *rationalism* and the role it played for Western civilization as one of his most important discoveries."[1]

In this chapter we are interested in Weber's understanding of science as a "cultural construct" having intrinsic value and the decisive part played by the sciences in the "rational mastery of the world."[2] At the center of this interest stand the "intellectuals" as carriers of "the process of intellectualization which we have been undergoing for thousands of years." Weber's own position is always revealed in such an assertion, for he includes himself among the "intellectuals" who allow themselves "to be integrated into this specialized organization, running on *ad infinitum*" and who embrace as their vocation "this intellectualist rationalization, created by science and by scientifically oriented technology."[3]

Which scholars have stood on Weber's shoulders in order to think about science as a vocation and intellectual praxis? As a starting point we should emphasize the special status of Weber's reflections on the complex of "science," "scholars," and "intellectuals"— for nowhere else are life and work so closely connected. Weber always argued from a double perspective: from a universal historical perspective he explicitly assigned "rational science" to the "elements of a specifically *modern* rationalism that were constitutive of Western culture."[4] As a scholar he understood himself as an active participant in this rationalization process and thus engaged in self-critical inquiry into the activity of social scientists and intellectuals. This unusual connection between life and work should receive much closer scrutiny.

Intellectualization and the Formation of Science in Modern Culture

"The fate of our times is characterized by rationalization and intellectualization and, above all, by the 'disenchantment of the world.'"[5] As Weber understood this fact, intellectualization, the growth of a scientific worldview, and reflexive social interpretation of the world belong to the basic processes of the modern. To this day they continue to be the subject of investigation throughout the world.

Weber himself spent his entire life investigating the formation and growth of science, scientism, and scientistic ways of thinking. His view of the intellectuals within the sphere of public debate grew out of this concern, as well as his view of the role of scholars in academic institutions, and above all the achievements that "science as a vocation" could bring in a "godless" world of contradictory value positions, worldviews, and life orientations. In this respect the work and the person are closely bound together. From the standpoint of his intellectualized habitus, Weber critically examined the "intellectuals" as "switchmen" and as carriers of "a systematically rationalized 'image of the world [*Weltbild*].'"[6] From his ethical self-understanding as a scholar, he drew a precise boundary between politics and science: "The politician should and *must* make compromises. But by vocation I am a *scholar*."[7] And his work as a social and cultural scientist proceeded under the question, "What is the *vocation of science* within the total life of humanity? And what is its value?"[8]

What does the value of science consist of? When in November 1917 Weber confronted academic youth in Munich with his speech "Science as a Vocation," the United States had decided to enter the Great War, the Bolsheviks had brought about the Russian Revolution, and in Weber's view the "pseudo-constitutional" political system of the German Kaiserreich had begun to disintegrate. The students demanded spiritual leadership and an answer to the question, "what should we do?" Max Weber's answer has often been cited. In the disenchanted world of rationalism and intellectualism science could not show the "way to true being," the "way to true art," the "way to true nature," the "path to God," or the "way to true happiness."[9] Instead, for human beings living within the modern orders of life it becomes increasingly difficult to ponder the world and consciously take a position toward it. In addition, it is not simply a matter of coming to terms with the internal and lawful autonomy of the heterogeneous orders of life and spheres of value but precisely also a question of acknowledging and wanting to have science as an autonomous value: "scientific truth is only that which *claims* validity for all who *seek* truth."[10]

The value of modern science, as the Weberian sociologist Wolfgang Schluchter has repeatedly emphasized, consists when "properly conceived of insight into factual relationships, along with its demand for clarity and a sense of responsibility."[11] On the one hand, that is less than Weber's audience of 1917 expected for their needs for orientation, for conferring meaning on a shattered world. On the other hand, it demands more, as witnessed in Weber's own time by many theoretical and methodological modes of thought—for a complex modernity would demand a complex social and cultural scientific paradigm, in order to be able to understand and grasp "the reality in which we are placed." Weber endeavored constantly to clarify the value and the powerful capabilities of science, from his programmatic essay of 1904 "The 'Objectivity' of Knowledge in Social Science and Social Policy" to "Science as a Vocation."

There are specific methodological and theoretical demands that confer a fundamental value on science in Weber's sense and allow it to proceed as a self-conscious "science of reality."[12] Methodologically, as a first step, science requires that we analyze "the reality in which we are placed" according to specific "points of view," thereby acknowledging the primacy of the way of looking at a problem for factual knowledge. As a second step, science demands the construction of precise concepts in order comparatively "to understand *the distinctive character* of the reality of the life in which we are placed and which surrounds us—on the one hand: the interrelation and the cultural *significance and importance* of its individual elements as they manifest themselves today; and, on the other: the reasons why the[se elements] historically developed as they did and not otherwise."[13]

The "Weberian paradigm" rests on this theoretical foundation.[14] It demands that the social and cultural sciences grasp three dimensions of the social world in their reciprocal relationships: individual human conduct of life, guided by interests and ideas; social orders of life that are institutionally established; and cultural orientations that are formed symbolically and mediated through communication. The Weberian paradigm offers the historian the opportunity to write the history of contemporary Europe from a global-historical perspective as the history of tension-filled rationalization dynamics in a world of bureaucratized constitutional states, capitalist economic systems, and pluralistic cultural values.

In the twentieth century has a habitus taken shape in the history of science that can be identified as Weberian? What power of attraction does such a habitus possess in comparison with the impressive systems of thought in Marxism and critical theory, logical positivism and empiricism, or structuralism and poststructuralism in their many variations after the cultural turn? How can we track down the presence of Weber's scientific ethos from the twentieth century to the present?

In the sections that follow we can only investigate a few examples of the way in which, following Weber's death, his conception of intellectualization and the growth of scientific knowledge has assisted in shaping various sectors of modern thought—in Germany, in Europe, and increasingly in other parts of the world. Today Weberian intellectuals form a rather small minority in contentious public discourse. But scientific convocations repeatedly served critically to test the "Weberian paradigm" and its usefulness for analyses of the present.[15] In particular, the international academic community used anniversaries of Weber's birth and death to ascertain the validity of his ethos for science.

The Weber Circle before 1933 and the Worldwide Transfer of His Ideas

Talk of a "Max Weber circle" appeared immediately after Weber's death. Emil Lederer, the editor of the *Archiv für Sozialwissenschaft und Sozialpolitik*, the periodical that Weber helped found, characterized the "circle that gathered around the 'Archiv'" as a "circle around Max Weber."[16] In addition to Lederer himself, this included especially the co-editors at the time: Werner Sombart, Edgar Jaffé, Robert Michels, Alfred Weber, and Joseph A. Schumpeter. Shortly thereafter Weber's student, Paul Honigsheim, even proposed expounding a "sociology of the Max Weber Circle."[17]

The decisive characteristic for belonging to this circle was not a particular worldview but rather a rigorous intellectual way of life, or *Lebensführung*. Entry was satisfied by "possession of the spirit" to the point of "tragicomedy."[18] Thus, for Honigsheim the Weber circle formed the decisive opposite to the powerful cultural milieu of the era found in the Stefan George circle: that is, an objectively oriented association committed to systematic scientific thought and a rational conception of the world, as opposed to a subjectively infused community emphasizing religious, mystical, and fraternal bonds. In exemplary fashion the "scientific outlook" had set up the Weber circle and the George circle as opponents. "If one speaks of the Heidelberg of the twenties, this tension between the Max Weber circle and the academic Georgians is probably the most interesting event.... I believe one can say, without overlooking other considerations, that...in this Athens of Germany there was a struggle over the concept of science as either a democratizing science, or a science determined by heroes and a heroic image." Thus, once again in the 1980s did the philosopher of religion Jacob Taubes revive this opposition in describing the Berlin Wissenschaftskolleg founded in 1981.[19]

Emil Lederer, the organizer of the Weber circle, was correct. A history of the "validity" of Weber's understanding of science must take the *Archiv für Sozialwissenschaft und*

Sozialpolitik as its starting point. The *Archiv* placed itself in the service of the "historical and theoretical knowledge of the *general cultural significance of capitalist development*,"[20] a problematic that Weber investigated throughout his life. The most important authors were represented in the *Archiv*, and they also published articles on Weber's questions in the commemorative *Hauptprobleme der Soziologie*, edited by Melchior Palyi in 1923. Similarly, the *Archiv* was the forum for contributors to the *Grundriss der Sozialökonomik*, whose conception Weber himself proposed and for which he drafted *Wirtschaft und Gesellschaft*. The *Grundriss* was published in nine sections between 1914 and 1929, conveying a Weberian spirit. Moreover, the majority of its authors were participants in the Verein für Sozialpolitik, an association in which Weber was actively engaged from 1892 until his death.[21]

The *Archiv* was also the location and starting point for the debate over Weber's scientific theories and philosophy of science. A fundamental theoretical debate over Marx and Kant, which the *Archiv* had already critically promoted before the First World War, affected the young philosopher Karl Löwith in his major *Archiv* essay of 1932, "Max Weber and Karl Marx"—an essay that inaugurated a new theoretical comparison, which persists to this day. For Löwith it was a comparison with an anthropological intent, in which he expressed a preference for Weber's "science of reality" or *Wirklichkeitswissenschaft* over Marx's revolutionary goals. Weber had made the theme of the problematic of the modern world of humanity even more central than Marx. His idea of human "freedom" encouraged him to engage in social science in the sense of "an open system of 'possibilities' " rather than "a closed dogmatism of particularities," such as the "world-formulae" for class struggle.[22]

In the *Archiv* ten years prior to Löwith's essay, Alexander von Schelting had already introduced the debate over Weber's methodology with the full publication of his comprehensive Heidelberg dissertation on the "logical theory of the historical and cultural science of Max Weber."[23] Subsequently, Schelting worked until 1932 at the *Archiv* as Lederer's editorial assistant, having considerable influence on the acceptance and rejection of manuscripts. In addition, his stay in the United States from 1934 to 1939 had great significance for Weber's reputation in the anglophone world. Talcott Parsons had already become acquainted with Schelting earlier in Heidelberg, as he was writing his dissertation "Capitalism in Recent German Literature: Sombart and Weber." The relationship was renewed while Parsons was working on *The Structure of Social Action* (1937), as well as his translations of *The Protestant Ethic and the Spirit of Capitalism* (1930) and *Economy and Society*, part one, which he retitled *The Theory of Social and Economic Organization* (1947). Translations always contribute importantly to a new discourse. For the English-language world Lawrence A. Scaff has described in thorough detail the history of the appropriation of Weber's work as a history of interpretation and selection.[24] Similarly, for Japan Wolfgang Schwentker has published a study with a wealth of material.[25] Thus, already in the 1920s and 1930s Weberian thought was being disseminated in the world beyond Europe, with the United States and Japan staging a true competition over translations.[26]

Raymond Aron and Ralf Dahrendorf: The Committed Observer in the Genealogy of Max Weber

The committed observer (*spectateur engagé*) represents a special type in the history of the intellectuals. This figure was created by Raymond Aron, the French philosopher, sociologist, and political scientist, and proposed as an alternative to the French tradition of the "universal intellectual" as masterfully incorporated in the persona of his rival, Jean-Paul Sartre. In his memoir of 1983, Aron explicitly identified Max Weber as the model for the habitus of the "committed observer." He saw himself "linked to [Weber] by a *Wahlverwandtschaft*, an elective affinity" in three ways: he was struck by Weber's "vision of world history." He affirmed theoretically and in practice Weber's "enlightened perspective on the originality of modern science." And he was inspired by Weber's "reflection on the historical and political condition of mankind."[27] In Weber Aron saw the philosophical seeker after truth in the modern world: "He was looking for a universal truth, in other words a form of knowledge that would be valid for everyone in search of such a truth."[28]

One must recognize this close connection to Weber in order to understand Aron's famous expression of belief, locating his own position in the history of modern intellectuals: "Since I had devoted myself to the role of committed observer, I owed it to myself to bring into the open the relationship between the historian and the man of action, between the knowledge of history-in-the-making and the decisions that a historical being is condemned to make."[29]

In this respect Aron appropriated Weber's maxims regarding the separation between scientific knowledge and political action for use in the ideological conflicts during the second half of the twentieth century. In the French discussions Aron introduced Weber's understanding of science, above all in his *German Sociology* of 1935 where Weber "took up more than one-third of the book,"[30] and he charted a course in opposition to the Parisian mainstream. This occurred in a larger social context, in which with Weber in mind he put forward a new type of intellectual. Within the narrower confines of science, Aron's recovery of German sociology offered an alternative to the dominant Durkheimian school that recognized "as scientific only those disciplines which establish laws."[31] More than anything else, Aron valued in Weber's work "a method that established the freedom of the individual within the realm of science. Weber's theories always have, in fact, this three-fold significance: polemical, methodological and philosophical."[32]

Relying on Weber, Aron adopted the habitus of presenting himself both as a scholar and as a political writer under the sign of the "duality of imperatives." This meant one had to maintain the dual tension between the will "to know the truth, to grasp reality" and the will "to act," as Aron expressed his basic idea of the "committed observer" in a conversation with two Parisian intellectuals on the left.[33] The only person who consistently appropriated this habitus and at the same time turned it into an object of theoretical reflection was Aron's close friend Ralf Dahrendorf. The sociologist, politician, and publicist Dahrendorf, a traveler between German and British culture, shared with Aron the lifelong engagement with Max Weber.

Committed observation of the "*distinctive character* of the reality of the life in which we are placed and which surrounds us"[34] rested on "an inner engagement that the actor cannot match in intensity." A "certain obsession with the thematics of the time" was indispensable. For the intellectual the special demands consisted of coming to terms intellectually with the tension between the stance of the scientific analyst, the diagnosticians and interpreters of the present, and the political actors—in sum, bearing up under the antinomies of observation and intervention. Committed observers are "regularly seated between the stools."[35]

Dahrendorf delivered the commendation when Raymond Aron was awarded the prestigious Goethe Prize of the city of Frankfurt in 1979. Both speakers hardly mentioned Goethe, the prize's namesake, but without hesitation instead gave prominence to Max Weber. Aron admitted "not having studied Montesquieu and Tocqueville seriously," while by contrast "Kant, Marx and Max Weber influenced my education decisively." He saw himself "following in the footsteps of Marx and Weber."[36] In his prior acknowledgments, Ralf Dahrendorf had highlighted Aron's critical distance from Marx and his equally critical appropriation of Weber: "Raymond Aron is the only social scientist of the last decades whose significance can be compared with Max Weber in terms of the range of his interests, the combination of analysis and the passion for action, engagement along with the power of understanding, and the blending of critical indignation and critical reserve."[37] This is a characterization that Dahrendorf would undoubtedly have applied to himself.

Like Aron in France, Dahrendorf also applied Weberian thinking to the social sciences in Britain and Germany. At one of the most stimulating international Weber conferences, convened by Wolfgang J. Mommsen in 1984 at the German Historical Institute in London, Dahrendorf delivered advice for "modern Weberians" in his pointed concluding remarks. Weber taught "how too literal an application of the logic of scientific discovery to things social can become arid." It was "above all the explosive unity of his ambiguities that modern social science should remember." Foremost among them were the "ambiguities of fact and value, science and responsibility." And to learn from Weber's ambiguities meant that "one has to live with these conflicts."[38] From Weber's philosophy of science Dahrendorf adopted the conflict-oriented theoretical outlook on the social world and paved the way for "a seat in the modest pantheon" that he constructed in his book *The Modern Social Conflict*, which he saw as the "summation of my social science." Weber was chosen because, like Aron, he took the "duality of imperatives" as his model. He considered Weber a "straddler, precariously combining in his life scholarship and politics, theory and practice. Weber suffered more than the others from the conflicting demands of these worlds."[39] As a central concept of his social theory Dahrendorf also borrowed the notion of "life chances"

(*Lebenschancen*) from Weber. Together with "life conduct" (*Lebensführung*) and "life orders" (*Lebensordnungen*) the concept has been widely used in advancing Weber's "research program."[40]

Already in 1984 Dahrendorf had hoped for a biography of Weber that would emphasize the "nucleus of power" so characteristic of Weber's intellectual personality, instead of the tendency toward hero worship found in the writings of Marianne Weber and Karl Jaspers.[41] When one considers the biographies published thirty years later by the 150th anniversary of Weber's birth, Jürgen Kaube's life of Weber "between the epochs" comes closest to satisfying this wish. Kaube's biography is written with Weber's scientific thirst for reality in full view. The Weberian "science of reality," or *Wirklichkeitswissenschaft*, assists modern humanity in achieving consciousness of the fact "that every reality contains an infinitude of causal relations, a thousand possible reasons."[42] Science makes the decisive contribution to the "disenchantment" of the world, as a result of which religion is transformed from an opponent of science into an object for its knowledge of the world. If there is an inner meaning to "science as a calling," then it lies in the demagification of the self (*Selbstentzauberung*) of the modern cultural being, or the enlightenment of the self through the critique of illusions, a matter-of-fact view of life, and a "striving for logical consistency." In Kaube's summation, Weber wanted to bind the social and cultural sciences to a specific maxim: "For him their most important contribution to culture was not to solve the problems of life, but rather to combat the falsehoods about life.[43]

HEIDELBERG AND THE "WEBER PARADIGM" IN 1964 AND 2014

Weber's academic home in Heidelberg has seen itself up to the present as the defender of his legacy for international sociology. The fifteenth meeting of the German Sociological Association, held in Heidelberg on the centennial of Weber's birth, can serve as a starting point. It was a prelude down to the present day for numerous international conferences devoted to debating controversies about the validity, achievements, and potential of a Weberian science. At the Heidelberg conference the task was "to discover the significance of Weber's life-work for present-day sociology, for the social sciences in the broader sense of the term, and for the relationship between science and political and social practice, as they appear to us today."[44] Every generation of social scientists seeks its own new answer to this question, from the older conferences in Milwaukee and London to the more recent gatherings in Rome, Mexico City, and Tokyo.

The Heidelberg conference of 1964 has remained exceptional, for here the important opposed directions in the thought of the time clashed with each other, as would no longer be the case subsequently in a scientific landscape that was becoming increasingly pluralistic. For instance, for Ernst Topitsch and Hans Albert and their "critical rationalism" it was a matter of advancing the philosophy of the Vienna circle. Assigned the introductory lecture, Topitsch finished with a eulogy for Weber's scientific ethos: "But what remains typical in this man is the researcher's passion, elemental and yet held in incorruptible control, the passion of the researcher striving for new truths against external and internal opposition—well aware that that which today has to be fought for with Promethean strength, will tomorrow be taken for granted or indeed be out of date. As long as there are men who live by science, they will experience in this way both the limits and the fulfillment of their existence."[45] By contrast, Herbert Marcuse, Max Horkheimer, Theodor W. Adorno, and Jürgen Habermas confronted Weber with their "critical theory" in a reflexive return to Marx and Hegel. For Marcuse, Weber's "bourgeois reason" did not avoid the constraints of capitalist rationality. Against this failure, a critical science had to show the way to escape the shell or "house of bondage," a path which must not be disqualified as a "utopia."[46] Addressing Weber's defense of value-freedom in science, Max Horkheimer found it merely "an expression of his own times."[47] Finally, on the especially contentious topic of "value-freedom and objectivity," Talcott Parsons argued that his structural-functional theory of social action was based on Weber. For Parsons Weber was anything other than obsolete. On the contrary, for him Weber had transcended the old European systems of thought of idealism and Marxism, as well as English utilitarianism, opening the social sciences to a new perspective: "He understood, as hardly any of his contemporaries did, the fact and nature of the break-up of the older system, and he contributed more than any single figure to the outline of a new intellectual orientation which promises to be of constitutive importance in defining the situation for the emerging social world."[48]

What scientific orientation did Weber offer for comprehending the social world? Parsons had asked the right question, and in Heidelberg it became clear how much the famous "positivism dispute" of the time was an extension of the "value judgment dispute" before the First World War, as well as a dispute about Weber. The intellectual dominance of critical theory in combination with Western Marxism led to a situation in which the "ultra-positivist" Weber, as Habermas labeled him in 1963, was ushered to the sidelines about the time of the revolutionary movements of 1968.

From a long-term perspective Weber's thought became increasingly recognized for its capacity to provide orientation for scientific and theoretical inquiry. "Critical rationalism" as represented by Karl Popper and especially Hans Albert distinguished itself with increasing clarity from "logical positivism," and in doing so it adopted Weber's position that empirical investigations always assume a starting point in epistemological perspectives and an ordering of problems in the mind of the investigator. Even in the later work of Jürgen Habermas, Weber was promoted "to the most often cited and most extensively and affirmatively used author."[49]

The Heidelberg conference was a disappointment for those in search of a fundamental reorientation in the social sciences, guided by the spirit of Max Weber, for "in a precise sense scarcely any sociological content entered the discussion."[50] Faced with conflicting accounts of the work, in Germany the rather small circle of Weber scholars set forth two goals aimed at promoting a Weberian conception of science.

First, in order to put the debate on a firm textual foundation, they recognized the need for a complete edition of all of Weber's writings, speeches, lectures, and letters. This marked the origin in the middle of the 1970s of the project to publish a comprehensive historical-critical collected works, the *Max Weber-Gesamtausgabe* (*MWG*). It was not planned, as is often claimed, as a reaction to the *Marx-Engels Gesamtausgabe*, and thus as a continuation of the Cold War through editorial means. The leading idea was instead to present, through Weber, a more compelling analytic conception of the self-understanding of capitalist industrial societies. The founding editors of the *MWG*—Horst Baier, M. Rainer Lepsius, Wolfgang J. Mommsen, Wolfgang Schluchter, and Johannes Winckelmann—acted nevertheless with the conscious intention of presenting a convincing alternative to the varieties of Western Marxism, an alternative that was unable to assert itself during the earlier positivism dispute.[51] The first *MWG* volumes appeared in 1984; a total of forty-seven volumes is projected for completion by 2020, the centennial of Weber's death. The last edited volumes include Weber's methodological writings and philosophy of science.[52] They should give a new impetus to the debate over the paradigmatic status of Weber's way of thinking.

Precisely this was the second goal for all those who cherished the independent value of science in the spirit of Weber, who wanted to promote scientific inquiry and longed to leave the positivism debate behind.[53] Following the great caesura of the 1970s, efforts were devoted to reframing Weber's understanding of science as an epistemological model, a "Weber paradigm." This occurred as naive expectations regarding increasing affluence and rising living standards in the West began to collapse, along with progress-oriented theories of modernization.

A Heidelberg emphasis returned once again with publication of the book *Das Weber-Paradigma* (*The Weber Paradigm*).[54] But what should we understand by "Weber paradigm"? At the beginning of his exposition of basic sociological concepts, the result of lifelong reflections, Weber himself explained why he practiced science in the name of "value freedom" and "objectivity." It was the task of the cultural sciences, sociology among them, both to achieve an "interpretive understanding" of the "subjective meaning" of social action and to be concerned "thereby with a causal explanation of its course and consequences."[55] Thus, the Weber paradigm is composed of hermeneutic-interpretative, typological-comparative, and causal-inferential methods. It is never a matter of historical and philosophical narrative and certainly not a master narrative of "disenchantment" in thrall to "the risky and dangerous process-concept of 'rationalization.'"[56] Instead, Weberian analysis is always a matter of a specific "concatenation" or "combination of circumstances"[57] in open-ended historical situations, whether the subject is economic action under capitalism or engagement with a socialist party.

The most succinct definition of the Weber paradigm has come from M. Rainer Lepsius, whose Weber-accented research was bound together effectively under the heading "interests, ideas and institutions."[58] The paradigm "takes its shape in a certain sense within a tripartite space of sequences of action, structural formations, and complexes of meaning. Each one has an effect on the others, and none is reducible to the others. The constitution of the object of knowledge gives Weberian sociology its inner dynamic, and this dynamic requires a constant examination and testing of the constellations within which social action occurs, coordination of action takes place, and meaning is established. Thus, the complexity in the approach is enormous."[59]

Intellectual competition over Weber can have its own complexity. Heidelberg sociologists have noted with pride that "Max Weber is internationally the most read author of our discipline.... All the work that made him famous was written in Heidelberg."[60] But what kind of recognition can Weber attain in comparison with the rival paradigms of the present day in social and cultural theory? In 2003 Ralf Dahrendorf expressed the hope, with Weber, of putting an end to the "great flight into the clouds, into the world of communication free from domination, into the world of systems."[61] But he had not taken into account the depictions of the world in postmodernism and poststructuralism, dominant not only in France and the United States but also in Germany. Does the return to Weber offer a more adequate understanding of the "crisis of modernity" and the demands of the present? Herein lies what may actually prove to be the crucial test for the "Weber paradigm."

Let us return to our original question: "What is the *vocation of science* within the total life of humanity? What is the value of science?"[62] Weber had raised the question during the monumental crisis of 1917 as the issue of the day became the reordering of Germany, Europe, and the world. In her investigation into the worldwide extension of Weber's work, Edith Hanke has emphasized that intellectuals always turned to Weber when processes of change in their societies intensified political crises. From Russia to China and from Iran to Lebanon such crises enhanced Weber's relevance for "critically addressing radical changes within their own cultures."[63]

This trend has focused attention on "efforts to expound Weber's sociology and develop it further in confrontation with contemporary problems." But according to what scientific ideals should such efforts be guided?[64] Since the 1970s the erosion of "Western modernity" has created a caesura, a radical break. Weber had still understood himself as a "son of modern European civilization" in the singular.[65] Since the 1970s, however, plurality has ruled, with "postmodern" intellectuals paving the way. Macro-sociology now speaks of "multiple modernities," while history makes "multiple globalizations" its field of study.

The shift in perspective has enormous consequences for the "Weber paradigm," especially one that takes as its basic subject matter the universal-historical relations between individual life-conduct (*Lebensführung*) and the social life-orders (*Lebensordnungen*), and seeks to clarify the genesis of the modern life-world and its antinomies. A debate begun once again in Heidelberg suggests two intellectual strategies for deploying the "Weber paradigm."

A large number of scholars borrow particular Weberian concepts and use them in their own empirical investigations. In this manner Weber's concept of charisma can be used to assess neoliberal financial markets, or his understanding of "bureaucratization" can be applied to the European Union. A smaller group of scholars is predominantly oriented toward critical engagement with Weber's historical theory of modernity and his interpretation of "occidental rationalism." In the concluding section let us consider the intellectual potential in these appropriations of Weber.

POSTMODERNISM, MULTIPLE MODERNITIES, AND GLOBAL HISTORIES

Weber's concept of the intellectualization and rationalization of the world through science was always controversial. For some it did not go far enough, whereas for others it was deficient as an expression of European hegemony. For the representatives of critical theory it offered too little, those who like Herbert Marcuse wanted to employ the social sciences politically to advance their emancipatory goals. In opposition, Reinhard Bendix reminded scholars of a necessary basic purpose of Weberian inquiry: "It is relevant to ask whether researchers in the same field possess a common foundation. This is to be found not only in belief in the value of the science.... It is primarily created by the ability of the scholar in questions of formation of concepts and of methods of research to aim at a temporary unity from one case to another, which will make it possible to continue the work."[66]

Such a foundation was much less evident in postmodernism's understanding of science as it celebrated its victory march through the Western academic world during the 1970s. Reduced to its most elemental principles, postmodernism or poststructuralism was characterized by a self-understanding and cultural-analytical view of the world that emphasized the fragmentary, radical plurality, and absolute difference. One of postmodernism's protagonists, Jean-François Lyotard, delivered the programmatic statement in *The Postmodern Condition*, in which he demanded an end to scientific "master narratives."[67] The sciences of the social world possess no higher claim to truth than other forms of knowledge but are only one among many language games. Humankind in the postmodern era must liberate itself from the straightjacket of the rational narratives about civilization in modernity, while "deconstructing" its contents. This amounts to a fundamental repudiation of Weber, particularly evident from the fallout in postcolonial studies.[68]

Postmodern discourse has sensitized us a great deal to the increasing plurality and variety of ways of life in the twentieth century. But its analytic potential has its limits when it comes to new global-historical explanations of the "transformation of the world" since the nineteenth century. The new discourse about the modern, originating in the sphere of global history, shows itself to be closely tied to Max Weber. Thus, in an undeniable paraphrase of Weber, Jürgen Osterhammel underscores the key role of nineteenth-century Europe in the genesis of a global modernity: "But the new thinking, technologies, institutions and 'dispositives' that were supposed to achieve universality over time, and that by 1930 at the latest appeared as a hallmark of global 'modernity,' all came into being in the west in the nineteenth century and began their various global careers from there."[69] Similar references to Weber can be found in the global histories of Christopher Bayly and John Darwin, where it is a matter of looking at scientific, techni-cal, or artistic exports from Europe in a complicated intertwining of transfers from imperial powers and borrowings from local cultures.[70]

In this way Weber remains a central point of reference for the new combination of macro-sociological with global-historical research and for the intellectual controversies over the origin of the "peculiarity" of the modern world. This "peculiarity" is indeed one of the "most important discoveries" that Weber pointedly formulated in the "Preface" to his *Collected Essays in the Sociology of Religion*: it was "a question of the specific and peculiar rationalism of Western culture...hence our first concern [is] to work out and to explain genetically the special peculiarity of Occidental rationalism, and within this field that of the modern Occidental form." As a "son of modern European civilization" he concentrated on nothing so much as the question, "to what combination of circum-stances the fact should be attributed that in Western civilization, and in Western civili-zation only, cultural phenomena have appeared which (as we like to think) lie in a line of development having *universal* significance and value."[71]

All discussions of modernity depart from the hypothesis of a distinctive European "peculiarity" that Weber wanted to keep in view. To be sure, a Weberian "science of real-ity" had to free itself from exegetical "routine patterns of thought always pursuing the same themes,"[72] while orienting itself to new problems and coming to terms with new intellectual challenges. From this perspective I would like to suggest that there are three important approaches to reading Weber with fresh eyes.

Multiple Modernities Instead of "Modern European Civilization"

In 1997 the Israeli sociologist Shmuel N. Eisenstadt delivered the Max Weber lecture in Heidelberg, published with the title "The Varieties of Modernity." The ensuing discus-sion took place under a heading that emphasized plurality even more clearly: multiple modernities.[73] Eisenstadt summed up his life work on the great "Axial civilizations" in China, India, and Europe; compared them with Japan; and investigated their conse-quences for "Western modernity." For this purpose he stood firmly on the shoulders of Max Weber, though recommending "another way of reading Weber's work that is highly significant for the understanding of modernity's variety. To do this one must reflect on his *Collected Essays in the Sociology of Religion* as studies of the inner dynamic of the different major civilizations."[74]

While Weber had presented only asymmetrical comparisons of China and India in order to delineate the world-altering power of sixteenth-century Puritan economic eth-ics, Eisenstadt sought to grasp empirically the two thousand–year-old history of these three "Axial civilizations." He called them Axial civilizations because in the "Axial Age" (Karl Jaspers) between 800 and 200 BCE the sacred and the secular were separated from each other in all three civilizations, although each was completely independent of the others. In large-scale empirical studies Eisenstadt investigated their religious and cultural development, their characteristic rationality, and their distinctive paths to modernity. He contrasted these civilizations with Japan, which did not experience an "Axial Age" and where the emperor's divinity as "heavenly sovereign" (*Tennō*) survived. For Eisenstadt, just as for Weber, the intellectuals play a decisive role in mediating religious ideas and in rationalizing the conduct of life (*Lebensführung*). Eisenstadt intentionally avoids the collective expression "modern civilization" and speaks instead programmatically of "multiple modernities" through history and into the present.

Eisenstadt's erudite work places him within the canon of historical sociology. Viewed critically, however, one can object to his presentation from the inside of religiously grounded developmental paths, hardly affected by external influences, and even in the nineteenth century scarcely acknowledging the interrelationships with European imperialism. Combining comparative history with a shared or "entangled" history of interrelationships belongs to the central methodological task of global history. That combination also provokes a new reading of Weber.

"Occidental Rationalism" and Great Britain's "Great Divergence"

As we have seen in his "Preface" to the *Collected Essays in the Sociology of Religion*, Weber had presented the rationalization of the state and law, of capitalist economic enterprise, and of the exact sciences as a clearly established "peculiarity" of European history that occurred "only here." The claim has encouraged Weberians to differentiate Europe and its achievements in general from the rest of the world. But what has Europe's manifest difference actually accomplished?[75] In the continuing debates over the "great divergence" scholars have tried to interpret more precisely the geographical spaces and the historical periods in which "European categories of thought, forms of scientific inquiry, interpretations of the past, ideas of social order, models of public morality, concepts of crime and justice, and modes of literary expression" led in the "non European world" to an "alarming disparity in knowledge and power."[76] To trace the "great divergence" throughout the world between winners and losers, rich and poor, global historians have proposed to look not at Europe generally but more specifically at the imperialism of Great Britain. They are not interested in following a special or exceptional path up to the Middle Ages, much less into antiquity, but instead want to emphasize the concrete combination of circumstances evident in the nineteenth century. It is the century of Max Weber, and briefly stated, it was the excessive utilization of fossil fuels and the forcible acquisition of colonies that made the "great divergence" possible.

Critical interpreters of Weber's concept of "universal history," like the Italian historian Pietro Rossi, have reacted to this state of affairs. "The exceptional character that Weber ascribed to European development in the course of universal history must be relativized today, and it must be restricted to a particular phase of development," according to Rossi.[77] If one accepts this limitation, then, following Weber, one can certainly pursue the intellectualization of modern culture and its global interconnections in another way: "The historical peculiarity of the Occident consists not in the rationalization process as such, but in the tendency toward domination of the world through scientific knowledge and its technical application."[78]

It would prove beneficial to revisit Weber's intellectual biography once again and to reassess his view of England in light of more recent research developments. England was at the height of its world power as Weber the "would be Englishman" (Guenther Roth) delivered his lectures on political economy and as a capitalism dominated by Britain celebrated its fateful victory march "until the last ton of fossil fuel is burned up."[79] For Weber the combination of Britain's imperial power with a democratic order served intellectually as a model for the future of Germany. The goals of the war that he publicly supported did not include territorial annexations, but he demanded a recognition of Germany's position among the "European world powers," especially by Great Britain. He composed the "Preface" that referred to a distinctive European development "having *universal* significance and value" exactly at the moment when the Treaty of Versailles sealed the fate of European dominance and "the world came to terms with America's new centrality, through the struggle to shape a new order."[80] In his intellectual habitus Weber was more a diagnostician of the times than a macro-level theorist. What fascinated him as a scholar was to be able as concretely as possible to unravel and reconstruct historical change as a "combination of circumstances."

The Contingency of History and the "Combination of Circumstances"

Max Weber made the historical processes of intellectualization and rationalization not simply the subject matter of his investigations. In his intellectualized habitus he actively advanced the "scientifically driven process" of the modern.[81] As an intellectual he experienced his own times as the emergence of a pluralistic and democratic modernity, and he involved himself passionately in its ideological struggles. As a scholar he fought against a science that in the name of Marx promoted social revolutions according to scientific principles or in Darwin's name reduced politics to laws of nature. Instead, following Kant he ascribed an independent value to science and for that purpose worked out a distinctive conception of science. Along with the "critique of concepts" and the "ordering of facts,"[82] his conception rested on the permanent testing of one's own "presuppositions of thought" in order "in the service of clarity" to be able to explain phenomena that "historically developed as they did and not otherwise."[83] That was the central message of "Science as a Vocation."

The impetus for a Weberian science is obvious. The philosopher Dieter Henrich characterized this science as an "empirical science" for "the diagnosis of a situation."[84] That puts in a nutshell what Weber himself called the "combination of circumstances" so as to highlight the contingency of history in face of the infinite "multiplicity" of historical life. Today we speak of historical and social analysis of "constellations." In an insightful essay on the "new global history, Max Weber and the concept of 'multiple modernities,'" the social theorist Wolfgang Knöbl has appealed to Weberians to mine Weber's historical and comparative work "more fruitfully." Considering the many global conflicts underway, global historians and macro-sociologists are being challenged to discover a new way of relating the empirical and the theoretical. In this respect, "it must surely be the Weberians who should feel especially committed to the historical-comparative interests of their master."[85]

Taking on this challenge in Edinburgh in December 2015, a group of "young Weber scholars" formed a "network on Max Weber for the present day." This group with its worldwide connections was convinced that "a number of political and social upheavals since 2008 have again brought questions Weber raised throughout his work to the fore-front of public and scholarly discussion."[86] Both the radical changes in our own time as well as Weber's intellectual problematics and impulses point to the truth in the young Weber scholars' insight.

Translated from the German by Lawrence A. Scaff

Notes

1. Marianne Weber, *Max Weber: A Biography*, trans. Harry Zohn (New Brunswick, NJ: Transaction, 1988), 333 (translation modified); *Max Weber. Ein Lebensbild* (Tübingen, Germany: Mohr Siebeck, 1984), 348–349.
2. Marianne Weber, *Biography*, 333; *Lebensbild*, 348.
3. Max Weber, "Science as a Vocation," in *From Max Weber: Essays in Sociology* (hereafter *FMW*), ed. H. H. Gerth and C. W. Mills (New York: Oxford University Press, 1946), 138–139; *Wissenschaft als Beruf 1917/1919—Politik als Beruf 1919, Max Weber-Gesamtausgabe* (hereafter *MWG*) I/17, ed. W. J. Mommsen and W. Schluchter with B. Morgenbrod (Tübingen, Germany: Mohr [Siebeck], 1992), 86.
4. Max Weber, *The Religion of China: Confucianism and Taoism*, trans. H. H. Gerth (New York: Free Press, 1951), 152 (translation modified); *Die Wirtschaftsethik der Weltreligionen. Konfuzianismus und Taoismus. Schriften 1915–1920, MWG* I/19, ed. H. Schmidt-Glintzer with P. Kolonko (Tübingen, Germany: Mohr [Siebeck], 1989), 345.
5. Weber, "Science as a Vocation," *FMW*, 155; *MWG* I/17, 109.
6. Weber, "The Social Psychology of the World Religions," *FMW*, 280; "Introduction to the Economic Ethics of the World Religions," in *The Essential Weber: A Reader*, ed. Sam Whimster (London: Routledge, 2004), 69; *MWG* I/19, 101.
7. Letter to Carl Petersen, April 14, 1920, in Weber, *Briefe 1918–1920, MWG* II/10, ed. G. Krumeich and M. R. Lepsius with U. Hinz et al. (Tübingen, Germany: Mohr [Siebeck], 2012), 986.
8. Weber, "Science as a Vocation," *FMW*, 140 (translation modified); *MWG* I/17, 88.
9. Weber, "Science as a Vocation," *FMW*, 142–143; *MWG* I/17, 92–93.
10. Max Weber, "The 'Objectivity' of Knowledge in Social Science and Social Policy," in *Collected Methodological Writings* (hereafter *CMW*), ed. H. H. Bruun and S. Whimster, trans. H. H. Bruun (London: Routledge, 2012), 121; *Zur Logik und Methodik der Sozialwissenschaften. Schriften 1900–1907, MWG* I/7, ed. G. Wagner with C. Härpfer et al. (Tübingen, Germany: Mohr [Siebeck], 2018), 193.

11. Wolfgang Schluchter, *Die Entzauberung der Welt. Sechs Studien zu Max Weber* (Tübingen, Germany: Mohr Siebeck, 2009), 14.

12. Weber, "'Objectivity,'" *CMW*, 114; *MWG* I/7, 174.

13. Weber, "'Objectivity,'" *CMW*, 114; *MWG* I/7, 174.

14. See in particular Gert Albert et al., eds., *Das Weber-Paradigma. Studien zur Weiterentwicklung von Max Webers Forschungsprogramm* (Tübingen, Germany: Mohr Siebeck, 2003).

15. Compare Thomas Schwinn and Gert Albert, eds., *Alte Begriffe–Neue Probleme. Max Webers Soziologie im Lichte aktueller Problemstellungen* (Tübingen, Germany: Mohr Siebeck, 2016).

16. Emil Lederer, "Max Weber," *Archiv für Sozialwissenschaft und Sozialpolitik* 48 (1920/21): IV.

17. Paul Honigsheim, "Der Max-Weber-Kreis in Heidelberg," *Kölner Vierteljahrshefte für Soziologie* 5 (1926): 270–287.

18. Ibid., 271.

19. "Elite oder Avantgarde? Jacob Taubes im Gespräch mit Wolfert von Rahden und Norbert Kampferer," *Zeitschrift für Verkehrswissenschaft* 4 (1982): 67.

20. Edgar Jaffé, Werner Sombart, and Max Weber, "Accompanying Remarks," *CMW*, 997 (translation modified); "Geleitwort," *Archiv für Sozialwissenschaft und Sozialpolitik* 19 (1904): V; *MWG* I/7, 130.

21. Melchoir Palyi, ed., *Hauptprobleme der Soziologie. Erinnerungsgabe für Max Weber*, 2 vols (Munich: Duncker & Humblot, 1923): *Grundriss der Sozialökonomik*, 9 Abteilungen (Tübingen, Germany: Mohr Siebeck, 1914–1929). See *MWG* I/7, for Weber's role in founding the *Archiv* (new series), editing the *Grundriss*, and supporting the *Verein für Sozialpolitik*.

22. Karl Löwith, "Max Weber und Karl Marx," *Archiv für Sozialwissenschaft und Sozialpolitik* 67 (1932): 212–214; *Max Weber and Karl Marx*, ed. T. Bottomore and W. Outhwaite, trans. Hans Fantel (London: Allen & Unwin, 1982), 104–106.

23. Alexander von Schelting, "Die logische Theorie der historischen Kulturwissenschaft von Max Weber und im besonderen sein Begriff des Idealtypus," *Archiv für Sozialwissenschaft und Sozialpolitik* 49 (1922): 623–752.

24. Lawrence A. Scaff, *Max Weber in America* (Princeton, NJ: Princeton University Press, 2011), 197–252.

25. Wolfgang Schwentker, *Max Weber in Japan. Eine Untersuchung zur Wirkungsgeschichte 1905–1995* (Tübingen, Germany: Mohr Siebeck, 1998).

26. Edith Hanke, "Max Weber weltweit. Zur Bedeutung eines Klassikers in Zeiten des Umbruchs," in *Europäische Wissenschaftskulturen und politische Ordnungen in der Moderne (1890–1970)*, ed. G. Hübinger (Munich: Oldenbourg, 2014), 285–305, with a statistical summary, 287.

27. Raymond Aron, *Memoirs: Fifty Years of Political Reflection* (New York: Holmes & Meier, 1990), 45.

28. Ibid., 46.

29. Ibid., 79; on the genealogy of the "committed observer" as a type of intellectual, see Gangolf Hübinger, *Engagierte Beobachter der Moderne. Von Max Weber bis Ralf Dahrendorf* (Göttingen, Germany: Wallstein, 2016).

30. Aron, *Memoirs*, 76.

31. Raymond Aron, *German Sociology*, trans. Mary and Thomas Bottomore (New York: Free Press, 1964), 68, and more generally, chapter 3 on Max Weber.

32. Ibid., 69 (translation modified).

33. Raymond Aron, *Der engagierte Beobachter. Gespräche mit Jean-Louis Missika und Dominique Wolton* (Stuttgart, Germany: Klett-Cotta, 1983), 31.

34. Weber, "'Objectivity,'" *CMW*, 114; *MWG* I/7, 174.

35. Ralf Dahrendorf, *Versuchungen der Unfreiheit. Die Intellektuellen in Zeiten der Prüfung* (Munich: Beck, 2006), 68–70.

36. Raymond Aron, "Zeuge und Kritiker des Geschehens," in *Verleihung des Goethepreises der Stadt Frankfurt am Main an Raymond Aron am 28. August 1979 in der Paulskirche* (Frankfurt am Main, Germany: Amt für Wissenschaft und Kunst, 1979), 22–23.

37. Ralf Dahrendorf, "Lebendiger Geist geht von ihm aus," in *Verleihung des Goethepreises*, 11.

38. Ralf Dahrendorf, "Max Weber and Modern Science," in *Max Weber and His Contemporaries*, ed. W. J. Mommsen and J. Osterhammel (London: Allen & Unwin, 1987), 574, 578, 580.

39. Ralf Dahrendorf, *The Modern Social Conflict: An Essay on the Politics of Liberty* (Berkeley: University of California Press, 1990), 54.

40. Ralf Dahrendorf, *Lebenschancen* (Frankfurt am Main, Germany: Suhrkamp, 1979), esp. "Der Begriff der 'Chance' bei Max Weber," 93–106; also Hans-Peter Müller, "Lebensführung. Eine systematische Skizze im Anschluss an Max Webers Forschungsprogramm," in *Alte Begriffe—Neue Probleme*, ed. G. Albert and T. Schwinn (Tübingen, Germany: Mohr Siebeck, 2016), 249–267.

41. Ralf Dahrendorf, "Max Weber and Modern Social Science," in *Max Weber and His Contemporaries*, 580.

42. Jürgen Kaube, *Max Weber. Ein Leben zwischen den Epochen* (Berlin: Rowohlt, 2014), 152.

43. Ibid., 377.

44. Otto Stammer, "Introduction," in *Max Weber and Sociology Today*, ed. O. Stammer, trans. K. Morris (New York: Harper & Row, 1971), 6, a translation of the proceedings of the 1964 German Sociological Association conference.

45. Ernst Topitsch, "Max Weber and Sociology Today," in *Max Weber and Sociology Today*, 25.

46. Herbert Marcuse, "Industrialization and Capitalism," in *Max Weber and Sociology Today*, 151.

47. Max Horkheimer, "Discussion on Value-Freedom and Objectivity," in *Max Weber and Sociology Today*, 52.

48. Talcott Parsons, "Value-Freedom and Objectivity," in *Max Weber and Sociology Today*, 49.

49. Johannes Weiß, "Max Weber und die Kritik der Kritischen Theorie," in *Das Faszinosum Max Weber. Die Geschichte seiner Geltung*, ed. Karl-Ludwig Ay and Knut Borchardt (Constance, Germany: UVK Verlagsgesellschaft, 2006), 310; also Reinhard Neck, ed., *Was bleibt vom Positivismusstreit?* (Frankfurt am Main, Germany: Lang, 2008).

50. A comment by M. Rainer Lepsius, quoted in Guenther Roth, "Heidelberg und Montreal: Zur Geschichte des Weberzentenariums 1964," in *Das Faszinosum Max Weber*, 377. The American Sociological Association met in Montreal in 1964 and devoted a session to Max Weber.

51. Edith Hanke, Gangolf Hübinger, and Wolfgang Schwentker, "The Genesis of the Max Weber-Gesamtausgabe and the Contribution of Wolfgang J. Mommsen," *Max Weber Studies* 12, no. 1 (2012): 59–94.

52. Max Weber, *Zur Logik und Methodik der Sozialwissenschaften. Schriften und Reden 1900–1907*, *MWG* I/7, ed. G. Wagner, and *Verstehende Soziologie und Werturteilsfreiheit. Schriften und Reden 1908–1920*, *MWG* I/12, ed. J. Weiß.

53. Weber's conception of an empirical science free from value judgments is based not only on the proposition "to make possible the 'success' of empirical scientific knowledge under the conditions of a world of antagonistic values." It is also based "on wanting to have 'successful' empirical scientific knowledge. Empirical science should be shielded against the

unresolveable struggle among values, because only in this sense can independent science possess value." Wolfgang Schluchter, *Wertfreiheit und Verantwortungsethik* (Tübingen, Germany: Mohr Siebeck, 1971), 20–21.

54. Albert et al., *Das Weber-Paradigma*, a collection of articles resulting from a colloquium commemorating M. Rainer Lepsius' seventy-fifth and Wolfgang Schluchter's sixty-fifth birthdays.

55. Max Weber, *Economy and Society. An Outline of Interpretive Sociology*, ed. G. Roth and C. Wittich (New York: Bedminster Press, 1968), 4; *Wirtschaft und Gesellschaft. Soziologie. Unvollendet 1919–1920, MWG* I/23, ed. K. Borchardt, E. Hanke, and W. Schluchter (Tübingen, Germany: Mohr [Siebeck], 2013), 149.

56. Hans Joas, *Die Macht des Heiligen. Eine Alternative zur Geschichte der Entzauberung* (Frankfurt am Main, Germany: Suhrkamp 2017), 414.

57. Max Weber, "[Preface]," in *The Protestant Ethic and the Spirit of Capitalism* (hereafter *PESC*), trans. Talcott Parsons (New York: Scribner's, 1958), 13 (translation modified according to the original); "Vorbemerkung," in *Die protestantische Ethik und der Geist des Kapitalismus/ Die protestantische Sekten und der Geist des Kapitalismus. Schriften 1904–1920, MWG* I/18, ed. W. Schluchter with U. Bube (Tübingen, Germany: Mohr [Siebeck], 2016), 101; "It is always substantive problems that must drive inquiry" and must be "considered from a pragmatic point of view," writes Lawrence A. Scaff "Jenseits des heiligen Textes: Max Webers Fragestellung und die Perspektiven für ein weberianisches Denken," *Berliner Journal für Soziologie* 24, no. 4 (2015): 478.

58. M. Rainer Lepsius, *Interessen, Ideen und Institutionen* (Opladen, Germany: Westdeutscher Verlag, 1990).

59. M. Rainer Lepsius, "Eigenart und Potenzial des Weber-Paradigmas," in *Das Weber-Paradigma*, 33.

60. Gert Albert and Thomas Schwinn, "Einleitung," in *Alte Begriffe—Neue Probleme*, 1.

61. Dahrendorf is cited in the foreword to *Das Weber-Paradigma*, VII.

62. Weber, "Science as a Vocation," *FMW*, 140 (translation modified); *MWG* I/17, 88.

63. Edith Hanke, "Max Weber weltweit," 286.

64. Gert Albert and Thomas Schwinn, "Einleitung," in *Alte Begriffe—Neue Probleme*, 5.

65. Weber, "[Preface]", *PESC*, 13 (a more literal translation than Parsons'); *MWG* I/18, 101.

66. Reinhard Bendix, "Discussion on Industrialization and Capitalism," in *Max Weber and Sociology Today*, 156.

67. Jean-François Lyotard, *The Postmodern Condition: A Report on Knowledge*, trans. G. Bennington and B. Massumi (Minneapolis: University of Minnesota Press, 1984).

68. See Andrew Zimmerman, "Decolonizing Weber," *Postcolonial Studies* 9 (2006): 53–79.

69. Jürgen Osterhammel, *The Transformation of the World: A Global History of the Nineteenth Century*, trans. P. Camiller (Princeton, NJ: Princeton University Press, 2014), 44.

70. Christopher Bayly, *The Birth of the Modern World, 1780–1914. Global Connections and Comparisons* (Oxford: Blackwell, 2004); John Darwin, *After Tamerlane: The Rise and Fall of Global Empires, 1400–2000* (London: Penguin, 2008).

71. Weber, "[Preface]", *PESC*, 26, 13; *MWG* I/18, 116, 101; Marianne Weber, *Biography*, 333.

72. Gert Albert and Thomas Schwinn, "Einleitung," in *Alte Begriffe—Neue Probleme*, 6.

73. Shmuel N. Eisenstadt, *Die Vielfalt der Moderne* (Weilerswist, Germany: Velbrück, 2000); and as editor, *Multiple Modernities* (New Brunswick, NJ: Transaction, 2002).

74. Eisenstadt, *Vielfalt*, 12.

75. On this point see Osterhammel, *Transformation of the World*, 650–672; also Geoffrey Ingham, "The Great Divergence: Max Weber and China's 'Missing Links,'" *Max Weber Studies* 15, no. 2 (2015): 160–191.
76. Darwin, *After Tamerlane*, 339.
77. Pietro Rossi, "Universalgeschichte und interkultureller Vergleich," in *Das Weber-Paradigma*, 119.
78. Ibid., 116.
79. *PESC*, 181 (translation modified); *MWG* I/18, 487.
80. Adam Tooze, *The Deluge: The Great War, America and the Remaking of the Global Order, 1916–1931* (New York: Penguin, 2014), 7.
81. Wolfgang Schluchter, "Die Moderne—eine neue Achsen(zeit)kultur?" in *Alte-Begriffe—Neue Probleme*, 200.
82. Weber's understanding of science is vividly described in a letter to Ferdinand Tönnies, February 19, 1909, in Weber, *Briefe 1909–1910, MWG* II/6, ed. M. R. Lepsius and W. J. Mommsen with B. Rudhard and M. Schön (Tübingen, Germany: Mohr [Siebeck], 1994), 63–66.
83. Weber, " 'Objectivity,'" *CMW*, 114; *MWG* I/7, 174.
84. Dieter Henrich, "Discussion on Value-Freedom and Objectivity," in *Max Weber and Sociology Today*, 71.
85. Wolfgang Knöbl, "Die neue Globalgeschichte, Max Weber und das Konzept der 'multiple modernities,'" in *Alte Begriffe—Neue Probleme*, 416–417.
86. Victor Strazzeri, "What Comes Next in the Global Max Weber Reception? Call for Participation in the Young Weber Scholars Network," *Max Weber Studies* 16, no. 1 (2016): 95, 97.

....

CHAPTER 30

THE IRON CAGE IN THE INFORMATION AGE

Bureaucracy as Tangible Manifestation of a Deep Societal Phenomenon

....

JOS C. N. RAADSCHELDERS

M A X Weber observed that people would increasingly live in a society enveloped in an "iron cage" of material desires as well as one that was heavily circumscribed by rules. He believed that in this modern society both goods and rules had become ends in themselves and were produced in and by bureaucratic organizations where the employee was merely part of a large "machine." The future would belong to bureaucratization, and he vigorously expressed his concern about whether democracy would still be possible in light of this inexorable march forward of bureaucratic mechanization.[1] Schumpeter echoed the same sentiment when writing about bureaucracy that "Its expansion is the one certain thing about our future."[2] To many of Weber's and Schumpeter's contemporaries, the great challenge was how to balance democracy and bureaucracy. In the words of Leonard White, author of the first American handbook of public administration in 1926: "The reconciliation of democratic institutions and a professional bureaucracy operating still in the shadows of the spoils system is one of the major perplexities of the future."[3] Today, one cannot but conclude that bureaucracy as a type of organizational structure and personnel system has triumphed in the public, private, and nonprofit sectors. In his ideal type, a heuristic instrument and method for research, Weber listed seventeen characteristics of bureaucracy as an organization and as a personnel system; and these included continuous administrative activity, formal rules and procedures, hierarchical organization of offices, non-ownership of office, personnel appointed on the basis of knowledge and expertise, reward in regular salary and pension in money, and working in a career system.[4] Bureaucracy, though, is mostly identified with the public sector, and some ink has been spilled arguing that the "old bureaucratic order [is] now creaking under the strain of the mighty assault being waged against it" and that the state is being hollowed out by privatization and contracting-out.[5]

What is the role and position of public bureaucracy in contemporary Western, democratic societies? In this chapter I argue that the state, and by extension its bureaucracy, cannot be hollowed out and supplanted by other types of organization such as enterprise governance and network governance, as Considine and Lewis have suggested. Has Weber's worry come true that democracy is marginalized by bureaucratization? Do we still live in an "iron cage," and if so, is it similar to Weber's conception? And to what extent is the iron cage imposed upon us and/or created by us?

These questions and that of bureaucracy's role and position in contemporary Western societies are big questions. Bureaucratization is inevitable in sedentary societies, especially in those that have been subjected to the forces of industrialization, urbanization, and population growth. It is especially in this modern societal context that bureaucracy has been labeled an "iron cage." This concept is Parsons' translation of Weber's *stahlhartes Gehäuse* and has become a highly recognized metaphor for bureaucracy. Translating it as "shell as hard as steel" is correct but is a lot less evocative.[6] The "iron cage" may be less constraining than one would think. Finally, the contemporary relevance of the "iron cage" metaphor will be explored, and it will be illustrated with three examples concerning the economy in society and work.

Bureaucratization Is Inevitable and Necessary in Complex Society

Despite ample evidence that public bureaucracies have been unbelievably successful in delivering a larger range and scope of services than ever before,[7] the stereotype that government is too big and that bureaucracy is too cumbersome endures. One and a half to two centuries of bureaucracy for and by the people is not enough to eradicate the collective memory of millennia of (ab)use of bureaucracy by the elites.

Bureaucracy as dominant type of organization is inevitable in complex societies where people live in sedentary, imagined communities and in close proximity to one another.[8] These imagined communities are no longer shaped by their natural environment in an organic manner, bottom up, and without direction or intention. Instead, people consciously mold and shape society through functional and structural means. In terms of functioning, the public policy making process and the content of policies vary with national culture and traditions. With regard to structuring government, convergence is predominant in two ways.[9] First, all states and governments have circumscribed territorial jurisdictions from the local up to the national level. Today, almost the entire globe is administered space (Antarctica excepted).[10] More important for the purpose of this chapter, second, is to note that all governments, from those in the few remaining city states (e.g., Vatican City, Monaco, San Marino) and the small island states in the

Caribbean and the Pacific to those of large countries, have organized their functions via bureaucracy, a horizontally and vertically differentiated organizational structure that facilitates a more or less clear division of labor.

Why this territorial and bureaucratic structure is inevitable is quite simple. People communicate most effectively in face-to-face, physical communities. Communication becomes much harder, if not impossible, in imagined communities of millions and hundreds of millions of people. It is thus that a system of nested organizations emerges. Organizations are nested in a scalar hierarchy, where the structure of these organizations can partially be understood as a function of their component physical parts at the biological and molecular levels.[11] In a frequently cited article, and focusing on the social levels of organizational nestedness in a scalar hierarchy, Herbert Simon noted that all social systems are nearly decomposable to subsystems, which in turn can be further subdivided. Social systems in that respect are not different from physical–chemical systems. He observed that hierarchical systems will sooner emerge in complex human societies than in small-scale human societies, simply because hierarchy simplifies communication.[12] Furthermore, such hierarchical systems are also a function of increased political control over a territory. That is, the larger the territory to be governed, the more formal political authority has to be partially delegated to the regional and local levels; and that is evidence of the bureaucratization of power.[13]

However, organizations can also be partially understood as being nested in a control heterarchy, functioning in a self-organizing system where the various organizations are unranked vis-à-vis each other but together form the components of social life.[14] One illustration of this can be found in the various functions that cities or towns have in the larger society: one city can be a primary political center, another a primary religious center and a politically secondary center, and yet another a trade/craft center and only a fourth-tier religious center.[15] A second illustration is that in democratic societies formal political power and sovereignty are channeled through and centralized in government (in unitary states in national government, in a federal system shared between federal and subnational governments), but informal political power is shared with other societal associations such as those of religious denominations, labor unions, sports associations—in short, with all sorts of organized interests. Some scholars have argued that the iron cage of bureaucratized politics, that is, a politics where most, if not all, power is concentrated in the state, is undermined by the emergence of active subpolitics.[16] Politics narrowly defined as the concentration of power in the state has in a democratic institutional superstructure always had to deal with politics broadly defined as the associations of people around specific collective interests. While the big civic organizations of the nineteenth century have lost their appeal, the single-issue associations have increased significantly in the past half-century.[17] So, hierarchically structured bureaucracies operate in a heterarchy of bureaucracies, and any organization with more than, say, fifty or a hundred employees operates as a bureaucracy. Thus, bureaucracies are found in the public, nonprofit, and private sectors. As for interest groups, in the effort to influence public policy they also have bureaucratized. They operate in and around that network of bureaucratic organizations and, dependent upon funding and ownership, can be either a nonprofit or a private agent. As for Weber, he analyzed bureaucratic organization (and not particularly interorganizational networks) but did so as part of a much larger interest in what he regarded as one of history's major drivers: the rationalization process affecting politics, economics, and life itself, a process through which people had placed themselves increasingly in an iron cage.

WEBER'S IRON CAGE

To Weber the most obvious development in the Western world was the process of rationalization that touched all aspects of human life (i.e., family life, sexuality, architecture, religion, music, science, politics, capitalism, and organization). In his view, knowledge and beliefs were increasingly commodified: "there are no mysterious incalculable forces that come into play...one can, in principle, master all things by calculation."[18] Rationalization was the process through which people acquired control over social and material life and was a function of the intellectualization and disenchantment of the world and possibly of the Puritan desire of self-discipline and -control. What he called value-rationality (*Wertrationalität*) was matched by purposive or instrumental rationality (*Zweckrationalität*), as expressed by the extent to which individuals work in social, economic, and political systems that are primarily driven by efficiency, calculation, and control.[19] Bureaucracy is without doubt the primary organizational expression of instrumental rationality. In Weber's view bureaucracy's efficiency makes it an inevitable and irreversible phenomenon; it is a "congealed spirit" (*geronnener Geist*) where the lifeless machine is combined with the living machine of bureaucratic organization which is in the

> process of manufacturing the housing of that future serfdom to which, perhaps, men may have to submit powerlessly, just like the slaves in the ancient state of Egypt, *if they consider that the ultimate and only value by which the conduct of their affairs is to be decided is good administration and provision for their needs by officials (that is "good" in the purely technical sense of rational administration).* (italics in original)[20]

In this modern organizational environment that is focused on the calculability of actions, outputs, and outcomes, the individual is but an instrument to be exploited in such a way that the best possible result is achieved. The "iron cage" is mentioned in a much-quoted passage at the end of his *The Protestant Ethic*.[21] Close reading suggests that this metaphor does not simply and only refer to an overpowering temptation of, submission to, and care for external, material goods, a pursuit that placed Bunyan's man in an iron cage, but also to an unprecedented objectification of all aspects of work and life.[22] In the course of the twentieth century the "iron cage" concept increasingly connotes formal organizational structure, an industrial, mechanistic approach to production and action in general, a "cage of bondage," a solid enclosure. The iron cage is then the metaphor for "bureaucracy," "regulatory structure," "rationalized form of action," and "administrative technology" that, through its goal-directedness and purposeful-ness, enables people to deal with some of life's uncertainties.[23]

Law is an element in the "closing of the iron cage."[24] It expands in scope and range and becomes increasingly refined and then not so much as primary law, which is debated in and enacted by a legislature, but in secondary law which is written and issued by admin-istrative agencies.[25] Driven to its extreme, modern law becomes a technically rational machine with the judge operating as an automaton who is expected to apply the law as a technical and intellectual procedure.[26] Just as economic and bureaucratic systems, the legal system operates upon formal rationality; it is merely procedural when taking only unambiguous general characteristics of the facts of a case into regard.[27]

Bureaucratization is global and has permeated society at large.[28] It can even be seen as representing a worldview in which everything functions in a systematic and ratio-nalized manner, where the workplace has been reduced to a series of well-defined activities, where the individual no longer is responsible for the production process from raw beginning (material) to end product,[29] and where people are solely occupied with means rather than tending to ends.[30] The "iron cage" is not just "bureaucracy"; it is life bureaucratized in the sense that people expect predictability in mechanical as well as in personal relations.[31] Weber's critique of bureaucracy culminated in a strongly worded comment at the September 1909 meeting in Vienna of the Verein für Sozialpolitik against the ideas of the *Kathedersozialisten* (the Dutch use the term "salon socialists") that challenges of industrial society could best be solved by a bureaucratic organization populated by experts. He fumed about the possibility that employees would consider themselves as a mere cog in a machine, holding "a small position" and merely striving for a "somewhat larger position."[32]

Some claim that Weber's influence on the sociology of organizations began in a soci-etal context where the pace of change was less punishing.[33] However, people, including scholars, have the tendency to evaluate the pace and scope of change as larger in their own time than what their ancestors experienced in the past.[34] Royston Greenwood and Thomas Lawrence note that the hierarchical type of organizational structure that Weber captured in his ideal type is at odds with the knowledge-based organizational structures we find today.[35] But hierarchy in and of itself does not prohibit, let alone replace, more organic and informal arrangements.[36] In fact, informal arrangements are probably very productive since colleagues can "use" those to work through the organizational challenges and tensions that hierarchy inevitably brings.[37]

Weber may have shuddered at the idea that human beings lived in an "iron cage," but he also recognized that individuals may not experience the "iron cage" as a prison because they accept the rules and expectations on the basis of legal authority.[38] While the metaphor of an "iron cage" is associated with loss of freedom and individual auton-omy, people accept the legality of many public regulations. However, the iron cage metaphor is no longer only associated with limitation of freedom and autonomy (i.e., a prison) but also as a "prerequisite structure," a "playground" for action, as well as a necessary "scaffold for thought."[39] With regard to the notion of "prerequisite structure," the iron cage metaphor is also used to refer to the production of goods and services at an unprecedented scale and with an unparalleled rational and technical efficiency.[40]

The "Iron Cage" Today: Dominant Organizational Structure in Societal Context

Weber hypothesized that bureaucratization was the outcome of three intertwined processes: competition between capitalist firms in the market, the need of the ruler to enhance control over the territory and competition among states, and citizen demand for services and equal protection under the law. These three are still at play, and the organizational structures of public, nonprofit, and private organizations are increasingly similar (cf. institutional isomorphism).[41] Thus, Weber's observation that the future belongs to bureaucratization has certainly come true, but he understood that as an extrapolation of a longue durée rather than as a new phenomenon. What about the "iron cage?" Was that a new phenomenon in Weber's age, and is that concept still helpful when assessing features of and trends in our time?[42]

The Iron Cage in Everyday Life

At the level of day-to-day activity it is abundantly clear that the "iron cage" does not belong to a bygone era, as some scholars have suggested.[43] First, we live in a society where many actions are assessed in terms of their calculability. Performance management and measurement (e.g., new public management) thrive as never before, expressed in scorecards and dashboards, in rankings, and in *public meta-policy*, which is policy that assesses the outputs of other policies. The American Government Performance and Results Act (GPRA) (1993; and the GPRA 2010 Modernization Act) and the Program Assessment Rating Tool (2002) are examples of this type of policy. Performance measures are pervasive in most occupations. For instance, academics annually report publications, citations, and the impact factor of journals in which they have published. In recent years, American scholars have to report the "guesstimated" percentage of authorship of any co-authored pieces! Whether a publication makes a difference in the real world seems less important. Second, we live in a surveillance society surrounded by a "steel web of surveillance,"[44] with cameras at street corners, on police uniforms, and in department stores; with satellites encircling the globe in a dense web of observations; and with companies monitoring our purchasing (e.g., Amazon) and physical activity (e.g., Fitbit) behaviors. Since March of 2017, Internet providers (e.g., AT&T, Verizon, Comcast) in the United States can provide user information directly to companies that mine personal data; restrictions imposed in October of 2016 by the Federal

Communications Commission that aimed at protecting consumer interests are no longer in play.[45] Third, people place themselves increasingly in a "virtual cage" by posting all sorts of information about their lives on Facebook, YouTube, Twitter, and so on, thus, inadvertently, giving others (e.g., marketing businesses) insight into and control over their lives. The National Conference of State Legislatures in the United States actively seeks to prohibit private companies as well as colleges and universities from demanding an individual's Facebook username and password when assessing a job or student application.[46] Public-sector employees should keep in mind that personal emails sent via a public email account are subject to requests under an open information act. This trend toward a society where many things and actions are commodified, standardized, measured, and monitored has been aptly characterized as the "McDonaldization" of society by the sociologist George Ritzer.[47]

The Iron Cage and Decision-Making

At the organizational and decision-making level it is clear that communication technology makes for a rapid-response culture, where people take less and less time to think about what it is that they are texting or emailing. Especially in the public realm, texts and emails may be interpreted as decisions and thus influence responses that may not have been intended or thought through. At the same time, the virtual cage of technology has made public bureaucracy, organization, and management much more transparent, allowing for negotiable and reflexive authority. *Negotiable authority* exists when decisions are considered authoritative on the basis of (1) an open and participative process of interaction, (2) an accessible decision-making arena, and (3) the knowledge that a decision can be changed when the circumstances change.[48] The *reflexive authority* mentioned by Marcel Hoogenboom and Ringo Ossewaarde only concerns the process of interaction and the decision-making arena.[49]

The Iron Cage as Feature of Society at Large

Finally, we should look for major trends in politics, economics, and society. With regard to politics, it must be clear by now that bureaucracy is less a threat and rather a benefit to and guardian of democracy. First, it is a benefit in the sense that public bureaucracies today offer more goods and services to citizens than ever before in history. Second, public bureaucracy is so fragmented into hundreds of thousands of units[50] that it cannot possibly be dominated, let alone abused, by one ruler or by a small elite and is thus quite incapable of overshadowing democracy. Third, we may live in an age where many suggest we have "moved" from government to governance, emphasizing that other societal actors pursue activities and make decisions that have consequences for people and perhaps even for the entire citizenry. Perhaps this is so, but let us not forget that these other societal actors do not have, nor can or should have in a democratic system, the authority to make binding decisions in the name of all citizens and other people (il)legally residing in a country. *Government is the only actor left in contemporary Western and democratic societies that has the authority to make binding decisions on behalf of an entire population.* In that sense the state is not hollowed out, and privatization and contracting-out merely mean that government shifts from being a service provider (the welfare state) to being the regulator and supervisor of services provided by market parties (the enabling and ensuring state).[51] If anything, we ought to consider whether the pendulum has not swung too much to the market when deciding who is to provide services (see the following section, "The 'Iron Cage' in Economic Policy and at Work). Fourth, within a democratic polity, large bureaucracy may very well assure that unilateral actions by political officeholders are not possible, thus avoiding a slide into unconstitutional or even totalitarian actions. At the same time, public bureaucracy may well be able to assure that market-inspired actions by private actors (i.e., corporations) will not harm society.

The "Iron Cage" in Economic Policy and at Work

In real life, examples of the existence of an "iron cage" show that these elements are very much intertwined. This can be illustrated with two examples from, respectively, economic policy and work.

The Iron Cage beyond the Grasp of Many: Deregulation for Rent-Seeking Entrepreneurs

The "iron cage" metaphor is mostly used as a metaphor for bureaucracy and government regulation. All too often this metaphor as well as the concept of bureaucracy are regarded in a negative light. Can there be a positive perspective? Does the "iron cage" of public regulation issued by government actually serve societal, public interests vis-à-vis the interests of private businesses, multinational corporations, and all sorts of interest groups and lobbyists?

In all of history, there have been about thirty years in which the gap between rich and poor narrowed, and the French economist Jean Fourastié labeled these as *Les Trente Glorieuses.*[52] They were glorious because all boats were rising. Everywhere in the Western world, the income inequality gap narrowed significantly. Since the mid- to late 1970s, the situation has reversed because the economy is now run on the principle of maximizing profits. Also, the income of top executives is rising much faster than that of the rank and file, especially in the United States where CEO income is more than three hundred times the median income. People accept and understand income inequality but not to the point that the fruits of economic growth benefit mainly the upper income levels. As early as 1613, the Italian philosopher and mercantilist economist Antonio Serra outlined the secret of economic growth and social well-being: a combination of public spending for education, infrastructure, and technology, together with developing a diversified economy.[53] This is also advocated by some contemporary economists such as Nobel Prize winner Joseph Stiglitz,[54] but it is not guiding policy and is not part of the education of economists in general. In American business schools this type of economic policy is also no longer part of the curriculum, as we learned from the study by sociologist Rakesh Khurana. In the words of Khurana,

> The resulting corporate oligarchy has no role-defined obligation other than to self-interest. The unintended consequences of this revolution, first evident in the anomalies of executive pay in relation to individual and corporate performance first noted in the late 1990s, have since the beginning of the current decade come to include the long string of corporate scandals involving misstated earnings, back-dated stock options, and various exotic variances on such themes that have as their common thread the enrichment of individual executives at the expense of share-holders, employees, and the public trust in the essential integrity and fairness of the system on which democratic capitalism itself depends.[55]

The French economist Thomas Piketty showed recently how the upper centile's share of national income increased less in Europe and Japan than it did in English-speaking countries since 1980. The United States leads the pack: between 1977 and 2007 the richest 10 percent absorbed 75 percent of growth and the richest 1 percent about 60 percent of growth.[56] The consequence of this increasing inequality is virtual stagnation of purchasing power of the lower and middle classes. Since the late 1970s people have seen a very one-sided shift to market-based economics. Whatever happened with Karl Polanyi's observation that the free market can only exist by the grace of public regulatory oversight?[57] A market without oversight becomes an arena where some can plow the profits of their companies into their own pockets rather than invest in their human capital and their companies' technical assets. One can argue that where deregulation reduces government oversight, citizens are placed in an iron cage of the desires dictated by big corporations and legislated by those in public authoritative positions. Indeed, democracy is in jeopardy when private interests manage to "capture" government regulation via financial support of electoral campaigns of political officeholders and where multinational corporations can escape the reach of the territorial state.[58]

In Western democracies market-based approaches appear to drive the economy, in some countries more than in others. This is expressed in a blanket preference for market-based services over government production of services and extends to collective services for which the market-based profit motive is (much) less clear. What short- and long-term profit does society gain when privatizing prisons (as in the United Kingdom and the United States), when advocating private over public education (as in the United States), when opting for health management organizations rather than universal healthcare (again, as in the United States), when privatizing pensions (as in Chile), when privatizing utilities (as in several parts of the United States)? Who gains most from contracting-out and privatization? The citizen or the entrepreneur? There are many examples across the globe where the rationale for privatization can be questioned.[59] As for contracting-out, knowing that this requires an adequate system of public regulatory oversight, what has the taxpayer gained when contract waste and fraud are more common than we like or hear about?[60] Indeed, contracting-out without adequate oversight can well be a threat to democracy.[61] In Western economies the two main drivers of economic growth are ever-increasing profits combined with expanding consumer demand.[62] In such a society it is "imperative to sell more goods, to innovate continually, to stimulate higher and higher levels of consumer demand.... Product lifetimes plummet as durability is designed out of consumer goods and obsolescence is designed in. Quality is sacrificed relentlessly to volume throughput." That the strong materialist desire "even offers some kind of substitute for religious consolation" was already recognized by Bunyan and Weber.[63]

If government and its regulation are regarded as an "iron cage," then let it be said that in the context of a democratic political system this "iron cage" is not just one of restraint. It is also one that establishes and protects the freedom of citizens from manipulation of the democratic process and the market by self-interested private actors. Let's keep in mind that Alexis de Tocqueville's "self-interest properly understood"[64] concerns the notion that advancing common welfare is a precondition for individual well-being. Weber might have liked Tocqueville, for he could then have appreciated that escaping from the "iron cage" is not only possible through aesthetic expression, intellectual pursuit, and erotic experience[65] but also through solidarity with one another as if living in a physical community of people where everyone knows all members.[66]

The Iron Cage at Work for and of the Many: Expectation of Constant Accessibility

As far as deep societal trends are concerned, we live not only in a consumer society but also in an increasingly information-rich and an increasingly fast-communication society; and this is apparent at the workplace as well as in private life. Individuals are reported to be increasingly overwhelmed at the workplace, and this is a function of the hyperconnectedness made possible by technology. As a consequence, people may have and/or take fewer opportunities to step away from their desk or laptop and iPhone to spend some time thinking.[67] It has been suggested that people take or need about twenty-four minutes to return to a task after having allowed themselves to be interrupted by an email.[68] The neuroscientist Daniel Levitin and the science journalist Nicholas Carr report that people who rapidly switch from one task to another often feel exhausted.[69] At the societal level there is an accelerated production and more efficient distribution of information than ever before; and this leads at the organizational level to challenges regarding what information to use, and at the personal level it has led to information overload and thoughtless communication.[70] And technology permits that we work not only at the office but also when away from the office. It is reported that 21 percent of people work daily also outside their workplace, while 59 percent of the population does so occasionally.[71]

"Iron Cage" and "Virtual Cage": Benefit and Risk

The iron cage as John Bunyan used it is different from how Max Weber approached it, and we have seen that the "iron cage" metaphor has been given meanings in the late twentieth century that are different from those of Bunyan and Weber. In the introduction to this chapter several questions were raised to which I now return.

With regard to the role and position of public bureaucracy in contemporary Western democratic societies, it is clear that governments have been able to provide many more services since the late nineteenth century simply because of massive bureaucratization, a process that, with regard to government, refers to (1) the dominance of bureaucracy as organizational type, (2) the vastly increased standardization of organizational actions and services, and (3) the professionalization of the civil service (with manual functions at the national level generally contracted out or privatized), Keep in mind, though, that bureaucracy in this day and age is the organizational type that dominates in the public, the private, and the nonprofit sectors. We may not think of Microsoft, Boeing, United Airlines, WalMart, Target, the Red Cross, and Boy and Girl Scouts of America as bureaucracies; but they are.

Has Weber's worry come true that democracy is marginalized by bureaucratization?

Bureaucracy and the "iron cage" are tangible manifestations of rationalization, and were Weber able to look around today he might see that bureaucratization has become even more pervasive as the standard structure for any organization. He would also find that public bureaucracy has not overpowered democracy in Western countries. Instead, bureaucracy has proven to be a great support to democracy. Democracy and its elected legislators cannot make decisions or policies without the expert input of so-called policy bureaucrats.[72] Now, we do not usually "see" those policy bureaucrats, but we do see all those street-level bureaucrats, that is, public servants who interact with citizens on a daily basis.[73] They include public school teachers, trash collectors, judges, police officers, social workers, the people who mow the grass in the parks and make sure the playgrounds are safe, the people working in the water management plant, etc. The threat to democracy does not come from bureaucracy but from self-interested private parties, be they corporate businesses or lobbying interest groups.

Do we still live in an "iron cage," and if so, is it similar to Weber's conception? Weber would see not only that we live in an "iron cage" of material desires and (bureaucratic) rules to a far larger degree than a century ago but also that these bureaucratic rules are a product of rationalization in terms of people seeking larger control over social and material life. Weber would also see that people have created a "virtual cage" of almost constant monitoring and targeting of people and almost continuous messaging by people. Clearly, this virtual cage is also a product of rationalization, which is a function of the scientific research that produced new technologies of communication. In this case, "rationalization" refers to science conducted according to accepted methods and within an existing and explicit framework of reference. People are thus not simply victims but also creators of "cages"; we experience them as imposed but must recognize that we make them as well. The various manifestations of an "iron cage," whether it is regulation, science, logical thought, or literally making oneself "visible" in a virtual cage, are artificial, that is, created by humans. Some of these manifestations can only be influenced by the few, such as deregulation that benefits private businesses or the planned obsolescence of products in order to generate consumer demand.[74] Other manifestations, though, are within the grasp of people at large, namely the extent to which they allow email to drive the structure of the workday, the extent to which they respond to work-related emails outside of the workday, and the extent to which they make their personal lives public knowledge.

Rationalization as a societal trend is most visible in this incessant drive for quantifying as much as is possible. It invites rent-seeking behavior, and these rents are not just in money (as the rent that property owners receive from their tenants) but also in numbers and rankings that testify to the extent and reach of an individual's or organization's activities. It is also visible in the pursuit of personal monetary and/or power gains in the public, nonprofit, and private worlds. With regard to the organizational world, the introduction of rankings of organizations and individuals has led to a decline in the exchange of best practices. Why would an organization or individual share the "secrets" of success when that could result in a drop in the rankings next year? Why would an employee not open unauthorized bank accounts, when the number of accounts opened will determine the size of the end-of-year bonus (e.g., Wells Fargo)? Why not manipulate economic policy at home and abroad when such is "allowed" because of limited regulatory oversight?

Finally, can we escape the "iron cage" of public bureaucracy and government regulation? The answer is unambiguous: we cannot and, more importantly, we should not want to. The time that people lived in small physical communities of thirty to fifty individuals is long past. Instead, we live in imagined communities of people, where we only know a few others well enough to trust them. In these imagined communities, it is government through which society is regulated. Ideally, and mainly in democratic political systems, a fair degree of local self-government is possible, not just allowed but actually encouraged. And it is in democratic political systems that bureaucracy is not the handmaiden to those in power but actually the agent that performs and provides many tasks, functions, and services to the people. As far back as the early nineteenth century, Georg Friedrich Wilhelm Hegel wrote about bureaucrats as the new guardians of democracy who forgo "the selfish and capricious satisfaction of their subjective ends" and serve in a "dispassionate, upright, and polite demeanor."[75] Without the "iron cage" of government oversight, there is a serious danger that the freedoms gained since the American and

French Revolutions are eroded by private interests. We may not always like it, but in democracies we cannot live without the "iron cage" of bureaucracy and government regulation. Keep in mind that bureaucracy is merely a type of organizational structure that has been put to benevolent use in the context of democratic political systems, serving and advancing the interests of citizens. In the hands of totalitarian political systems bureaucracy simply is and will continue, as it has through most of history, to serve only as an instrument (ab)used by those in power for their own ends only.

NOTES

1. In Weber's phrases, "The future belongs to bureaucratisation" because of the "unstoppable advance of bureaucratic mechanization." Max Weber, "Parliament and Government in Germany under a New Political Order," in *Political Writings* (hereafter *PolW*), ed. P. Lassman and R. Speirs (Cambridge: Cambridge University Press, 1994), 130–271, 156; *Zur Politik im Weltkrieg. Schriften und Reden 1914–1918, Max Weber-Gesamtausgabe* (hereafter *MWG*) I/15, ed. W. J. Mommsen with G. Hübinger (Tübingen, Germany: Mohr [Siebeck], 1984), 432–596, 462; and "Die wirtschaftlichen Unternehmungen der Gemeinden. Diskussionsbeitrag auf der Generalversammlung des Vereins für Sozialpolitik am 28. September 1909," in *Wirtschaft, Staat und Sozialpolitik. Schriften und Reden 1900–1912, MWG* I/8, ed. W. Schluchter with P. Kurth and B. Morgenbrod (Tübingen, Germany: Mohr [Siebeck], 1998), 360–366, 361.
2. Joseph A. Schumpeter, *Capitalism, Socialism and Democracy*, 3rd ed. (New York: Harper & Row, 1950), 294.
3. Leonard D. White, *Trends in Public Administration* (New York: McGraw-Hill, 1933), 20.
4. Max Weber, *Economy and Society*, ed. G. Roth and C. Wittich (Berkeley: University of California Press, 1978), 217–226; *Wirtschaft und Gesellschaft. Soziologie. Unvollendet 1919–1920, MWG* I/23, ed. K. Borchardt, E. Hanke, and W. Schluchter (Tübingen, Germany: Mohr [Siebeck], 2013), 455–468; these were expanded to twenty by A. van Braam, "Bureaucratiseringsgraad van het plaatselijk bestuur van Westzaandam ten tijde van de Republiek," *Tijdschrift voor de Geschiedenis* 90 (1977): 459; translated in Jos C. N. Raadschelders and Mark R. Rutgers, "The Evolution of Civil Service Systems," in *Civil Service Systems in Comparative Perspective*, ed. H. Bekke et al. (Bloomington: Indiana University Press, 1996), 92.
5. Mark Considine and Jennifer M. Lewis, "Governance at the Ground Level: The Frontline Bureaucrat in the Age of Markets and Networks," *Public Administration Review* 59, no. 6 (1999): 467–480; see also Mark Considine and Jennifer M. Lewis, "Bureaucracy, Network, or Enterprise? Comparing Models of Governance in Australia, Britain, the Netherlands, and New Zealand," *Public Administration Review* 63, no. 2 (2003): 131; Bob Jessop, "Towards a Schumpeterian Workfare State? Preliminary Remarks on Post-Fordist Political Economy," *Studies in Political Economy* 40, no. 1 (1993): 10; Brent H. Milward and Keith G. Provan, "Governing the Hollow State," *Journal of Public Administration Research and Theory* 10, no. 2 (2000): 359–379; Larry J. Ray and Michael Reed, "Weber, Organizations and Modernity: An Introduction," in *Organizing Modernity. New Weberian Perspectives on Work, Organization and Society*, ed. L. J. Ray and M. Reed (London: Routledge, 1994), 7.
6. Peter Baehr, "The 'Iron Cage' and the 'Shell as Hard as Steel': Parsons, Weber, and the stahlhartes Gehäuse metaphor in The Protestant Ethic and the Spirit of Capitalism," *History and*

Theory 40, no. 2 (2001): 153; Gordon C. Wells, "Issues of Language and Translation in Max Weber's Protestant Ethic Writings," *Max Weber Studies* 2, no. 1 (2001): 36. John Bunyan describes a man in an iron cage for having indulged himself with the lusts, pleasures, and profits of this world: "Interpreter: [he] took [Christian] by the hand, and led him into a very dark Room, where sat a man in an Iron Cage.... Christian: For what did you bring yourself into this condition?... Man: For the lusts, pleasures, and profits of this world" (Bunyan, *The Pilgrim's Progress* [New York: W. W. Norton, 2009], 29–30). Weber mentions Bunyan several times in *The Protestant Ethic*, and it could be that Talcott Parsons chose to use the image since it was so well known among English Puritans. Parsons' recollection of his translation choice is ambivalent: see Baehr, "The 'Iron Cage,' " 158.

7. Charles T. Goodsell, *The New Case for Bureaucracy* (Los Angeles: CQ Press, 2015); Paul C. Light, *Government's Greatest Achievements. From Civil Rights to Homeland Security* (Washington, DC: Brookings Institution, 2002); Max Neiman, *Defending Government: Why Big Government Works* (Englewood Cliffs, NJ: Prentice Hall, 2000).

8. The term "artificial societies" is coined by Bertrand Russell, *The Scientific Outlook* (New York: W. W. Norton, 1962), chap. 12; the term "imagined communities" by Benedict Anderson, *Imagined Communities. Reflections on the Origins and Spread of Nationalism* (New York: Verso, 2006).

9. Jos C. N. Raadschelders and Eran Vigoda-Gadot, *Global Dimensions of Public Administration and Governance: A Comparative Voyage* (San Francisco: Jossey-Bass/Wiley, 2015), chaps. 2 and 3.

10. James C. Scott, *The Art of Not Being Governed. An Anarchist History of Upland Southeast Asia* (New Haven, CT: Yale University Press, 2009).

11. Rupert Riedl, "Über die Biologie des Ursachen-Denkens: Ein evolutionistischer, system-theoretischer Versuch," in *Mannheimer Forum—Ein Panorama der Naturwissenschaften*, ed. H. von Ditfurth (Mannheim, Germany: Boehringer, 1978–1979), 9–70; for brief discussion of Riedl, see Jos C. N. Raadschelders, *Public Administration: The Interdisciplinary Study of Government* (Oxford: Oxford University Press, 2011), 51.

12. Herbert A Simon, "The Architecture of Complexity," *Proceedings of the American Philosophical Society* 106, no. 6 (1962): 468, 475.

13. Charles S. Spencer, "Territorial Expansion and Primary State Formation," *Proceedings of the National Academy of Sciences* 107, no. 16 (2010): 7125; and "A Mathematical Model of Primary State Formation," *Cultural Dynamics* 10, no. 1 (1998): 6.

14. Carole L. Crumley, "Heterarchy and the Analysis of Complex Societies," *Archeological Papers of the American Anthropological Association* 6, no. 1 (1995): 3.

15. Joyce Marcus and Gary M. Feinman, "Introduction," in *Archaic States*, ed. G. M. Feinman and J. Marcus (Santa Fe, NM: School of American Research Press, 1998), 11.

16. Boris Holzer and Mads P. Sørensen, "Rethinking Subpolitics. Beyond the 'Iron Cage' of Modern Politics?" *Theory, Culture & Society* 20, no. 2 (2003): 95.

17. Robert Putnam, *Bowling Alone: The Collapse and Revival of American Community* (New York: Simon and Schuster, 2000); Theda Skocpol, *Diminished Democracy: From Membership to Management in American Civic Life* (Norman: University of Oklahoma Press, 2003).

18. Max Weber, "Science as a Vocation," *From Max Weber: Essays in Sociology*, ed. H. H. Gerth and C. W. Mills (Oxford: Oxford University Press, 1946), 139; *Wissenschaft als Beruf 1917/1919—Politik als Beruf 1919*, M WG I/17, ed. W. J. Mommsen and W. Schluchter with B. Morgenbrod (Tübingen, Germany: Mohr [Siebeck], 1992), 71–111, 87.

19. Stewart R. Clegg, "Puritans, Visionaries and Survivors," *Organization Studies* 26, no. 4 (2005): 533; Terry Maley, "Max Weber and the Iron Cage of Technology," *Bulletin of Science, Technology & Society* 24, no. 1 (2004): 70.

20. Weber, "Parliament and Government," in *PolW*, 158; *MWG* I/15, 464.

21. Weber, *The Protestant Ethic and the Spirit of Capitalism*, trans. Talcott Parsons (New York: Scribner's, 1958), 181; *Die protestantische Ethik und der Geist des Kapitalismus/Die protestantischen Sekten und der Geist des Kapitalismus. Schriften 1904–1920*, *MWG* I/18, ed. W. Schluchter with U. Bube (Tübingen, Germany: Mohr [Siebeck], 2016), 487.

22. David Chalcraft, "Bringing the Text Back In: On Ways of Reading the Iron Cage Metaphor in the Two Editions of *The Protestant Ethic*," in *Organizing Modernity: New Weberian Perspectives on Work, Organization and Society*, ed. L. J. Ray and M. Reed (London: Routledge, 1994), 26–27; Lawrence A. Scaff, "Fleeing the Iron Cage: Politics and Culture in the Thought of Max Weber," *American Political Science Review* 81, no. 3 (1987): 741.

23. See Asok Sen, "Weber, Gramsci and Capitalism," *Social Scientist* 13, no. 1 (1987): 8; Stephen A. Kent, "Weber, Goethe, and the Nietzschean Allusion: Capturing the Source of the 'Iron Cage' Metaphor," *Sociological Analysis* 44, no. 4 (1983): 300; Stewart R. Clegg, "Max Weber and Contemporary Sociology of Organizations," in *Organizing Modernity: New Weberian Perspectives on Work, Organization and Society*, ed. L. J. Ray and M. Reed (London: Routledge, 1994), 53–54.

24. P. Devereaux Jennings et al., "Weber and Legal Rule Evolution: The Closing of the Iron Cage?" *Organization Studies* 26, no. 4 (2005): 621.

25. Jos C. N. Raadschelders, "The United States of America as *Rechtsstaat*: State and Administrative Law as Key to Understanding the Administrative State," *Public Administration Review* 77, no. 3 (2017): 458–465.

26. Peter Ghosh, *Max Weber and The Protestant Ethic: Twin Histories* (Oxford: Oxford University Press, 2014), 121.

27. Jon Elster, "Rationality, Economy, and Society," in *The Cambridge Companion to Weber*, ed. S. P. Turner (Cambridge: Cambridge University Press, 2000), 22.

28. Henry Jacoby, *The Bureaucratization of the World* (Berkeley: University of California Press, 1976); Larry J. Ray and Michael Reed, "Max Weber and the Dilemmas of Modernity," in *Organizing Modernity*, 167.

29. Joshua Derman, *Max Weber in Politics and Social Thought: From Charisma to Canonization* (Cambridge: Cambridge University Press, 2016), 69, 98.

30. Zygmunt Bauman, *Liquid Modernity* (Cambridge: Polity Press, 2000), 59.

31. Alan Sica, *Max Weber and the New Century* (New Brunswick, NJ: Transaction, 2004), 139.

32. Weber, "Die wirtschaftlichen Unternehmungen der Gemeinden," *MWG* I/8, 363; also discussed in Derman, *Max Weber in Politics*, 51; see also comments on Weber's critique of bureaucracy in Lawrence A. Scaff, *Weber and the Weberians* (London: Palgrave Macmillan, 2014), 108.

33. Royston Greenwood and Thomas B. Lawrence, "The Iron Cage in the Information Age: The Legacy and Relevance of Max Weber for Organization Studies," *Organization Studies* 26, no. 4 (2005): 494.

34. Jos C. N. Raadschelders and Marie-Louise Bemelmans-Videc, "Political (System) Reform: Can Administrative Reform Succeed Without?" in *The Civil Service in the 21st Century: Comparative Perspectives*, ed. Jos C. N. Raadschelders, Theo A. J. Toonen, and Frits M. Van der Meer (Basingstoke, UK: Palgrave Macmillan, 2015), 334–335.

35. Greenwood and Lawrence, "The Iron Cage," 495.

36. Catherine L. Wang and Pervaiz K. Ahmed, "Structure and Structural Dimensions for Knowledge-Based Organizations," *Measuring Business Excellence* 7, no. 1 (2003): 55.

37. Chris Argyris, *Personality and Organization* (New York: Harper & Row, 1957).

38. Marcel Hoogenboom and Ringo Ossewaarde, "From Iron Cage to Pigeon House: The Birth of Reflexive Authority," *Organization Studies* 26, no. 4 (2005): 602. It is striking how often Weber's *legale Herrschaft* is translated as "legal-rational authority," even though Weber never wrote *legal-rationale Herrschaft*!

39. Gareth Morgan, *Images of Organizations* (Thousand Oaks, CA: Sage, 2006), chap. 7; Jay Klagge, "Approaches to the Iron Cage: Reconstructing the Bars of Weber's Metaphor," *Administration & Society* 29, no. 1 (1997): 63–77; Hunter Crowther-Heyck, *Herbert A. Simon: The Bounds of Reason in Modern America* (Baltimore, MD: Johns Hopkins University Press, 2005), 117.

40. Ghosh, *Max Weber and The Protestant Ethic*, 389.

41. Paul J. DiMaggio and Walter W. Powell, "The Iron Cage Revisited: Institutional Isomorphism and Collective Rationality in Organizational Fields," *American Sociological Review* 48, no. 2 (1983): 157.

42. Scaff, *Weber and the Weberians*, 151–156, discusses the relevance of the "iron cage" in the context of Shmuel Eisenstadt's "multiple modernities" concept.

43. Hoogenboom and Ossewaarde, "From Iron Cage to Pigeon House," 603; Larry J. Ray and Michael Reed, "Conclusion: Autonomy, Pluralism and Modernity," in *Organizing Modernity*, 203.

44. See Frank Pasquale, *The Black Box Society. The Secret Algorithms That Control Money and Information* (Cambridge, MA: Harvard University Press, 2015), 42; Ronnie D. Lipschutz, "The Assemblage of American Imperium. Hybrid Power, World War and World Government(ality) in the Twenty-First Century," in *Legacies of Empire: Imperial Roots of the Contemporary Global Order*, ed. Sandra Halperin and Ronen Palan (Cambridge: Cambridge University Press, 2015), 235.

45. Brian Fung, "The House Just Voted to Wipe Away the FCC's Landmark Internet Privacy Protections," *Washington Post*, March 28, 2017, www.washingtonpost.com/news/the-switch /wp/2017/03/28/the-house-just-voted-to- (accessed March 31, 2017).

46. Jonathan Dane, "Will Employers Still Ask for Facebook Passwords in 2014," *USA Today*, January 5, 2014; see also National Conference of State Legislatures, "Access to Social Media Usernames and Passwords," http://www.ncsl.org/research/telecommunications -and-information-technology/employer-access-to-social-media-passwords-2013.aspx.

47. George Ritzer, "The 'McDonaldization' of Society," *Journal of American Culture* 6, no. 1 (1983): 100–107; see also Lawrence A. Scaff, "Weber on the Cultural Situation of the Modern Age," in *The Cambridge Companion to Weber*, 104.

48. The term "negotiable authority" was introduced in Jos C. N. Raadschelders, *Government. A Public Administration Perspective* (Armonk, NY: M. E. Sharpe, 2003), 57–59, and is discussed in more depth in Jos C. N. Raadschelders and Richard J. Stillman, "Toward a New Conceptual Framework for Studying Administrative Authority," *Administrative Theory & Praxis* 29, no. 1 (2007): 4–40.

49. Hoogenboom and Ossewaarde, "From Iron Cage to Pigeon House," 614; see also Holzer and Sørensen, "Rethinking Subpolitics," 95, on reflexive modernity.

50. For a nice illustration of this, see the organizational diagrams and discussion in Jos C. N. Raadschelders, *Public Administration*, 83–97.

51. Eberhard Bohne, John D. Graham, and Jos C. N. Raadschelders, "Concluding Observations. The State Is Here to Stay: We Cannot Live with It, We Cannot Live without It," and "Introduction," in *Public Administration and the Modern State: Assessing Trends and Impact*, ed. E. Bohne et al. (Basingstoke, UK: Palgrave MacMillan, 2014), 257–264, 1–14.

52. Jean Fourastié, *Les Trente Glorieuses ou la Révolution invisible de 1946 à 1975* (Paris: Librairie Arthème Fayard, 1979).

53. Erik S. Reinert, *How Rich Countries Got Rich and Why Poor Countries Stay Poor* (London: Constable & Robinson, 2007), 95.

54. Joseph E. Stiglitz, *The Euro: How a Common Currency Threatens the Future of Europe* (New York: W. W. Norton, 2016), 137.

55. Rakesh Khurana, *From Higher Aims to Hired Hands. The Social Transformation of American Business Schools and the Unfulfilled Promise of Management as a Profession* (Princeton, NJ: Princeton University Press, 2007), 364; Khurana received the 2008 Max Weber prize from the American Sociological Association's Organizations, Occupations, and Work Section. See also Duff McDonald, *The Golden Passport: Harvard Business School, the Limits of Capitalism, and the Moral Failure of the MBA Elite* (New York: HarperCollins, 2017).

56. Thomas Piketty, *Capital in the Twenty-First Century*, trans. A. Goldhammer (Cambridge, MA: Belknap Press, 2017), 297.

57. Karl Polanyi, *The Great Transformation* (New York: Rinehart, 1944), 130, 141.

58. The term "regulatory capture" can be found in Joseph Stiglitz, *The Price of Inequality: How Today's Divided Society Endangers Our Future* (New York: W. W. Norton, 2013), 59; on the erosion of freedom of the state by multinational corporations, see Bauman, *Liquid Modernity*, 186.

59. For examples see Jos C. N. Raadschelders and Eran Vigoda-Gadot, *Global Dimensions of Public Administration and Governance* (Hoboken, NJ: John Wiley & Sons, 2015).

60. Trevor L. Brown, Matt Potoski, and David M. van Slyke, *Complex Contracting. Government Purchasing in the Wake of the US Coast Guard's Deepwater Program* (Cambridge: Cambridge University Press, 2013); Steven Cohen, William Eimicke, and Tanuya Heikkila, *The Effective Public Manager: Achieving Success in Government Organizations* (San Francisco: Jossey-Bass, 2015), 142.

61. Jody Freeman and Martha Minow, *Government by Contract: Outsourcing and the American Democracy* (Cambridge, MA: Harvard University Press, 2009); Paul R. Verkuil, *Outsourcing Sovereignty: Why Privatization of Government Functions Threatens Democracy and What We can Do about It* (Cambridge: Cambridge University Press, 2007); Paul R. Verkuil, "The Case for Bureaucracy," *New York Times*, October 3, 2016.

62. T. Jackson, *Prosperity without Growth: Foundations for the Economy of Tomorrow* (London: Routledge, 2017), 104.

63. Ibid., 113, 115.

64. Alexis de Tocqueville, *Democracy in America*, ed. and trans. H. Mansfield and D. Winthrop (Chicago: University of Chicago Press, 2000), 502.

65. Scaff, "Fleeing the Iron Cage," 743; Jos C. N. Raadschelders, "Did Max Weber's Agony and Ecstasy Influence His Scholarship?" *Public Administration Review* 70, no. 2 (2010): 304–316.

66. Amitai Etzioni, "Communitarian Antidotes to Populism," *Society* 54, no. 2 (2017): 95–99.

67. Tom Hodson et al., "The Overwhelmed Employee: Simplify the Work Environment," in *Global Human Capital Trends 2014. Engage the 21st Century Workforce*, ed. P. N. Raja Junankar et al. (Westlake, TX: Deloitte University Press, 2014), 97–104.

68. Paul Hemp, "Death by Information Overload," *Harvard Business Review*, September 2009.

69. Daniel J. Levitin, *The Organized Mind: Thinking Straight in the Age of Information Overload* (New York: Random House, 2014); Nicholas Carr, *The Shallows: What the Internet Is Doing to Our Brain* (New York: W. W. Norton, 2010).

70. Martin J. Eppler and Jeanne Mengis, "The Concept of Information Overload: A Review of Literature from Organization Science, Accounting, Marketing, MIS and Related Disciplines," *The Information Society* 20, no. 5 (2004): 325–344.

71. World Economic Forum, *Digital Media and Society: Implications in a Hyperconnected Era* (Geneva: World Economic Forum, 2016), 27.

72. Edward C. Page and Bill Jenkins, *Policy Bureaucracy: Government with a Cast of Thousands* (Oxford: Oxford University Press, 2005); Edward C. Page, *Policy without Politicians: Bureaucratic Influence in Comparative Perspective* (Oxford: Oxford University Press, 2012).

73. Michael Lipsky, *Street-Level Bureaucracy: The Dilemmas of Individuals in Public Services* (Cambridge, MA: MIT Press, 1980).

74. Examples of processes mainly outside the influence of most people include an ideology of free-market economy, a consumptive economy possible through planned obsolescence, technological change, and growth of governmental power upon political and popular demand for security and social welfare; see Scaff, *Weber and the Weberians*, 110.

75. G. W. F. Hegel, *Hegel's Philosophy of Right*, trans. T. M. Knox (1821; Oxford: Oxford University Press, 1967), 191, 193.

CHAPTER 31

CAUSATION, VALUE JUDGMENTS, *VERSTEHEN*

STEPHEN P. TURNER

MAX Weber's methodological writings are some of the most influential parts of his work. A number of its basic ideas and formulations have passed into common usage, just as concepts like charisma and the Protestant ethic have. These include the concept of the ideal type, methodological individualism and the rejection of collective concepts, causal and meaning adequacy, *Verstehen*, value-freedom or ethical neutrality, the distinction between normative and empirical sciences, the idea that the objects of science and social science are constituted by presuppositions that have a valuative character, and the definition of sociology in terms of socially meaningful action. In the course of passing into common usage, these ideas have been removed from their original context, so understanding them requires putting them back in the context of Weber's whole methodological conception and the development of his thinking on these topics.

The reception of Weber's methodological writings has also complicated the problem of interpretation, in part as a result of his complicated and not entirely positive relation to the neo-Kantian philosophy that supplied much of the terminological framework for these writings and in part as a result of the selective appropriation of particular ideas by influential interpreters, such as Talcott Parsons, and by the creative but largely unattributed exploitation of his ideas. These uses include those by such figures as Joseph Schumpeter, who developed his methodological individualism out of Weber. Schumpeter paraphrases Weber's value theory, whose formulation is quoted without attribution in a paper that is regarded as one of the two or three most important political theory papers of the twentieth century, Isaiah Berlin's "Two Concepts of Liberty."

> "To realise the relative validity of one's convictions," said an admirable writer of our time, "and yet stand for them unflinchingly, is what distinguishes a civilized man from a barbarian." To demand more than this is perhaps a deep and incurable metaphysical need; but to allow it to determine one's practice is a symptom of an equally deep, and more dangerous, moral and political immaturity.[1]

Similarly, Karl Popper's "logic of the situation" explanation[2] resembles Weber's account of instrumental action but is not cited, despite the fact that Popper cites the methodological writings elsewhere.[3] Gunnar Myrdal's influential reflections on the role of values in social science, similarly, rearticulated Weber's views.[4]

Misinterpretation, creative misinterpretation, and misrepresentation through application in novel contexts go hand in hand with influence, so it is not surprising that some of the popular understanding of Weber has strayed far from the original. The view of Weber as an interpretivist reflects the attempt to reinterpret Weber in terms of phenomenology by Alfred Schutz. The rise and subsequent critical rejection by philosophy of logical positivism entangled Weber's legacy in the "positivist dispute."[5] The shift in influence from German to American and English-speaking academic thought is a major factor in these transformations: many of Weber's ideas were restated or appropriated to serve the purposes of the social science of the postwar era, purposes that differed from Weber's own or applied to novel controversies. In particular, Weber's ideal types, which he did not propose as "theories," were often restated as theories, for example, as his "theory of bureaucracy." In this overview, the emphasis will be on the basic concepts, but the issues over interpretation and the reception of these ideas, which are important, will be discussed at the end.

Facts and Values

The distinction between facts and oughts, what is and what should be done, or *Sein* and *Sollen*, is deeply rooted both in philosophy and in legal theory, both of which are sources for Weber's "methodological" writing.[6] Weber's neo-Kantian contemporaries tended to conceptualize it in terms of a distinction between fact and value and to regard value in a Kantian way as part of the constitutive framework in which reasoning about the world occurred. This reasoning combined two powerful but problematic ideas, values and presuppositions, into what we now would call frameworks. Weber's first general statement of his methodological views, in "The 'Objectivity' of Knowledge in Social Science and Social Policy" relied on these concepts.[7] He used them to explain two things: the historically variable construction of reality and the distinctive disciplinary construction of subject matter. For Weber, common sense was a worldview, a framework, which was also valuative.

Our worldview is not the same as the worldview of others, especially people from other cultures or historical periods, so the way we organize reality and discern particulars is different from theirs. Nevertheless, we are compelled to start with our ordinary daily worldview, which is infused with values, and to communicate with our contemporaries in terms of it. "Science," including social science, or what Weber called the historical sciences, refines these categories in light of their "interest" or what aspect of the phenomenon mattered from the point of view of their purposes. Science, like common sense, is selective. The world itself, however, is "meaningless chaos" without our doing, consciously or unconsciously, this work of selecting and categorizing.

Central to this argument was the idea that the sciences were necessarily selective and, in the case of the social sciences, dependent on culture, which contained value presuppositions. Culture, as he put it, is "a finite segment of the meaningless infinity of the world process, a segment on which human beings confer meaning and significance."[8] Particular historical problems necessarily and properly reflect our own concerns as human beings, which are informed by our own culture, which consists of values or of valuative ideas that themselves fade in and out of significance and meaningfulness in the course of history. So Weber argued that the cultural sciences were selective *in a different way* from natural science.

> From the point of view of astronomy, only the quantitative relationships of the celestial bodies, which can be measured with precision, engage our interest; [but] what matters to us in the social sciences is the qualitative aspect of events. Moreover, the social sciences are concerned with the influence of processes in the human mind; and the re-experiencing "understanding" of such processes is of course a task that is specifically different from that which the formulas building on the exact knowledge of the natural world are at all able, or designed, to solve.[9]

The historical sciences were compelled to deal with the small selection of possible descriptions that were culturally meaningful and meaningful to us as contemporaries with a common cultural outlook; the natural sciences started with these kinds of descriptions but replaced them with the kinds of descriptions that could be formulated in terms of scientific laws—the relationships that could be measured with quantitative precision, whether or not they were culturally meaningful or even intelligible to the nonscientist.

Historical sciences thus operate under a double constraint. Not only was there a high degree of cultural selectivity about what could be discussed—the objects of explanation— but there was additional selectivity about *how* it could be made sense of. The explanation, whether understood as a narrative or as Weber would put it an ideal type, had itself to be intelligible to an audience located in similar historical and cultural circumstances. For Weber it was this latter selectivity that precluded history from becoming a science like chemistry or astronomy and prevented historical causality from resembling the law-constructing causality found in the natural sciences.

The language we customarily use to describe and explain primary social reality, actions, and events is "valuative" or involves appraisal because its basic facts are described in terms of a worldview that was itself valuative: "in the field of the empirical social sciences of culture, the possibility of gaining meaningful knowledge of what is important to us in the infinite multitude of occurrences is tied to the unremitting application of viewpoints that have a specifically particular character and that are all in the last resort oriented towards value ideas."[10] The dilemma for a science of social reality in the face of the fact–value distinction was that it could not be value-free, in the sense of being without "valuative" presuppositions. But valuative positions or presuppositions were not on the fact side of the distinction, or as he put it, "value ideas may be established and experienced empirically as elements of all meaningful human action, but their validity cannot be proved on the basis of the empirical material."[11]

The standard neo-Kantian solution to this problem was to guarantee the objectivity of historical knowledge through the objectivity of values. Weber simply rejected this approach, for reasons we will discuss in connection with the question of his value theory. He instead stressed that the topics of interest to us and the questions we ask as historians or as the practitioners of "sciences" such as sociology that deal with historical phenomena are bound up with our culture, which in turn is specific to our historical period, contains unexamined and unexaminable presuppositions, and is always subject to change. But he still wanted to resolve the following problem: if valuative presuppositions cannot be grounded, to what extent can our treatment of the subject matter we constitute with our valuative language be objective? His answer was that it cannot be free of values at the point of the original formulation of research problems but that we can recognize this and decline the drawing of valuative conclusions or the making of valuative appraisals on the basis of these descriptions in the name of science or history. But it also cannot be free of values with respect to the goals of inquiry.

These goals are themselves subjective, or on the value side of the fact–value distinction. This means that "our" science, in the case of "Objectivity," the field of social economics, has "nothing to offer a person to whom this truth is of no value—and belief in the value of scientific truth is the product of certain cultures, and is not given to us by nature."[12] But while these values are culture-specific, the products of these value commitments have special features: no other truth can "take the place of science with respect to those features that *it* alone can provide: concepts and judgments that are neither empirical reality, nor reproductions of empirical reality, but that allow empirical reality to be *ordered intellectually* in a valid manner" (italics in original).[13] The values of science, then, are the source of objectivity itself: "The 'objectivity' of knowledge in social science depends on something else, [namely] that the empirically given is constantly oriented towards those value ideas that are the only source of its cognitive *value*" (italics in original).[14]

Taken together, these two roles of values in social science, the selecting and problem constituting, on the one side, and the valuative goals of science, on the other, produce a paradoxical result. "We all harbour some form of *belief* in the supra-empirical validity of those fundamental and sublime value ideas in which we anchor the meaning of our existence; but this does not exclude—on the contrary, it includes—the constant change in the concrete points of view from which the empirical reality derives its significance" (italics in original).[15] The selection that occurs on the first level is always in flux:

> the irrational reality of life, and its store of *possible* meanings, are inexhaustible; the *concrete* configuration of the value relation therefore remains fluid and subject to change far into the dim future of human culture. The light shed by those sublime value ideas falls on a constantly changing, finite part of the immense, chaotic stream of occurrences churning its way through the ages.[16] (italics in original)

This might be thought to imply "that the real task of social science is a ceaseless chase after new points of view and conceptual constructions." But the goals do not change: "helping to acquire knowledge of the *cultural significance and importance of concrete historical relationships* is the single, exclusive, ultimate goal" (italics in original).[17]

CAUSALITY

Weber realized that the idea of causal laws like those in natural science was unworkable in social science, for reasons he drew from his discussion of the role of values in constituting the subject matter of social science. Fields like chemistry or astronomy could abandon and replace the folk concepts that had originally motivated them. Social science, however, was bound to the interests of the present and to its concepts: the causal questions that it asked could not be answered by causal laws in an entirely different conceptual frame, even if there could be such laws. So he needed a way of thinking about causation that was consistent with the fact that it had to employ ordinary concepts. He found it in the work of his colleague from his Freiburg years Johannes von Kries, who constructed a probabilistic theory of causation influential in legal contexts, which were faced with the same issues about concepts.[18]

The reasoning of the theory worked like this: one could choose, for the purposes of analysis that suited the questions you were asking, a set of potential background causal influencers and define, presumably based on some information, a probability of the outcome of interest, such as a historical event, given these influences. This was called its "objective possibility." One could then define a probability of the same outcome with a particular cause from this set eliminated. By subtracting the second probability from the first, one could get an estimate of the causal contribution of the potential causal influencer. If it was above a certain threshold, it could be said to be an "adequate cause." Weber used this technical language to the end of his life.

This model of causal thinking had quite radical implications. In the first place, it made causation relative to questions, to the concepts in terms of which the questions were constructed, and to the analyst's choice of background potential causes from which to subtract the causal influence in order to make a judgment of causal adequacy. This had two important implications. The first was that there could be no one "causal" answer to a question like the one that motivated Weber, namely "what produced capitalism." The answer depended on the background of potential causes one selected. And, indeed, Weber answered this question in at least three different ways: in the *Protestant Ethic* he identified a religious factor which his argument established as an adequate cause in relation to the religious background of the time[19]; in his late lectures on general economic history, he added such considerations as the development of rational law, rational accounting, and the rational organization of labor[20]; and in one of his final writings at the level of civilizational comparison, which explained the emergence of capitalism in the West in terms of the distinctive rational characteristics that appeared in Western antiquity.[21] The second implication was that these causal analyses necessarily worked with idealizations: the causes and the outcomes were constructions of a diverse set of historical facts made to look comparable for the purpose of constructing a class of "same" causes. This was needed to construct the estimates of the probability of outcomes which had to be compared to establish "adequacy."

Moreover, the "objective possibility" was itself normally not actually calculated from anything; it was a plausible estimate of the probability that was "objectively" present but for which data normally did not exist (though Weber did employ actual statistical data when he could). This meant that "objective" causal analysis normally had the character of a thought experiment but a thought experiment about objective probabilistic facts. The objective core to this kind of analysis included the relevant calculations themselves. These (hypothetical) calculations were not themselves relative to cultural presuppositions and could be performed objectively on data once they were broken down into classifications representing outcomes and potential causes.

IDEAL TYPES

Weber was sensitive to the implications of the fact that to provide a causal analysis, as well as to understand a historical phenomenon, such as the mind of the Middle Ages, one was forced to construct idealizations: the actual causal world was heterogeneous, and the thoughts and outlooks of individual people were also diverse. The problem of abstraction is exemplified for him by the case of medieval Christianity. Historians can construct a meaningful, meaning understandable, ideal-typical representation of the beliefs of medieval Christians that is intelligible and extremely clear; but it would be an error to think that this mental model is actually part of, or constitutive of, the subjective reality of any given medieval Christian, much less all of them.[22] Nevertheless, this kind of abstraction was essential for historical exposition. But it was especially important to work with conceptually clear categories, categories that were understood because they were clear. One could then identify deviations from this ideal, but one needs a clear idealization to start with. But it was a fatal error to confuse these idealizations with reality.

He applied the same reasoning about idealizations to "abstract economic theory." As he characterizes this theory,

> It presents us with an ideal image of what goes on in a market for goods when society is organized as an exchange economy, competition is free, and action is strictly rational. This mental image brings together certain relationships and events of historical life to form an internally consistent cosmos of imagined interrelations. The substance of this construct has the character of a utopia obtained by the theoretical accentuation of certain elements of reality. Its only relation to the empirically given facts of [real] life is the following: if it is established or assumed that interrelations of the same kind as those represented in abstract form in the construct (that is to say: occurrences that depend on the "market") to some extent operate.[23]

This paragraph captures some key Weberian ideas. He treats the economists' theory of the market as an ideal type which selectively abstracts from reality by taking mental images or concepts that are in fact derived from culture or common experience and purifying or simplifying them, accentuating certain aspects, to produce an internally consistent image. For Weber, then, the theory is a cultural artifact: it is composed of elements of culture that we already understand but that are presented back to us in a clarified form, which we can then use as a tool to understand the less than clear empirical world, but which we should never confuse with the empirical reality it is abstracted from.

Economic theories assuming rational agents are obviously idealizations of human behavior that was messier and more complex. Yet the decisions and calculations made by the idealized agents of economic theory were transparently understandable, unlike the often obscurely motivated actions of actual people. So understanding actions in terms of clear concepts and explaining why people deviated from these idealized concepts not only makes sense but seems to be an inevitable strategy in the face of such problems as explaining the wrong and right choices made by a general in battle. This did not, however, mean that there was a standard of correctness for action. Right and wrong here are relative to the ideal type we choose in order to understand, but the ideal type has no claim to normative correctness itself: it is simply a tool for understanding.

But there is an important qualification that comes with this recognition: that there is a radical degree of underdetermination in the relation between empirical reality and intelligible abstractions from it.

> Now, it is possible (or rather: it must be regarded as certain) that more than one utopia of this kind—in fact, surely a great many—can be drawn up in any given case. *None* of these utopias will resemble any other, and, even more definitely, *none* of them will be observable in empirical reality as an actually prevailing ordering of social conditions; but *each* of them will claim to represent the "idea" of capitalist culture, and *each* of them *can* advance this claim, insofar as each of them in fact [contains] certain features of our culture that are *significant* in their *distinctive* character and that have been selected from reality and combined into a consistent ideal image. [This is a reflection of the fact that] when we are interested in cultural phenomena, our interest in these phenomena—their cultural *significance*—will as a rule be derived from quite disparate value ideas, to which we can relate them. Just as there are therefore many different "viewpoints."[24] (italics in the original)

Weber's use of the concept of the ideal type, which he regarded with pride as his own contribution, was more extensive than this, however. He used it in two ways: positively, to characterize his own conceptual constructions, and critically, to show that other social and historical thinkers had made the mistake of confusing their concepts with reality. Weber recharacterized their constructions as idealizations, He also identified kinds of ideal types, particularly "genetic" ideal types, which included not only his own account of the stages which led from Protestant religious ideas to the lifestyle of worldly asceticism of the early capitalists but also the many developmental schemas that were found in the German historical school economics and, most significantly, of the histori-cal theory of Marx.

His negative point against historical genetic ideal types involved causality: Marx presented his scheme as a representation of inexorable laws of history. For Weber, the inexorability was an illusion that resulted from the failure to acknowledge that the scheme was an abstraction from a complex, probabilistic underlying reality consisting in part of individual agents whose conduct was understandable on its own terms and a failure to acknowledge our limitations as analysts. We can do no better than to construct concepts that strive for the clarity we need for our intellectual purposes, for example, to answer questions which we need to acknowledge are based on our historically limited cultural horizon.

His positive use of the concept of ideal type is exemplified by his classification of legitimate orders. This was based on three ideal types of legitimacy: traditional, rational-legal, and charismatic. He suggested that the clarity we gained with these concepts came at a price in descriptive historical details and that they did not have validity beyond their utility for the historical analyst with their particular historical purposes. Ideal types did not need to be fully realized in historical reality in order to be useful in this sense: it was valuable to construct a clarified idealization of the causal patterns and meanings attrib-uted to events that were characteristic of the rise and fall of the ideal-typical charismatic leader in order to understand the careers of actual leaders in history that resembled this pattern but deviated from it in details. The value came from the clarity that was possible to achieve with such idealizations, but whether the concepts were in fact useful to the historian depended on their intellectual purposes or "interests." Thus, Weber rejected the absolutization of his types, as well as the criticism that they represented just another historical system or theory of history of the kind that had failed in the past.[25]

The Definition of Sociology
and Collective Concepts

Weber defined sociology as "science that seeks to understand social action interpretatively, and thereby to explain it causally in its course and its consequences."[26] This definition was given in the same spirit as his account of ideal types: it was one possible definition among others and could not be grounded in a deeper truth, such as a metaphysics of society or of the individual. It was rather an expression of our interest, in the sense that he articulated in "Objectivity." Nevertheless, the definition had an important polemical point. It raised the question of what was left unexplained by a serious application of the concepts of subjective meaning and individual social action. Given the profound signif-icance in his intellectual milieu and in German culture itself of the German theory of the state, which attributed a metaphysical status to the state, the obvious question raised by such a definition was whether sociology could accommodate, or say anything about the state. But the same question could be raised for other collective concepts, such as the nation or, for that matter, society, which he reinterpreted in terms of forms of association.

Weber defines *verstehende* (i.e., understanding or interpretive) sociology in terms of its object of study: "behavior that is interpretable in terms of meaning and related to (inner or external) objects" or actions, which is also in some way oriented to others, and thus in this specific sense "social." Actions are a particular kind: "action appears in the guise of a persistent being, an objective structure or one that is 'personified' and lives its own life."[27] There are other such structures, such as the state; but they have a peculiar property. As his contemporary Hans Kelsen pointed out, the acts of the state are always acts of individuals. This was Weber's thought as well. And it implied that the task of sociology in understanding such "products of joint human action" was to "reduce them to action that can be understood, which without exception means: the action of the participating human beings."[28] Different disciplines could proceed differently: in jurisprudence, the state can be treated as a "legal person" because this is useful for the purposes of jurisprudence.[29]

Weber acknowledged that, for the purposes of certain disciplines, it was advantageous, and a conceptual convenience, to treat the state as real. But this did not mean that the state was some sort of special entity which had properties or powers that could not be accounted for by sociology as he defined it, that is to say in terms of meaningful action. The reason for this was simple: not only does the "state" always and only "act" through individuals: judges, legislators, bureaucrats, police officers, and so forth; they attribute meanings to their acts and the acts of others. It is in terms of these meanings that one can get an explanation of these actions. The type of legitimating belief in the actions of, for example, state officials explains obedience to them. This type of action is what "the state" consists of, and there is nothing empirical about the state left over to explain. The contrast Weber has in mind here, and repeatedly returns to in his methodological writings, is with juridical, normative concepts and between reality sciences and normative sciences. The empirical concept of the state, as distinct from the juridical one, is an idealization of a mass of individual actions which have particular meanings for the people acting.

This was a formulation of an idea that his contemporary Joseph Schumpeter labeled "methodological individualism," a term not used by Weber himself. A common view is that this doctrine was introduced as a methodological precept for the social sciences by Max Weber, most importantly in the first chapter of *Economy and Society* (1922). It amounts to the claim that social phenomena must be explained by showing how they result from individual actions, which in turn must be explained through reference to the intentional states that motivate the individual actors.[30]

Weber never formulated it in precisely this way, but he did reject the use of collective concepts and provided analyses of collective concepts in terms of individual actions and beliefs about the actions, or meaning.[31] Instead of formulating precepts, he did something apparently more modest: provided a definition of sociology, which he did not ground in metaphysical considerations, such as a claim that only individuals were real (that would have been metaphysical individualism). Nor did he engage in a controversy about the meaning of the term "sociology." Instead, he simply stipulated a meaning:

> Sociology (in the sense in which this highly ambiguous word is used here) is a science concerning itself with the interpretive understanding of social action and thereby with a causal explanation of its course and consequences. We shall speak of "action" insofar as the acting individual attaches a subjective meaning to his behavior—be it overt or covert—omission or acquiescence. Action is "social" insofar as its subjective meaning takes account of the behavior of others and is thereby oriented in its course.[32]

This was not a methodological precept, but rather a characterization of the problem of accounting for what he called meaningful action in relation to an account of the relationship of sociology to other disciplines. This was a new topic for him. The term "sociology" does not appear in his earlier writings. But defining it provided him with a way to focus on issues of explanation.

VERSTEHEN, ADEQUACY ON THE LEVEL OF MEANING, AND CAUSAL ADEQUACY

Weber expanded on his definition of sociology by creating a standard for explanation: explanations should be adequate both on the level of cause and on the level of meaning. What these two requirements mean, and how they relate, requires some explanation. Weber did not intend to create a metaphysics of meanings, though some of his contemporaries did just that (e.g., Ernst Cassirer). His own account of meaningful action was explained in terms of the concept of *Verstehen*, and he called his sociology *Verstehende Soziologie*, or "understanding sociology." What the term meant for him was, however, quite specific. He defined action in these terms: "We shall speak of action insofar as an individual attaches a subjective *meaning* to his behavior—be it overt or covert, omission or acquiescence."[33] The reference to omissions reflects the origins of these definitions in the law. But Weber's use of "subjective meaning" differentiates him from the legal tradition, which is concerned with the purpose of an action and its intentional character. Weber's definition avoids both of these concepts. But what was "subjective meaning" for him, and how did the concept relate to understanding or *Verstehen*?

Weber's account of *Verstehen* employed two then novel philosophical concepts: *Einfühlung* (in-feeling) or empathy, a term taken from Theodore Lipps, and *Evidenz*, meaning transparently evident to anyone.[34] His account of understanding identified two categories that he considered to be "direct." The first was the understanding of action whose meaning was apparent: the case he gave was a man chopping wood. This meaning is a primary historical fact, in contrast to indirect interpretations involving motives or other off-stage facts, such as the wood chopper's desire to warm his family or sell the wood, which could be made evident to a lesser degree.[35] Attaining *Evidenz* was possible for these kinds of cases. Going beyond the meaningful act of chopping wood to explain the action, appealing to what Weber called a motive explanation that produced "explanatory understanding," required bringing facts together, such as the fact that the man took the wood to market, in order to infer a motive, and was therefore indirect and not fully evident. This departed from the normal use of *Evidenz* by suggesting that *Evidenz* was a matter of degree. Thus, the motive explanations in explanatory understanding that involved inferences were capable of a degree of *Evidenz*: adequacy on the level of meaning meant having a sufficient degree of *Evidenz*. The other place it was possible to attain *Evidenz* was in the understanding of logical systems of thought, such as mathematics and the logically closed system of Roman law.

CAUSAL ADEQUACY

Adequacy on the level of cause, in the case of single actions, is not problematic: a reasonable motive explanation would have a high enough probability to be "adequate" in terms of the von Kries theory. For complex historical sequences, however, the situation is different, and the criterion of adequacy on the level of meaning has a different role.

History presents us with a vast array of probabilistic relationships, some of which are, as Weber put it, meaningful and others not. The historian's task is not predictive: the events have already occurred. Nor is it a matter of seeking the determinate causes of events: low-probability causes are also causes of events. It is, rather, to pull, from the mass of probabilistic causal relevances that can be constructed, the ones that answer the questions that there is a historical interest in answering and selecting those that make narrative sense of the actions of individuals. More than one such account will always be possible: historical narrative is necessarily selective, even beyond the selection required by our cultural presuppositions, given the vast mass of historical fact that might be causally relevant. This is what Weber acknowledged in his own work at the end of the *Protestant Ethic*, when he wrote that "it is, of course, not my aim to substitute for a one-sided materialistic an equally one-sided spiritualistic causal interpretation of culture and of history. Each is equally possible, but each, if it does not serve as the preparation, but as the conclusion of an investigation, accomplishes equally little in the interest of historical truth."[36]

There is a crucial relationship between the two types of adequacy. When we lower the standards for causation to allow for low-probability relationships, these correlations become numerous and unmanageable. The probabilities themselves are thus useless as a guide to historical analysis. There are low-probability statistical associations everywhere, most of which make no sense or are not of interest to us. Adequacy on the level of meaning is an alternative ground for eliminating a large class of these probabilistic relations: those that conflict with this meaning and for which there is no "subjective meaning" evidence. This joint relation of the two kinds of adequacy is thus fundamental to historical analysis. Considerations of meaning are also a constraint with respect to causal chains. Requiring that chains, where they involve actions, include only actions that can be adequately accounted for at the level of meaning selects very significantly from the set of chains made up of all statistically relevant relations strong enough to be causally adequate. But Weber's account of probabilistic causality goes beyond the problem of chains to address the problem of relevance.

VALUE THEORY

The term "values" plays a large role in this account of the nature of social scientific and historical knowledge. What was Weber's own philosophy of values? He is normally characterized as a kind of relativist, in that he stressed the impossibility of grounding values in anything more basic, such as reason, and the necessity of choosing values. Understanding this requires some understanding of the historical circumstances in which this idea arose. The term "values" and its related usages, such as valuation, are not a part of the longer history of philosophy or ethics but a product of a particular moment in nineteenth-century philosophy. The idea was a response to the "scientific" under-standing of a human as subject to the laws of causation, which was thought to rob the human of moral responsibility: "it opposed a sphere of values, as a realm of ideal valua-tions, to a sphere of being that was only causally understood."[37] With this conceptual novelty, as Martin Heidegger pointed out, "One could talk of vital values, eternal values, about the hierarchy of values, spiritual values, which one claimed to have discovered in antiquity, for example."[38] The notion lent itself to systematization through the ranking and logical ordering of values, and much of the writing of neo-Kantianism was devoted to the construction of philosophical systems involving this kind of systematization.[39] The goal of the neo-Kantians was to avoid relativism and for the values to be themselves validated by their analyses. But this ran into the conspicuous problem that moral ideas varied from culture to culture and historically.

One quirk of this system of ideas was that the values that existed in this separate realm had to be the subject of "valuation" by persons to be effective: a valuation was a commit-ment of some kind to a value. And this raised the question of whether there was anything to values beyond the fact of their valuation, or their embrace, by individuals. Weber's interpreters and critics took Weber to have answered this question in the negative. As Schmitt said, "according to Weber it is the individual human being, who, in full and genu-inely subjective freedom of decision, sets up the values."[40] Weber himself said many things that fit this characterization. He commented that "the 'free trade argument' is ridiculous" as "a *world view* or as a valid *norm*."[41] This implies, however, that it is a *possible* world view or valuation. And this also suggests that the range of possible valuations is very wide.

There is nothing like a formal statement of a theory of value in Weber, so although the concept is important to him, it must be reconstructed from his usages in other contexts, most of which are outside of his specifically "methodological writings."

These are nevertheless coherent. His stress is typically on the rational irreconcilability of value claims or worldviews. The cases of genuine irreconcilability that impressed him most came from religious ethics, where the demands were absolute. And these typically produced conflicts between the demands of different spheres, such as the religious sphere and the political sphere. Thus, he says that

> The religion of brotherliness has always clashed with the orders and values of this world, and the more consistently its demands have been carried through, the sharper the clash has been. The split has usually become wider the more the values of the world have been rationalized and sublimated in terms of their own laws.[42]

The rationalization of worldly values, in short, sharpens the conflict between them and the ethic of brotherliness.

But on some important occasions his reasoning was more elaborate than this kind of sociological observation and more specifically ethical. In "Politics as a Vocation"[43] he argued that certain value conflicts were irreconcilable, such as the conflict between the ethics of conviction and the ethics of responsibility. In this case, the conflict was between an "other-worldly" and a "this-worldly" ethics.[44] For the former, the ethical good was governed by a lack of concern for the consequences of action in this world, which is to say by the principle *Fiat justitia, pereat mundus* or "Let justice be done, though the world perish," the latter by the principle that one is responsible for the consequences of one's action in this world. No rational or empirical argument could resolve this conflict. (See Bruun, "Politics and Ethics, and the Ethic of Politics," in this handbook.)

But Weber did not think that this implied that ordinary ethical reasoning was immune from rational and empirical considerations. He argued, in the different context of discussing the role of values in university teaching, that teachers should clearly separate fact and value in their presentation of these issues and limit themselves to causal facts, such as the relation of means to particular desired ends or values, and logical questions about the consistency of a valuative position. Endorsing a valuative position as grounded in science was a violation of the principles of science because the valuative grounds themselves were not a matter of fact but the result of an ungroundable decision that lay outside of science. But he also argued that although it was not the business of professors to inculcate values, especially on the pretense that they could be derived from "science," it was their proper business to show (1) that particular value choices were inconsistent with one another, (2) that some value choices which appeared to be this-worldly or realizable in practice were not, and (3) unnoticed consequences of some value choices for the achievement of other values or ends that would be unacceptable to the chooser. His point was that *ultimate* value choices were ungroundable, not that reasoning about values and clarifying both them and the consequences of pursuing them was impossible.

But this also needs to be qualified. The cases of rational irreconcilability that he discusses are about "ultimate" values and involve somewhat artificial conflicts produced by extreme religious values, such as those that would allow the world to perish. Some values could be taken to be instrumental values, such as free trade as an instrument to bring about greater wealth. And Weber warns against the confusion that arises from rejecting the value as a worldview and failing to see its instrumental value, as when, in "our discussions of commercial policy...we have underestimated the heuristic value of the ancient wisdom of the greatest merchants of the world, encapsulated in such ideal-typical formulas."[45] Rejecting the worldview but accepting the intermediate or instrumental value is possible, and there is a role of rational analysis here: we can and should clarify our value commitments by making them consistent with one another and with the causal relation between means and ends. Moreover, although Weber stressed the rational irreconcilability of certain values with others, he nevertheless did not regard all value conflicts as implying the necessity of choice between extremes: consistent Christianity, he thought, placed particular demands. But when he commented that the middle course is no more scientific than the extremes, he implied that in some cases the middle course could be an option, and in one of the few footnotes to his discussions of value he cites his ally Gustav Radbruch's discussion of the value conflicts in the sphere of law (1913),[46] which are between justice, certainty, and expediency.[47] In this context, legal action needs to balance between the values, not to choose one over the others.

VALUE-FREEDOM OR ETHICAL NEUTRALITY

With this complex background in mind, we can consider one of Weber's most influential ideas, the idea of value-freedom or ethical neutrality. Weber himself tried to forestall misunderstandings in his key paper on the subject, but the concept became subject to serious misunderstandings, by virtue of its extensive discussion, its peripheral but important role in later disputes over positivism, and its application in new contexts. The core of Weber's argument was directed at what he saw as a kind of misrepresentation that occurred when policy ideas were presented as based on "science" without acknowledging that they were also based on values. He saw this kind of misrepresentation as characteristic of the work of the Social Policy Association (Verein für Sozialpolitik). The recommendations made by this organization often sought a middle course and typically reflected a preference for state action and hostility to economic liberalism. Weber also thought that this preference was reflected in their factual determinations on such subjects as mining and led to falsehoods.[48] But Weber's stated concern in his main text on the subject is the conventions of academic life, and particularly the role of the professor.

Weber was himself active in political causes and published on political topics, and he considered this an appropriate activity for professors speaking in public for themselves. He considered the task of the professor in the lecture hall to be different: to carefully separate valuative matters from factual ones and to examine valuative questions as such. The professor could facilitate the students' choices of values through the kind of examination involving realizabilty and consistency discussed earlier, but had no "scientific" grounds for presenting a value as the correct one.

This sounds limiting, but as Weber understood the political and social positions of the time, it provided the professor with powerful tools of criticism. A full commitment to, for example, Christian values of peace could be shown to be inconsistent with political participation because the state is defined by its potential use of the means of violence and thus, as he put it, contracts with diabolical power. This implies that Christian pacifism in politics is confused: one either adheres to the Sermon on the Mount and excludes oneself from politics or fails to be truly Christian. There is no middle ground. Thus, the kind of analysis Weber considered appropriate could be highly critical of common ethical viewpoints despite refusing to promote an ultimate value. (See Bruun, "Politics and Ethics, and the Ethic of Politics," in this handbook.)

Subsequent discussions of value-freedom typically concerned a different but related set of questions, such as the problem of bias in social research, the ineliminability of bias, and the consequent need to take sides. In the philosophical literature, the term was associated with the question of whether there were elements of value within science, such as in the decision to accept a hypothesis, typically concluding that there were and that therefore science could not be value-free. Weber, however, claimed that the choice of topics and the perspective taken that informed the framing of research questions is "valuative." He did not consider such questions as inductive risk, but to the extent that such value commitments are relative to the perspective of the researcher, it is still possible to be value-free, on his terms. It is only necessary to avoid (1) misrepresenting the facts disclosed from the relevant perspective and (2) drawing conclusions, for example, about policy, that conceal the valuative aspects of the perspective framing the research problem. All social science problematics were perspectival, for Weber, and all perspectives had valuative elements. The values involved in the problem of inductive risk can be understood in terms of perspectives as well. Weber's point would be that the values should be recognized, not eliminated, which he agreed was not possible. This is distinct, however, from the idea that there are values, such as emancipation, that are intrinsic to social science and should guide it. For him, this is merely a value choice that informs a value-laden perspective, which honesty requires us to disclose rather than pass off as a product of scientific inquiry.[49] More generally, he did not believe that social science *as science* should take a "side" in social conflicts. To do this would be to misrepresent a value position and the policy conclusions that could be drawn from it as "scientific."

THE HISTORICAL BACKGROUND AND THE RECEPTION OF WEBER'S METHODOLOGICAL WRITINGS

Understanding Weber's writings on these subjects presents many difficulties, some of which come from the fact that the context of their composition is no longer familiar to readers, partly as a result of the changed context in which he was received, especially by

American social science in the mid-twentieth century.[50] Several of the longest methodological texts are polemics against important figures of his own generation and the one preceding him. These figures are almost unknown today and came from fields—historical school economics and the philosophy of law, for example—in which they are obsolete. But the greatest difficulty comes from the problem of Weber's relation to neo-Kantianism, a topic which has been a matter of controversy since Weber's funeral itself.

Neo-Kantianism has a convoluted history, but the core was the idea that various sciences had their own distinctive presuppositions. These presuppositions, however, could not be grounded in anything more fundamental. They were validated by what was called "the fact of science." The solid reality of a body of thought, such as physics or law, was taken to support the validity of the presuppositions on which the body of thought was based: the presuppositions that made physics, or law, possible had to be true if physics or law were valid. The presuppositions could presumably be revealed by philosophical analysis using transcendental or "conditions for the possibility" arguments: these arguments purported to identify the unique set of presuppositions that was logically necessary for the science in question. This provided the basic framework in which such thinkers as Wilhelm Windelband approached the problem of distinguishing historical knowledge, about unique individual facts, from the knowledge of generalizations characteristic of natural science. Weber combined this concern with an issue that grew out of Wilhelm Dilthey's historical approach to knowledge. Dilthey argued that the intellectual construction of the world in history was governed by processes that involved the creation of values and that the objects of interest to us bear "the stamp of spirit."[51] The problem of relativism was deeply rooted in the neo-Kantians' fundamental ideas about the groundlessness of basic presuppositions, and they constantly struggled to neutralize it by limiting the scope of what was relative and overcome it by finding higher-order universal "necessary" presuppositions of cognition. This problematic generated a wide variety of conflicting philosophical systems and, together with the recognition in neo-Kantian philosophy of physics that alternative mathematical frameworks for physical theory were possible (which meant that neither alternative was a necessary presupposition), ultimately produced the demise of neo-Kantianism as a philosophical project.

Variant assumptions about Weber's sources have had an important effect on the secondary literature. Much of this literature has focused on Weber's relation to his childhood friend Heinrich Rickert.[52] This was based in part on a passage quoted in Marianne Weber's biography of Weber which quoted a letter from Weber in which he claims to find a work of Rickert's to be impressive.[53] This, however, was followed by another note on Rickert ("the Nervi Fragment"[54]), which was highly critical, making the point that Rickert had not achieved his purpose of settling the issue of the status of historical knowledge but merely produced another philosophical system.[55] The Rickert-oriented interpretation was bolstered by an influential book by von Schelting,[56] which was particularly important because its basic interpretation was accepted by Parsons and repeated in his major work on Weber, *The Structure of Social Action*.[57] However, von Schelting's book contains a major oddity, which is repeated in Parsons: although the book mentions the terms "objective possibility" and "adequate cause," they are explained without reference to the technical complexities of von Kries' theory.

The problem of causality was largely neglected in the early literature on the methodological writings. Alfred Schutz, who admired Weber, nevertheless considered him to lack a philosophical framework and attempted to supply one taken from phenomenology.[58] A slogan of phenomenology was that it was concerned with "the foundation of the foundation"—that is to say the level of ultimate presuppositions on which neo-Kantian constructions were based.[59] As we have seen, Weber rejected any such grounding and offered his constructions as potentially useful to the interpreter of social life. Schutz nevertheless was influential for treating Weber as an interpretive sociologist and reinterpreted his concern with causality in interpretive terms.

There are many other potential sources for Weber's basic concerns, especially during the period of the writing of his three major methodological essays published in 1903–1907; he was in constant contact with the young philosopher Emil Lask, who had already moved beyond Rickert in a direction contrary to phenomenology.[60] Lask, who was killed in World War I, presumably made Weber aware of the contemporary philosophical options, including the anti-neo-Kantian views of Franz Brentano. His later philosophical follower and explicator was Karl Jaspers, who publicly disagreed with Rickert's attempt to take credit as Weber's philosophical source and himself developed a form of existentialism that reflected Weber's view of the meaningless chaos and the ubiquity and significance for experience of the flow of historical change.

The Logical Positivist Otto Neurath was highly critical of Weber, who he regarded as an idealist in his interpretation of history, against Neurath's own historical materialism.[61] But as the writings of Weber were repurposed and reinterpreted in relation to American social science, they were understood in terms of positivist problematics. His value ideas were reinterpreted in terms of emotivism,[62] and his account of value-freedom was assimilated to the logical positivists' rejection of metaphysics. In social science itself, *Verstehen* was reinterpreted not as empathy that potentially attained *Evidenz* but as a source of hypotheses that could then be tested statistically.[63] The tendency to transform Weber's ideal types into "theories," against his intentions but in conformity with the practices of American behavioral science, even affected the translations, in which the term "theoretical" was inserted in place of Weber's original language.

In the confused "positivism dispute" of the 1960s, themes of an earlier dispute over Weber reappeared.[64] The original dispute had to do with the potential of philosophy to provide a worldview. The critical theorists of the Frankfurt school took the side, against Weber, of a Hegelian revelation of the meaning of history which could underwrite a "correct" worldview. In the 1960s the issues were debated in terms of the self-limitation of science represented by Weber's denial that values could be established scientifically. In this debate the admirers of Weber, such as Raymond Aron, faced off against such critical theorists as Herbert Marcuse and Jürgen Habermas. Subsequently, the discussion of these issues became professionalized and historical, as portrayed in such collections as those by Wagner and Zipprian (1994) and Wagner and Härpfer (2016).[65]

The issues that motivated Weber's methodological writings have not been resolved and constantly reappear in different guises. The considerations Weber advanced and his arguments for them remain relevant. His critical analysis of the role of values in constituting problems and his view that one cannot get normative conclusions from social science without having started with normative premises remain important tools for understanding the divergences between perspectives in social science. His project in the methodological writings was a form of de-ideologization: revealing the concealed premises of social science analyses is an ongoing task, and Weber's methodological writings continue to provide a basis for challenging essentialisms and ontologizations of collective concepts.

Weber remains relevant in positive ways as well. The von Kriesian approach to probability is undergoing a revival of interest in the philosophy of science.[66] Weber's account of *Verstehen* with its emphasis on the role of direct observational understanding has been validated by contemporary discussions of empathy in cognitive neuroscience, especially in connection with the discovery of mirror neurons.[67] His account of the character of ideal types as abstractions illuminates such contemporary issues as the problem of the status of rational-choice explanations and of the nature of social construction. Despite their difficulty and the archaic philosophical vocabulary in which they are expressed, they remain a powerful source for methodological reflection and establish and define the fundamental issues of social science methodology.

Notes

1. Isiah Berlin, *Two Concepts of Liberty* (Oxford: Clarendon Press, 1958), 33–34.
2. Karl Popper, *The Open Society and Its Enemies* (1945; New York: Harper & Row, 1962), 2:149.
3. Karl Popper, *The Poverty of Historicism* (1945; New York: Harper & Row, 1964), 97, 324–397.
4. Gunnar Myrdal, *Value in Social Theory: A Selection of Essays and Methodology*, ed. Paul Streeten (London: Routledge & Keegan Paul, 1958).
5. Theodor Adorno et al., *The Positivist Dispute in German Sociology*, trans. Glyn Adey and David Frisby (1969; New York: Harper & Row, 1976).
6. Max Weber, *Collected Methodological Writings* (hereafter *CMW*), ed. H. H. Bruun and S. Whimster, trans. H. H. Bruun (London and New York: Routledge, 2012); the texts are now published in two volumes of the *Max Weber-Gesamtausgabe* (hereafter *MWG*).
7. Max Weber, "The 'Objectivity' of Knowledge in Social Science and Social Policy," in *CMW*, 100–138; *Zur Logik und Methodik der Sozialwissenschaften. Schriften 1900–1907*, *MWG* I/7, ed. G. Wagner with C. Härpfer et al. (Tübingen, Germany: Mohr [Siebeck], 2018), 142–234.
8. Weber, "The 'Objectivity' of Knowledge," *CMW*, 119; *MWG* I/7, 188.
9. Weber, "The 'Objectivity' of Knowledge," *CMW*, 115; *MWG* I/7, 178.
10. Weber, "The 'Objectivity' of Knowledge," *CMW*, 137; *MWG* I/7, 232.
11. Weber, "The 'Objectivity' of Knowledge," *CMW*, 137; *MWG* I/7, 232.
12. Weber, "The 'Objectivity' of Knowledge," *CMW*, 137; *MWG* I/7, 231.
13. Weber, "The 'Objectivity' of Knowledge," *CMW*, 137; *MWG* I/7, 232.

14. Weber, "The 'Objectivity' of Knowledge," *CMW*, 137; *MWG* I/7, 232.

15. Weber, "The 'Objectivity' of Knowledge," *CMW*, 137; *MWG* I/7, 232.

16. Weber, "The 'Objectivity' of Knowledge," *CMW*, 137; *MWG* I/7, 232–233.

17. Weber, "The 'Objectivity' of Knowledge," *CMW*, 137; *MWG* I/7, 233.

18. Michael Heidelberger, "From Mill via von Kries to Max Weber: Causality, Explanation, and Understanding" in *Historical Perspectives on Erklären and Verstehen*, ed. Uljana Feest (Heidelberg, Germany: Springer, 2010), 241–266. Stephen P. Turner and Regis A. Factor, "Objective Possibility and Adequate Causation in Weber's Methodological Writings," *Sociological Review* 29 (1981): 5–29. Stephen P. Turner, *The Search for a Methodology of Social Science* (Dordrecht, the Netherlands, and Boston: Reidel, 1986). Gerhard Wagner and Heinz Zipprian, "The Problem of Reference in Max Weber's Theory of Causal Explanation," *Human Studies* 9 (1986): 21–42. (Reprinted in Peter Hamilton, ed., *Max Weber. Critical Assessments* [London: Routledge, 1991], 4:273–289.)

19. Max Weber, *The Protestant Ethic and the Spirit of Capitalism* (hereafter *PESC*), trans. Talcott Parsons (1905; New York: Scribner, 1958); *Die protestantische Ethik und der Geist des Kapitalismus/Die protestantischen Sekten und der Geist des Kapitalismus. Schriften 1904–1920, MWG* I/18, ed. W. Schluchter with U. Bube (Tübingen, Germany: Mohr [Siebeck], 2016), 123–492.

20. Max Weber, *General Economic History*, trans. Frank H. Knight (1927; New York: Collier Books, 1961); *Abriß der universalen Sozial- und Wirtschaftsgeschichte. Mit- und Nachschriften 1919/20, MWG* III/6, ed. W. Schluchter with J. Schröder (Tübingen, Germany: Mohr [Siebeck], 2011).

21. Max Weber, "Introduction," in *PESC*, 13–31; "Vorbemerkung," in *MWG* I/18, 101–121.

22. Weber, "The 'Objectivity' of Knowledge," *CMW*, 128–131; *MWG* I/7, 212–215.

23. Weber, "The 'Objectivity' of Knowledge," *CMW*, 124; *MWG* I/7, 202–203.

24. Weber, "The 'Objectivity' of Knowledge," *CMW*, 125; *MWG* I/7, 205.

25. Cf. Uta Gerhardt, *Idealtypus: zur methodologischen Begründung der modernen Soziologie* (Frankfurt am Main, Germany: Suhrkamp, 2001).

26. Max Weber, *Economy and Society: An Outline of Interpretive Sociology* (hereafter *E&S*), 3 vols., ed. Guenther Roth and Claus Wittich (1922; Berkeley: University of California Press, 1978); quoted and translated in *CMW*, xxviii; *Wirtschaft und Gesellschaft. Soziologie. Unvollendet 1919–1920, MWG* I/23, ed. K. Borchardt, E. Hanke, and W. Schluchter (Tübingen, Germany: Mohr [Siebeck], 2013), 149.

27. Max Weber, "On Some Categories of Interpretive Sociology" (1913), *CMW*, 280; *Verstehende Soziologie und Werturteilsfreiheit. Schriften und Reden 1908–1917, MWG* I/12, ed. J. Weiß with S. Frommer (Tübingen, Germany: Mohr [Siebeck], 2018), 404.

28. Weber, "On Some Categories," *CMW*, 280–281; *MWG* I/12, 404.

29. Weber, "On Some Categories," *CMW*, 280–281; *MWG* I/12, 404.

30. Joseph Heath, "Methodological Individualism," *Stanford Encyclopedia of Philosophy* (2015), https://plato.stanford.edu/entries/methodological-individualism/.

31. For a review of current controversies in relation to forms of individualism, see Francesco Di Iorio and Catherine Herfeld, "Review of Brian Epstein *The Ant Trap: Rebuilding the Foundations of the Social Sciences*," *Philosophy of the Social Sciences* 48, no. 1 (2018): 105–128, http://journals.sagepub.com/doi/full/10.1177/0048393117724757.

32. Weber, "Basic Sociological Terms," *E&S*; *MWG* I/23, 149.

33. Weber, "Basic Sociological Terms," *E&S*; *MWG* I/23, 149. (Emphasis added).

34. Stephen P. Turner, "Review of *Max Weber: Collected Methodological Writings*," *Archives Européennes de Sociologie* 53 (2012): 455–460.

35. Weber, "Basic Sociological Terms," *E&S*, 8–9; *MWG* I/23, 155.
36. Weber, *PESC*, 183; *MWG* I/18, 490–491.
37. Carl Schmitt, *The Tyranny of Values*, ed. and trans. Simona Draghici (1979; Washington, DC: Plutarch Press, 1996), 19.
38. Schmitt, *Tyranny of Values*, 19.
39. Guy Oakes, "The Antinomy of Values," *Journal of Classical Sociology* 1 (2001): 195–212; "Weber on Value Rationality and Value Spheres," *Journal of Classical Sociology* 3 (2003): 27–46.
40. Schmitt, *Tyranny of Values*, 19.
41. Weber, "The 'Objectivity' of Knowledge," in *CMW*, 137; *MWG* I/7, 231.
42. Max Weber, "'*Zwischenbetrachtung*'. Religious Rejections of the World and Their Directions," in *From Max Weber: Essays in Sociology* (hereafter *FMW*), trans. H. H. Gerth and C. Wright Mills (1915; New York: Oxford University Press, 1946), 330; "Zwischenbetrachtung: Theorie der Stufen und Richtungen religiöser Weltablehnung," in *Die Wirtschaftsethik der Weltreligionen. Konfuzianismus und Taoismus. Schriften 1915-1920*, *MWG* I/19, ed. H. Schmidt-Glintzer with P. Kolonko (Tübingen, Germany: Mohr [Siebeck], 1989), 479–522, 487.
43. Max Weber, "Politics as a Vocation" (1919), in *FMW*, 77–128; *Wissenschaft als Beruf 1917/1919—Politik als Beruf 1919*, *MWG* I/17, ed. W. Schluchter and W. J. Mommsen with B. Morgenbrod (Tübingen, Germany: Mohr [Siebeck], 1992), 159–252, 237ff.
44. Wolfgang Schluchter, "Value-Neutrality and the Ethic of Responsibility," in Guenther Roth and Wolfgang Schluchter, *Max Weber's Vision of History* (Berkeley: University of California Press, 1979), 65–116.
45. Weber, "The 'Objectivity' of Knowledge," in *CMW*, 137; *MWG* I/7, 231.
46. Gustav Radbruch, *Einführung in die Rechtswissenschaft*, 2nd ed. (Leipzig, Germany: Quelle & Meyer, 1913).
47. Max Weber, "The Meaning of 'Value Freedom' in the Sociological and Economic Sciences," *CMW*, 310n; "Der Sinn der 'Wertfreiheit' in den soziologischen und ökonomischen Wissenschaften," *MWG* I/12, 445–512, 460n4.
48. J. P. Mayer, *Max Weber and German Politics: A Study in Political Sociology*, 2nd rev. enl. ed. (London: Faber and Faber, 1956), 128–129.
49. Myrdal, *Value in Social Theory*, 215–216.
50. Sven Eliaeson, *Max Weber's Methodologies* (Cambridge: Polity, 2002). Stephen P. Turner and Regis A. Factor, *Max Weber and the Dispute over Reason and Value* (London: Routledge & Kegan Paul, 1984).
51. Rudolf Makkreel, *Dilthey: Philosopher of the Human Studies* (Princeton, NJ: Princeton University Press, 1992), 307.
52. Thomas Burger, *Max Weber's Theory of Concept Formation* (1976; Durham, NC: Duke University Press, 1987). Thomas Burger, "Max Weber's Methodology in Its Place," *International Journal of Politics, Culture and Society* 12 (1998): 277–291. Peter-Ulrich Merz, *Max Weber und Heinrich Rickert. Die erkenntniskritischen Grundlagen der verstehenden Soziologie* (Würzburg, Germany: Königshausen & Neumann, 1990). Guy Oakes, "Weber and the Southwest German School: The Genesis of the Concept of the Historical Individual," in *Max Weber and His Contemporaries*, ed. Wolfgang J. Mommsen and Jürgen Osterhammel (London: Unwin Hyman, 1987), 434–446; *Weber and Rickert. Concept Formation in the Cultural Sciences* (Cambridge, MA: MIT Press, 1988); "Reading Max

Weber's *Wissenschaftslehre*: Remarks on the Recent German Literature," *Sociological Forum* 3 (1988): 301–307; "Value Theory and the Foundations of the Cultural Sciences. Remarks on Rickert," in *Methodology of the Social Sciences, Ethics, and Economics in the Newer Historical School*, ed. Peter Koslowski (Berlin and Heidelberg, Germany: Springer, 1997), 59–78. Gerhard Wagner, *Geltung und normativer Zwang: Eine Untersuchung zu den neukantianischen Grundlagen der Wissenschaftslehre Max Webers* (Freiburg, Germany: Alber, 1987). Gerhard Wagner and Heinz Zipprian, "Oakes on Weber and Rickert," *International Journal of Politics, Culture and Society* 3 (1990): 559–563.

53. Marianne Weber, *Max Weber: A Biography*, trans. Harry Zohn (1975; Abingdon, UK, and New York: Routledge, 2017), 260; Weber's postcard to Marianne Weber from April 11, 1902, in *Briefe 1895–1902, MWG* II/3, ed. R. Aldenhoff-Hübinger with U. Hinz (Tübingen, Germany: Mohr [Siebeck], 2015), 826.

54. Weber, "Rickert's 'values,'" *CMW*, 413–414; *MWG* I/7, 623–626.

55. Hans Henrik Bruun, "Weber on Rickert: From Value Relation to Ideal Type," *Max Weber Studies* 1 (2001): 138–160; *Science, Values and Politics in Max Weber's Methodology*, new exp. ed. (Aldershot, UK: Ashgate, 2007), 26–27.

56. Alexander von Schelting, *Max Webers Wissenschaftslehre* (Tübingen, Germany: Mohr [Siebeck], 1934).

57. Talcott Parsons, *The Structure of Social Action* (1937; Glencoe, IL: Free Press, 1968).

58. Alfred Schutz, *The Phenomenology of the Social World*, trans. George Walsh and Frederick Lehnert (1932; Evanston, IL: Northwestern University Press, 1967).

59. Leo Strauss, "Philosophy as a Rigorous Science and Political Philosophy," *Interpretation* 2 (1972): 1–9.

60. Karl Schumann and Barry Smith, "Two Idealisms: Lask and Husserl," *Kant-Studien* 83 (1993): 448–466.

61. Otto Neurath, "Sociology and Physicalism," in *Logical Positivism*, ed. A. J. Ayer (1931–1932; Chicago: Free Press, 1959), 282–317.

62. Alasdair MacIntyre, *After Virtue: A Study in Moral Theory*, 3rd ed. (1981; Notre Dame, IN: University of Notre Dame Press, 2007).

63. Theodore Abel, "The Operation Called Verstehen," *American Journal of Sociology* 54, no. 3 (1948): 211–218.

64. Peter Lassman, Irving Velody, and Herminio Martins, eds., *Max Weber's "Science as a Vocation"* (London: Unwin Hyman, 1989). Peter Lassman and Irving Velody, "Max Weber on Science, Disenchantment and the Search for Meaning," in *Max Weber's "Science as a Vocation,"* 159–220.

65. Gerhard Wagner and Heinz Zipprian, eds., *Max Webers Wissenschaftslehre. Interpretation und Kritik* (Frankfurt am Main, Germany: Suhrkamp, 1994). Gerhard Wagner and Claudius Härpfer, eds. *Max Webers vergessene Zeitgenossen (Max Weber's Forgotten Contemporaries): Beiträge zur Genese der Wissenschaftslehre* (Wiesbaden, Germany: Harrassowitz Verlag, 2016).

66. Cf. Jacob Rosenthal and Carsten Seck, "Johannes von Kries's Conception of Probability, Its Roots, Impact, and Modern Developments: Introduction," special section "Kries and Objective Probability" in *Journal for General Philosophy of Science* 47 (2016): 105–107.

67. Vittorio Gallese, "Before and Below 'Theory of Mind': Embodied Simulation and the Neural Correlates of Social Cognition," *Philosophical Transactions of the Royal Society B* 362 (2007): 659–669.

CHAPTER 32

....

REALISM AND REALITY
IN MAX WEBER

....

SÉRGIO DA MATA

THE PRIMACY OF REALITY
....

MAX Weber viewed science not so much as a destiny for modern humanity but, rather, as a choice. Whoever chooses the way of science must be clear that in science nothing can replace hard work, even though contingencies are inevitable. Above all it is necessary to bear in mind science's limitations. Responsibility is not an imperative for the politician alone but equally so for the scientist. In short, to Weber the exercise of science was strictly related to a sense of reality. While he declares in his famous article of 1904 that "the social science that *we* want to pursue is a *science of reality*," he also acknowledges that "nowhere is science worse off in the long run than in the hands of those who refuse to face uncomfortable facts and the tough realities of life."[1]

Much has been written about the concept of *Wirklichkeitswissenschaft*, but it has not always been the object of careful reflection. Before examining Weber's realism, it is surely important to elucidate what Weber meant by the term "reality." Without doubt, he never problematized the concept in his historical studies, his sociology, or even his theoretical writings. Actually, the "crisis of reality" had not yet appeared on the horizon during his lifetime so that Weber was more concerned with questions like the role of values in historical–social analysis, the heuristic importance of the concepts, and the limits of the principle of causality. In his research into the history of the concept of reality, Hans Blumenberg showed how, in the Western world, four concepts associated with it had been developed: reality as momentary evidence, metaphysically guaranteed reality, reality as context, and reality as resistance. In Weber's theoretical writings there is a clear predominance of reality as effective evidence, although the notion of reality as resistance is by no means absent. For him realism in science and realism in politics are deeply interconnected, as two sides of the same coin. If the vocation of the researcher hinders him or her from avoiding "uncomfortable facts," a competent politician should have "the ability to maintain one's inner composure and calm while being receptive to realities." Thus, reality can be understood, as an influential sociologist once wrote, as that "which happens anyway and can not be changed."[2]

There can be no doubt that the interest in Kant's philosophy he expressed ever since he was quite young left lasting marks on Weber's thinking.[3] In his copy of Kant's *Prolegomena to Any Future Metaphysics*, Weber underscored in pencil a part of the text in which Kant establishes a relationship between reality and experience: "Cognition of that which cannot be an object of experience would be hyperphysical, and here we are not concerned with such things at all, but rather with that cognition of nature the reality of which can be confirmed through experience."[4] As is well known, that particular passage merely synthesizes what Kant had previously set out in his *Critique of Pure Reason*.

Nevertheless, the concept of a science of reality in Weber owes less to Kant than to the historicist tradition and, more precisely, to the neo-Kantian theory of history. In his article on Wilhelm Roscher, written in 1903, Weber repeatedly quotes from the book about Thucydides that the founding father of the Historical School of economics had published in 1842. From the methodological standpoint, Roscher was following the lessons of Wilhelm von Humboldt. The famous essay entitled "On the Historian's Task," which according to Weber "has recently again been the subject of much discussion," would have decisively influenced Roscher.[5] Humboldt affirmed that one of the historian's central concerns should be to "stimulate a sensibility for reality" because "the element in which history operates is the sense of reality" (*Sinn für die Wirklichkeit*).[6] That postulate had a strong influence on Leopold von Ranke and his disciple, Roscher, who added that the historian had to "illuminate the present by means of the past and bring the past to life by means of the present."[7]

While Georg Simmel seems to have been the first to use the concept of a "science of reality,"[8] it was actually with Wilhelm Windelband and Heinrich Rickert that the notion acquired a clearer delineation. Weber's position seems to have oscillated between the point of view of Windelband and that of Rickert. In other words, it oscillated between a broader definition and another more restricted one as to what the "sciences of reality" were. When developing his ideal-type theory in his essay "Objectivity," Weber writes, "What, then, is the importance of such ideal-typical concepts for a science of *empirical* experience as we want to conduct it?"[9] In that regard, in his well-known rectorial address in 1894, Windelband had stated that the empirical sciences (*Erfahrungswissenschaften*) could be distinguished from philosophy and from mathematics by the fact that they "undertake to establish knowledge of reality which is somehow given and accessible to observation."[10] Empirical sciences embrace a vast set of disciplines, and basically, what differentiates one from another is its tendency either to generalize or to individualize. In that sense, both Friedrich Gottl and Max Weber make use of the *Erfahrungswissenschaft* concept to characterize both political economy and history, though strictly speaking this does not say much about their ontological contents.[11] Further developing Windelband's contribution, Rickert prefers to designate the human sciences as "cultural sciences," with history being their paradigmatic case. In its aspect as a science directed, above all, at the study of phenomena approached in the condition of singularities and in which generalizations take second place from the methodological point of view, Rickert considers history to be the science of reality par excellence. It is the "proper science of reality" (*die eigentliche Wirklichkeitswissenschaft*), the "proper empirical science" (*die eigentliche Erfahrungswissenschaft*), because, as Weber puts it, "the 'pure'... reality" is "always individual."[12]

Up until this moment, it would seem that we have been moving within the bounds of the old concept of reality in its aspect as evidence, but it is important to bear in mind that in Rickert's perception it is impossible to apprehend reality directly, exactly as it is, because reality is infinitely complex and multifaceted. To use his terminology, it is "irrational."[13] In the theory of systems jargon of today, we would say that for Rickert the function of concepts would be to foster the reduction of the complexity of the real. However, complexity is not the only distinctive feature of reality: historical thinking is always confronting "the resistance of a lusterless world."[14] Emil Lask, the young philosopher whom Weber considered to be "a very gifted student of Rickert" and who actually came to enjoy the privilege of reading the galley proofs of Weber's essay "Objectivity," formulated the second concept of reality—that of reality as resistance—in such a way that in its pathos it seems to draw a little closer to Weber's own perspective. In his book about Fichte, Lask writes that "brutality is actually the 'law' of reality."[15]

What we need to know is how the science of reality proposed by Weber is actually practiced. We do not believe its originality lies in the passionate defense of value-freedom and even less in the ideal types,[16] but instead, it lies in the fact that it is, in essence, *historical*.

> We want to understand *the distinctive character* of the reality of the life in which we are placed and which surrounds us—on the one hand: the interrelation and the cultural *significance and importance* of its individual elements as they manifest themselves today; and, on the other: the reasons why these elements historically developed as they did and not otherwise.[17]

It therefore concerns (1) the identification of a specific aspect, a manifest singularity in the present reality, which is only possible (2) if we are clear about the values and connections that determine the relevance of the respective problem in such a way that it can then (3) be explained in a historical perspective. It should be noted that what is stated here is not to be confused with the proposal that Weber was to develop later in *Economy and Society*. Comprehensive sociology is based on different premises: in its aspect as an "empirical science of action," the primary concerns are the effort to interpret subjective meaning of human actions and the elaboration of conceptual taxonomies, thereby making it a "generalizing science."[18] The concept of a science of reality is not even mentioned in *Economy and Society*.

However that may be, at least up until 1909 not even the program set out in the article "Objectivity" gives a clear description of the methodology Weber employed. The challenge however is to see how Weber himself deploys his methodology in his own empirical studies.

The strategy of taking his methodological writings as the basis for analysis of Weber's empirical investigations is one that can induce errors or, rather, that can obscure the fact that no researcher habitually remains as faithful to his or her own methodological premises as would appear at first sight. Thus, it is a case of inverting the way conventionally used by the interpreters and reading Max Weber's science of reality not on the basis of the theory exhibited above all in his essay "Objectivity" but instead by slowly and carefully examining the concrete rules of his scientific activity based on his practice. Only in that way can any eventual contradictions be demonstrated between the "idea" and the "reality" in the trajectory of this and other great social scientists. Inverting the perspective in this way, in the final analysis, draws us closer to the spirit of his *Wirklichkeitswissenschaft*: because here too "nothing is more dangerous than ... *mixing up* theory with history."[19]

Reading some of his more important historical, comparative, economic, and observational empirical studies reveals a common pattern rather than any given themes or concepts. This pattern can be identified in the way Weber endeavors to solve the problem his doctoral thesis addressed (the origins of the differences between general and limited commercial partnerships), in the study presented at the universal exhibition in St. Louis (the causes of the contrasts that existed between agrarian structures in the east and the west of Germany), in *The Protestant Ethic and the Spirit of Capitalism* (the emergence of worldly asceticism), and even in the prefatory remarks to *Economic Ethics of the World Religions* (the uniqueness of Western rationalism).[20] Indeed, there was nothing exactly revolutionary about the nucleus of the Weberian science of reality, and it had been developed earlier in an analogous form by Johann Gustav Droysen in 1857. To the author of *Historik*, "there is no doubt that we will completely understand what is, only as soon as we realize how it came into being."[21] We do know that in his undergraduate days Weber was an enthusiastic participant in the seminars given by a disciple of Droysen's, Bernhard Erdmannsdörffer, at Heidelberg University.[22]

The elements that make up the real (and not strictly formally logical) nucleus of Max Weber's science of reality may vary a little from case to case, but they recur to such an extent that we can safely list them, as follows:

- a point of departure which is constituted by "the primacy of the problem"[23] ("problem" here is taken to mean an unexpected singularity which can be perceived in the present)
- a return to the past and use of the historical method as the most suitable for explaining the reasons for the said singularity
- a meticulous use of generalizing concepts, the *ideal types*, not as the aim but as an instrument of inquiry[24]
- the use of the comparative method to complement the genetic approach
- a preference for a morphological form of presentation rather than the conventional narrative form
- a multilevel approach of the causality relations and at the same time a tendency to isolate and emphasize certain macro-determinations according to the specific problem to be elucidated.[25]

The Limits of Max Weber's Science of Reality

It is trivial to say that Weber's oeuvre still has a prominent place among the great achievements in the humanities of the last hundred years. The clarity and rigor with which he theoretically grounded the social sciences find parallels only in classics such as those by Émile Durkheim or Niklas Luhmann. But no less trivial is to recognize that Weber was not too distant from some ideas and assumptions that one could hardly accept today. If, as he believed, the main feature of the historical disciplines is their "eternal youth," then the Weberian science of reality must be critically appraised if we wish to preserve its full potential. In this regard, we will now turn to two problems that in our view characterize the *Wirklichkeitswissenschaft*: the conventional character of Weber's concept of culture and the (weak) teleology behind his vision of human history. In order to explore these two different issues, we must take some of Weber's minor studies into account.

The four decades from 1880 to 1920 were the "heroic" period of modernity and of the European sciences' great conquests. In that sense, it could be said that Weber lived in perfect tune with the *Zeitgeist*. Friedrich Meinecke remarked on the saying that Weber never withdrew from "naked investigation with no illusions" of the causes of social phenomena.[26] Even though Nietzsche's and Freud's critiques of culture were conquering an increasing number of adepts, those authors only had very slight impacts on the author of *Protestant Ethic and the Spirit of Capitalism*. From 1909 on, Weber openly criticized the "neo-romantics," opposing all efforts to mistake science for a worldview. For him the disenchantment stemming from the burgeoning intellectualism was as inevitable as the "triumphal progress of capitalism" so that all that was left for the "cultivated man" was resignation in the face the senselessness of the world and of history.[27]

The limitations of Weber's perspective largely stem from his theory about the rationalization process. He was convinced that the West and the West alone developed a rational work ethic, a rational socialism, and even rational music. Art, law, political and economic life forms of bureaucratic organization, in short, all spheres of life testified to the existence of a rationalizing impulse which it was useless to oppose. Regarding that theory, *grosso modo* two schools of opinion have formed. There are those who deny that in it one can descry a "philosophy of universal history," while others note that a spontaneous philosophy of history actually ends up entering Weber's work by the back door, by means of the category "fate," for example. The rationalization thesis was not one in the usual style of the speculative theories of the eighteenth century but, instead, a modality of what Odo Marquard referred to as "a resigned form of philosophy of history." There were even some (Freyer was probably the first one) who identified a philosophy of history tout court in Weber. Coming from the very different background of a "peripheral modernity," philosopher and essayist José Guilherme Merquior stated that "Weber's mistake was to think that rationalization and disenchantment would not entail chronic, near-institutionalized backlashes of re-enchantment creeds and trends."[28]

Johannes Weiß considers that the famous last paragraphs of *Protestant Ethic* contain nothing that would reveal "a 'fatalistic' posture in regard to history." That impression would be different, however, if the text were submitted to a synoptic reading with the speech presented in St. Louis in 1904 and the first of his studies on the Russian Revolution of 1906. It is precisely in the conclusions of these two "minor" texts that the seduction of historical inevitability shows itself more clearly. The temptation of prognosis seems to constitute a facet of the science of reality that Weber never formulated explicitly but which, nevertheless, reveals its presence now and then: "as far as our weak eyes can see into the impenetrable mists of mankind's future," he says, both Russia and the United States will follow the same European tendency to bureaucratize politics and form an aristocracy of landowners. In what is an almost dystopic vision, Weber believes that the Enlightenment "seems also to be irretrievably fading" and that "all *economic* auguries point in the direction of a growing *loss* of freedom."[29]

Only a philosophy of history explains why Weber evaluates societies located outside of western Europe using occasionally the rhetoric of backwardness and even of ahistoricity. As other chapters in this handbook show, he speaks of the risks of "Chinese ossification of intellectual life" and of a "Chinese petrification" (*chinesische Versteinerung*) of our civilization, he attributes absolute stability to the caste system and states that there is no autochthonous historiography in India, and he considers that an archaic social environment prevails in Russia.[30] At age twenty-four we find him complaining about his stay in Posen: the peasants' faces appeared to him to be more like those of "Tartars." When he takes up his post as professor in Freiburg, Weber declares that thanks to "his habitually low physical and intellectual standard of living," the Polish rural laborer is gaining space in eastern Germany because "he is prepared even to eat grass."[31] It is true that as time went by his tone softened somewhat, but the essence of his argument remained the same. In the same year that he published the first part of *Protestant Ethic*, Weber declared that due to the constant introduction of Polish workers into German lands, "the advance of *Kultur* towards the east... has reversed completely."[32] Wilhelm Hennis and Peter Steinbach tried to minimize Weber's proximity to the "spirit" of turn-of-the century social Darwinism in Germany,[33] but the language of his writings in the 1890s is sufficiently clear. In Weber's view, the "de-Germanization" of Germany's eastern provinces "is in no way a mere question of nationality, but rather it means that: our cultural level is being... brought down to the level of a culture that is lower, oriental."[34] He suggests that from the point of view of the theory of evolution, modern agrarian capitalism would lead to a paradoxical result, for in the *struggle for existence* in a free-market economy, the "superior" cultures would be in a disadvantageous situation. The German peasants would be unable to compete with agricultural workers endowed with "differently constituted stomachs," with the disproportionately low maintenance costs of Argentinean "nomadic barbarians" or "the itinerant Polish workers, nomadic treks (*Nomadenzüge*)."[35] Weber sketches a somber vision of agrarian capitalism's development insofar as he foresaw there would be an increased demand for "elements without *Kultur* in the occidental *Kulturnationen*" (he also mentions the "coolies" in California). A contingent of foreign workers with very slender chances of becoming culturally assimilated would, in Weber's opinion, put the North American democratic tradition at risk.[36]

It would be only too easy, but tedious, to evoke all the criticism of those two points of view made by later generations.[37] A fairer way would be to confront them not with the current "state of the art" but instead with the vision of a contemporary of his, of someone who belonged to the same generation as Weber but who had developed a distinct and, to some extent, "heroic" sensitivity in the face social Darwinism's influence at that time[38] in regard to the luxuriant cultural diversity of human societies. Just six years older than Weber, Franz Boas had emigrated to the United States in 1887. They both took part in the great academic event of 1904, the Congress of Arts and Science, in St. Louis.[39] Boas, who had spent some time among the Eskimos and had recently participated in the founding of the journal *American Anthropologist*, reconstructed the trajectory of anthropology from its primordial moments, whereas Weber made a sophisticated historical–comparative analysis of rural capitalism's development in the United States and in Germany. What is important here is to observe how the two erudite men handled an issue that was at once so simple and so up to date as cultural otherness. While Weber's essay was marked by the principle of historical inevitability and made use of the temporal–normative concept of "backwardness,"[40] Boas used a language that is in this respect far more value-free:

> Of greater educational importance is its power to make us understand the roots from which our civilization has sprung, to impress us with the relative value of all forms of culture, and thus serve as a check to an exaggerated valuation of the standpoint of our own period, which we are only too liable to consider the ultimate goal of human evolution, thus depriving ourselves of the benefits to be gained from the teachings of other cultures, and hindering an objective criticism of our own work.[41]

It is a moot point whether by relinquishing the dialogue with ethnography in his developmental history—"because human powers of work are restricted"[42]—Weber did not close against himself the very door that had enabled Boas to get around the "elitist" conception of culture which predominated in the German *Bildungsbürgertum* at that time.[43] Attempts to elucidate Weber's concept of culture[44] have been tangential to what seems to us to be the decisive aspect of the question, namely, its ambivalence. At one moment, Weber uses a "logical" definition, thereby drawing close, for better or for worse, to Rickert, for whom "our concept of culture is formal and must remain so."[45] It is everything that the life of a group is imbued with "value." As that is not saying much, it was inevitable that Weber would frequently use a substantive concept which, however, reveals itself to be restrictive and hierarchic precisely because it is structured on the basis of the category "value."[46] The use of terms like *Kulturvölker*, *Kulturmensch*, and *Kulturnation*; his great narrative of the Western *Sonderweg*; his omission of popular forms of religiosity from his sociology of religion[47]; the difficulty he had in perceiving the autochthonous historicity of certain societies; his vision of Polish and Argentinean peasants as being culturally inferior—all of that shows that throughout a considerable period of his life Weber kept his distance from an effectively modern concept of the significance of cultures in themselves. His definition of culture is one of those rare moments in his oeuvre when one would be justified in saying, as Kant would, that "this may be true in theory, but it does not apply in practice."[48]

REALITY AS A VOCATION

Weber wrote in "Science as a Profession and a Vocation" that science "*demands* to be surpassed and rendered obsolete," echoing the last page of the "Objectivity" essay.[49] In fact, he never imagined that his works could escape this fate. As we have seen, his method operates far more genetically than contextually. Weber's resistance to Dilthey and hermeneutics up to the point he formulated an interpretive sociology (*verstehende Soziologie*) of his own, in his 1913 essay for *Logos*, meant that re-evaluation of what was by then almost mainstream social theory occurred relatively late in his intellectual career. As a consequence, some analytical problems arose, less in his extensive historical–sociological studies than in the theoretical fundaments of comprehensive sociology, as shown by Alfred Schütz in the 1930s. On the other hand, other aspects emphasized by him remain important for us: the recognition that, in analyzing cultural phenomena, individuals can be as important as social groups; the emphasis on cultural and historical "problems"; the necessity of putting limits on what Ricoeur once called "bad subjectivity"; the rejection of any kind of determinism or theoretical *hybris*; and so on. Simply put, as in other classics of Western thought, not everything we learn from Max Weber demands to be surpassed and rendered obsolete.

This leads us to a last question: What does a Weberian science of reality have to say to us nowadays? Has it survived—and, if so, to what extent—all the developments and crises that occurred in the social sciences since his death?

A possible way to find answers to these questions is to observe how three of the most celebrated German sociologists of the twentieth century related to Weber's heritage and in particular to his science of reality—not least because of the societal crises of their own time. Let us begin with the founder of the Leipzig school, Hans Freyer. Although he belonged to a younger generation and was close to the so-called conservative revolution that helped to deepen the Weimar Republic's legitimation crisis, we can understand Freyer's work as a continuation of the Weberian approach. Freyer's distinction between the science of reality and "sciences of logos" is based on the assumption that the most stimulating in Weber is not exactly to be found in the countless typifications presented in *Economy and Society*, and much less in his ideal of value-freedom, but on the historicity that underlies almost all dimensions of Weberian social science. Freyer firmly believed that sociology should avoid assimilating the hypersystematic model of the "sciences of logos," which have their ultimate goal in the elaboration of classificatory systems and typologies (according to him, a trend already to be found in Dilthey). Those who believe that the task of sociology is to move away from concrete, empirical reality, in order to attain higher levels of abstraction, only "denaturalize social facts, divest them of their attributes of reality." If the core of Weberian sociology was indeed in *Economy and Society*, he suggests, then the logical consequence would be a conventional "morphology" in a classificatory sense. But if Weber's work is still alive and continues to stimulate new generations of researchers, it is, argues Freyer, because it preserved a radical historical consciousness: historical not only is the method of the science of reality but also includes its heuristic tools, especially its self-understanding. A science of reality has no "pure" concepts. They are rather, as Freyer claims, "historically saturated." Only thus does it fulfill its "systematic goal": to ground a "theory of the present."[50]

Following in the footsteps of the German Historical School of economics and its leading proponent, Gustav Schmoller, who died in 1917, historical sociology reaches a peak during the Weimar Republic. Its rapid decline, as Volker Kruse has convincingly shown, was provoked mainly by the rise of Nazism and the fact that most of the younger talents (Karl Mannheim, Franz Oppenheimer, Norbert Elias, Alexander Rüstow, Karl Polanyi) had to leave the country. Nevertheless, and from a more philosophical perspective, this process had been prepared by the increasing rejection to historicism since the early 1930s, an attitude which—despite the protests of authors such as Benedetto Croce, Friedrich Meinecke, and Theodor Litt—defined the dominant sociological style of thought of the following decades.[51]

Based on a fundamentally historical approach to social phenomena, the old science of reality gradually gave way to the conception of sociology as a "science of the present" (*Gegenwartswissenschaft*). In the 1950s, the sociological presentism of René König, Hans Albert, and Helmut Schelsky seemed to indicate the definitive overcoming of the Weberian science of reality. Not by chance, at that time Weber exerted less influence in Germany than in the United States or in Latin America. Schelsky writes in one of his books that "where sociology becomes essentially historical ... it loses—for instance in Max Weber—very fast its capacity of providing orientation." In a rapidly changing world the main task of social science would be to rediscover the threads that bind collective consciousness to social structure. For Schelsky, sociology could only achieve this goal and provide effective orientation if it renounces entirely the historical perspective and becomes an "empirical" discipline. Inverting the precepts of the science of reality and reflecting the existentialist fashion of the postwar years, he was convinced that the loss of the past is the only antidote to the "loss of reality."[52]

With Friedrich Tenbruck, an important name in the sociology of culture and one of the most renowned interpreters of the Weberian legacy, there is a clear change of attitude. The first half of his academic career reveals a strong synergy with König's and Schelsky's views, so much so that he asserts in 1959 that "Max Weber's methodology as a whole has nothing more to tell us."[53] The intellectual atmosphere changed significantly in the mid-1970s, when history and sociology repeatedly gave signs of reconciliation. At the same time, and in part as a response to the politicization of the German academic environment, the organization of the immense publication project of Weber's complete writings was taking its first steps. In 1975, Tenbruck publishes his revolutionary article "Das Werk Max Webers," in which he demonstrates that the work of Weber has its fugue point not in *Economy and Society* but in the long series of studies on the *Economic Ethics of World Religions* and in the problem of rationalization. With Tenbruck (and Wilhelm Hennis shortly after in his essay "Max Webers Fragestellung"), the historical dimension redeems a central place in the analysis of Weberian thought. In fact, Tenbruck renounces sociological presentism and retakes the essence of the science of reality, which Freyer was the last to explore in a consistent basis. In 1986, Tenbruck goes further and criticizes his own habilitation thesis, saying that a structural analysis only builds constellations of ideal types that are meant to replace history, rather than providing tools that enable an understanding of historical processes. In this sense, structural sociology loses sight of all that is historically and culturally specific, that is, "reality itself." Only his studies on Weber, he admits, "have taught me to the full extent that we got entangled in our own concepts."[54] In the same year, Tenbruck asserts that any interpretation "that neglects the *Wissenschaftslehre*, with its concept of science of reality, will…only contribute to sow more confusion," since "Weber's work can not be deciphered without the concept of the science of reality."[55]

Last but not least, we have to ask whether this almost "forgotten concept"[56] still deserves to receive attention from the human sciences in the twenty-first century. Now, if the social sciences are still engaged in the search for reality, it was because they are in risk of losing it. Such a risk has never been entirely absent from modern societies' existential horizons. This problem, of course, deserves a sociological examination. One of the paradoxes that emerged throughout occidental rationalization is that it from time to time generates its opposite. The negative of rationalization has assumed countless faces throughout the last two centuries, from early romanticism through postmodernism. Some of these cultural phenomena and intellectual movements have left us with an extraordinary legacy and others, little more than tautology. As we do not have available those statistics of imposture once claimed by Thomas Carlyle, we limit ourselves to only one of these less fortunate forms, seeing that its effects are also felt in the social sciences. Arnold Gehlen called it the "aesthetic–irrationalistic reaction against the rationalization process."[57] Its typical representative proclaims both the soteriological attributes of fine arts and the impossibility of a rigorous reconstruction of reality, but, as soon as he or she is confronted with the most trivial problems and needs of daily life, he or she acts and thinks exactly the opposite. This incessant zigzagging between theoretical relativism and a mere "instrumental" realism is not only explained by a certain taste for *Kulturkritik* or novelty at whatever cost. This patent inconsistency, which is usually lived in an absolutely non-problematic way, is, in fact, characteristic of that kind of irrationalism. He is a relativist not because he believes in the validity of "anything goes" but because he obeys the dictates of the market of ideas. As often is the case in our societies, disillusionments also become goods, and there are many willing to buy them. In sum, that which best defines this attitude is its inauthenticity. Since the true relativist is incapable of establishing compromises, he or she refuses to raise a wall between the ideas he or she professes and his or her life.

Nothing similar is to be found in Max Weber. With his aversion to all self-stylization and all "diplomacy of imprecision,"[58] he always defends a *Realpolitik* of knowledge. Both politicians and intellectuals must orient themselves by an ethic of responsibility. This means the following to the social scientist: while he or she is capable of relating in a consistent and prudent way to the world *and* his or her discipline, he or she has to recognize in it a science of reality.

Reality, for many ears today, is an overrated concept. To reflect about how the disenchantment of our era could arrive at such a point and what this means in practice, it is worth thinking historically about it. In an important study, Otto Gerhard Oexle showed how the topos of a "crisis of reality" gained force in Germany in the 1930s, both in the natural sciences and in philosophy.[59] An emblematic passage in the novel *The Sleepwalkers*, written by Hermann Broch in those days, is suggestive enough: "Can this age be said still to have a reality? . . . In what haven has reality found its refuge? In science, in law, in duty, or in the uncertainty of an ever-questioning logic whose point of plausibility has vanished into the infinite?"[60]

As a matter of fact, the immediate outcome of this thought style—characterized by a "vote of ontological distrust"[61]—was the loss of the capacity for rational orientation in the public sphere. In the course of the First World War, Weber seems to predict those later developments, when he repeatedly criticizes pacifists and his country's intelligentsia. Pacifism as an absolute value is for him nothing more than naivety and indicates the ignorance of what he calls the "responsibility before history" of every *Machtstaat*. Even German academic mandarins showed a similar unfamiliarity with the "diabolical nature of power"[62]:

> I myself belong to this stratum, and have examined its new generation both in Berlin, and later, in another state, and have come to know the products of our different factories of final exams. For this reason, I can emphatically state: *In Germany, there is simply no* stratum which, on average, could be less politically qualified than this. What academic professors have demonstrated in terms of lack of political perception [*Augenmaß*], above all during this war, surpasses, notoriously, any other precedent.[63]

Weber clearly realizes that disconnection to reality leads to the decline of political judgment and, with this, a conscious and responsible *engagement*. For him, specific intellectual fashions have the potential of leading social actors to take the way of a "mystical escape of the world" (*mystische Weltflucht*) so that they are not "a match for the world as it really is."[64] Individuals become then mere passengers on the train of history, with the silence—sometimes the blessing—of intellectuals. The famous appeals to reason of Julien Benda and Thomas Mann, made a decade later and in the same spirit as that of Weber, were not heard on either side of the Rhine.

Reality finally reappeared, or imposed itself, before the ruins of the Second World War. Those who did not want to lose sight of it in the years that followed were to be called the "sceptical generation." In the 1960s, however, as Spaemann has shown, the balance that had been postulated by Freud was broken once again: authors like Herbert Marcuse announced the end of the reality principle and the unconditional supremacy of the pleasure principle.[65] The revolutionary romanticism of Europe's youth suffered its first serious blow only with the oil crisis of 1973. Reality, however, tends to be seen as something excessively prosaic by the literati. Shortly thereafter, a new way of re-editing the preceding crisis of reality appeared, by means of its specific postmodern configuration: the fictionalization of the world.

Philosopher Odo Marquard attributed such a phenomenon to the growing civilizational acceleration of contemporary societies. In a world that is being transformed with increasing speed, past experiences would be no longer capable of providing us with sufficient orientation. More than ever, it is difficult to evaluate correctly the content of reality of the information we receive, and thus, the difference between reality and fiction tends to disappear. "For this reason," Marquard concludes, "it is now very easy to ignore actual terrible things, and remain convinced of fictitious positivities, and almost easier to believe in terrible fictions, while remaining blind to real, positive things."[66]

Nonetheless, that intellectuals not infrequently show themselves ready to go *even* further than ordinary individuals in their obstinate denial of the "absolutism of reality" is something that puts into question their very reason for being. The Weberian sociologist and former Brazilian president Fernando Henrique Cardoso accurately diagnosed this dilemma when he said that "the usual danger facing an intellectual is the risk of seeing himself as a demiurge, as he could substitute reality."[67] Thus, we can generally see the fictionalization of the world as the most recent expression of a quite long history of human struggle against the absolutism of reality. As Blumenberg observed, "if, in theory of history, there's no place but for weak actions, it can happen that their esthetic promotion will be strongest amongst the weak."[68]

If the social sciences still can be seen as sciences of reality, then it can be said that *Mut vor der Realität*, that "courage in the face of reality" that Nietzsche admired so much in Thucydides, will continue to exist.[69] Vis-à-vis the fictionalization of the world—which persists in academic circles as much by means of aestheticism as by repeated efforts to rehabilitate utopia—those who responsibly look at the study of humans in society have but one alternative: make reality a vocation and a profession. This, among other important epistemic virtues, was what Max Weber taught us. It is sufficient reason to believe his legacy is neither surpassed nor obsolete, especially in a moment when a "new realism" is gradually gaining traction in contemporary philosophy.[70]

There are, of course, those who hesitate to believe this, even in the Weber studies community. Some years ago, someone who enjoys international recognition in this field said to me that Weber's sun was probably going to wane in the near future. At that occasion, I did not know how to reply. Only a few days later, I remembered the words of Marianne Weber, when she describes her conversations with Else Jaffé after the death of the "myth of Heidelberg":

> We talked about him, days, weeks, months; we repeated his way of speaking, his gestures; we forced him to return. If we speak of him, then he is "among us," if we cease talking, he disappears. There will come a time in which we leave locked inside us the greater part of what now leaves our lips. The capacity to make present in our

feelings he who has left will wane. Slowly he will disappear from us. In a sad dream, I hear him saying: "Look, I have to continue to decay."[71]

In the face of the enduring influence of Weberian *Wirklichkeitswissenschaft* and its refreshed potential in a world yearning for reality, Marianne's fears remain unfounded.

NOTES

1. Max Weber, "The 'Objectivity' of Knowledge in Social Science and Social Policy," in *Collected Methodological Writings* (hereafter *CMW*), ed. H. H. Bruun and S. Whimster, trans. H. H. Bruun (London: Routledge, 2012), 114, 105; *Zur Logik und Methodik der Sozialwissenschaften. Schriften 1900–1907*, Max Weber-Gesamtausgabe (hereafter *MWG*) I/7, ed. G. Wagner, with C. Härpfer et al. (Tübingen, Germany: Mohr [Siebeck], 2018), 174, 154.

2. Hans Blumenberg, "Wirklichkeitsbegriff und Möglichkeit des Romans," in *Nachahmung und Illusion*, ed. H. R. Jauß (Munich: Fink, 1964), 9–27, Peter Lassman and Ronald Speirs, "Introduction," in Max Weber, *Political Writings* (hereafter *PolW*), ed. P. Lassman and R. Speirs (Cambridge: Cambridge University Press, 2003), 22; Max Weber, "The Profession and Vocation of Politics," in *PolW*, 353; *Wissenschaft als Beruf 1917/1919—Politik als Beruf 1919*, *MWG* I/17, ed. W. J. Mommsen and W. Schluchter, with B. Morgenbrod (Tübingen, Germany: Mohr [Siebeck], 1992), 227–228; Helmut Schelsky quoted by Volker Kemp, *Wider die Wirklichkeitsverweigerung. Helmut Schelsky. Leben—Werk—Aktualität* (Munich: Olzog, 2012), 30.

3. Marianne Weber, *Max Weber: A Biography*, trans. H. Zohn (New Brunswick, NJ: Transaction, 1988), 45, 156.

4. Immanuel Kant, *Prolegomena to Any Future Metaphysics*, trans. G. Hatfield (Cambridge: Cambridge University Press, 2004), 48. Weber's copy is in the Bavarian Academy of Sciences and Humanities in Munich. See also Kant's *Critique of Pure Reason*, trans. P. Guyer and A. W. Wood (Cambridge: Cambridge University Press, 1998), 321, 325.

5. Weber, "Roscher's 'Historical Method,'" in *CMW*, 16n1; *MWG* I/7, 71n53.

6. Wilhelm von Humboldt, "On the Historian's Task," *History and Theory* 6 (1967): 60.

7. Wilhelm Roscher, *Leben, Werk und Zeitalter des Thukydides* (Göttingen, Germany: Vandenhoeck und Ruprecht, 1842), 44. Cf. Wilhelm Hennis, *Max Weber und Thukydides* (Tübingen, Germany: Mohr Siebeck, 2003), 3–52.

8. Georg Simmel, *Die Probleme der Geschichtsphilosophie* (Leipzig, Germany: Duncker & Humblot, 1892), 43.

9. Weber, "Objectivity" in *CMW*, 126; *MWG* I/7, 205.

10. Wilhelm Windelband, "Rectorial Address, Strassbourg, 1894," trans. G. Oakes, *History and Theory* 19 (1980): 173.

11. Friedrich Gottl, *Die Herrschaft des Wortes* (Jena, Germany: Gustav Fischer, 1901), 69.

12. Heinrich Rickert, *Die Grenzen der naturwissenschaftlichen Begriffsbildung* (Tübingen, Germany: Mohr [Siebeck], 1896–1902), 255, 634; Weber, "Objectivity" in *CMW*, 62n3; *MWG* I/7, 313–314n54. Ontology is for both Weber and Rickert clearly *no* problem at that time: reality is taken for granted. In his *Habilitationsschrift*, the philosopher writes, "Chemistry, biology, psychology, history, and all other disciplines presuppose a real world as an 'object.'" Heinrich Rickert, *Der Gegenstand der Erkenntnis*, 3rd ed. (1892; Tübingen, Germany: Mohr [Siebeck], 1915), 356.

13. Rickert, *Die Grenzen*, 321, 507, 511.

14. Ibid., 653.

15. Weber's comment about Lask is in "Roscher's 'Historical Method,'" *CMW*, 12n2; *MWG* I/7, 63n29; Emil Lask, *Fichtes Idealismus und die Geschichte* (Tübingen, Germany: Mohr [Siebeck], 1902), 169.

16. Peter Ghosh, "Max Weber and Georg Jellinek: Two Divergent Conceptions of Law," *Saeculum* 59 (2008): 299–347; Marcos César Seneda, "Uma leitura equívoca de Jellinek: Weber e a elaboração da noção de tipo ideal," in *Max Weber: religião, valores, teoria do conhecimento*, ed. M. C. Seneda and H. F. Custódio (Uberlândia, Brazil: Edufu, 2016), 201–234.

17. Weber, "Objectivity" in *CMW*, 114; *MWG* I/7, 174.

18. Max Weber, *Economy and Society*, ed. G. Roth and C. Wittich (Berkeley: University of California Press, 1978), 4, 20; *Wirtschaft und Gesellschaft. Soziologie. Unvollendet 1919–1920*, *MWG* I/23, ed. K. Borchardt, E. Hanke, and W. Schluchter (Tübingen, Germany: Mohr [Siebeck], 2013), 149, 170.

19. Weber, "Objectivity" in *CMW*, 127; *MWG* I/7, 209.

20. Max Weber, "Author's Introduction," in *The Protestant Ethic and the Spirit of Capitalism* (hereafter *PESC*), trans. T. Parsons (New York: Scribner's, 1930), 13; "Vorbemerkung," in *Die Protestantische Ethik und der Geist des Kapitalismus*, *MWG* I/18, ed. W. Schluchter, with U. Bube (Tübingen, Germany: Mohr [Siebeck], 2016), 18, 101; "The Relations of the Rural Community to Other Branches of Social Science," *History of European Ideas* 31 (2005): 337; *Wirtschaft, Staat und Sozialpolitik. Schriften und Reden 1900–1912*, *MWG* I/8, ed. W. Schluchter, with P. Kurth and B. Morgenbrod (Tübingen, Germany: Mohr [Siebeck], 1998), 227–229.

21. Quoted by Arthur Alfaix Assis, *What Is History For? Johann Gustav Droysen and the Functions of Historiography* (New York: Berghahn, 2014): 75; cf. Hermann Lübbe, *Geschichtsbegriff und Geschichtsinteresse* (Basel, Switzerland: Schwab, 2012), 49–61.

22. Sérgio da Mata, *A fascinação weberiana. As origens da obra de Max Weber* (Belo Horizonte, Brazil: Fino Traço, 2013), 26.

23. Cf. Gangolf Hübinger, *Engagierte Beobachter der Moderne. Von Max Weber bis Ralf Dahrendorf* (Göttingen, Germany: Wallstein, 2016), 118; Otto Gerhard Oexle, "Max Weber—Geschichte als Problemgeschichte," in *Das Problem der Problemgeschichte*, ed. O. G. Oexle (Göttingen, Germany: Wallstein, 2001), 11–37.

24. Weber, "Objectivity," in *CMW*, 118; *MWG* I/7, 187.

25. Cf. Lawrence A. Scaff *Weber and the Weberians* (Basingstoke, UK: Palgrave Macmillan, 2014), 4.

26. Friedrich Meinecke, "Drei Generationen deutscher Gelehrtenpolitik," *Historische Zeitschrift* 125 (1922): 273.

27. Max Weber, "Relations of the Rural Community," 335; *MWG* I/8, 224; "Religious Rejections of the World and Their Directions," in *From Max Weber: Essays in Sociology* (hereafter *FMW*), trans. and ed. H. H. Gerth and C. W. Mills (New York: Oxford, 1946), 356; *Die Wirtschaftsethik der Weltreligionen. Konfuzianismus und Taoismus. Schriften 1915–1920*, *MWG* I/19, ed. H. Schmidt-Glintzer with P. Kolonko (Tübingen, Germany: Mohr [Siebeck], 1989), 519; Paul Honigsheim, *The Unknown Max Weber* (New Brunswick, NJ: Transaction, 2003), 143.

28. Wolfgang Schluchter, *Die Entstehung des modernen Rationalismus* (Frankfurt am Main, Germany: Suhrkamp, 1998), 66; Heinz Dieter Kittsteiner, "Geschichtsphilosophie nach

der Geschichtsphilosophie. Plädoyer für eine geschichtsphilosophisch angeleitete Kulturgeschichte," *Deutsche Zeitschrift für Philosophie* 48 (2000): 75; Odo Marquard, *Schwierigkeiten mit der Geschichtsphilosophie* (Frankfurt am Main, Germany: Suhrkamp, 1982), 118; Hans Freyer, *La sociología ciencia de la realidad. Fundamentación lógica del sistema de la sociología* (Buenos Aires, Argentina: Losada, 1944), 181–183; José Guilherme Merquior, "Georges Sorel and Max Weber," in *Max Weber and His Contemporaries*, ed. W. J. Mommsen and J. Osterhammel (London: Routledge, 1987), 168. If the recourse to the concept of "development" offers a non-teleological alternative here is another question. Troeltsch believed that "the concept of historical development has an universal and philosophical meaning, that again and again needs to burst out." Ernst Troeltsch, "Der Historismus und seine Probleme" (1922), in *Ernst Troeltsch. Kritische Gesamtausgabe*, vol. 16,2, ed. F. W. Graf with M. Schloßberger (Berlin: Walter de Gruyter, 2008), 963. On this complex topic, see also Julius Löwenstein, "Die verborgene Geschichtsphilosophie Max Webers," *Jahrbuch des Instituts für Deutsche Geschichte* 6 (1977): 337–384; Wolfgang J. Mommsen, "Max Webers Begriff der Universalgeschichte," in *Max Weber, der Historiker*, ed. J. Kocka (Göttingen, Germany: Vandenhoeck & Ruprecht, 1986), 51–72; Joachim Vahland, *Max Webers entzauberte Welt* (Würzburg, Germany: Königshausen & Neumann, 2001), 118; Charles F. Keyes, "Weber and Anthropology," *Annual Review of Anthropology* 31 (2002): 235–236; Eduardo Weisz, *Racionalidad y tragedia. La filosofía histórica de Max Weber* (Buenos Aires, Argentina: Prometeo Libros, 2011), 321–340.

29. Johannes Weiß, *Vernunft und Vernichtung. Zur Philosophie und Soziologie der Moderne* (Opladen, Germany: Westdeutscher Verlag, 1993), 144; Max Weber, "On the Situation of Constitutional Democracy in Russia," in *PolW*, 71, 69; Weber, *Zur Russischen Revolution von 1905. Schriften und Reden 1905–1912, MWG* I/10, ed. W. Mommsen, with D. Dahlmann (Tübingen, Germany: Mohr [Siebeck], 1989), 272, 270; Weber, "Relations of the Rural Community," 344; *MWG* I/8, 240–241.

30. Weber, "Objectivity," *CMW*, 121; *MWG* I/7, 194; Max Weber, *The Protestant Ethic and the "Spirit" of Capitalism and Other Writings*, ed. and trans. Peter Baehr and Gordon C. Wells (New York and London: Penguin Books, 2002), 121; *Asketischer Protestantismus und Kapitalismus. Schriften und Reden 1904–1911, MWG* I/9, ed. W. Schluchter, with U. Bube (Tübingen, Germany: Mohr [Siebeck], 2014), 423; Max Weber, *The Religion of India. The Sociology of Hinduism and Buddism*, trans. and ed. Hans H. Gerth and Don Martindale (Glencoe, IL: Free Press, 1958), 161; *Die Wirtschaftsethik der Weltreligionen. Hinduismus und Buddhismus. 1916–1920, MWG* I/20, ed. H. Schmidt-Glintzer, with K.-H. Golzio (Tübingen, Germany: Mohr [Siebeck], 1996), 259; Max Weber, "Russia's Transition to Pseudo-constitutionalism," in *The Russian Revolutions*, trans. and ed. Gordon C. Wells and Peter Baehr (Cambridge: Polity Press, 1995), 187; *MWG* I/10, 477.

31. Max Weber's letter to his mother, August 15, 1888, *Briefe 1887–1894, MWG* II/2, ed. R. Aldenhoff-Hübinger, with T. Gerhards and S. Oßwald-Bargende (Tübingen, Germany: Mohr [Siebeck], 2017), 170, 172; Weber, "The Nation State and Economic Policy," in *PolW*, 10; Weber, *Landarbeiterfrage, Nationalstaat und Volkswirtschaftspolitik. Schriften und Reden 1892–1899, MWG* I/4, ed. W. J. Mommsen, with R. Aldenhoff (Tübingen, Germany: Mohr [Siebeck], 1993), 553.

32. Weber, "Relations of the Rural Community," 345; *MWG* I/8, 241.

33. Peter Steinbach, "Sozialdarwinismus: Der politische Kampf ums Dasein. Ein Leitmotiv der Freiburger Antrittsrede Max Webers—interdisziplinär komplexer interpretiert," in *Max Weber 1864–1920. Politik—Theorie—Weggefährten* (Cologne, Germany: Böhlau, 2016), 83;

Wilhelm Hennis, *Max Webers Wissenschaft vom Menschen* (Tübingen, Germany: Mohr Siebeck, 1996), 24.

34. Max Weber, "Die ländliche Arbeitsverfassung," *MWG* I/4, 176 (translated by the author).

35. *MWG* I/4, 1, 182–183, 298 (translated by the author); "The Nation State and Economic Policy," *PolW*, 9; *MWG* I/4, 552.

36. Weber, "Relations of the Rural Community," 345; *MWG* I/8, 242; *The Protestant Ethic Debate. Max Weber's Replies to His Critics 1907–1910*, ed. D. J. Chalcraft and A. Harrington (Liverpool, UK: Liverpool University Press, 2001), 33; *MWG* I/9, 481; Weber, "On the Situation of Constitutional Democracy in Russia," *PolW*, 71; *MWG* I/10, 272–273.

37. Cf. Kenneth Pomeranz, *The Great Divergence* (Princeton, NJ: Princeton University Press, 2000), 269–274; Godfrey Muriuki, "Western Uniqueness? Some Counterarguments from an African Perspective," in *Western Historical Thinking. An Intercultural Debate*, ed. J. Rüsen (New York: Berghahn, 2002), 142–147; Romila Thapar, *The Past Before Us: Historical Traditions in Early North India* (Cambridge, MA: Harvard University Press, 2013); Marta Bucholc, "Die Reaktion polnischer Soziologen auf Max Webers Polenschriften—der Verlust an Schärfentiefe," in *Max Weber in der Welt. Rezeption und Wirkung*, ed. M. Kaiser and H. Rosenbach (Tübingen, Germany: Mohr Siebeck, 2014), 103–124.

38. Hübinger, *Engagierte Beobachter*, 68.

39. Cf. Lawrence A. Scaff, *Max Weber in America* (Princeton, NJ: Princeton University Press, 2011), 54–69.

40. Weber, "Relations of the Rural Community," 335, 344; *MWG* I/8, 225, 240. Cf. Reinhart Koselleck, *Zeitschichten. Studien zur Historik* (Frankfurt am Main, Germany: Suhrkamp, 2003), 363.

41. Franz Boas, "The History of Anthropology," in *Congress of Arts and Science*, ed. H. J. Rogers (Boston: Houghton Mifflin, 1906), 5:482.

42. Weber, "Author's Introduction," *PESC*, 30; *MWG* I/18, 120.

43. Wilfried Witte, "Populär oder elitär: Anmerkungen zum Kulturbegriff in der Geschichtswissenschaft," *Berichte zur Wissenschaftsgeschichte* 25 (2002): 254; Gangolf Hübinger, *Kulturprotestantismus und Politik* (Tübingen, Germany: Mohr Siebeck, 1994), 22–23.

44. Cf. Friedrich Jaeger, "Der Kulturbegriff im Werk Max Webers und seine Bedeutung für eine moderne Kulturgeschichte," *Geschichte und Gesellschaft* 18 (1992): 371–393; Lawrence A. Scaff, "Max Webers Begriff der Kultur," in *Max Webers Wissenschaftslehre. Interpretationen und Kritik*, ed. Gerhard Wagner and Heinz Zipprian (Frankfurt am Main, Germany: Suhrkamp, 1994), 678–699.

45. Rickert, *Die Grenzen*, 596.

46. Cf. the excellent chapter by Johannes Weiß, " 'Der Begriff der Kultur ist ein Wertbegriff'— Über einen problematischen Grundsatz Max Webers," in *Kultursoziologie. Paradigmen, Methoden, Fragestellungen*, ed. Monika Wohlrab-Sahr (Wiesbaden, Germany: VS, 2010), 53–71.

47. Cf. Stanley Tambiah, "Buddhism and This-Worldly Activity." *Modern Asian Sudies* 7 (1973): 1–20; Hubert Knoblauch, *Populäre Religion. Auf dem Weg in eine spirituelle Gesellschaft* (Frankfurt am Main, Germany: Campus, 2009).

48. Immanuel Kant, "On the Common Saying: This May Be True in Theory, But It Does Not Apply in Practice," in *Kant Political Writings*, ed. H. S. Reiss (Cambridge: Cambridge University Press, 1991), 61–92.

49. Weber, "Science as a Profession and Vocation," *CMW*, 341; *MWG* I/17, 85. "Objectivity," *CMW*, 138; *MWG* I/7, 234.

50. Freyer, *La sociología ciencia de la realidad*, 100, 249, 197.

51. Volker Kruse, *"Geschichts- und Sozialphilosophie" oder "Wirklichkeitswissenschaft"? Die deutsche historische Soziologie und die logischen Kategorien René Königs und Max Webers* (Frankfurt am Main, Germany: Suhrkamp, 1999); Volker Kruse, *Soziologie und "Gegenwartskrise." Die Zeitdiagnosen Franz Oppenheimers und Alfred Webers. Ein Beitrag zur historischen Soziologie der Weimarer Republik* (Wiesbaden, Germany: DUV, 1987). On the undeniable importance of the historical school of economics for Max Weber and Werner Sombart, see Wilhelm Hennis *Max Webers Fragestellung* (Tübingen, Germany: Mohr Siebeck, 1987), 117–166; Hinnerk Bruhns, *Max Webers historische Sozialökonomie* (Wiesbaden, Germany: Harrassowitz, 2014), 147–168. Since the theme of historicism remains often misunderstood, see Gunter Scholtz, "Das Historismusproblem in der Geisteswissenschaften im 20. Jahrhundert," in *Zwischen Wissenschaftsanspruch und Orientierungsbedürfnis*, ed. G. Scholtz (Frankfurt am Main, Germany: Suhrkamp, 1991), 130–157; and Frank Ankersmit, "The Necessity of Historicism," *Journal of the Philosophy of History* 4 (2010): 226–240.

52. Helmut Schelsky, *Auf der Suche nach der Wirklickkeit. Gesammelte Aufsätze zur Soziologie der Bundesrepublik* (Munich: Wilhelm Goldmann, 1979), 394–396, 441, 462–463. On Schelsky's relation to Weber, see Carsten Klingemann, "Zur Rezeption Max Webers durch Helmut Schelsky im Kontext der 'Leipziger Schule der Soziologie,'" in *Helmut Schelsky— Der politische Anti-Soziologe. Eine Neurezeption*, ed. A. Gallus (Göttingen, Germany: Wallstein, 2013), 39–49.

53. Friedrich Tenbruck, *Das Werk Max Webers. Gesammelte Aufsätze zu Max Weber* (Tübingen, Germany: Mohr Siebeck, 1999), 52–53.

54. Friedrich Tenbruck, *Geschichte und Gesellschaft* (Berlin: Duncker & Humblot, 1986), 6.

55. Tenbruck, *Das Werk Max Webers*, 159, 173.

56. Ibid., 174.

57. Arnold Gehlen, "Formen und Schicksale der Ratio," in *Studien zur Anthropologie und Soziologie*, ed. H. Mauss and F. Fürstenberg (Berlin: Luchterhand, 1963), 93–139, here 138.

58. Weber, "Addendum to the Essay on R. Stammler," *CMW*, 233; *MWG* I/7, 597.

59. Otto Gerhard Oexle, "Wirklichkeit—Krise der Wirklichkeit—Neue Wirklichkeit. Deutungsmuster und Paradigmenkämpfe in der deutschen Wissenschaft vor und nach 1933," in *Die Rolle der Geisteswissenschaften im Dritten Reich 1933-1945*, ed. F.-R. Hausmann, with E. Müller-Luckner (Munich: Oldenburg, 2002), 1–20. It is well known that such a topos was employed both in sociology (by Mannheim) and in biology (by Fleck). Cf. Karl Mannheim, *Ideology and Utopia. An Introduction to the Sociology of Knowledge* (New York: Harcourt, Brace & Co., 1954), 87; Ludwig Kleck, "On the Crisis of 'Reality,'" in *Cognition and Fact. Materials on Ludwig Fleck*, ed. R. S. Cohen and T. Schnelle (Dordrecht, The Netherlands: D. Reidel, 1986), 47–57.

60. Hermann Broch, *The Sleepwalkers* (New York: Vintage Books, 1996), 605.

61. Arnold Gehlen, *Die Seele im technischen Zeitalter und andere sozialpsychologische, soziologische und kulturanalytische Schriften* (Frankfurt am Main, Germany: Vittorio Klostermann, 2004), 57.

62. Weber, "Between Two Laws," in *PolW*, 75; Weber, *Zur Politik im Weltkrieg. Schriften und Reden 1914-1918*, *MWG* I/15, ed. W. J. Mommsen, with G. Hübinger (Tübingen, Germany: Mohr [Siebeck], 1984), 95.

63. Weber, "Das preußische Wahlrecht," *MWG* I/15, 229–230 (translated by the author).

64. Weber, "The Profession and Vocation of Politics," *PolW*, 368–369; *MWG* I/17, 251.

65. Robert Spaemann, *Grenzen. Zur ethischen Dimension des Handelns* (Stuttgart, Germany: Klett-Cotta, 2002), 508.

66. Odo Marquard, *Apologie des Zufälligen* (Stuttgart, Germany: Reclam, 2001), 86.

67. Quoted by Celso Lafer, "FHC: o intelectual como político," *Novos Estudos* 83 (2009): 39–63, here 43.

68. Hans Blumenberg, *Tiempo de la vida y tiempo del mundo* (Valencia, Spain: Pre-Textos, 2007), 210.

69. Friedrich Nietzsche, *The Anti-Christ, Ecce Homo, Twilight of the Idols* (Cambridge: Cambridge University Press, 2005), 226. See also Karl-Siegbert Rehberg, "Soziologie als 'Wirklichkeitswissenschaft' jenseits Naturalismus und Virtualitälseuphorie," in *Die Natur der Gesellschaft: Verhandlungen der 33. Kongresses der Deutschen Gesellschaft für Soziologie,* ed. K.-S. Rehberg (Frankfurt am Main, Germany: Campus, 2008), 23–41; and Jens Hacke, "Wirklichkeitswissenschaft? Realistisches Denken in analytischen Kontexten," *Merkur* 62, no. 704 (2008): 82–85.

70. Cf. Daniel Plenge, "Realist Turn?," *Zeitschrift für philosophische Forschung* 68, no. 3 (2014): 400–422; Jan Faye, *After Posmodernism. A Naturalistic Reconstruction of the Humanities* (Basingstoke, UK: Palgrave Macmillan, 2012); Graham Harman, "Realism Without Materialism," *SubStance* 40, no. 2 (2011): 52–72; Lee Braver, *A Thing of This World. A History of Continental Anti-Realism* (Evanston, IL: Northwestern University Press, 2007).

71. Marianne Weber, *Lebenserinnerungen* (Bremen, Germany: Johs. Storm, 1948), 116.

Index